A Commentary on *The Old English and Anglo-Latin Riddle Tradition*

SUPPLEMENTS TO THE
DUMBARTON OAKS MEDIEVAL LIBRARY

A Commentary on *The Old English and Anglo-Latin Riddle Tradition*

Andy Orchard

Supplement to DOML LXIX

The Old English and Anglo-Latin Riddle Tradition
Edited and translated by Andy Orchard
published by Harvard University Press

SUPPLEMENTS TO THE
DUMBARTON OAKS MEDIEVAL LIBRARY

A Commentary on *The Old English and Anglo-Latin Riddle Tradition*

ANDY ORCHARD

DUMBARTON OAKS RESEARCH LIBRARY AND COLLECTION
WASHINGTON, DC

Printed in the United States of America.

LIBRARY OF CONGRESS CATALOGING-IN-PUBLICATION DATA

NAMES: Orchard, Andy, author.
TITLE: A commentary on The Old English and Anglo-Latin Riddle Tradition / Andy Orchard.
OTHER TITLES: Dumbarton Oaks medieval library ; 69 supplement.
DESCRIPTION: Washington, DC : Dumbarton Oaks Research Library and Collection, [2021] | Series: Supplements to the Dumbarton Oaks medieval library; supplement to DOML 69 | "Supplement to DOML LXIX, Old English and Anglo-Latin Riddle Tradition, edited and translated by Andy Orchard, published by Harvard University Press"—Series title page. | Includes bibliographical references and indexes. | Summary: "This volume is a companion to The Anglo-Saxon Riddle Tradition. Its extensive notes and commentary on hundreds of Latin, Old English, and Old Norse-Icelandic riddles illuminate and clarify the multifaceted and interconnected nature of a broad, international tradition. Within this commentary, readers will encounter a deep reservoir of knowledge about riddles produced in both Latin and Old English during the Anglo-Saxon period, and the literatures with which they were in dialogue. Riddles range from those by prominent authors like Aldhelm, Bede, Alcuin, and Boniface to those presented anonymously in collections such as the Exeter Book. All are fully discussed, with particular attention paid to manuscript traditions, subject matter, solutions, style, sources, parallels, and recommendations for further reading. Consideration is given to running themes throughout the collection, comparisons to other riddles and to other literature more broadly, and important linguistic observations and manuscript readings. The commentary also lists the manuscripts and earlier editions for each riddle, extensive catalogues of proposed solutions, and additional bibliographic references. Following the general discussion of each riddle there is detailed line-by-line annotation. This authoritative commentary is the most comprehensive examination to date of the bilingual riddle tradition of Anglo-Saxon England and its links to the wider world"—Provided by publisher.
IDENTIFIERS: LCCN 2020032089 | ISBN 9780884024774 (cloth)
SUBJECTS: LCSH: Riddles, English (Old)—History and criticism. | Riddles, Latin—England—History and criticism. | Riddles, English (Old)—Themes, motives. | Riddles, Latin—England—Themes, motives. | English poetry—Old English, ca. 450-1100—History and criticism.
CLASSIFICATION: LCC PR1764 .O73 2021 | DDC 829/.1009—dc23
LC record available at https://lccn.loc.gov/2020032089

TEXT COMPOSITION: Melissa Tandysh

For Oscar, the enigmatic,
and god's own private mystery

·ᚠᛏᛈᚷᚠ·
·ᚾᚾᛚᚠᛏᛈᚾᚾ·
·/\/\/\/·

Contents

Preface ix

A Note on This Commentary xiii

Abbreviations of Riddles and Riddle Collections xvii

Abbreviations of Previous Editions, Translations, and Commentaries xix

Manuscript Sigla xxiii

Bibliographical Abbreviations xxvii

COMMENTARY

THE ANGLO-LATIN TRADITION 1

Aldhelm 1

Bede 113

Tatwine 131

Hwætberht, The Riddles of Eusebius 172

Boniface 230

Alcuin 257

The Lorsch Riddles 289

The Abingdon Riddle 300

The High-Minded Library 302

The Old English Tradition 315
The Franks Casket Riddle 315
The Leiden Riddle 317
The Exeter Book Riddles 321
The Old English Rune Poem 489
The Riddles of Solomon and Saturn II 501
The Old English Prose Riddle 505

Sources and Analogues of the Tradition 509
Symphosius 509
The Bern Riddles 573
The Verses of a Certain Irishman on the Alphabet 607
The Old Icelandic Rune Poem 624
The Riddles of Gestumblindi 630
Various Riddles 648

Bibliography 655
Index of Solutions 685
Concordance of Parallels with Isidore's Etymologiae 697
General Index 701

Preface

Frige mec frodum wordum. Ne læt þinne ferð onhælne,
degol þæt þu deopost cunne. Nelle ic þe min dyrne gesecgan,
gif þu me þinne hyge-cræft hylest. ond þine heortan geþohtas.
Gleawe men sceolon gieddum wrixlan.

Maxims I 1–4a

Question me with wise words. Don't keep your soul concealed,
the deepest secret that you know. I don't want to tell you my
mysteries,
if you hide from me the power of your mind and the thoughts of
your heart.
The smart should swap riddles.

It is in the nature of riddles to highlight unlikely or unusual combinations and contrasts, and in that spirit, I can only apologize for the combination and contrast of this volume of notes and commentary with the somewhat leaner, slimmer lines of the DOML volume of *The Old English and Anglo-Latin Riddle Tradition (OEALRT)* from which it grew, and with which it is necessarily paired. I have endeavored to keep the inevitable overlap to a minimum, while intending each volume to stand alone, with this one in particular potentially useful alongside all earlier editions of the relevant texts and translations.

Whether there was indeed such a thing as an Anglo-Saxon riddle tradition at all, as I argue here, I leave to others to judge.[1] But if this book and its companion serve any useful purpose, it may be again to underline the benefits of considering Anglo-Saxon culture in the widest possible context, and to highlight the dangers of simply speaking of Anglo-Saxon riddles (or indeed Anglo-Saxon literature as a whole) in the monoglot manner that the current study of the subject, overwhelmingly within university Departments of English, has inevitably, if inadvertently, encouraged. I have deliberately cast my net wider, and, mindful of the delightful manner in which riddles can level playing fields and eclipse both academic qualifications and book-learning in general, have also attempted to consult and incorporate as many relevant unpublished dissertations, comparative discussions, and other often web-based material as I have been able to identify. Here, I should particularly highlight the tools available through my own ongoing project, "A Consolidated Library of Anglo-Saxon Poetry," funded by the European Research Council (www.clasp.eu), several of which were employed and tested here.

I am indebted to many individuals for specific suggestions, most of all to my mighty longtime mentor, Michael Lapidge, who has as always kept me grounded and corrected numerous errors, and to my sometime student, Rob Getz, who with typical flair and panache far exceeded all expectations in his role as research assistant. I have also benefited from the impressively effective DOML machine, and would highlight in particular the sterling and unstinting help of Bob Babcock, Raquel Begleiter, Dan Donoghue, Nicole Eddy, Drew Jones, Katherine O'Brien O'Keeffe, and Jan Ziolkowski. Their exemplary aid is gratefully acknowledged, and where we have disagreed, I hope they will forgive me. Likewise, I also happily acknowledge the many debts I owe to successive generations of students on both sides of the Atlantic who have sat through classes on the Anglo-Saxon riddle tradition over many years. Riddles are a team sport, after all,

1 Throughout this work, "Anglo-Saxon" is used in specific reference to the history and culture of the English-speaking people in what is now England from the sixth to the eleventh century CE.

one in which there is not always a clear winner, and part of the point of these books is to argue that riddles are not only competitive and collaborative, but also within the Anglo-Saxon tradition quintessentially comprise a contact sport, one in which significant relationships can be traced between riddles from different periods and places, even those that were composed and have survived in quite different and mutually unintelligible languages.

At all events, and as will be evident from the notes and necessarily extensive bibliography, this volume is in large part a compilation and a combination of the words and works of many others with far more specialized and specific knowledge of each of the collections and individual texts considered here. If the happy solution of a riddle routinely involves the juxtaposition of uncanny and alien elements, then I hope to have done some service simply by bringing all these scattered collections together, and fully expect that further research, which I trust will be stimulated thereby, will only expose both the local and broken nature of this volume. But then again, another of the joys of riddling is that there can still be considerable benefit and a number of teachable moments in reading and engaging with these texts: I wish all readers the same blend of pleasure, puzzlement, outrage, and indignation as these texts have given me and so many others through the years.

DOML volumes are rightly stripped down for the general reader, but here I offer this rather more myopic volume to a more specialized audience, and dedicate it to those who have taught me so much, so happily; beginning with my sometimes puzzling, often challenging, but always entertaining and enlightening (and now towering) boy, who for more than a decade and a half has given me so much bright and beautiful son-shine. If this is a book that he and his friends may quite rightly never choose to read, it is nevertheless dedicated to Oscar, the enigmatic, and to god's own private mystery, with love—the biggest riddle of them all.

The Rose and Crown, Oxford
November 29, 2018

A Note on This Commentary

The multifaceted, complex, and interconnected nature of the Anglo-Saxon riddle tradition can seem bewildering, and in devising a set of abbreviations and manuscript sigla I have striven for simplicity and transparency, always in order to emphasize the many different kinds of links that can be traced between the texts and collections presented here. The principles of abbreviation are as follows:

1. The major texts and collections are abbreviated in upper case, using three letters where possible, with pseudonymous material prefaced by ps-, where relevant.
2. Earlier texts, translations, and commentaries are abbreviated by suitable combinations of upper- and lowercase letters, restricted where feasible to two-letter forms, necessarily augmented to avoid ambiguity.
3. Manuscripts are represented by sigla consisting of a single uppercase letter, augmented where necessary by a superscript number. I have tried to retain the same sigla used in earlier editions, though this has not always been possible.

Apart from these abbreviations, I have indicated preferred and suggested solutions in uppercase italics, and also used the sign "→" to indicate where logogriphs (those riddles that rely on changes in spelling to offer more than one solution) are involved. While the various texts and collections differ significantly, often from manuscript to manuscript, as well as from text to text, about whether or not solutions are given at all, or circulate separately or in alternative forms, here I have deferred all suggested solutions (or indeed titles, as they are sometimes presented) to the relevant notes and headnotes, and leveled their forms to the nominative, rather than preferring the versions with Latin *DE* + ablative which I believe to be a secondary development aligning the Latin *aenigmata* with other didactic and encyclopedic texts, alongside which they often circulate. In presenting the texts, I have followed the usual conventions: acrostics and telestichs are signaled in capitals, and interpolations, especially interpolated solutions, whether right or wrong, in italics; runes are generally transliterated in lowercase. In general, in presenting a text I have followed existing editions more slavishly and silently in Sources and Analogues of the Tradition than in the Anglo-Latin Tradition and the Old English Tradition, where I have (occasionally) attempted originality, and the notes and markup reflect this accordingly.

I have translated the poems line by line, where reasonable, and in as neutral a manner as I could, in order to preserve the inherent ambiguity and developing revelation of these tricky, enigmatic texts. In introducing the relevant texts and collections, I have used the same basic template, again to facilitate direct comparison, considering in turn: authorship and date; manuscript context; subject matter and solutions; style; sources and parallels; idiosyncrasies of this text and translation; and further reading. For individual texts, including those within larger collections, I have adopted a similar basic structure, reporting individual manuscripts, earlier editions and translations, and solutions both accepted and suggested. For brevity and focus, in cases where there are multiple manuscript witnesses, I have deliberately favored the reporting of manuscripts written or owned in Anglo-Saxon England, and though I am well aware that this gives a highly skewed picture, it is at least a bias accurately reflected in the title. In a more inclusive manner, I report previous editions and translations so that their readings and renderings can be checked against mine, and have tried to include the whole range of suggested solutions, both modern and medieval, even those that remain baffling, unlikely, impossible, or overly imaginative. Within the notes, I have taken particular care to highlight comparisons, both verbal and conceptual, that link the various texts and collections, the better to emphasize what binds this material together. In the same vein, and to the extent that much of what makes the Anglo-Saxon riddle tradition appears to be a developing set of mutually reflexive texts with many shared themes and strategies, I have endeavored to offer exhaustive listings in the various introductions and headnotes, with cross-references where appropriate. By contrast, verbal parallels from outside the particular texts and collections showcased here are not intended to be comprehensive, but rather again to reflect the milieu within which the literate Anglo-Saxons who composed the vast majority of texts considered here taught and worked.

Abbreviations of Riddles and Riddle Collections

ABI anon., *The Abingdon Riddle*

ALC Alcuin, *Aenigmata*

- ALC D Alcuin, *Disputatio regalis et nobilissimi Pippini cum Albino scholastico*
- ps-ALC pseudo-Alcuin, *Aenigma*

ALD Aldhelm, *Aenigmata*

- ALD PR Aldhelm, *Aenigmata, Praefatio*

ALF anon., *De alfabeto*

BED Bede, *Aenigmata*

- ps-BED pseudo-Bede, *Aenigmata*

BER anon., *Aenigmata Bernensia*

- ps-BER pseudo-*Aenigma Bernense*

BIB anon., *Bibliotheca magnifica*

BON Boniface, *Aenigmata*

- BON PR Boniface, *Aenigmata, Praefatio*

EUS Hwætberht, *Aenigmata Eusebii*

EXE anon., *The Exeter Book Riddles*

FRA anon., *The Franks Casket Riddle*

GES anon., *Gestumblindagátur*

LEI anon., *The Leiden Riddle*

LOR anon., *Aenigmata Laureshamensia*

OEP Ælfwine (?), *The Old English Prose Riddle*

OER anon., *The Old English Rune Poem*

OIR anon., *The Old Icelandic Rune Poem*

ONR anon., *The Old Norwegian Rune Poem* (found in notes to OIR)

SOL anon., *The Riddles of "Solomon and Saturn II"*

SYM Symphosius, *Aenigmata*

- SYM PR Symphosius, *Aenigmata, Praefatio*
- ps-SYM pseudo-Symphosius, *Aenigmata*

TAT Tatwine, *Aenigmata*

- TAT PR Tatwine, *Aenigmata, Praefatio*
- TAT EP Tatwine, *Aenigmata, Epilogus*

XMS anon., *Aenigmata varia*

- XMS P anon., *Aenigmata* from P^5 (Paris, Bibliothèque nationale de France, lat. 8071 [s. x]) and S^1 (London, British Library, Harley 3020, fols. 95–132 [provenance Glastonbury, s. x/xi, Winchester?])
- XMS S anon., *Aenigmata* from S (Edinburgh, National Library of Scotland, Advocates 18. 6. 12 [provenance Thorney, s. $xi^{ex.}$ or $xii^{in.}$])
- XMS X anon., *Aenigmata* from X (St Gallen, Stiftsbibliothek 196 [s. x^{med}]) and X^1 (St Gallen, Stiftsbibliothek 446 [s. x])
- XMS Y anon., *Aenigma* from P^2 (Paris, Bibliothèque nationale de France, lat. 10861 [Canterbury CC?; s. $ix^{1/4}$ or ix^1])
- XMS Z anon., *Aenigmata* from Z (Karlsruhe, Badische Landesbibliothek, Aug. perg. 205 [Reichenau, s. x])

Abbreviations of Previous Editions, Translations, and Commentaries

Ab	Abbott, *Riddles of the Exeter Book* (EXE)
An	Anlezark, *Old English Dialogues of Solomon and Saturn* (SOL)
Ba	Baum, *Anglo-Saxon Riddles of the Exeter Book* (EXE)
Be	Bergamin, *Aenigmata Symposii* (SYM)
BL	Bayless and Lapidge, *Collectanea Pseudo-Bedae* (ps-BED; ALD; SYM)
Bu	Burrows, *Heiðreks gátur* (GES)
By	Bayless, "Alcuin's *Disputatio Pippini*" (ALC D)
CH	Crossley-Holland, *Exeter Book Riddles* (EXE)
Di	Dickins, *Runic and Heroic Poems* (OER; OIR; ONR)
DB	du Bois, *Hundred Riddles of Symphosius* (SYM)
DS	Daly and Suchier, *Altercatio Hadriani Augusti et Epicteti philosophi* (ALC D)
DüA	Dümmler, *Carmina Alcuini* (ALC)
DüB	Dümmler, *Aenigmata Bonifatii* (BON)
DüL	Dümmler, *Aenigmata anglica* (BER)
Eh	Ehwald, *Aldhelmi opera* (ALD)
ES	Erhardt-Siebold, *Die lateinischen Rätsel* (ALD; BER; BON; EUS; LOR; SYM; TAT)
Fi	Finnur Jónsson, *Heiðreks saga* (GES)
Gi	Giles, *Anecdota Bedæ* (BIB)
Gl	Glorie, *Collectiones aenigmatum merovingicae aetatis* (ALD; ALF; BER; BON; EUS; LOR; SYM; TAT)

Ha	Halsall, *Old English Rune Poem* (OER; ALF)
Hi	Hickes, *Linguarum veterum septentrionalium thesaurus* (OER; OIR; ONR)
HoA	Howlett, "*Versus cuiusdam Scotti de alphabeto*" (ALF)
HoP	Howlett, "'Tres Linguae Sacrae'" (OEP)
Ju	Juster, *Saint Aldhelm's Riddles* (ALD)
KD	Krapp–Dobbie, *Exeter Book* (EXE)
La	Lapidge, *Bede's Latin Poetry* (BED)
Le	Leary, *Symphosius, The "Aenigmata"* (SYM)
Lo	Love, *The Reception of "Hervarar saga ok Heiðreks"* (GES)
LR	Lapidge and Rosier, *Aldhelm: The Poetic Works* (ALD)
Ma	Mackie, *Exeter Book* (EXE)
MS	Müllenhof and Scherer, *Denkmäler deutscher Poesie und Prosa* (XMS)
MSB	Salvador-Bello, *Isidorean Perceptions* (ABI; ALD; BER; EUS; EXE; LOR; SYM; TAT; XMS Z)
Mu	Muir, *Exeter Anthology* (EXE)
Ni	Niles, *Old English Enigmatic Poems* (EXE)
Oh	Ohl, *Enigmas of Symphosius* (SYM)
Or	Orchard, "Alcuin's Educational Dispute" (ALC D)
Pa	Page, "The Icelandic Rune Poem" (OIR)
Pi	Pitman, *Riddles of Aldhelm* (ALD)
PL	Migne, Patrologia Latina (ALD; SYM)
Po	Porter, "Double Solution" (ABI)
PZ	Pinsker and Ziegler, *Die altenglischen Rätsel* (EXE)
Se	Sebo, *In Enigmate* (ALD 100; SYM)
Sk	Stork, *Through a Gloss Darkly* (ALD)
Sm	Smith, *Three Northumbrian Poems* (LEI; EXE 33)
St	Strecker, *Aenigmata hexasticha* (BER)
To	Tolkien, *The Saga of King Heidrek the Wise* (GES)
Tr	Trautmann, *Die altenglischen Rätsel* (EXE)
Tu	Tupper, *Riddles of the Exeter Book* (EXE)

TuB	Tupper, "Riddles of the Bede Tradition" (BED)
Ve	Vernet, "Notice et extraits d'un manuscrit d'Edimbourg" (XMS)
Wh	Whitman, *Old English Riddles* (EXE)
Wi1	Wilbur, "Three Riddles from Symphosius" (SYM)
Wi2	Wilbur, "Some Riddles from Symphosius" (SYM)
Wi3	Wilbur, "Some Riddles in Symphosius" (SYM)
WiC	Williamson, *Complete Old English Poems* (EXE)
WiF	Williamson, *Feast of Creatures* (EXE)
WiR	Williamson, *Old English Riddles* (EXE)
Wl	Williams, "The Riddles of Tatwine and Eusebius" (TAT; EUS)
Wy	Wyatt, *Old English Riddles* (EXE)

Manuscript Sigla

Note: Here I focus on those manuscripts that were written or owned in England up to 1100 (and so are listed in G–L).

A St. Petersburg, Russian National Library, Q. v. I. 15 (SW England, s. viii^{2}; prov. Corbie) [G–L 845: contains SYM and ALD]

A^{1} Aberystwyth, National Library of Wales, 735 C, fols. 1–26 (France [Limoges?], s. xi^{1}; provenance England or Wales, s. xi) [G–L 1.5: contains BON]

B London, British Library, Royal 15. A. XVI (s. ix$^{4/4}$ or ix/x, perhaps N France or England, with additions made s. x$^{med.}$ or x$^{3/4}$, England; both parts Canterbury St. Augustine's by s. x^{2} [provenance ibid.]) [G–L 489: contains ALD]

C London, British Library, Cotton Vitellius E. xviii (Winchester New Minster (provenance Winchester OM), s. xi$^{med.}$ or xi$^{3/4}$) [G–L 407: contains OEP]

C^{1} Cambridge, Corpus Christi College, 422, pp. 1–26 (s. x^{1} or x$^{2/4}$ or x$^{med.}$) [G–L 110: contains SOL]

D Leiden, Universiteitsbibliotheek, Vossianus Lat. Q. 106 (W France [provenance Fleury], s. ix$^{2/4}$) [contains SYM, ALD, and LEI]

E Exeter, Cathedral Library, 3501 (s. x^{2}, prob. SW England [or Canterbury Christ Church??], prov. Exeter by s. xi$^{3/4}$) [G–L 257: contains EXE]

F^{1} Brussels, Bibliothèque royale, 10615–729 (perhaps from Trier, s. xii) [contains ALD and ALF]

F^{2} Brussels, Bibliothèque royale, 9799–809 (s. xii) [contains ALD and ALF]

G Cambridge, University Library, Gg. 5. 35 (Canterbury St. Augustine's, s. xi med.) [G–L 12: contains SYM, ALD, TAT, EUS, BED, BIB, and ALF]

H Bern, Burgerbibliothek 611 (s. viii^{1}) [contains BER]

H^{1} Reykjavík, Stofnun Árna Magnússonar, AM 544, 4º ("Hauksbók"; Norway and Iceland, 1306–8) [contains GES] (see http://handrit.is/en/manuscript/view/AM04-0544)

H^{2} Reykjavík, Stofnun Árna Magnússonar, AM 281 4º (paper; 17th century) [contains GES]

H^{3} Reykjavík, Stofnun Árna Magnússonar, AM 597b 4º (paper; 17th century) [contains GES]

I Berlin, Staatsbibliothek zu Berlin, Preussischer Kulturbesitz, Phillipps 1825 (Verona, s. viii/ix) [contains SYM and BER]

K Leiden, Universiteitsbibliotheek, Vossianus Lat. O. 15 (Limoges, Saint-Martial, s. x/xi) [contains SYM and ALD]

L London, British Library, Royal 12. C. XXIII (Christ Church, Canterbury, s. x^{2} or x/xi) [G–L 478: contains SYM, ALD, TAT, EUS, and ALF]

L^{2} London, British Library, Royal 15. B. XIX (a composite manuscript: fols. 36–78 s. ix$^{4/4}$, Rheims area, provenance England s. x? or not in England before s. xii or xiii; fols. 79–199 s. x, Rheims; in England not before s. xii or xiii?) [G–L 492 and 493: contains part of SYM and (on fols. 204–5, so not in the English part) a different part of SYM and BON 1–10]

M Grand Haven, Michigan, The Scriptorium, VK 861 (Canterbury CC?, provenance N France s. xi [doubtful]) [G–L 829.8: contains three verse riddles, the third of which is listed as SK 3618 (beginning with ALC 6.4–5)]

N [Rome], Città del Vaticano, Biblioteca Apostolica Vaticana, Reg. lat. 1553 (s. ix in.) [contains SYM, ALD, BON, and BER]

O Oxford, Bodleian Library, Rawlinson C. 697 (NE Francia, s. ix$^{3/4}$) [G–L 661: contains SYM, ALD, and ALF]

P^{2} Paris, Bibliothèque nationale de France, lat. 10861 (Canterbury CC?; s. ix$^{1/4}$ or ix^{1}) [G–L 898: contains XMS Y (add. s. x or xi)]

P^{3} Paris, Bibliothèque nationale de France, lat. 2773 (s. ix) [contains SYM, ALD, and ALF]

P^{4} Paris, Bibliothèque nationale de France, lat. 8440 (s. x) [contains SYM and ALD]

P^{5} Paris, Bibliothèque nationale de France, lat. 8071 (s. x) [contains XMS P1–3]

Q Antwerp, Plantin-Moretus Museum, M. 16. 2 (47) (with London, British Library, Add. 32246) (probably Abingdon [or Continent?], s. xi$^{in.}$ and xi^{1}) [G–L 775: contains ABI]

R St. Petersburg, Russian National Library, F. v. XIV. 1 and Paris, Bibliothèque nationale de France, lat. 13048, fols. 31–58 (Corbie, s. viii/ix) [contains SYM, ALD, and BON]

R^{1} Copenhagen, GKS 2845 4º (late 14th or early 15th century) [contains GES]

S Edinburgh, National Library of Scotland, Advocates 18. 6. 12 (provenance Thorney, s. xi$^{ex.}$ or xii$^{in.}$) [G–L 252: contains SYM (incomplete), plus XMS S1–3]

S^{1} London, British Library, Harley 3020, fols. 95–132 (provenance Glastonbury, s. x/xi, Winchester?) [G–L 433.3: contains XMS P2]

T [Rome], Città del Vaticano, Biblioteca Apostolica Vaticana, Pal. lat. 1719 (s. ix^{1}) [contains SYM and ALD] (http://digi.vatlib.it/view/bav_pal_lat_1719)

U [Rome], Città del Vaticano, Biblioteca Apostolica Vaticana, Pal. lat. 1753 (Lorsch, s. viii$^{ex.}$) [contains SYM and the *Epistola ad Acircium* as a whole, including ALD and LOR] (http://digi.vatlib.it/view/bav_pal_lat_1753)

U^{1} Uppsala, University Library, R715 (paper; mid-17th century) [contains GES]

V [Rome], Città del Vaticano, Biblioteca Apostolica Vaticana, Reg. lat. 2078 (Rheims, s. ix) [contains SYM and ALD]

W Wolfenbüttel, Herzog August Bibliothek, Gud. lat. 331 (s. x/xi) [contains SYM and ALD]

X St. Gallen, Stiftsbibliothek 196 (s. x^{med}) [contains SYM and XMS X1–3] (http://www.e-codices.unifr.ch/en/description/csg/0196)

X[1] St. Gallen, Stiftsbibliothek 446 (s. x) [XMS X4] (http://www.e-codices.unifr.ch/en/description/csg/0446)

Y Reykjavík, Stofnun Árna Magnússonar, AM 687d, 4° (Iceland, *c.* 1500) [contains OIR]

Z Karlsruhe, Badische Landesbibliothek, Aug. perg. 205 (Reichenau, s. x) [contains XMS Z1–6 (the so-called *Reichenau Riddles*)]

Bibliographical Abbreviations

Abbreviations for Old English texts follow those provided in *DOE*.

AL	Riese, Alexander, ed. *Anthologia Latina, pars prior: Carmina in codicibus scripta*. 2nd ed., 2 vols. Leipzig: Teubner, 1894–1906.
BCLL	Lapidge, Michael, and Richard Sharpe. *A Bibliography of Celtic-Latin Literature, 400–1200*. Dublin: Royal Irish Academy, 1985.
CCSL	Corpus Christianorum, Series Latina. Turnhout, 1953–.
CPL	Dekkers, Eligius, and Aemilius Gaar. *Corpus Patrum Latinorum*. 3rd ed. Steenbrugge, 1995.
DMLBS	Latham, R. E., D. R. Howlett, and R. K. Ashdowne. *Dictionary of Medieval Latin from British Sources*. Oxford: British Academy, 1975–2013.
DOE	*Dictionary of Old English: A–I online*. Ed. Antonette diPaolo Healey, et al. Toronto, 2018.
G–L	Gneuss, Helmut, and Michael Lapidge. *A Bibliographical Handlist of Manuscripts and Manuscript Fragments Written or Owned in England up to 1100*. Toronto: University of Toronto Press, 2014. [cited by entry number]
ICUR	Rossi, Giovanni Battista de, ed. *Inscriptiones Christianae Urbis Romae*. 2 vols. Rome, 1861–88.
MGH	Monumenta Germaniae Historica. AA — Auctores Antiquissimi. PLAC — Poetae Latini Aevi Carolini.

OEALRT Orchard, Andy. *The Old English and Anglo-Latin Riddle Tradition*. Dumbarton Oaks Medieval Library LXIX. Cambridge, MA: Harvard University Press, 2019.

PN Mastandrea, P., and Luigi Tessarolo. *Poetria Nova 2: A CD-ROM of Latin Medieval Poetry (650–1250 A.D.), with a Gateway to Classical and Late Antique Texts*. Florence: SISMEL, 2010.

PSLMA Walther, H. *Proverbia Sententiaeque Latinitatis Medii Aevi*. 5 vols. Göttingen, 1963–69.

SK Schaller, Dieter, and Ewald Könsgen. *Initia carminum Latinorum seculo undecimo antiquiorum*. Göttingen: Vandenhoeck and Ruprecht, 1977.

SK Sup. Schaller, Dieter, and Ewald Könsgen, with Thomas Klein. *Initia carminum Latinorum seculo undecimo antiquiorum: Supplementband*. Göttingen: Vandenhoeck and Ruprecht, 2005.

The Anglo-Latin Tradition

ALDHELM

Authorship and Date

Aldhelm (b. 639 or 640, d. 709 or 710) is one of the most important, prolific, and widely read authors of the Anglo-Saxon period, a deeply learned and innovative scholar whose writings were rightly celebrated in his own lifetime. His works were highly prized by later generations, to judge not only from the number of manuscripts that survive, but also by the sheer amount of indebtedness to him of later Anglo-Saxons, both at the verbal and thematic levels. It appears that Aldhelm was a son of the West Saxon King Centwine (676–685), but that, like several other members of his family, he chose the church above a potential (or, in some cases, continuing) royal career. Nonetheless, his royal connections may well have contributed to his ultimate preferment, as he became abbot of Malmesbury around 685, and traveled to Rome in 688 accompanying his kinsman Ceadwalla, a successor to Centwine, who had abdicated his throne sometime between 682 and 685 and retired (also to Malmesbury). Aldhelm ultimately became the first bishop of the newly created see of Sherborne in 705/6, which he held until his death. We know from Aldhelm's own letters that he was initially educated by an Irish teacher (presumably at Malmesbury), but that he considered his education to have been completed rather later in life when he attended the celebrated school established at Canterbury sometime after 670 by Archbishop Theodore (602–690), a Greek-speaking monk from

Tarsus, and Abbot Hadrian (d. 709), a North African with a reputation as a superb scholar of Latin.

Aldhelm himself describes the *aenigmata* as among his earliest works, and ALD seems to have been sent as part of the composite *Epistola ad Acircium* sent to King Aldfrith of Northumbria (685–705) shortly after his accession in 685. In the *Epistola,* which survives complete in five manuscripts and three fragments, ALD appears third in a sequence of four texts, following a treatise on the significance of the number seven and another "on meters" *(De metris),* and preceding another "on the rules of metrical feet" *(De pedum regulis).* Such a context is important for understanding certain features of ALD, which seems sometimes designed to illustrate aspects of Latin poetics rather than to promote any sense of enigmatic mystery. This is particularly clear when the metrical patterning of ALD is compared with that found in his other major verse works, namely the 428 lines of the *Carmina ecclesiastica* ("ecclesiastical poems") and the 2941 lines of the *Carmen de virginitate* ("poem on virginity"). Not only do the 801 lines of ALD display markedly greater metrical variety than the other works, but they have a clear preponderance of patterns that Aldhelm rarely uses elsewhere. Likewise, several of the aenigmata in ALD comprise either entirely or mostly different metrical patterns, or conversely repeat the same metrical pattern: both strategies would of course be useful in a classroom context (for some particularly striking examples, see further the headnotes to ALD 56, ALD 76, and ALD 92). If the focus on metrical patterning essentially offers practical illustration of the theoretical material that makes up the treatise *De metris* which precedes ALD in the relevant manuscripts, another aspect does the same for the further treatise *De pedum regulis,* which follows in the same manuscripts. In composing *De pedum regulis,* Aldhelm performed a signal service for would-be composers of Latin poetry, by providing (apparently for the first time) lists of words that fit particular metrical patterns, so allowing them to be inserted at the appropriate place in the line.

Likewise, several of the aenigmata contain sequences of synonyms or near-synonyms scanned variously, thereby offering the same flexibility and service to aspiring poets. Some of the synonyms are found in aenigmata whose solutions may offer clues to their content, such as the synonyms for "fire" and "water" in ALD 54 (*COCUMA DUPLEX*, "double boiler"), but in other cases the connection between solutions and synonyms is more oblique. ALD 70 (*TORTELLA*, "loaf of bread"), for example, has a series of synonyms for "shield," presumably prompted by the shared round shape of both in Anglo-Saxon England.

Set in the larger context of the didactic project of using ALD to teach meter, the *Prose Preface* gives an interesting perspective on Aldhelm's attitudes: he cites three basic models for his aenigmata, namely the Bible (quoting only from the Old Testament), Aristotle, and Symphosius, and it is surely notable that these three ideals are in Hebrew, Greek, and Latin respectively, the so-called *tres linguae sacrae* ("three holy languages") of Christian theology. In other words, as is clear also from the range and trajectory of the subjects, as well as the manuscript transmission, in composing his aenigmata Aldhelm sought to teach not only the principles of Latin poetry, but an encyclopedic attitude, based largely, but not entirely, on Isidore, towards appreciating the wider world both within and beyond the classroom.

Manuscript Context(s)

ALD survives in two quite distinct recensions, one of which appears to be a revised version of the other, and in general corrects metrical infelicities in what is presumed to be the original version. The first recension is found in only three manuscripts, one from the early eighth century (A) and two from the twelfth (F^1F^2, where the second is an apograph of the first). Apart from a number of distinctive readings highlighting the difficulties that composing Latin metrical verse presents for a nonnative speaker, it is characterized both by lacking any numbering of the constituent aenigmata and by giving the titles/solutions in the nominative case; the second recension uniformly employs the preposition *DE* ("about"), followed by the ablative case, perhaps after the model of the two treatises *De metris* and *De pedum regulis,* which contain many subsections similarly titled. The second recension is extant in part or in whole in no fewer than twenty separate manuscripts, and there are a number of further fragmentary or now-lost witnesses. While the metrical improvements are most likely by Aldhelm himself, the rubrics cannot be, since several of them are problematic or demonstrably wrong (see, for example, the headnote to ALD 7 (*FATUM,* "fate"). Although there is considerable doubt whether the solutions originally traveled alongside the aenigmata or not, in offering my preferred solutions I have chosen here to follow Aldhelm's first-recension manuscripts by adopting the nominative form. At least seventeen relevant manuscripts considered here contain ALD (ABDF^{1}F^{2}GKLNOP^{3}P^{4}RTUVW), and in no fewer than fifteen of them (the exceptions are F^{1}F^2), ALD circulates alongside SYM, including in the earliest manuscript, A (s. viii^2), and in the two important Anglo-Saxon compendia G and L. It is likewise important to note that in seven of those manuscripts the only aenigmata from the Anglo-Saxon riddle tradition are those of ALD and SYM (ABKP^{4}TVW); the figure rises to thirteen if the parameters are extended to include just one other text (D also contains the *Leiden Riddle,* OP^3 ALF, R BON, and U LOR). The only other text from the tradition that travels alone alongside ALD is ALF (in the two related twelfth-century manuscripts containing the first recension F^{1}F^2). Such a significant presence across such a range and variety of manuscripts only emphasizes Aldhelm's central role in the Anglo-Saxon riddle tradition.

Five of the aenigmata in ALD are also found in the pseudo-Bede *Collectanea* (see the headnotes to ALD 2, 3, 4, 9, and 90), again interspersed with five from SYM (see the headnotes to SYM 1, 4, 7, 10, and 12). It is striking that the preponderance of these selections should come from the beginning of both collections, and such a choice may again emphasize the extent to which the texts in the Anglo-Saxon riddle tradition tended to circulate in a classroom context, where a particular focus tends to be placed on the beginnings of texts.

Subject Matter and Solutions

It has long been noted that several of the aenigmata in ALD appear sequentially connected: see, for example, the headnotes to ALD 63 (*CORBUS,* "raven"), ALD 64 (*COLUMBA,* "dove"), ALD 76 (*MELARIUS,* "apple tree"), and ALD 77 (*FICULNEA,* "fig tree"). It is only recently, however, that an attempt has been made (by Salvador-Bello, "Patterns of Compilation") to offer an overarching narrative to explain the structure of the collection as a whole, and to connect it to similar sequences more readily perceived in (for example) BON, TAT, and EUS, as well as elsewhere in the Anglo-Saxon riddle tradition, notably SYM and EXE.

There are a significant number of aenigmata in ALD where the solutions are given in both Latin and Greek, or where the solutions given include what seem to be glosses (the total proportion is 35%); see further the headnote to ALD 5 (*IRIS,* "rainbow"), where several clusters and sequences, elsewhere commonplace throughout the tradition, are highlighted. The aenigmata gradually increase in length, with a range of solutions that is grand indeed, beginning with the briefest (four lines, presumably a conscious decision to outdo the three-line aenigmata of Symphosius) and culminating in the eighty-three lines of the last, ALD 100 (*CREATURA,* "creation").

Style

Aldhelm's verse is generally end-stopped and rhythmically repetitive; he shows a marked aversion to such metrical niceties as elision, notwithstanding the fact that the aenigmata are presented in the context of two metrical treatises that are themselves highly original, and indeed more practical than many of their putative models in offering nonnative speakers essential assistance in the composition of Latin verse. Aldhelm's verse as a whole is highly formulaic, whether borrowing freely and frequently from the phrasing of previous poets, recasting earlier words in a distinctive style of his own, or simply repeating idiosyncratic and favored combinations. An analysis of compound adjectives, together with those formed from the (mostly poetic) suffixes *-abilis, -alis, -eus, -fer, -ficus, -genus, -ger,* and *-osus,* reveals Aldhelm's deep fondness for these rather flamboyant forms, some much rarer than others, but including several rare forms such as *aethralis* (100.12), *aquosus* (38.2), *arcitenens* (100.19; also BON 5.13), *astrifer* (35.4 and 86.3; also EUS 40.4), *biformis* (28.1), *brumalis* (92.10; also EUS 47.5), *campester* (47.8), *cenosus* (43.1), *discolor* (82.1), *flammiger* (92.9; also EUS 49.3, BON 10.11), *fluctivagus* (73.7), *frondiger* (91.6), *fructifer* (84.8), *glandifer* (100.49), *horrisonus* (2.3), *latebrosus* (100.56), *lucifluus* (PR.2 and 6.3; also EUS 58.2, BON 2.11 and

20.6, LOR 3.2, SYM 95.1), *melliger* (32.1), *memphiticus* (36.6), *mulcifer* (27.4; also LOR 5.6), *naviger* (92.4), *nemorosus* (84.9), *ostriger* (98.1), *pedester* (84.5), *penniger* (26.3; also EUS 40.1 and 43.1), *pinifer* (93.7), *piscosus* (16.2), *pruinosus* (67.1), *ramosus* (45.1), *raucisonus* (22.1 and 35.5), *retrogradus* (37.3; also BON 12.15), *rubicundus* (47.4), *rugosus* (40.1 and 86.1), *setiger* (17.2, 33.2, 36.5, 39.1, 100.10; also EUS 52.2, SYM 36.1), *spumifer* (37.2), *spumosus* (83.1), *squamiger* (31.4), *squamosus* (19.1 and 24.4), *versicolor* (3.1; also TAT 9.1, BON 20.1, SYM 58.2), *versificus* (PR.14), none of which appears more than ninety times throughout the whole 900,000 lines of the assembled corpus of Latin poetry up to 1250 in *PN* (so less than 0.01% of the total). If we include all such compound adjectives, from the rarest to the most banal, there are ninety-four such adjectives found here, or roughly one per *aenigma*, a frequency somewhat higher than that found in other collections, with the striking exceptions of BON and LOR (see further the comments on style in the relevant headnotes).

Sources and Parallels

Aldhelm tells us explicitly in his *Prose Preface* that among his models was Symphosius, twelve of whose aenigmata he quotes on thirteen separate occasions in the course of his two metrical treatises *De metris* and *De pedum regulis*. The one hundred aenigmata that constitute SYM evidently encouraged Aldhelm to produce a hundred of his own, and some subtle recognition of the numerical debt may be seen in the fact that the penultimate line of ALD 100, just before the closing challenge, speaks of a "reader" potentially considering the aenigmata as "frivolous things" *(frivola lector),* two terms that are found with some prominence in SYM PR (at lines 10 and 17). Aldhelm's primary debt to Symphosius, clearly acknowledged in the *Prose Preface* to ALD, is also apparent in the many conceptual and verbal parallels linking aenigmata on closely related themes in the two collections, such as ALD 3 (*NUBES,* "cloud") and SYM 8 (*NEBULA,* "cloud"), ALD 11 (*POALUM,* "bellows") and SYM 73 (*UTERFOLLIS,* "bellows"), ALD 12 (*BOMBIX,* "silkworm") and SYM 17 (*ARANEA,* "spider"), ALD 30 (*ELEMENTUM,* "letter of the alphabet") and SYM 1 (*GRAPHIUM,* "stylus"), ALD 32 (*PUGILLARES,* "writing tablets") and SYM 1

(*GRAPHIUM,* "stylus"), ALD 34 (*LOCUSTA,* "locust") and SYM 24 (*CURCULIO,* "weevil"), ALD 44 (*IGNIS,* "fire") and SYM 67 (*LANTERNA,* "lantern"), ALD 46 (*URTICA,* "nettle") and SYM 44 (*CAEPA,* "onion"), ALD 49 (*LEBES,* "pot") and SYM 89 (*STRIGILIS AENEA,* "bronze strigil"), ALD 58 (*VESPER SIDUS,* "evening star") and SYM 28 (*VESPERTILIO,* "bat"), ALD 66 (*MOLA,* "mill") and SYM 79 (*ROTAE,* "wheels"), ALD 75 (*CRABRO,* "hornet") and SYM 65 (*SAGITTA,* "arrow"), ALD 90 (*PUERPERA GEMINAS ENIXA,* "woman bearing twins") and SYM 93 (*MULIER QUAE GEMINOS PARIEBAT,* "mother of twins"), ALD 96 (*ELEFANS,* "elephant") and SYM 49 (*EBUR,* "ivory"). Likewise, ALD 99 (*CAMELLUS,* "camel") is based on a terrible pun on the name of the Roman consul Camillus, just as SYM 25 (*MUS,* "mouse") and SYM 32 (*TAURUS,* "bull") have similarly painful puns on the names of two other famous Romans. Other aenigmata have a less obviously direct connection, explored in the notes below, but Aldhelm has apparently bridged the gap through a verbal link, so allowing us an interesting insight into the way his mind must have worked, apparently prompting such odd associations as ALD 1 (*TERRA,* "earth") and SYM 11 (*NIX,* "snow"), ALD 2 (*VENTUS,* "wind") and SYM 58 (*CAPILLUS,* "hair"), ALD 11 (*POALUM,* "bellows") and SYM 31 (*PHOENIX,* "phoenix"), ALD 22 (*ACALANTIDA,* "nightingale") and SYM 59 (*PILA,* "ball"), ALD 29 (*AQUA,* "water") and SYM 14 (*PULLUS IN OVO,* "chick in egg"), ALD 30 (*ELEMENTUM,* "letter of the alphabet") and SYM 26 (*GRUS,* "crane"), ALD 36 (*SCNIFES,* "midge") and SYM 33 (*LUPUS,* "wolf"), ALD 74 (*FUNDIBALUM,* "sling") and SYM 35 (*CAPRA,* "she-goat"), ALD 78 (*CUPA VINARIA,* "wine cask") and SYM 42 (*BETA,* "beet").

In a different manner, Aldhelm's etymological interest is particularly apparent in those aenigmata that refer directly to the specific word for the creature in question in Latin or Greek or both; there are fifteen such aenigmata: ALD 1 (*TERRA,* "earth"), ALD 18 (*MYRMICOLEON,* "ant lion"), ALD 28 (*MINOTAURUS,* "Minotaur"), ALD 33 (*LORICA,* "armor"), ALD 35 (*NYCTICORAX,* "night-raven"), ALD 37 (*CANCER,* "crab"), ALD 43 (*SANGUISUGA,* "leech"), ALD 47 (*HIRUNDO,* "swallow"), ALD 50 (*MYRIFYLLON,* "milfoil, yarrow"), ALD 51 (*ELIOTROPUS,* "heliotrope"), ALD 58 (*VESPER SIDUS,* "evening star"), ALD 60 (*MONOCERUS,* "unicorn"), ALD 65 (*MURICEPS,* "mouser"), ALD 91 (*PALMA,* "palm"), and ALD 95 (*SCILLA,* "Scylla"). A different kind of interest in words, and one which influenced many subsequent collections, is evinced in the three logogriphs ALD 63 (*CORBUS,* "raven" → *ORBUS,* "widow"), ALD 70 (*TORTELLA,* "loaf of bread," where *spelta,* "grain" → *pelta,* "shield"), and ALD 86 (*ARIES,* "ram" → *PARIES,* "wall of a house"), all of which play on the spellings of the creatures in question, and indeed elsewhere Aldhelm talks of "playful letters" (Eh, 75: *ludibundis apicibus*); see further the headnote to ALD 63. In his focus on such bookish aspects of words, Aldhelm simply echoes his immediate sources, of which Isidore is clearly the most significant (see in particular the *Index of Parallels* with Isidore's *Etymologiae* below).

In this context, Sk notes that manuscript L contains no fewer than forty-one extended glosses on the text of ALD that can be traced back, often verbatim, to Isidore, *Etymologiae,* as is made clear here in the headnotes to ALD 1, 5, 8, 9, 12, 15, 17, 18, 20, 24, 25, 37, 40, 42, 46, 49, 51, 53, 56, 61, 82, 98, and 99; further extended glosses are noted at PR.4 and PR.13; ALD 1.4, 4.3, 13.1, 14.4, 25.5, 28.4, 36.6, 45.5 and 6, 47.9, 88.3, 89.4; and 100.47, 49, 65, and 82. The total tally of all those aenigmata in ALD that either focus explicitly on etymological factors, or can be otherwise explained by reference to Isidore's *Etymologiae* (or both) accounts for forty-three out of the one hundred in the collection. Sk (at 48–54) also discusses the Old English glosses in L, which appear in two hands. There are sixty-seven of them, including two in the *Prose Preface,* where *cola* is glossed as *lim,* "members, limbs," and *commata* as *limes dæl,* "parts of members," "parts of limbs." Twenty-four of the one hundred aenigmata that make up ALD cover all eight chapters of Book 12 (Isidore, *Etym.* 12.1.8–8.14), but are somewhat scattered throughout the collection (see the individual notes at ALD 12, 15–18, 20, 28, 31, 35–37, 39, 42–43, 56, 60, 63, 65, 82, 86, 88, 96, 99, and 100).

This Text and Translation

This edition essentially follows that of Eh, which gives an extensive recording of manuscript variants which I have much simplified here, focusing on the four most important Anglo-Saxon manuscripts containing multiple collections of aenigmata, namely BGLO, as well as D, which contains ALD, SYM, and LEI. Eh gives priority to the readings of the so-called first recension, especially the witness of the eighth-century manuscript A, but I have highlighted in the notes changes (generally correcting faulty scansion) made in the course of the second recension; for examples, see the notes at ALD 6.4, 12.2, 14.1, 18.4, 19.4, 30.1, 42.3, 44.8, 52.7, 53.8–9, 54.1–2, 58.4–5, 60.3, 74.3, 82.1, 95.5, and 100.37. I have also made extensive use of the translations in LR, St, and Ju (with whom I shared a first draft of what follows).

Further Reading

Manitius, "Zu Aldhelm und Beda"; Cook, "Aldhelm's Legal Studies"; Pitman, *Riddles of Aldhelm*; Campbell, "Some Linguistic Features"; Lagorio, "Aldhelm's Aenigmata"; Winterbottom, "Aldhelm's Prose Style"; Howe, "Aldhelm's *Enigmata*"; Lapidge and Rosier, *Aldhelm: The Poetic Works;* Cameron, "Aldhelm as Naturalist"; Orchard, "After Aldhelm"; Orchard, *Poetic Art;* Scott, "Rhetorical and Symbolic Ambiguity"; Stork, *Through a Gloss Darkly;* Crane, "Describing the World"; Milanović-Barham, "Aldhelm's *Enigmata* and Byzantine Riddles"; Rusche, "Isidore's *Etymologiae*"; Thornbury, "Aldhelm's Rejection of the Muses"; Ruff, "Metrics"; Salvador-Bello, "Patterns of Compilation"; Salvador-Bello, "Sexual Riddle Type"; Lapidge, "Career of Aldhelm"; Lapidge, "Aldhelmus Malmesberiensis Abb. et Scireburnensis ep"; Salvador-Bello, *Isidorean Perceptions,* 177–221 and 460–61.

ALD PR

MANUSCRIPTS: D, fol. 10v–11r; L, fol. 83; G, fol. 394v–95r; B, fol. 59v; O, fol. 1r–v.

EARLIER EDITIONS AND TRANSLATIONS: Eh, 97–99; Gl, 377–81; LR, 70–71; Sk, 93–99; Ju, 2–7 and 77–85. (SK 961)

The *Preface,* with its ambitious hexameter acrostic-telestich spelling out (albeit with some slight numerical exaggeration) the notion that

"Aldhelm has sung songs in thousands of verses" *(ALDHELMUS CECINIT MILLENIS VERSIBUS ODAS),* is a highly crafted poem and a fitting tour de force to begin the collection. It is notable that Aldhelm leads off with his own name, just as he concludes the *Preface* with two lines asking God for forgiveness of sins, presumably primarily his own; it is worth pointing out that the Old English poet Cynewulf uses a similar technique in his own runic signatures. Aldhelm exploits the exigencies of the acrostic-telestich form to his own advantage, so that the larger structure of the poem provides sentence breaks that coincide neatly with the first three words of the resulting hexameter. In seeking out words which end in the required final letter for each line, Aldhelm is led to some odd choices, including the proper names *Uehemoth, Iob* (evidently scanned imaginatively as disyllabic with first syllable long: *Īob*), and *David,* as well as the Hebrew-derived *cephal* (a usage evidently imitated later in EUS 45.3 [*DE CAMELEONE,* "about a camelopard"]). It is striking that he never repeats a final word, despite the difficulty of finding (for example) four words ending in *-l* and two each in *–c* and *–d.* Similarly varied are all the many different words employed here for "poem," "song," "singing," or "poet" *(metrorum carmina . . . versibus aenigmata . . . cantibus . . . versificum . . . carmen . . . metrica . . . carmina vatem . . . cecinisse . . . psalmista canens metrorum cantica . . . aenigmata versu . . . ritu dactilico . . . cecinit . . . carmine),* with barely a repeated word in the whole display. The range of possibilities for scansion and metrical placement offers a kind of *gradus* or collection of alternative forms for the aspiring poet, just as many of Aldhelm's other aenigmata seem to do; see for example the notes at ALD 13 (*BARBITA,* "organ"), 37 (*CANCER,* "crab"), 39 (*LEO,* "lion"), 40 (*PIPER,* "pepper"), 69 (*TAXUS,* "yew"), 70 (*TORTELLA,* "loaf of bread"), and 75 (*CRABRO,* "hornet"). This listing is very much in the spirit of his *De pedum regulis,* which dul(l)y catalogs different words with the same metrical pattern, and immediately follows the *Aenigmata* in several manuscripts.

As if to underline that part of the purpose of the piece is poetic training, Aldhelm displays here a much wider range of caesura-patterning than is his norm: lines 7, 8, 11, 13, 18, 23, and 29 all deviate from the strong masculine caesura that Aldhelm employs almost universally elsewhere. In a similar vein, Aldhelm's use of unusual monosyllabic and quadrisyllabic endings in lines 12, 19, and 26 marks this passage as a set piece; the single example of hiatus in line 25 is likewise striking (there are no elisions at all in the poem, unless the reading *almi,* found in L, is accepted for *prisci* in line 18).

The Old Testament references to Behemoth, Moses, Job, and David are balanced very carefully by classical ones to Castalian nymphs and the twin peaks of Parnassus and Cynthus. It is notable that here *lucifer* (ALD PR.23) is simply the morning star, and part of a wider pattern of poetic light-shedding and wandering that is enshrined in the Latin verb *lustro* (which implies both), and lies at the heart of the play of word and image in the middle passage of the poem, where the words *perlustro . . . illustria . . . lustrat* (lines 12, 19, and 20) clearly echo each other; see further the note at ALD 5.4 (*IRIS,* "rainbow"). The allusion to Persius in lines 12–13 is at once a gesture toward a somewhat obscure (during the early Medieval period, at least) classical poet whose works Aldhelm cites by name on no fewer than three occasions in the metrical treatises *De metris* (Eh 78.12–14 and 88.2–3) and *De pedum regulis* (Eh 168.7).

The middle section (ALD PR.10–13) details four kinds of classical pagan poetic inspiration: by Muses, by eating nectar, by wandering on Cynthus, by sleeping, and by dreaming on Parnassus. It is notable that this passage is not only bracketed by references to "God" (*Deus:* ALD PR.9 and 14), but also spells out "blind ones" (*CECI*) in the acrostic-telestich form: in such ways Aldhelm expresses his disapproval. God is referred to by four different designations: *Arbiter, praesul, deus* (twice), and *genitor,* and acts in four different ways: *disponis, largire, rependis, servas;* such numerological exposition is matched elsewhere in the *Epistola ad Acircium,* where the number in question is not four but seven.

See also Crane, "Describing the World," 59–64; Orchard, "Performing Writing and Singing Silence," 75–77; Thornbury, "Aldhelm's Rejection of the Muses"; Salvador-Bello, *Isidorean Perceptions,* 175–77.

PR.1 Compare BON 5.15 *(Arbiter, aethereus)*; ALD 7.4 *(Sceptra regens mundi)* and 99.2 *(regni sceptra regebat)*.

PR.4 For Behemoth, see Job 40:15–24; Enoch 60:7–8. The extended gloss in L derives from Isidore, *Etym.* 8.11.27 *(Behemoth)*.

PR.7 Compare Corippus, *Iust.* 3.145 *(Tot divinarum miracula pandere rerum)*.

PR.9 Compare Prudentius, *Apotheosis* 632 *(quae dona rependam)*.

PR.10 Compare Aldhelm, *Carmen de virginitate* 24 *(Nec peto Castalidas metrorum cantica nimphas)*; Paulinus of Nola, *Carmen* 15.30 *(Non ego Castalidas vatum phantasmata Musas)*. Eh notes several instances where Aldhelm seems to use *istuc* in the sense "to here" rather than the usual "to there."

PR.10–14 For Parnassus, see too Isidore, *Etym.* 14.8.11.

PR.11 See further Thornbury, "Aldhelm's Rejection of the Muses," 80.

PR.12 For the monosyllabic ending here *(nec)*, compare ALD PR.19 *(sol)*, 67.8 *(nix)*; Aldhelm, *Carmen ecclesiasticum* 2.26 (= *Carmen de virginitate* 1704); *Carmen de virginitate* PR.21, 556, and 1460.

PR.12–13 Compare Persius, *Preface to the Satires* 3 *(nec in bicipiti somniasse Parnaso)*.

PR.13 Compare Ovid, *Metamorphoses* 9.475 *(somnia vidi)*. The extended gloss in L derives from Isidore, *Etym.* 14.8.11 *(Parnassus)*.

PR.15 Compare Cyprianus Gallus, *Genesis* 196 *(munera mentis)*.

PR.16 For the biblical story, see Exodus 15:1–18; compare Venantius Fortunatus, *Vita S. Martini* 4.453 *(corde rependit)*.

PR.17 Compare ALD 57.2 *(carmine vates)*, 79.2 *(carmina vatum)*, and 97.3 *(NOX*, "night": *carmine vates)*; BON 13.44 *(carmina vatum)*; BIB 5.7 *(carmina vatum)*; Aldhelm, *Carmen de virginitate* praef. 1, virg. 2010 *(metrica . . . carmina)*.

PR.18 On Aldhelm's occasional use of anomalous scansion, in this case *prĭsci,* see Orchard, *Poetic Art of Aldhelm,* 74–79. Compare Aldhelm, *Carmen de virginitate* 1104 and 2900 *(vexilla tropei).*

PR.19 Compare *Miracula S. Nyniae* 10 *(late per populos),* 98 *(late per populos lustravit),* and 155 *(late per populos).* On the monosyllabic ending *sol* here, see the note at PR.12 above.

PR.20 The unusual and ultimately Greek-derived term *cephal* is also found at EUS 41.1 and 45.3; as well as in Aldhelm, *Carmen de virginitate* 1016 and the anonymous *Miracula S. Nyniae* 144. It is interesting to note that while Aldhelm and the *Miracula S. Nyniae* scan the word *cēphal,* EUS has variously *cĕphăl* and *cĕphāla.*

PR.21 See further Psalms 109:3 (*ex utero ante luciferum genui te,* "from the womb before the day star I begot thee"); Caelius Sedulius, *Carmen paschale* 1.23–26. For variants on the phrase *psalmista canens,* compare Aldhelm, *Carmen de virginitate* 33, 458, 885, 1644, and 2581. See too Aldhelm, *Carmen de virginitate* 24 *(metrorum cantica).*

PR.24 Compare BON 2.11 *(lumina saeclis)* and 5.2 *(splendida . . . saeclis);* Bede, *Vita S. Cudbercti* 1 *(fulgescere lumina saeclis)* and 503 *(lumina saeclis); Miracula S. Nyniae* 16 *(lumina seclis).*

PR.26–29 Compare Thornbury, "Aldhelm's Rejection of the Muses," 76–79.

PR.26 For the unusual pentasyllabic ending here *(rusticitate),* compare ALD 30.2 *(annumerandas),* as well as the quadrisyllabic endings at ALD 4.1 *(moderante),* 13.2 *(modulentur),* 30.3 *(moribundae),* 57.1 *(Ganimidis),* 84.3 *(duodenis),* and 100.47 *(calamistro); Carmen de virginitate* 325, 2502, and 2699. In producing such polysyllabic endings apparently as a rhetorical flourish or ornament, Aldhelm seems to have inspired imitation: it is notable that BED has six in only 32 lines (see the note at BED 1.3

below) and TAT contains twelve examples of quadrisyllabic endings in only 213 verses (see the note at TAT 1.10 below). In employing such exotic forms, Aldhelm seems to have been ahead of his time: not until the ninth century did poets regularly begin to exploit such forms.

PR.28 Compare Juvencus, *Evangelia* 1.521 and 2.308 *(molimina mentis)*; also Lucan, *Bellum civile* 9.612 *(vana specie)*.

PR.30 Compare *Miracula S. Nyniae* 107 *(moderans eternis legibus illas)*.

PR.32–34 For the biblical story, see Psalms 77:16 and 106:9; Exodus 14:37–15:21. The phrasing from Psalms 77:16 seems closest: *et eduxit aquam de petra et deduxit tamquam flumina aquas*, "He brought forth water out of the rock: and made streams run down as rivers."

PR.33 Compare Cyprianus Gallus, *Exodus* 1029 *(marmore rubro)*.

PR.34 Compare BON 1.8 *(cecinit quod carmine David)*; Alcuin, *Carmen* 1 603 *(cecinit . . . David)*. See too Aldhelm, *Carmen ecclesiasticum* 4.9.10 *(Ut quondam cecinit psalmorum carmine vates)*; Aldhelm, *Carmen de virginitate* 1158 *(cecinit sponsali carmine vatis)*, 1912 *(Ut cecinit dudum famosus carmine vates)*; 2139 *(Ut cecinit quondam famoso carmine princeps)*; 2772 *(cecinit quod carmine vates)*.

PR.35 Compare ALD 8.3 *(arce poli)* and 53.7 *(arce polorum)*.

ALD 1

MANUSCRIPTS: D, fol. 11r; L, fol. 84r; G, fol. 395r; B, fol. 60r; O, fol. 1v.

EARLIER EDITIONS AND TRANSLATIONS: Eh, 99; Gl, 382–83; LR, 71; Sk, 100–101; Ju, 4–5 and 85. (SK 681)

SOLUTION: *TERRA* (earth), although Aldhelm seems in his use of the imagery of suckling to toy with the potential solution *SAPIENTIA* (wisdom), which opens other riddle collections, such as ps-BED 1 (see the note there). See further Sebo, *In Enigmate*, 73–74.

The feminine nature of the solution here is made grammatically plain in the opening word: *altrix*. The extended gloss in L derives from Isidore, *Etym.* 14.1.1 *(terra).*

1.2 The deponent form *nuncupor* is rare; compare BON 10.6 (*VIRGINITAS,* "virginity").

1.3 Compare Bede (?), *De die iudicii* 105 *(lacerant . . . dentibus).*

1.4 Compare SYM 11.2 *(Sole madens, aestate fluens);* ALD 22.5 *(bruma . . . aestate);* ALD 77.7 *(brumae . . . tempore);* ALC 9.1 *(tempore brumae);* Bede, *Vita S. Cudbercti* 185 *(sub tempore brumae);* Frithegod, *Breviloquium S. Wilfridi* 567 *(tempora brumae).* The extended gloss in L derives from Isidore, *Etym.* 5.35.6 *(bruma).*

ALD 2

MANUSCRIPTS: D, fol. 11r; L, fol. 84r; G, fol. 395r; B, fol. 60r; O, fol. 1v.

EARLIER EDITIONS AND TRANSLATIONS: Eh, 99–100; Gl, 384–85; LR, 71; Sk, 102–95; Ju, 4–5 and 85–86. See further Crane, "Describing the World," 68–75; Hill, "Saturn's Time Riddle"; Orchard, "Enigma Variations," 294–95; Anlezark, *Solomon and Saturn.* (SK 2106)

SOLUTION: *VENTUS* (wind), although on the face of it others are feasible, including *DEUS* (God).

In this context, EXE 1 (*GODES WIND,* "the wind of God") looks very much like an extended reverie on ALD 2, while in the parallel riddle in SOL 2, a quite different solution, "old age," is explicitly given. See too ALC D46, BER 41, ps-BED 5 (all *VENTUS*). There are also some broad parallels to be found in *Hisperica famina* A479–96 (*DE VENTO,* "on wind"; see further Herren, *Hisperica Famina: The A-Text;* Orchard, "*Hisperica famina* as Literature").

2.1 Compare SYM 58.1 *(Findere me nulli possunt);* TAT 1.8 *(Nulla manus poterit nec me contingere visus)* and 2.5 *(cernere que nullus nec pandere septa valebit);* BON 1.1 *(Vincere me nulli possunt).* See too Aldhelm, *Carmen de virginitate* 1730 *(prendere palmis).*

2.3 Compare BON 12.5 *(Viribus . . . valeo).*

2.3–4 Compare Aldhelm, *Carmen rhythmicum* 39–44, describing a mighty storm *(Cumque flatus victoriae / non furerent ingloriae / tremebat tellus turbida / atque eruta robora / cadebant cum verticibus / simul raptis radicibus).*

2.4 Compare BON 1.4 and LOR 2.6 *(rura peragro).*

ALD 3

MANUSCRIPTS: D, fol. 11r; L, fol. 84r–v; G, fol. 395r; B, fol. 60r; O, fol. 1v.

EARLIER EDITIONS AND TRANSLATIONS: Eh, 100; Gl, 384–85; LR, 71; Sk, 103; Ju, 4–5 and 86. (SK 17143)

SOLUTION: *NUBES* (cloud). SYM 8 (*NEBULA,* "cloud") has a similar answer.

The sympathetic reference to exile aligns this aenigma with a large part of the extant Old English tradition, here given a twist by the fact that this exile has no place in heaven or on earth, a feature emphasized by the chiastic arrangement of "heaven . . . earth . . . earth . . . heaven" in ALD 3.1–2 *(caelum terramque . . . tellure . . . parte polorum).*

3.1 The form *versicolor* also appears in SYM 58.2, TAT 9.1, and BON 20.1 (as *vericolor*). Compare ALD 49.2 *(caelum . . . terramve)* and 97.16 *(caeli . . . terraeque);* ps-ALC 8.2 *(caeli terraeque);* BON 19.7 *(caelum terramve);* Statius, *Thebaid* 11.692 *(caelum terramque reliqui).*

ALD 4

MANUSCRIPTS: D, fol. 11r–v; L, fol. 84v; G, fol. 395r; B, fol. 60r; O, fol. 1v.

EARLIER EDITIONS AND TRANSLATIONS: Eh, 100; Gl, 386–87; LR, 71; Sk, 104; Ju, 6–7 and 86–87. (SK 2848)

SOLUTION: *NATURA* (nature). See further Sebo, *In Enigmate,* 73–74.

The phrase *crede mihi* is a loaded one, since it is so closely associated with Christ's identical exclamation in the Vulgate (John 4:21). The combination of natural phenomena and the question of their controller which are shot through ALD 1–4 have many parallels in EXE 1.

4.1 Compare Lucan, *Bellum civile* 8.504 *(nulla manet).*
4.3 The extended gloss in L derives from Isidore, *Etym.* 13.5.6 (note the use of *convexa* here).
4.4 Compare Lucan, *Bellum civile* 9.6 *(lunaeque meatus)* and 9.693 *(lunaeque meatibus);* Wulfstan Cantor of Winchester, *Vita S. Swithuni* 1.392 *(lunaeque meatum).*

ALD 5

MANUSCRIPTS: D, fol. 11v; L, fol. 84v; G, fol. 395r; B, fol. 60r; O, fol. 1v–2r.

EARLIER EDITIONS AND TRANSLATIONS: Eh, 100; Gl, 386–87; LR, 71; Sk, 105; Howe, "Aldhelm's Enigmata," 54–57; Ju, 6–7 and 87–88. (SK 16040)

SOLUTION: *IRIS* (rainbow); second-recension manuscripts include a Latin gloss (*DE IRI VEL ARCU CAELESTI,* "on the rainbow, which is to say the bow in the sky").

This is one of several aenigmata, generally clustering around the theme of heavenly bodies, in which Aldhelm appeals to an ancient etymology that is held to be false; the others are ALD 7 (*FATUM,* "fate"), 8 (*PLIADES,* "Pleiades"), 37 (*CANCER,* "crab"), and 79 (*SOL ET LUNA,* "sun and moon"). In other cases, too, the second-recension manuscripts include glosses, notably ALD 11–13, 15–18, 20, 21–24, 27, 30, 38, 41, 45, 49–51, 56, 59–62, 65, 67, 72, 76, 88, 92, and 95. There are some obvious sequences to be seen here, notably ALD 11–13, 15–18, 21–24, 49–51, and ALD 59–62; such clusters and sequences are commonplace throughout the tradition. The further extended gloss in L derives from Isidore, *Etym.* 13.10.1 *(Iris).*

5.1 On Thaumas, see too Virgil, *Aeneid* 9.2; Ovid, *Metamorphoses* 4.479. Compare BON 13.16 *(famine ficto).*

5.3 Compare Virgil, *Aeneid* 8.429 and Ovid, *Metamorphoses* 4.622 *(nubis aquosae).*

5.4 Note Aldhelm's customary wordplay on *lustro* in the double sense "wander" and "illuminate" (an ambiguity amply exploited by Boniface, as at BON 8.9 and 11.4); see too, for example, ALD PR.12 *(Cynthi . . . perlustro)* and 65.2 *(lustrabo latebras),* 81.2 *(lustrat qui limpidus orbem),* and 97.8 *(saecula dum lustrat lampas Titania Phoebi).* The same wordplay is also found at BED 17.

ALD 6

MANUSCRIPTS: D, fol. 11v; L, fol. 84v; G, fol. 395r; B, fol. 60r; O, fol. 2r.

EARLIER EDITIONS AND TRANSLATIONS: Eh, 101; Gl, 388–89; LR, 72; Sk, 106; Ju, 6–7 and 88. (SK 10730)

SOLUTION: *LUNA* (moon).

6.3 Compare ALD 96.9 *(gloria formae).*

6.4 Reading *cumulatus* with the second-recension manuscripts; the first recension has *rēdundans,* with false quantity: the normal scansion is *rĕdundans* (see further ALD 99.2). Retaining *red<u>undan</u>s* preserves an apparently original pun on the word *unda,* "wave," which reinforces the other two watery words in the same line, namely *latex* and *gurgite;* all three words scan in different ways.

ALD 7

MANUSCRIPTS: D, fol. 11v; L, fol. 84v; G, fol. 395v; B, fol. 60r–v; O, fol. 2r.

EARLIER EDITIONS AND TRANSLATIONS: Eh, 101; Gl, 388–89; LR, 72; Sk, 107; Ju, 6–7 and 88–89. (SK 4925)

SOLUTION: The solution given is *FATUM* (fate); a broad clue is offered by the use of the term *fortuna* in line 2, who is presumably the feminine *dominam* of ALD 7.3. O has the rather problematic rubric *FATUS VEL GENESIS,* which is ungrammatical, but offers the alternative solution "Genesis." See further Howe, "Aldhelm's Enigmata," 54–57; Sebo, *In Enigmate,* 73–74.

This is one of several riddles from across the Anglo-Saxon tradition where the solution is heavily hinted at through embedded clues, often etymological; other examples are found at ALD 25, 26, 28, 50, 52, 67, 88, and 92; BED 1; TAT 18 and 21; EUS 2, 9, 14, 19, 37, and 39; LOR 11; SYM 44 and 64; EXE 5, 6, 45, 51, 53, 55, 62, and 73; BER 19. This aenigma is noteworthy for its insistent use of alliteration, especially on *c-/q-, d-, f-/v-,* and *s-* in the first three lines, which deal with the classical and pagan past, and polyptoton on *regens . . . regnet* in the last, which turn to Christ (compare the similar polyptoton on *regmine . . . regale* in ALD PR.1–2). This is one of several aenigmata in which Aldhelm appeals to ancient etymology; see the note at ALD 5 (*IRIS,* "rainbow").

7.1 Compare Virgil, *Eclogue* 10.7 *(cecinisse poetam).*

7.2 The line quoted is Virgil, *Aeneid* 12.677 *(quo deus et quo dura vocat fortuna sequamur).* For the use of direct quotation within riddles, compare ALD 57.1 (quoting Virgil); ALD 63.7 (quoting Caelius Sedulius), ALD 97.12–16 (quoting Virgil). See too EXE 31.9–13 (alluding to ps-SYM 1) and EXE 36.6–7 (apparently alluding to EUS 37.3–4).

7.4 Compare ALD PR.1 *(regmine sceptra);* ALD 99.2 *(regni sceptra regebat).* Note the polyptoton on *regens . . . regnet.*

ALD 8

MANUSCRIPTS: D, fol. 11v; L, fol. 84v–85r; G, fol. 395v; B, fol. 60v; O, fol. 2r.

EARLIER EDITIONS AND TRANSLATIONS: Eh, 101–2; Gl, 390–91; LR, 72; Sk, 108–9; Howe, "Aldhelm's Enigmata," 54–57; Ju, 6–7 and 89–90. (SK 10555)

SOLUTION: *PLIADES* (Pleiades).

This is one of several aenigmata in which Aldhelm appeals to ancient etymology (see the note on ALD 5). This aenigma seems connected to the preceding one by a number of factors, including its classical references *(Athlante... Tartara)* and its echoing of the notion of an erroneous ancient name ALD 7.3 *(Me veteres... falso... vocitare solebant)* in the opening line *(Nos . . . stolidi dixere priores)*. A further link is suggested by the implicit reference to Virgil (who is actually quoted in ALD 7.2) via the alternative name for the Pleiades *(Vergiliae)* noted by Isidore, *Etym.* 3.71.13, alluded to in the first element of "the time of spring" (ALD 8.5: *verno... tempore*). See further Aldhelm, *Epistola ad Acircium* (Lapidge and Herren, 42–43), quoting Job 38:31. The extended gloss in L derives from Isidore, *Etym.* 3.71.13 *(Pliades)*.

See further Murphy, *Unriddling the Exeter Riddles,* 49.

8.1 Compare BON 13.61 *(dixere priorum);* Virgil, *Aeneid* 3.693 and Ovid, *Metamorphoses* 15.332 *(dixere priores)*.

8.2 Compare LOR 7.3 *(vix... cernitur una)*.

8.3 Compare ALD PR.35 *(arce poli)* and ALD 53.7 *(arce polorum)*.

8.5 Compare ALD 100.23 *(tempora prisca)*.

ALD 9

MANUSCRIPTS: D, fol. 11v; L, fol. 85r; G, fol. 395v; B, fol. 60v; O, fol. 2r.

EARLIER EDITIONS AND TRANSLATIONS: Eh, 102; Gl, 390–91; LR, 72; Sk, 110; Ju, 8–9 and 90. (SK 4412)

SOLUTION: *ADAMAS* (diamond); second-recension manuscripts add a specifying description (*DE ADAMANTE LAPIDE* "on the diamond, a stone"). See further Salvador-Bello, *Isidorean Perceptions,* 184–85.

Note the envelope pattern based on the elements of fear and iron which link the first line with the last *(vereor . . . ferri . . . ferrea . . . pavescit)*. All the essential information is given in Isidore, *Etym.* 16.13.2:

> Hic [= adamas] nulli cedit materiae, nec ferro quidem nec igni, nec umquam incalescit; unde et nomen interpretatione Graeca indomita vis accepit. Sed dum sit invictus ferri ignisque contemptor, hircino rumpitur sanguine recenti et calido maceratus, sicque multis ictibus ferri perfrangitur.

> The diamond yields to no substance, not even to iron or fire, nor does it ever grow warm, and from that fact it takes its name, which is translated from Greek as "unconquerable force." But although it is invulnerable to iron and spurns fire, it breaks apart after it has been soaked in fresh warm goat's blood, and in that way it is shattered by many iron blows.

This passage is clearly Aldhelm's immediate source, even down to specific wording: where Isidore has *indomita vis,* Aldhelm opts for *virtus indomiti rigoris.* The notion that a diamond dissipates the force of a magnet, found in the section of Isidore immediately following (*Etym.* 16.13.3), is employed in ALD 25.5 (*MAGNES FERRIFER,* "magnet"). See further ES, 149–50. The extended gloss in L derives from Isidore, *Etym.* 16.13.2 *(adamans).*

9.1 Compare Aldhelm, *Carmen de virginitate* 1748 *(discrimina ferri);* Frithegod, *Breviloquium S. Wilfridi* 886 *(rigidi . . . ferri).*

9.2 For goat's blood melting diamonds, compare Augustine, *De civitate Dei,* 21.4. See too Orchard, *Pride and Prodigies,* 111–12 (on *Liber monstrorum* 2.23).

ALD 10

MANUSCRIPTS: D, fol. 11v; L, fol. 85r; G, fol. 395v; B, fol. 60v; O, fol. 2r.

EARLIER EDITIONS AND TRANSLATIONS: Eh, 102; Gl, 392–93; LR, 72; Sk, 111; Ju, 8–9 and 90–91. (SK 15284)

SOLUTION: *MOLOSUS* (mastiff). See further ES, 173–74.

It may be relevant that the word *molosus* also signifies a metrical foot consisting of three long syllables, such as *iamdudum* in line 1, immediately following *me,* "me."

10.1 Compare Lucan, *Bellum civile* 5.537; Juvencus, *Evangelia* 4.684 *(veneranda potestas); Miracula S. Nyniae* 1 and 185 *(veneranda potestas).*

10.3 For the notion of a weapon-bearing creature, compare ALD 26.4 *(GALLUS,* "cockerel": *arma ferens pedibus).* The idea is considerably developed in other riddle collections: see the note on EXE 12.1a *(HORN,* "horn": *Ic wæs wæpen wigan).*

ALD 11

MANUSCRIPTS: D, fol. 12r; L, fol. 85r; G, fol. 395v; B, fol. 60v; O, fol. 2r–v.

EARLIER EDITIONS AND TRANSLATIONS: Eh, 102–3; Gl, 392–93; LR, 72; Sk, 112; Ju, 8–9 and 91–92. (SK 5174)

SOLUTION: *POALUM* (bellows); O has *FOLLES* (bellows); second-recension manuscripts include a Latin gloss (*DE POALEIS ID EST FOLLIBUS FABRORUM,* "on bellows, which is to say smiths' bellows"). See further ES, 13–14; see Lapidge and Rosier, *Aldhelm: The Poetic Works,* 249, n. 9; Lapidge, "Career of Aldhelm," 41.

The rare term *poalum* derives from confusion arising from a glossary entry. See also SYM 73 *(UTER FOLLIS).*

11.1 Compare BON 13.9 *(fratre gemello).*

11.2 Compare SYM 31.1 *(Vita mihi mors est);* BER 30.3 *(Vita mihi mors est),* BER 50.4 *(mihi mors est);* Aldhelm, *Carmen ecclesiasticum* 3.30 and 4.3.15 *(mortalis clausit spiracula vitae).*

11.3 Compare TAT 3.3 *(ornata metallis);* BON 17.8 *(ars mea escarum).*

ALD 12

MANUSCRIPTS: D, fol. 12r; L, fol. 85r–v; G, fol. 395v; B, fol. 60v; O, fol. 2v.

EARLIER EDITIONS AND TRANSLATIONS: Eh, 103; Gl, 394–95; LR, 73; Sk, 113; Ju, 8–9 and 92–93. (SK 833)

SOLUTION: *BOMBIX* (silkworm); second-recension manuscripts include a Latin gloss (*DE BOMBICIBUS ID EST VERMIBUS QUI SERES DICUNTUR,* "on silkworms, which is to say the worms that are called 'Chinese'"). See further ES, 214–20; Cavell, *Weaving Words,* 63. See too Leahy, *Anglo-Saxon Crafts,* 62.

In his discussion of silkworms, Isidore (*Etym.* 12.5.8) speaks of their being emptied out in the course of spinning thread, a notion that seems to underlie the final line of this aenigma; the extended gloss in L derives from two passages in Isidore, *Etym.* 9.2.40 *(Seres)* and *Etym.* 12.5.8 *(bombex).*

12.1 Compare SYM PR.3 *(Annua . . . tempora);* SYM 17.1–2 *(ARANEA,* "spider": *texendi . . . / . . . telae).* Note the alliteration on *t-* in the final three words.

12.2 Reading *replentur,* as in the second-recension manuscripts (see further the notes at ALD 6.4 and 19.1); the first-recension manuscripts have *redundant.* Two of the first-recension manuscripts also have *redeant* for *redeunt* in 12.1; the echo between the two verbs is in any case clear, as is the golden line pattern here. Aldhelm is particularly fond of the compound *setiger,* which also appears in five further aenigmata, at ALD 17.2, 33.2, 36.5, 39.1, and 100.10. Elsewhere in the Latin tradition of the aenigmata, the compound appears at SYM 36.1 and EUS 52.2. Twenty-one of the riddles refer to *viscera,* "guts," according to Lapidge and Rosier at 65, specifically ALD 12.2, 13.3, 27.1, 33.1, 40.6, 52.2, 52.8, 54.3, 55.6, 62.4, 67.2, 68.4, 72.5, 78.5, 80.2, 82.6, 89.1, 94.7, 97.2, 100.42, as well as ALD PR.31. There is a similar focus on the "belly" *(womb)* of the creature in question in EXE, on which see the note at EXE 1.78a.

12.3 Cameron, "Aldhelm as Naturalist," 123–24, argues that Aldhelm is describing the Oak Eggar *(Lasiocampa quercus quercus)*.

12.3 Compare TAT 17.4 *(cacumina scando)*.

12.4 Compare Aldhelm, *Carmen ecclesiasticum* 4.8.17 *(fatali sorte quiescit)*.

ALD 13

MANUSCRIPTS: D, fol. 12r; L, fol. 85v; G, fol. 395v; B, fol. 60v; O, fol. 2v.
EARLIER EDITIONS AND TRANSLATIONS: Eh, 103; Gl, 394–95; LR, 73; Sk, 114; Ju, 8–9 and 93–94. (SK 13021)
SOLUTION: *BARBITA* (organ); second-recension manuscripts include a Latin gloss with a variant on the grammatical gender of the solution (*DE BARBITO ID EST ORGANO,* "on the organ, which is to say the musical instrument organ"). See further ES, 120–31; Crane, "Describing the World," 142–43.

This aenigma is notable for the number of words for "musician" and "musical instrument" mentioned *(salpictae classica . . . citharae . . . tubae)* in the first two lines, each scanned in a different way. Compare the description of an organ by Wulfstan Cantor of Winchester, lines 146–76 (ed. and trans. Lapidge, 382–87).

13.1 Compare *Versus Sibyllae* 23 *(spiritus aere cavo mugebit ab aethere cornu)*. The phrase *aere cavo* is a commonplace. The phrasing here is particularly Aldhelmian; alongside 96.5 *(clangenti . . . classica)*, compare Aldhelm, *Carmen ecclesiasticum* 4.5.18 *(clanget classica salpix)*; Aldhelm, *Carmen de virginitate* 1549 *(salpix classica clangit)*, 2459 *(clangit classica salpix)*, and 2613 *(Salpicis et clangor necnon et classica)*. The extended gloss in L derives from Isidore, *Etym.* 18.4.5 *(classica)*.

13.3 Compare BER 16.6 *(eructant exta)*; Paulinus of Nola, *Carmen* 15.27 *(mea viscera cantu)*.

ALD 14

MANUSCRIPTS: D, fol. 12r; L, fol. 85v; G, fol. 395v–96r; B, fol. 60v–61r; O, fol. 2v.

EARLIER EDITIONS AND TRANSLATIONS: Eh, 103–4; Gl, 396–97; LR, 73; Sk, 115; Ju, 10–11 and 94.

SOLUTION: *PAVO* (peacock). See further ES, 194–95. (SK 15763)

14.1 Reading *pulcher et* with the second-recension manuscripts; the first recension has *sum namque,* as, however, at ALD 86.1 *(sum namque).* Compare Wulfstan Cantor of Winchester, *Vita S. Swithuni* 1.43 *(mirandus in orbe).*

14.2 Compare ALD 43.4 *(Ossibus et pedibus);* Lucretius, *De rerum natura* 1.866 *(Ossibus et nervis sanieque et sanguine mixto);* Alcuin, *Carmen* 1 419 *(ossibus et nervis).* Both *sanguine rubro* and *sanguine cretus* are commonplace.

14.4 Compare LOR 2.13 *(pulpa putrescens).* Augustine, *De civitate Dei* 21.4, notes that peacock flesh does not rot, an idea that Aldhelm echoes in his prose *De virginitate* 9 (Eh, 237.16–18: *beatus Augustinus in libro civitatis Dei, quod pulpa pavonis inputribilis naturae sit, experimentis se comprobasse testatur*) and *Carmen de virginitate* 231 *(Sic caro mirandum fatu putrescere nescit).* The same chapter of *de civitate Dei* also discusses both the salamander and the lodestone, as in ALD 15 (*SALAMANDRA,* "salamander") and ALD 25 (*MAGNES FERRIFER,* "magnet"). The extended gloss in L derives from Isidore, *Etym.* 11.1.81 *(pulpa).*

ALD 15

MANUSCRIPTS: D, fol. 12r; L, fol. 85v; G, fol. 396r; B, fol. 61r; O, fol. 2v.

EARLIER EDITIONS AND TRANSLATIONS: Eh, 104; Gl, 396–97; LR, 73; Sk, 116; Ju, 10–11 and 94–95. (SK 7684)

SOLUTION: *Salamandra* (salamander); second-recension manuscripts include a Latin gloss (*DE SALAMANDRA QUAE SIMILIS EST LACERTAE,* "on the salamander, which is like a lizard").

Here again, it is notable that Aldhelm employs many synonyms for "fire," "flames," "furnace," and "burning" without repeating forms, and with considerable metrical variety (*Ignibus . . . flammas . . . rogi . . . crepitante foco . . . scintillante favilla ardeo . . . flammae . . . flagranti torre*). It is instructive to compare the account by Isidore, *Etym.* 12.4.36, on which Aldhelm doubtless drew, and which has far less variety of form and diction (*incendia . . . incendia . . . ignes . . . flammis*). An even more impressive example of employing strings of synonymous nouns, adjectives, and verbs is found in a section of *Hisperica famina* A426–51, entitled *De igne,* "concerning fire," where we find the following astonishing sequence: *laricomi torriminis . . . rogus . . . torridum . . . ardore . . . flammeas . . . flammeo torret . . . incendio . . . fomite . . . pira . . . aestibus favillam . . . fornace . . . camino . . . viricomis calificat . . . flammiuomi . . . inflammator focile . . . scintillosus exarsit . . . incentor . . . scintilla . . . faccem . . . pira flammis . . . flammisonus . . . clibanus . . . torrida . . . incendia . . . uricomo concremaret focus.* Note how many of the forms here are poetic coinages; on the relationship of the *Hisperica famina* to the Anglo-Saxon riddle tradition, see Orchard, "*Hisperica famina* as Literature" and Corrigan, "Hisperic Enigma Machine."

See further ES, 205; Orchard, *Pride and Prodigies,* 312–13 (*Liber monstrorum* 3.14).

The extended gloss in L derives from Isidore, *Etym.* 12.4.36 (*salamandra*).

15.1 Compare Prudentius, *Apotheosis* 1.154 (*Ignibus et mediis*).

15.2 For the use of the verb *faxo,* compare ALD 26.4 and ALD 31.3; EUS 55.1.

ALD 16

MANUSCRIPTS: D, fol. 12r; L, fol. 85v–86r; G, fol. 396r; B, fol. 61r; O, fol. 2v (*LUGILLUS*).

EARLIER EDITIONS AND TRANSLATIONS: Eh, 104; Gl, 398–99; LR, 73; Sk, 117; Ju, 10–11 and 95–96. (SK 10723)

SOLUTION: *LULIGO* (flying fish); second-recension manuscripts include a Latin gloss (*DE LULIGINE ID EST PISCE VOLANTE,* "on the *luligo,* which is to say flying fish"). See further ES, 204; Klein, "Of Water and the Spirit."

After an aenigma which focuses on fire, this one turns to the elements of air and water. Aldhelm's immediate source is likely Isidore, *Etym.* 12.6.47, although a similar account is given in Pliny, *Nat. Hist.* 9.45 and 32.6. The notion of a creature that plumbs the depths and scours the skies is recurrent in the riddle tradition, often with regard to celestial signs such as Cancer the crab and Pisces the fish; see, for example, the headnote to EXE 1.

16.1 Compare Aldhelm, *Carmen de virginitate* 2052 *(spectacula vitae).*

16.3 Compare ALD 42.3 *(trano per aethera pennis)* and ALD 48.6 *(pennis aethera tranet);* Virgil, *Georgics* 1.406 and 409, *Aeneid* 11.272 *(aethera pinnis).*

16.4 Compare EUS 42.8 *(aethereum flatum).*

ALD 17

MANUSCRIPTS: D, fol. 12r–v; L, fol. 86r; G, fol. 396r; B, fol. 61r; O, fol. 2v.

EARLIER EDITIONS AND TRANSLATIONS: Eh, 105; Gl, 398–99; LR, 73; Sk, 118; Ju, 10–11 and 96. (SK 4116)

SOLUTION: *PERNA* (ham, fan mussel); second-recension manuscripts include a Latin gloss (*DE PERNA QUAE MULTO MAIOR EST OSTREIS EX CUIUS VELLERIBUS CONFICITUR VESTIS,* "on the bivalve mollusk, which is bigger than the oysters and from whose skin clothing is made"). See further Dale, *Natural World,* 131.

The aenigma plays on notions of twinning and doubling, and the fact that the creature in question supplies both food and clothing connects it directly to ALD 77 (*FICULNEA,* "fig tree") and ALD 91 (*PALMA,* "palm"), where the same feature is emphasized. See further ES, 202–4. The extended gloss in L derives from Isidore, *Etym.* 12.6.50 (which, however, is on *muricae*).

17.1 Compare Virgil, *Aeneid* 10.209 *(caerula concha).*

17.2 Compare ALD 33.2 *(setigero . . . vellere).* On *setiger,* see the note at ALD 12.2.

17.3 Compare ALD 30.4, 31.1, 49.3, 56.7, 61.7, and 100.58 *(necnon et).*

17.4 Compare TAT 6.3 *(persolvo tributum);* Juvencus, *Evangelia* 3.395 *(duplex dissolve tributum).*

ALD 18

MANUSCRIPTS: D, fol. 12v; L, fol. 86r; G, fol. 396r; B, fol. 61r; O, fol. 3r.

EARLIER EDITIONS AND TRANSLATIONS: Eh, 105; Gl, 400–401; LR, 73–74; Sk, 119–20; Ju, 10–11 and 96–97. (SK 3940)

See further Howe, "Aldhelm's Enigmata," 47–50.

SOLUTION: *MYRMICOLEON* (ant lion, "ant-eater"); second-recension manuscripts give a Latin version closer to that found in Isidore, Aldhelm's source (*DE FORMICA LEONE,* "on the ant lion").

This is one of several aenigmata that play explicitly on perceived Greek etymology; the others are ALD 35 (*NYCTICORAX,* "night-raven"), ALD 51 (*ELIOTROPUS,* "heliotrope"), and ALD 60 (*MONOCERUS,* "rhinoceros"). See further ES, 212–13; Gregory the Great, *Moralia in Iob,* 5.20.40. The extended gloss in L derives from Isidore, *Etym.* 12.3.10 *(formicoleon)*:

> Formicoleon ob hoc vocatus, quia est vel formicarum leo vel certe formica pariter et leo. Est enim animal parvum formicis satis infestum, quod se in pulvere abscondit, et formicas frumenta gestantes interficit. Proinde autem leo et formica vocatur, quia aliis animalibus ut formica est, formicis autem ut leo est.

> The "ant lion" is named thus either because it is the lion *(leo)* of the ants or, more likely, because it is equally an ant and a lion, for it is a small animal very dangerous to ants, since it hides itself in the dust and kills the ants as they are carrying grain. And so it is called both an "ant" and a "lion," because

to the rest of the animals it is like an ant, but to ants it is like a lion.

18.2 Compare ALD 33.6 *(sermone vocabor)*. The use of the adjective *Pelasgus*, "Greek" (the term derives from the name of the oldest inhabitants of Greece, and was popularized by Virgil) is characteristic of Aldhelm's aenigmata: compare ALD 35.6 and 60.10; see too Aldhelm, *Carmen de virginitate* 2150 and EUS 53.1 and 57.1.

18.4 Reading *rescindere* with the second-recension manuscripts; the first recension has *resistere*, but with false quantity: the normal scansion is *rĕsistere.*

18.5 Compare ALD 26.3 *(nomine fungor)* and ALD 100.83 *(fungar . . . nomine)*, and especially XMS P1.9 *(scrutetur sapiens, lector, quo nomine fungit)*; compare Venantius Fortunatus, *Carmen* 4.20.3 *(nomine functum)*. See further the note to BON 19.4, and Orchard, *Poetic Art*, 208, n. 307.

ALD 19

MANUSCRIPTS: D, fol. 12v; L, fol. 86r; G, fol. 396r; B, fol. 61r; O, fol. 3r.

EARLIER EDITIONS AND TRANSLATIONS: Eh, 105–6; Gl, 400–401; LR, 74; Sk, 121; Ju, 12–13 and 97–98. (SK 3941)

SOLUTION: *SAL* (salt). See further ES, 147. For another aenigma on the same topic, see BER 3 (*SAL*, "salt").

19.1 Compare Aldhelm, *Carmen de virginitate* 223 *(squamosis piscibus)* and Venantius Fortunatus, *Carmen* 3.13a.1 *(pisce redundant)*. See further the notes at ALD 6.4 and ALD 12.2.

19.3 Compare BON 13.33 *(horrida pestiferis cumulat tormenta maniplis)*.

19.4 Reading *constat* with the second-recension manuscripts (some of which have *fulget*); the first recension has *nitet*, but with false quantity: the normal scansion is *nĭtet*. Compare ALD 80.4 *(glacieque simillima lucet)*.

ALD 20

MANUSCRIPTS: D, fol. 12v; L, fol. 86r–v; G, fol. 396r; B, fol. 61r–v; O, fol. 3r.

EARLIER EDITIONS AND TRANSLATIONS: Eh, 106; Gl, 401–2; LR, 74; Sk, 122; Ju, 12–13 and 98. (SK 9676)

SOLUTION: *APIS* (bee); second-recension manuscripts give the plural, and note the predominance of five-line aenigmata in what follows (*DE APIBUS ENIGMATA QUINQUE VERSIBUS DECURRUNT,* "on bees; aenigmata with five verses follow on"). See further ES, 206–8; Casiday, "St. Aldhelm's Bees"; Murphy, *Unriddling the Exeter Riddles,* 167–68; Taylor, "Enigma Variations," 73–74.

The extended gloss in L derives from Isidore, *Etym.* 12.8.1 *(apes),* with the added twist that while Isidore traces the etymology of "bees" *(apes)* to the fact that they are "without a foot" *(a-pes),* Aldhelm, perhaps considering that bees clearly have legs, focuses instead on the amazing craftsmanship of the bee, building "without hands" *(carens manibus).* The martial flavor of the closing lines of ALD 20.4–5, echoed in so many of EXE, also springs directly from Isidore, who speaks of bees having "fortifications" *(castra),* "an army" *(exercitum),* and "kings" *(reges);* and "waging war" *(proelia movent).* See too BER 21 (*APIS,* "bee"), which, however, approaches the topic from an entirely different angle.

20.1 Compare BER 19.2 *(nullo virili creta de semine)* and 55.1 *(Semine nec ullo patris creatus);* BIB 1.5 *(ternae patrio sine semine),* 3.1 *(patrio sine semine),* and 8.1 *(Sunt mihi . . . patrio sine semine ternae);* Ovid, *Metamorphoses* 15.760 *(semine cretus);* Juvencus, *Evangelia* 4.242 *(semine cretas).*

20.3 Note the lengthening before mute and liquid in next word of the final syllable of *crocea* here; there are other examples at ALD 37.3, 41.2, 51.4, 61.2, 77.7, 81.1, 82.6, 86.8, 87.3, 100.6, 100.13, and 100.59. See further Orchard, *Poetic Art of Aldhelm,* 76. Compare BON 7.10, 15.11, and 20.10 *(Arte mea);* ALD 51.2 *(croceo flavescunt).* For the reference to how the creature in question can benefit kings, compare BER 22.6 (*OVIS,* "sheep"), 24.5 (*MEMBRANUM,* "parchment"), and 28.6 (*DE SERICO,* "on a silkmoth"); EXE 47.7–8a (*BÆC-OFEN,* "baking-oven").

20.5 Other aenigmata focus on the lack of specific body parts, notably EUS 40.2 *(manibus pedibusque carens);* see too BON 10.14 *(vinco . . . metalla).*

ALD 21

MANUSCRIPTS: D, fol. 12v; L, fol. 86v; G, fol. 396r–v; B, fol. 61v; O, fol. 3r.

EARLIER EDITIONS AND TRANSLATIONS: Eh, 106; Gl, 402–3; LR, 74; Sk, 123; Ju, 12–13 and 98–99. (SK 2803)

SOLUTION: *LIMA* (file); second-recension manuscripts offer a rather baffling gloss (*DE LIMA QUAE ROSCINA DICITUR,* "on the file which is called *roscina*"), on which see the headnote to ALD 22 below. See too Leahy, *Anglo-Saxon Crafts,* 119–21; Riley, *Anglo-Saxon Tools,* 49–51.

This aenigma is linked to the preceding by the notion that both creatures in question are "lacking" something (ALD 20.5, *carens;* ALD 21.5, *carens;* and see the note below); it is linked to the one following by the twin notions of "voice" and "harshness" in the last line of ALD 21 (21.5, *voce . . . rauco*) and in the opening lines of ALD 22 (22.1–3, *Vox . . . raucisonis*).

21.3 Compare BON 13.8 *(Auri materiem . . . metalla).*

21.5 Compare ALD 31.3 *(voce carens);* Ovid, *Metamorphoses* 13.567 *(rauco cum murmure).*

ALD 22

MANUSCRIPTS: D, fol. 12v (ALD 22.4 is missing); L, fol. 86v; G, fol. 396v; B, fol. 61v; O, fol. 3r.

EARLIER EDITIONS AND TRANSLATIONS: Eh, 106–7; Gl, 404–5; LR, 74; Sk, 124; Ju, 12–13 and 99. (SK 17531)

SOLUTION: *ACALANTIS* (nightingale); second-recension manuscripts include a Latin gloss (*DE ACHALANTIDA QUAE LATINE LUSCINIA DICITUR,* "on the nightingale, which is called *luscinia* in Latin").

In fact, the solution given is misleading: Greek ἀκαλανθίς (more commonly ἀκανθίς) generally signifies a goldfinch, and is found in Virgil, *Georgics* 3.338 *(acalanthida dumi),* where it appears in the form given in the first-recension manuscripts *(acalantida).* In the context of the odd gloss found in second-recension manuscripts to the previous aenigma *(DE LIMA QUAE ROSCINA DICITUR),* it is intriguing to note that in the preceding line in Virgil, *Georgics* 3.337, we find the phrase *roscida luna,* which in a confused form may underlie *(LIMA . . . ROSCINA).* See further ES, 182–83. Compare ALD 68.7–8 (*SALPIX,* "trumpet": *aut arguta simul cantans luscinia ruscis / quam lingua propria dicunt acalantida Graeci*). The final line of the previous aenigma speaks of a creature "lacking a voice" *(voce carens),* while the very first word of this one focuses on the superabundance of its "voice" *(Vox).* Note the rather intrusive end rhyme on *-o* and *-is;* if this is intended as a gesture towards the musicality of the bird, it is a somewhat clumsy one. Alcuin evidently made use of this aenigma in composing his own nightingale poems, as the notes below make clear. For another riddle with the same solution, see EXE 6 *(NIHTE-GALE).*

22.1 Compare LOR 1.1 *(mihi diverso varia sub tempore fata)* and 11.8 *(mea diversis variantur fata sub annis).*

22.2 Compare Alcuin, *Carmen* 58.12 *(modulans . . . carmina rostro).*

22.3 Several manuscripts (including L) read *spreta* for *spurca;* compare Alcuin, *Carmen* 61.7 *(spreta colore tamen . . . non spreta canendo),* which presumably derives from a manuscript containing just such a variant. For the form of the line, compare SYM 59.1 *(Non sum cincta comis et non sum compta capillis).*

22.4 Compare LOR 4.4 *(fato terrente).*

ALD 23

MANUSCRIPTS: D, fol. 12v–13r; L, fol. 91r (no. 50); G, fol. 399r (no. 50); not in B; O, fol. 3r–v.

EARLIER EDITIONS AND TRANSLATIONS: Eh, 107; Gl, 404–5; LR, 74; Sk, 163; Ju, 14–15 and 99–100. (SK 10562)

SOLUTION: *TRUTINA* ("scales"); second-recension manuscripts include a gloss (*DE TRUTINA QUAE MOMENTANA DICITUR EO QUOD AD MOMENTUM INCLINATA VERGIT,* "on a pair of scales, which is called *momentana,* for the reason that it tips and turns for the moment"). See further ES, 21–22; Scull, "Scales and Weights."

The gloss in the second-recension manuscripts derives ultimately from Isidore, *Etym.* 16.25.4:

> Trutina est gemina ponderum lances aequali examine pendens, facta propter talenta et centenaria adpendenda; sicut momentana pro parva modicaque pecunia. Haec et moneta vocata. Idem et statera nomen ex numero habens, quod duobus lancis et uno in medio stilo librata aequaliter stet.

> A pair of scales is an instrument that suspends two weighted plates from a balance-tongue. It is made for weighing talents and hundred-pound weights, just as a *momentana* [that is, a smaller-sized scale] is made for small change. This is also called a *moneta.* It also has the name *statera* from its number, because it stands evenly balanced with two plates and a single point in the middle.

It seems clear from the parallels noted below that both BON 4 (*MISERICORDIA,* "mercy") and BON 6.9 (*IUSTITIA,* "justice") are modeled on this aenigma, with Boniface evidently making the obvious connection between "scales" and both "mercy" and "justice."

23.1 Compare BON 4.1 *(geminae . . . sorores);* BIB 9.1 *(geminae sorores);* Ovid, *Metamorphoses* 4.774; Aldhelm, *Carmen de virginitate* 2279 *(geminas . . . sorores).*

23.4 Compare BON 4.14 *(mortalibus aevi)* and BON 8.1 *(fieret mortalibus aevum)*; Virgil, *Georgics* 3.66 *(mortalibus aevi)*; Lucan, *Bellum civile* 9.981 *(mortalibus aevum)*.

23.5 Compare BON 6.9 *(normam servarent)*.

ALD 24

MANUSCRIPTS: D, fol. 13r; L, fol. 86v (no. 23); G, fol. 396v (no. 23); B, fol. 61v; O, fol. 3v.

EARLIER EDITIONS AND TRANSLATIONS: Eh, 107; Gl, 406–7; LR, 75; Sk, 125–26; Ju, 14–15 and 100–101. (SK 9475)

SOLUTION: *DRACONTIA* (dragon-stone, draconite); second-recension manuscripts include a gloss (*DE DRACONTI GEMMA ID EST SANGUIS DRACONIS*, "on the dragon, a gemstone, which is to say dragon's blood"). See further ES, 153–55.

Aldhelm draws heavily on Isidore, *Etym.* 16.14.7 (where the stone in question is called *dracontites*):

> Dracontites ex cerebro draconis eruitur. Quae nisi viventi abscisa fuerit, non ingemmescit; unde et eam magi dormientibus draconibus amputant. Audaces enim viri explorant draconum specus, spargunt ibi gramina medicata ad incitandum draconum soporem, atque ita somno sopitis capita desecant et gemmas detrahunt. Sunt autem candore translucido. Usu earum orientis reges praecipue gloriantur.

> *Dracontites* is snatched from a dragon's brain, and it does not develop into a gemstone, unless it has been cut from a living creature; and so magicians extract it from sleeping dragons. So brave men seek out the caves of dragons, and sprinkle drugged herbs there to cause the dragons to fall asleep, and then they cut off their heads when they are fast asleep and take out the gemstones: they are translucent white. The kings of the East especially glory in their use.

The extended gloss in L derives from the same chapter of Isidore. Compare the Old English gloss *gim-rodor* or *gim-hroþor*, "glorious gem," which appears nine times glossing *dracontia* (see Meritt, 72), on which see *DOE*.

24.2 Compare *Miracula S. Nyniae* 146; Venantius Fortunatus, *Carmen* 6.1.102 and *Vita S. Martini* 3.512 *(gemmarum . . . lumina)*.

24.3 Compare Venantius Fortunatus, *Carmen* 7.24.25 *(rigida virtute)* and Aldhelm, *Carmen de virginitate* 1101 *(virtute potestas)* and 1347 *(rigida virtute)*.

24.4 Compare Juvencus, *Evangelia* 2.519 *(squamoso corpore lepra)*; *Miracula S. Nyniae* 252 *(squamoso corpore)*.

24.5 Compare ALD 26.5 *(capitis gestans in vertice)*, ALD 91.8 *(summo capitis . . . vertice)*; EUS 30.2 *(gestabar vertice)*.

ALD 25

MANUSCRIPTS: D, fol. 13r; L, fol. 86v–87r (no. 24); G, fol. 396v (no. 24); B, fol. 61v; O, fol. 3v.

EARLIER EDITIONS AND TRANSLATIONS: Eh, 108; Gl, 406–7; LR, 75; Sk, 127–28; Howe, "Aldhelm's Enigmata," 46; Ju, 14–15 and 101. (SK 17390)

SOLUTION: *MAGNES FERRIFER* (magnet). The extended gloss in L derives from Isidore, *Etym.* 16.4.1 *(magnes)*. It is notable that the word *ferrifer* is restricted in verse to a single occurrence in Aldhelm, *Carmina ecclesiastica* 4.7.22.

25.4 Aldhelm drops a broad clue about the solution in the phrase *ferrea fata*; compare Prudentius, *Contra Symmachum* 2.463 *(ferrea fata)*.

25.5 A false quantity: *potentiā* is the normal usage. The idea that diamonds cause magnets to lose their strength is found in Isidore, *Etym.* 16.13.3 (see the note on ALD 9 *ADAMAS*, "diamond"). The extended gloss in L derives from Isidore, *Etym.* 14.6.14 *(Ciprus)*.

ALD 26

MANUSCRIPTS: D, fol. 13r; L, fol. 87r (no. 25); G, fol. 396v (no. 25); B, fol. 61v–62r; O, fol. 3v.

EARLIER EDITIONS AND TRANSLATIONS: Eh, 108; Gl, 408–9; LR, 75; Sk, 129; Ju, 14–15 and 101–2. (SK 5488)

SOLUTION: *GALLUS* (cockerel). See further ES, 178–80; Howe, "Aldhelm's Enigmata," 47.

There is an obvious pun here on the homonyms *gallus,* "cockerel," and *Gallus,* "Gaul, Frank"; the opening line offers another linguistic clue for those sensitive enough to see an echo of the solution in the very first word *Garrulus.* Note too the martial imagery, emphasized by the loans from heroic verse; a similar strategy is also employed occasionally elsewhere in ALD, for example ALD 56 (*CASTOR,* "beaver"), 75 (*CRABRO,* "wasp"), 82 (*MUSTELA,* "weasel"), and 96 (*ELEFANS,* "elephant"), as well as in several riddles of EXE (on which see further Stanley, "Heroic Aspects of the Exeter Book Riddles").

26.2 Compare ALD 57.8 *(lumine Phoebi);* TAT 1.5 *(clarior et Phoebi radiis);* EUS 11.1 and 58.2 *(lumine Phoebi).*

26.3 Compare ALD 18.5 *(nomine fungar).*

26.4 Compare Virgil, *Georgics* 1.511 *(arma ferunt);* Lucan, *Bellum civile* 8.389 *(in discrimina belli);* Aldhelm, *Carmen de virginitate* 2626 *(discrimina belli).*

26.5 In L, *serratas* is glossed in Old English as *gecyrnode* and *cristas* is glossed in OE as *cambas.* Compare ALD 24.5 *(summo . . . capitis de vertice),* ALD 91.8 *(summo capitis . . . vertice);* EUS 30.2 *(gestabar vertice);* Virgil, *Aeneid* 6.779 *(vertice cristae),* 9.732 *(in vertice cristae),* 10.701 *(vertice . . . cristas),* and 12.493 *(vertice cristas);* Ovid, *Metamorphoses* 6.672 *(in vertice cristae);* Statius, *Thebaid* 5.587 *(vertice cristas);* Prudentius, *Psychomachia* 1.117 *(galeato in vertice cristas).*

ALD 27

MANUSCRIPTS: D, fol. 13r; L, fol. 87r (no. 26); G, fol. 396v (no. 26); B, fol. 62r; O, fol. 3v.

EARLIER EDITIONS AND TRANSLATIONS: Eh, 108–9; Gl, 408–9; LR, 75; Sk, 130; Ju, 16–17 and 102–3. (SK 5381)

SOLUTION: *COS* (whetstone).

The two solutions given in both the first- and second-recension manuscripts (*COTICULA*, "touchstone," "small stone mortar," and *DE COTICULO* respectively) offer conflicting and indeed potentially misleading signals, being divided even about the gender of the creature in question (signaled as unequivocally masculine in the opening word *Frigidus*, yet the apparently correct solution *COS* [whetstone] is also feminine). Isidore, *Etym.* 16.3.6, discusses the "whetstone" *(cos)*, but there is little overlap with Aldhelm's account.

27.1 Compare the related ALD 33.1 *(LORICA,* "armor": *me genuit gelido de viscere);* TAT 31.2 *(DE SCINTILLA,* "about a spark": *nasci gelido natum de viscere matris)* and 39.1 *(DE COTICULO,* "about a whetstone": *Natam me gelido terrae de viscere);* LOR 4.1 *(DE GELU,* "about ice": *me . . . ex gelido generat . . . tergore matris).*

27.3 Compare EUS 50.1 *(senectutis . . . discrimina).*

27.4 *Mulcifer* is a rare variant of *Mulciber,* an alternative name for Vulcan, here used metonymically for "fire"; on such *-b-* for *-f-* spellings, see the headnote on LEI below. See further Postgate, "Etymological Studies."

27.5 Compare BON 16.11 *(torribus atris);* Aldhelm, *Carmen de virginitate* 1753 and 1991 *(torribus atris).*

ALD 28

MANUSCRIPTS: D, fol. 13r–v; L, fol. 87v (no. 27); G, fol. 396v–97r (no. 27); B, fol. 62r; O, fol. 3v–4r.

EARLIER EDITIONS AND TRANSLATIONS: Eh, 109; Gl, 410–11; LR, 75; Sk, 131–32; Howe, "Aldhelm's Enigmata," 42; Ju, 16–17 and 103. (SK 15761)

SOLUTION: *MINOTAURUS* (Minotaur). See too ES, 237–38; Crane, "Describing the World," 148–54; Orchard, *Pride and Prodigies*, 284–85 (*Liber monstrorum* 1.50).

Some (but by no means all) of the material here is also found in Isidore, *Etym.* 11.3.38. The pun on *Gnossia* is emphasized by the evident pun on *Creta . . . creatus* in ALD 28.4, which, via "Crete" *(Creta)*, offers a broad clue to the solution.

28.1 Note the spelling *acerbis* for the usual *acervis*, and see the note on PR.4 above.

28.2 Compare ALD 36.1 *(SCNIFES,* "midge": *stimulis armatus acerbis)*; ALD 86.1 *(ARIES,* "ram": *armatus . . . cornibus)*. The notion of a creature "armed with horns" is repeated in EXE 12.1 *(OXA,* "ox": *Ic wæs wæpen wigan)*, and is also given by Isidore, *Etym.* 12.1.8 as an etymology for the word *armentum*, "cattle."

28.3 Compare ALD 36.6 *(SCNIFES,* "midge": *famosus . . . Memphitica rura)*.

28.4 Compare Ovid, *Metamorphoses* 5.145 and 11.295; Cyprianus Gallus, *Genesis* 191 and 1056. The extended gloss in L derives from Isidore, *Etym.* 9.5.23–24 (which, however, is on *nothus*).

28.5 Compare Virgil, *Aeneid* 6.728 *(hominum pecudumque)*; Virgil, *Aeneid* 1.530, 3.163, 3.702, and 12.845 *(cognomina dicunt)*.

ALD 29

MANUSCRIPTS: D, fol. 13v; L, fol. 87r–v (no. 28); G, fol. 397r (no. 28); B, fol. 62r; O, fol. 4r.

EARLIER EDITIONS AND TRANSLATIONS: Eh, 109; Gl, 410–11; LR, 75–76; Sk, 125–26; Ju, 16–17 and 103–4. (SK 13678)

SOLUTION: *AQUA* (water). See further Dale, *Natural World*, 179.

29.1 Two of the three first-recension manuscripts read *quisne obstupescat*, so preserving a false quantity: the normal scansion is *obstŭpescat*.

29.2 For the notion, compare SYM 72.3 (*TUBA*, "pipe").

29.3 Aldhelm commonly has short syllables before -*s*-groups, as here in *gestamina;* see further Orchard, *Poetic Art of Aldhelm,* 74–76. There are other examples at ALD 100.37 and 58.

29.5 Compare SYM 14.1 *(primordia vitae);* Juvencus, *Evangelia* 2.202 *(primordia vitae);* Aldhelm, *Carmen de virginitate* 176 *(primordia vitae).*

29.6 Compare LOR 12.3 *(Tertia pars mihimet);* Ovid, *Metamorphoses* 5.372 *(pars tertia mundi);* Corippus, *Iohannid* 1.47 *(tertia pars mundi).*

ALD 30

MANUSCRIPTS: D, fol. 13v; L, fol. 87v (no. 29); G, fol. 397r (no. 29); B, fol. 62r; O, fol. 4r.

EARLIER EDITIONS AND TRANSLATIONS: Eh, 110; Gl, 412–13; LR, 76; Sk, 134–35; Ju, 16–17 and 104. (SK 10557)

SOLUTION: *ELEMENTUM* (letter of the alphabet); second-recension manuscripts include a Latin gloss (*DE ELEMENTO VEL ABECEDARIO,* "on the alphabet or *abecedarium*"). Compare O'Brien O'Keeffe, *Visible Song,* 52; Bitterli, *Say What I Am Called,* 144; Fell, "Wax Tablets of Stone," 261; Ooi, "Speaking Objects," 54–57.

This is the first of a large group of aenigmata and riddles connected with the classroom and scriptorium; compare ALD 32 (*PUGILLARES,* "writing tablets"), ALD 59 (*PENNA,* "pen"), ALD 89 (*ARCA LIBRARIA,* "book chest"); TAT 5 (*MEMBRANUM,* "parchment"), TAT 6 (*PENNA,* "quill pen"), TAT 10 (*RECITABULUM,* "lectern"); EUS 14 (*X LITTERA,* "the letter x"), EUS 30 (*ATRAMENTORIUM,* "inkhorn"), EUS 32 (*MEMBRANUM,* "parchment"), EUS 33 (*SCETHA,* "book satchel"), EUS 35 (*PENNA,* "quill pen"); LOR 9 (*PENNA,* "quill pen"), LOR 12 (*ATRAMENTUM,* "ink"). This aenigma also opens a closely connected sequence comprising ALD 30–32; the links are explored in the following headnotes. Isidore, *Etym.* 1.4.10, discusses the seventeen "letters" (*litterae,* grammatically feminine, hence "sisters") of the original Latin alphabet, usually understood as the "mutes" (*mutae,* littera-ly [as it were] "silent"). The aenigma plays upon the conceit of "silent speech," and so is filled with words and phrases for sound and hearing *(sine voce . . . non dicimus . . . audire . . . silenter)*. The theme of silent speech is particularly frequent in riddles and aenigmata dealing with reading and writing.

30.1 Reading *denae* with the second-recension manuscripts; the first recension has *decem,* but with false quantity (or perhaps hiatus); the normal scansion is *dĕcem*.

30.2 For *annumerandas* as a polysyllabic cadence, see the note on ALD PR.26 above.

30.3 The notion that these creatures are born and killed through iron echoes SYM 1.3 (*GRAPHIUM,* "stylus"), and is again reflected in ALD 32.8 (*PUGILLARES,* "writing tablets").

30.4 Compare ALD 17.3, ALD 31.1, ALD 49.3, ALD 56.7, ALD 61.7, ALD 100.58 *(necnon et)*; SYM 26.1 *(penna . . . volantis)*, SYM 28.2 *(penna volantis)*; ALF X.2 *(penna volantis)*. The pun on *volucris . . . volitantis* emphasizes the connection to other riddles focusing on quill pens.

30.5 Compare TAT 18.2 *(nos . . . matre creatos)*; BER 25.2 *(tres unito simul nos crearunt ictu parentes)*. The "three brothers" are the two fingers and thumb that hold the writing-implement; see further BED 18; EXE 29 and 49.

ALD 31

MANUSCRIPTS: D, fol. 13v–14r; L, fol. 87v (no. 30); G, fol. 397r (no. 30); B, fol. 62r–v; O, fol. 4r.

EARLIER EDITIONS AND TRANSLATIONS: Eh, 110–11; Gl, 414–15; LR, 76; Sk, 136; Ju, 18–19 and 104–5. (SK 1870)

SOLUTION: *CICONIA* (stork). See further ES, 186–89.

Much of the information given here is also found in Isidore, *Etym.* 12.7.16. This aenigma connects to the last through the notions of both voicelessness (ALD 30.1: *sine voce;* ALD 31.3: *voce carens*) and feathers (ALD 30.4: *penna;* ALD 31.2: *pennae*); the legendary link between the flight of cranes and the invention of the alphabet by

Mercury is intriguing here, as is the specific contrast of black and white noted in the opening line, which is also common in riddles dealing with script (see further the note on ALD 59.3–5 below).

31.1 Compare TAT 9.1 (*forma nitescit*); Caelius Sedulius, *Carmen paschale* 3.282 (*candida forma nivis*).
31.2 Compare BON 20.3 (*varia . . . imagine*).
31.3 Compare ALD 21.5 (*voce carens*); EUS 56.2 (*crepacula rostro*).
31.4 Compare Aldhelm, *Carmen de virginitate* 545 (*squamigerum . . . draconem*) and 2399 (*squamigerum . . . celydrum*).
31.5 Compare ALD 46.4 (*turgescunt membra*); Ovid, *Metamorphoses* 15.359 (*membra venenis*).
31.6 Compare ALD 47.5 (*Post teneros fetus et prolem*).

ALD 32

MANUSCRIPTS: D, fol. 14r; L, fol. 88r (where it is no. 31); G, fol. 397r (no. 31); B, fol. 62v (with ALD.3–4 transposed); O, fol. 4r–v.

EARLIER EDITIONS AND TRANSLATIONS: Eh, 111; Gl, 416–17; LR, 76; Sk, 137–38; Ju, 18–19 and 105–6. (SK 9525)

SOLUTION: *PUGILLARES* (writing tablets). See further ES, 63–67, and in general, see Stevenson, "Literacy in Ireland," 136–38; Milanović-Barham, "Aldhelm's *Enigmata* and Byzantine Riddles," 58–60; Fell, "Wax Tablets of Stone," 261. There are some broad parallels in *Hisperica famina* A531–46 (*DE TABULA*, "on a writing tablet"; see further Herren, *Hisperica Famina: The A-Text*; Orchard, "*Hisperica famina* as Literature").

For other aenigmata connected with the classroom and scriptorium, see the note at ALD 30. The term *pugillaris* (literally "what can be held in the hand or fist") has, as its etymology suggests, inherently pugilistic overtones, and echoes comparisons between scholars and warriors elsewhere in Aldhelm's works and within the wider Anglo-Saxon riddle tradition, as well as in (for example) the Hiberno-Latin aenigmata embedded in the *Hisperica famina*. Such a notion would link this aenigma more closely to the next, ALD 33 (*LORICA*, "armor"); on the idea of writing as a form of fighting, and of scholars as warriors, see further Orchard, "*Hisperica famina* as Literature."

32.8 Compare ALD 88.3 *(seges diris);* see further the notes at SYM 1.3 (*GRAPHIUM,* "stylus") and ALD 30.3 (*ELEMENTUM,* "letter of the alphabet").

ALD 33

MANUSCRIPTS: D, fol. 14r; L, fol. 88r (no. 32); G, fol. 397r–v (no. 32); B, fol. 62v; O, fol. 4v.

EARLIER EDITIONS AND TRANSLATIONS: Eh, 111–12; Gl, 416–17; LR, 76; Sk, 139; Howe, "Aldhelm's Enigmata," 53–54; Ju, 18–19 and 106–7. (SK 14386)

SOLUTION: *LORICA* (armor). See further ES, 87–88; Hyer and Owen-Crocker, "Woven Works"; Owen-Crocker, "'Seldom . . . does the deadly spear rest for long'"; Weber, "Isidorian Context"; Soper, "Count of Days," 78–82; Cavell, *Weaving Words,* 54–67; Taylor, "Enigma Variations," 74–77. See too Leahy, *Anglo-Saxon Crafts,* 131–33.

Aldhelm's aenigma (in effect, a single sentence) represents a considerable expansion on what he may have gleaned from Isidore, *Etym.* 18.13.1–2 (see further Klein, "Old English Translation"; Weber, "Isidorian Context"). This aenigma is the source for both EXE 33 and LEI. It is notable for its use of the technical vocabulary of weaving enshrined in the middle three lines *(Licia . . . fila . . . texunt . . . radiis . . . pectine),* with the opening pair of lines stressing the fact that the creature in question is both earth-born and not made of wool, and the closing pair highlighting its martial life *(Spicula . . . faretris).* The notion that the creature is, despite the six preceding denials *(Non . . . nulla . . . nec . . . nec . . . nec . . . nec),* nonetheless referred to as "clothing" *(vestis)* in "common speech" *(vulgi sermone vocabor)* is intriguing with regard to the insistent alliteration on *v-*. The reference here to China (ALD 33.4: *Seres)* begins a series of deceptively exotic aenigmata that also extend to the worlds of Egypt (ALD 34.6 [*LOCUSTA,* "locust": *Nilotica regna*] and ALD 36.6

[SCNIFES, "midge": *Memphitica rura]*), Greece, and Rome (ALD 35.6 *[NYCTICORAX*, "night-raven"]: *romuleis . . . biblis . . . voce Pelasga*).

33.1 Compare ALD 27.1 *(ex gelido . . . viscere);* TAT 31.2 *(nasci gelido natum de viscere matris)* and 39.1 *(Natam me gelido terrae de viscere);* LOR 4.1 *(me . . . ex gelido generat . . . tergore matris);* SYM 7.3 *(me genuit);* ps-SYM 1 *(Mater me genuit);* ALD 59.1 *(Me . . . genuit)* and 97.1 *(me genuit);* TAT 11.1 *(me genuit);* BON 14.1 *(me genuit);* BIB 1.1 *(me . . . genuit)* and 2.1 *(me genuit).*

33.2 See note on ALD 12.2 above. Compare ALD 17.2 *(Vellera setigero).*

33.4 Compare BON 20.20–21 *(lanugine texunt . . . / Seres vermes).*

33.5 Compare Virgil, *Aeneid* 6.647 *(pectine pulsat);* Aldhelm, *Carmen de virginitate* 67 *(pulset pectine).* The "wheel" and "hard comb" are parts of a spinning wheel.

33.6 Compare ALD 18.2 *(vocor sermone Pelasgo);* Aldhelm, *Carmen de virginitate* 1808 *(vulgi sermone).* For the future form *vocabor* used in place of the present tense, compare BON 7.9 *(vocabor),* BON 8.7 *(vocabor),* BON 11.5 *(depingent),* BON 13.34 *(dominabor),* and BON 19.1 *(vocabor);* BER 54.4 *(requiret);* ALF E.1 *(habebor),* ALF G.1 *(habebor),* ALF G.2 *(habebor),* and ALF K.1 *(habebar).* It is tempting to connect such usage with the fact that Old English does not distinguish formally between the present and future tenses (the latter is often formed with auxiliary verbs). An alternative might be to emend to the imperfect *vocabar.*

33.7 Compare Aldhelm, *Carmen de virginitate* 2276 *(spicula . . . longis exempta faretris).*

ALD 34

MANUSCRIPTS: D, fol. 14r; L, fol. 88r–v (no. 33); G, fol. 397v (no. 33); B, fol. 62v; O, fol. 4v.

EARLIER EDITIONS AND TRANSLATIONS: Eh, 112; Gl, 418–19; LR, 77; Sk, 140–41; Ju, 20–21 and 107. (SK 13024)

SOLUTION: *LOCUSTA* (locust). See further ES, 221–22.

For the biblical story, see Exodus 10:5 and 14. The reference to the plagues of Egypt connects this aenigma to ALD 36 (*SCNIPHES*, "gnat, midge") which follows.

34.1 Compare SYM 24.1 *(Non . . . agricolis . . . utilis hospes).*

34.2 Compare ALD 50.2 *(viridi de cespite);* Virgil, *Aeneid* 3.304; Ovid, *Metamorphoses* 10.166, 13.395, and 15.573 *(viridi . . . caespite);* Aldhelm, *Carmen de virginitate* 118 and 172 *(cespite ruris).*

34.3 Aldhelm is very fond of the adverb *catervatim,* which he employs many times, always (as here) in the second foot, such as at Aldhelm, *Carmen de virginitate* 662, 1579, 1609, 2349, 2454, 2878, and 2901; ALD 36.2, 62.6, and 75.9.

34.4 Compare Aldhelm, *Carmen de virginitate* 1452 and 1505 *(Nilotica tellus).*

34.6 Compare Prudentius, *Hamartigenia* 1.918 *(carcere saeptus)* and Aldhelm, *Carmen ecclesiasticum* 4.7.24 *(carcere saeptas).*

34.7 While most manuscripts clearly read *plagae,* the accusative *plagas,* witnessed in the earliest (eighth-century) manuscript, St. Petersburg, Russian National Library, Q. v. I. 15, seems far preferable.

ALD 35

MANUSCRIPTS: D, fol. 14r–v; L, fol. 88v (no. 34); G, fol. 397v (no. 34); B, fol. 63r; O, fol. 4v.

EARLIER EDITIONS AND TRANSLATIONS: Eh, 112; Gl, 418–19; LR, 77; Sk, 142–43; Howe, "Aldhelm's Enigmata," 47–50; Ju, 20–21 and 107–8. (SK 4093)

SOLUTION: *NYCTICORAX* (night-raven). See further ES, 190–92; Whitman, "Birds of Old English Literature"; Kitson, "Old English Bird-Names."

This is one of several aenigmata that play explicitly on perceived Greek etymology; the others are ALD 18 (*MYRMICOLEON,* "ant lion"), ALD 51 (*ELIOTROPUS,* "heliotrope"), and ALD 60 (*MONOCERUS,* "rhinoceros"). While the previous aenigma focuses attention on the exotic Nile kingdoms of Egypt, this one makes capital of the combined Latin and Greek elements in the name of the creature, the undoubted solution of which is *nycticorax*. The double element is, appropriately enough, stressed twice, first in the opening line *(Duplicat . . . geminis)*, and again in the penultimate line, which offers exotic circumlocutions to cover both the Latin and Greek worlds *(Romuleis . . . Pelasga)*. Precisely what kind of bird Isidore intends by a *nycticorax* (the word also appears in the Vulgate Psalm 101:7) is a different matter: the Old English *niht-hrefn* is a simple calque. Commentators have argued over whether this "night-raven" is more properly to be identified as a screech owl or a heron; Isidore, *Etym.* 12.7.39–42, distinguishes a *nycticorax* from a *strix*, "screech owl" and a *noctua*, "night-owl." In the Old English glosses *nycticorax* is glossed as *niht-hraefn*. See further the headnotes to EUS 58 (*NOCTUA*, "owlet") and EUS 60 (*BUBO*, "horned owl"). Compare Isidore, *Etym.* 12.7.41:

> Nycticorax ipsa est noctua, quia noctem amat. Est enim avis lucifuga, et solem videre non patitur.

> The *nycticorax* is also a night owl, because it loves the night. It is a bird that flees the light and cannot bear to look at the sun.

35.1 The phrase *mihi nomen* (or *nomen mihi*) is commonplace in the aenigmata; compare SYM 25.3; ALD 37.1, 58.1, 60.10, and 95.1; EUS 55.2; Arator, *De actibus apostolorum* 1.795 *(rite figuram)*.

35.4 Compare ALD 82.6; EUS 55.3 *(Quin magis)*.

35.6 Compare ALD 18.2 *(MYRMICOLEON*, "ant lion": *sermone Pelasgo)*, ALD 60.10 *(MONOCERUS*, "unicorn": *lingua Pelasga)*; EUS 53.1 *(YPOTAMA*, "hippopotamus": *voce Pelasga)*; ALF A.2 *(voce Pelasga)*; Juvencus, *Evangelia* 1.480; Aldhelm, *Carmen ecclesiasticum* 3.66; *Carmen de virginitate* 500. The phrase *Romulei bibli*, "Roman fables," presumably refers not to the *Fables* of Aesop directly, but to their various reflexes in, for example, Avianus, whose *Fabulae* are preserved in three manuscripts written or owned in Anglo-Saxon England (G–L

252 [here manuscript S], 535, and 664); see further Lapidge and Mann, "Reconstructing the Anglo-Saxon Aesop."

ALD 36

MANUSCRIPTS: D, fol. 14v; L, fol. 88v (no. 35); G, fol. 397v (no. 35); B, fol. 63r; O, fol. 4v–5r.

EARLIER EDITIONS AND TRANSLATIONS: Eh, 113; Gl, 420–21; LR, 76; Sk, 144; Howe, "Aldhelm's Enigmata," 47; Ju, 20–21 and 108. (SK 2804)

SOLUTION: *SCNIFES* (midge). See further ES, 208; Foxhall Forbes, "Book-Worm or Entomologist?"; Murphy, *Unriddling the Exeter Riddles,* 81–82.

The usual spelling is *cinifes,* but the *sc-* spelling (properly *SCINIFES*) is supported by an apparent etymological pun on *scando* in ALD 36.2, and backed up by Isidore, *Etym.* 12.8.14:

> Sciniphes muscae minutissimae sunt, aculeis permolestae. Qua tertia plaga superbus Aegyptiorum populus caesus est.

> *Sciniphes* are very tiny flies, very irritating with their stinging. The proud people of Egypt were struck down by these in the third plague.

The reference to the plagues of Egypt connects this aenigma to ALD 34 (*LOCUSTA,* "locust"); the biblical tale is told in Exodus 8:16–18 and Psalms 104:31. Aldhelm makes a further reference to the *scniphes* at ALD 93.9. Various forms of *scniphes* are glossed as both *mycg,* "midge," and *gnæt,* "gnat."

36.1 Compare ALD 66.5 *(stimulis . . . acerbis)* and TAT 34.2 *(stimulis . . . acervis);* Aldhelm, *Carmen de virginitate* 1818 *(stimulis . . . acerbis);* Alcuin, *Carmen* 59.25 *(stimulis armatus acutis).*

36.2 Compare TAT 17.4 *(ardua ceu pennis)*; SYM 35.2 *(peragrans super ardua gressu)*; Virgil, *Aeneid* 12.892 *(ardua pinnis)*. For the use of *catervatim* here, see the note at ALD 34.3 above.

36.3 Compare SYM 33.2 *(sanguineas praedas)*; Aldhelm, *Carmen de virginitate* 1749 *(mucrone cruento)*.

36.4 Compare ALD 75.9 *(spicula trudunt)*.

36.6 Compare ALD 28.3 *(fama clarus per Gnossia rura)*. Aldhelm is fond of the adjective *Memphitica*, which he perhaps derives from Paulinus of Nola, *Carmen* 27.39, and employs at Aldhelm, *Carmen de virginitate* 751, 971, 1469, 2477, and 2558. The extended gloss in L derives from Isidore, *Etym.* 15.1.31 *(memphitica)*.

36.7 Given the false quantity in *toros* (the usual scansion is *tŏros*), it is tempting to emend to *Namque toros*, as a single manuscript does, especially as the correct scansion *tŏr-* is attested no fewer than thirteen times in Aldhelm, *Carmen de virginitate* (at 88, 121, 242, 443, 617, 1175, 1287, 1722, 1800, 1844, 2016, 2127, and 2524). But the manuscripts are consistent, and elsewhere in ALD *Nam* opens the line eighteen times (PR.14, 2.4, 8.2, 19.4, 22.5, 29.4, 35.2, 43.2, 48.5, 60.8, 61.6, 63.8, 84.3, 85.3, 93.6, 100.7, 100.23, and 100.42), while opening *Namque* is comparatively rare (only 88.6); I have therefore retained the predominant reading, and assume that Aldhelm realized his mistake and corrected it in later composition. Compare ALD 43.3 *(SANGUISUGA*, "leech": *sanguine vescor)*. The insistent soundplay on *toros terebrans taurorum* is notable.

ALD 37

MANUSCRIPTS: D, fol. 14v; L, fol. 88v–89r (no. 36); G, fol. 397v–98r (no. 36); B, fol. 63r; O, fol. 5r.

EARLIER EDITIONS AND TRANSLATIONS: Eh, 113; Gl, 420–21; LR, 77; Sk, 145–46; Howe, "Aldhelm's Enigmata," 54–57; Ju, 22–23 and 108–9. (SK 10159)

SOLUTION: *CANCER* (crab); second-recension manuscripts include a gloss that is indeed more obscure than what it seeks to gloss, and may be the original lemma (*DE CANCRO QUAE NEPA VOCATUR,* "on the crab that is called a *nepa*"). See further ES, 200–202; Lockhart, "Everyday Wonders and Enigmatic Structures," 58–60.

This is one of several aenigmata in which Aldhelm appeals to ancient etymology; see the note at ALD 5 (*IRIS,* "rainbow"). This aenigma is an oddity, in that the creature in question declares itself openly in the very first line, if only the reader is sufficiently learned to identify the antique form *nepa,* which actually refers to a scorpion, and which several Anglo-Saxon glossaries (perhaps attempting to elucidate ALD) helpfully render *hæfern* or *crabba.* It is striking how closely *nepa,* when rendered backwards according to the retro-movement of the crab itself, approximates (in the form *apen*) the Old English solution *(h)æfe(r)n.* The traveling of the creature over earth and sea and sky is emphasized by three different verbs *(spatior . . . transeo . . . scando),* each of which is scanned differently, presumably as an *aide-mémoire* to poets looking for alternative forms to suit different verses; the same technique is also apparent in the aenigma that follows. The association of the creature in question with all three of the elements earth, sea, and sky is a theme common in the Anglo-Saxon riddle tradition: see further, for example, ALD 48.6–7 (*VERTICO POLI,* "sphere of the heavens"). Compare also Isidore, *Etym.* 11.4.3 and 12.6.51: the latter passage describes the particular antipathy of crabs and oysters, and how the former prevent the closing of the shell of the latter by cunning placement of a hard pebble, so allowing leisurely consumption. For other crab/oyster pairs, see the notes on EXE 74 (*OSTRE,* "oyster") and EXE 75 (*CRABBA,* "crab") below. Compare too the extended gloss in L, which derives from Isidore, *Etym.* 12.6.51–52 *(cancri . . . ostrea).*

37.1 Compare ALD 60.11 *(dixerunt voce Latini);* EUS 54.6 *(nomen dixere Latini).* For the use *metri gratia* of the form *dixere,* compare ALD 44.1 *(genuere);* for the outright declaration of the name, albeit in an unusual form, compare EXE 21 (*BOGA,* "bow": *Agof is min noma).*

37.2 Compare Ovid, *Metamorphoses* 11.397 and 15.507; Lucan, *Bellum civile* 1.693; Aldhelm, *Carmen ecclesiasticum* 4.3.5; *Miracula S. Nyniae* 30 *(litora ponti).*

37.3 Note the lengthening of the final syllable of *retrograda* here before mute and liquid in next word; there are other examples at ALD 20.3, 41.2, 51.4, 61.2, 77.7, 81.1, 82.6, 86.8, 87.3, 100.6, 100.13, and 100.59. See further Orchard, *Poetic Art of Aldhelm,* 76.

37.4 Compare Aldhelm, *Carmen ecclesiasticum* 4.6.21 and *Carmen de virginitate* 1224 *(aethereum . . . Olimpum).*

37.5 Compare BON 1.10 *(sidera scandam).*

37.6 Compare Isidore, *Etym.* 12.6.51. See too Salvador-Bello, "The Oyster and the Crab" (primarily on EXE 74 and 75).

ALD 38

MANUSCRIPTS: D, fol. 14v–15r; L, fol. 89r (no. 37); G, fol. 398r (no. 37); B, fol. 63r; O, fol. 5r.

EARLIER EDITIONS AND TRANSLATIONS: Eh, 114; Gl, 422–23; LR, 77; Sk, 147; Ju, 22–23 and 109–10. (SK 11903)

SOLUTION: *TIPPULA* (water strider); second-recension manuscripts include a gloss (*DE TIPPULA ID EST VERMIS QUI NON NANDO SED GRADIENDO AQUAS TRANSIT,* "on the water strider, which is to say the insect that crosses water not by swimming but by walking"). See further ES, 201–11; Sorrell, "Like a Duck to Water," 29–34; Meccariello, "Echo of Nonius Marcellus"; Lockhart, "Everyday Wonders and Enigmatic Structures," 58–60.

This aenigma is related to the one immediately preceding by the motif of movement across more than one element: while the crab both as a creature and as a constellation covers land, sea, and sky, so here the "water strider" or "pond skater" traverses water as if it were dry land. The extraordinary variety of words and phrases for the key concepts of water *(latices . . . limphas . . . aquosas . . . flumina . . . amnem . . . fluvios . . . aequora)* and traveling *(Pergo . . . calco . . . transire . . . gradior)* offer an aspiring poet a useful stock of expressions with different shades of meaning and (at least as important in the composition of metrical verse) different metrical footprints. Meccariello argues that Aldhelm uses Nonius Marcellus, *De compendiosa doctrina* 264.8 (which describes the *tippula*), as a source, both here and at ALD 100.40–41 (where of course the word *tippula* appears at ALD 100.41).

38.6 Compare ALD 42.4 *(potius pedibus spatior),* ALD 84.3 *(gradior pedibus),* ALD 100.68 *(pedibus gradior).* There is a close parallel in Ovid, *Metamorphoses* 14.50 *(Summaque decurrit pedibus super aequora siccis),* describing the jouney of the enchantress Circe. The lightly dactylic meter presumably mimics the insect's gentle step.

ALD 39

MANUSCRIPTS: D, fol. 15r; L, fol. 89r (no. 38); G, fol. 398r (no. 38); B, fol. 63r–v; O, fol. 5r.

EARLIER EDITIONS AND TRANSLATIONS: Eh, 114; Gl, 422–23; LR, 78; Sk, 148; Ju, 22–23 and 111. (SK 14518)

SOLUTION: *LEO* (lion). See further ES, 222–23; Orchard, *Pride and Prodigies,* 290–91 (*Liber monstrorum* 2.1).

This aenigma, connected conceptually and verbally to the preceding by a lack of fear (ALD 38.2, *nec . . . vereor* matches ALD 39.5, *haud vereor*), is unusual in its evident enumeration of four different kinds of animal that are emphatically *not* the subject, namely boars, stags, bears, and wolves *(apros . . . cervos . . . ursorum . . . luporum):* the masculine and aggressive nature of the creature in question is emphasized, as well as the alternative scansions for the creatures named, in either the accusative or genitive case. The reference in the final lines to the open eyes of the sleeping lion *(patulis . . . lumina gemmis)* gestures towards the Old English kenning for eyes as "head-gems" *(heafod-gimmas),* as in *Andreas* 31b, *ChristC* 1330a, and *Maxims I* 44a. On the lion in general, see Isidore, *Etym.* 12.2.3–5.

39.1 Compare EUS 53.4 *(dentibus apri);* Ovid, *Metamorphoses* 10.550 *(dentibus apri).*

39.2 Compare ALD 88.5 *(cornigeri . . . cervi);* Ovid, *Metamorphoses* 7.701 *(cornigeris . . . cervis).*

39.4 Compare Caelius Sedulius, *Carmen paschale* 4.296 *(ora cruentatum);* Aldhelm, *Carmen de virginitate* 362 *(rictus morsusque),* 992 *(rictusque luporum),* and 1038 *(rictus morsusque luporum).*

39.5 Compare Venantius Fortunatus, *Carmen* 6.5.237 *(regali culmine).*

39.6 Compare Claudian, *Epithalamium Laurentii* 36 *(non . . . nam . . . lumina gemmis).* The phrase *claudens lumina* is a commonplace. On the redundant use of *nam* here, one might compare the idiosyncratic redundant use of *iam* throughout TAT, detailed in the headnote there.

ALD 40

MANUSCRIPTS: D, fol. 15r; L, fol. 89r–v (no. 39); G, fol. 398r (no. 39); B, fol. 63v; O, fol. 5r.

EARLIER EDITIONS AND TRANSLATIONS: Eh, 114–15; Gl, 424–25; LR, 78; Sk, 149; Ju, 24–25 and 111. (SK 15764)

SOLUTION: *PIPER* (pepper). See further ES, 147–49. See also Salvador-Bello, *Isidorean Perceptions,* 200–201.

Pepper was an exotic luxury for Anglo-Saxons: Bede left some among his few effects when he died (see *Cuthbert's Letter on the Death of Bede,* ed. Colgrave and Mynors, 584–85). ALD 40.3 gives three different ways of designating fine dining, each demonstrating a different scansion *(dilicias epulas . . . luxusque ciborum),* and ALD 40.4 does the same for common fare such as soups, stews, and sauces *(ius . . . pulpas . . . battutas).* The extended gloss in L derives from Isidore, *Etym.* 17.8.8 (that section, however, is on *serpentes*).

40.1 Compare Ovid, *Metamorphoses* 7.626 *(rugosoque . . . cortice);* Virgil, *Georgics* 2.304 *(cortice tectus).*

40.3 Compare Aldhelm, *Carmen de virginitate* 2487 *(luxusque ciborum).*

ALD 41

MANUSCRIPTS: D, fol. 15r; L, fol. 89v (no. 40); G, fol. 398r (no. 40); B, fol. 63v; O, fol. 5v.

EARLIER EDITIONS AND TRANSLATIONS: Eh, 115; Gl, 424–25; LR, 78; Sk, 150; Ju, 24–25 and 112. (SK 10304)

SOLUTION: *PULUILLUS* (pillow); second-recension manuscripts include a gloss (*DE PULUILLO ID EST MINIMUM CERVICAL*, "on a pillow, which is to say a very small cushion"). See further ES, 54–57; Bayless, "Alcuin's *Disputatio Pippini* and the Early Medieval Riddle Tradition," 170–71; Lockhart, "Everyday Wonders and Enigmatic Structures," 62–63.

For a rather different treatment of the same object, see ALC D83 (*PULUILLUS*, "pillow").

41.1 Compare BON 12.14 (*IRACUNDIA LOQUITUR*, "anger declares": *Inrita dicta*); Virgil, *Aeneid* 10.244 (*non inrita dicta putaris*). The Virgilian phrase is, appropriately enough, addressed to the sleeping Aeneas.

41.2 Note the lengthening of the final syllable of *pande* here before mute and liquid in the next word; there are other examples at ALD 20.3, 37.3, 51.4, 61.2, 77.7, 81.1, 82.6, 86.8, 87.3, 100.6, 100.13, and 100.59. See further Orchard, *Poetic Art of Aldhelm*, 76. Compare Aldhelm, *Carmen ecclesiasticum* 4.3.12 (*credula pandentes . . . praecordia*) and 4.8.14 (*credula . . . pandit praecordia*); *Carmen de virginitate* 1396 (*pandit praecordia*), 1531 (*credula . . . praecordia*), 2393 (*credula . . . pandant praecordia*); *Miracula S. Nyniae* 23 (*credula pandentes*).

41.5 Compare Juvencus, *Evangelia* 2.786 (*mole gravatis*).

41.6 Compare Virgil, *Aeneid* 8.67 (*ima petens*); Caelius Sedulius, *Carmen paschale* 3.206 (*ima petunt*).

ALD 42

MANUSCRIPTS: D, fol. 15r; L, fol. 89v (no. 41); G, fol. 398r (no. 41); B, fol. 63v; O, fol. 5v.

EARLIER EDITIONS AND TRANSLATIONS: Eh, 115; Gl, 426–27; LR, 78; Sk, 151; Ju, 24–25 and 112–13. (SK 5665)
SOLUTION: *STRUTIO* (ostrich). See further ES, 195–96.

There are several possible sources for this aenigma, including Pliny, *Nat. Hist.* 10.1 and Isidore, *Etym.* 12.7.20; Job 39:13–18. See further the headnote to EUS 57 (*STRUTIO,* "about an ostrich"). The extended gloss in L derives from Isidore, *Etym.* 12.7.20 *(strutio).*

42.2 Compare ALD 66.3 *(Par . . . dispar);* Caelius Sedulius, *Carmen paschale* 5.206 *(par . . . sed dispar causa).*
42.3 Reading *nam summa* with the second-recension manuscripts; the first-recension manuscripts read *summa dum,* so creating a hiatus that Aldhelm seems to have corrected. Compare ALD 16.3 *(scando per aethera pennis)* and 48.6 *(pennis aethera tranet);* LOR 3.1 *(per aethera trano);* Virgil, *Georgics* 1.406 and 409 *(secat aethera pennis).*
42.4 Compare ALD 38.6 *(potius pedibus gradior);* Aldhelm, *Carmen de virginitate* 642 *(per squalida rura)* and 757 *(squalida . . . rura).*

ALD 43

MANUSCRIPTS: D, fol. 15r–v; L, fol. 89v–90r (no. 42); G, fol. 398v (no. 42); B, fol. 63v; O, fol. 5v.
EARLIER EDITIONS AND TRANSLATIONS: Eh, 116; Gl, 426–27; LR, 78; Sk, 152; Howe, "Aldhelm's Enigmata," 45–46; Ju, 24–25 and 113. (SK 9098)
SOLUTION: *SANGUISUGA* (leech). See further ES, 211.

The source of this aenigma seems to be Isidore, *Etym.* 12.5.3:

> Sanguisuga vermis aquatilis, dicta quod sanguinem sugit. Potantibus enim insidiatur, cumque labitur faucibus vel ubi uspiam adhaerescit, sanguinem haurit; et cum nimio cruore maduerit, evomit quod hausit, ut recentiorem denuo sugat.

The leech is a kind of water-dwelling vermin, so called because it sucks blood. It lies in wait for creatures when they are drinking, and when it slips into their throat, or attaches itself somewhere, it gorges on their blood. When it is drenched by too much blood, it vomits out what it has gorged so that it may again suck fresher blood.

43.3 Compare TAT 4.2, BON 16.1, and LOR 5.5 *(bibulis . . . buccis);* ALD 36.7 *(sanguine vescor).* For the phrase *rubro . . . sanguine,* see the note on 14.2 above.

43.4 Compare ALD 14.2 *(Ossibus ac nervis);* ALD 72.6 *(geminis . . . lacertis).* The motif of listing missing body parts or attributes is a common one in the riddles: see elsewhere, for example, ALD 20.5 and EUS 40.2.

ALD 44

MANUSCRIPTS: D, fol. 15v; L, fol. 90r (no. 43); G, fol. 398v (no. 43); B, fol. 64r; O, fol. 5v–6r.

EARLIER EDITIONS AND TRANSLATIONS: Eh, 116; Gl, 428–29; LR, 79; Sk, 153; Ju, 24–25 and 113. (SK 9491)

SOLUTION: *IGNIS* (fire).

The last two lines of this aenigma seem also to fit a description of Lucifer, although several of the texts in ALD seem to invite more than one solution: see the headnotes to ALD 1 and ALD 2 above. Many of the same themes are repeated in ALD 93 (*SCINTILLA,* "spark"). There are some broad parallels in *Hisperica famina* A426–51 (*DE IGNE,* "on fire"; see further Herren, *Hisperica Famina: The A-Text;* Orchard, "*Hisperica famina* as Literature"). See too Soper, "Count of Days," 78–82.

44.1 Compare LOR 1.2 *(me pater),* LOR 4.1 *(Me pater . . . gelido);* BER 3.1 *(Me pater);* TAT 31.2 *(gelido . . . matris);* BER 23.1 *(pater . . . me generat mater).* The phrase *gelido. . . rigore* is best solved as "flint," so offering a riddle within a riddle, such as is found elsewhere in the Anglo-Saxon riddle tradition in (for example) ALD 67, 70, and 77; EXE 1, 3, 9, 24, 76, 77, and 83.

44.4 Compare Ovid, *Metamorphoses* 2.617 and 15.799 *(vincere fata).*

44.6 Compare LOR 11.3 *(naturae iura rescidi);* Virgil, *Aeneid* 2.157 *(resolvere iura)* and 4.27 *(iura resolvo);* Aldhelm, *Carmen ecclesiasticum* 4.7.28 *(penitus naturae iura resolvens); Carmen de virginitate* 54 *(naturae iura relaxas),* 1139 *(naturae iura resolvens),* and 1920 *(naturae iura rescindens).*

44.7 Compare SYM 67.2 *(sideris instar);* Arator, *De actibus apostolorum* 1.1068 *(sideris . . . instar).*

44.8 Reading *post haec* with the second-recension manuscripts; the first recension has *postmodum et,* with hiatus. Compare BON 9.2 *(nigrior exsto);* Ovid, *Metamorphoses* 12.402 *(pice nigrior).*

ALD 45

MANUSCRIPTS: D, fol. 15v; L, fol. 90r (no. 44); G, fol. 398v (no. 44); B, fol. 64r; O, fol. 5v–6r.

EARLIER EDITIONS AND TRANSLATIONS: Eh, 117; Gl, 430–31; LR, 79; Sk, 154–55; Ju, 26–27 and 113–14. (SK 7918)

SOLUTION: *FUSUM* (spindle); second-recension manuscripts include a Latin gloss (*DE FUSO QUO FILA TORQUENTUR,* "on a spindle, on which threads are twisted"). See further ES, 47–48, and in general Owen-Crocker, "Weapons and Armour," 272–316.

It is striking that the seven lines of this aenigma exhibit six different metrical patterns, just as the five lines of the aenigma that follows exemplify five different patterns of scansion, so suggesting their combined utility in teaching Latin meter. For the general usefulness of the creation of fabrics to make people warm, see too TAT 11.3 *(ACUS,* "needle": *sed constat nullum sine me iam vivere posse).* This aenigma shares many of the same themes as ALD 74 (*FUNDIBALUM,* "sling").

45.1 Compare ALD 94.1 *(EBULUS,* "dwarf elder": *fronde virescit).*

45.3 Given the false quantity in *molam* (the usual scansion is *mŏlam*), it is tempting to emend to *mōlem* ("mass, weight"), but compare Aldhelm, *Carmen de virginitate* 1464 *(vehit in collo tereti vertigine molam)*. It may be that Aldhelm simply confused the forms and the senses.

45.5 The extended gloss in L derives from Isidore, *Etym.* 8.11.93 *(Parcae)*.

45.6 The extended gloss in L derives from Isidore, *Etym.* 19.26.1 *(stragula)*.

ALD 46

MANUSCRIPTS: D, fol. 15v (ALD 46.5 is missing); L, fol. 90r–v (no. 45); G, fol. 398r (no. 45); B, fol. 64r; O, fol. 6r.

EARLIER EDITIONS AND TRANSLATIONS: Eh, 117; Gl, 433–27; LR, 79; Sk, 156; Howe, "Aldhelm's Enigmata," 40–41; Ju, 26–27 and 114. (SK 16408)

SOLUTION: *URTICA* (nettle). See further ES, 157.

This aenigma seems to be an adaptation of SYM 44 (*CEPA,* "onion"), with the pun there on *adurat* that offers a clue to the solution likely derived from Isidore, *Etym.* 17.9.44, but here focused on the single word *fervida.* See Rusche, "Isidore's *Etymologiae* and the Canterbury Aldhelm Scholia," 439. The extended gloss in L derives from Isidore, *Etym.* 17.9.44 *(urtica)*:

> Urtica ex eo vocata quod tactus eius corpus adurat. Est enim igneae omnino naturae et tactu perurit, unde et pruriginem facit.

> The nettle *(urtica)* is so called because contact with it burns the flesh, for it is altogether of a fiery nature and it inflames *(perurere)* through touch, whereby it also causes an itch *(prurigo)*.

46.1 Compare SYM 44.1 *(mordeo mordentes ultro non mordeo quemquam)*.

46.3 For the notion of "plucking a bright-green stalk," compare EXE 23.8 (*CIPE,* "onion": *ræseð mec on reodne* "rushes me to redness"); the phallic significance of the stalk may have been suggested by a perceived pun on *vir,* "man, manliness," in *viridem,* "bright green."

46.4 Compare ALD 31.5 *(turgescunt membra).*

46.5 Compare Aldhelm, *Carmen de virginitate* 2070 *(stimulis . . . acutis).*

ALD 47

MANUSCRIPTS: D, fol. 16r; L, fol. 90v (no. 46); G, fol. 398v–99r (no. 46); B, fol. 64r–v; O, fol. 6r.

EARLIER EDITIONS AND TRANSLATIONS: Eh, 117–18; Gl, 433–44; LR, 79; Sk, 157–58; Ju, 26–27 and 114–15. (SK 69)

SOLUTION: *HIRUNDO* (swallow). See further ES, 180–82; Pliny, *Nat. Hist.* 8.41.

The immediate source of this aenigma is probably Isidore, *Etym.* 17.9.36:

> Chelidonia ideo dicitur vel quod adventu hirundinum videtur erumpere, vel quod pullis hirundinum si oculi auferantur, matres eorum illis ex hac herba mederi dicantur.

> The celandine *(chelidonia)* is so called either because it seems to burgeon with the coming of swallows [compare χηλιδών, "swallow"] or because if the eyes of swallow chicks are picked out, their mothers are said to heal them with this herb.

47.2 In L, the whole line is glossed in Old English as *wa,* "woe" (the manuscript has ƿ*a*); note too the Old English gloss ƿ (*wynn,* "joy") at ALD 40.3. Compare Venantius Fortunatus, *Carminum appendix* 30.1 *(ieiunia longa parari).*

47.3 Compare ALD 100.68 *(gramina ruris).*

47.4 Compare Virgil, *Georgics* 4.307 *(garrula . . . hirundo).*

47.5 Compare ALD 31.6 *(Sic teneros pullos prolemque);* Virgil, *Aeneid* 1.431 *(gentis adultos).*

47.6 Compare ALD 51.1 and SYM 99.1 *(Sponte mea);* compare Juvencus, *Evangelia* 2.582.

47.7–9 These lines play on the connection between Latin *chelidonia,* "the plant celandine," and the adjective *chelidonius,* "pertaining to swallows," from which it was derived.

47.8 Compare Aediluulf, *De abbatibus* 11.71 *(medicans . . . cataplasma salutis).*

47.9 Compare TAT 7.1 *(proprio sub nomine);* ALF T.3 *(proprio me nomine).* The extended gloss in L derives from Isidore, *Etym.* 17.9.36 (which, however, is on celandine, *chelidonia*).

ALD 48

MANUSCRIPTS: D, fol. 16r; L, fol. 90v–91r (no. 47); G, fol. 399r (no. 47); B, fol. 64v; O, fol. 6r.

EARLIER EDITIONS AND TRANSLATIONS: Eh, 118; Gl, 434–35; LR, 79–80; Sk, 159–60; Ju, 28–29 and 115. (SK 15282)

SOLUTION: *VERTICO POLI* (sphere of the heavens). See further Salvador-Bello, *Isidorean Perceptions,* 203–4.

The phrase *vertigo poli* also appears in Juvencus, *Evangelia* praef. 13 and Aldhelm, *Carmen de virginitate* 2690.

48.6 Compare ALD 16.3 *(scando per aethera pennis)* and ALD 42.3 *(trano per aethera pennis);* LOR 3.1 *(per aethera trano);* Virgil, *Aeneid* 10.265 *(aethera tranant);* Virgil, *Georgics* 1.406 and 409 *(secat aethera pennis);* Aldhelm, *Carmen de virginitate* 47 *(pedibus pergant).*

48.6–7 Many of the riddles focus on the earth/sea/sky triad, as here. See further the headnote at ALD 37 (*CANCER,* "crab").

ALD 49

MANUSCRIPTS: D, fol. 16r; L, fol. 91r (no. 48); G, fol. 399r (no. 48); B, fol. 64v; O, fol. 6v.

EARLIER EDITIONS AND TRANSLATIONS: Eh, 119; Gl, 436–37; LR, 80; Sk, 161; Ju, 28–29 and 115–16. (SK 7205)

SOLUTION: *LEBES* (pot), although several manuscripts prefer *CACCABUS* (cauldron). Both ultimately derive from Greek, whether λέβης, "kettle, cauldron," or κακκάβος, "three-legged pot." See further ES, 22–26.

For the conflict between fire and water described here, compare ps-BED 10 (*LEBES,* "cauldron"); ALC D76 (*LEBES,* "cauldron"). See too Isidore, *Etym.* 20.8.4 (on *lebes*), although the extended gloss in L derives from Isidore, *Etym.* 20.8.3 *(caccabus).*

49.1 Compare SYM 88.1 *(Rubida, curva, capax);* ALD 93.8 *(Truxque rapaxque capaxque feroxque).*

49.2 Compare ALD 3.1 *(caelum terramque),* ALD 97.16 *(caeli . . . terraeque);* ps-ALC 1.2 *(caeli terraeque);* BON 19.7 *(caelum terramve).* The idea of hanging between heaven and earth links this *aenigma* to TAT 7 (*TINTINABULUM,* "bell").

49.3 Compare ALD 17.3, ALD 30.4, ALD 31.1, ALD 56.7, ALD 61.7, ALD 100.58 *(necnon et).*

49.4 Compare ALD 82.7 *(patitur discrimina),* ALD 87.2 *(patiens discrimina);* BON 4.1 *(geminae variis);* EUS 58.6 *(patior discrimina).*

ALD 50

MANUSCRIPTS: D, fol. 16r–v; L, fol. 91r (no. 49); G, fol. 399r (no. 49); B, fol. 64v; O, fol. 6v.

EARLIER EDITIONS AND TRANSLATIONS: Eh, 119; Gl, 436–37; LR, 80; Sk, 162; Ju, 28–29 and 116. (SK 12676)

SOLUTION: *MYRIFYLLON* (milfoil yarrow); second-recension manuscripts include a Latin gloss (*DE MIRIFOLIO GRECE QUOD EST MILLEFOLIUM LATINE,* "on the milfoil, its Greek name, which is *millefolium* in Latin"). See further ES, 157–59.

The phrase *mille . . . folium* at ALD 50.2 offers the broadest of hints at the solution, and such an obvious clue, mentioned in the context of both Greek and Latin terms, may indicate that in fact the real solution is a double one, in both languages.

50.2 Compare ALD 34.2 *(viridi de cespite)*; Ovid, *Metamorphoses* 13.395 *(viridi genuit de caespite florem)*, though *viridi de cespite* is a commonplace phrase.

50.3 Compare SYM 100.1, 27.2 (both *nomen habens*), 36.3 *(nomine numen habens)*, and 74.3 *(nomen habebo)*; ALD 65.9 and 91.2 *(nomen habendum)*; TAT 8.6 *(nomen habere)*; EUS 46.4 *(nomen habendo)*, 57.1 *(nomen habebo)*, and 58.3 *(nomen habens)*; ALF A.2, D.2, and H.1 *(nomen habens)*.

50.5 Compare Virgil, *Aeneid* 2.697 *(limite sulcus)*.

ALD 51

MANUSCRIPTS: D, fol. 16v; L, fol. 91r–v; G, fol. 399r–v; B, fol. 64v; O, fol. 6v.

EARLIER EDITIONS AND TRANSLATIONS: Eh, 119–20; Gl, 438–39; LR, 80; Sk, 164; Howe, "Aldhelm's Enigmata," 47–50; Ju, 28–29 and 116–17. (SK 15638)

SOLUTION: *ELIOTROPUS* (heliotrope); second-recension manuscripts include a Latin gloss (*DE ELIOTROPO GRECE QUOD EST SOLSEQUIUM LATINE*, "on a heliotrope, its Greek name, which is called *solsequium* in Latin"). See further Erhardt-Siebold, "Heliotrope Tradition"; ES, 159–60; Murphy, *Unriddling the Exeter Riddles*, 49–50.

The double Latin–Greek names here link this aenigma to the one immediately preceding; this is one of several aenigmata that play explicitly on perceived Greek etymology; the others are ALD 18 (*MYRMICOLEON*, "ant lion"), ALD 35 (*NYCTICORAX*, "night-raven"), and ALD 60 (*MONOCERUS*, "rhinoceros"). The extended gloss in L derives from Isidore, *Etym.* 17.9.37 *(eliotropi)*. Further parallels can be found in Pliny, *Nat. Hist.* 2.41; 22, 29.

51.1 Compare ALD 47.6 and SYM 99.1 *(Sponte mea)*; Ovid, *Metamorphoses* 1.63 *(occiduo . . . sole tepescunt)*.

51.2 Compare ALD 20.3 *(crocea flavescunt)*, ALD 52.4 *(flavescunt . . . flore)*.

51.4 Note the lengthening of the final syllable of *unde* here before mute and liquid in next word; there are other examples at ALD 20.3, 37.3, 41.2, 61.2, 77.7, 81.1, 82.6, 86.8, 87.3, 100.6, 100.13, and 100.59. See further Orchard, *Poetic Art of Aldhelm*, 76.

ALD 52

MANUSCRIPTS: D, fol. 16v; L, fol. 91v; G, fol. 399v; B, fol. 64v–65r; O, fol. 6v.

EARLIER EDITIONS AND TRANSLATIONS: Eh, 120; Gl, 440–41; LR, 80; Sk, 165; Howe, "Aldhelm's Enigmata," 47; Ju, 30–31 and 117. (SK 9425)

SOLUTION: *CANDELA* (candle). See further ES, 26–29.

As in other aenigmata, such as ALD 50 above, Aldhelm here offers an etymological clue in ALD 52.2 *(interiora mihi candescunt)*.

52.1 Compare Frithegod, *Breviloquium S. Wilfridi* 1133 *(palmis . . . apertis)*.

52.4 Compare ALD 51.2 *(flavescunt . . . flore)*.

52.7 Reading *extinguo* with the second-recension manuscripts; the first recension has *repello*, but with false quantity: the normal scansion is *rĕpello*.

52.8 Compare Virgil, *Aeneid* 8.180 *(viscera tosta)*.

ALD 53

MANUSCRIPTS: D, fol. 16v; L, fol. 91v–92r; G, fol. 399v; B, fol. 65r; O, fol. 6v–7r.

EARLIER EDITIONS AND TRANSLATIONS: Eh, 120–21; Gl, 442–43; LR, 80–81; Sk, 166–67; Howe, "Aldhelm's Enigmata," 51–53; Ju, 30–31 and 117–18. (SK 15346)

SOLUTION: *ARCTURUS* (Arcturus). See further Bitterli, *Say What I Am Called,* 63–64; Murphy, *Unriddling the Exeter Riddles,* 118.

For a riddle on the same topic, see EXE 20 (*CARLES WÆN,* "Charles's Wain"), and ALC D66–71 on the classical motif of the wagon of the heavens. Likewise, the extended gloss in L derives from Isidore, *Etym.* 3.71.6 (which, however, is on *Septentrio*). Aldhelm's source here is Isidore, *De rerum natura* 26.3.

53.2 The use of the rare word *esseda* (here ironically described as "in common speech") plays on the notion that Arcturus is also represented as a wagon; compare the reading of L: *famosum nomen gesto cognomine vulgi.*

53.3 For the spelling *giro* (rather than the usual *gyro*), see too ALD 98.7; BER 1.4 and 26.5.

53.4 Compare *Miracula S. Nyniae* 302 *(celorum lumina).*

53.6 Compare Virgil, *Aeneid* 3.644 *(montibus errant); Eclogues* 6.52 *(in montibus erras);* Caelius Sedulius, *Carmen paschale* 1.211 *(montibus errans).*

53.7 Compare ALD PR.35 and ALD 8.3 *(arce poli).* The term *Vergilias* here is a classical poetic term for the Pleiades, sandwiched handily between two echoes of the poet Virgil.

53.8 Compare Virgil, *Aeneid* 6.323 *(stygiamque paludem)* and 6.369 *(stygiamque innare paludem).*

53.8–9 The first recension has *pars cuius . . . manibus nigris,* with false quantities; the usual scansion is *cūius . . . mānibus.* The second recension substitutes the more metrically acceptable *cui pars . . . fundo . . . nigro.*

ALD 54

MANUSCRIPTS: D, fol. 16v–17r; L, fol. 92r; G, fol. 399v; B, fol. 65r; O, fol. 7r.

EARLIER EDITIONS AND TRANSLATIONS: Eh, 121; Gl, 444–45; LR, 81; Sk, 168; Ju, 30–31 and 118–19. (SK 2854)

SOLUTION: *COCUMA DUPLEX* (double boiler). See further ES, 22–26 and Erhardt-Siebold, "Archaeological Find."

This aenigma exhibits considerable alliteration on *f-*/*v-*. For the conflict between fire and water, sec ALD 49 (*LEBES*, "cauldron") above. Aldhelm emphasizes the antagonism not only by offering a range of terms for both fire *(larem . . . incendia . . . ignibus . . . flammas)* and water *(laticem . . . undantes . . . limphae . . . flumina fontis . . . undas)*, displaying considerable metrical variety, but also by juxtaposing and alternating them in the middle four lines of the *aenigma (larem laticem . . . undantes . . . incendia limphae ignibus . . . flumina fontis . . . flammas . . . undas)*. The gloss in L, with what may be a reference to Viking double cooking-pots, is intriguing: *Quam pyrate in navibus solent habere vel tantis vel rerum vel causis.*

54.1–2 Reading (with L and the second-recension manuscripts) *tantarum foedera rerum . . . morum;* the first-recension manuscripts read *tantis spectacula causis . . . rerum.* Compare BON 5.1 *(cernere quis poterit).*

54.2 Compare SYM 75.2 *(contraria fato);* Virgil, *Aeneid* 1.239; Aldhelm, *Carmen de virginitate* 1171 *(fatis contraria fata).*

54.3 Compare ALD 93.5 *(gestant . . . ventris).* In L, *ventris* is glossed in Old English as *wambe.*

54.4 Compare Caelius Sedulius, *Carmen paschale* 1.203 *(vincunt incendia poenae);* for the participle *undantes,* see too ALD 48.4 and 92.2.

54.5 Compare ALD 100.74 *(flumine fontis).* The phrase *ignibus atris* is a commonplace. Compare Caelius Sedulius, *Carmen paschale* 3.300 *(aut ignibus atris).*

54.6 Compare ALD 75.6 *(foedera pacis);* Aldhelm, *Carmen de virginitate* 2628 *(foedera pacis).*

ALD 55

MANUSCRIPTS: D, fol. 17r; L, fol. 92r; G, fol. 399v–400r; B, fol. 65r–v; O, fol. 7r.

EARLIER EDITIONS AND TRANSLATIONS: Eh, 122; Gl, 446–47; LR, 81; Sk, 169; Ju, 32–33 and 119–21. (SK 584)

SOLUTION: *CRISMAL* (chrismal). See further ES, 94–104; Erhardt-Siebold, "Aldhelm's Chrismal"; Crane, "Describing the World," 139–41.

55.1 Compare Caelius Sedulius, *Carmen paschale* 5.4 *(munere plenam);* Arator, *De actibus apostolorum* 1.477 *(munere plenos),* 2.321 *(plenus munere).*

55.2 Compare Virgil, *Aeneid* 7.613 *(reserat . . . limina);* Caelius Sedulius, *Carmen paschale* 1.287 *(reserantur limina);* see too Virgil, *Aeneid* 6.525; Paulinus of Nola, *Carmen* 32.163; Aldhelm, *Carmen de virginitate* 571 and 2821 *(limina pandit).*

55.3 Glosses suggest that "corners" may be the best translation of *aulis.*

55.5 Compare ALD 96.11 *(auri fulvis . . . metallis),* BON 13.8 *(Auri . . . fulvo . . . metalla);* Aldhelm, *Carmen de virginitate* 1341 *(Aurea . . . fulva);* Eucheria, *Carmen* 1 *(Aurea concordi quae fulgent fila metallo).*

55.7 *Versus Sibyllae* 28 *(species flagrat pulcherrima Christi).*

55.8 The phrase *gloria rerum* is a commonplace. Compare ALD 91.3 *(florescit gloria).*

55.9 Compare Statius, *Thebaid* 7.44 *(tecta columnis).*

ALD 56

MANUSCRIPTS: D, fol. 17r; L, fol. 92r–v; G, fol. 400r; B, fol. 65v; O, fol. 7r.

EARLIER EDITIONS AND TRANSLATIONS: Eh, 122; Gl, 448–49; LR, 81; Sk, 170–71; Ju, 32–33 and 121–22. (SK 7255)

SOLUTION: *CASTOR* (beaver); second-recension manuscripts include a Latin gloss (*DE CASTORE QUI LATINE FIBER DICITUR,* "on a beaver, which is called *fiber* in Latin"). See further ES, 175–77;

Pliny, *Nat. Hist.* 8.47; the extended gloss in L derives from Isidore, *Etym.* 12.2.21 *(castores).*

56.1 Compare Ovid, *Metamorphoses* 1.729; Statius, *Thebaid* 4.703 *(margine ripae).*

56.2 Compare Venantius Fortunatus, *Vita S. Martini* 1.111 and 458; Aldhelm, *Carmen de virginitate* 2850 *(belliger armis).*

56.4 The "axes" in question are of course teeth; on the mock-heroic aspect here, see the note on ALD 26 (*GALLUS*, "cockerel") above.

56.7 Compare ALD 17.3, 30.4, 31.1, 49.3, 61.7, and 100.58 *(necnon et).*

ALD 57

MANUSCRIPTS: D, fol. 17r–v; L, fol. 92v; G, fol. 400r; B, fol. 65v; O, fol. 7v.

EARLIER EDITIONS AND TRANSLATIONS: Eh, 123; Gl, 450–51; LR, 81–82; Sk, 172–73; Ju, 32–33 and 122–23. (SK 1055)

SOLUTION: *AQUILA* (eagle). See further ES, 192–94.

57.1 Compare Virgil, *Aeneid* 1.28 *(et rapti Ganymedis)* and 5.255 *(rapuit Iovis armiger).* For the use of direct quotations within riddles and aenigmata, see the note at ALD 7.2 (*FATUM*, "fate") above.

57.1–3 The reference is to Zeus in the form of an eagle abducting Ganymede.

57.2 Compare ALD PR.17 *(carmina vatem),* 79.2 *(carmina vatum),* and 97.3 *(carmine vates);* BON 13.44 *(carmine vatum);* BIB 5.7 *(carmine vatum);* ALF Z8 *(carmine . . . vates);* Aldhelm, *Carmen ecclesiasticum* 2.18 and 4.9.10; Aldhelm, *Carmen de virginitate* 1912 and 2772.

57.4 Compare ALD 65.7 *(agitare fugaces).*

57.5 Compare Virgil, *Aeneid* 2.512 and 8.28 *(sub aetheris axe);* Virgil, *Aeneid* 10.265 *(grues . . . aethera tranant).*

57.8 Compare ALD 26.2; EUS 11.1 and 58.2 *(lumine Phoebi);* Juvencus, *Evangelia* 2.482; Aldhelm, *Carmen de virginitate* 180 *(praeclaro . . . lumine).*

ALD 58

MANUSCRIPTS: D, fol. 17v; L, fol. 92v–93r; G, fol. 400r; B, fol. 65v; O, fol. 7v.

EARLIER EDITIONS AND TRANSLATIONS: Eh, 123; Gl, 452–53; LR, 82; Sk, 174–75; Ju, 34–35 and 123–24. (SK 1055)

SOLUTION: *VESPER SIDUS* (evening star).

58.1 Compare SYM 28.1 *(Nox mihi . . . nomen primo de tempore noctis)*; EUS 55.2 *(mihi nomen adhesit)*.

58.2 Compare ALD 100.8 *(complector . . . cardine)*.

58.3 Lapidge and Rosier, 102, note that Aldhelm equates Titan with Christ in his *Carmen de virginitate*.

58.4 Compare Virgil, *Aeneid* 10.307 *(unda relabens)*; Ovid, *Metamorphoses* 1.570 *(volvitur undis)*.

58.4–5 Reading *descendens . . . abscondens* with the second-recension manuscripts; the first recension has *relabens . . . recondens*, with false quantities: the usual scansion is *rĕlabens . . . rĕcondens*.

58.5 Compare Caelius Sedulius, *Carmen paschale* 3.235; Aldhelm, *Carmen de virginitate* 813 *(per vitreos . . . campos)*.

58.6 Compare BON 17.16 *(ab aethra)*.

58.7 Compare Bede, *Vita S. Cudbercti* 237 *(noctis cum pelleret umbras)*; Juvencus, *Evangelia* 4.149; Aldhelm, *Carmen de virginitate* 908 *(furvis . . . umbris)*; 2321 and 2453 *(furvas . . . umbras)*.

ALD 59

MANUSCRIPTS: D, fol. 17v; L, fol. 93r; G, fol. 400r–v; B, fol. 65v–66r; O, fol. 7v.

EARLIER EDITIONS AND TRANSLATIONS: Eh, 124; Gl, 454–55; LR, 82; Sk, 176; Ju, 34–35 and 124–25. (SK 16185)

SOLUTION: *PENNA* (pen); second-recension manuscripts include a glossing elucidation (*DE PENNA SCRIPTORIS*, "on a writer's pen"). See further ES, 57–63; Bitterli, *Say What I Am Called*, 143; Murphy, *Unriddling the Exeter Riddles*, 88–89; Dale, *Natural World*, 89–91.

The pelican imagery may connect this aenigma to the previous one, through a shared Christological theme. Another rhetorical conceit in this aenigma is the constant contrast between white (note the initial chiasmus *candens . . . albam . . . albentes . . . candenti*) and black *(nigratis fuscans),* a theme also picked up elsewhere, as the note at 59.3–5 makes clear. For other aenigmata connected with the classroom and scriptorium, see the headnote to ALD 30 (*ELEMENTUM,* "letter of the alphabet").

59.1 Compare SYM 7.3 *(me genuit);* ps-SYM 1 *(Mater me genuit);* ALD 33.1 *(me genuit)* and 97.1 *(me genuit);* TAT 11.1 *(me genuit);* BON 14.1 *(genuit me);* BIB 1.1 *(me . . . genuit)* and 2.1 *(me genuit).*

59.2 Compare Virgil, *Aeneid* 9.23 *(hausit de gurgite lymphas);* Aldhelm, *Carmen de virginitate* 410 *(in gurgite limphis).*

59.3 Compare LOR 9.2 *(PENNA,* "quill pen": *per albentes . . . campos);* Juvencus, *Evangelia* 2.313 *(albentes . . . campos);* Aldhelm, *Carmen de virginitate* 645 and 872 *(directo tramite);* Alcuin, *Carmen* 1 1029 *(per angustam quas recto tramite callem).*

59.3–5 For the "black on white" theme in the context of writing, see TAT 4.3 (*APICES,* "letters"); EUS 7.2 (*LITTERAE,* "letters"), 32.3 (*MEMBRANUM,* "parchment"), and 35.4 (*PENNA,* "quill pen"); LOR 12.4–5 (*ATRAMENTUM,* "ink"); BER 25.1 (*LITTERAE,* "on letters"); EXE 49.3 (*FEÐER OND FINGRAS,* "quill pen and fingers") and 55.2–3 (*STAFAS,* "letters").

59.6 Compare Bede, *Vita S. Cudbercti* 378 *(pandere callem).*

59.7 Compare Aldhelm, *Carmen de virginitate* 763 *(tramite tendunt),* 1315 *(tramite tendens),* 2275 *(tramite . . . tendens),* and 2677 *(tramite tendant).*

59.8 Compare ALD 86.4 and 100.3; TAT 40.4; BON 3.3, 4.12, 8.8, 14.1, 16.12, and 17.7 (all variations on *caeli culmina, culmina caelorum, culmina caeli,* or *culmine caeli*).

ALD 60

MANUSCRIPTS: D, fol. 17v–18r; L, fol. 93r–v; G, fol. 400v; B, fol. 66r; O, fol. 7v–8r.

EARLIER EDITIONS AND TRANSLATIONS: Eh, 124–25; Gl, 456–57; LR, 82; Sk, 177–78; Howe, "Aldhelm's Enigmata," 47–50; Ju, 34–35 and 125–26. (SK 2458)

SOLUTION: *MONOCERUS* (unicorn); second-recension manuscripts include a Latin gloss (*DE MONOCEROTE GRECE UNICORNU LATINE,* "on a unicorn, its Greek name, *unicornus* in Latin"). See further ES, 229–31; Pliny, *Nat. Hist.* 8.31; Crane, "Describing the World," 148–56.

This is one of several aenigmata that play explicitly on perceived Greek etymology; the others are ALD 18 (*MYRMICOLEON,* "ant lion"), ALD 35 (*NYCTICORAX,* "night-raven"), and ALD 51 (*ELIOTROPUS,* "heliotrope"). The immediate source is likely Isidore, *Etym.* 12.2.12–13:

> Rhinoceron a Graecis vocatus. Latine interpretatur in nare cornu. Idem et monoceron, id est unicornus, eo quod unum cornu in media fronte habeat pedum quattuor ita acutum et validum ut quidquid inpetierit, aut ventilet aut perforet. Nam et cum elephantis saepe certamen habet, et in ventre vulneratum prosternit. Tantae autem esse fortitudinis ut nulla venantium virtute capiatur; sed, sicut asserunt qui naturas animalium scripserunt, virgo puella praeponitur, quae venienti sinum aperit, in quo ille omni ferocitate deposita caput ponit, sicque soporatus velut inermis capitur.
>
> The rhinoceros *(rhinoceron)* is named by the Greeks; in Latin it means "horn on the nose." The same creature is a *monoceron,* that is, a unicorn *(unicornus),* because it has a single horn four feet long in the middle of its forehead, so sharp and strong that whatever it attacks it tosses in the air or impales. It often fights with the elephant and after wounding it in the belly throws it down to the ground. It has such strength that it can

be captured by no hunter's ability, but, as those who have written about the natures of animals claim, if a virgin girl is placed before it, as the beast approaches, she may open her lap and it will lay its head there with all its fierceness set aside, and thus lulled and disarmed it may be captured.

Note the extraordinary amount of alliteration on (for example) *f-/v-*, *p-*, and *c-* in this aenigma.

60.1 Compare SYM 26.2 *(discrimine Martis);* TAT 17.5 *(discrimina Martis);* Virgil, *Aeneid* 7.608 *(saevi . . . Martis);* Lucan, *Bellum civile* 3.336 *(discrimina Martis),* 4.770 *(discrimine Martis),* and 5.723; Cyprianus Gallus, *Genesis* 247 *(celsis . . . collibus).*

60.3 Reading *arciferi* with the second-recension manuscripts; the first recension has *arcister,* a rare term which Aldhelm uses elsewhere in his *Epistola* 5 to Heahfrith (Eh 493/7, *belliger arcister*); see further Lapidge, "Career of Aldhelm," 41. Compare Virgil, *Aeneid* 7.165 *(spicula contorquent);* Aldhelm, *Carmen de virginitate* 2701 *(spicula ferri).*

60.5 Compare BON 20.8 *(vulnera sterno).*

60.6 Compare Aldhelm, *Carmen de virginitate* 1897 *(arte fefellit).*

60.10 Compare ALD 95.1 *(nomen mihi).* For the phrase *nomen mihi,* see the note at 35.1.

60.11 Compare ALD 37.1 *(nomen . . . dixere Latini);* EUS 54.6 *(nomen dixere Latini).*

ALD 61

MANUSCRIPTS: D, fol. 18r; L, fol. 93v; G, fol. 400v; B, fol. 66r; O, fol. 8r.

EARLIER EDITIONS AND TRANSLATIONS: Eh, 125; Gl, 452–53; LR, 83; Sk, 179–80; Ju, 36–37 and 126. (SK 3394)

SOLUTION: *PUGIO* (dagger); second-recension manuscripts include a Latin gloss (*DE PUGIONE VEL SPATA,* "on a dagger or short sword"). See further ES, 77–85; Lendinara, "Aspetti della società germanica."

The extended gloss in L derives from Isidore, *Etym.* 18.6.6 *(pugio).*

61.2 Note the lengthening of the final syllable of *materia* before mute and liquid in next word here; there are other examples at ALD 20.3, 37.3, 41.2, 51.4, 77.7, 81.1, 82.6, 86.8, 87.3, 100.6, 100.13, and 100.59. See further Orchard, *Poetic Art of Aldhelm,* 76.

61.4 Compare ALD 100.6 *(clauduntur lumina);* Virgil, *Aeneid* 10.746 and 12.310; Juvencus, *Evangelia* 2.761; Aldhelm, *Carmen de virginitate* 959 *(clauduntur lumina).*

61.5 Compare ALD 97.10 *(nitor defendere).*

61.7 Compare ALD 17.3, ALD 30.4, ALD 31.1, ALD 49.3, ALD 56.7, ALD 100.58 *(necnon et).*

ALD 62

MANUSCRIPTS: D, fol. 18r; L, fol. 93v; G, fol. 400v; B, fol. 66r–v; O, fol. 8r.

EARLIER EDITIONS AND TRANSLATIONS: Eh, 125–26; Gl, 454–55; LR, 83; Sk, 181; Ju, 36–37 and 126–27. (SK 3360)

SOLUTION: *FAMFALUCA* (bubble); second-recension manuscripts include a Latin gloss (*DE FAMFALICA GRECE BULLA AQUATICA LATINE,* "on a bubble, its Greek name, in Latin a watery ball").

62.1 Compare Aldhelm, *Carmen ecclesiasticum* 4.9.8; *Carmen de virginitate* 1989 *(aethera guttis).*

62.2 Compare Claudian, *In Rufinum* 1.159 *(flumina lapsu).*

62.4 Compare BON 13.49 *(viscera rumpant).*

62.5 Compare ALD 74.9 *(tenues . . . in auras);* Ovid, *Metamorphoses* 8.179, 8.834; Arator, *De actibus apostolorum* 1.92.

ALD 63

MANUSCRIPTS: D, fol. 18r; L, fol. 93v–94r; G, fol. 400v–401r; B, fol. 66v; O, fol. 8r–v.

EARLIER EDITIONS AND TRANSLATIONS: Eh, 126; Gl, 462–63; LR, 83; Sk, 183–84; Ju, 36–37 and 127. (SK 4013)

SOLUTION: *CORBUS* (raven). See further ES, 183–85.

This is the spelling of the solution found in the manuscripts; the usual spelling is *CORVUS* (on such *-b-* for *-f-* or *-v-* spellings, see the headnote on LEI below); the reference to the Flood is from Genesis 8:6–7, but otherwise, the likely source is Isidore, *Etym.* 12.7.43:

> Corvus, sive corax, nomen a sono gutturis habet, quod voce coracinet. Fertur haec avis quod editis pullis escam plene non praebeat, priusquam in eis per pinnarum nigredinem similitudinem proprii coloris agnoscat; postquam vero eos tetros plumis aspexerit, in toto agnitos abundantius pascit. Hic prior in cadaveribus oculum petit.

> The raven *(corvus)*, or *corax*, takes its name from the sound of its throat, because it croaks *(coracinare)* with its voice. It is said that this bird does not provide food fully for the young it has hatched until it recognizes in them a similarity to its own color through the blackness of their feathers, but after it sees that they are grim-feathered it nourishes them more abundantly, as fully acknowledged offspring. This bird seeks the eyes of a corpse before any other part.

This is one of at least twenty-three logogriphs in the aenigmata; others include: ALD 70 (*TORTELLA*, "loaf of bread"): *spelta* → *pelta*, ALD 86 (*ARIES*, "ram"): *aries* → *paries*; BED 11 (*ONUS*, "burden"): *bonus* → *onus*, BED 12 (*NAVIS*, "ship"): *navis* → *avis*; EUS 34 (*FLUMEN*, "river"): *flumen* → *lumen*, EUS 44 (*PANTER*, "panther"): *panter* → *pater*; TAT 4 (*APICES* "letters"): *nomen* → *omen*, TAT 35 (*PRUNA*, "ember"): *pruna* → *pruina*; ALC 2 (*MALUM*, "evil" → *MULAM*, "mule"), ALC 3 (*VIRTUS*, "power" → *TUS*, "incense" → *VIR*, "man" → *VIRUS*, "venom"), ALC 4 (*CANUS*, "white-haired man" → *ANUS*, "old woman" → *SUS*, "swine"), ALC 5 (*MAGNUS*, "mighty" → *AGNUS*, "lamb" → *MANUS*, "hand" → *MAGUS*, "magician" → *MUS*, "mouse" → *ANUS*, "old woman"), ALC 6 (*SIC ET NON*, "yes and no" → *MEUM ET TUUM*, "mine and yours" → *EGO ET TU*, "I and you" → *NOS ET VOS*, "we and you" [?]); LOR 7 (*DE CASTANEA*, "about the chestnut"): *castanea* → *casta*; SYM 36 (*PORCUS*, "pig"):

porcus → *orcus*, SYM 74 (*LAPIS*, "stone"): *lapis* → *apis*; ALF F: *flumen* → *lumen*, ALF M: *mater* → *ater*, ALF N: *nomen* → *omen*; XMS P2 (*TURTUR*, "turtledove"), XMS P3 (*ARIES* → *PARIES*, "ram" → "wall of a house"), XMS S2 (*REX*). There is an evident biblical connection to the aenigma that follows.

63.1 Compare TAT 4.5 (*littera tollatur*); EUS 34.6 (*littera subtrahitur post haec*); BON 5.6 (*humanum . . . in aevum*). The rhyming of *truculenta fluenta* is matched by Aldhelm, *Carmen de virginitate* (*fluenta cruenta*).

63.2 Aldhelm, *Carmen de virginitate* 2503 (*multarent aequora flustris*).

63.4 Compare BON 10.20 (*foedera iuris*).

63.5 Compare Prudentius, *Peristephanon* 11.9 (*subdere colla*).

63.6 Compare Aldhelm, *Carmen de virginitate* 29 (*quondam . . . fertur dixisse poeta*).

63.7 This is another direct quotation from a curriculum-poet, in this case Caelius Sedulius, *Carmen paschale* 1.175 (*abluit in terris quidquid deliquit in undis*). For other examples, elsewhere, see the note at ALD 7.3 above.

63.10 Compare ALC 3.4 and 5.2; TAT 4.5 (*Littera tollatur*); EUS 34.6 (*Littera subtrahitur*); the wordplay implied in the logograph turns on *corvus* or *corbus*, "raven," vs. *orbus*, "bereaved, childless" (on such *-b-* for *-v-* spellings, see the headnote on LEI below). See too the reference to logographs in the headnote to ALD 86.

ALD 64

MANUSCRIPTS: D, fol. 18r–v; L, fol. 94r; G, fol. 401r; B, fol. 66v; O, fol. 8v.

EARLIER EDITIONS AND TRANSLATIONS: Eh, 126; Gl, 464–65; LR, 83; Sk, 184; Ju, 38–39 and 127–28. (SK 3014)

SOLUTION: *COLUMBA* (dove). See further ES, 185–86; Isidore, *Etym.* 7.3.22.

There is a good parallel at XMS Y1 (*NOE ET COLUMBA,* "Noah and the dove"). The reference to the Flood is to Genesis 8:8–9; the connection with the preceding aenigma is obvious.

64.2 Compare Lucan, *Bellum civile* 3.322 *(scelerum contagia).*

64.3 Compare BON 5.5 and 7.10 *(conplentur iussa superna);* Virgil, *Aeneid* 7.368 *(iussa parentis);* Juvencus, *Evangelia* 3.697 *(iussa parentis).* The phrase is a commonplace.

64.4 Compare Caelius Sedulius, *Carmen paschale* 1.203 *(vincunt incendia).*

64.5 Compare ALD 89.2 *(gestant praecordia);* BER 45.4 *(semper praecordia restant).*

ALD 65

MANUSCRIPTS: D, fol. 18v; L, fol. 94r–v; G, fol. 401r; B, fol. 66v; O, fol. 8v.

EARLIER EDITIONS AND TRANSLATIONS: Eh, 127; Gl, 466–67; LR, 84; Sk, 185; Ju, 38–39 and 128–29. (SK 5107)

SOLUTION: *MUSIO* (mouser); the various manuscripts give, with various degrees of glossing, *MURICEPS,* "mouse-catcher," and *DE CATTO VEL MURICIPE VEL PILACE,* "on a cat or a mouse-catcher or a kitty." See further ES, 174–75.

The source is likely Isidore, *Etym.* 12.2.38:

> Musio appellatus, quod muribus infestus sit. Hunc vulgus cattum a captura vocant. Alii dicunt, quod cattat, id est videt. Nam tanto acute cernit ut fulgore luminis noctis tenebras superet. Unde a Graeco venit catus, id est ingeniosus, APO TOU KAIESTHAI.

> The mouser *(musio)* is so called because it is hateful to a mouse *(mus).* Common people call it the cat *(cattus)* from "catching" *(captura).* Others say it is so named because *cattat,* that is, "it sees"—for it can see so keenly *(acute)* that with the brightness

of its eyes it overcomes the darkness of night. Hence "cat" comes from Greek, that is, "clever," from καίεσθαι ["to be lit up," i.e. the passive form of καίειν, "to kindle"].

65.2 Compare ALD 89.2 *(gestant praecordia).* Note Aldhelm's customary wordplay on *lustro* in the double sense "wander" and "illuminate" (an ambiguity amply exploited by Boniface); see the note at ALD 5.4: the root of the form is picked up in ALD 65.6 *(lustra).*

65.4 Compare Virgil, *Aeneid* 4.402 and *Georgics* 1.185 *(farris acervum).* Note the ambiguity of *invisus,* in its twin sense "unseen" and "hateful."

65.5 Compare ps-SYM 2.1 (*Insidiis tacite dispono scandala mortis*).

65.6 Compare Virgil, *Georgics* 2.471 *(lustra ferarum);* Juvencus, *Evangelia* 1.364 *(lustra ferarum).*

65.7 Compare ALD 57.4 *(agitabo fugaces).*

65.8 Compare Dracontius, *De laude Dei* 3.501 *(crudelia bella);* Frithegod, *Breviloquium S. Wilfridi* 390 *(crudelia bella lacessunt).*

65.9 For the parallel notion of "having a name," see the note at ALD 50.3.

ALD 66

MANUSCRIPTS: D, fol. 18v; L, fol. 94v; G, fol. 401r; B, fol. 67r; O, fol. 8v.

EARLIER EDITIONS AND TRANSLATIONS: Eh, 127; Gl, 468–69; LR, 84; Sk, 186; Ju, 38–39 and 129–30. (SK 10575)

SOLUTION: *MOLA* (mill). See further ES, 17–19; Rahtz and Bullough, "Anglo-Saxon Mill."

66.1 Compare SYM 77.1 *(aequales . . . sorores)* and EUS 48.1 *(sumus aequales . . . sorores);* BON 9.9 *(sorte sororum).*

66.3 Compare ALD 42.2 *(Par . . . dispar);* Caelius Sedulius, *Carmen paschale* 5.206 *(par . . . sed dispar causa).*

66.5 Compare ALD 36.1 *(stimulis . . . acerbis)* and TAT 34.2 *(stimulis . . . acervis);* Arator, *De actibus apostolorum* 2.1

(stimulis agitata); Aldhelm, *Carmen de virginitate* 1818 *(stimulis . . . acerbis)*.

66.7 Compare BON 13.53, 14.9, and 17.1 *(fraude maligna* or *fraude malignum)*; Juvencus, *Evangelia* 2.112 *(sine fraude maligna)*.

ALD 67

MANUSCRIPTS: D, fol. 18v–19r; L, fol. 94v; G, fol. 401r–v; B, fol. 67r; O, fol. 8v–9r.

EARLIER EDITIONS AND TRANSLATIONS: Eh, 127–28; Gl, 470–71; LR, 84; Sk, 187; Ju, 40–41 and 130. (SK 15326)

SOLUTION: *CRIBELLUS* (sieve); second-recension manuscripts are more fulsome (*DE CREBELLO QUO FURFURAE A FARINA SEQUESTRANTUR*, "on a sieve, by which the husks are removed from flour"). See further ES, 19–21; Howe, "Aldhelm's Enigmata," 47.

The solution seems enshrined in an etymological pun in the opening line *(crebris . . . fenestris)*, which offers a broad hint.

67.1 Compare Cyprianus Gallus, *Judices* 307 *(sicca pruinosos)*.

67.5 Compare Cyprianus Gallus, *Exodus* 296 *(funera leti)*.

67.7 Compare BON 13.13 *(limina Ditis)*. Note the pun *ditati . . . Ditis*, linking the riches and death.

67.8 The double monosyllabic ending *haec nix* is rare, but not unparalleled elsewhere; see, for example, ALD PR.12 *(sed nec)*.

67.9 Compare TAT 11.4 and 14.3 *(Est mirum dictu)*; Aldhelm, *Carmen de virginitate* 384 and 1216.

ALD 68

MANUSCRIPTS: D, fol. 19r; L, fol. 94v–95r; G, fol. 401v; B, fol. 67r; O, fol. 9r.

EARLIER EDITIONS AND TRANSLATIONS: Eh, 128; Gl, 472–73; LR, 84; Sk, 188; Ju, 40–41 and 131. (SK 15753)

SOLUTION: *SALPIX* (trumpet).

This aenigma divides easily into three parts: the opening couplet stresses the martial context of the creature in question, but is then followed by three lines emphasizing the creature's essential emptiness, expanding on the opening words *(sum cava)*; the final three lines inject a rather learned note.

68.1 Note the extensive alliteration on *c-/q-* in this line.

68.3 Compare Virgil, *Aeneid* 4.411 *(tantis clamoribus)* and 5.150 *(clamore resultant)*; Prudentius, *Apotheosis* 1, 386 *(Quidquid in aere cavo reboans tuba curva remugit)*.

68.5 Compare Venantius Fortunatus, *Vita S. Martini* 3.100 *(in toto regnaret corpore)*.

68.7 Compare Alcuin, *Carmen* 59.5 and 61.1 *(luscinia ruscis)*. Note that Alcuin borrows from this aenigma in his own poems on nightingales; see further ALD 22.

68.8 Compare ALD 60.11 *(propria dixerunt voce Latini)*.

ALD 69

MANUSCRIPTS: D, fol. 19r; L, fol. 95r; G, fol. 401v; B, fol. 67r–v; O, fol. 9r.

EARLIER EDITIONS AND TRANSLATIONS: Eh, 128–29; Gl, 474–75; LR, 85; Sk, 189; Howe, "Aldhelm's Enigmata," 43–44; Ju, 40–41 and 131–32. (SK 14865)

SOLUTION: *TAXUS* (yew). See further ES, 164–65; Crane, "Describing the World," 103–7.

Note the extensive alliteration on *f-/v-* in this aenigma.

69.1 Compare Caelius Sedulius, *Carmen paschale* 4.55 *(semper habens frondes)*.

69.4 Compare BON 13.2 *(visibus horrendum)*.

69.5 Compare Venantius Fortunatus, *Vita S. Martini* 2.76 *(quod Boreas Aquilo Libs Circius Auster et Eurus)*. Aldhelm here offers an abbreviated version of the tour de force line produced by Venantius Fortunatus, who lists six wind-names in a single hexameter; Aldhelm has selected just three, each exhibiting a different scansion.

69.7 Compare EUS 52.2 *(rictibus ora).*

69.8 Compare Juvencus, *Evangelia* 4.751; Aldhelm, *Carmen de virginitate* 470 and 698 *(cadavera leto).* It is tempting to see this final line as another variant on the "biter bitten" motif (on which see the introduction to *OEALRT,* under "Shared Themes across the Collections").

ALD 70

MANUSCRIPTS: D, fol. 19r; L, fol. 95r–v; G, fol. 401v; B, fol. 67v; O, fol. 9r.

EARLIER EDITIONS AND TRANSLATIONS: Eh, 129; Gl, 476–77; LR, 85; Sk, 190; Ju, 42–43 and 132–33. (SK 3395)

SOLUTION: *TORTELLA* (loaf of bread). See further ES, 90–93.

This aenigma offers a useful list of different words for "shield" *(pelta . . . scuta . . . clipei . . . umbo . . . parma),* which, even if they do not suggest wholly different scansions, nonetheless offer a variety of synonyms matched in Isidore, *Etym.* 18.12.1–6 *(clipeus . . . scutum . . . umbo . . . ancile . . . pelta . . . cetra . . . parma).* Aldhelm is clearly thinking of the circular shape of the standard Anglo-Saxon shield, whereas Isidore is describing a variety of different shield shapes used in the Greco-Roman world; the classical references here to both Vulcan and Hades bridge that gap, as do the clear verbal borrowings from Virgil.

70.1 Compare Virgil, *Aeneid* 9.563 *(candenti corpore).*

70.2 The term *nive,* "snow," is a reference to flour, and ties this aenigma back to ALD 67.2 *(CRIBELLUS,* "sieve": *nivem);* in both cases we find another riddle within a riddle.

70.3 Compare BON 13.17 *(CUPIDITAS AIT,* "greed speaks": *carior et multis).*

70.7 Compare Virgil, *Aeneid* 2.50 and 5.500 *(validis . . . viribus);* Juvencus, *Evangelia* 3.201 *(viribus . . . validis).*

ALD 71

MANUSCRIPTS: D, fol. 19r–v; L, fol. 95v; G, fol. 402r; B, fol. 67v; O, fol. 9r–v.

EARLIER EDITIONS AND TRANSLATIONS: Eh, 129; Gl, 478–79; LR, 85; Sk, 191; Ju, 42–43 and 132–33. (SK 9496)

SOLUTION: *PISCIS* (fish). See further ES, 198–99.

The idea that the creature in question represents both a mundane creature and a constellation is matched elsewhere, notably ALD 86 (*ARIES*, "ram"), while the combined ideas of flying, swimming, and breathing are also explored in ALD 16 (*LULIGO*, "flying fish").

71.1 Compare SYM 39.1 *(pedibus manibusque)*; EUS 40.2 *(manibus pedibusque)*; Juvencus, *Evangelia* 3.769 and 4.394; Cyprianus Gallus, *Judices* 15 *(manibus pedibusque)*.

71.3 Compare Statius, *Thebaid* 2.39 *(praepetis alae)*.

71.4 Compare Prudentius, *Contra Symmachum* 2.815 *(corpora flatu)*.

71.5 Compare TAT 17.4 *(convecta cacumina)*; the line refers to the constellation Pisces. Note the extensive alliteration on *c-*/*q-*.

71.6 Compare ALD 100.75 *(marmora ponti)*; Aldhelm, *Carmen de virginitate* 825.

ALD 72

MANUSCRIPTS: D, fol. 19v; L, fol. 95v; G, fol. 402r; B, fol. 67v; O, fol. 9v.

EARLIER EDITIONS AND TRANSLATIONS: Eh, 130; Gl, 480–81; LR, 85; Sk, 192; Ju, 42–43 and 133–34. (SK 11257)

SOLUTION: *COLOSUS* (Colossus); second-recension manuscripts include a rather puzzling gloss (*DE COLOSO VEL TORACICLO*, "on the Colossus, or *toraciclus*"). See further ES, 156; Pliny, *Nat. Hist.* 34.18; Crane, "Describing the World," 137–39; Orchard, *Pride and Prodigies*, 258–61 (*Liber monstrorum* 1.3).

72.2 Compare ALD 89.3 *(tamen ex isdem)*; Juvencus, *Evangelia* 1.744 *(membrorum munia)*; Cyprianus Gallus, *Judices* 4 *(munia sumit)*.

72.3 Compare Aldhelm, *Carmen ecclesiasticum* 4.1.21 and Aldhelm, *Carmen de virginitate* 473 *(pergere plantis).*

72.4 Compare Aldhelm, *Carmen de virginitate* 958 *(geminis sub fronte fenestris)* and 2869 *(patulis . . . sub fronte fenestris);* Caelius Sedulius, *Carmen paschale* 4.38 *(reserans sub fronte fenestras).*

72.5 Compare Bede, *Vita S. Cudbercti* 73 *(viscera flatus).*

72.8 Compare Prudentius, *Psychomachia* 7 *(turbatis sensibius intus).*

ALD 73

MANUSCRIPTS: D, fol. 19v; L, fol. 95v–96r; G, fol. 402r; B, fol. 67v–68r; O, fol. 9v.

EARLIER EDITIONS AND TRANSLATIONS: Eh, 130; Gl, 482–83; LR, 85; Sk, 193; Ju, 44–45 and 134–35. (SK 11839)

SOLUTION: *FONS* (spring).

Note the evident echoing of ALD 73.6–7 in close proximity in the *Miracula S. Nyniae* 26 and 30, where this aenigma has apparently supplied consecutive phrases in quite a different context.

73.4 Compare BON 5.1 *(numero aut quis calculo aequat)* and BON 13.20 *(numerus aut calculus aequat).*

73.6 Compare *Miracula S. Nyniae* 26 *(rutilantia sidera celi).*

73.7 Compare Aldhelm, *Carmen de virginitate* 5 and 423; *Miracula S. Nyniae* 30 *(fluctivagi . . . ponti).*

ALD 74

MANUSCRIPTS: D, fol. 19v; L, fol. 96r; G, fol. 402r; B, fol. 68r; O, fol. 9v.

EARLIER EDITIONS AND TRANSLATIONS: Eh, 131; Gl, 484–85; LR, 86; Sk, 194; Ju, 44–45 and 135–36. (SK 5603)

SOLUTION: *FUNDIBALUM* (sling). See further ES, 71–75.

The primary source is of course the biblical tale of David and Goliath, told in 1 Samuel 17:40–50.

74.1 Compare TAT 6.4 *(aequora campos)*; Virgil, *Aeneid* 7.781 and 12.710 *(aequore campi)*.

74.3 Reading *nam brachia loro* with the second-recension manuscripts; the first-recension manuscripts read *retinacula filo*.

74.7 Compare Virgil, *Aeneid* 5.208 *(ferratasque . . . cuspide contos)*.

74.8 Compare SYM 35.2 *(peragrans super ardua gressu)*. See too the headnote to BED 19 (*DIGITI SCRIBAE*, "a scribe's fingers").

74.9 Compare ALD 62.5 *(tenues . . . in auras)*; Ovid, *Metamorphoses* 8.179, 8.834; Arator, *De actibus apostolorum* 1.92.

ALD 75

MANUSCRIPTS: D, fol. 20r; L, fol. 96r–v; G, fol. 402r–v; B, fol. 68r; O, fol. 10r.

EARLIER EDITIONS AND TRANSLATIONS: Eh, 131–32; Gl, 486–87; LR, 86; Sk, 195–96; Ju, 44–45 and 136. (SK 386)

SOLUTION: *CRABRO* (hornet). See further ES, 208–10; Murphy, *Unriddling the Exeter Riddles*, 163–64.

This is another aenigma playing on mock-heroic themes, on which see the headnote to ALD 26 (*GALLUS*, "cockerel") above. Note that the first seven lines all end in *-is*, albeit for different grammatical reasons.

75.1 Compare SYM 65.2 *(pinnis / aera per medium)* and 95.2 *(aera per medium)*.

75.2 Compare Ovid, *Metamorphoses* 12.49 *(murmura vocis)*.

75.3 Compare Aldhelm, *Carmen de virginitate* 2165 and 2348 *(densis . . . turmis)*.

75.4 Compare Aldhelm, *Carmen de virginitate* 342 *(dulcia . . . alimenta)*.

75.6 Compare ALD 54.6 *(foedera . . . pacis)*; Aldhelm, *Carmen de virginitate* 442 *(disrupit foedera fratris)*, 779 *(disrumpens foedera pacis)*, 2628 *(disrumpit foedera pacis)*, 2722 *(disrupit foedera)*.

75.8 Compare Cyprianus Gallus, *Numeri* 777 *(sociasque . . . in bella cohortes)* and *Iosua* 230 *(socias . . . in bella cohortes)*.

75.9 Compare ALD 36.4 *(spicula trudo).*

75.9–11 Note that here again Aldhelm includes three synonyms (in this case *spicula . . . iaculis . . . tela*) each of which offers a different scansion.

75.11 Compare Lucan, *Bellum civile* 3.567 *(torquentur tela).*

75.12 Compare BON 17.3 *(per tetra venena);* Aldhelm, *Carmen de virginitate* 1017 *(tetrum . . . venenum),* 1093 *(tetra venena);* Virgil, *Aeneid* 7.341; Dracontius, *De laude Dei* 3.303; Venantius Fortunatus, *Carmen* 2.7.17 *(infecta venenis).*

ALD 76

MANUSCRIPTS: D, fol. 20r; L, fol. 96v; G, fol. 402v; B, fol. 68r–v; O, fol. 10r.

EARLIER EDITIONS AND TRANSLATIONS: Eh, 132; Gl, 488–89; LR, 86; Sk, 197; Howe, "Aldhelm's Enigmata," 47; Ju, 46–47 and 136–38. (SK 4956)

SOLUTION: *MELARIUS* (apple tree); second-recension manuscripts include a gloss (*DE MELARIO VEL MALO,* "on an apple tree, or an apple"). See further ES, 168–69; Crane, "Describing the World," 107–10.

The common etymological pun on *mălum,* "evil" and *mālum,* "apple," is embodied in 76.1–2 (especially with regard to the word *maligni*). Note that ALD 76.1–4 refers to the Old Testament and ALD 76.5–7 refers to the New (with the Tree of Life necessarily supplanting the Tree of Death), a contrast embodied in the very metrics: each of the seven lines of this aenigma is scanned differently, with the heavier spondees dominating 3:1 over the lighter dactyls in the first four feet of the Old Testament lines, and the ratio reversed to 2:1 dactyls over spondees in the same feet of the New Testament lines. The subject matter links this aenigma to the one that follows.

76.1 Compare Corippus, *Iohannid* 3.45 *(fuerit belli nascentis origo);* Aldhelm, *Carmen ecclesiasticum* 4.10.9 *(nascentis origine saecli);* Aldhelm, *Carmen de virginitate* 744 *(mundi nascentis origo).*

76.5 Compare Juvencus, *Evangelia* 1.748 *(remeare salutem)* and 2.343 *(remeasse salutem).*

76.6 The phrase *arbiter orbis* is a commonplace; compare too BON 11.11 and BON 13.66; Aldhelm, *Carmen ecclesiasticum* 4.3.14 *(in patulo suspensus stipite); Carmen de virginitate* 452 *(in patulo suspensum stipite).*

76.7 Compare Juvencus, *Evangelia* 3.455 *(lueret . . . poenis);* Juvencus, *Evangelia* 4.672 *(soboles veneranda tonantis)* and 4.786 *(proles veneranda tonantis);* Aldhelm, *Carmen ecclesiasticum* 4.6.13 *(soboles . . . veneranda Tonantis).*

ALD 77

MANUSCRIPTS: D, fol. 20r; L, fol. 96v; G, fol. 402v; B, fol. 68v; O, fol. 10r.
EARLIER EDITIONS AND TRANSLATIONS: Eh, 132; Gl, 490–91; LR, 86–87; Sk, 198; Ju, 46–47 and 138. (SK 13686)
SOLUTION: *FICULNEA* (fig-tree). See further ES, 165–66; Crane, "Describing the World," 110–14.

On background and likely sources, see Genesis 3:7; 1 Kings 4:25; Matthew 21:18–22; Caelius Sedulius, *Carmen paschale* 4.45–56. Note the extensive alliterative patterning, focusing on *f-/v-, c-,* and *p-*. The subject matter links this aenigma to the one that precedes.

77.1 Compare Juvencus, *Evangelia* 4.651 *(ducebat tegmina vestis).*

77.3 Compare ALD 85.1 *(referam verbis);* Aldhelm, *Carmen de virginitate* 930 *(frivola fingam)* and 997 *(fingentes frivola).*

77.5 Compare Aldhelm, *Carmen de virginitate* 789 *(sub frondibus altis).*

77.6 The "Carian fruit" is a kind of dried fig, and is mentioned in Isidore, *Etym.* 17.7.17 *(ficus),* so providing a further riddle within a riddle.

77.7 Note the lengthening of the final syllable of *agricola* before mute and liquid in next word here; there are other examples at ALD 20.3, 37.3, 41.2, 51.4, 61.2, 81.1, 82.6, 86.8, 87.3, 100.6, 100.13, and 100.59. See further Orchard, *Poetic Art of Aldhelm,* 76.

ALD 78

MANUSCRIPTS: D, fol. 20r–v; L, fol. 96v–97r; G, fol. 402v–403r; B, fol. 68v; O, fol. 10r–v.

EARLIER EDITIONS AND TRANSLATIONS: Eh, 133; Gl, 492–93; LR, 87; Sk, 199; Ju, 46–47 and 138–39. (SK 4444)

SOLUTION: *CUPA VINARIA* (wine cask). See further ES, 41–44; Salvador-Bello, *Isidorean Perceptions,* 202–3; Dale, *Natural World,* 162–65.

As with ALD 70 (*TORTELLA,* "loaf of bread") above, which partly comprises a list of synonyms for "shield" drawn from Isidore, so too here Aldhelm employs a sequence of words scanned in a variety of ways, all relating to viticulture *(vinitor . . . uvis / pampinus . . . palmite botris / . . . vite)* and largely matched in Isidore, *Etym.* 17.5.10 and 13–14 *(pampinus . . . vitis . . . pampinus . . . de palmite; uvae; botrus).* The Christological themes of the preceding two aenigmata may have suggested this extended meditation on the benefits of the vine. Note how this aenigma makes particularly heavy use of phrases drawn from just two curriculum-authors, namely the pagan Virgil and the Christian Cyprianus Gallus, here combined.

78.1 Compare Virgil, *Aeneid* 3.354 and *Ciris* 229 *(pocula bacchi).*

78.2 Compare Virgil, *Eclogue* 10.36 *(vinitor uvae);* Caelius Sedulius, *Carmen paschale* 1.91 *(impressas . . . vinitor uvas).*

78.3 Compare Cyprianus Gallus, *Exodus* 895 *(pampineasque . . . palmite vites);* Dracontius, *De laude Dei* 2.235 *(palmite . . . pampinus admovet uvas);* Aldhelm, *Carmen de virginitate* 178 *(pampinus . . . palmite botros)* and 2792 *(palmite botros).*

78.4 Compare SYM 42.2 *(cauponis . . . tabernam).*

78.5 Compare Cyprianus Gallus, *Judices* 531; Aldhelm, *Carmen ecclesiasticum* 2.29 and *Carmen de virginitate* 1707 *(turgescunt viscera fetu).*

78.7 Reading *hauserit;* several manuscripts, including two from the first recension, read *auxerit.* In L, *hoc nectar* is glossed in Old English as *ða swe,* presumably for *ða swetnysse.*

78.10 Compare Virgil, *Aeneid* 11.136 *(fraxinus evertunt actas ad sidera pinus)* and *Georgics* 1.256 *(evertere pinum).*

ALD 79

MANUSCRIPTS: D, fol. 20v; L, fol. 97r; G, fol. 403r; B, fol. 68v–69r; O, fol. 10v.

EARLIER EDITIONS AND TRANSLATIONS: Eh, 133–34; Gl, 494–95; LR, 87; Sk, 200–201; Howe, "Aldhelm's Enigmata," 54–57; Ju, 48–49 and 139–40. (SK 10451)

SOLUTION: *SOL ET LUNA* ("sun and moon").

This is one of several aenigmata in which Aldhelm appeals to ancient etymology (see the note at ALD 5). This aenigma is also notable for the number and variety of classical references *(Saturni . . . Delo . . . Latona . . . Cynthia . . . Apollo . . . Olimpi . . . Erebi . . . Tartara),* and presumably offered a number of teachable moments in the Anglo-Saxon classroom.

79.1 Compare Aldhelm, *Carmen de virginitate* 1330 *(spurcissima proles).*

79.2 See the note on ALD PR.17 *(carmina vatem).*

79.3 Compare Aldhelm, *Carmen de virginitate* 27 *(Delo . . . Latona creatrix).*

79.5 Compare Virgil, *Aeneid* 7.558 *(summi regnator Olympi); Miracula S. Nyniae* 304 *(regnator Olimpi);* Frithegod, *Breviloquium S. Wilfridi* 12 *(summi volvit regnator Olimphi).*

79.7 Compare Damasus, *Epigramma* 3.3 *(communi lege).*

79.9 Compare ALD 100.19 *(iure guberno);* Aldhelm, *Carmen ecclesiasticum* 2.15, 3.37; Aldhelm, *Carmen de virginitate* 1693 *(iure gubernat),* 2067 *(iure gubernant).*

79.10 Compare Juvencus, *Evangelia* 1.613 *(cunctaque . . . latebris)* and 2.480 *(cuncta latebris).* A false quantity: *clauděret* is the normal usage, unless we suppose that Aldhelm confused *clauděre,* "to close," with *claudēre,* "to limp"; certainly, the meter limps here.

79.11 Compare BON 6.12 *(Erebi . . . nigri / Tartara);* BON 14.4 *(trudens in Tartara nigra);* Venantius Fortunatus, *Carmen* 2.7.48 and 4.26.88; Aldhelm, *Carmen de virginitate* 849 *(Tartara nigra).*

ALD 80

MANUSCRIPTS: D, fol. 20v; L, fol. 97r–v; G, fol. 403r; B, fol. 69r; O, fol. 10v.

EARLIER EDITIONS AND TRANSLATIONS: Eh, 134; Gl, 496–97; LR, 87; Sk, 202; Ju, 48–49 and 140. (SK 3382)

SOLUTION: *CALIX VITREUS* (glass cup). See further ES, 29–39; Murphy, *Unriddling the Exeter Riddles,* 205; Salvador-Bello, *Isidorean Perceptions,* 210–11. See too Leahy, *Anglo-Saxon Crafts,* 106–7.

This aenigma introduces the notion of kissing, which becomes something of a leitmotif throughout the Anglo-Saxon riddle tradition, and is found further, for example, at BON 6; LOR 5; EXE 12, 28, and 61; BER 5–6, 35, 42, 46; GES 4.

80.3 Compare Bede, *De die iudicii* 73 *(ignis ubique suis ruptis regnabit habenis).*

80.4 Compare SYM 52.3; TAT 8.1, TAT 9.1, TAT 12.5; ALF X.1 *(mihi . . . forma).*

80.5 Compare Aldhelm, *Carmen de virginitate* 2332 *(collum constringere).*

80.8 Compare TAT 4.2 *(dulcia quod bibulis praestamus pocula buccis);* LOR 5.5 *(Dulcia . . . bassia buccis);* Aldhelm, *Carmen de virginitate* 2137 *(dulcia . . . compressit labra labellis).*

80.9 The way that alcohol trips up the unwary is a focus of several riddles: compare BON 16.3–6 *(EBRIETAS,* "drunkenness": *Rixas irarum iugiter conturbo feroces, / Ignavos oculos et linguam famine trico, / Et pedibus tardis somnos et somnia dira);* BER 13.6 *(DE VITE,* "on a vine": *sanguine dum fuso lapsis vestigia versant);* BER 50.6 *(DE VINO,* "on wine": *et iniqua reddo me quoque satis amanti).*

ALD 81

MANUSCRIPTS: D, fol. 21r; L, fol. 97v; G, fol. 403r; B, fol. 69r; O, fol. 10v–11r.

EARLIER EDITIONS AND TRANSLATIONS: Eh, 134–35; Gl, 498–99; LR, 88; Sk, 203–4; Ju, 48–49 and 140–42. (SK 14863)

SOLUTION: *LUCIFER* (morning star).

On background and likely sources, see Isaiah 14:3–20; 2 Peter 1:19.

81.1 Note the lengthening of the final syllable of *ego* before mute and liquid in the next word here; there are other examples at ALD 20.3, 37.3, 41.2, 51.4, 61.2, 77.7, 82.6, 86.8, 87.3, 100.6, 100.13, and 100.59. See further Orchard, *Poetic Art of Aldhelm*, 76. The phrase *lumine lumen* is commonplace: compare Caelius Sedulius, *Carmen paschale* 1.313 *(patris de lumine lumen)*; Aldhelm, *Carmen ecclesiasticum* 2.5 *(lumen de lumine patris)*, *Carmen de virginitate praefatio* 24 *(lumine lumen)*, *Carmen de virginitate* 1686 *(lumen de lumine patris)*, and 1950 *(clarum . . . lumine lumen)*.

81.2 Note Aldhelm's customary pun on *lustro* in the double sense "wander" and "illuminate"; see further the note at ALD 5.4 *(lustro polos)*.

81.3 Compare ALD 92.6 *(tramite flexo)*; Aldhelm, *Carmen de virginitate* 181 *(obliquo tramite Titan)*.

81.6 Compare SYM 45.3 *(O felix)*.

81.7 Compare BON 15.9 and 20.24 *(mente superba)*.

81.8 Compare Aldhelm, *Carmen de virginitate* 2591 *(Ultio quapropter letali calce)*.

81.9 Compare ALD 16.3 *(scando per aethera)*. The "six friends" are the other six planets of the seven known in the seventh century.

81.10 Compare ALD 100.81 *(pandere quae poterit gnarus)*.

ALD 82

MANUSCRIPTS: D, fol. 21r; L, fol. 97v–98r; G, fol. 403r–v; B, fol. 69r; O, fol. 11r.

EARLIER EDITIONS AND TRANSLATIONS: Eh, 135; Gl, 500–501; LR, 88; Sk, 205–6; Ju, 50–51 and 142. (SK 3784)

SOLUTION: *MUSTELA* (weasel). See further ES, 177–78.

This is another aenigma playing on mock-heroic themes, on which see the headnote to ALD 26 (*GALLUS*, "cockerel") above. The likely source is Isidore, *Etym.* 12.3.3:

> Mustela dicta, quasi mus longus; nam telum a longitudine dictum. Haec ingenio subdola in domibus, ubi nutrit catulos suos, transfert mutatque sedem. Serpentes etiam et mures persequitur. Duo autem sunt genera mustelarum; alterum enim silvestre est distans magnitudine, quod Graeci ἴκτιδας vocant; alterum in domibus oberrans. Falso autem opinantur qui dicunt mustelam ore concipere, aure effundere partum.

> The weasel *(mustela)* is so called as if it were a long mouse *(mus)*, for a dart *(telum)* is so called due to its length. This creature, by its nature, practices deceit in the houses where it nurses its pups, and it moves and changes its dwelling. It hunts snakes and mice. There are two kinds of weasels: one, which the Greeks call ἴκτις, lives in the wild and is different in size, while the other wanders into houses. Those people are mistaken who suppose that the weasel conceives through its mouth and bears its young through its ear.

The extended gloss in L derives from Isidore, *Etym.* 12.3.3 *(mustelae)*. There are several parallels with EXE 13 (*FOX*, "fox").

82.1 Reading *curvas deflecto membra cavernas* with the second-recension manuscripts; the first recension has *curvis conversor quadripes arvis* (usually read as *antris*).

82.2 The martial and heroic tenor here (likely derived from the Isidorian etymological focus on *telum*, "dart") can be matched elsewhere: see the note at ALD 26 (*GALLUS*, "cockerel").

82.6 Note the lengthening of the final syllable of *aure* before mute and liquid in next word here; there are other examples at ALD 20.3, 37.3, 41.2, 51.4, 61.2, 77.7, 81.1, 86.8, 87.3, 100.6, 100.13, and 100.59. See further Orchard, *Poetic Art of Aldhelm*, 76. Compare ALD 35.4; EUS 55.3 (both *Quin magis*); Juvencus, *Evangelia* 1.14; Cyprianus Gallus, *Judices* 531; Venantius Fortunatus, *Carmen* 8.3.325; Aldhelm, *Carmen ecclesiasticum* 2.29, *Carmen de virginitate* 1707 (all *viscera fetu*). At issue is the reading of *ore* or *aure*, and whether birth or conception is in question.

82.7 Compare ALD 49.4 *(patior discrimine)*, ALD 87.2 *(patiens discrimina)*; EUS 58.6 *(patior discrimina)*; Paulinus of Nola, *Carmen* 16.252; Aldhelm, *Carmen de virginitate* 269 *(discrimina mortis)*, 352, 706, 1253, 2213, 2351, and 2563 *(mortis discrimina)*.

82.7–8 The idea that one weasel can revive another weasel, even at the point of death, is found elsewhere both in the French *Eliduc* of Marie de France and in the Old Norse *Vǫlsunga saga*; see further Clover, "*Vǫlsunga saga* and the Missing Lai."

ALD 83

MANUSCRIPTS: D, fol. 21r; L, fol. 98r; G, fol. 403v; B, fol. 69v; O, fol. 11r.

EARLIER EDITIONS AND TRANSLATIONS: Eh, 136; Gl, 502–3; LR, 88; Sk, 207; Howe, "Aldhelm's Enigmata," 43; Ju, 50–51 and 142–43. See further Orchard, "Enigma Variations," 297–99; Stanley, "Riddling: A Serious Pursuit," 25–26; Cavell, *Weaving Words*, 160; Dale, *Natural World*, 69–73 and 80–85. (SK 1035)

SOLUTION: *IUVENCUS* (bullock).

This aenigma has close ties with those other riddles on the same or similar theme, such as EUS 37; LOR 11; ps-BED 8; EXE 12 and 36; compare Wl, 77–80.

83.1 Compare Virgil, *Aeneid* 5.200 *(aridaque ora).*
83.2 Compare TAT 8.3 *(bis binis);* LOR 11.1 *(bis binis fontibus hausi);* Aldhelm, *Carmen de virginitate* 1613 *(bis binis).*
83.3 Compare Virgil, *Georgics* 2.53 *(stirpibus . . . imis)* and 209 *(cum stirpibus imis).*

ALD 84

MANUSCRIPTS: D, fol. 21r–v; L, fol. 98r–v; G, fol. 403v; B, fol. 69v; O, fol. 11r–v.
EARLIER EDITIONS AND TRANSLATIONS: Eh, 136; Gl, 502–3; LR, 88; Sk, 208; Ju, 50–51 and 143. (SK 7542)
SOLUTION: *SCROFA PRAEGNANS* (pregnant sow).

This aenigma divides easily into a section (ALD 84.1–5) comprising a numerological riddle on body parts, which incidentally demonstrates the flexibility of Latin verse depicting numbers through multiples and combinations of both cardinals and ordinals *(bis seni . . . bis ternumque . . . bis duodenis . . . decies novem);* and another (ALD 84.6–9) which lists no fewer than six different kinds of tree *(populus . . . taxus . . . salicta . . . fagos . . . quercus . . . ilex),* all of which appear, albeit in a different order, in Isidore, *Etym.* 17.7.26–47. The enumerative qualities of the first section are echoed elsewhere, both within and beyond this collection, and include (for example) ALD 90 (*PUERPERA GEMINAS ENIXA,* "woman bearing twins"), SYM 95 (*LUSCUS ALIUM VENDENS,* "one-eyed garlic-seller"), EXE 34 (*BAT,* boat"), and EXE 82 (*AN-EAGEDE GAR-LEAC-MONGER,* "one-eyed garlic-seller"). There is a close analogue in the Norse GES 12 (*SÚ OK GRÍSIR,* "sow and piglets"). Other riddles within the tradition which focus on body parts include ALD 20, 43, 90, and 95; EUS 40 and 45; BON 10; ALC D10–37; EXE 37, 56, and 77.

84.1 Compare ALD 90.1 *(sunt mihi . . . oculi)*; BIB 6.2 *(mihi sunt oculi)*.

84.2 Compare Paulinus of Nola, *Carmen* 23.190 *(membra gubernans)*.

84.3 Compare ALD 38.6 *(pedibus gradior)*, ALD 100.68 *(CREATURA*, "Creation": *pedibus gradior)*.

84.5 On the ninety-six different kinds of meter, see Isidore, *Etym.* 1.17.1; Aldhelm, *De pedum regulis* 112 (Eh, 150).

84.6 Compare Virgil, *Georgics* 2.13 *(populus et . . . fronde salicta)*.

84.8 Compare *Carmen Flavii Felicis* 219 *(florenti vertice)*; Aldhelm, *Carmen ecclesiasticum* 2.20 and *Carmen de virginitate* 1698 *(florenti vertice vernans)*.

ALD 85

MANUSCRIPTS: D, fol. 21v; L, fol. 98v; G, fol. 403v–4r; B, fol. 69v; O, fol. 11v.

EARLIER EDITIONS AND TRANSLATIONS: Eh, 137; Gl, 504–5; LR, 88–89; Sk, 209; Ju, 52–53 and 143–44. (SK 7542)

SOLUTION: *CAECUS NATUS* (man born blind).

Note the many words for "gift" and "giving" here, clustered in lines 3–6 *(munuscula . . . tradere . . . munere . . . dono)*, and offering a variety of different scansions.

85.1 Compare ALD 77.3 *(referam verbis)*.

85.5 Compare ALD 89.4 *(fraudabor munere)*.

ALD 86

MANUSCRIPTS: D, fol. 21v; L, fol. 98v; G, fol. 404r; B, fol. 69v–70r; O, fol. 11v.

EARLIER EDITIONS AND TRANSLATIONS: Eh, 137; Gl, 504–5; LR, 89; Sk, 210; Ju, 52–53 and 144. (SK 15762)

SOLUTION: *ARIES* (ram). See further ES, 88–90; Lendinara, "Aspetti della società germanica."

There are rather vague parallels with Isidore, *Etym.* 12.1.11 *(aries)* and *Etym.* 18.11.1–4 *(De ariete).* See further Orchard, *Poetic Art of Aldhelm,* 208, and XMS P3 below.

86.1 Compare ALD 28.2 *(cornibus armatus).*

86.3 Compare Aldhelm, *Carmen de virginitate* 2432 *(stipantes agmine).*

86.4 Compare BON 9.8 *(caelorum conscendet culmina);* ALD 59.8, ALD 100.3; TAT 40.4; BON 3.3, BON 4.12, BON 8.8, BON 14.1, BON 16.12, BON 17.7 *(caeli culmina, culmina caelorum, culmina caeli* or *culmine caeli);* Aldhelm, *Carmen de virginitate* 268 *(caelorum . . . culmina),* 873 *(scandens caelorum . . . culmina),* and 1667 *(culmina caelorum . . .scandunt).* The phrase *culmina celsa* is a commonplace; compare Aldhelm, *Carmen de virginitate* 953, 112, 1386, and 2759.

86.5–6 Note the insistent alliteration on *c-/q-* in these lines.

86.7 Compare ALD 100.60 *(CREATURA,* "Creation": *stamina pepli).*

86.8 Note the lengthening of the final syllable of *quindecima* before mute and liquid in the next word here; there are other examples at ALD 20.3, 37.3, 41.2, 51.4, 61.2, 77.7, 81.1, 82.6, 87.3, 100.6, 100.13, and 100.59. See further Orchard, *Poetic Art of Aldhelm,* 76. Removing *p* from *paries,* "wall," produces *aries,* "ram"; for more on these logogriphs within the Anglo-Saxon riddle tradition, see the note at ALD 63 (*CORBUS,* "raven"); there is a precise parallel at XMS P3. False quantity: the genitive is usually *domūs.*

ALD 87

MANUSCRIPTS: D, fol. 21v; L, fol. 98v–99r; G, fol. 404r; B, fol. 70r; O, fol. 11v.

EARLIER EDITIONS AND TRANSLATIONS: Eh, 137–38; Gl, 506–7; LR, 89; Sk, 211; Ju, 52–53 and 144. (SK 3383)

SOLUTION: *CLIPEUS* (shield); O has the solution *SCUTUM* (shield). See further ES, 85–87; Stephenson, *Anglo-Saxon Shield.*

There are several parallels with EXE 3 (*BORD*, "shield"), notably with regard to the rather wry and doleful depictions of both of the creatures in question as battle-scarred warriors.

87.2 Compare ALD 49.4 *(patior discrimine)*, ALD 82.7 *(patitur discrimina)*; EUS 58.6 *(patior discrimina)*.

87.3 Note the lengthening of the final syllable of *ego* before mute and liquid in next word here; there are other examples at ALD 20.3, 37.3, 41.2, 51.4, 61.2, 77.7, 81.1, 82.6, 86.8, 100.6, 100.13, and 100.59. See further Orchard, *Poetic Art of Aldhelm*, 76.

87.3 Compare Ovid, *Metamorphoses* 15.89 *(corpore corpus)*.

ALD 88

MANUSCRIPTS: D, fol. 21v–22r; L, fol. 99r; G, fol. 404r; B, fol. 70r; O, fol. 11v–12r.

EARLIER EDITIONS AND TRANSLATIONS: Eh, 138; Gl, 506–7; LR, 89; Sk, 212; Ju, 54–55 and 144–45. (SK 1842)

SOLUTION: *BASILISCUS* (serpent); second-recension manuscripts include a Latin gloss (*DE ASPIDE VEL BASILISCO*, "on a snake, or serpent"). See further ES, 232–33.

There are vague parallels with Isidore, *Etym.* 12.1.18 *(cervus)* and *Etym.* 7.1.27. This aenigma has a fascinating bilingual connection with ALD 87 (*CLIPEUS*, "shield"), which immediately precedes, since whereas Latin *aspis* commonly means "snake," and rarely "shield," Greek ἀσπίς more often means "shield" than "snake." The whole of the first sentence (ALD 87.1–4) is bounded by heavy alliteration on *c-* *(Callidior cunctis . . . cornigeri certamina cervi)*, and the phrases highlighted by alliteration both drop heavy hints as to the solution; high levels of sibilance and assonance on *s-* fulfill the same function.

88.1 Compare Genesis 3:1, the account of the Fall of Man.

88.3 Compare ALD 32.8 *(seges diris)*; Aldhelm, *Carmen de virginitate* 2500 *(Unde seges . . . succrevit aristis)*. The extended gloss in L derives from Isidore, *Etym.* 16.3.11 *(arista)*.

88.5 Compare ALD 39.2 *(cornigeros . . . cervos).*

88.5–6 The antagonism between stags and snakes is described by Pliny, *Nat. Hist.* 8.20; 22.37.

ALD 89

MANUSCRIPTS: D, fol. 22r; L, fol. 99r; G, fol. 404r; B, fol. 70r; O, fol. 12r.

EARLIER EDITIONS AND TRANSLATIONS: Eh, 138; Gl, 508–9; LR, 89; Sk, 213; Ju, 54–55 and 145–46. (SK 10751)

SOLUTION: *ARCA LIBRARIA* (book chest). See further Lapidge, *Anglo-Saxon Library,* 61–62; Crane, "Describing the World," 142–43. There are some broad parallels in *Hisperica famina* A513–30 (*DE TABERNA,* "on a book-container"; see further Herren, *Hisperica Famina: The A-Text;* Orchard, "*Hisperica famina* as Literature").

Given the common notion of snakes or dragons guarding various kinds of hoards, and their association with wisdom, there seems to be a connection between this aenigma and the one that precedes it. For other aenigmata connected with the classroom and scriptorium, see the headnote at ALD 30 (*ELEMENTUM,* "letter of the alphabet").

89.1 Compare TAT 34.1 *(complent mea viscera).*

89.2 Compare ALD 64.5 *(semper praecordia gesto);* BER 45.4 *(semper praecordia restant).*

89.3 Compare ALD 72.2 *(tamen ex isdem);* Juvencus, *Evangelia* 4.224 *(cognoscere quisquam).*

89.4 Compare ALD 85.5 *(fraudaret munere);* BON 18.6 *(Infelix fatum . . . fraude).* The extended gloss in L derives from Isidore, *Etym.* 8.9.93 (which, however, is on *Parcae*).

ALD 90

MANUSCRIPTS: D, fol. 22r; L, fol. 99r; G, fol. 404r; B, fol. 70r; O, fol. 12r.

EARLIER EDITIONS AND TRANSLATIONS: Eh, 139; Gl, 508–9; LR, 90; Sk, 214; Ju, 54–55 and 146. (SK 15869)

SOLUTION: *PUERPERA GEMINAS ENIXA* (woman bearing twins).

This aenigma is evidently based on the similar SYM 92 (*MULIER QUAE GEMINOS PARIEBAT*, "mother of twins"). A similar set of enumerative descriptions is found in ALD 84.1–5 (*SCROFA PRAEGNANS*, "pregnant sow"); see further the headnote there.

90.1 Compare ALD 84.1; BIB 6.2 *(mihi sunt oculi)*; EUS 12.3 *(et segetes colui nec potus ebrius hausi)*; Virgil, *Aeneid* 4.359; Ovid, *Metamorphoses* 13.787 and 14.309 *(auribus hausi)*; Aldhelm, *Carmen de virginitate* 1132 *(auribus hausisset)* and 1277 *(auribus hausit)*.

90.2 Compare Prudentius, *Contra Symmachum*, 2.301 *(corpore gestent)*; Cyprianus Gallus, *Leviticus* 209 *(corpore gestat)*; ALD 87.3 *(gestantis corpore)*; BER 57.4 *(gestare corpore)*.

ALD 91

MANUSCRIPTS: D, fol. 22r; L, fol. 99v; G, fol. 404v; B, fol. 70r–v; O, fol. 12r.

EARLIER EDITIONS AND TRANSLATIONS: Eh, 139; Gl, 510–11; LR, 90; Sk, 215–16; Ju, 54–55 and 146–47. (SK 11310)

SOLUTION: *PALMA* (palm). See further ES, 166–68; Howe, "Aldhelm's Enigmata," 44–45; Crane, "Describing the World," 114–16.

There are parallels and potential sources in John 12:13 and Isidore, *Etym.* 17.7.1 *(palma)*, part of which reads:

> Est enim arbor insigne victoriae, proceroque ac decoro virgulto, diuturnisque vestita frondibus, et folia sua sine ulla successione conservans.

> The tree is the symbol of victory, with lofty and luxuriant growth, clothed in long-lasting leaves, and preserving its leaves without any succession of foliage.

91.1 Compare BON 13.50 *(conditor excelsus dudum qui saecla creavit);* the phrase *cuncta creavit* is a commonplace; compare Aldhelm, *Carmen de virginitate* 35.

91.2 For the parallel notion of "having a name," see note at ALD 50.3.

91.3 Compare ALD 55.8 *(floret gloria);* EUS 39.2 *(nempe mearum),* EUS 43.4 *(Nomine nempe meo);* BON 4.9 *(Regmine nempe meo),* BON 19.2 *(Germine nempe meo);* Aldhelm, *Carmen ecclesiasticum* 1.1 *(florescit gloria);* Aldhelm, *Carmen de virginitate* 636 *(nomine nempe tuo)* and 2281 *(nomine nempe).*

91.4 Compare Aldhelm, *Carmen de virginitate* 2022 and 2465 *(proelia mundi).*

91.5 Compare BON 10.18 and 20.6 *(praemia vitae);* Caelius Sedulius, *Carmen paschale* 1.341; Arator, *De actibus apostolorum* 1.471; Aldhelm, *Carmen de virginitate* 1226, 2019, and 2275.

91.7 Compare Virgil, *Aeneid* 5.493 *(certamine victor);* Aldhelm, *Carmen de virginitate* 197 *(victor certamine).*

91.8 Compare ALD 24.5 *(summo . . . capitis de vertice),* ALD 26.5 *(capitis gestans in vertice);* EUS 30.2 *(gestabar vertice).*

91.11 Compare Juvencus, *Evangelia* 3.207; Aldhelm, *Carmen de virginitate* 342 and 1610 *(alimenta ciborum).*

ALD 92

MANUSCRIPTS: D, fol. 22r–v; L, fol. 99v–100r; G, fol. 404v; B, fol. 70v; O, fol. 12r–v.

EARLIER EDITIONS AND TRANSLATIONS: Eh, 140; Gl, 512–13; LR, 90; Sk, 217; Howe, "Aldhelm's Enigmata," 41–42; Ju, 56–57 and 147–48. (SK 14408)

SOLUTION: *FARUS EDITISSIMA* (very tall lighthouse); second-recension manuscripts include a gloss (*DE PHARO EDITISIMO* [for *EDITISSIMO*] *IN RUPIBUS PELAGI POSITO,* "about a very tall lighthouse situated on the rocks of the sea") which evidently derives from a description in Aldhelm's prose *De virginitate* 9 (Eh, 238; cf. Gwara, 108–9), describing virginity itself "as if a lofty lighthouse, situated on a tall promontory of rock, shone out" *(quasi praecelsa farus in edito rupis promontorio posita splendescit).* See further ES, 155; Crane, "Describing the World," 135–37.

For the notion that there was indeed a lighthouse in Aldhelm's time at a chapel in Dorset, see Barker and Le Pard, "St. Aldhelm and the Chapel at Worth Matravers." The memorial that Beowulf has constructed for himself (*Beowulf* 2802–8 and 3156–62) seems to be described rather like a lighthouse (and note that in the passage from Aldhelm's prose *De virginitate* cited above, *farus* is glossed by Old English *here-becn,* "army-beacon, army-monument"); see further Orchard, *Critical Companion to "Beowulf,"* 36–37. There is also an intriguing passage in Bede, *Historia Ecclesiastica,* which describes Roman remains, including at least one lighthouse (the form given is singular, though the context seems to require a plural, as if Bede thought that *farus* was fourth declension), still standing in his day (*HE* 1.11):

> Habitabant autem intra vallum quod Severum trans insulam fecisse commemoravimus, ad plagam meridianam, quod civitates, farus, pontes, et stratae ibidem factae usque hodie testantur: ceterum ulteriores Brittaniae partes, vel eas etiam quae ultra Brittaniam sunt insulas iure dominandi possidebant.

> Yet they [the Romans] used to live within the rampart which we have noted that Severus built across the island to the south, as it attested to the present day by cities, lighthouses, bridges, and paved roads that were created; and yet they used to control by right of conquest the farther parts of Britain and the islands beyond Britain.

The aenigma uses the same metrical form (DSSS) for nine out of ten lines; note too the consistent medial verbs, and fixed caesura-patterning emphasizing an unchanging metrical *molossus* (three long syllables) in the middle of the line, which can perhaps imaginatively be taken to mimic the form of the lighthouse itself. The aenigma offers variations on a few key themes, namely tall structures *(rupibus in celsis . . . summis . . . molibus . . . arcibus ex celsis . . . in turribus altis),* waterways *(caerula . . . salis undantes . . . aequore fluctus . . . navigeros calles . . . maris aequoreos . . . campos . . . pontum . . . tramite flexo . . . fluctibus),* and flames *(flammiger . . . torres . . . ignea)* which together offer a broad clue to the solution. Further clues are provided on the one hand by a rather obvious pun on "torches on towers" *(torres in turribus),* and on the other by a further example of Aldhelm's favorite wordplay involving the double sense of the verb *lustro* as both to "wander" or "travel" and to "illuminate," highlighted in the only line offering different scansion from the rest (line 5), and so perhaps reminding the audience of the role of the creature in question offering light to those wandering on stormy seas. For the subject matter in general, compare Isidore, *Etym.* 15.2.37 *(farus).*

92.2 Compare Juvencus, *Evangelia* 3.98 *(in aequore fluctus).*
92.3 Compare Cyprianus Gallus, *Exodus* 1 *(substructis molibus).*
92.4 Compare Bede, *Vita S. Cudbercti* 285 *(navigero . . . calle).*
92.5 Compare Aldhelm, *Carmen ecclesiasticum* 3.21 *(maris aequoreos lustrabat remige campos).*
92.6 Compare ALD 81.3 *(tramite flector).*
92.7 Compare EUS 54.2 *(et tamen inmensas);* Virgil, *Aeneid* 1.333 *(vastis et fluctibus acti)* and 7.213 *(nec fluctibus actos).*
92.9 Compare Virgil, *Aeneid* 4.187, 9.470, 10.121; Aldhelm, *Carmen de virginitate* 646 *(turribus altis).*
92.10 Compare Juvencus, *Evangelia praefatio* 3 *(ignea sidera).*

ALD 93

MANUSCRIPTS: D, fol. 22v (ALD 93.7 is missing); L, fol. 100r; G, fol. 404v–5r; B, fol. 70v; O, fol. 12v.

EARLIER EDITIONS AND TRANSLATIONS: Eh, 140–41; Gl, 514–15; LR, 90; Sk, 218; Ju, 56–57 and 144–45. (SK 12873)

SOLUTION: *SCINTILLA* (spark).

93.2 Compare BON 9.15 *(viribus audax);* Virgil, *Aeneid* 5.67; Aldhelm, *Carmen de virginitate* 2740; Aediluulf, *De abbatibus* 2.9 *(viribus audax).*

93.3 Compare SYM 25.1 *(Parva mihi);* Juvencus, *Evangelia* 2.190; Prudentius, *Apotheosis* 1.169 *(exordia vitae);* Arator, *De actibus apostolorum* 1.244 *(prima . . . exordia vitae).*

93.4 Compare TAT 32.2 *(sternere leto);* Juvencus, *Evangelia* 4.406 *(prosternere leto).*

93.5 Compare ALD 54.3 *(gesto . . . ventris);* Juvencus, *Evangelia* 3.394 *(penetralia ventris);* Aldhelm, *Carmen de virginitate* 2491 *(gestit . . . penitralia ventris).*

93.6 Compare Venantius Fortunatus, *Carmen* 7.4.17 *(nemorum saltusque).*

93.8 Compare SYM 88.1 *(Rubida, curva, capax);* ALD 49.1 *(Horrida, curva, capax).*

93.10 A fertile concept, here the frozen mother and her hard belly are references to flint; compare SYM 14.2 *(genitricis in alvo)* and 36.1 *(matris . . . natus in alvo);* ALD 100.24 *(matris . . . generabar ab alvo);* TAT 15.5 *(matris . . . in alvum),* TAT 17.1 *(nascor . . . matris in alvo);* BER 34.1 *(mater concipit alvo).*

93.11 Compare Lucan, *Bellum civile* 9.906 *(pignora gentis).*

ALD 94

MANUSCRIPTS: D, fol. 22v–23r; L, fol. 100r–v; G, fol. 405r; B, fol. 70v–71r; O, fol. 12v.

EARLIER EDITIONS AND TRANSLATIONS: Eh, 141; Gl, 516–17; LR, 91; Sk, 219; Ju, 56–57 and 149–50. (SK 14590)

SOLUTION: *EBULUS* (dwarf elder). See further ES, 162–64; Crane, "Describing the World," 116–18.

94.1 Compare ALD 45.1 *(fronde virescens).*

94.3 Reading *fronte* rather than *fronde,* which seems to derive by eye-skip from 94.1.

94.7 Compare Lucan, *Bellum civile* 9.742; Juvencus, *Evangelia* 1.733 *(viscera tabe)*; Cyprianus Gallus, *Leviticus* 53; *Miracula S. Nyniae* 330 *(viscera tabo)*.

94.8 Compare Aldhelm, *Carmen de virginitate* 2569 *(ne possit serpere virus)*.

94.9 Compare Aldhelm, *Carmen ecclesiasticum* 5.7 *(fibras olidas)*.

ALD 95

MANUSCRIPTS: D, fol. 23r; L, fol. 100v; G, fol. 405r; B, fol. 71r; O, fol. 12v–13r.

EARLIER EDITIONS AND TRANSLATIONS: Eh, 142; Gl, 518–19; LR, 91; Sk, 220–21; Ju, 58–59 and 150–51. (SK 4171)

SOLUTION: *SCILLA* (Scylla); second-recension manuscripts include a Latin gloss (*DE SCILLA ID EST MARIS NIMPHA*, "on Scylla, which is to say a sea nymph"). See further Page, "The Study of Latin Texts (2): The Evidence of English Glosses," 160–64; Crane, "Describing the World," 149–60; Orchard, *Pride and Prodigies*, 98–102, as well the text and translation of the *Liber monstrorum* 1.14, 2.20, and 2.32 (266–67, 298–99, and 304–5).

On Scylla and Charybdis, see for example Ovid, *Metamorphoses* 14.248–308. Aldhelm's likely source is Isidore, *Etym.* 11.3.32:

> Scyllam quoque ferunt feminam capitibus succinctam caninis, cum latratibus magnis, propter fretum Siculi maris, in quo navigantes verticibus in se concurrentium undarum exterriti latrari aestimant undas, quas sorbentis aestus vorago conlidit.

> They say that Scylla is a woman girt about with the heads of dogs and their mighty barking, since sailors, scared by whirlpools dashing against each other in the straits of the sea of Sicily, reckon that the waves, which the cleft of the sucking tide forces together, are barking.

95.1 Compare ALD 60.10 *(nomen mihi).*

95.2 Compare TAT 10.3 *(lingua loquendi);* EUS 59.4 *(lingua loquax);* Caelius Sedulius, *Carmen paschale* 4.63 *(lingua loquellas);* Aldhelm, *Carmen ecclesiasticum* 4.9.6; *Carmen de virginitate* 1913 *(lingua loquelis).*

95.5 Reading *cruraque cum coxis* with the second-recension manuscripts; the first recension has *femora cum cruribus,* with false quantity: the usual scansion is *crūribus.* The whole line is a list of body parts, all from the lower limbs.

95.6 Note the use of the word *virago* (perhaps suggested by Isidore's *vorago* above) for *virgo* here; the same conflation of terms is found in Aldhelm's verse *De virginitate* 1895, 1908, 2183, and 2534, and becomes something of a verbal tic in, for example, BON 9.24, 10.13, and 16.2.

95.8 Compare Venantius Fortunatus, *Vita S. Martini* 4.275 *(caerula findens).*

95.8–10 This parenthetical set-piece description of seafaring is studded with ornamental alliteration on *t-, c-, f-/v-,* and *p-.*

95.11 Compare Ovid, *Metamorphoses* 14.6 *(latrantibus inguina).*

ALD 96

MANUSCRIPTS: D, fol. 23r–v; L, fol. 100v–101r; G, fol. 405r–v; B, fol. 71r–v (ALD 96.5–6 are transposed); O, fol. 13r.

EARLIER EDITIONS AND TRANSLATIONS: Eh, 142–43; Gl, 520–21; LR, 91; Sk, 222–23; Ju, 58–59 and 151–52. (SK 5046)

SOLUTION: *ELEFANS* (elephant). See further ES, 223–24; Orchard, *Pride and Prodigies,* 290–91 (*Liber monstrorum* 2.2); Salvador-Bello, *Isidorean Perceptions,* 317–18.

For general parallels, compare Isidore, *Etym.* 12.2.14 *(elephans)* and *Etym.* 18.4.5 *(classica).* The heroic language of the battlefield is self-evident in the early part of this aenigma (ALD 96.1–7), and seems something of a set-piece description. For other examples in the Anglo-Saxon riddle tradition, see the headnote at ALD 26 (*GALLUS,* "cockerel"); with regard to parallels in the vernacular tradition, see further Stanley, "Heroic Aspects of the Exeter Book Riddles."

96.1 Compare Cyprianus Gallus, num. 394 *(densoque . . . milite turmas)*; Aldhelm, *Carmen de virginitate* 1187 *(denso milite)*, 1408, 2573, and 2670 *(milite denso)*; Prudentius, *Cathemerinon* 48; Cyprianus Gallus, *Iudices* 203 *(ferratasque acies)*; Arator, *De actibus apostolorum*, *Epistola ad Florianum* 21 *(ferratas acies)*; Wulfstan Cantor of Winchester, *Epistola specialis* 522 *(ferratas acies)*.

96.1–5 This lengthy set-piece description of battle follows hard on the heels of a similar set piece of seafaring in the preceding aenigma.

96.3 Compare TAT 34.3 *(pia . . . foedera frangam)*; Lucan, *Bellum civile* 1.4 *(acies et rupto foedere regni)* and 86 *(foedera regni)*.

96.4 Compare Cyprianus Gallus, *Iudices* 7 *(ventosis flatibus)*.

96.5 Compare Aldhelm, *Carmen de virginitate* 1549 *(salpix classica clangit)* and 2613 *(clangor . . . classica sistri)*.

96.6 Compare BON 13.5 *(murmure Martis)*.

96.7 Compare Arator, *De actibus apostolorum* 1.540 *(fecerit auctor)*; *Miracula S. Nyniae* 165 *(fecerat auctor)*.

96.8 The phrase *munera vitae* is a commonplace; compare BON 20.15 *(munera vitae)*; Juvencus, *Evangelia* 2.229, 2.769, 4.346; Paulinus of Nola, *Carmen* 32.227; Caelius Sedulius, *Carmen paschale* 5.290; Arator, *De actibus apostolorum* 1.591 and 1.845; Aldhelm, *Carmen de virginitate* 752 and 2688.

96.9 Compare ALD 6.3 *(gloria formae)*.

96.9–13 Compare SYM 49 (*EBUR*, "ivory").

96.10 Note the sound-play in the almost anagrammatic phrase *serpat apertas*.

96.11 Compare ALD 55.5 *(Aurea . . . fulvis . . . metallis)*, BON 13.8 *(Auri . . . fulvo . . . metalla)*.

96.15 Compare Cyprianus Gallus, *Genesis* 1058 *(curvo cum poplite)*; Aldhelm, *Carmen de virginitate* 375 and 1513 *(curvo poplite)*.

96.15–16 According to the medieval *Physiologus* traditions, elephants are notoriously light sleepers, and only sleep standing up.

96.16 Aldhelm is fond of the phrase *quin potius,* especially at the beginning of verses: compare Aldhelm, *Carmen de virginitate* 2769; ALD 38.6, 56.3, 59.7. Compare too LOR 2.5 and EUS 56.5.

ALD 97

MANUSCRIPTS: D, fol. 23v; L, fol. 101r–v (nos. 97 and 98); G, fol. 405v; B, fol. 71v; O, fol. 13r–v (nos. 97 and 98).

EARLIER EDITIONS AND TRANSLATIONS: Eh, 143–44; Gl, 522–23; LR, 92; Sk, 224–26; Ju, 60–61 and 152. (SK 5226)

SOLUTION: *NOX* (night). See further Salvador-Bello, *Isidorean Perceptions,* 215–16.

The fact that Aldhelm here quotes verbatim six lines from Virgil (*Aeneid* 12.846, 4.177 and 181–84) is intriguing in two ways: first, because Isidore, one of his great models, likewise quotes verbatim four lines from Virgil (*Etym.* 5.31.1–14, *De nocte*); and second, because in his embedding of poetry within poetry he sets a pattern followed by others in the Anglo-Saxon riddle tradition. Later manuscripts divide this aenigma into two, with *De fama,* "On Fame," beginning at line 11 of the original *De nocte;* compare Stork, *Through a Gloss Darkly,* 44–45. See too Orchard, "Performing Writing and Singing Silence," 77–78.

97.1 Compare SYM 7.3 *(me genuit);* ps-SYM 1 *(Mater me genuit);* ALD 33.1 *(me genuit)* and 59.1 *(Me . . . genuit);* TAT 11.1 *(me genuit),* BON 14.1 *(me genuit),* BIB 1.1 *(me . . . genuit)* and 2.1 *(me genuit);* Virgil, *Aeneid* 12.9 *(corpora tellus).*

97.2 Note the alternative spelling *stereli* here; elsewhere, Aldhelm appears to use the more usual *sterili* (*Carmen ecclesiasticum* 4.12.18; *Carmen de virginitate* 418).

97.3 Compare ALD PR.17 *(carmina vatem),* ALD 57.2 *(carmine vates),* ALD 79.2 *(carmina vatum),* BON 13.44 *(carmina vatum),* BIB 5.7 *(carmina vatum);*Aldhelm, *Carmen ecclesiasticum* 2.18 and 4.9.10; Aldhelm, *Carmen de virginitate* 1912 and 2772.

97.7 Compare Virgil, *Aeneid* 1.67 *(gens inimica mihi).*

97.8 Compare BON 13.1 *(lustrans per saecula monstrum)* and BON 20.1 *(migrans per saecula lustro).* This is another example of Aldhelm's customary wordplay on *lustro* in the double sense "wander" and "illuminate," on which see the note at ALD 5 (*IRIS,* "rainbow").

97.10 Compare ALD 61.5 *(nitor defendere).*

97.12–16 For the use of direct quotations within riddles and aenigmata, see the note at ALD 7.2 (*FATUM,* "fate") above.

97.12 Compare Virgil, *Aeneid* 4.177 and 10.767 *(ingrediturque solo et caput inter nubila condit).*

97.13 Compare Virgil, *Aeneid* 4.181 *(monstrum horrendum ingens cui quot sunt corpore plumae).*

97.14 Compare ALD 100.62 *(mirabile fatu);* TAT 27.1 *(mirabile dictu);* Virgil, *Aeneid* 4.182 *(tot vigiles oculi subter mirabile dictu).*

97.15 Compare Virgil, *Aeneid* 4.183 *(tot linguae totidem ora sonant tot subrigit auris).*

97.16 Compare ALD 3.1 *(caelum terramque),* ALD 49.2 *(caelum . . . terramve);* ps-ALC 1.2 *(caeli terraeque);* BON 19.7 *(caelum terramve);* Virgil, *Aeneid* 4.184 *(nocte volat caeli medio terraeque per umbram).*

ALD 98

MANUSCRIPTS: D, fol. 23v–24r; L, fol. 101v (no. 99); G, fol. 405v; B, fol. 71v–72r; O, fol. 13v (ALD 98.7 is missing).

EARLIER EDITIONS AND TRANSLATIONS: Eh, 144; Gl, 524–25; LR, 92; Sk, 227–28; Ju, 60–61 and 152–53. (SK 11500)

SOLUTION: *ELLEBORUS* (hellebore). See further ES, 160–62; Erhardt-Siebold (1936), 161–70; Cameron, "Aldhelm as Naturalist."

For the notion that the plant in question is really woody nightshade *(Solanum dulcamara),* see Hall, "Madness, Medication—and Self-Induced Hallucinogen? *Elleborus* and Woody Nightshade in Anglo-Saxon England," and note the gloss *wede-berge.* Aldhelm seems to have invented the term *ostriger* (the apparently parallel *ostrifer* means "oyster-bearing," and is found in Virgil, *Georgics* 1.207), and may have taken the word *conquilium* (with false quantity: the usual form is *conquīlium*) from a variant of SYM 18.3 (*COCLEA*, "snail"). There are certain similarities with EXE 9 (*WIN-FÆT*, "cup of wine"). The extended gloss in L derives from Isidore, *Etym.* 17.9.24 *(elleborus).*

98.2 Compare Caelius Sedulius, *Carmen paschale* 5.165 *(rubri sub tegmine cocci);* Aldhelm, *Carmen de virginitate* 228 *(rubro murice).*

98.2 In L, *conquilio* is glossed in Old English as *weolc-scille;* see further *conchilium* at SYM 18.3, and the note there.

98.6 Compare Corippus, *Iohannid* 6.414 *(dementia cordis).*

98.7 For the spelling *giro* (rather than the usual *gyro*), see the note at ALD 53.3.

ALD 99

MANUSCRIPTS: D, fol. 24r; L, fol. 101v (no. 100); G, fol. 406r; B, fol. 72r; O, fol. 14v.

EARLIER EDITIONS AND TRANSLATIONS: Eh, 145; Gl, 526–27; LR, 92; Sk, 229–30; Ju, 60–61 and 153–54. (SK 2681)

SOLUTION: *CAMELLUS* (camel). See further ES, 227–28.

There is a pun here on the name of the Roman consul Camillus; see further the notes on SYM 25 (*MUS*, "mouse") and SYM 32 (*TAURUS*, "bull"), which have similar and equally cringe-making puns on famous Romans. The extended gloss in L derives from Isidore, *Etym.* 12.1.35 *(camelus).*

99.2 Compare ALD PR.1 *(regmine sceptra);* ALD 7.4 *(sceptra regens mundi);* Aldhelm, *Carmen ecclesiasticum* 4.12.4 *(regni sceptra regebat).* Note *rēportant,* with false quantity: the normal scansion is *rĕportant* (see further the note on ALD 6.4).

99.5 Compare Virgil, *Aeneid* 6.591 *(cornipedum . . . equorum);* Venantius Fortunatus, *Vita S. Martini* 3.328 *(agmen equorum).*

99.6 Compare Virgil, *Aeneid* 8.596 *(quadripedante putrem);* Paulinus of Nola, *Carmen* 19.492 *(trepidi fugiuntque).*

99.7 The phrase *corporis artus* is a commonplace; compare EUS 55.8 *(corporis artus);* Appendix Vergiliana, *Ciris* 198; Ovid, *Metamorphoses* 7.317; Paulinus of Périgueux, *Vita S. Martini* 5.287 and 432; Corippus, *In laudem Iustini* 2.193.

ALD 100

MANUSCRIPTS: D, fol. 24r–25v; L, fol. 101r–v (no. 101); G, fol. 406r–7r (no. 101); B, fol. 72r–73v; O, fol. 15r–16r (no. 101). In O, the rest of fol. 16r is cut out; the metrical *Preface* to Aldhelm's *Carmen de virginitate* follows on fol. 17r.

EARLIER EDITIONS AND TRANSLATIONS: Eh, 145–49; Gl, 528–39; LR, 92–94; Sk, 231–38; Ju, 62–67 and 154–58. (SK 2552)

SOLUTION: *CREATURA* (Creation). See further Orchard, "Enigma variations," 286–87; Murphy, *Unriddling the Exeter Riddles,* 154–56; Crane, "Describing the World," 132–35; Stanley, "Riddling: A Serious Pursuit," 20–23; Cavell, *Weaving Words,* 253–56; Soper, "Count of Days," 78–82; Lockhart, "Everyday Wonders and Enigmatic Structures," 63–65; Sebo, *In Enigmate,* 71–91. Compare Stork, *Through a Gloss Darkly,* 17, who notes a particular interest in ALD 100 by the glossators in the English manuscripts, LG, perhaps suggesting that it was a particular classroom text; certainly, it was ultimately the source of EXE 38, 64, and 90 (all solved *GESCEAFT,* "creation").

There are vague parallels in Isidore, *Etym.* 13.6.1–7 *(De circulis caeli)* and 13.2.1–4. The closing lines recall SYM PR *(frivola lector).*

100.1 Compare BON 13.50 *(conditor . . . qui saecla).*

100.1–3 Compare EXE 38.1–5 *(Ece is se scyppend . . . swa he ymb þas utan hweorfeð).*

100.3 Compare ALD 59.8, ALD 86.4; TAT 40.4; BON 3.3, BON 4.12, BON 8.8, BON 14.1, BON 16.12, BON 17.7 *(caeli culmina, culmina caelorum, culmina caeli* or *culmine caeli).* The phrase *culmina caeli* is a commonplace; compare Juvencus, *Evangelia* 3.456; Paulinus of Nola, *Carmen* 10.120; Aldhelm, *Carmen ecclesiasticum* 3.15, 4.1.36; Aldhelm, *Carmen de virginitate* 2, 764, 1445, 2816, 2877 (on its use in Aldhelm in particular, see Lapidge, "Aldhelm's Latin Poetry and Old English Verse," 226–28).

100.4 Compare EXE 38.6–7 *(He mec wrætlice . . . ærest sette);* Lucan, *Bellum civile* 2.577; Prudentius, *Hamartigenia* 1.338; Aldhelm, *Carmen de virginitate* 741 *(conderet orbem).* The most significant parallel is with Virgil, *Aeneid* 1.5 *(dum conderet urbem).*

100.5 Compare EXE 38.8–9 *(heht mec wæccende . . . siþþan æfre);* Paulinus of Périgueux, *Vita S. Martini* 5.789; Arator, *De actibus apostolorum* 1.754 *(pervigil excubiis); Miracula S. Nyniae* 45; Frithegod, *Breviloquium S. Wilfridi* 846 *(pervigil excubias).*

100.6 Note the lengthening of the final syllable of *extemplo* before mute and liquid in the next word here; there are other examples at ALD 20.3, 37.3, 41.2, 51.4, 61.2, 77.7, 81.1, 82.6, 86.8, 87.3, 100.13, and 100.59. See further Orchard, *Poetic Art of Aldhelm,* 76. Compare EXE 38.10–11 *(ond mec semninga slæp . . . ofestum betyned);* ALD 61.4 *(clauduntur lumina);* Virgil, *Aeneid* 10.746 and 12.310; Juvencus, *Evangelia* 2.761; Aldhelm, *Carmen de virginitate* 959; Virgil, *Georgics* 4.414, *Aeneid* 4.185; Cyprianus Gallus, *Genesis* 34, 912, and 1129; Paulinus of Périgueux, *Vita S. Martini* 4.132, 313, 428, 5.833; Corippus, *Iohannid* 3.3 *(lumina somno).*

100.7 Compare EXE 38.12–13 *(þisne middan-geard . . . æghwær styreð);* Prudentius, *Hamartigenia* 281 *(dicione gubernat);* Venantius Fortunatus, *Carmen* 9.1.91 *(dicione gubernas);* Aldhelm, *Carmen de virginitate* 1 *(mundum dicione gubernans).*

100.8 Compare EXE 38.14–15 *(swa ic mid wealdendes . . . utan ymbclyppe);* Aldhelm, *Carmen de virginitate* 1887 *(sub caeli cardine).*

100.9 Compare EXE 38.16–17 *(Ic eom to þon bleað . . . grima abregan)*; Ovid, *Metamorphoses* 7.792 *(invictos . . . certamine cursu)*, 10.56 *(certamine cursus)*; TAT 9.2 *(larbula servis)*. The word *larvula* (also spelled *larbula* with the customary -*b*- for -*f*- or -*v*- spelling, see EXE 21.1 and the headnote on LEI below) appears in several glossaries as *eges-grima*, rendered by the *DOE* as "ghost, (terrifying) specter, (evil) spirit."

100.10 Compare EXE 38.18–19 *(ond eofore eom . . . bid-steal giefeð)*; ALD 39.1 *(setiger . . . apros)*.

100.11 Compare EXE 38.20–21a *(ne mæg mec oferswiþan . . . ænig ofer eorþan)*; TAT 8.2; BER 3.4 *(Nullus me)*; Statius, *Thebaid* 8.238; Aldhelm, *Carmen ecclesiasticum* 1.2 *(vexilla triumphi)*.

100.12 Compare EXE 38.21b–22 *(nymþe se ana god . . . healdeþ ond wealdeþ)*; BON 13.45 *(summa qui regnat in arce)*; Aldhelm, *Carmen ecclesiasticum* 4.5.9 *(qui regnat in arce)*; Aldhelm, *Carmen de virginitate* 1393, 1587, and 2287.

100.13 Note the lengthening of the final syllable of *ture* before mute and liquid in next word here; there are other examples at ALD 20.3, 37.3, 41.2, 51.4, 61.2, 77.7, 81.1, 82.6, 86.8, 87.3, 100.6, and 100.59. See further Orchard, *Poetic Art of Aldhelm*, 76.

100.13–16 These lines contain references to the subjects of many other aenigmata found in close proximity in other collections, notably SYM 45 and 47–48 (*ROSA*, "rose," *TUS*, "incense," and *MURRA*, "myrrh"); BER 34–35 (*DE ROSA*, "on a rose," and *DE LILIIS*, "on lilies").

100.13–17 Compare EXE 38.23–32 *(Ic eom on stence . . . adelan stinceð)*.

100.14 Compare Aldhelm, *Carmen de virginitate* 1402 *(olfactum ambrosiae)*.

100.15 Compare Caelius Sedulius, *Carmen paschale* 1.278 *(lilia purpurei)*; Claudian, *Epithalamium Laurentii* 32 *(lilia . . . commixta rosetis)*; Venantius Fortunatus, *Carmina* 9.2.122 *(candida ceu rubeis lilia mixta rosis)* and 6.1.108 *(lilia mixta rosis)*.

100.16 Compare Venantius Fortunatus, *Carminum appendix* 13.11 *(dulcedine plenus);* BON PR.8 *(spirantes replet nardi ... nares).*

100.17 Compare Caelius Sedulius, *Carmen paschale* 3.82 *(sordibus atque olido ... caeno);* Aldhelm, *Carmen de virginitate* 2014 *(caeni squalentis).*

100.18–20 Compare EXE 38.33–37 *(Eal ic under heofones ... æghwær healde).*

100.19 Compare ALD 79.9 *(iure gubernent);* Aldhelm, *Carmen ecclesiasticum* 2.15 and 3.37, *Carmen de virginitate* 1538 *(sator arcitenens),* 1693 *(iure gubernat),* and 2067 *(iure gubernant).*

100.21 Compare EXE 38.38–39 *(Hyrre ic eom heofone ... dyre bihealdan).*

100.21–22 Compare TAT 24.5 *(inferior terris et celis altior exsto).*

100.22 Compare EXE 38.40–41 *(eac ic under eorþan ... wraþra gæsta).*

100.23 Compare ALD 8.5 *(tempore prisca);* EXE 38.42–43 *(Ic eom micle yldra ... meahte geweorþan).*

100.24 Compare EXE 38.44–45 *(ond ic giestron wæs ... þurh minre modor hrif);* see too the note at ALD 93.10 *(genetrix ... generaret ab alvo).*

100.25 Compare Aldhelm, *Carmen de virginitate* 207 *(auratis ... fibula bullis);* EXE 38.46–47 *(Ic eom fægerre ... wirum utan).*

100.26 Compare EXE 38.48–49 *(Ic eom wyrslicre ... þe her aworpen ligeð);* Virgil, *Eclogue* 7.42 *(horridior ... vilior alga).*

100.27 Compare EXE 38.50–51 *(Ic eorþan eom ... þonne þes wong grena).*

100.28 Compare EXE 38.52–53 *(folm mec mæg bifon ... ealle ymbclyppan).*

100.29 Compare EXE 38.54–55 *(Heardra ic eom ond caldra ... þonne he to hrusan cymeð).*

100.30 Compare EXE 38.56–57 *(Ic eom Ulcanus ... lege hatra);* BON 7.8 *(PATIENTIA AIT,* "patience speaks": *torribus ardens);* Virgil, *Aeneid* 6.550 *(flammis ... torrentibus).*

100.31 Compare EXE 38.58–59 *(Ic eom on goman . . . blende mid hunige);* BON PR.7 *(mulso . . . nectaris haustu),* BON 13.53 *(mulsum . . . nectaris haustum),* BON 17.2 *(nectaris haustus).*

100.32 Compare EXE 38.60–61 *(swylce ic eom wraþre . . . heasewe stondeþ).*

100.33 Compare EXE 38.62–63 *(Ic mesan mæg . . . ealdum þyrse).*

100.34 Compare EXE 38.64–65 *(ond ic gesælig . . . æfre to feore).*

100.35 Compare TAT 1.4 *(sum salamone sagacior et velocior euro);* Venantius Fortunatus, *Vita S. Martini* 1.288 *(australis . . . velocibus alis).* In L, *zephiri* is glossed in Old English as *suðernes.*

100.35–36 Compare EXE 38.66–69 *(Ic mæg fromlicor . . . feran æghwær).*

100.36 In L, *properantior* is glossed in Old English as *hor,* presumably for *horsc.*

100.37 Reading *testudo tarda* with the second-recension manuscripts; the first recension has *et tarda testudo,* with false quantity: *tēstudo* is the normal usage, although elsewhere in his verse, Aldhelm does not necessarily lengthen vowels before *-st* (see Orchard, *Poetic Art of Aldhelm,* 75–76).

100.37–39 Compare EXE 38.70–73 *(me is snægl swiftra . . . wordum nemnað).*

100.39 Compare Ovid, *Metamorphoses* 7.792 *(invictos . . . certamine cursus),* 10.560 *(certamine cursus).* The tag *dicto citius* is ultimately Virgilian (*Aeneid* 1.142), but Aldhelm makes it his own, employing it, for example, no fewer than nine times in his *Carmen de virginitate* (lines 1021, 1100, 1135, 1473, 1754, 1777, 1797, 1962, and 2395), always (as here, and in contrast to Virgil) immediately after an opening monosyllable.

100.40–41 The influence of Nonius Marcellus, *De compendiosa doctrina* 264.8 (which discusses the *tippula*), both here and in ALD 38 (which is actually on the *tippula*) has been argued by Meccariello, "An Echo from Nonius Marcellus in Aldhelm's *Enigmata.*"

100.40 Compare EXE 38.74–75 *(Hefigere ic eom micle . . . leades clympre).*

100.41 Compare EXE 38.76–77 *(leohtre ic eom micle . . . fotum dryge).*

100.42 Compare EXE 38.78–79 *(Flinte ic eom heardre . . . style heardan);* TAT 11.1 *(viscere flammae),* TAT 14.3 *(mea viscera flammis),* TAT 34.1 *(mea viscera flammae);* LOR 10.4 *(viscera matris);* Virgil, *Aeneid* 6.253 *(viscera flammis).*

100.43 Compare EXE 38.79–80 *(of þissum strongan . . . micle halsre-feþre);* Ovid, *Metamorphoses* 14.712 *(durior et ferro);* Aldhelm, *Carmen de virginitate* 1983 *(durior ut ferro).*

100.44–45 Compare EXE 38.98–99 *(Nu hafu ic in heafde . . . scyppend eallum).*

100.44–47 Note the extensive alliteration in this passage on elaborate coiffure *(Cincinnos capitis . . . cacumine . . . cum . . . caesaries . . . crispae . . . calamistratis . . . comunt quae calamistro).*

100.46 Compare EXE 38.102–3 *(nu me wrætlice . . . wundne loccas);* Virgil, *Aeneid* 6.779 *(vertice cristae),* 9.732 *(in vertice cristae),* and 12.493 *(vertice cristas);* ALD 26.5 *(vertice cristas).*

100.46–49 On the range of hairstyles in the period, see James, "Bede and the Tonsure Question," 85–98.

100.47 The extended gloss in L derives from Isidore, *Etym.* 20.13.5 *(calamistrum).* In L, *calamistratis* is glossed in Old English as *gewalcudum,* and *calamistro* as *of wolc-spinle.*

100.48–49 Compare EXE 38.105–7 *(Mara ic eom ond fættra . . . wynnum lifde).*

100.49 The extended gloss in L derives from Isidore, *Etym.* 17.7.28 *(fagus).*

100.52 Compare BON 13.36 *(dapibus . . . opimis);* Virgil, *Aeneid* 3.224 *(dapibusque . . . opimis);* Juvencus, *Evangelia* 3.87; Aldhelm, *Carmen de virginitate* 1604 and 2489. In L, *pallida* is glossed in Old English as *æ,* presumably for *æ-blæce.*

100.53 Compare TAT 1.5 *(clarior et Phoebi radiis);* BON 17.1 *(Limpida sum, fateor).*

100.54 Compare Ovid, *Metamorphoses* 8.371 *(nive candidioribus)*; Venantius Fortunatus, *Vita S. Martini* 2.26 *(sine vellere nimbi)*.

100.55 Compare Juvencus, *Evangelia* 4.334 *(atris . . . tenebris)*; Bede, *De die iudicii* 53 *(tenebris obducitur atris)*.

100.57 Compare Horace, *Sermones* 86 *(teres atque rotundus)*.

100.58 Compare ALD 17.3, ALD 30.4, ALD 31.1, ALD 49.3, ALD 56.7, ALD 61.7 *(necnon et)*. In L, *sperula* is glossed in Old English as *sinewea*, presumably for *sine-wealt*. Aldhelm commonly has short syllables before *-s*-groups, as here in *cristalli*; see further Orchard, *Poetic Art of Aldhelm*, 75–76. There are other examples at ALD 29.4 and 100.37.

100.59 Note the lengthening of the final syllable of *vice* before mute and liquid in next word here; there are other examples at ALD 20.3, 37.3, 41.2, 51.4, 61.2, 77.7, 81.1, 82.6, 86.8, 87.3, 100.6, and 100.13. See further Orchard, *Poetic Art of Aldhelm*, 76. Compare BER 31.3 and 46.3 *(Versa mihi . . . vice)*; BER 58.3 *(Versa vice)*.

100.59–60 Compare EXE 38.84–85 *(ic uttor eaþe . . . wundor-cræfte)*.

100.60 Compare ALD 86.7 *(stamine pepli)*.

100.61–62 Compare EXE 38.81–83 *(seo her on winde . . . þonne þes wong grena)*.

100.62 Compare ALD 97.14; TAT 27.1 *(mirabile dictu)*.

100.63 Compare EXE 38.86–88 *(Nis under me . . . ealra gesceafta)*. Caelius Sedulius, *Carmen paschale* 5.420; Aldhelm, *Carmen de virginitate* 658, 1593 *(mirabile fatu)*, and 2029 *(latus qua tenditur orbis)*.

100.64 Compare EXE 38.89–91 *(þara þe worhte . . . þæt ic onþunian ne sceal)*; Juvencus, *Evangelia praefatio* 4; Caelius Sedulius, *Carmen Paschale* 4.13 *(genitor rerum)*.

100.65 Compare EXE 38.92–94 *(Mara ic eom ond strengra . . . ic eom swiþre þonne he)*. The extended gloss in L derives from Isidore, *Etym.* 12.6.7 *(ballenae)*.

100.66 Compare EXE 38.95–97 *(swylce ic eom on mægene . . . seaxe delfað)*.

100.67 Compare TAT 1.5 *(Phoebi radiis).*

100.68 Compare ALD 38.6 *(pedibus gradior),* ALD 84.3 *(gradior pedibus);* ALD 47.3 *(gramine rura).*

100.69 Compare EUS 40.1 *(vago rura pedester).*

100.70 Compare ALD 100.83 *(sciscitor inflatos fungar quo nomine sofos).*

100.71 Compare Aldhelm, *Carmen de virginitate* 1032 *(per biblos descripsit littera).*

100.74 Compare SYM 11.2 *(Sole madens);* ALD 54.5 *(flumina fontis);* Virgil, *Aeneid* 5.854 *(rore madentem);* Lucan, *Bellum civile* 4.316 *(rore madentis)* and 6.369 *(rore madentem);* Prudentius, *Cathemerinon* 5.13 *(rore madentibus).*

100.75 Compare ALD 71.6 *(marmora ponti);* Cyprianus Gallus, *Exodus* 761; Aldhelm, *Carmen de virginitate* 825.

100.76 Compare SYM 75.3 *(lymphis gelidis).*

100.78 Compare Aldhelm, *Carmen de virginitate* 158 *(ex quibus ornatur praesentis machina mundi)* and 196 *(ex quibus ornatus).*

100.80–83 Note the extensive alliteration in the challenge *(famina verbi . . . infitians . . . frivola . . . inflatos . . . fungar).*

100.81 Compare ALD 81.10 *(gnarus quos poterit per biblos pandere lector).* See too Paulinus of Nola, *Carmen* 19.286; Venantius Fortunatus, *Carmen* 3.19.7 *(ore magister).*

100.82 The extended gloss in L derives from Isidore, *Etym.* 10.49 (which, however, is on *negator*).

100.83 Compare ALD 18.5 *(scrutetur sapiens gemino cur nomine fungar),* ALD 26.3 *(nomine fungor),* and ALD 100.70 *(sic mea prudentes superat sapientia sofos),* as well as, and perhaps especially, XMS P1.9 *(scrutetur sapiens, lector, quo nomine fungit);* compare Venantius Fortunatus, *Carmen* 4.20.3 *(nomine functum).*

BEDE

Authorship and Date

Bede (b. ca. 673, d. 735) was among the most deeply learned and well-read authors of the Anglo-Saxon period. Although he spent all but the first seven years of his life in the monastery at Monkwearmouth-Jarrow, his scholarly horizons were extended exponentially through its extraordinary library, in great part thanks to the diligent book-collecting of the much-traveled Benedict Biscop (d. 689), who brought a wealth of Mediterranean learning back with him from his frequent trips to Rome. Given Bede's colossal stature in Anglo-Saxon England, it is hardly surprising that a collection of aenigmata has been attributed to him. This collection is preserved only in G, a manuscript that also contains several other collections central to the Anglo-Saxon riddle tradition (see the introduction to *OEALRT,* under "Manuscript Contexts").The so-called *Collectanea pseudo-Bedae,* now preserved only in Herwagen's editio princeps of Bede of 1563 (see BL for the most recent edition), also includes several anonymous aenigmata, as well as a number that can be attributed to both SYM and ALD (there are ten in total, with five from each collection), appearing in three clusters (at BL §101–3, 132–33; BL §200, 144–45; BL §239–44, 150–53), with a range of solutions. The first cluster comprises three aenigmata, as follows: SYM 1 (*GRAPHIUM,* "stylus"), SYM 7 (*FUMUS,* "smoke"), ALD 3 (*NUBES,* "cloud"). The second contains just a single aenigma: ALD 90 (*PUERPERA GEMINAS ENIXA,* "woman bearing twins"). The third cluster is the densest, comprising six aenigmata, with three drawn from each collection, as follows: SYM 4 (*CLAVIS,* "key"), SYM 12 (*FLUMEN ET PISCIS,* "river and fish"), SYM 10 (*GLACIES,* "ice"), ALD 2 (*VENTUS,* "wind"), ALD 4 (*NATURA,* "nature"), and ALD 9 (*ADAMAS,* "diamond"). Further support for a collection of aenigmata attributed to Bede can be found in the works of the antiquary John Leland (ca. 1503–1552), who reported having seen a "very ancient manuscript of epigrams" *(antiquissimum codex epigrammatum)* at Malmesbury, and although the manuscript is now lost (except for a single bifolium, G–L 938), an opening epigram identifies its owner as Bishop Milred of Worcester

(745–775). Leland cites several of the relevant poems, and otherwise gives a list of contents, including several clearly genuine poems by Bede and Aldhelm. In such a context, and from such an early collection, albeit one only witnessed much later and at second hand, the reference to some *Enigmata Bedae* is tantalizing indeed, and is matched by the same title given in G for the texts reproduced here.

Manuscript Context(s)

BED is found on fols. 418v–19r of G, a manuscript that also contains SYM, ALD, TAT, EUS, ALF, and BIB (see the introduction to *OEALRT*, under "Manuscript Contexts") and so links BED intimately to the broader tradition. BED is heavily glossed in G, suggesting intensive study.

Subject Matter and Solutions

Given Bede's linguistic and didactic interests, it is fitting that so many of the riddles in BED should focus on such grammatical and classroom subjects as individual letters and grammatical topics. The opening aenigma (BED 1) deals first with metrical quantity, then syllable count, while the nine succeeding aenigmata (BED 2–10) focus in turn on a letter (2), a monosyllable (3), a trio of fungible disyllables (4–6), and a sequence of four vowels (7–10). It is tempting to try to wring out the missing fifth vowel as the solution for the otherwise obscure 11, but that seems hard to do. BED 13 (*OVA,* "eggs") and 18 (*DIGITI SCRIBAE,* "a scribe's fingers") are also both explicitly connected with letters and writing, an overwhelming focus for the collection as a whole which sits well with Bede's interests. One might compare the similar use of logogriphs elsewhere in the Anglo-Saxon riddle tradition, on which see further the note at ALD 63 (*CORBUS,* "raven"). Three of the remaining aenigmata share a marine theme, namely BED 12 (*NAVIS,* "ship"), BED 15 (*MARE,* "sea"), and BED 17 (*CETUS,* "a whale"); but the other two are harder to place within the sequence, comprising BED 14 (*SAGITTA,* "arrow") and BED 16 (*AETAS HOMINIS,* "the age of man").

Style

Bede has by far the smoothest and most fluent style of any of the Anglo-Saxon poets who chose to compose Latin verse, combining elegance and eloquence with an evident desire to distinguish his own style from that of others, notably Aldhelm. Where Aldhelm's Latin is heavily end-stopped, spondaic, and repetitive, often metrically idiosyncratic and eschewing such features as elision, Bede's verse is in many aspects the direct opposite, demonstrating a keen sense of the form's plastic possibilities. Bede's verses are fluid and in general highly varied in terms of form and formulas. In that context, the over-representation of quadrisyllabic endings in BED (see the note at BED 1.2 below), as well as the close repetition of words and ideas, might militate against the idea that these are genuine compositions by Bede. For example, there are six quadrisyllabic endings in the 32 lines of BED (see the note at BED 1.2), while in the 977 hexameters of Bede's metrical *Life of Cuthbert (Vita S. Cudbercti),* I count only two such quadrisyllabic endings, at lines 492 *(adunatis)* and 682 *(superaddit);* it is striking, by contrast, that there are few of the poetic adjectives and usages here that characterize the rest of the Anglo-Saxon riddle tradition, on which see the headnote to ALD.

Sources and Parallels

In general, the difference between BED and ps-BED can be characterized in terms of a marked originality in theme and presentation in the former, and a distinct set of broader connections between the latter and the wider tradition. Even where there are parallels for the specific topics outlined in BED (and several are noted in the companion volume in the Dumbarton Oaks series), it is striking how different the treatment is here, while a good many of those in ps-BED can be traced directly to particular sources.

This Text and Translation

I have consulted La, TuB, and LB freely, while also (in the case of BED) going back to the original manuscript, G; I am also grateful to Rob Getz and Bob Babcock for specific advice at many points. The main subject matter of BED, namely the Latin language and Latin spellings, makes it particularly problematic to translate: in some cases it seems impossible not to introduce Latin forms into the translation, to add some degree of clarity to what would otherwise be utterly baffling and intransigent material.

Further Reading

Bayless, "The *Collectanea* and Medieval Dialogues and Riddles"; Lapidge, "Some Remnants of Bede's Lost *Liber Epigrammatum*"; Lapidge, *Bede the Poet.*

BED 1

MANUSCRIPT: G, fol. 418v.
PREVIOUS EDITIONS: TuB 1–2, 568; La 316–17. (SK10204)
SOLUTION: *LIBRA* (scales). See further in general, Scull, "Scales and Weights in Early Anglo-Saxon England." The solution *TRUTINA* (scales), as at ALD 23 and BER 53 (see also ABI), would also be possible, but the use of the word *trutinando* in BED 1.3 perhaps lends a rather broader hint than is customary in aenigmata.

TuB prints BED 1.1–2 as two separate aenigmata. As the notes in the associated *OEALRT* make clear, what is being measured here is metrical and linguistic quantity (for example, numbers of metrical beats or *tempora,* or simply syllabic weight), so providing a fitting opening to a collection largely concerned with specific properties of the Latin language.

1.1 Reading *nil* (G has *sic*), as indeed a gloss (unreported by TuB) suggests.

1.2 BED contains no fewer than six polysyllabic endings in only thirty-two hexameters, of which *trutinando* is only the first; see further BED 7.1 *(copulatum),* 13.2 *(pepererunt),* 17.1 *(tenebrosa)* and 2 *(numerosum),* and 18.2 *(vagitando).* See further the notes at ALD PR.26 and TAT 1.10.

1.3 Reading *titivillitium* for manuscript *titivicillium.* The word is attested in Plautus, *Casina* 2.5.39 (where it is variously spelled *titt-* and *titi-*), but was presumably known via a grammarian; the best suggestion is Fulgentius, *Sermones antiqui* (ed. Helm, 117). Note the quadrisyllabic ending here *(trutinando),* as frequently in the aenigmata; such quadrisyllabic endings are rare in Bede's *Vita S. Cudbercti* (682, *superaddit*), and may have been viewed as a specific hallmark of aenigmata: Aldhelm's *Carmen de virginitate* has few examples when compared with his aenigmata. What is described here is metrical quantity, with *titivillitium* (scanned as ˘˘¯˘˘¯), which comprises eight *tempora* or *morae,* taking up twice as much of the hexameter as *plumbum* (scanned as ¯¯), which comprises four.

1.4 In this line, it is apparently the syllables that are being counted, with the six of *titivillitium* being three times as many as the two of *plumbum*. Compare Virgil, *Aeneid* 4.690, and Caelius Sedulius, *Carmen paschale* 2.199 *(Ter sese attollens).*

1.5 Reading *oneris* (G has *honeris*); compare Horace, *Epistola* 2.1.170 *(Plus oneris).* The words *plus honeris* are glossed *maioris ponderis; aggravat* is glossed *onerat; orcam,* "tun, dice-box," is glossed *lancem vel stateram,* "the scale of a balance or a steelyard." The last word seems to have come into Old English in the form *orcas,* "goblets, drinking-bowls," and to signify there archaic or exotic vessels (compare *Beo* 2760b, *orcas stondan,* and 3047b, *bune ond orcas; Jud* 18b *bune ond orcas*; the phrase may be borrowed from *Beowulf*); see further Frank, "Sharing Words with *Beowulf,*" 6–7 and "Three 'Cups' and a Funeral in *Beowulf,*" 410–11. Note that the *h-* of *hoc* lengthens the final syllable of *oneris,* a license sanctioned by Bede in his *De arte metrica;* compare Lapidge, "How 'English' Is pre-Conquest Anglo-Latin?," 7–9.

BED 2

MANUSCRIPT: G, fol. 418v.
PREVIOUS EDITIONS: TuB 3, 568; La 318–19.
SOLUTION: *F LITTERA* (the letter *f*).

The fullest gloss explains the likely solution: *Fel acerbum saporem habet; muta f. in m. et mutabis saporem quia erit mel,* "*fel,* 'gall,' has a bitter taste; change the *F* to *M* and you will change the taste, since it will be *mel,* 'honey.'" Another simpler gloss summarizes: *F. M. MEL.*

BED 3

MANUSCRIPT: G, fol. 418v.
PREVIOUS EDITIONS: TuB 4, 568; La 318–19.
SOLUTION: *OS* (mouth; bone).

The gloss explains the likely solution: *os monosilliba est: sive significet* [G has *significes*] *os oris aut os ossis et non mutat litteraturam in nominativo vel sensum,* "*Os* is a monosyllable: whether it means *os, oris,* 'mouth,' or *os, ossis,* 'bone,' and it does not change its spelling in the nominative, but its sense." Another simpler gloss summarizes: *OS.* For reversal as an instrument either to reveal or to conceal the solution, see for example EXE 21.1 (BOGA, "bow"), and the note there.

BED 4

MANUSCRIPT: G, fol. 418v.
PREVIOUS EDITIONS: TuB 5, 569; La 318–19.
SOLUTION: *AMOR* (love) → *ROMA* (Rome).

The gloss explains the likely solution: *Amor dissillabus est: verte sillabas et fiet Roma,* "*Amor* is disyllabic: reverse the syllables and it will become *Roma.*" The word *patrabit* is glossed *faciet.* Another simpler gloss summarizes: *AMOR.*

4.1 The same strategy of turning around a two-syllable word is found not only in the two aenigmata that follow, but also in EXE 21.1 *(Agof is min noma eft onhwyrfed).*

BED 5

MANUSCRIPT: G, fol. 418v.
PREVIOUS EDITIONS: TuB 6, 569; La 318–19.
SOLUTION: *NEMO* (no one) → *OMEN* (omen).

The gloss explains the likely solution: *Verte has sillabas et fiet omen, i. augurium—omnipresens deus non amat augurium nec observantes,* "Reverse these syllables and it will become *omen,* that is, 'augury': omnipresent God does not love augury nor those who observe it." Another simpler gloss summarizes: *NEMO. OMEN.*

BED 6

MANUSCRIPT: G, fol. 418v.
PREVIOUS EDITIONS: TuB 7, 569; La 318–19.
SOLUTION: *SEGES* (field of grain).

The gloss explains the likely solution: *Muta sillabam, semper seges erit—ideo datur meanti hac et illac,* "Change a syllable; it will always be *seges,* 'grainfield': so it is granted to one wandering this way and that." Another simpler gloss summarizes: *SEGES.* It is tempting to connect this chaste and learned riddle with the somewhat more risqué EXE 45 (*DAH,* "dough"), based on double entendre, since both focus on the back-and-forth motion associated with bread-making, here enshrined in the very solution.

BED 7

MANUSCRIPT: G, fol. 418v.
PREVIOUS EDITIONS: TuB 8, 569; La 318–19.
SOLUTION: *A LITTERA* (the letter *a*).

This aenigma begins a sequence devoted to the vowels, with the exception of *e,* which may have dropped out. See further EUS 9 (*DE ALPHA,* "about alpha"); ALF A; ALD 20 (*APIS,* "bee"); LOR 21 (*APIS,* "bee").

7.1 Reading *tollit sine sanguine quod* (G has *sine sanguine quod tollit*). There are three glosses; the one above the line reads: *Si littera a preponit pedi erit apes—i. sine pede et declinat apes-apedis—et sine concisione,* "If one places the letter *a* in front of *pes,* 'foot,' it will be *apes,* 'bees'—that is, 'without foot,' and it declines *apes, apedis*—and without cutting." A second gloss in the margin reads *Ideo littera copula pedi et tollis pedem sine sanguinem.* A third gloss in the inner margin reads: *Tollit pedem cum datur apes—absque ped. Apes-apedis—sine pede et inde apes datur quia sine pede.* Another, simpler gloss summarizes: *Apes.*

BED 8

MANUSCRIPT: G, fol. 418v.
PREVIOUS EDITIONS: TuB 9, 569; La 318–19.
SOLUTION: *I LITTERA* (the letter *i*).

The gloss explains the likely solution: *I littera sola recta est in alphabetis,* "*i* is the only upright letter in the alphabet." Another, simpler gloss summarizes: *.I.* Compare EUS 39 (*DE I LITTERA,* "about the letter *I*"), although the treatment there is quite different.

8.1 Reading *potest stans* (G has *est*); the line is too short as it stands, although there are other possible corrections, such as *manet stans.*

BED 9

MANUSCRIPT: G, fol. 418v.
PREVIOUS EDITIONS: TuB 10, 569; La 318–19.
SOLUTION: *O LITTERA* (the letter *o*).

The gloss explains the likely solution: *Estque* [G *etque*] *culus ani dorsi quae minime videt, antepone O littera et videbit ut oculus utpote quia erit oculus,* "The *culus* is the backside of the anus, which hardly sees; put the letter *O* in front and it will see just like an eye, since it will be *oculus,* 'eye.'" Another simpler gloss summarizes: *.O.* The syncopated spelling *oclus* is unusual here, and replicated only in the ninth-century *oclorum* of Lios monachus, *Libellus scaerdotalis* 99 and 127. On syncopation in general, see Bede, *De arte metrica* 14 (ed. Kendall, 122–31), and the notes on EUS 2.2 and 23.2; BON PR.6, 15.12, 17.13, and 20.23; BER 14.5, 32.2, 45.5, 52.3, and 57.2.

BED 10

MANUSCRIPT: G, fol. 418v.
PREVIOUS EDITIONS: TuB 11, 569; La 318–19.
SOLUTION: *V LITTERA* (the letter *u/v).*

In this case, the gloss is misleading, simply restating the sense of the aenigma: *Si tollis b. litera fiet bonus statim gravat,* "If you take away the letter *b, bonus,* 'a good man,' will immediately become heavy." If we accept the preceding sequence of vowel-solutions to imply that this is another, then it is indeed true that when the letter *u* appears at the beginning of words (in other words, has lost its head), it is written with straight lines as *v* and becomes a consonant (so taking up that burden). The problem is that the use of *bonus* implies a masculine solution, while of the two words previously used *littera* is feminine and *gramma* is neuter; perhaps *apex* is intended? There are a number of glosses: *amittit* is glossed *perdit;* and *artat* is glossed *gravat vel stringit vel aliter.*

BED 11

MANUSCRIPT: G, fol. 418v.
PREVIOUS EDITIONS: TuB 12, 569; La 320–21.
SOLUTION: *ONUS* (load, burden).

Both the syntax and the aenigma are obscure, although the repetition of both *bonus* and *onus* from the previous aenigma may connect them; the suggested solution seems rather awkward. The gloss is unhelpful (though perhaps instructive in suggesting that the glosses are not by Bede): *Quisquis perversus est ex levitate mentis est, tolle primam sillabam que caput est eius i. per et sit versus i. bonus,* "A perverse man is so from lightness of mind; take away the first syllable, which is his 'head,' that is, *per,* and let him be changed *(versus),* that is, good." The gloss to the previous aenigma may be of more pertinence, if we assume another logogriph on *BONUS* → *ONUS,* in which case the absence of a "head of shortness" (i.e., the beginning of the word *breviatis,* namely *b-*) lends heft to the result.

11.1 Reading *brevitatis* for manuscript *levitati,* and assuming haplography of *-s* due to the following *s-;* alternatively, we can read *brevitati,* and consider it a dative of purpose ("if the beginning is absent for brevity"): I am grateful to Michael Lapidge for the suggestion.

BED 12

MANUSCRIPT: G, fol. 418v.
PREVIOUS EDITIONS: TuB 13, 569; La 320–21.
SOLUTION: *NAVIS* (ship).

The gloss explains the likely solution: *Navis prora et puppis sicce erunt quando mare innatant,* "The prow and the stern of a ship will be dry when they swim upon the sea." In later Latin aenigmata this solution would be part of a broader logogriph on *NAVIS* → *AVIS,* a feature that would link this aenigma to the next.

12.1 Compare BED 6.1 *(meanti);* TuB wrongly reads *ineat.*

BED 13

MANUSCRIPT: G, fol. 418v.
PREVIOUS EDITIONS: TuB 14, 570; La 320–21. (SK 16465)
SOLUTION: *OVA* (eggs).

13.1 The gloss explains the likely solution: *Ista est constructio tres iunctae sorores i. tres litterae o. v. a. genuere nantes proles i. tres pullos et iterum maturi pulli genuere easdem scilicet litteras o. v. a. que iuncta ova exprimunt,* "This is the construction: three joined sisters, that is, the three letters *o, u,* and *a,* begot three swimming children, that is, three chicks, and in turn the mature chicks begot 'the same,' that is, the letters *o, v,* and *a,* which signify the joined eggs."

13.2 Reading *post hae maturae* (G has *he mature post*). The gloss has: *S. sorores i. o. v. a.; mature* is glossed *ova sana; post* is glossed *postea.*

13.3 The gloss reads *Si quem somniat manducasse ova dum evigilaverit, intelligent non esse somnium bonum,* "If anyone dreams of eating eggs, when he awakes he will understand that it is not a good dream." The notion that a dream of eating eggs betokens bad luck is enshrined in several versions of the *Somniale Danielis;* compare Liuzza, ed., *Anglo-Saxon Prognostics,* 186 (T9/88): *Gif him þince þæt he henna æiru hæbbe oððe þicge, ne deah him þæt,* "If it seems to him that he sees or eats hens' eggs, that will do him no good." Liuzza helpfully gives the parallel Latin version in Trinity College, Cambridge, O.1.57, no. 244: *ova gallinarum habere vel videre, nullum bonum significat.*

BED 14

MANUSCRIPT: G, fol. 419r.
PREVIOUS EDITIONS: TuB 15, 570; La 320–21. (SK 17219)
SOLUTION: *SAGITTA* (arrow).

This is obviously an "I saw" riddle, of a type well attested in Old English (see the note on EXE 3.1), but also in Anglo-Latin (see the note on BON 13.1); several aenigmata in the pseudo-Bede *Collectanea* have the same structure. Compare SYM 65; TAT 32; ALC D98 (all *SAGITTA*).

14.1 Reading *cornutam in celo* (G has *in celo cornutam*). For the unusual form *petiisse*, compare Virgil, *Aeneid* 2.25 and 3.603. The gloss explains the likely solution: *Cornigeratam catapulta volantem in aere avem appetit, que minime posset attingere, si ipsa catapulta suis pennis sublevaret ante*, "A missile seeks a horn-bearing bird flying in the air, which it could not reach at all, if the missile itself were not lifted up by its feathers." Likewise, *in aere* is glossed *in celo; cornutam* is glossed *catapultam; petiise* is glossed *apetisse; volantem* is glossed *avem.*

14.2 Reading *minime* (G has *minimum*). The gloss reads: *Si pennata catapaulta non fuerit, non potest longe* (G has *longi*) *iaci*, "Unless the missile is feathered, it cannot be cast far." Likewise, *minimum* is glossed *s. volantem; peteret* is glossed *attingeret; iuvaret* is glossed *s. cornutam.*

BED 15

MANUSCRIPT: G, fol. 419r.
PREVIOUS EDITIONS: TuB 16, 570; La 320–21.
SOLUTION: *MARE* (sea).

The gloss explains the likely solution: *Semper mare accedit et recedit, quando cessaverit in die iudicii magnum portentum erit*, "The sea always ebbs and flows; when it stops on Doomsday that will be a mighty portent." Likewise, *cedit* is glossed *percutit; siverit* is glossed *cessaverit; omen* is glossed *signum*. For the signs before Doomsday, see in general Heist, *Fifteen Signs*. There are some broad parallels in *Hisperica famina* A381–425 (*DE MARI*, "on the sky"; see further Herren, *Hisperica Famina: The A-Text;* Orchard, "*Hisperica famina* as Literature").

BED 16

MANUSCRIPT: G, fol. 419r.
PREVIOUS EDITIONS: TuB 17, 570; La 320–21
SOLUTION: *AETAS HOMINIS* (the age of man).

The gloss explains the likely solution: *Aetas hominis quanto magis crescat vicinior erit morti,* "Man's age will come the closer to death the more it grows." Likewise, *curtior extat* is glossed *defectior per senium.* Compare ps-BED 21 (*AETAS HOMINIS,* "age").

16.1 Supplying *tanto* for the sake of the meter; one might equally supply *semper.*

BED 17

MANUSCRIPT: G, fol. 419r.

PREVIOUS EDITIONS AND TRANSLATIONS: TuB 18, 570–71; La 320–21. (SK 13676)

SOLUTION: *CETUS* (a whale).

The same solution is given explicitly for FRA, although little else connects the texts. The notion of the "eater eaten" here parallels that of the theme of the "biter bitten" (on which see the introduction to *OEALRT,* under "Shared Themes across the Collections").

17.1 The wordplay here on *(-)lustro* in the joint sense of "illuminates" and "wanders" is a commonplace that is particularly appropriate in the case of a creature that travels while alive and supplies oil for lighting after its demise; see further the note above, at ALD 5.4. The gloss explains: *Occisus certe magnum praebet sagine augmentum lichnis et nolens quia invitus moritur,* "When it is killed it certainly provides with its fat a great boon for lanterns; and unwilling, because it dies against its will."

17.2 Note alliteration on *p-*. The gloss explains: *A nullo populo pascitur et tamen multitudinem populi satiat suis carnibus,* "It is fed by no people, and yet it fills a multitude of people with its flesh."

17.3 Reading *at* (G has *et*). The gloss explains: *Unus homo potest eum decipere sed non unus potest eum devorare,* "A lone man can catch it, but is not able alone to devour it."

17.4 The gloss explains: *Nunquam abibit i. consumetur in una die,* "Will never pass away, that is, be consumed, in a single day." Likewise, *abibit* is glossed *consumetur vel recedet.*

BED 18

MANUSCRIPT: G, fol. 419r.
PREVIOUS EDITIONS AND TRANSLATIONS: TuB 15, 571; La 322–23. (SK 16454)
SOLUTION: *DIGITI SCRIBAE* (a scribe's fingers).

The same conceit is a commonplace of the riddle tradition: in the pseudo-Bede *Collectanea* (BL 305, 164–65 and 261–62), which reads *Non laboriosum est opus scribendi: tres digiti scribunt, totum corpus laborat,* "The task of writing is not arduous: three fingers write, but the whole body labors"; see too ALD 74.8 (*FUNDIBALUM,* "sling": *Tres digiti totum versant super ardua corpus,* "Three fingers swing my whole body up in the air"). BED 18 attracts the greatest range of glosses, several of which are themselves glossed, as the following notes show.

18.1 The line is glossed *Tres digiti discurrunt in pagina stimulati .i. cum acuta penna vel graphio vel planitie,* "Three fingers run back and forth across the page, goaded, that is, by a sharp pen or stylus or on a flat surface." The word *stimulati* is glossed *stimulis armati,* "armed with goads," and the word *pellis* is glossed *campi,* "field." The "twins" in question are individual fingers, each of which has a "twin" on the other hand. It is tempting to emend *gemini* (which may have been influenced by the *geminas* of the following line), especially in view of the parallel phrase at ALD 74.8 *(Tres digiti),* but since the solution requires the term *digiti,* it seems unlikely that it would appear in the aenigma itself (though compare BED 8 *[BONUS → ONUS]* above).

18.2 The line is glossed *Discurrendo huc et illuc duas vias ostendunt .i. bonam et malam quia tam bene scribunt vias sequendas quam vitandas,* "By running here and there they show two paths, namely a good one and a bad one, since they describe paths that should be followed just as well as those that should be shunned."

18.3 The line is glossed *Et ipsi muti digiti loquentes et sunt ceci et ostendunt viam videntibus,* "And those very mute fingers are speaking, while they are blind they show the way to those who can see"; the words *cecique videntes* are glossed *docent,* "they teach."

18.4 Reading *it* for manuscript *id* and *ubi* for manuscript *ibi.* Note that the *h-* of *haud* does not make position here. The line is glossed *Sepe decipiunt scriptorem quia scribunt quae non debent et non servant quod scribunt,* "Often they deceive the writer, because they write what they should not and do not retain what they write"; the words *moventem, fallunt,* and *quod id haud* are further glossed *scriptorem,* "writer," *decipiunt,* "deceive," and *quia vadit non,* "because it does not go." In the outer margin is yet another gloss: *Cum digiti scribunt que sancta sunt et scriptor non servat que scribit, tunc decipit quia non vadit viam quam docet scribendo,* "When the fingers write what is holy, and the writer does not retain what he writes, then he deceives (or perhaps better is deceived *[decipitur]*, since he does not walk the path he teaches when he writes."

18.5 The line is glossed *Sepe seipsos decipiunt ut puta moneta, quia falsum? Numisma sculpit et pro hoc amputantur ei manus,* "Often they deceive themselves. So, for example, money (or a minter *[monetarius]?*): because he engraves a false coin, and so his hands are cut off." Æthelstan issued a decree (2 As 14.1) around 928 at Grateley, specifying the following punishment for issuing light coins: "And if a moneyer is found guilty the hand shall be cut off with which he committed the crime, and then fastened up on the mint."

PS-BED 1

EARLIER EDITIONS AND TRANSLATION: BL 1 (122–23 and 199).
SOLUTION: *SAPIENTIA* (wisdom). Compare BIB 1 (*SAPIENTIA,* "wisdom").

This is, appropriately enough, the first item in a large collection of wisdom material that incorporates aenigmata from both SYM and ALD, and also has close parallels and analogues in ALC D and EXE.

PS-BED 2

EARLIER EDITION AND TRANSLATION: BL 18 (122–23 and 205–6).
SOLUTION: *PULLUS* (chick).

Compare SYM 14 (*PULLUS IN OVO,* "chick in egg"); ALC D78 (*PULLUS IN OVO,* "chick in egg"); EXE 11 (*TEN CICCENU,* "ten chickens"); LOR 8 (*PULLUS IN OVO,* "chick in egg"); XMS X2 (*PULLUS,* "chick").

PS-BED 3

EARLIER EDITION AND TRANSLATION: BL 19 (122–23 and 206).
SOLUTION: *EQUI PICTURA* (a drawing of a horse [?]). See too Tupper, "Riddles of the Bede Tradition," 3.

This aenigma is linked to the previous one by the mother-son theme; the "mother" in question is presumably the "pen" *(penna).* An alternative solution might be *NAVIS,* "ship," given the common association in Anglo-Saxon England of ships and horses, on which see the note on EXE 12.6; in that case, the "mother" in question would presumably be a wooden tiller.

PS-BED 4

EARLIER EDITION AND TRANSLATION: BL 21 (122–23 and 207–8).
SOLUTION: *AETAS HOMINIS* (age).

Compare BED 16 (*AETAS HOMINIS,* "age of man"). See too Tupper, "Riddles of the Bede Tradition," 3 and 10.

PS-BED 5

EARLIER EDITION AND TRANSLATION: BL 79 (130–31 and 219).
SOLUTION: *VENTUS* (wind).

Compare ALD 2 (*VENTUS,* "wind"), of which this is clearly a prose version. There are some broad parallels in *Hisperica famina* A479–96 (*DE VENTO,* "on wind"; see further Herren, *Hisperica Famina: The A-Text;* Orchard, "*Hisperica famina* as Literature"). See too Hill, "Saturn's Time Riddle"; Wright, "The Three 'Victories' of the Wind"; Orchard, "Enigma Variations"; Anlezark, *Solomon and Saturn,* 84–85 and 125–26.

PS-BED 6

EARLIER EDITION AND TRANSLATION: BL 122 (136–37 and 227–28).
SOLUTION: *GLACIES* (ice).

Compare ps-SYM 1 *(GLACIES),* of which this is evidently a prose version. There are a number of riddles that share this or similar solutions, including SYM 10; BER 38 and 42 (all *GLACIES*); LOR 4 *(GELU);* EXE 31 and 66 (both *IS*).

PS-BED 7

EARLIER EDITION AND TRANSLATION: BL 194 (144–45 and 243).
SOLUTION: *IUVENCUS* (bullock).

This is one of the many "bullock" riddles in the tradition, on which see ALD 83 (*IUVENCUS,* "bullock") above.

PS-BED 8

EARLIER EDITION AND TRANSLATION: BL 195 (144–45 and 243–45).
SOLUTION: *HOMO SEDENS SUPER TRIPODEM* (man sitting on a three-legged stool).

See too Tupper, "Riddles of the Bede Tradition," 4; Hill, "Riddle on the Three Orders."

PS-BED 9

EARLIER EDITION AND TRANSLATION: BL 196 (144–45 and 243–44).
SOLUTION: *CUCULUS* (cuckoo).

Compare EXE 7 (*GEAC,* "cuckoo"), with which it shares a number of key features. See too Tupper, "Riddles of the Bede Tradition," 4; Daly and Suchier, *Altercatio,* 142, no. 96; Bitterli, "The 'Cuckoo' in the *Collectanea* of Pseudo-Bede."

PS-BED 10

EARLIER EDITION AND TRANSLATION: BL 197 (144–45 and 245).
SOLUTION: *LEBES* (cauldron).

For other aenigmata that play on the same opposition of fire and water in cooking-pots, compare ALD 49; ALC D76; XMS X1 (all *LEBES,* "cauldron").

PS-BED 11

EARLIER EDITION AND TRANSLATION: BL 198 (144–45 and 245).
SOLUTION: *PENNA* (quill pen). Daly and Suchier, *Altercatio,* 144, n. 3; Tupper, "Riddles of the Bede Tradition," 1 and 3.

For other riddles in the tradition that deal with writing and the scriptorium, see the note at ALD 30 (*ELEMENTUM,* "letter of the alphabet"). See too XMS X3 (*PENNA,* "quill pen").

PS-BED 12

EARLIER EDITION AND TRANSLATION: BL 199 (144–45 and 246).
SOLUTION: *PUERPERA GEMINAS ENIXA* (woman bearing twins).

This is a prose version of ALD 90 (*PUERPERA GEMINAS ENIXA,* "woman bearing twins"), which immediately follows in the *Collectanea* (BL 200). Note that this "I saw" riddle seems to derive from an "I am" original.

PS-BED 13

EARLIER EDITION AND TRANSLATION: BL 246 (152–53 and 250).
SOLUTION: *CUPA* (clay beer-mug).

Several riddles in the tradition focus on the notion of a creature with only one foot; see further, for example, the note at TAT 10.6 (*RECITABULUM,* "lectern") below.

TATWINE

Authorship and Date

Tatwine is best known as a scholar and grammarian who also held the post of Archbishop of Canterbury from 731 until he died in 734. He was apparently born in Mercia, and was for a time a priest in the monastery of Breedon-on-the-Hill in Leicestershire; his elevation to Archbishop of Canterbury through the patronage of the mighty and long-reigning King Æthelbald of Mercia (r. 716–757) is described by Bede in his *Historia ecclesiastica* (*HE* 5.23):

> Anno eodem factus est archiepiscopus vocabulo Tatwini . . . vir religione et prudentia insignis, sacris quoque litteris nobiliter instructus.

> In the same year [731] a man by the name of Tatwine became archbishop. . . . He was outstanding in terms of religion and thoughtfulness, and also brilliantly learned in sacred letters.

Tatwine's death is noted alongside that of Bede in the *Anglo-Saxon Chronicle* for the year 734, and both deaths are heralded portentously:

> Her wæs se mona swelce he wære mid blode begoten, and ferdon forþ Tatwine and Bieda.

> In this year, the moon was as if it were suffused with blood, and Tatwine and Bede passed away.

An anonymous and rather anodyne epitaph for Tatwine is preserved in a collection of inscriptions (a so-called *sylloge*) apparently put together by Bishop Milred of Worcester (d. 774); alas, it makes little reference to Tatwine's writings. Apart from aenigmata, Tatwine was also the author of an elementary Latin grammar, the *Ars de partibus orationis,* and there is some sign of this in TAT: of particular relevance to his grammatical interests are TAT 4 (*APICES,* "letters") and 16 (*PREPOSITIONES UTRIUSQUE CASUS,* "prepositions that take two cases").

Manuscript Context(s)

Tatwine's aenigmata appear in only two manuscripts, the clearly related L and G, both of which contain several other collections of aenigmata (see the introduction to *OEALRT,* under "Manuscript Contexts"), where in each case they are preceded by EUS (see too the headnote there). In G, the titles/solutions are given in the same hand in the outer margins. Mnemonics giving the first letter of the solution are also written in the margins at the beginning of TAT 2–7, 9–10, 12, 14–21, 23–29, and 31–40. These are of a sort that is also found in EXE, especially for the first few riddles of that collection; the parallel is the more intriguing given that in other respects E, the manuscript containing EXE, has been held to resemble G in its combination of long poems with religious themes at the beginning, followed by shorter collections of aenigmata and riddles. Even though EUS comes before TAT in both G and L, it is generally assumed that EUS was composed after TAT, so bringing their combined total of aenigmata (60 + 40) up to the "canonical" 100 of ALD and SYM. This putative comparative chronology is based on the presumed authorship of EUS by Abbot Hwætberht of Monkwearmouth-Jarrow, who seems to have been much younger than Tatwine. At all events, the 40 aenigmata that make up TAT are fixed in both number and order by a complicated acrostic-telestich which itself spells out two lines of Latin verse, and thus offer a useful insight into how Tatwine perceived his own position within what he at least seems to have seen as a developing tradition.

Subject Matter and Solutions

Given the way in which the precise order of the aenigmata is fixed by the acrostic-telestich, TAT offers a useful control for evaluating the extent to which transmitted titles/solutions can be trusted as either reliable or original, as well as how far runs or clusters of related themes can be said to be intended by individual compilers. TAT combines, both in sequence and in a more scattered manner, a number of clearly overarching themes which might be characterized as relating to the world of abstract learning (TAT 1–3), the scriptorium (TAT 4–6), church furniture and accoutrements (TAT 7–10 and 12), embroidery (TAT 11 and 13), eyes (TAT 18–20), humility and pride (TAT 25–26), blacksmithing (TAT 27–28, 31, 33, 35, 38–39), weaponry (TAT 30, 32, 34), and sowing (TAT 36–37). Particularly pleasing from a conceptual perspective is the apparent interpenetration of the last three sequences, while the final aenigma, 40, on the rays of the sun, offers a suitably overarching climax. To be sure, however, not all of the aenigmata in TAT can be attached to one or another of these groupings, including TAT 16 (*PRAEPOSITIONES UTRIUSQUE CASUS*, "about prepositions that take two cases"), which at least fits delightfully with what is known of Tatwine as a grammarian. Other possible links are explored in the notes below, but a general pattern of association is as evident throughout this collection as in others, and surely invites a search for similar patterns elsewhere. Salvador-Bello ("Patterns of Compilation") has made a particularly cogent attempt to do just that for ALD, TAT, EUS, and EXE 1–40, and her work can be extended further with regard to SYM in particular, as the headnote there seeks to explain.

In general, the arc of the topics covered, from philosophy to the rays of the sun, has a Christological basis that one might expect from an Archbishop of Canterbury. The further ordering of abstract knowledge through scribal activity via the Church follows a coherent sequence which is doubly instructive: suggesting both that Tatwine, in tying the order of his aenigmata through the acrostic-telestich form, may have perceived similar structural collocations and sequences in earlier collections with which he can be directly connected (specifically those of Aldhelm and Symphosius); and that later authors, with or without direct knowledge of Tatwine's possible perceptions, may have done the same. Whereas Aldhelm and Boniface and perhaps even Bede looked at their predecessors and models, but then moved on in their own individual directions, it is with Tatwine that the notion of a coherent Anglo-Saxon riddle tradition is born.

The collection is also intertwined with other linking themes, such as the notion that the creature in question was born from a single mother, a theme that appears in no fewer than eleven of the aenigmata in the collection: TAT 2 (*SPES, FIDES, CARITAS,* "Hope, Faith, Charity"), TAT 3 (*HISTORIA ET TROPOLOGIA ET ALLEGORIA ET ANAGOGE,* "historical, tropological, allegorical, and anagogical meaning"), TAT 4 (*APICES,* "letters"), TAT 15 (*NIX, GRANDO, ET GLACIES,* "about snow, hail, and ice"), TAT 16 (*PRAEPOSITIONES UTRIUSQUE CASUS,* "prepositions that take two cases"), TAT 18 (*OCULI,* "eyes"), TAT 19 (*STRABI OCULI,* "squinting eyes"), TAT 20 (*LUSCUS,* "one-eyed man"), TAT 26 (*QUINQUE SENSUS,* "the five senses"), TAT 31 (*SCINTILLA,* "spark"), TAT 39 (*COTICULUM,* "whetstone").

There also seems to be some rationale to the compilation in terms of a generally decreasing length, with only TAT 4 (*NATURA,* "nature") and TAT 40 (*RADII SOLIS,* "the rays of the sun") breaking what is otherwise a clear sequence: TAT 1 is fourteen lines long, TAT 2 precisely half that length, TAT 3 and 5–10 are all six lines long, TAT 4, 11–30, and 40 all five lines long, and TAT 31–39 all four lines long. Similar patterning (albeit not quite so neat) is also evident in ALD and EUS, as the headnotes to those collections make clear.

Style

In general, Tatwine's aenigmata are distinguished by a far greater use of elision than any other Anglo-Latin poet's (see Table A4 in Orchard, *Poetic Art of Aldhelm,* 295), as well as some odd linguistic quirks, such as colorless or redundant use of *iam* (as at TAT 7.2, 9.2, 9.4, 10.5, 11.3, 15.1, 21.5, 23.2, 25.5, 27.1 and 35.4), where the word functions more or less as a metrical filler. The collection's overall debt to Aldhelm is clear from both the general acrostic-telestich form (see the note to TAT PR) and very specific parallels at the beginning and end of the sequence (see the notes to TAT 1 and TAT 40). An analysis of compound adjectives, together with those formed from the (mostly) poetic suffixes *-abilis, -alis, -eus, -fer, -ficus, -genus, -ger,* and *-osus,* reveals an intriguing distribution: there are twenty such adjectives comprising sixteen different words, with twelve of these compound adjectives in the opening line whose first and last letters form the acrostic-telestich, and ten of these comprise the opening word that spells out the acrostic, presumably because Tatwine wished to highlight their importance. There are also eight false quantities in the combined 213 lines of TAT, a strikingly high ratio that only emphasizes the difficulty that composing Latin verse posed for nonnative speakers, even those with grammatical interests; see the notes at 1.7, 21.3, 23.2, 23.5, 29.3, 36.4, 38.4, and 40.5.

Sources and Parallels

Most of the verbal parallels noted below are with ALD and SYM; and it is clear that ALD in particular offers further parallels of both style and structure. Perhaps more surprising, in view of their close physical association and the assumption that the two collections were composed to produce a total of one hundred aenigmata, is the relative scarcity of such links between TAT and EUS (an interesting exception is the treatment of the connected themes of humility and pride in TAT 25–26 on the one hand, and EUS 27 on the other), as well as the often unique perspectives offered within this collection. It is instructive, for example, to compare TAT 32 (*SAGITTA*, "arrow") with three other more obviously closely related aenigmata on the same theme (SYM 65; BED 14; ALC D98), or TAT 5 (*MEMBRANUM*, "parchment") with similar riddles (EUS 32; BER 24; EXE 24); in each case, the aenigma in TAT takes a distinctive approach.

This Text and Translation

Here I have revised and updated the edition given by Gl, adding a number of conjectures of my own, and relying heavily on the excellent doctoral dissertation by Williams, "The Riddles of Tatwine and Eusebius," as well as the unpublished work of Rob Getz; several individual debts are acknowledged in the notes.

Further Reading

See in general Ebert, "Die Räthselpoesie der Angelsachsen"; Hahn, "Die Rätseldichter Tatwin und Eusebius"; Cobbs, "Prolegomena to the *Ars Grammatica Tatuini*"; Williams, "Riddles of Tatwine and Eusebius"; Whitman, "Aenigmata Tatwini"; Orchard, "After Aldhelm"; Marco, *Tatwine: Ars Grammatica;* Salvador-Bello, *Isidorean Perceptions,* 221–34 and 462–63.

TAT PR

MANUSCRIPTS: L, fol. 121v; G, fol. 374v.
EARLIER EDITIONS AND TRANSLATIONS: Gl, 167; Wl, 101–2. (SK 15708)

See further Cavell, *Weaving Words,* 299–300.

In both manuscripts the two-line *Preface,* which explains the acrostic-telestich that fixes the order of the aenigmata, is written as the opening lines of the aenigma that follows. If we take it as a separate text which has become attached to the original TAT 1, in a manner not unlike that suggested for EXE 21 (*BOGA*, "bow"), then the first letters of the opening line of each of the forty aenigmata, read in sequence, spell *SUB DENO QUATER HAEC DIVERSE AENIGMATA TORQUENS;* while the final letters of the same line, read in reverse, spell *STAMINE METRORUM EXSTRUCTOR CONSERTA RETEXIT.* Somewhat in the same spirit, I have reversed the order of the two lines as reported in both manuscripts (which are, however, related), in order to preserve the acrostic-telestich sequence. Aldhelm's *Preface* to his own aenigmata consists of a much simpler acrostic-telestich, in which the opening and closing letters of each line are the same, and spell out in sequence *ALDHELMUS CECINIT MILLENIS VERSIBUS ODAS*, "Aldhelm has sung songs in thousands of verses," while in the *Preface* to his *Carmen de virginitate* he employs a more elaborate acrostic-telestich (and one more likely to have provided Tatwine with his immediate model): the first letters of each line spell out in sequence the opening line, *METRICA TIRONES NUNC PROMANT CARMINA CASTOS*, "May metrical poems celebrate chaste beginners," while the final letters of each line, read in reverse, spell out the same.

PR.1 Glosses in both manuscripts explain *deno* as *numero*.

PR.2 The form *retexit* seems deliberately ambiguous: it can be taken as the perfect of *retego* (so "has uncovered") or the present of *retexo* ("unravels"); given the metaphor of the "thread of verses" connecting the forty aenigmata, I have preferred the latter. The term *exstructor*, "compiler," is unusual, being used elsewhere, for example in Jerome's *Commentary on Isaiah*, 18.6.1 18, but fits well with the notion of Tatwine carefully building his collection.

TAT 1

MANUSCRIPTS: L, fol. 121v; G, fol. 374v.

EARLIER EDITIONS AND TRANSLATIONS: Gl, 168; Wl, 101–3. (SK 14909)

SOLUTION: *SAPIENTIA* (Wisdom); the solution given is *DE PHILOSOPHIA* (about Philosophy). See further Lockett, *Anglo-Saxon Psychologies*, 264–65; Salvador-Bello, *Isidorean Perceptions*, 224–25.

Several collections of riddles begin with "philosophy" or "wisdom," notably BIB 1 (*SAPIENTIA*, "wisdom") and ps-BED 1 (*SAPIENTIA*, "wisdom"). To judge from the verbal and structural parallels noted below, at TAT 1.4 and TAT 1.8, Tatwine seems also here to be alluding to two of Aldhelm's aenigmata, at either end of that collection, namely ALD 2 (*VENTUS*, "wind") and ALD 100 (*CREATURA*, "creation"); the opening and (now) closing riddles in the Exeter Book, EXE 1 (*GODES WIND*, "wind of God") and EXE 91 (*BOC*, "book"), share some similar themes. TAT 1–3 form a clear sequence focusing on the world of learning, and there is even a gesture toward the world of pagan poetry in the penultimate line of this opening aenigma (TAT 1.11), with its evident echo of Virgil.

1.1 The "sevenfold apparatus of wings" has been taken as a reference to the seven liberal arts of the trivium (grammar, rhetoric, dialectic) and quadrivium (arithmetic, geometry, music, and astronomy), as noted for example by Isidore, *Liber numerorum* 44. Elsewhere, Aldhelm, in the course of a discussion of the number seven in the opening section of his *De metris* 3 (Eh, 71), another part of the larger work to which his aenigmata are attached, and apparently relying on Isidore, *Liber numerorum* 44, says that *Saeculares quoque et forasticae philosophorum disciplinae totidem supputationum partibus calculari cernuntur, arithmetica scilicet, geometrica, musica, astronomia, astrologia, mechanica, medicina*, "Likewise the secular and learned disciplines of the philosophers are observed to be divided into the same number of parts of study, namely arithmetic, geometry, music, astronomy, astrology, mechanics, medicine." Many of the same themes are developed in the same sequence in BIB 3 (*ARITHMETICA*, "arithmetic"), 4 (*GEOMETRICA*, "geometry"), 5 (*MUSICA*, "music"), and 6 (*ASTRONOMIA*, "astronomy"). A more elegant solution seems simply to connect this aenigma with the two that follow—TAT 2 (*SPES, FIDES, CARITAS*, "Hope, Faith, Charity") and TAT 3 (*HISTORIA ET TROPOLOGIA ET ALLEGORIA ET ANAGOGE*, "historical, tropological, allegorical, and anagogical sense")—which detail three and four sisters respectively related to a *mater* (TAT 2.1) and *dominatrix* (TAT 3.1), who is glossed both times in both manuscripts as *trinitate* or *trinitas*, but seems just as likely to be

Wisdom *(Sapientia)* or Philosophy *(Philosophia)* herself. The word *circumstantia* is rare, but also appears in TAT 30.2.

1.2 Despite the fact that the phrase *alma poli,* "holy (places?) of the sky," is attested in both manuscripts, it seems sensible to emend to the more usual *alta poli,* "heights of heaven" attested elsewhere (for example at ALD 4.4). A gloss in G explains *quis* as standing for *quibus.*

1.2–3 Here is an example of what might be called the "both high(er) and low(er)" motif also found in ALD 100.21–22; TAT 24.5; EUS 1.1 and 1.3, 3.4; LOR 2.4–5. The creature in question can traverse earth and sea and sky; compare EXE 1, which also employs a variant of the "both high(er) and low(er)" motif, found likewise in the various Exeter Book riddles that derive directly or indirectly from ALD 100, notably EXE 38, 64, and 90 (*GESCEAFT,* "creation").

1.3 Preferring *atque* G to *et* L, for reasons of meter and allowing for Tatwine's great fondness for elision. Compare BON 11.12 and 16.13 *(ima profundi).*

1.4 Compare ALD 100.35 *(Plus pernix aquilis Zephiri velocior alis).*

1.5 Compare ALD 26.2 *(radios et lumina Phoebi),* ALD 100.53 *(Titanis clarior orbe)* and 100.67 *(Phoebi radiis).* Tatwine is much more reticent about naming classical gods than either Aldhelm or Eusebius; Phoebus appears only here, and Mars (employed metonymically for "war") only at TAT 17.5 *(discrimina Martis)* and TAT 32.1 *(Martis . . . bella);* the Romans are mentioned only at TAT 39.2 *(romanis).* It is notable that in each case, Tatwine is borrowing the phrase in question from Aldhelm, so emphasizing his arms-length approach.

1.7 A false quantity: *făvo* is the normal usage.

1.8 Compare ALD 2.1 *(Cernere me nulli possunt nec prendere palmis).*

1.10 Glosses in both manuscripts explain *Mordentem* as *bonum lectorem.* The line looks like an interesting twist on the "biter bitten" motif (on which see the introduction to *OEALRT,* under "Shared Themes across the Collections"); the twist being that here it also alludes to the notion of the "teats of wisdom," on which see the note on ps-BED 1. The notion of restricted or favored access to wisdom is repeated at TAT 2.5–7, TAT 3.5–6, and TAT 8.4–5; the theme forms an obvious link between the first three aenigmata. Note too the quadrisyllabic ending here *(viduabo)*, as at TAT 3.1 *(dominatrix)*, 5.1 *(spoliavit)*, 6.2 *(penetrabam)*, 6.5 *(lacrimarum)*, 19.2 *(uterinos)*, 20.2 *(comitatu)*, 22.1 *(vocitabant)*, 25.2 *(spoliavi)*, 36.1 *(rogitanti)*, 39.2 *(vocitabar)*, and EP.4 *(coloratas)*. See further the note at ALD PR.26 above; Aldhelm certainly favors polysyllabic endings in ALD, proportionately far more than throughout the rest of his poetic corpus.

1.11 An obvious echo of Virgil, *Georgics* 2.490 *(felix qui potuit rerum cognoscere causas)*; compare TAT 2.2 *(Est felix . . . cui)*.

1.12 Presumably the line contains a reference to the fact that the disciples of *Sapientia* are *sapientes*, "wise men." Glosses in both manuscripts explain *rebor* as *vocabo*.

TAT 2

MANUSCRIPTS: L, fol. 121v–22r; G, fol. 374v.
EARLIER EDITIONS AND TRANSLATIONS: Gl, 169; Wl, 104. (SK 16729)
SOLUTION: *SPES, FIDES, CARITAS* (Hope, Faith, and Charity).

This aenigma is connected to the previous one by a shared allusion to ALD 2 (*VENTUS*, "wind"), as well as implicitly, if the "wise mother" *(mente sagaci)* mentioned in the opening line can be associated with the Sapientia of Ecclesiasticus 24:24, who says *Ego mater pulchrae dilectionis et timoris et agnitionis et sanctae spei*, "I am the mother of fair love, and of fear, and of knowledge, and of holy hope." See too the *Collectanea* of pseudo-Bede, in a section replete with enigmatic material (Bayless and Lapidge, *Collectanea Pseudo-Bedae*, no. 248), which reads *tres sunt filiae mentis: fides, spes, et charitas*, implying that the "mother" in question can also be construed as "mind."

2.1 The opening word *Una* can be translated either as "single" or "together"; given that Tatwine has presumably chosen deliberately to juxtapose the two elements of *Una tres* (since *Tres natae una*... scans just as well), we might take the collocation as an allusion to the undivided Trinity, as do both manuscripts, which gloss *natae* as *filiae* and *matre* as *trinitate.*

2.2 Compare TAT 1.11 *(Est felix).*

2.3 Both manuscripts gloss *numine* as *potestate.*

2.4 Compare TAT 9.1 *(nitescit); nitescit* is glossed *rutilat* in G.

2.5 Compare ALD 2.1 *(cernere me nulli possunt nec prendere palmis).* A gloss in G explains *septa* as *thalami.*

2.5–7 On the motif of restricted and favored access here, see the note on TAT 1.10 above.

TAT 3

MANUSCRIPTS: L, fol. 122r; G, fol. 374v.

EARLIER EDITIONS AND TRANSLATIONS: Gl, 170; Wl, 105–6. (SK 1692)

SOLUTION: *HISTORIA ET TROPOLOGIA ET ALLEGORIA ET ANAGOGE* (historical, tropological, allegorical, and anagogical meaning); the solution given is *DE HISTORIA ET SENSU ET MORALI ET ALLEGORIA.* This is a good example of where the solution transmitted makes no grammatical sense, though there are the required four elements. There are several possible sources for Tatwine; the most likely, given the prevalence of his influence elsewhere, is Aldhelm, *De virginitate* 4 (Eh, 232): *nunc quadrifaria evangelicae relationis dicta . . . secundum historiam, allegoriam, tropologiam, anagogen digesta.*

3.1 Both manuscripts gloss *dominatrix* as *trinitas.*

3.2 Reading *sorores* for *sorori* LG (noting that a gloss in G supplies *sapientiae* after *sorori),* to offer a link to the parallel speaking sisters in TAT 2 (*SPES, FIDES, CARITAS,* "Hope, Faith, Charity") and TAT 15 (*NIX, GRANDO, ET GLACIES,* "snow, hail, and ice"). Note that this is a four-word hexameter; a rare type practically unparalleled in the Anglo-Saxon riddle tradition.

3.3 Reading *diversis quae* for *diversisque* LG; *ornata* for *ornamenta* G, although compare ALD 11.3 *(ornamenta metallis)*; Aldhelm, *Carmen de virginitate* 337 *(diversis . . . metallis)*.

3.5–6 On the motif of restricted access here, see the note on TAT 1.10 above.

3.6 Glosses in both manuscripts explain *ingratisque* as *malis lectoribus*.

TAT 4

MANUSCRIPTS: L, fol. 122r; G, fol. 374v–75r.
EARLIER EDITIONS AND TRANSLATIONS: Gl, 171; Wl, 107–9. (SK 3970)
SOLUTION: *APICES* (letters); the solution given is *DE LITTERIS* (about letters). See further ES, 249–51.

For other aenigmata connected with the classroom and scriptorium, see the note on ALD 30 (*ELEMENTUM,* "letter of the alphabet") above. This aenigma is linked both to the preceding three (on knowledge and wisdom) and to the next two, which also deal with literacy. This is another example where the transmitted title/solution seems inadequate: the requirements of TAT 4.5 simply cannot be satisfied by what appears in both manuscripts, especially since the line in question contains the very word *(littera)* that is held to be the answer. Rather, this line seems to align the aenigma with the many other logogriphs found in the Anglo-Saxon riddle tradition (on which see the headnote to ALD 63 [*CORBUS,* "raven"]). The general solution "letters" or "writing," however, seems clearly correct, and one wonders whether the transmitted text is itself a gloss on (for example) *APICES,* since the removal of the first letter of the noun would give *PICES,* the first syllable of which is shared with *pix, picis,* "pitch." While the term *apices* for "letters" is common enough, and indeed the form *apicibus* appears frequently in glossaries (most often glossed as *stafum*), the plural form of Latin *pix,* "pitch," is otherwise unattested, which is presumably why the grammarian Tatwine emphasizes that it is the beginning of the word *(pic-)* that does not shine, so again highlighting the "black on white" trope that is found in many riddles on writing (see the note on TAT 4.3 below). This is the fourth aenigma in a row where Tatwine stresses a feminine (and in three out of four cases plural) solution, and here the idea of the female riddle-creatures serving at tables speaks directly to Anglo-Saxon cultural stereotypes.

4.1 The notion of a *pia genitrix* connects this aenigma to the three preceding; compare ALD 30.5 *(incerta matre).* The mother in question could be the mind *(mens)* of the scribe, his hand *(manus),* his pen *(penna),* or wisdom itself *(sapientia),* since in each case the noun in question is feminine in grammatical gender.

4.2 Compare ALD 43.3; BON 16.1; LOR 5.5 *(bibulis . . . buccis).*

4.3 The word *tosta,* "cooked," presumably refers to the blackened letters on the parchment, here "snow-white tables" *(nitidis . . . mensis).* For the "black on white" theme in the context of writing, see the note at ALD 59.3–5 (*PENNA,* "pen") above.

4.5 Compare SYM 74.3 *(littera decedat [lapis → apis]);* ALD 63.10 *(littera tollatur [corbus → orbuss]);* EUS 34.6 *(littera subtrahitur [flumen → lumen])* and EUS 44.4 *(littera . . . cedat [panter → pater]);* ALC 3.4 and ALC 5.2 *(Littera tollatur).* On such logogriphs in general, see the headnote to ALD 63 (*CORBUS,* "raven").

TAT 5

MANUSCRIPTS: L, fol. 122r–v; G, fol. 375r.

EARLIER EDITIONS AND TRANSLATIONS: Gl, 172; Wl, 110–11. (SK 4271)

SOLUTION: *MEMBRANUM* (parchment). See further ES, 67–68; Bitterli, *Say What I Am Called,* 173–74; Murphy, *Unriddling the Exeter Riddles,* 94; Cavell, *Weaving Words,* 169; Dale, *Natural World,* 88–89 and 96. See too Leahy, *Anglo-Saxon Crafts,* 89–93.

The lengthy description of the painful process by which a living creature becomes a piece of parchment has a close parallel in EXE 24.1–6, for which TAT 5 looks a likely source. The link between "parchment" *(membranum)* and the "limbs" *(membra)* of the animal from which it is made is in any case enshrined in Isidore, *Etym.* 6.11.1 *(Haec et membrana dicuntur, quia ex membris pecudum detrahuntur).* For other aenigmata connected with the classroom and scriptorium, see the note on ALD 30 (*ELEMENTUM,* "letter of the alphabet") above; there is a particular connection to EUS 32 (*MEMBRANUM,* "about parchment"). In general, the notion that the creature in question suffers grief, life, and death to become a posthumous tool of humanity is a commonplace of the Anglo-Saxon riddle tradition, being found also at, for example, TAT 6, 28, and 29; EXE 2, 26, 77; BER 5, 13, and 18.

5.1 A gloss in G adds *et* to *vitalis.* Tatwine exploits the twin senses of *exuviae* (both "spoils" and "hide").

5.4 Glosses in both manuscripts explain *cultor* as *scriptor.*

5.5–6 The natural connection of writing on parchment with the salvific effects of holy scripture forms a further tantalizing link with EXE 24.

5.6 Glosses in both manuscripts supply *messe* after *qua* and explain *lesis* as *peccatoribus.*

TAT 6

MANUSCRIPTS: L, fol. 122v; G, fol. 375r.
EARLIER EDITIONS AND TRANSLATIONS: Gl, 173; Wl, 112. (SK 10017)
SOLUTION: *PENNA* (pen). See further ES, 57–63; Cavell, *Weaving Words,* 169.

The concept of a cruel enemy despoiling the speaker and setting it to a new purpose links this aenigma to the one preceding (TAT 5), but also to several of the Exeter Book riddles, such as EXE 24–26 (*CRISTES BOC,* "Gospel book," *MEDU,* "mead" or *BEOR,* "beer," and *BOC-FELL,* "parchment") and EXE 77 (*BOC,* "book"). For other aenigmata connected with the classroom and scriptorium, see the note on ALD 30 (*ELEMENTUM,* "letter of the alphabet") above; compare particularly TAT 6 and both ALD 59 (*PENNA,* "pen") and EUS 35 (*PENNA,* "pen").

6.3 Both manuscripts gloss *tribus* as *digitis* and *persolvo* as *redo,* and supply *scribendi* after *tributum.* The "three fingers" motif is also found at ALD 30.5 and BER 25.2. There also exists in many manuscripts a scribal colophon comprising a single hexameter *(Tres digiti scribunt totum corpusque laborat* or [with false quantity] *Tres digiti scribunt et totum corpus laborat),* which is found in corrupt form in the pseudo-Bede *Collectanea* (ed. Bayless and Lapidge, no. 304, with useful annotation); compare too ALD 74.8 *(FUNDIBALUM,* "sling": *tres digiti totum versant super ardua corpus).* For the ending of TAT 6.3, compare ALD 17.4 *(persolvo tributum).* This line in particular also gestures towards Isaiah 40:12: *Quis mensus est pugillo aquas, et caelos palmo ponderavit? Quis appendit tribus digitis molem terrae, et liberavit in pondere montes, et colles in statera?* "Who hath measured the waters in the hollow of his hand, and weighed the heavens with his palm? Who hath poised with three fingers the bulk of the earth, and weighed the mountains in scales, and the hills in a balance?"

6.4 Both manuscripts gloss *aequora* as *cartas.* Compare ALD 74.1 *(FUNDIBALUM,* "sling": *aequore campi).*

6.5 Reading *amor is* for *amoris* LG, to preserve the masculine caesura that is elsewhere invariable in Tatwine's verse. Both manuscripts gloss *fontes* as *atramentum.*

6.6 A gloss in L supplies *atramentum* after *infundere.*

TAT 7

MANUSCRIPTS: L, fol. 122v; G, fol. 375r.

EARLIER EDITIONS AND TRANSLATIONS: Gl, 174; Wl, 113–14. (SK 11190)

SOLUTION: *TINTINNABULUM* (bell). See further ES, 131–47, who gives a detailed history of Anglo-Saxon bells and bell-making; Murphy, *Unriddling the Exeter Riddles,* 74.

The notion (first suggested by Buecheler, "Coniectanea," 342) that, having once had the name "Caesar," the original bronze of a Roman statue or collection of Roman coins depicting some pagan Caesar has been repurposed for the casting of a bell would connect this aenigma to the two preceding. That such an old pagan, transformed, should be strung up to summon the Christian faithful would certainly have been pleasing to an Anglo-Saxon cleric, and the bell's former human form with real teeth and lips may help to explain the otherwise rather clumsy use of the "biter bitten" motif, on which see further Wl, 75–77 (see too the introduction to *OEALRT,* under "Shared Themes across the Collections"). As befits a grammarian, Tatwine plays on several different grammatical forms, notably *Caesar . . . caesus; cursibus . . . recurrit; mordeo mordentem* (with a further pun on *dentibus*). For another aenigma on a somewhat smaller bell, compare SYM 81 *(TINTINNABULUM).*

7.1 Compare ALD 47.9 *(proprio de nomine).*

7.4–5 The insistently spondaic nature of the lines, together with the thumpingly heavy elision of the monosyllable in *cum ad luctum,* may be an attempt to convey the lugubriousness of the sentiments, or simply the tolling of the bell.

7.6 Another example of the "biter bitten" motif; compare SYM 44.1 *(CAEPA,* "onion": *Mordeo mordentes);* BER 37.5 *(PIPER,* "pepper": *Mordeo mordentem).*

TAT 8

MANUSCRIPTS: L, fol. 122v–23r; G, fol. 375r.

EARLIER EDITIONS AND TRANSLATIONS: Gl, 175; Wl, 115–16. (SK 12824)

SOLUTION: *ALTARE* (altar); the solution given is *DE ARA* (about an altar). See further ES, 115–17; Okasha and O'Reilly, "Anglo-Saxon Portable Altar"; Teviotdale, "Latin Verse Inscriptions."

This aenigma is linked to the last by the twin notions of loftiness and a high name. Indeed, the name of the object is concealed in the last line, since what is at issue is undoubtedly an *alta . . . re* (TAT 8.6), to be interpreted as both a "lofty task" and (through tmesis) an *altare,* "altar," according to Isidore, *Etym.* 15.4.13–14. Note that Isidore explicitly excludes the word *ara* from being linked (at least "properly"!) to the notion of height, and one wonders whether here again the transmitted title/solution is the original one. The opening lines seem to play on the notion of the altar as a nourishing quadruped, so aligning this aenigma with many of the riddles on "bull" or "bullock," on which see the note on ALD 83 (*IUVENCUS*, "bullock") above; TAT 29 (*MENSA*, "table") plays on the same idea. Here and in the next two aenigmata, all of which focus on church furniture, the notion of spiritual nourishment is prominent, so harking back to similar themes in TAT 1, 4, and 5.

8.1 Compare SYM 52.3; ALD 80.4; TAT 9.1, TAT 12.5; ALF X.1 *(mihi . . . forma).*

8.1–2 Tatwine uses the same motif of a creature with one or more feet but unable to walk also at TAT 10.6 (*RECITABULUM*, "lectern") and TAT 28.3 (*INCUS*, "anvil").

8.2 Note here another elision of a monosyllable, as well as the assonance of *nullus . . . usquam lustrare*. Compare ALD 100.11; BER 3.4 *(Nullus me).* A gloss in G explains *lustrare* as *ambulare.*

8.3 For the notion of a creature armed with horns, compare EXE 12.1 *(OXA*, "ox": *Ic wæs wæpen wigan).* Tatwine is fond of describing the creatures in question as "armed" or facing "arms": compare TAT 25.5 *(SUPERBIA*, "pride": *prostraverat armis),* TAT 27.2 *(FORCEPS*, "pair of tongs": *geminis . . . armis),* TAT 30.1 *(ENSIS ET VAGINA*, "sword and sheath": *armigeri . . . cordis),* TAT 32.1 *(SAGITTA*, "arrow": *armigeros inter).* The theme is shared elsewhere; cf. for example EUS 18.2 *(INIQUITAS ET IUSTITIA*, "iniquity and justice": *armatos),* EUS 21.2 *(TERRA ET MARE*, "land and sea": *non stantibus armis),* EUS 30.1–2 *(ATRAMENTORIUM*, "inkhorn": *armorum . . . in armis . . . armigeri),* EUS 51.3 *(SCORPIO*, "scorpion": *armari).* With specific regard to the "horns" of an altar, compare Exodus 27:1–2: *Facies et altare de lignis setthim quod habebit quinque cubitos in longitudine et totidem in latitudine id est quadrum et tres cubitos in altitudine cornua autem per quattuor angulos ex ipso erunt et operies illud aere,* "Thou shalt make also an altar of setim wood, which shall be five cubits long and as many broad, that is, foursquare, and three cubits high. And there shall be horns at the four corners of the same: and thou shalt cover it with brass."

8.4 A gloss in G explains *quosque* as *quoscumque;* glosses in both manuscripts explain *dapibus* as *corpus Christi vel sanguis.*

8.4–5 On the motif of restricted access here, see the note on TAT 1.10 above.

8.6 For the notion of "having a name," see the note at ALD 50.3; for the idea that the creature in question has a "famous name," compare EXE 24.27b–28 *(Nama min is mære / hæleþum gifre, ond halig sylf).* Further examples of the tmesis of *alta ... re* here are found at TAT 22.4–5 *(circum ... cinxit);* EUS 37.1 *(post ... quam);* BON 1.10 *(Trans ... fugiens).*

TAT 9

MANUSCRIPTS: L, fol. 123r; G, fol. 375r–v.
EARLIER EDITIONS AND TRANSLATIONS: Gl, 176; Wl, 117–18. (SK 17142)
SOLUTION: *CRUX XRISTI* (Christ's cross). See further ES, 107–15.

Several commentators, such as Bolton, "Tatwine's *De cruce Christi,*" have connected this aenigma with *The Dream of the Rood* (see further Orchard, "*The Dream of the Rood:* Cross-References"). Compare EUS 17 (*CRUX,* "cross").

9.1–3 Compare *Dream* 21b–23 *(Geseah ic þæt fuse beacen / wendan wædum ond bleom; hwilum hit wæs mid wætan bestemed, / beswyled mid swates gange, hwilum mid since gegyrwed).*

9.1 Compare SYM 52.3; ALD 80.4; TAT 8.1, TAT 12.5; ALF X.1 *(mihi ... forma).*

9.2 Compare ALD 100.9 *(larbula terret).*

9.5 Glosses in both manuscripts supply *corporibus* after *insanis.*

9.6 Another elision of a monosyllable. Compare *Dream* 117–18 *(Ne mæg þær ænig unforht wesan / for þam worde þe se wealdend cwyð);* Revelation 9:4 speaks of those *qui non habent signum Dei in frontibus suis,* words which are reflected in the baptismal rite.

TAT 10

MANUSCRIPTS: L, fol. 123r; G, fol. 375v.

EARLIER EDITIONS AND TRANSLATIONS: Gl, 177; Wl, 119. (SK 769)

SOLUTION: *RECITABULUM* (lectern). See further ES, 117–20.

The description is clearly of an eagle-shaped lectern, and concludes the sequence of ecclesiastical furniture in TAT 7–10. The animal imagery here matches that of TAT 8 (*ALTARE,* "altar"), with which it shares the motif of "feet without walking" (on which see the note at TAT 8.1–2), but is continued throughout the aenigma, which also contains at TAT 10.2–3 the motif of "speech without tongue." In general, this aenigma has much in common with other riddles enumerating body parts, on which see the headnote on ALD 84 above. For other aenigmata connected with the classroom and scriptorium, see the headnote on ALD 30 (*ELEMENTUM,* "letter of the alphabet") above.

10.2–3 For the motif of "speech without tongue," compare EUS 7.3 (*LITTERAE,* "letters") and EUS 32.1–2 (*MEMBRANUM,* "parchment").

10.3 Compare ALD 95.2 *(lingua loquelis);* EUS 59.4 *(lingua loquax).*

10.4 The description of being supported on wings links this aenigma back to TAT 1 (*SAPIENTIA,* "wisdom"). The form *fulci* is used here for metrical reasons in place of *fulciri.*

10.5 A gloss in G explains *quis* as *quibus,* and supplies *alis.*

10.6 For the theme of the single-footed creature, see for example TAT 28 (*INCUS,* "anvil"); ps-BED 13 (*LEBES,* "cauldron"); EXE 29 (*SALTERE,* "psaltery"), 30 (*CEAP-SCIP,* "merchant ship"), 56 (*ROD,* "pole, cross"), 77 (*WEDER-COC,* "weathercock"), and 88 (*BOC,* "book; beech"); SYM 40 (*PAPAVER,* "poppy").

TAT 11

MANUSCRIPTS: L, fol. 123r–v; G, fol. 375v.
EARLIER EDITIONS AND TRANSLATIONS: Gl, 178; Wl, 120. (SK 16410)
SOLUTION: *ACUS* (needle). See further ES, 48–54. See too Leahy, *Anglo-Saxon Crafts,* 76–78.

The connection of this aenigma to the last is unclear, but compare TAT 13 (*ACUS PICTILIS,* "embroidery needle").

11.1 A gloss in G explains *Torrens* as *ardens.* Compare ALD 100.42 *(viscere flammas),* TAT 14.3 *(mea viscera flammis),* TAT 34.1 *(mea viscera flammae);* LOR 10.4 *(viscera flamma);* Aldhelm, *Carmen de virginitate* 1384 *(viscera flammis).*

11.2 Both manuscripts gloss *luscam* as *cum uno oculo.*

11.3 Reading *sine me iam* for *iam sine me* LG. Compare TAT 21.2 *(me sine vivere);* TAT 33.2 *(qua sine vivere possunt).* See the headnote above on the colorless sense of *iam* here, as commonly in TAT. The idea that sewing and clothing save mankind from death repeats ALD 45.7 *(FUSUM,* "spindle": *frigora dura viros sternant ni forte resistam).*

11.4 Compare ALD 67.9; TAT 14.3 *(mirum dictu).*

11.6 Both manuscripts gloss *condere* as *ostendere.*

TAT 12

MANUSCRIPTS: L, fol. 123v; G, fol. 375v.
EARLIER EDITIONS AND TRANSLATIONS: Gl, 179; Wl, 121–22. (SK 4882)
SOLUTION: *PATENA* (paten). If the title/solution is correct, what is depicted appears to be a highly ornate paten of the footed type more common in the Eastern Church than that of the West, so leading to speculation that Tatwine may be describing a specific paten brought over by Theodore, one of his predecessors as Archbishop of Canterbury.

Compare in general ALD 55 (*CRISMAL,* "chrismal").

12.2 Both manuscripts gloss *caros* as *amicos.*

12.3 Compare BIB 2.7 *(PHYSICA,* "physics": *tot lumina lucent).* Both manuscripts gloss *lumina* as *gemmae* G *dilicias vel gemmas* L.

12.5 Compare SYM 52.3; ALD 80.4; TAT 8.1, TAT 9.1; ALF X.1 *(mihi . . . forma).*

TAT 13

MANUSCRIPTS: L, fol. 123v; G, fol. 375v.

EARLIER EDITIONS AND TRANSLATIONS: Gl, 180; Wl, 123. (SK 14130)

SOLUTION: *ACUS PICTILIS* (embroidery needle). See further ES, 48–54.

This is the second of Tatwine's aenigmata to deal with needles and sewing, if the given solution is correct; a theme that of course also links the whole collection, according to the wording of the *Preface.* It is hard, however, to see what links this particular aenigma either to the one preceding or following, unless it is the echo of SYM 55.2–3 (*ACULA,* "needle") in TAT 14.1–2. The language is certainly titillating and rich, and the theme seems a curious choice. Perhaps the preferred solution should be "embroidery" itself, given the use of the term *polymitarius* to signify an embroiderer in the Vulgate Exodus 35:35, 36:35, and 38:23. Compare TAT 11 (*ACUS,* "needle"); SYM 55 (*ACULA,* "needle").

13.1 Note here the cadence ending in a double monosyllable, which is rare but not unparalleled within the Anglo-Saxon riddle tradition: see, for example, the note at ALD PR.12.

TAT 14

MANUSCRIPTS: L, fol. 123v; G, fol. 375v.

EARLIER EDITIONS AND TRANSLATIONS: Gl, 181; Wl, 124. (SK 6158)

SOLUTION: *CARITAS* (love). See further Lockett, *Anglo-Saxon Psychologies,* 273–74.

The whole aenigma is predicated on a double paradox of binding and loosing, and burning and enjoying being consumed. With regard to the aspect of binding and loosing, it is notable that there seems little to connect this aenigma with the notion of Peter and the keys of heaven, as expressed in Matthew 16:19 and 18:18. Compare BON 5 (*CARITAS,* "love").

14.1 Both manuscripts gloss *gemino* as *dilectio dei et proximi.*

14.1–2 Compare SYM 5.2 *(vincior ipsa prius sed vincio vincta vicissim)* and SYM 55.2–3 *(mollia duco levi comitantia vincula ferro / et faciem laesis et nexum reddo solutis).* The second of these parallels may have suggested a link to the preceding TAT 11 (*ACUS,* "needle") and TAT 13 (*ACUS PICTILIS,* "embroidery needle").

14.2 Note the awkward elision at the caesura, as well as the scansion of *resolvŏ,* presumably to preserve the parallel syntax and the dactylic meter; reading *vincta ligata resolve* barely improves things.

14.3 Compare ALD 67.9; TAT 11.4 *(mirum dictu);* ALD 100.42 *(viscere flammas);* TAT 11.1 *(viscere flammae),* TAT 34.1 *(mea viscera flammae);* LOR 10.4 *(viscera flamma).*

14.5 A gloss in G explains *mulcent* as *blandificant.* Compare Virgil, *Georgics* 4.101 *(dulcia mella),* although the tag is also picked up by later poets, notably Venantius Fortunatus.

TAT 15

MANUSCRIPTS: L, fol. 123v–24r; G, fol. 375v–76r.
EARLIER EDITIONS AND TRANSLATIONS: Gl, 182; Wl, 125. (SK 438)
SOLUTION: *NIX, GRANDO, ET GLACIES* (snow, hail, and ice).

Presumably the "mother" of TAT 15.2 and 15.5 is *aqua,* "water," following the gloss (*aqua et pluvia* LG; *pluviae* G); the "father" is most likely *ventus,* "wind," or perhaps *nimbus,* "cloud." Compare LOR 4 (*GELU,* "ice"), which shares a number of parallels with this aenigma.

15.1 Note the monosyllabic ending, unique here in Tatwine's corpus, and presumably solely for the sake of the telestich.

15.2 Both manuscripts gloss *matre* as *aqua et pluviae.*

15.5 Both manuscripts gloss *matris* as *pluviae.* For more examples of the mother and womb motif, see the note at ALD 93.10.

TAT 16

MANUSCRIPTS: L, fol. 124r; G, fol. 376r.

EARLIER EDITIONS AND TRANSLATIONS: Gl, 183; Wl, 126. (SK 4371)

SOLUTION: *PREPOSITIONES UTRIUSQUE CASUS* (prepositions that take two cases). See further Lockett, *Anglo-Saxon Psychologies,* 262–63.

This aenigma clearly derives from Tatwine's interest in grammar, and indeed Tatwine is true to his own grammatical treatise; compare *Ars Tatuini* 1.54 (ed. De Marco, CCSL 133, 22): *ACCUSATIVUS quod per ipsum accusamus aliquem aut aliquis nos accusat . . . ABLATIVUS dictus est quia per ipsum aut quiddam ab aliquo auferamus aut a nobis auferatur,* "[The case is called] ACCUSATIVE because through it we accuse someone, or someone accuses us. . . . [The case] is called ABLATIVE because through it either we take something from someone or something is taken from us," and *Ars Tatuini* 7.4 (ed. De Marco, CCSL 133, 86): *Praepositiones utriusque casus, accusativi scilicet et ablativi, hae quattuor communes sunt:* in sub super subter, "The prepositions taking both cases, namely accusative and ablative, are the following four: *in, under, above, beneath.*" Here, in indicating those prepositions that take different cases according to whether they follow static verbs (ablative) or verbs of motion (accusative), Tatwine uses the synonyms *tollo* and *causo* for *aufero* and *accuso* respectively. Note the closeness of this passage to the gloss on TAT 16.4 in G below.

16.3 The insistent alliteration *(causanti contra cursus comitamur)* is more characteristic of Aldhelm: see, for example, the notes to ALD 7, 12, 33, 54, 60, 68, 69, 71, 77, 86, 87, and 95.

16.4 The phrase *bis binae* is glossed *in sub subter super* G; both manuscripts supply *casibus* in glosses after *ambis*. Compare BER 56.3 *(coniungimur ambo)*.

16.5 Note the lengthening of the final syllable of *decreta* before the *st-* of *stat*.

TAT 17

MANUSCRIPTS: L, fol. 124r; G, fol. 376r.
EARLIER EDITIONS AND TRANSLATIONS: Gl, 184; Wl, 127–28. (SK 2071)
SOLUTION: *SCIURUS* (squirrel). See further ES, 178.

Compare the mock-heroic tone of ALD 26 (*GALLUS*, "cockerel") and 75 (*CRABRO*, "hornet"). The resolutely dactylic rhythm presumably mimics the creature's perky antics.

17.1 Compare SYM 14.2 *(PULLUS IN OVO*, "chick in egg": *natus in alvo)* and SYM 36.1 *(PORCUS*, "pig": *matris . . . natus in alvo)*; ALD 93.10 *(SCINTILLA*, "spark": *genetrix . . . generaret ab alvo)*; ALD 100.24 *(CREATURA*, "Creation": *matris . . . generabar ab alvo)*; TAT 15.5 *(NIX, GRANDO, ET GLACIES*, "about snow, hail, and ice": *matris . . . in alvum)*; BER 34.1 *(ROSA*, "on a rose": *mater concipit alvo)*. The word *alvus* is one of the few second-declension nouns that is feminine, a point that the grammarian Tatwine here underlines (hence *foecunda*).

17.3 A gloss in G explains *astu* as *arrogantia*.

17.4 A gloss in L explains *ceu* as *si*. Compare ALD 12.3 *(cacumina scando)*; ALD 36.2 *(super ardua pennis)*; ALD 71.5 *(convexa cacumina cernam)*.

17.5 Both manuscripts gloss *Martis* as *proelii*. Compare SYM 26.2 *(discrimine Martis)*; ALD 60.1 *(discrimina Martis)*; Aldhelm, *Carmen de virginitate* 1377 *(vitans discrimen acerbi)*.

TAT 18

MANUSCRIPTS: L, fol. 124r; G, fol. 376r.
EARLIER EDITIONS AND TRANSLATIONS: Gl, 185; Wl, 129–30. (SK 3758)
SOLUTION: *OCULI* (eyes). See further ES, 240.

By contrast with the highly dactylic meter of the previous aenigma, this one is ploddingly spondaic. The solution is broadly hinted at by the various forms of the two verbs *video* and *cerno* (employing the device of polyptoton), both signifying "I see" *(Discernens . . . vidi . . . viderat . . . cernit . . . cerno)*, with the final four examples arranged chiastically within their respective lines for greater emphasis. This aenigma begins a short sequence of three on eyes (TAT 18–20: *OCULI*, "eyes," *STRABI OCULI*, "squinting eyes," and *LUSCUS*, "a one-eyed man"). For a strikingly parallel riddle in the Middle Welsh *Branwen Ferch Lŷr*, together with a discussion of a number of other analogues in various languages and cultures, see Sims-Williams, "Riddling Treatment of the 'Watchman Device,'" especially 83. The Welsh version describes how Irish watchmen see a marvelous forest traveling on the sea, and close by the forest, and also traveling, a big mountain with a ridge, and a lake on either side of that ridge *(ac eskeir aruchel ar y mynyd, a llynn o pop parth y'r eskeir)*. The riddle is solved as the approach of the British giant Bendigeidfran (the mountain in question) with his forest of ships, and "his two eyes, one on each side of his nose, are the two lakes on either side of the ridge" *(y deu lygat ef o pop parth y drwyn yw y dwy lynn o bop parth y'r eskeir)*.

18.2 Both manuscripts gloss *matre* as *capite vel creatore*. On the single mother, compare TAT 19.2 (*STRABI OCULI*, "squinting eyes"), and the headnote to TAT. Note the twin oxymorons *geminos una* and *magno parvi*. Compare ALD 30.5 *(nos . . . matre crearunt)*.

18.3 A gloss in G supplies *sumus* after *divisi*; another in L explains *haud magno* as *parvo*.

18.4–5 Compare TAT 19.3–4 (*STRABI OCULI*, "squinting eyes").

TAT 19

MANUSCRIPTS: L, fol. 124r–v; G, fol. 376r.
EARLIER EDITIONS AND TRANSLATIONS: Gl, 186; Wl, 131. (SK 8213)
SOLUTION: *STRABI OCULI* (squinting eyes).

This aenigma is the second of three on eyes (TAT 18–20). See further ES, 240. Compare ALD 85 (*CAECUS NATUS,* "man born blind"); EUS 19 and 20.

19.2 On the theme of the single mother, compare TAT 18.2.
19.3–4 Compare TAT 18.4–5 (*OCULIS,* "eyes").
19.5 Both manuscripts gloss *amor* as *videndi.*

TAT 20

MANUSCRIPTS: L, fol. 124v; G, fol. 376r.
EARLIER EDITIONS AND TRANSLATIONS: Gl, 187; Wl, 132–33. (SK 16798)
SOLUTION: *LUSCUS* (one-eyed man). See further ES, 240.

This aenigma concludes the sequence on sight and seeing (TAT 18–20). Compare ALD 85 (*CAECUS NATUS,* "man born blind"); SYM 95 (*LUSCUS ALIUM VENDENS,* "one-eyed garlic-seller").

20.1 Both manuscripts read *ducifer,* but *dulcifer* (as in TAT 4.1) seems preferable.
20.4 Both manuscripts supply *oculum* in glosses after *quem;* a gloss in G explains *creverat* as *viderat.* Compare Matthew 18:9 *bonum tibi est unoculum in vitam intrare quam duos oculos habentem mitti in gehennam ignis,* "It is better for thee having one eye to enter into life, than having two eyes to be cast into hell fire," and Mark 9:47 *bonum est tibi luscum introire in regnum Dei quam duos oculos habentem mitti in gehennam ignis,* "It is better for thee with one eye to enter into the kingdom of God than having two eyes to be cast into the hell of fire."

TAT 21

MANUSCRIPTS: L, fol. 124v; G, fol. 376r–v.
EARLIER EDITIONS AND TRANSLATIONS: Gl, 188; Wl, 134. (SK 4614)
SOLUTION: *MALUM* (evil).

The repetition of "the good" in three different grammatical cases *(bono . . . bonum . . . boni)* in TAT 21.3–5 again underlines Tatwine's main interests, and offers a broad clue to the solution. The word *privatim* (TAT 21.3) may suggest that Tatwine's immediate source is Augustine, *Confessiones* 3.7.12: *Quia non noveram malum non esse nisi privationem boni usque ad quod omnino non est,* "because I did not know that evil was nothing but a taking away of good, until at last something utterly ceases to be."

21.1 A gloss in G supplies *mirum* after *malum;* another in L supplies *mirum* after *ingrato.*

21.2 Both manuscripts contain glosses that supply *sit* after *rarum.* Compare TAT 11.3 *(me sine vivere posse),* TAT 33.2 *(qua sine vivere possunt).*

21.3 False quantity: Tatwine scans the first word *nĕc;* the temptation to emend to *nēve* is strong, but given other false quantities and the absence of *nēve* elsewhere in his verse, it seems feasible to accept the received reading. Both manuscripts gloss *privatim* as *specialiter* and *constare* as *malum.*

TAT 22

MANUSCRIPTS: L, fol. 124v–25r; G, fol. 376v.
EARLIER EDITIONS AND TRANSLATIONS: Gl, 189; Wl, 135. (SK 14107)
SOLUTION: *ADAM* (Adam).

The juxtaposition of Adam and Evil, while clearly biblical, is not exploited in either TAT 21 or 22; if the suggested connection between TAT 22 and 23 seems fruitful, there seems also to be an implicit link between *mălum,* "evil," and *mālum,* "apple."

22.3 The juxtaposition of the two exclamations *pro dolor* and *heu,* which can both broadly be translated as "alas!," surely brings to mind a third, namely *vae,* the traditional anagrammatic etymology of *Eva,* "Eve"; compare Isidore, *Etym.* 7.7.5: *Eva interpretatur vita sive calamitas sive vae. Vita, quia origo fuit nascendi: calamitas et vae, quia praevaricatione causa extitit moriendi. A cadendo enim nomen sumpsit calamitas,* "Eve is interpreted as life or calamity or woe *(vae).* Life, because it was the origin of being born: calamity and woe, because through her deception the cause of dying occurred, since calamity took its name from falling." The reinterpretation of *vae* as *Eva* requires the word to be "reduced" or "redacted" *(redactus).* Eve is of course the *socia,* "mate," specified in the word that follows, as the glosses clearly show. Both manuscripts gloss *socia* variously as *Eva* L *Æva* G.

22.4–5 Note tmesis of *circum . . . cinxit* and polyptoton of *servis servire,* both emphasized by insistent alliteration on *c-* and *s-*. On tmesis, see the note at TAT 8.6 above.

TAT 23

MANUSCRIPTS: L, fol. 125r; G, fol. 376v.
EARLIER EDITIONS AND TRANSLATIONS: Gl, 190; Wl, 136–37. (SK 14736)
SOLUTION: *TRINA MORS* (threefold death).

The motif of the threefold death here has a parallel in the pseudo-Bede *Collectanea* 77: *Dic mihi quot mortes peccatoribus reputantur? Mors in peccato, et separatio animae et corporis, et mors poenae,* "Tell me, how many deaths are reckoned for sinners? Death in sin, and the separation of the soul and body, and the death of torment"; Bayless and Lapidge (1998), 130–31 and 218. Presumably the notion of the threefold death is linked implicitly to Adam, the subject of the preceding aenigmata, through the motif of the Fall. The biting motif so prevalent throughout *(morsibus . . . dente . . . dentum . . . mordet)* may perhaps recall the biting of the apple in Eden, as Isidore explains, in a variant passage (here underlined), *Etym.* 11.2.31–32: *Mors dicta, quod sit amara, vel a Marte, qui est effector mortium sive mors a morsu hominis primi, quod vetitae arboris pomum mordens mortem incurrit. Tria sunt autem genera mortis: acerba, inmatura, naturalis. Acerba infantum, inmatura iuvenum, merita, id est naturalis, senum,* "Death *(mors)* is so called, because it is bitter *(amarus)*, or because it stems from Mars, who is the author of death; or else death is derived from the bite *(morsus)* of the first human, because when he bit the fruit of the forbidden tree, he incurred death. There are three kinds of death: bitter, untimely, and natural. That of children is bitter, and of young people untimely, and of old people fitting, which is to say natural."

23.1 Both manuscripts use glosses to supply *vitiorum* after *morsibus.*

23.2 Reading *perimo* after L; note that G has *perunco,* but glosses it as *perimo (DMLBS* suggests *perintro).* In adopting the reading *perimo,* I assume the same false quantity as in TAT 23.5: *perĭmo* is the normal usage; it is possible that Tatwine is confusing present-tense forms of *perĭmo* with similar future-tense forms of *perībo,* as at EUS 4.2 *(peribit),* TAT 21.4 *(peribo),* and TAT 24.3 *(peribit).* The same false quantity is also to be found at BON 14.15 *(SUPERBIA LOQUITUR,* "pride speaks": *perīmo).*

23.5 A false quantity: *perĭmit* is the normal usage; compare TAT 23.2. Perhaps read *peremit*?

TAT 24

MANUSCRIPTS: L, fol. 125r; G, fol. 376v.
EARLIER EDITIONS AND TRANSLATIONS: Gl, 191; Wl, 138. (SK 4324)
SOLUTION: *HUMILITAS* (humility).

The final line seems obviously to be indebted to ALD 100 (*CREATURA,* "Creation"). Gl and Wl cite a variety of biblical parallels, including Deuteronomy 4:29; 2 Chronicles 30:19 and 31:21; Luke 14:11; Matthew 18:14; Psalms 17:28 and 112:16; Job 5:11; the connection here to the aenigma that follows is obvious. For quite different treatments of the same theme, compare BON 9 (*HUMILITAS CRISTIANA,* "Christian humility") and EUS 27 (*HUMILITAS ET SUPERBIA,* "humility and pride").

24.1 Another rather clumsy elision of a monosyllable.

24.3 On *peribit,* see the note on TAT 23.2.

24.4 Compare LOR 1.12 *(sine fine manendus).*

24.5 Compare ALD 100.21–22 *(Altior, en, caelo . . . inferior terris);* see too TAT 1.4–5, and the note above.

TAT 25

MANUSCRIPTS: L, fol. 125r; G, fol. 376v.

EARLIER EDITIONS AND TRANSLATIONS: Gl, 192; Wl, 139–40. (SK 4811)

SOLUTION: *SUPERBIA* (pride); the given solution is the same. Note that the customary *DE* is missing in both manuscripts, again supporting the notion that the "original" solutions (if indeed they traveled alongside the aenigmata at all) were in the nominative.

In giving Pride seven sisters, Tatwine seems influenced here by Aldhelm, who, following Cassian, concludes his *Carmen de virginitate* with an extended passage, itself derived from Prudentius's *Psychomachia,* which has no counterpart in the twinned Prose *De virginitate,* and in some later manuscripts is given the separate title *De octo vitiis principalibus* (On the eight principal vices [*Carmen de virginitate* 2446–761]). The rubrics in *Carmen de virginitate* at this point appear to have been added in the tenth century, perhaps by Dunstan. This aenigma is heavily adorned with wordplay (essentially, paronomasia) on three separate elements, namely *par-, reg-,* and *sept- (parente . . . partier . . . parabam . . . parvulus; regno . . . reginas; septenas . . . septas).* Pride and her seven sisters here also match Wisdom and her seven daughters in TAT 1–3.

25.1 Both manuscripts gloss *Eximio* as *alto* and *parente* as *diabolo.* The reading is *seclis* in G, *sedis* L; here I prefer *sedis.*

25.2 The reading is *regna* in both G and L; for metrical reasons, other editors have emended to *regno,* which makes better grammatical sense, but violates the meter (as indeed the *sp-* might in any case be argued to make position). It seems more likely that Tatwine thought *spolio* took a double accusative.

The polysyllabic ending appears twelve times in TAT, as elsewhere in the tradition; see the notes at ALD PR.26 and TAT 1.10 above.

25.5 The reading is *Parvulus* in G, *Parvus* in L; here I prefer *Parvulus* for metrical reasons. A gloss in G explains *Parvulus* as *humilis Christus;* another in L explains *parvus* as *humilis.* Compare Aldhelm, *Carmen de virginitate* 2493 *(prosternitur armis).* There is an interesting parallel with EUS 1.4 *(agmina devastans avertor laesus ab uno).*

TAT 26

MANUSCRIPTS: L, fol. 125r–v; G, fol. 376v.
EARLIER EDITIONS AND TRANSLATIONS: Gl, 193; Wl, 141. (SK 10570)
SOLUTION: *QUINQUE SENSUS* (the five senses).

Presumably the previous enumeration of Pride and her seven sisters sparks off this aenigma on the five senses, here depicted as brothers. The paronomasia here is less insistent that in the previous aenigma, focusing here on the single element *(-)fer(-)* (*fero fercula . . . aufert*).

26.1 Both manuscripts gloss *templum* as *corpus.*

26.3 Both manuscripts gloss *thuris* (*turis* in L) as *odoratus dicit,* and explain *ille saporis* as *gustus.*

26.4 Both manuscripts gloss *hic totum* variously as *tactus* G *tactum* L, and *ille videndum* as *visus.*

26.5 A gloss in G explains *quintus* as *auditus;* another in L supplies *auditus* at *ministrat.*

TAT 27

MANUSCRIPTS: L, fol. 125v; G, fol. 376v–77r.
EARLIER EDITIONS AND TRANSLATIONS: Gl, 194; Wl, 142. (SK 7591)
SOLUTION: *FORCEPS* (pair of tongs). See too Leahy, *Anglo-Saxon Crafts,* 117; Riley, *Anglo-Saxon Tools,* 46–48.

This aenigma in clearly connected to the following one, TAT 28 (*INCUS,* "anvil").

27.1 Compare ALD 97.14 *(NOX,* "night": *mirabile dictu)* and ALD 100.62 *(CREATURA,* "Creation": *mirabile fatu).*

27.3 A gloss in G supplies *et* at *est.*

TAT 28

MANUSCRIPTS: L, fol. 125v; G, fol. 377r.

EARLIER EDITIONS AND TRANSLATIONS: Gl, 195; Wl, 143. (SK 5662)

SOLUTION: *INCUS* (anvil). See too Leahy, *Anglo-Saxon Crafts,* 117; Riley, *Anglo-Saxon Tools,* 44–45.

This aenigma in clearly connected to the preceding one, TAT 27 (*FORCEPS,* "pair of tongs").

28.1 Compare SYM 87.3 *(MALLEUS,* "hammer" : *caput est)* and SYM 40.1 *(PAPAVER,* "poppy": *Grande mihi caput est).* Note the insistent alliteration on *c-*.

28.3 For the fixed-foot motif, see the note on TAT 8.1–2 (*ALTARE,* "altar") above.

28.3–4 The clearly masculine forms *fixus . . . sinitūrus* seem to belie the title/solution *incus,* which is grammatically feminine. It is possible that Tatwine was misled by the *-us* ending of the nominative, although the noun is third declension, and in any case that would be an odd error for a grammarian. Or perhaps the given solution masks an original *INCUDIS MALLEUS,* as Bob Babcock has suggested to me.

28.5 The theme of the suffering creature is a commonplace throughout the riddle tradition; see especially the two sequences TAT 5–6 and here TAT 28–29.

TAT 29

MANUSCRIPTS: L, fol. 125v; G, fol. 377r.
EARLIER EDITIONS AND TRANSLATIONS: Gl, 196; Wl, 144. (SK 9857)
SOLUTION: *MENSA* (table). See further ES, 44–47.

The closest general parallel here is with BER 5 (*MENSA,* "table"), and indeed, several specific details (notably those of clothing, nakedness, and ingratitude) seem to correspond.

29.1 Reading *multiferis,* which is rare, but attested in Pliny, and may have come into Anglo-Saxon England through grammatical sources. L has *mulciferis;* the scribe of G writes an initial word *(dulciferis)* that ruins the acrostic. Compare LOR 5.6 *(mulcifer).*

29.2 A harsh elision, where in this case it is the monosyllable that causes it.

29.3 A false quantity: the usual form is *fătim,* though the word itself is extremely rare; both manuscripts gloss it as *habunde.*

TAT 30

MANUSCRIPTS: L, fol. 125v–26r; G, fol. 377r.
EARLIER EDITIONS AND TRANSLATIONS: Gl, 197; Wl, 145. (SK 1056)
SOLUTION: *ENSIS ET VAGINA* (sword and sheath). See further ES, 77–85; Lendinara, "Aspetti della società germanica."

Compare ALD 61 (*PUGIO,* "dagger") and EUS 36 (*GLADIUS,* "sword"); EXE 18 (suggested solution: "sword"). The thematic resemblance to ALD 61 in particular is striking: in both, the sheath is described as a "house" or "hall," though in TAT 30 the speaker is the sheath; in ALD 61 it is the weapon. In general, one might also compare EXE 59 (*CYRTEL,* "shirt, garment"), which shares with this aenigma a propensity to double entendre and a sexual interpretation.

30.2 The form *circumstantia* is rare, but it also appears in TAT 1.1 (*SAPIENTIA,* "Wisdom").

TAT 31

MANUSCRIPTS: L, fol. 126r; G, fol. 377r.
EARLIER EDITIONS AND TRANSLATIONS: Gl, 198; Wl, 146. (SK 16321)
SOLUTION: *IGNIS* (fire); the solution given is *DE SCINTILLA* (about a spark).

The aenigma focuses on aspects of both birth and life, highlighted by word- and sound-play. Note the insistent alliteration on *v-* and *s-* *(vult . . . viscere . . . vere . . . vitae . . . vivens . . . ventre; sensit spiramina . . . sepultus).* The final word *sepultus,* "buried," forms a fitting reminder through reversal of the birth-and-life theme. The gender of the title/solution seems belied by the forms *ipse* and *sepultus* in TAT 31.4; one wonders whether *IGNIS,* "fire," or *CAMINUS,* "forge," is intended instead; note that TAT 33 has the given solution *IGNIS.* Compare TAT 28 (*INCUS,* "anvil"), which has a similar disconnection of grammatical gender. See further ES, 245.

Compare ALD 93 (*SCINTILLA,* "spark"), though the treatment is very different.

31.1 The form *crevi* could derive either from *cerno,* "I perceive," or from *cresco,* "I grow"; note the sibilance on *-sc-* in the following line *(nasci . . . viscere).*

31.2 Compare ALD 27.1 *(ex gelido . . . viscere)* and 33.1 *(me genuit gelido de viscere);* TAT 39.1 *(Natam me gelido terrae de viscere);* LOR 4.1 *(me . . . ex gelido generat . . . tergore matris);* EUS 38.4 *(viscera matris);* Aldhelm, *Carmen de virginitate* 311 *(quod dudumquam nascatur de viscere matris).*

31.4 Preferring *ipse* L over *ipsa* G. A gloss in L explains its reading, *mansi,* as *mansit.* Compare SYM 76.1 *(semper inest intus, sed raro cernitur ignis)* and SYM 77.3 (*SILEX,* "flint," which repeats SYM 76.1 almost verbatim); see too Virgil, *Aeneid* 6.6–7 *(quaerit pars semina flammae / abstruse in venis silicis).*

TAT 32

MANUSCRIPTS: L, fol. 126r; G, fol. 377r.
EARLIER EDITIONS AND TRANSLATIONS: Gl, 199; Wl, 147. (SK 1057)
SOLUTION: *SAGITTA* (arrow).

The aenigma explains the threefold role of archery in war, hunting, and (presumably) target practice. Compare SYM 65 *(SAGITTA);* BED 14 *(SAGITTA);* ALC D98 *(SAGITTA).* There is a natural link with TAT 34 (*FARETRA,* "quiver").

32.1 Compare TAT 34.4 *(subire duellum),* so connecting this aenigma verbally to another already connected conceptually.
32.2 Reading *iubent* for *iuvant* LG; note the implied *b/v* conflation, on which see further the note at ALD 63 *(CORBUS).* Compare ALD 93.4 *(prosternere leto),* a verbal parallel which links this aenigma to the last.
32.3 Note the paronomasia on *inferre ferino,* and compare *leto . . . letos* in 32.2 and 32.4 for the figure; see Bede, *De scematibus et tropis* 1.9 (ed. Kendall, 174–77).
32.4 A gloss in G explains its reading, *cętus,* as *coetus.*

TAT 33

MANUSCRIPTS: L, fol. 126r; G, fol. 377r.
EARLIER EDITIONS AND TRANSLATIONS: Gl, 200; Wl, 148. See further ES, 245. (SK 16319)
SOLUTION: *IGNIS* (fire).

Some broad parallels are to be found in *Hisperica famina* A426–51 (*DE IGNE,* "on fire"; see further Herren, *Hisperica Famina: The A-Text;* Orchard, "*Hisperica famina* as Literature").

The notion of a threefold form for fire (so connecting this aenigma to the one preceding) perhaps derives from Isidore, *Etym.* 19.6.3–5, who specifies one kind of domestic fire for human use, and two stemming from divine causes, whether in the form of lightning or volcanic eruption: *Habet quoque et aliam in se diversitatem ignis. Nam alius est qui usui humano, alius qui iudicio apparet divino, sive qui de caelo fulmen adstringit, sive qui de terra per vertices montium eructuat,* "[Fire] has another inherent variation: for there is one kind for human use, and a second which appears from divine judgement, whether appearing as a lightning bolt from the sky or belching from the earth through the tops of mountains." Compare ALD 44 (*IGNIS,* "fire"); EUS 15 (*DE IGNE ET AQUA,* "about fire and water").

33.1 The juxtaposition of *simplex* and *triplicem* naturally brings to mind the notion of the Triune god of Christianity.

33.2 Compare TAT 11.3 *(me sine vivere posse);* TAT 21.2 *(me sine vivere).*

33.4 Whichever of the manuscript readings is accepted (G has *haut sum,* L *sum haut*), elision of a monosyllable arises; G is preferred here, since that of L has the added disadvantage of not producing a metrical line. The sense of *exorsus* (or indeed, with emendation, *exortus*) seems to be that fire is a primordial element that existed before mankind, the "them" noted here.

TAT 34

MANUSCRIPTS: L, fol. 126r–v; G, fol. 377r–v.

EARLIER EDITIONS AND TRANSLATIONS: Gl, 201; Wl, 149. (SK 11227)

SOLUTION: *FARETRA* (quiver). See further Cavell, *Weaving Words,* 180–81.

The connection of this aenigma to those surrounding it derives from the repeated mention of flames *(flammae . . . flamma),* emphasized through insistent alliteration on *f-* and *v-* *(viscera flammae . . . flamma ferox . . . devastat . . . foedera frangam).* In particular, there is a clear conceptual connection to TAT 32 (*SAGITTA,* "arrow").

34.1 Compare ALD 89.1 *(complentur viscera)* and 100.42 *(viscere flammas);* TAT 11.1 *(viscere flammae)* and 14.3 *(mea viscera flammis);* LOR 10.4 *(viscera flamma);* Aldhelm, *Carmen de virginitate* 1384 *(viscera flammis).* The readings *Miles* and *flammis* in G for the first and last words ruin the acrostic-telestich, and have necessitated the scribe's correcting his original *complent* to *complet,* as well as reading *diris* to agree with *flammis.* A gloss in G doubles down, explaining *Miles* as *bellator.* The reading of L *(Omnis enim dirae complent mea viscera flammae)* prompts mine, which in reading *Omnia* restores an elision (a feature for which Tatwine is well known), as well as the structure of a golden line.

34.2 Reading *acerbis* for *acervis,* which appears in both manuscripts (on such *-b-* for *-f-* spellings, see EXE 21.1 and the headnote on LEI below). Compare ALD 36.1 and 66.5 *(stimulis . . . acerbis);* Aldhelm, *Carmen de virginitate* 1818 *(stimulis cedebat acerbis).*

34.3 Compare ALD 96.3 *(pia foedera);* Aldhelm, *Carmen de virginitate* 2628 *(piae . . . foedera pacis).*

34.4 Glosses in both manuscripts explain *duellum* as *discordiam vel pugnam;* that in G supplies *discordiam* over an erasure that originally read *victoriam.*

TAT 35

MANUSCRIPTS: L, fol. 126v; G, fol. 377v.

EARLIER EDITIONS AND TRANSLATIONS: Gl, 202; Wl, 150. (SK 14395)

SOLUTION: *PRUNA* (ember); the solution given is *DE PRUINA* (about rime, about hoarfrost). The given solution points only to the last two lines, given that "the ninth letter" is *i,* and given some leeway with regard to whether hoarfrost can properly be described as "snowy hail." See further ES, 150–53.

This is the second of Tatwine's aenigmata to feature a logogriph (on which in general see the headnote to ALD 63 (*CORBUS,* "raven"); the other is TAT 4, where it is suggested above that the title/solution in both manuscripts (*LITTERAE,* "letters") precisely fails to answer the challenge posed by the logogriph in TAT 4.5 *(littera tollatur, non fulget nominis ortus).* There it was argued that the correct solution was *APICES,* "about letters." In such a context, it seems significant that the word used here in TAT 35.3 to denote the addition of a letter to form the logogriph is *apex*. This aenigma is connected to the previous one by the notion of burning, and the repeated themes of flames *(flammor flagrat . . . flammae)*; a further theme here is the redness of a gem *(rubricolor . . . gemma rubore . . . gemma rubens)*. For the further connection of heat, burning, and "hoarfrost" *(pruina)*, compare Isidore, *Etym*. 13.10.8:

> Pruina est matutini temporis frigus, quae inde pruina nomen accepit quia sicut ignis urit; πῦρ enim ignis. Urere enim et ad frigus et ad solem pertinet.
>
> Hoarfrost is the freezing in the morning, and from that indeed hoarfrost took its name, namely that it burns like fire, since Greek πῦρ is "fire," and burning is a feature of both freezing and the sun."

35.1 A gloss in G gives an alternative to its reading, *Rubricolor flammae*, as *vel flammor*, which it further glosses as *incendior*.

TAT 36

MANUSCRIPTS: L, fol. 126v; G, fol. 377v.
EARLIER EDITIONS AND TRANSLATIONS: Gl, 20–23; Wl, 151. (SK 12850)
SOLUTION: *VENTILABRUM* (winnowing fan).

Here again, the grammatical gender of the title/solution (which is neuter) does not fit the clues: both manuscripts read masculine *captus* at TAT 36.2; given that in this case the transmitted solution seems correct, it seems appropriate to emend to *captum*. The final line turns to a biblical allusion with regard to seeds sown in the heart; of the possible passages that might have given the poet his impetus, that from Matthew 3:12 (compare Luke 3:17) actually includes the word *ventilabrum* in a verse describing John the Baptist: *cuius ventilabrum in manu sua et permundabit aream suam et congregabit triticum suum in horreum paleas autem conburet igni inextinguibili*, "whose fan is in his hand, and he will thoroughly cleanse his floor and gather his wheat into the barn; but the chaff he will burn with unquenchable fire." The reference to "unquenchable fire" links this aenigma to the one preceding; the link to the aenigma that follows is also very clear.

See further ES, 19–21; Lendinara, "Aspetti della società germanica."

36.4 The usual spelling is *pullulent,* although that would not scan; this might be viewed as another false quantity, but compare EUS 41.7 *(pululans),* transmitted in the same two manuscripts. The piety of the metaphorical reading is both underlined and undermined by the literal interpretation. Despite the fact that *solo* is found in both manuscripts, it seems better to interpret *quod* as functioning like *ut* in a purpose clause, and so emend to *sola.*

TAT 37

MANUSCRIPTS: L, fol. 126v; G, fol. 377v.
EARLIER EDITIONS AND TRANSLATIONS: Gl, 204; Wl, 152. (SK 17080)
SOLUTION: *SEMINANS* (sower).

The link with the preceding aenigma is obvious, and may explain the reading *mente* found in both manuscripts at TAT 37.4 (compare *in pectore* at TAT 36.4), where emendation to *monte* seems preferable. The notion of seeds and sowing and living and dying is enshrined centrally in biblical passages such as John 12:24–25 and, more succinctly, in 1 Corinthians 15:36: *insipiens tu quod seminas non vivificatur nisi prius moriatur,* "Senseless man, that which thou sowest is not quickened, except it die first."

Compare BER 12 (*GRANUM,* "grain of corn").

37.1 Reading *destino* for *destina* LG.
37.2 Glosses in both manuscripts supply *seminando* after *perdam.*
37.3 Glosses in both manuscripts supply *in terra* after *moriantur.*
37.4 Reading *monte* for *mente* LG.

TAT 38

MANUSCRIPTS: L, fol. 126v–27r; G, fol. 377v.
EARLIER EDITIONS AND TRANSLATIONS: Gl, 205; Wl, 153. (SK 4856)
SOLUTION: *CARBO* (charcoal). See further ES, 150–53.

This aenigma links back to TAT 35 (*PRUNA,* "ember"); compare Isidore, *Etym.* 19.6.7:

> Pruna est quamdiu ardet; quum autem extincta fuerit, carbo nominatur. Pruna autem a perurendo dicta est; carbo vero, quod flamma caret. Qui dum interisse creditur, maioris fit virtutis; nam iterum accensus fortiori luce calescit.
>
> It is an ember for as long as it burns; when it has burnt out, it is called charcoal. For it is called an ember *(pruna)* from "burning up" *(perurendo),* but charcoal *(carbo),* because it lacks *(caret)* flames; and when it is thought to be used up, it becomes of greater power: for, being burnt a second time, it grows hot with a stronger light.

The "enemy" *(hostis)* in TAT 38.2 is "fire"; compare TAT 33 (*IGNIS,* "fire").

38.1 Reading *mutante* for *motante* LG.
38.4 A false quantity: the usual form is *officīnae.*

TAT 39

MANUSCRIPTS: L, fol. 127r; G, fol. 377v.
EARLIER EDITIONS AND TRANSLATIONS: Gl, 206; Wl, 154. (SK 10024)
SOLUTION: *COS* (whetstone); the given solution is *DE COTICULO* (whetstone). See further ES, 13–16.

Given the reference to a city in TAT 39.2, as well as the feminine forms *sordida* (39.3) and (by emendation) *natam* (39.1), the transmitted title/solution *DE COTICULO* cannot be correct: the capital city of the island Cos has the same name, and the correct solution must be *COS* (whetstone), especially given what seems in the final line of this aenigma (with its use of the noun *acumine*) to be a gesture towards the explanation given by Isidore, *Etym.* 16.3.6:

> Cotis nomen accepit quod ferrum ad incidendum acuat; κότις enim Graeco sermone incisio nominatur.
>
> The whetstone *(cotis)* took its name because it sharpens *(acuat)* iron for cutting, since *κότις* is the Greek word for cutting.

Compare ALD 27 (*COTICULA,* "whetstone"), with a change of gender.

39.1 Reading *natam* for *natum* LG, to agree with the preferred solution *COS*. Compare ALD 27.1 *(COTICULA,* "whetstone": *ex gelido . . . viscere)* and 33.1 *(LORICA,* "armor": *me genuit gelido de viscere);* TAT 31.2 *(SCINTILLA,* "about a spark": *nasci gelido natum de viscere matris);* LOR 4.1 *(GELU,* "about ice": *me . . . ex gelido generat . . . tergore matris).*

39.2 Compare Aldhelm, *Carmen de virginitate* 2097 *(inclita romanis).* This is the only place in TAT where the author alludes directly to the Romans.

TAT 40

MANUSCRIPTS: L, fol. 127r; G, fol. 377v.

EARLIER EDITIONS AND TRANSLATIONS: Gl, 207; Wl, 155. (SK 15805)

SOLUTION: *RADII SOLIS* (sun's rays). See further Lockett, *Anglo-Saxon Psychologies,* 264–65; Salvador-Bello, *Isidorean Perceptions,* 232–33.

There is wordplay here on the verb *lustro* (TAT 40.1), which means both "I wander" and "I illuminate," one that is repeated widely in the writings of Boniface (see further Orchard, "Old Sources, New Resources," 23).

40.2 The form *allecti* is found in L; glosses in G variously explain its reading, *at lectis,* as *vel tectis* and supply *me* after *curvo.*

40.4 Compare ALD 59.8, ALD 86.4, ALD 100.3; BON 3.3, BON 4.12, BON 8.8, BON 14.1, BON 16.12, BON 17.7 (in each case *caeli culmina, culmina caelorum, culmina caeli* or *culmine caeli*).

40.5 The final line clearly echoes the final line of Aldhelm's aenigmata (ALD 100.83: *sciscitor inflatos, fungar quo nomine, sofos*), even down to the false quantity: the usual scansion is *sŏphi.*

TAT E

MANUSCRIPTS: L, fol. 127r; G, fol. 377v.

EARLIER EDITIONS AND TRANSLATIONS: Gl, 208; Wl, 156. (SK 17141) See further Salvador-Bello, *Isidorean Perceptions,* 222–24.

E.1 Reading *vates* for *vatem* LG. The syntax here is complex: the simplest emendation is to *vates* in the opening line. It is far from clear that these closing four lines, which essentially repeat the directions of the opening couplet (which is established by the acrostic-telestich itself), are the work of Tatwine himself, although in terms of quadrisyllabic endings and elision, they are very like the style of Tatwine, as discussed in the headnote above.

HWÆTBERHT, THE RIDDLES OF EUSEBIUS

Authorship and Date

The two key questions with respect to EUS turn on the identity of the author and the integrity of the collection, with the second aspect also impinging on the issue of the order of the aenigmata both within the collection and in the two manuscripts G and L, as well as the relationship and comparative chronology of EUS and TAT. All depends on whether Eusebius can indeed be identified with the Hwætberht whom Bede addresses by the name "Eusebius" in the preface to the *Explanatio Apocalypsis,* and again in the preface to the *Expositio*

Actuum Apostolorum (Laistner, 3, lines 1–9); and (most importantly) on the fourth book of *In primam partem Samuhelis* (ed. Hurst, CCSL 119, 212, lines 1–22), as well as the *De temporum ratione* (ed. Jones, *Praefatio*, 176, lines 31–37). We know that Hwætberht followed Ceolfrith as abbot of Monkwearmouth-Jarrow in 716, an event detailed in both the anonymous *Vita S. Ceolfrithi* (ed. Plummer, 1, 398–99) and Bede's *Historia abbatum* (ed. Plummer, 1, 383–84). See further Williams, "Riddles of Tatwine and Eusebius," 44–52. In a letter dated 746/47 (*Epistola* 76, ed. Tangl, 158), Boniface wrote to Hwætberht requesting copies of several of the works of Bede. Also relevant in this context is Hwætberht's letter in *Historia abbatum* (ed. Plummer, 1, 383–84). In the same vein, it seems significant that Bede sent his highly technical treatise *De temporum ratione* to Hwætberht for correction, and that "Eusebius" (a name Bede tells us Hwætberht adopted, presumably in recognition of Eusebius the historian and chronographer) has two aenigmata on rather technical matters of computus: EUS 26 (*DIES BISSEXTILIS*, "bissextile day") and EUS 29 (*SALTUS*, "cycle and the moon's leap"), so again strengthening the association. The further attribution of several aenigmata both plausibly and implausibly to Bede himself (printed here as BED and ps-BED) may lend further support to the identification of Hwætberht as the Eusebius who penned this collection. Bede speaks of him several times, most clearly in the fourth book of *In primam partem Samuhelis* (ed. Hurst, CCSL 119, 212, lines 1–22):

> Hwetberctum iuvenem cui amor studiumque pietatis iam olim Eusebius cognomen indidit.

> The young Hwætberht, who was consumed with love and enthusiasm for piety, took on the nickname Eusebius.

And again, in his *Historia abbatum* 2:18, describing the aftermath of the death of Abbot Ceolfrith of Monkwearmouth-Jarrow in 716:

> Eligitur itaque abbas Huaetberctus, qui a primis pueritiae temporibus eodem in monasterio non solum regularis observantia

> disciplinae institutus, sed et scribendi, cantandi, legendi ac docendi fuerat non parva exercitatus industria. Romam quoque temporibus beatae memoriae Sergii papae accurrens, et non parvo ibidem temporis spatio demoratus, quaeque sibi necessaria iudicabat, didicit, descripsit, retulit; insuper et duodecim ante haec annos presbyteri est functus officio.
>
> And so Hwætberht was chosen as abbot, and he had not only been educated in the same monastery from the time of his earliest boyhood in the observance of the discipline of the Rule, but was also endowed with no small measure of achievement in writing, singing, reading, and teaching. Likewise, he visited Rome during the time of Pope Sergius of blessed memory, and stayed there for no small length of time; he learned and copied and brought back whatever he thought he needed, and on top of all that he had before his election performed the office of a priest for twelve years.

Hwætberht was consecrated by Bishop Acca of Hexham (710–732; d. 740), who was a close personal friend of Bede, and the latter dedicated to him a number of texts, just as he went on to dedicate to Hwætberht not only his commentaries on Acts and Revelation, but also his computistical treatise *De temporum ratione*. The fact that the number of TAT is fixed by the acrostic-telestich, combined with an impression that the final twenty aenigmata of EUS were somehow straining to combine with those of TAT to reach the canonical one hundred of SYM and ALD, has led to a suggestion that Eusebius wrote after Tatwine, although his collection precedes in both manuscripts.

Manuscript Context(s)

The aenigmata of Eusebius are preserved in only two manuscripts, designated here as L and G, which are, however, clearly related (see the introduction to *OEALRT,* under "Manuscript Contexts"), in each case following TAT. The younger G often contains improved or updated readings, but as with the other collections of aenigmata in these manuscripts the number of similar uncorrected errors that remain suggests that in many cases the earlier L has preserved the original reading, and it is generally preferred here. Both manuscripts have texts beginning with the phrase "The aenigmata of Eusebius begin" *(INCIPIUNT AENIGMATA EUSEBII),* and in general L gives solutions as titles, while G places them in the margins, although there are also mnemonic letters giving the first letter of the solution at the beginning of EUS 4–8, 10–11, 13, 15–16, 18, 20–22, 24, 26–27, 32–35, 37–38, 40, 43–44, 46–47, 51–54, and 57–59 (as indeed for TAT: see the headnote there). Various later hands added mnemonic clues to solutions, generally in the form of a single opening letter, in a fashion reminiscent of the occasional scribbles and scratched runes found for the first few riddles of EXE.

Subject Matter and Solutions

The aenigmata fall into two very distinct groups (EUS 1–40 and 48 on the one hand, and EUS 41–47 and 49–60 on the other); there is a pattern to EUS 1–6, as well as a number of clear pairs: EUS 10 (*SOL,* "sun") and EUS 11 (*LUNA,* "moon"); EUS 12 (*BOS,* "bull") and EUS 13 (*VACCA,* "cow"). Eusebius appears to have introduced an innovation in the Latin enigmatic tradition by demonstrating a fondness for single aenigmata solved by antithetical pairs: EUS 8 (*VENTUS ET IGNIS,* "wind and fire"), EUS 15 (*IGNIS ET AQUA,* "fire and water"), EUS 18 (*INIQUITAS ET IUSTITIA,* "iniquity and justice"), EUS 21 (*TERRA ET MARE,* "land and sea"), EUS 24 (*MORS ET VITA,* "death and life"), EUS 27 (*HUMILITAS ET SUPERBIA,* "humility and pride"), and EUS 48 (*DIES ET NOX,* "day and night"). Moreover, all of EUS 1–40 are composed of only four lines each, with the exception of the five-line EUS 34 (*FLUMEN,* "river"), which, however, may contain an interpolated line (see the headnote there). The mood and topics of the aenigmata change abruptly in the final third of the texts: EUS 41–60 (with the exception of EUS 48) all deal with outlandish and mythical creatures, with descriptions drawn from passages from Isidore's *Etymologiae* 11–12, almost in sequence (see Williams, "Riddles of Tatwine and Eusebius," 60); for the match to be perfect, the order would have to be EUS (41), 52, 43, 44, 46, 45,

42, 47, 49, (41), 50, 51, 53, 54, 55, 56, 57, 59, 60, and 58. See further Salvador-Bello, "Patterns of Compilation."

Style

The aenigmata of EUS, in stark contrast to the predominantly end-stopped style of ALD, TAT, and BON, demonstrate considerable use of enjambment, a feature particularly commended by Bede in his *De arte metrica.* Alas, there are a large number of metrical infelicities spread throughout the collection (see the notes to EUS 6–10, 20, 22–24, 27–30, 32–33, 38, 41–44, 46–47, 49, 52–53, 57, and 60), as well as a penchant for the type of anacoluthon known as the "hanging nominative" *(nominativum pendens),* on which see the note at EUS 6.1; again, however, such bloopers are found distributed throughout. Elisions (including several of monosyllables, for example, at EUS 1.1, 13.4, 32.3, and 39.1) are found more frequently in EUS 1–40 than in 41–60. A further interesting potential indicator of differences between the broader groupings of EUS 1–40 and 41–60 stems from an analysis of compound adjectives, together with those formed from the (mostly poetic) suffixes *-abilis, -alis, -eus, -fer, -ficus, -ger,* and *-osus:* there are thirty-eight such adjectives, of which all but ten occur in EUS 41–60; three more of these are in EUS 40. One could argue that the exotic subject matter triggers the ornate vocabulary, but the suspicion must still remain that despite the metrical and other verbal similarities between the first two-thirds and the last third of EUS, there is more than one mind at work here. However, some characteristic phrases and metrical infelicities do seem to link the two parts of Eusebius's aenigmata (see the notes below on EUS 43.3, 44.3–4, 50.1–2, 53.5–8, 57.3–5, and 58, largely drawn from Williams, "Riddles of Tatwine and Eusebius").

Sources and Parallels

While there are certain clusters in broad sequence, there is nothing like the close mirroring that occurs between Book 12 (Isidore, *Etym.* 12.2.7–7.42) and twenty of the twenty-one aenigmata in EUS 40–60 (the exception is EUS 48 [*DIES ET NOX,* "day and night"], which seems misplaced for other reasons), where many of the aenigmata map quite precisely onto Book 12, closely following the order of the definitions. There are also several parallels with SYM, as the notes to (for example) EUS 3 and 33 make clear, as well as with ALD, as is evident from the notes to EUS 33 again and 40.

This Text and Translation

Here I have revised and updated the edition given by Gl, adding a number of conjectures of my own, and relying heavily on the excellent doctoral dissertation by Williams, "The Riddles of Tatwine and Eusebius."

Further Reading

Ebert, "Die Räthselpoesie der Angelsachsen"; Hahn, "Die Rätseldichter Tatwin und Eusebius"; Tangl, *Epistolae Bonifatii et Lullii,* 158–60 (*Ep* 76); Williams, "Riddles of Tatwine and Eusebius"; Salvador-Bello, *Isidorean Perceptions,* 234–50 and 464–65.

EUS 1

MANUSCRIPTS: L, fol. 113v; G, fol. 370r.

EARLIER EDITIONS AND TRANSLATIONS: Gl, 211; Wl, 157–58. See further Lockett, *Anglo-Saxon Psychologies,* 266–68. (SK 3127)

SOLUTION: *DEUS* (God).

This aenigma, like many of those composed by Eusebius, and perhaps following the lead of Symphosius, is based on a series of paradoxes, in this case high/low and one/many. There seems to be an allusion to Psalms 139:8: *Si ascendero in caelum ibi es tu si iacuero in inferno ades,* "If I ascend into heaven, thou art there: if I descend into hell, thou art present." For the "both high(er) and low(er)" motif, see the note at TAT 1 (*SAPIENTIA,* "Wisdom"). Again, like many of Aldhelm's aenigmata, the collection offers a variety of alternative metrical forms for the same concept, such as *cunctos . . . omnibus,* "all," *sim . . . adsto,* "I am," and *domus . . . sedes,* "dwelling." Compare SYM 6.2 (*TEGULA,* "roof tile": *de terra nascor, sedes est semper in alto);* ALD 100.21–22 (*CREATURA,* "Creation": *Altior, en, caelo rimor secreta Tonantis / et tamen inferior terris tetra Tartara cerno);* TAT 1.2–3 (*SAPIENTIA,*

"Wisdom": *vecta per alta poli quis nunc volitare solesco / abdita nunc terrae penetrans atque ima profundi),* TAT 24.5 (*HUMILITAS,* "humility": *Inferior terris et celis altior exsto);* LOR 2.4–5 (*ANIMA,* "heart": *alta supernorum scrutans secreta polorum / omnia quin potius perlustro creata sub orbe).*

1.1 Note the elision of the monosyllable *sim*. This is another example of the higher-lower motif, on which see the headnote above.

1.2 Presumably *locus* has the second syllable lengthened at the caesura, on which practice see Bede, *De arte metrica* 3.4 (ed. Kendall, 50–53).

1.3 A gloss in G supplies *est* after *domus.*

1.4 Glosses in LG supply *peccatorum* after *agmina.*

EUS 2

MANUSCRIPTS: L, fol. 113v; G, fol. 370r.
EARLIER EDITIONS AND TRANSLATIONS: Gl, 212; Wl, 159. (SK 10786)
SOLUTION: *ANGELUS* (angel). See further Lockett, *Anglo-Saxon Psychologies,* 266–68.

As in other riddles—for example, EXE 21 (*BOGA,* "bow"), though there the entire first line may be interpolated—the opening word drops a heavy hint about the answer: the Greek form of *nuntius* is ἄγγελος, which essentially supplies the solution.

2.2 As it stands in the manuscripts, the line is metrically problematic. I assume that *taedium* is scanned as two syllables through synizesis, and that a *iam* has fallen out; alternatively, one might read *nec* after *taedium,* although such reinforcement of negative statements is common in Old English, but less so in Latin. Glosses supply *ullus* after *labor* and *ullum* after *tedium* in LG.

2.3 Compare SYM 13.3; BER 55.4 *(vestigia nulla).* Glosses supply *angeli* after *intrantis* in LG.

EUS 3

MANUSCRIPTS: L, fol. 113v–14r; G, fol. 370r.
EARLIER EDITIONS AND TRANSLATIONS: Gl, 213; Wl, 160. See further Murphy, *Unriddling the Exeter Riddles,* 129. (SK 8016)
SOLUTION: *DAEMON* (demon).

This aenigma plays on a developing set of paradoxes in much the same way as the previous two, and is clearly placed as part of a sequence; if we assume that the verbal parallel with SYM 18 (*COCLEA,* "snail") is deliberate, then Eusebius's view of the fallen angel is clear.

3.1 Compare SYM 18.2 *(sim miserabilis exul).*
3.2 Glosses specify *id est reges et principes mundi* after *viros fortes* in LG.
3.3 Reading *potenter* for *potentes* LG. Glosses supply *a regno dei* after *abiectoque* and explain *sunt . . . potestas* by *id est in potestate mea regna mundi sunt* in LG.
3.4 Compare Aldhelm, *Carmen de virginitate praefatio* 4 *(in sedibus altis).* The word *altis* could also be rendered "deep" here; see further the headnote to ALC.

EUS 4

MANUSCRIPTS: L, fol. 114r; G, fol. 370r.
EARLIER EDITIONS AND TRANSLATIONS: Gl, 214; Wl, 161. See further Lockett, *Anglo-Saxon Psychologies,* 266–68. (SK 5935)
SOLUTION: *HOMO* (humankind).

The double substance *(substantia bina)* of humankind, comprising both body and soul, aligns this aenigma with a number of other riddles, including (for example) EXE 41 (*GÆST OND LICHAMA,* "soul and body") and EXE 81 (*GÆST OND LICHAMA,* "soul and body").

4.1 A gloss supplies *et* after *materiae* in G.
4.2 Glosses supply variously *animal* L and *anima* G after *tenuior est alia.*

4.3 Although both manuscripts clearly read *helidrum,* sense requires a nominative and a *ch-* spelling: note that both *chelydrus* and *chelidrus* are attested, and indeed that Aldhelm, *Carmen de virginitate* 811 *(chelidrum)* and 2399 *(celydrum),* seems equally baffled. It is tempting to emend *fugax* to *sagax* in reference to the serpent, as Rob Getz suggests to me, but the association of the term *fugax* in Anglo-Saxon glossaries as (in Latin) *fugitivus, caduca, profugus,* and *fugiens,* and (in Old English) *flugol* and *earh,* may rather suggest the sense here to be "fugitive, outcast."

4.4 Compare TAT 24.4 *(sine fine manebit)* and LOR 1.12 *(sine fine manendus);* but see EUS 6.4 *(morte carebunt).*

EUS 5

MANUSCRIPTS: L, fol. 114r; G, fol. 370r.
EARLIER EDITIONS AND TRANSLATIONS: Gl, 215; Wl, 162. (SK 12928)
SOLUTION: *CAELUM* (heaven); the given solution in L is *DE CAELO,* although the scribe of G rather extraordinarily prefers *DE CAMELO* (about a camel), perhaps remembering ALD 99 (*CAMELLUS,* "camel"). See further ES, 245–46.

The insistent wordplay on concepts of "having," "holding," and "keeping" *(tenet . . . tenere tenax; habebit . . . habet),* emphasized by alliteration, quite apart from common sense and context, supports "heaven" as the solution. Compare ALD 48 (*VERTICO POLI,* "sphere of the heavens").

5.1 Preferring *avaris* L to *in arvis* G. Compare 1 Corinthians 6:10: *neque avari . . . regnum Dei possidebunt,* "nor covetous . . . shall possess the kingdom of God"; the alternative is to understand *vendor* in the figurative sense "be praised, be extolled," and translate "why I am extolled on earth."

5.2 Glosses explain *habebit* by *id est possidebit me* LG.

EUS 6

MANUSCRIPTS: L, fol. 114r; G, fol. 370r.
EARLIER EDITIONS AND TRANSLATIONS: Gl, 216; Wl, 163. (SK 14022)
SOLUTION: *TERRA* (earth). See further ES, 241–43.

This aenigma leads on naturally from the previous one, and depicts a world where the earth speaks of avenging itself on its ungrateful offspring. Compare ALD 1 (*TERRA*, "earth"); EUS 21 (*TERRA ET MARE*, "about the land and sea").

6.1 The syntax here is distinctly strained; the sense seems to require understanding *crescentibus . . . illis*, "I am torn apart when they are older by those I feed when young," but evidence elsewhere suggests that Eusebius is particularly prone to the type of anacoluthon known as the "hanging nominative" (*nominativum pendens*); compare EUS 11.4 (*deficiens*), EUS 22.2 (*venturus*, although emendation to *venturum* is possible), EUS 30.4 (*ructans*), EUS 42.3 (*cristatusque volans*), and EUS 50.1 (*fugiens*). Glosses explain *alo* by *nutria* LG.

6.2 False quantity: *subĭgunt* is the normal usage.

6.3 False quantity: *sēducam* is the normal usage.

EUS 7

MANUSCRIPTS: L, fol. 114r; G, fol. 370r.
EARLIER EDITIONS AND TRANSLATIONS: Gl, 217; Wl, 164. (SK 8122)
SOLUTION: *LITTERAE* (letters); the given solution is *DE LITTERA*. See further ES, 249–51; Bitterli, *Say What I Am Called*, 178–90; Murphy, *Unriddling the Exeter Riddles*, 101–2; Ooi, "Speaking Objects," 51–52.

This is a good example of a Latin aenigma where the solution given must technically be wrong, since a plural is explicit in the opening word; for a similar disparity, compare EUS 32. For other Anglo-Saxon riddles connected with the classroom and the scriptorium, see the note to ALD 30 (*ELEMENTUM*, "letter of the alphabet").

It first appears that the clear subject-based cosmological sequencing of EUS 1–6 is interrupted by EUS 7, which also separates the triad of "earth, wind, and fire" (EUS 6 and 8), and indeed seems better paired with EUS 9 (*ALPHA,* "alpha").

7.1 A gloss explains *Innumerae* as *multae* L.
7.2 False quantity: *nĕquit* is the normal usage. For the "black on white" theme in the context of writing, see the note at ALD 59.3–5 (*PENNA,* "quill pen") above.
7.3 Glosses explain *alta* as *misteria caelorum* G, *ministeria caelorum* L.

EUS 8

MANUSCRIPTS: L, fol. 114v; G, fol. 370r–v.
EARLIER EDITIONS AND TRANSLATIONS: Gl, 218; Wl, 165–66. (SK 3805)
SOLUTION: *VENTUS ET IGNIS* (wind and fire). See further ES, 245–46.

This is one of the aenigmata in which Eusebius takes his penchant for paradox to its natural conclusion, and requires a double solution involving opposites; see further EUS 15 (*IGNIS ET AQUA,* "fire and water"), EUS 18 (*INIQUITAS ET IUSTITIA,* "iniquity and justice"), EUS 21 (*TERRA ET MARE,* "land and sea"), EUS 24 (*MORS ET VITA,* "death and life"), EUS 27 (*HUMILITAS ET SUPERBIA,* "humility and pride"), and EUS 48 (*DIES ET NOX,* "day and night"). This aenigma and the two preceding seem to explore a grammatical notion, expressed by Tatwine as follows (*Ars Tatuini* 1.4): *Item omne quod nomine significatur corpus est aut corporale, vel incorporale: corpus est quicquid tangi et videri potest, ut "terra"; corporale quod tangi et non videri, ut "ventus," vel videri et non tangi, ut "caelum"; incorporale vero quod nec tangi nec videri valet, ut "sapientia,"* "Again, everything which can be designated by a noun is concrete or corporeal or abstract; concrete, whatever can be felt and seen, like 'earth'; corporeal, what can be felt but not seen, like 'wind,' or seen but not felt, like 'sky'; abstract what can neither be felt nor seen, like 'wisdom.'" Compare ALD 2 (*VENTUS*, "wind").

8.3 One must assume either a hiatus or a false quantity: *prŏpe* is the normal usage.

EUS 9

MANUSCRIPTS: L, fol. 114v; G, fol. 370v.
EARLIER EDITIONS AND TRANSLATIONS: Gl, 219; Wl, 167–68. (SK 4105)
SOLUTION: *ALPHA* (alpha). See further ES, 249–52; Murphy, *Unriddling the Exeter Riddles*, 100.

For other Anglo-Saxon riddles connected with the classroom and the scriptorium, see the note to ALD 30 (*ELEMENTUM*, "letter of the alphabet"). Compare ALF A; Isidore, *Etym.* 1.4.16:

> A autem in omnibus gentibus ideo prior est litterarum, pro eo quod ipsa prior nascentibus vocem aperiat.
>
> But *A* is the first letter among all peoples, for the reason that it is the first to open the voice for those being born.

9.2 The use of Greek A, marked with strokes above and below (A' and ͵A) to stand for the numbers 1 and 1000 respectively, is generally known, but its claimed use for 500 (for which the letter normally used is Φ) is highly unusual; it is a notion shared, however, with the eccentric Virgilius Maro Grammaticus, who was known to Aldhelm, at least, and who says in his *Epitomae* 2.73–74 (ed. Löfstedt [2003], 113): *Nam A sepe quincentos, sepe triginta, sepe X, sepe unum significant*, "For *A* often signifies 500, often 30, often 10, often 1." Bede, *De temporum ratione* 1 (ed. Jones, 181), contains a table of Greek numerals up to 900, but it does not support Eusebius's reading here.

9.3 In other words, the first letter of *Adam* is *a;* like all the letter-aenigmata in EUS, this one offers a broad clue; the others are EUS 14 (*X LITTERA,* "the letter *X*"), EUS 19 (*V LITTERA,* "the letter *V*"), and EUS 39 (*I LITTERA,* "the letter *I*").

9.4 False quantity: the nominative should be *domină.* Note the polysyllabic ending *(resonare);* on the use of such endings elsewhere in the Anglo-Latin aenigmata, see the note at TAT 1.10.

EUS 10

MANUSCRIPTS: L, fol. 114v; G, fol. 370v.
EARLIER EDITIONS AND TRANSLATIONS: Gl, 220; Wl, 169. (SK 11364)
SOLUTION: *SOL* (sun).

This aenigma is linked very clearly to the one that follows: note how EUS 10.1 *(pergit)* is picked up in EUS 11.1 *(pergenti)*. Compare ALD 79 (*SOL ET LUNA,* "sun and moon"); TAT 40 (*RADII SOLIS,* "rays of the sun"); BER 55–57 (*SOL,* "sun").

10.1 Note the polysyllabic ending *(requiescat);* on the use of such endings elsewhere in the Anglo-Latin aenigmata, see the note at TAT 1.10.

10.3 A gloss supplies *mihi* after *restat* G.

10.4 Preferring *et* L to *non* G. There are several metrical problems with the reading *non reges,* where *non* is glossed *et* in G, and *et* (which certainly scans, but is execrable Latin) appears as the reading in L.

EUS 11

MANUSCRIPTS: L, fol. 114v; G, fol. 370v.
EARLIER EDITIONS AND TRANSLATIONS: Gl, 221; Wl, 170–71. (SK 10435)
SOLUTION: *LUNA* (moon). See further ES, 247–49.

This aenigma leads on naturally from the preceding (see note above), and contains some characteristically Eusebian love of contrast (compare the chiasmus *in lumine . . . noctes . . . in noctes . . . lumina*). It is interesting to note that Bede, in a work dedicated to Hwætberht, gives a partial assertion concerning the light of the moon, quoting from Augustine's commentary on Psalm 10:3 (*De temporum ratione* 25 [ed. Jones, 227]): *Dicunt enim [lunam] non habere lumen proprium, sed a sole illustrari,* "For they say that the moon does not have its own light, but is illuminated by the sun." Compare ALD 6 (*LUNA,* "moon") and ALD 79 (*SOL ET LUNA,* "sun and moon"); BER 58–59 (*LUNA,* "on the moon").

11.1 Compare ALD 26.2 *(lumina Phoebi),* ALD 57.8; EUS 58.2 *(lumine Phoebi).* Glosses explain *in lumine* as *in die* LG; another explains *Phoebi* as *solis* G.

11.4 Reading *postea* for *post ego* LG. It is then necessary to read the first half of this line as completing the sense of the one preceding, in a form of enjambment, a feature specifically applauded by Bede in his *De arte metrica* 11 (ed. Kendall, 102–3). For the ungrammatical *deficiens,* see the note to EUS 6.1 above.

EUS 12

MANUSCRIPTS: L, fol. 114v–15r; G, fol. 370v.
EARLIER EDITIONS AND TRANSLATIONS: Gl, 222; Wl, 172–73. (SK 10717)
SOLUTION: *BOS* (bull). See further ES, 170–73; Bitterli, *Say What I Am Called,* 34.

This is one of several riddles that focus on the sorry plight of this much put-upon farm animal, and aligns it with others focusing on the motif of the "suffering servant," on which see the note at TAT 5. Compare ALD 83 (*IUVENCUS,* "bullock"); EUS 13 (*VACCA,* "cow") and 37 (*VITULUS,* "bullock").

12.2 A gloss in G explains *cereres* as *frumenta;* another (also in G) inserts *et* before *semper.*

12.3 Compare ALD 90.1 *(sunt mihi sex oculi totidem simul auribus hausi).* A gloss in G explains that *potus* is accusative. The suggestion that the ox is here drawing water that it is unable to drink is attractive, but unprovable; see further the note on EXE 56 below.

12.4 Compare EUS 59.4 *(verba sonabo);* Pliny, *Nat. Hist.* 8.70.183: *est frequens in prodigiis priscorum bovem locutum, quo nuntiato senatum sub diu haberi solitum,* "Among the prodigies of the ancients, a talking ox is common, and when this was reported, it was customary for the senate to be held in the open air." More interestingly, the talking ox is also found in the *Old English Martyrology* 1, where it is specifically attached to the reign of Augustus and given as a portent of Christ's birth (ed. Rauer, 34–35): "And an ox spoke to its ploughman in Rome, and said: 'Why do you goad me? Good wheat will grow this year, but you will not be around then, nor will you eat it'" *(And oxa spæc on Rome to þam ergendum, and he cwæð: "Tohwon sticest þu me? God hwæte geweaxeð togeare, ac ne bist ðu þonne, ne his ne abitest").* The detail is also found elsewhere in Anglo-Saxon contexts (see Hall, "Portents at Christ's Birth," 85–86), but if we adopt Michael Lapidge's suggestion that the materials for the *Old English Martyrology* were being gathered by Acca of Hexham, a close associate of Bede, sometime between 731 and 740 (Lapidge, "Acca of Hexham," 66–69), then we may have a further link between Eusebius and the circle surrounding Bede. Glosses in both manuscripts explain that the *urbs* in question is Rome; a further gloss in G explains *signo* as *tuba vel cornu.*

EUS 13

MANUSCRIPTS: L, fol. 115r; G, fol. 370v.

EARLIER EDITIONS AND TRANSLATIONS: Gl, 223; Wl, 174. (SK 15873)

SOLUTION: *VACCA* (cow). This aenigma is clearly linked to the one preceding, especially with respect to the multiple streams of EUS 13.4. See further ES, 170–73.

Compare ALD 83 (*IUVENCUS,* "bullock"); EUS 12 (*BOS,* "bull") and 37 (*VITULUS,* "bullock").

13.2 Glosses in both manuscripts explain *carneve vescor* as *si homines vescuntur carne mea.*

13.3 Note the insistent homoeoteleuton *(cibis aliis . . . aquis alienis).* Note too the polysyllabic ending *(alienis);* on the use of such endings elsewhere in the Anglo-Latin aenigmata, see the note at TAT 1.10.

13.4 Note the harsh elision of the monosyllable at *me et.* To add to the clunky (not to say bovine) scansion, there is no caesura in this line, and each foot coincides with a word-division. A gloss in G explains *flumina* as *lactis.*

EUS 14

MANUSCRIPTS: L, fol. 115r; G, fol. 370v.
EARLIER EDITIONS AND TRANSLATIONS: Gl, 224; Wl, 175. (SK 12191)
SOLUTION: *X LITTERA* (the letter *X*). See further ES, 249–53.

The explicit link with Augustus and the implicit one with Christ connect this aenigma with the talking ox of EUS 12, as above. Compare Isidore, *Etym.* 1.4.14:

> X littera usque ad Augusti tempus nondum apud Latinos erat, [et digne hoc tempore, quo Christi nomen innotuit, quod per eam, quae crucis signum figurat, scriptitatur,] sed pro ea C et S scribebant, unde et duplex vocatur, quia pro C et S ponitur, unde et ex eisdem litteris conpositum nomen habet.
>
> The letter *X* did not exist until the time of Augustus, and properly at that time, in which the name of Christ became known, since his name is written with this letter, which signifies the cross but they used to write *CS* instead, whence *X* is called a double letter, since it is used for *CS,* and therefore takes its composite name from the same letters.

For other Anglo-Saxon riddles connected with the classroom and the scriptorium, see the note to ALD 30.

14.1 Glosses in both manuscripts supply *litteras* after *reliquias*. The word *augustus* hides a reference to the Emperor Augustus, if the connection to Isidore, *Etym.* 1.4.14 noted above is sound, and is another example where a broad clue to a riddle-solution is enshrined in the first line. See further EUS 2 above.

14.2 The syntax of the transmitted text *(utor in alterius)* is problematic; here, I prefer *utor vi alterius,* following a clue in the gloss in G, which supplies *potestate* after *in alterius.*

14.3 Compare EUS 29.3 *(sola . . . videbor).*

14.4 A gloss in G inserts *litterarum* after *duarum* and explains them as *cs* or *gs.*

EUS 15

MANUSCRIPTS: L, fol. 115r; G, fol. 370v.
EARLIER EDITIONS AND TRANSLATIONS: Gl, 225; Wl, 176. (SK 12648)
SOLUTION: *IGNIS ET AQUA* (fire and water). See further ES, 245.

This aenigma employs wordplay in the form of polyptoton to emphasize the hostility between the two elements *(rebelles . . . bella . . . belligeramur).* The same paradox expressed here of fire and water battling but kept apart (TAT 15.4) is explored in ALD 54 (*COCUMA DUPLEX,* "double boiler"); a similar notion lies behind ps-BED 10. The double element is suggested by the *vim duarum* of the final line of the preceding aenigma. Perhaps "double cooking-pot" provides a preferable solution, and also connects more closely with the aenigma that follows. Compare ALD 44 (*IGNIS,* "fire"); TAT 33 (*IGNIS,* "fire").

15.1 Compare BER 56.3 *(coniungimur ambo).*

15.3 Note the pentasyllabic ending *(belligeramur);* on the use of such endings elsewhere in the Anglo-Latin aenigmata, see the note at TAT 1.10.

15.4 Glosses in both manuscripts explain the *murus* as *cac(c)abus.*

EUS 16

MANUSCRIPTS: L, fol. 115r–v; G, fol. 370v–71r.
EARLIER EDITIONS AND TRANSLATIONS: Gl, 226; Wl, 177. (SK 9508)
SOLUTION: *PHLASCA* (flask); the given solution in both G and L is in fact *DE PLASCA*. See further ES, 39–41.

If the parallel between the preceding aenigma and ALD 54 (*COCUMA DUPLEX,* "double boiler") is accepted, then there seems to be a further potential connection here. The more disagreeable aspects of drinking are emphasized here, as elsewhere (see the headnotes to EXE 9 and GES 1). Note the use of sound- and wordplay *(laetificans . . . laeta; osque . . . ore . . . oris).*

16.1 A gloss in G offers *refero* for *confero.*

16.2 There is a clear biblical echo with Psalms 103:15: "And that wine may cheer the heart of man. That he may make the face cheerful with oil: and that bread may strengthen man's heart" *(Et vinum laetificet cor hominis; ut exhilaret faciem in oleo, et panis cor hominis confirmet).*

16.3 False quantity: *ventrĕ* is the normal usage.

EUS 17

MANUSCRIPTS: L, fol. 115v; G, fol. 371r.
EARLIER EDITIONS AND TRANSLATIONS: Gl, 227; Wl, 178. (SK 11846)
SOLUTION: *CRUX* (cross). See further ES, 107–15.

Compare TAT 9 (*DE CRUCE XRISTI,* "about Christ's cross"), although many of the similarities seem fairly superficial and commonplace for what is, after all, a literally crucial symbol of the Christian faith.

EUS 18

MANUSCRIPTS: L, fol. 115v; G, fol. 371r.
EARLIER EDITIONS AND TRANSLATIONS: Gl, 228; Wl, 179. (SK 16191)
SOLUTION: *INIQUITAS ET IUSTITIA* (iniquity and justice).

As with EUS 8 (*VENTUS ET IGNIS,* "wind and fire") and EUS 15 (*IGNIS ET AQUA,* "fire and water"), there is an essential antipathy between the two elements.

18.3 Note the paronomasia in *seque sequentibus;* for the figure, see Bede, *De scematibus et tropis* 1.9 (ed. Kendall, 174–77). Glosses in both manuscripts explain *una* variously as *iniquitas* G, *altera* L.

18.4 Glosses in both manuscripts explain *altera* as *iustitia.*

EUS 19

MANUSCRIPTS: L, fol. 115v; G, fol. 371r.
EARLIER EDITIONS AND TRANSLATIONS: Gl, 229; Wl, 180–81. (SK 13624)
SOLUTION: *V LITTERA* (letter *V*). See further ES, 249–51 and 253–54; Murphy, *Unriddling the Exeter Riddles,* 94.

The first word, *Quinta,* "fifth," provides a broad clue to the solution, since of course the letter *V* signifies "five" in the Roman alphabet; the notion that it is "the prince of vocalization" again highlights the fact that the subject is also the fifth vowel, and that it derives its particular power from its position at the head of the key words *vox,* "voice, speech," and *verbum,* "word." The wordplay on *vocor . . . vocans* in EUS 19.1 highlights the first possibility, while that on *sonans . . . consono* in EUS 19.2 points up the word *verbis* at the end of the line. The opening of John 1:1 *(In principio erat verbum et verbum erat apud deum et deus erat verbum)* seems also in the poet's mind, and surely lies behind the reference to the heretic Arius in EUS 19.4. For other Anglo-Saxon riddles connected with the classroom and the scriptorium, see the note to ALD 30 (*ELEMENTUM,* "letter of the alphabet").

19.2 A gloss in G gives *verba* as an alternative for *verbis.*

19.2–3 Various grammatical descriptions of the letter *u* or *v* circulated widely, and many of them could have supplied the basic information here. With regard to the notion that in certain circumstances (after the letter *q*) the letter is "said to be considered nothing," however, it is noteworthy that Isidore, *Etym.* 1.4.8 says that *Ideoque quando nec vocalis, nec consonans est, sine dubio nihil est,* "Moreover, when it is neither a vowel nor a consonant, doubtless it is nothing."

19.4 The name of the third-century North African heretic Arius usually appears with only a single *r,* but is spelled as here *metri gratia* in (for example) Prudentius, *Psychomachia* 794; Caelius Sedulius, *Carmen paschale* 1.300 and 322; Venantius Fortunatus, *Vita S. Martini* 1.108 and 3.205; Aldhelm, *Carmen de virginitate* 976. It is not clear what is meant by the statement that Arius "banishes me from the rule of faith"; the Arian heresy emphasized the different divinity of God the Father from Christ the Son, against "the rule of faith," which insisted that they were "of one essence." The Greek term for the idea that they were of the "same being" (ὁμοούσιος; *homoousios*), while Arian belief held that they were merely of "similar being" (ὁμοιούσιος; *homoiousios*), where the difference is an iota.

EUS 20

MANUSCRIPTS: L, fol. 115v; G, fol. 371r.
EARLIER EDITIONS AND TRANSLATIONS: Gl, 230; Wl, 182. (SK 10772)
SOLUTION: *DOMUS* (house). See further ES, 156.

20.1 A gloss in G on *quis* explains that it stands for *quibus.* False quantity: *retrō* is the normal usage.

EUS 21

MANUSCRIPTS: L, fol. 115v–16r; G, fol. 371r.
EARLIER EDITIONS AND TRANSLATIONS: Gl, 231; Wl, 183–84. (SK 11521)
SOLUTION: *TERRA ET MARE* (land and sea); the given solution is *DE TERRA ET MARE,* although the more usual ablative of *mare* would be *mari.* See further ES, 241–43.

The notion of sea and land in perpetual conflict is highlighted here by the alternation of words for peace and war *(pacificari . . . bellum . . . pax . . . pugna).* The same notion underlies EXE 1 (*GODES WIND,* "wind of God": see especially EXE 1.20–23a, 49b–51a, and 55b–58a). For different treatments of a similar theme, see ALD 1 (*TERRA,* "earth") and EUS 6 (*TERRA,* "about earth").

21.1 Note the polysyllabic ending *(viduari);* on the use of such endings elsewhere in the Anglo-Latin aenigmata, see the note at TAT 1.10. Glosses in both manuscripts explain *viduari* as *separari* or *dividi.*

21.4 Glosses in both manuscripts explain that *insons* refers to *terra.*

EUS 22

MANUSCRIPTS: L, fol. 116r; G, fol. 371r.
EARLIER EDITIONS AND TRANSLATIONS: Gl, 232; Wl, 185. (SK 11944)
SOLUTION: *SERMO* (speech). See further Murphy, *Unriddling the Exeter Riddles,* 97.

The opening line is very different in the two manuscripts, as below, and it looks very much as if the scribe of L has attempted to tidy up the mess he has inherited.

22.1 Reading *valde celer currens per inania,* where G has *valde celer discurrens per inania* and L has *tam cito discurrens per aethera;* note that a gloss in G explains *inania* as *aethera.* False quantity: the usual form *valdē* is scanned *valdĕ* here and at EUS 43.3 and EUS 44.2.

22.2 It is tempting to emend to *venturum,* but for similar problems with participles elsewhere, see the note to EUS 6.1 above.

22.3 False quantity: *sēcurus* is the normal usage.

EUS 23

MANUSCRIPTS: L, fol. 116r; G, fol. 371r.
EARLIER EDITIONS AND TRANSLATIONS: Gl, 233; Wl, 186. (SK 9820)
Solution: *AEQUOR* (ocean). See further ES, 243–45.

Compare ALD 29 (*AQUA,* "water"), ALD 62 (*FAMFALUCA,* "bubble"), and ALD 73 (*FONS,* "spring"); EUS 34 (*FLUMEN,* "about a river"). This aenigma is notable for the number of finite verbs (nine in four lines), presumably echoing the sea's constant motion.

23.1 A gloss in G explains *motor* as *moveor.* The same notion of moving while staying in the same place is found in EUS 1–2 (*FLUMEN,* "about a river").

23.2 Here and at EUS 24.2 and EUS 59.3, *tam* seems to function simply as an intensifier. Note the oxymoron *vagumque manens,* as well as synizesis in *tenue,* which must presumably be scanned as disyllabic, with false quantity. The usual scansion is *tĕnuis,* although parallels are found, intriguingly enough, in Lucretius, *De rerum natura* 4.1242 and 6.1194. A gloss in G explains *grandia pondera* as *liburnas,* and the same gloss appears in L for the equivalent reading *gravia pondera.*

23.3 For this notion concerning snow and ice on the deep sea, compare Bede, *De temporum ratione* 35: *Nives aquarum vapore, necdum densato in guttas, sed gelu praeripiente formantur, quas in alto mari non cadere perhibent,* "Snow is formed from water vapor, when it has not yet condensed into drops, after it is caught up with cold; they say that it does not fall on the deep sea." Recall that this is the very treatise that is dedicated to Hwætberht.

EUS 24

MANUSCRIPTS: L, fol. 116r; G, fol. 371r–v.
EARLIER EDITIONS AND TRANSLATIONS: Gl, 234; Wl, 187. (SK 1691)
SOLUTION: *MORS ET VITA* (life and death).

Like many of Eusebius's aenigmata, this one too is centered on a series of paradoxes and parallel patterns, with sadness dominating lines 1 and 3 *(maesta . . . tristem)* and light and joy lines 2 and 4 (highlighted by the chiasmus of *lucida laetaque . . . laetifica . . . lumine*).

24.1 Although both manuscripts read *una sed,* the line as transmitted will not scan. Deleting *sed* certainly helps, although in any case we must assume *productio ob caesuram* in the final syllable of *sumus.*

24.4 Glosses in both languages explain *ridet* as *laetificet.*

EUS 25

MANUSCRIPTS: L, fol. 116r–v; G, fol. 371v.
EARLIER EDITIONS AND TRANSLATIONS: Gl, 235; Wl, 188. (SK 16795)
SOLUTION: *ANIMA* (soul); the solution given in G is *DE ANIMO* (about the mind), but *DE CORDE* (about the heart) in L. For a similar kind of conflation, compare LOR 5, and see Lockett, *Anglo-Saxon Psychologies,* 273–74.

The relationship to the various soul-and-body riddles is clear (see further the headnote to EUS 4 [*HOMO,* "mankind"]); less clear than between this aenigma and such fish-and-river riddles as SYM 12 and EXE 81.

25.1 Glosses in both manuscripts explain *homo* as *Christus;* another in L explains *clausa* as *misteria.*

25.2 Preferring *quique* L to *quisque* G; *quisque* is glossed *omnis* G.

25.3 Note the chiasmus *magna domus . . . accola magnus.*

EUS 26

MANUSCRIPTS: L, fol. 116v; G, fol. 371v.
EARLIER EDITIONS AND TRANSLATIONS: Gl, 236; Wl, 189. (SK 3098)
SOLUTION: *DIES BISSEXTILIS* (bissextile day). See further ES, 258–61.

The bissextile day is the one added every leap year to regularize the calendar. In modern times, this produces a February 29th every four years, but in the Julian calendar the extra day was inserted at February 24th, which in Roman reckoning was the sixth *(sextus)* day before the calends of March; in a leap year that sixth day would therefore occur twice, producing a second sixth day *(bissextilis)*. For another aenigma related to computus and chronology, see EUS 29 (*AETAS ET SALTUS*, "cycle and moon's leap"). No other riddle collection betrays such a computistical influence, and the double occurrence here strengthens the identification with Hwætberht, Abbot of Monkwearmouth-Jarrow, to whom Bede addressed his own treatise on computus, *De temporum ratione* (ed. Jones, 175–76).

26.1 A gloss in G explains *proprii* as *mei.*
26.2 Reading *creatur* for *creator* LG.

EUS 27

MANUSCRIPTS: L, fol. 116v; G, fol. 371v.
EARLIER EDITIONS AND TRANSLATIONS: Gl, 237; Wl, 190. (SK 3266)
SOLUTION: *HUMILITAS ET SUPERBIA* (humility and pride). In general, compare TAT 24 (*HUMILITAS*, "humility") and TAT 25 (*SUPERBIA*, "pride"); BON 9 *(HUMILITAS)*, although the treatments differ substantially.

This aenigma, like so many elsewhere within the tradition (see further the headnote to EXE 1), relies on a series of "high/low" comparisons, emphasized through chiasmus *(strata . . . exaltabo . . . sustollitur . . . sternit; depressa . . . exaltabo . . . alta . . . comprimit)*. Several biblical parallels suggest themselves, not least Luke 1:52, 14:11, and 18:14. Note too the extensive alliteration on *s-/st-*.

27.1 False quantity: *dēpressa* is the normal usage.
27.2 Note the final shortened syllable of *exaltabo.*
27.3 A gloss in G explains *Effera* as *ferox;* a further gloss in L explains *nimica* as *superbia.* False quantity: *meă* is the normal usage; the final syllable is presumably lengthened through *productio ob caesuram.*

EUS 28

MANUSCRIPTS: L, fol. 116v; G, fol. 371v.
EARLIER EDITIONS AND TRANSLATIONS: Gl, 238; Wl, 191. (SK 13969)
SOLUTION: *CANDELA* (candle). See further ES, 26–29.

For another aenigma on the same topic, compare ALD 52.

28.1 Glosses in both manuscripts explain *Quod* as *lumen.* False quantity: *dēfectum* is the normal usage.
28.2 Glosses explain *extinguor* as *deficio* G; *deficiendo* L.
28.3 Preferring *possim* L to *possum* G.
28.4 The *h* in *haec* makes position, contrary to Eusebius's practice elsewhere; compare EUS 39.4 *(regimen hominis),* 55.2 *(propter hoc),* and 58.3 *(visus hebetatur).* For such lengthening before *h-,* see Bede, *De arte metrica* 3.2 (ed. Kendall, 46–49).

EUS 29

MANUSCRIPTS: L, fol. 116v; G, fol. 371v.
EARLIER EDITIONS AND TRANSLATIONS: Gl, 239; Wl, 192–96. (SK 14340)
SOLUTION: *AETAS ET SALTUS LUNAE* (the age and the leap of the moon); the given solution is *DE AETATE ET SALTU* (G has *ETATE*). On grounds of sense, it seems clear that a reference to the moon has dropped out, hence the preferred solution. See further ES, 258–61.

This aenigma seeks to square the circle with regard to the disparity between solar and lunar calendars, which is at the heart of the problem of determining the date of Easter from the point of view of a solar calendar, whereas the Jewish festival of Passover, to which Easter is scripturally tied, is based on a lunar one. A solar year comprises 365.2422 days, a lunar month 29.3506 days; there are therefore 12.3683 lunar months in a solar year. The extra 0.3683 months over the standard twelve-month year can be variously expressed in fractions, but the one Bede chooses, namely 7/19 (= 0.3684) is astonishingly accurate: if seven extra lunar months are intercalated over every nineteen years, the cycles remain closely in sync. The *momenta* in question (EUS 29.3) are equivalent to 1/40 of an hour, according to Bede, *De temporum ratione* 3 (ed. Jones, 183), so "twenty times forty-eight *momenta*" equates to a normal twenty-four hour day. See further, in general, Bede, *De temporum ratione* 42 (*De saltu lunae* [ed. Jones, 255–57]). For another aenigma related to computus and chronology, see EUS 26 (*DIES BISSEXTILIS,* "bissextile day").

29.1 Reading *vĭcenis cum quadragiĕs octiĕs una,* so piling up the numerals, but with three false quantities: the normal forms are *vīcenis . . . quadragiēs octiēs.* Given the obscurity of the subject, such metrical lapses are perhaps forgivable.

29.2–3 Note tmesis of *una/quaque* over the line break.

29.3 False quantity: the usual form is *mōmentis.* Compare EUS 14.3 *(sola videbor).*

29.4 A gloss in G above the *non-* in *nondecimus* explains the element as *nonus.*

EUS 30

MANUSCRIPTS: L, fol. 116r; G, fol. 371v.

EARLIER EDITIONS AND TRANSLATIONS: Gl, 240; Wl, 197–98. (SK 1060)

SOLUTION: *ATRAMENTORIUM* (inkhorn). See further ES, 68–71; Lendinara, "Aspetti della società germanica"; Riddler and Trzaska-Nartowski, "Chanting upon a Dunghill"; Bitterli, *Say What I Am Called,* 151–52.

This aenigma is connected to the one following by the notion of writing, whether on wax tablets, as in EUS 31 (*CERA,* "about wax") or, as here, on parchment, and begins a sequence associated with the classroom. The parallels here with various riddles on horns in EXE are worth noting (EXE 12, 76, 84, and 89 [*BLÆC-HORN,* "inkhorn"]), especially the opening line of EXE 12 (*Ic wæs wæpen wigan,* "I was a warrior's weapon"), given the insistent emphasis on weapons in EUS 30.1–2 *(<u>arm</u>orum . . . <u>arm</u>is . . . <u>arm</u>igeri).* For other Anglo-Saxon riddles connected with the classroom and the scriptorium, see the note to ALD 30 (*ELEMENTUM,* "letter of the alphabet").

30.2 Compare ALD 24.5 *(summo . . . capitis de vertice),* ALD 26.5 *(capitis gestans in vertice),* ALD 91.8 *(summo capitis . . . vertice).*

30.3 False quantity: *intestīna* is the normal usage; it is also necessary to assume *intŭs,* where *intūs* is the normal usage; the same metrical license occurs at EUS 33.4.

30.4 False quantity: *nĭtor* is the normal usage. For the ungrammatical *ructans,* see the note to EUS 6.1 above. The emphasis on the value of writing here seems to be echoed in the damaged closing lines of EXE 84.31a–32 (*BLÆC-HORN,* "inkhorn"). I am grateful to Drew Jones for pointing out to me the further parallel in the combination of belching and seeing written words in Psalm 44:2: *Eructavit cor meum verbum bonum; dico ego opera mea regi. Lingua mea calamus scribae velociter scribentis,* "My heart hath uttered a good word; I speak my works to the king; My tongue is the pen of a scrivener that writeth swiftly."

EUS 31

MANUSCRIPTS: L, fol. 117r; G, fol. 371v.

EARLIER EDITIONS AND TRANSLATIONS: Gl, 241; Wl, 199. (SK 369)

SOLUTION: *PUGILLARES* (writing tablets); the given solution is *DE CERA* (on wax). See further ES, 63–67.

This aenigma leads on smoothly from the last, in that what is being described is not simply wax per se, but a wax tablet. Once again, there seems to be doubt about whether the title/solution in both manuscripts is the correct one. For another aenigma on a similar topic, see ALD 32, and the note on the connotations of the term there.

31.1 Glosses in both manuscripts explain *Aequalem* as *similem*.

31.4 Note the paronomasia on *tenens . . . tenebras;* for the figure, see Bede, *De scematibus et tropis* 1.9 (ed. Kendall, 174–77). The line is evidently influenced by the opening words of John 1:1.

EUS 32

MANUSCRIPTS: L, fol. 117r; G, fol. 371r–v.

EARLIER EDITIONS AND TRANSLATIONS: Gl, 242; Wl, 200–201. (SK 887)

SOLUTION: *MEMBRANA* (pieces of parchment); the given solution is *DE MEMBRANO* (on parchment). The subject speaks in the plural, hence the preferred solution; for a similar disparity, compare EUS 7. See further ES, 67–68; Hayes, "Talking Dead"; Bitterli, *Say What I Am Called,* 178–90; Murphy, *Unriddling the Exeter Riddles,* 86 and 94; Cavell, *Weaving Words,* 169; Ooi, "Speaking Objects," 52–53. See too Leahy, *Anglo-Saxon Crafts,* 89–93.

This aenigma again leads on in an obvious sequence from the previous, and connects it to several similar aenigmata in this and other collections. The "voiceless speaker" motif (emphasized here by the sequences *vox . . . verba . . . voce . . . verba; viva . . . mortua; nihil loquimur . . . famur*) is found, for example, in ALD 30.7; TAT 10.3; EUS 7.3, while the "black on white" theme is found in ALD 59.3–5; TAT 4.3; EUS 7.2 and 35.4; LOR 9.1 and 12.4–5; BER 25.1; EXE 49.2–3. For other aenigmata on similar topics, see TAT 5; BER 24; EXE 24.

32.1 False quantity: *anteā* is the normal usage, although there are parallels elsewhere; false quantity: *nēquaquam* is the normal usage.

32.2 A gloss in G explains *distincta* as ablative.

32.3 False quantity: *arvă* is the normal usage. Note the elision of the monosyllable *cum,* and the common wordplay on *lustro,* meaning both "traverse" and "illuminate," on which see the note at ALD 5.4 above. For the "black on white" theme in the context of writing, see the note at ALD 59.3–5 above. Glosses in both manuscripts explain *milibus* as *litteris*.

EUS 33

MANUSCRIPTS: L, fol. 117r; G, fol. 372r.
EARLIER EDITIONS AND TRANSLATIONS: Gl, 243; Wl, 202–3. (SK 7873)
SOLUTION: *SCETHA* (book-satchel). See further Salvador-Bello, *Isidorean Perceptions,* 362–63.

This aenigma follows on easily from the one before; here, however, the motif of "carrying wisdom that it cannot comprehend" is also found in SYM 16 (*tinea,* "bookworm"); ALD 89 (*Arca Libraria,* "book chest"); EXE 45 (**BOC-MOÐÐE,* "book moth"). There are some broad parallels in *Hisperica famina* A513–30 (*DE TABERNA,* "on a book-container"; see further Herren, *Hisperica Famina: The A-Text;* Orchard, "*Hisperica famina* as Literature").

33.1 False quantity: *multigenă* is the normal usage. Glosses in both manuscripts explain *multigene* as *multi libri*.

EUS 34

MANUSCRIPTS: L, fol. 117r–v; G, fol. 372r.
EARLIER EDITIONS AND TRANSLATIONS: Gl, 244; Wl, 204. (SK 11902)
SOLUTION: *FLUMEN,* "river." See further ES, 243–45.

EUS 1–33 and 35–40 all contain four lines, a pattern that seems to have confused the scribe of L, who leaves a blank line after EUS 34.4 and capitalizes the next line as if it began a new aenigma. Given the redundancy in EUS 34.3–4, it is tempting to suppose that one or the other (most likely EUS 34.4) is not original, and that the first group of EUS 1–40 is deliberately composed of four-line aenigmata. The position of this aenigma among a series all dealing with writing invites the suggestion that there is some misdirection here, and that the audience is at first invited to think that the solution is "ink." This rather bookish aenigma, which after a somewhat bland opening turns on the fact that the Latin words *flūmen* and *flŭvius* (both meaning "river") share an opening syllable distinguished only by quantity; the correct solution is revealed through a logogriph, with *FLUMEN* → *LUMEN* (light) by subtraction. On similar logogriphs, see the note on ALD 63 above. The connection between *flūmen* and *flŭvius* is also made, albeit in a different connection, by Isidore, *Etym.* 13.21.1. For other aenigmata on similar topics, see ALD 29 (*AQUA*, "water"), 62 (*FAMFALUCA*, "bubble"), and 73 (*FONS*, "spring").

34.4 Note the awkward elision in *syllaba et illud,* and compare the previous line.

34.6 Compare ALD 63.10; ALC 3.4 and 5.2; TAT 4.5 *(Littera tollatur);* the precise logogriph is revealed in ALF F3 *(Nox perit et tenebrae si me de flumine tollas).*

EUS 35

MANUSCRIPTS: L, fol. 117v; G, fol. 372r.

EARLIER EDITIONS AND TRANSLATIONS: Gl, 245; Wl, 205. (SK 10026)

SOLUTION: *PENNA* (quill pen). See further ES, 57–63; Murphy, *Unriddling the Exeter Riddles,* 88.

For similar aenigmata, see ALD 59, TAT 6, and LOR 9.

35.1–2 Compare EUS 33.1–2 (*SCETHA*, "book-wallet").

35.3 Reading *vagabar* in place of the future *vagabor* of LG. For other examples, see EUS 51.4 (reading *vocabar* for *vocabor* of LG).

35.4 For the "black on white" theme in the context of writing, see the note at ALD 59.3–5 above.

EUS 36

MANUSCRIPTS: L, fol. 117v; G, fol. 372r.
EARLIER EDITIONS AND TRANSLATIONS: Gl, 246; Wl, 206. (SK 14714)
SOLUTION: *GLADIUS* (sword). See further ES, 77–85; Murphy, *Unriddling the Exeter Riddles,* 209.

For other aenigmata on similar topics, see ALD 61 (*PUGIO,* "dagger") and TAT 30 (*ENSIS ET VAGINA,* "sword and sheath"). Just as EUS 34, in the immediate context of the surrounding aenigmata, seems to invite the extra solution "ink," so here there seems to be a conscious connection between the sword of the warrior and the stylus or pen of the scribe, a connection made explicitly in the *Hisperica famina,* on which see Orchard, "*Hisperica famina* as Literature."

36.2–3 Note the alliteration of *corpora . . . cruciare . . . curo . . . cum . . . coercent.*

36.3 A gloss in L supplies *digiti* after *quinque.*

36.4 The final line is problematic. It looks as if the transmitted phrase *tot pene* may mask an infinitive, as *possum* seems to require; *torquere* or *torpere* are the right shape, but confound both meaning and meter; perhaps one should read *tangere* instead.

EUS 37

MANUSCRIPTS: L, fol. 117v; G, fol. 372r.
EARLIER EDITIONS AND TRANSLATIONS: Gl, 247; Wl, 207. (SK 12101)
SOLUTION: *VITULUS* (bullock). See further ES, 170–73; Clemoes, *Interactions of Thought and Language,* 104; Orchard, "Enigma Variations," 297–99; Bitterli, *Say What I Am Called,* 26–30; Cavell, *Weaving Words,* 160.

The focus here is on living and dying, emphasized through both repetition *(vivere . . . vixero . . . vivos)* and oxymoron *(vivos moriens);* the notion is presumably highlighted by the visual pun of the first syllables of *vĭtulus,* "bullock," and *vīta,* "life," so offering a broad clue, despite their difference in vowel length. Even the verb tenses employed cover the gamut from past (EUS 37.1: *peperit*), through present (EUS 37.1: *solesco*), to future (EUS 37.3–4: *vixero . . . incipiam*). Note the enjambment here, a feature specifically applauded by Bede in his *De arte metrica* 11 (ed. Kendall, 102–3). For other riddles on similar topics, see ALD 83; EUS 12 and 13; EXE 36 (*HRYÐER*, "bullock").

37.1 For the spelling *genitrix* (and note that L has the more usual *genetrix*), compare EUS 44.3 and 46.1; there is also tmesis of *post . . . quam*, on which see further the note at TAT 8.6 above.

37.2 False quantity: *rīvos* is the normal usage. Given the emphasis of the young bullock drinking mother's milk in other similar aenigmata, Glorie's suggested emendation of *vivere*, "live," to *bibere*, "drink," is tempting, given the *-b-* for *-f-* or *-v-* spellings of the kind discussed in the headnote on LEI below. For the oxymoron *(vivos moriens)*, compare EUS 38.4 *(vivo sed exanimis)*.

EUS 38

MANUSCRIPTS: L, fol. 117v–18r; G, fol. 372r.
EARLIER EDITIONS AND TRANSLATIONS: Gl, 248; Wl, 208–10. (SK 2998)
SOLUTION: *PULLUS* (chick). See further Bitterli, *Say What I Am Called*, 115–21; Murphy, *Unriddling the Exeter Riddles*, 54–55.

Note the enjambment here, a feature specifically applauded by Bede in his *De arte metrica* 11 (ed. Kendall, 102–3). For other riddles on similar topics, see SYM 14; LOR 8; BER 8; ps-BED 2; EXE 11.

38.3 False quantity: *dētectus* is the normal usage. Compare Aldhelm, *Carmen de virginitate* 311 *(quod dudumquam nascatur de viscere matris)*; TAT 31.2 *(de viscere matris)*.

EUS 39

MANUSCRIPTS: L, fol. 118r; G, fol. 372r.
EARLIER EDITIONS AND TRANSLATIONS: Gl, 249; Wl, 211. (SK 4273)
SOLUTION: *I LITTERA* (the letter *I*). See further ES, 249–51 and 255–56.

In EUS 39.3 the word *sola* gives a clue to the solution, when it is remembered that in the Roman alphabet the number 1 is signified by an *I*. For other Anglo-Saxon riddles connected with the classroom and the scriptorium, see the note to ALD 30 (*ELEMENTUM*, "letter of the alphabet"), and compare ALF 1.3, which in turn depends on Matthew 5:18.

39.1 Note the elision of the monosyllable *sum*. The suggestion seems to be that *I* can stand for *IMPERATOR* or *IMPERIUM* or perhaps *IULIUS*. It may also be relevant that the imperative *i* means "go, depart."

39.2 Compare ALD 91.3 *(Nomine nempe meo)*; EUS 43.4 *(Nomine nempe meo)*; BON 4.9 *(Regmine nempe meo)*, BON 19.2 *(Germine nempe meo)*.

39.3 The two letters are either *IC* or *IX*, abbreviations of *IESUS CHRISTUS* or *IESUS XRISTUS*, the *I* of which in either case stands for *IESUS*.

39.4 The last syllable of *regimen* is lengthened by the following *h-*: compare EUS 28.4 *(lucet haec)*, 55.2 *(propter hoc)*, and 58.3 *(visus hebetatur)*, as well as Bede, *De arte metrica* 3.2 (ed. Kendall, 46–49). Similarly, the third syllable of *aliaque* must be assumed to be lengthened before *-q-*.

EUS 40

MANUSCRIPTS: L, fol. 118r; G, fol. 372r–v.
EARLIER EDITIONS AND TRANSLATIONS: Gl, 250; Wl, 212. (SK 10524)
SOLUTION: *PISCIS* (fish). See further ES, 198–99.

Compare ALD 71, with which there are many close parallels. This aenigma follows on naturally from the previous one, if we understand the repeated Christological references of EUS 39 to be extended here; the ancient association of Christ with the symbol of a fish seems to be invoked here too. EUS 40 works by parallelism and indirection, working with the motif of earth/sea/sky to establish in which spheres the creature does not usually travel *(non volo . . . non vago)* using either wings or feet *(penniger; pedester . . . pedibus),* before describing its normal watery home in terms of a different kind of "wing," used here presumably in the sense "fin" *(penniger . . . pennula),* and then again confounding expectations by indicating that it can travel the sky in another way as if walking the earth (I assume a pun linking the agricultural sense of *rura* in the first line to the rural overtones of *peragro* in the last). If Christ is intended as implied in the solution, this would be an excellent ending to a collection of forty aenigmata.

40.1 Compare ALD 100.69–70 *(per terram pergo pedester / Sic).*
40.2 Compare SYM 39.1; ALD 71.1 *(pedibus manibusque).*
40.4 Compare Aldhelm, *Carmen de virginitate* 2882 *(sublime tribunal).*

EUS 41

MANUSCRIPTS: L, fol. 118r; G, fol. 372v.
EARLIER EDITIONS AND TRANSLATIONS: Gl, 251; Wl, 213–15. (SK 1027)
SOLUTION: *HYDRA* (Hydra); the given solution is *DE CHELIDRO SERPENTE*. See further ES, 233–35.

Whereas in the previous aenigma mention is made of the earth/sea/sky, here the haunts of the creature in question are earth and water. The error in the given solution is made apparent once the source, which is clearly Isidore, *Etym.* 11.3.34–35, is identified (the specific parallels are in italics, following Wl):

> *Dicunt et Hydram serpentem cum* novem *capitibus, quae Latine excetra dicitur, quod uno caeso tria capita excrescebant. Sed constat Hydram locum fuisse evomentem aquas, vastantem vicinam civitatem,* in quo uno meatu clauso multi erumpebant. *Quod*

> *Hercules videns loca ipsa exussit,* et sic aquae clausit meatus. Nam hydra ab aqua dicta est. Huius mentionem facit Ambrosius in similitudinem haeresium, dicens: "Haeresis enim velut quaedam hydra fabularum vulneribus suis crevit; et dum saepe reciditur, *pullulavit* igni debita incendioque peritura."

> *They also say that the Hydra is a serpent with* nine *heads, which is called excetra in Latin, because when one head was cut off, three used to grow back. Yet it is established that Hydra was a place spewing up waters, ravaging the nearby city,* and when one of its conduits was closed, many others used to burst out. *When Hercules saw that, he burnt up the whole place,* and in that way sealed up the conduits of water. For it is called "Hydra" from water [Greek *ὕδωρ*]. Ambrose mentions this creature as resembling heresy, saying (*De fide* 1.4): "Heresy, just like the legendary Hydra, has grown back from its own wounds; and while it is often cut back, it *has welled back up,* destined for the flame and set to perish by fire."

There is a second mention of the creature in Isidore, *Etym.* 12.4.23, in almost identical terms. Immediately following this second account (*Etym.* 12.4.24), Isidore describes the *chelydros serpens,* and it is that which has erroneously been attached to this aenigma as a title/solution. Here and in several of the succeeding aenigmata there is a conflation of present and future tenses in the Latin that may ultimately reflect Old English vernacular usage, where the present tense can have future force: see further the note to ALD 33.6.

41.1 The exotic vocabulary used here can be matched elsewhere: *Argolici* can be seen in ALD 95.2 (*SCILLA,* "Scylla") and Aldhelm, *Carmen de virginitate* 2147, while *cephala* can be paralleled in ALD PR.20, Aldhelm, *Carmen de virginitate* 1016, and EUS 45.3 (*CAMELEON,* "chameleon"). Eusebius assumes that the word *cephal* is neuter, and thus produces a rare plural *cephala.* Glosses in both manuscripts explain *cephala* as *capita.* The seven heads seem to reflect the seven-headed dragon of

Apocalypse 12:3: *draco magnus rufus habens capita septem,* "a great red dragon, having seven heads," and may explain why this aenigma, describing a Satanic dragon, follows immediately after EUS 40, which deals with the Christological fish.

41.2 The form *scedra* is not found elsewhere, but seems to have been inspired by a manuscript variant of Isidore's *excetra* (both *excedra* and *exedra* are attested); the suggested emendation to *Hydra* cannot stand, since it would give away the "correct" solution.

41.4 A gloss in G supplies *capita* after *trina;* glosses in both manuscripts explain *manare* as *crescere.* False quantity: *mānare* is the normal usage.

41.6 For the notion of Hercules as a giant (one shared by Ælfric, for example), see Orchard, *Pride and Prodigies,* 115.

41.7 False quantity: *pūllulans* is the normal spelling and usage, although there is a parallel in TAT 36.4.

EUS 42

MANUSCRIPTS: L, fol. 118v; G, fol. 372v.
EARLIER EDITIONS AND TRANSLATIONS: Gl, 252; Wl, 216–17. (SK 7207)
SOLUTION: *DRACO* (dragon). See further ES, 231–32.

Whereas in the previous aenigma mention is made of the earth and water, here the haunts of the creature in question are earth and air. This aenigma follows on from the previous one in the common identification of the dragon of the Apocalypse with the devil; note that in the second passage cited above, Isidore describes the Hydra as a *draco.* Note too the change from the first to third person in EUS 42.6–8, and back again in the final line. The source is clearly Isidore, *Etym.* 12.4.4 (the specific parallels are italicized, following Wl):

> *Draco maior cunctorum serpentium,* sive omnium animantium super terram. Hunc Graeci δράκοντα vocant; unde et derivatum est in Latinum ut draco diceretur. *Qui saepe ab speluncis abstractus fertur in aerem, concitaturque propter eum aer. Est autem cristatus, ore parvo, et artis fistulis, per quas trahit*

spiritum et linguam exerat. *Vim autem non in dentibus, sed in cauda habet,* et verbere potius quam rictu nocet.

The dragon (draco) is the biggest of all the serpents, indeed of all the animals on the earth. The Greeks call this creature *δράκων,* whence also the derivative in Latin, so that it is called *draco. The creature is often driven out of caves and is borne into the air, and because of it the air is disturbed. It has a crest, and a small mouth and narrow airways through which it draws breath* and darts out its tongue. *It has its force not in its teeth but in its tail,* and it causes more damage through its thrashing about than through its maw.

42.1 Here I adopt the reading *Horridus* from the gloss to *Horrendus* in L; G has unglossed *Horrendus.* A further gloss in G supplies *per* before *horriferas.* Note the wordplay (polyptoton) in *horridus horriferas.*

42.3 For the ungrammatical *cristatusque volans,* see the note to EUS 6.1 above.

42.4 False quantity: *monstră* is the normal usage.

42.6–8 The change from first to third person is awkward, but is matched in EUS 46.4. Note too the insistent alliteration on *f-/v-* throughout *(volitans . . . volans . . . vipereas . . . vel . . . ferus . . . viscera venas . . . flatum . . . virtus . . . vim violentiam).*

42.8 Compare ALD 16.4 *(LULIGO: aethereo . . . flatu).*

42.9 Preferring *cauda* to *cruda* LG; the source strongly supports the emendation.

EUS 43

MANUSCRIPTS: L, fol. 118v; G, fol. 372v.
EARLIER EDITIONS AND TRANSLATIONS: Gl, 253; Wl, 218–19. (SK 3263)
SOLUTION: *TIGRIS* (tigress); the given solution is *DE TIGRI BESTIA.* See further ES, 224–25.

Whereas in the previous aenigmata mention is made of earth and water on the one hand, and earth and air on the other, here, while the creature in question clearly inhabits the earth, the references are to air and water. The etymology extends beyond Greek and Latin, and now encompasses Persian. The feminine form of *tigris* is reflected in the forms *fera* and *stellata*. The source is clearly Isidore, *Etym.* 12.2.7 (the specific parallels are in italics, following Wl):

> *Tigris vocata propter volucrem fugam; ita enim nominant Persae* et Medi *sagittam. Est enim bestia variis distincta maculis,* virtute et velocitate mirabilis; *ex cuius nomine flumen Tigris appellatur,* quod is rapidissimus sit omnium fluviorum.

> *The tigress (tigris) is so called because of its swift speed; and so that is what the Persians* and Medes *call an arrow. It is a beast identified by different markings,* amazing in its strength and speed, *and the river is called Tigris from its name,* because that is the quickest of all rivers.

The River Tigris itself is described in Isidore, *Etym.* 13.21.9, where again the connection with the speed of the tigress is made.

43.3 Compare SYM 38.1 (*TIGRIS,* "tigress"). False quantity: *valdē* is the normal usage; the same scansion is found at EUS 23.1; see the note there.

43.4 Compare ALD 91.3 *(Nomine nempe meo);* EUS 39.2 *(nempe mearum);* BON 4.9 *(Regmine nempe meo),* BON 19.2 *(Germine nempe meo).* Glosses in both manuscripts supply *me* after *dixere.*

EUS 44

MANUSCRIPTS: L, fol. 118v; G, fol. 372v.

EARLIER EDITIONS AND TRANSLATIONS: Gl, 254; Wl, 220–21. (SK 5252)

SOLUTION: *PANTER* (panther); the given solution is *DE PANTHERA,* presumably influenced by the feminine form of the solution for the aenigma that precedes this one. The preferred solution is *PANTER.* See further ES, 225–26.

The given solution for this aenigma cannot be correct as it stands, given the clearly masculine form of *alium* in EUS 44.3. A further problem arises from the logogriph implied in the final line: for a *genitor,* "father" (the usual word is *pater*), to be generated when the third letter is removed, the creature must be *panter* in the nominative, so throwing into doubt the whole pattern of titles/solutions of the form "*DE X.*" The thematic connection between this aenigma and the one immediately preceding is emphasized by the fact that just as EUS 43 draws on Isidore, *Etym.* 12.2.7, EUS 44 is dependent on Isidore, *Etym.* 2.2.8–9:

> Panther dictus . . . quod omnium animalium sit amicus, excepto dracone. . . . Haec semel omnino parturit.
>
> It is called the panther . . . because it is the friend of all the animals, except the dragon. . . . It only gives birth once.

The *Physiologus* tradition (preserved in Old English in the Exeter Book alongside the riddles) discusses in detail the animosity between the panther and the dragon. The theme of birth and generation is underlined by wordplay (polyptoton) here (*genitrix gestans . . . generare . . . genitor*).

44.2 False quantity: *valdē* is the normal usage, and the following *dr-* in *draconi* would normally lengthen by position; the same scansion is found at EUS 23.1: see the note there.

EUS 45

MANUSCRIPTS: L, fol. 118v–19r; G, fol. 372v–73r.
EARLIER EDITIONS AND TRANSLATIONS: Gl, 255; Wl, 222–23. (SK 9900)
SOLUTION: *CAMELEON* (chameleon); the given solution is *DE CAMELEONTE,* altered from *DE CANALEONE.*

Once again, the given solution as it stands cannot be strictly correct. This aenigma conflates two consecutive descriptions given by Isidore, namely that of the *Chamaeleon,* "chameleon," and *Camelopardus,* "giraffe," *Etym.* 12.2.18–19 (*de cameleonte* and *de camelopardo*; the specific parallels are in italics, following Wl):

> *Chamaeleon non habet unum colorem, sed diversa est varietate consparsus, ut pardus. . . . Huius chamaeleontis corpusculum ad colores quos videt facillima conversione variatur,* quod aliorum animalium non est ita ad conversionem facilis corpulentia. Camelopardus dictus, *quod dum sit ut pardus albis maculis superaspersus, collo equo similis, pedibus bubulis, capite tamen camelo est similis.* Hunc Aethiopia gignit.
>
> *The chameleon does not have a single color, but is speckled with various markings, like a leopard. . . . The small body of this chameleon changes by a very easy alteration to whatever colors it sees,* while the bigger bodies of other animals are not so prone to alteration. The giraffe *(camelopardus)* is so called *because while it is spattered over with white spots like the leopard, it has a neck like a horse, feet like an ox, but a head like a camel.* Ethiopia produces this animal.

This conflation may have occurred due to the repetition *ut pardus,* "like a leopard," denoting an animal that is itself often confused as being either a male panther (so linking this aenigma with EUS 44 [*PANTER,* "panther"]) or a leopard (so linking it with EUS 46 [*DE LEOPARDO,* "about a leopard"]). This is another body-part riddle; see further the headnote to ALD 84 above.

45.1 The word *orbiculis* is rare, but found again at EUS 47.1. The verb *muneror* is usually deponent, but is evidently to be regarded here as a proper passive; it is tempting to emend to *numeror,* "I am numbered," though that would involve a metrical infelicity: *nŭmeror* is the normal usage.

45.2 Glosses in both manuscripts explain *buballo* as *bubal.*

45.3 The term *cephal* is also found at ALD PR.20 and EUS 41.1.

EUS 46

MANUSCRIPTS: L, fol. 119r; G, fol. 373r.

EARLIER EDITIONS AND TRANSLATIONS: Gl, 256; Wl, 224–25. (SK 14520)

SOLUTION: *LEOPARDUS* (leopard). See further ES, 226–28. The connection with the previous aenigma is through the *pardus.*

The source is clearly Isidore, *Etym.* 12.2.10–11 (the specific parallels are in italics, following Wl):

> Pardus secundus post pantherem est, genus varium ac *velocissimum* et praeceps ad sanguinem. Saltu enim ad mortem ruit. *Leopardus ex adulterio leaenae et pardi nascitur,* et tertiam originem efficit; sicut et Plinius in Naturali Historia dicit, *leonem cum parda, aut pardum cum leaena concumbere et ex utroque coitu degeneres partus creari,* ut mulus et burdo.

> The pard (*pardus*) comes second after the panther, a breed which is spotted and *very swift* and keen for blood. It springs to slaughter with a leap. *The leopard (leopardus) is born from the filthy mating of a lioness and a pard,* and produces a third bloodline. Just as Pliny in his *Natural History* [8.42] says: *a lion mates with a female pard, or a male pard with a lioness, and from both couplings half-breed offspring are produced,* just like a mule or a hinny.

46.1 False quantities: *mihī* and *dēcreta* are the normal usages, though in the former case, lengthening at the caesura is not unusual. The use of the term *lena* highlights the sexualized imagery here: *lena,* "whore," and *leaena,* "lioness," seem deliberately conflated.

46.2 Note the alliteration: *pater pardus pardaeque.*

46.3 False quantity: *rōbustus* is the normal usage. Compare ALD 93.8 (*SCINTILLA,* "spark": *truxque rapaxque capaxque feroxque sub aethere spargo).*

46.4 For the notion of "having a name," see the note at ALD 50.3.

EUS 47

MANUSCRIPTS: L, fol. 119r; G, fol. 373r.
EARLIER EDITIONS AND TRANSLATIONS: Gl, 257; Wl, 226–27. (SK 1117)
SOLUTION: *SCITALE* (piebald serpent); the given solution is *DE SCITALI SERPENTE*. See further ES, 235–36.

A potential connection between this aenigma and the previous one lies in the apparent allusion in the latter to ALD 93 (*SCINTILLA*, "spark"), since the implied etymology of the serpent in this aenigma is precisely through *scintilla*. The source is clearly Isidore, *Etym.* 12.4.19 (the specific parallels are in italics, following Wl):

> Scytale serpens vocata, *quod tanta praefulget tergi varietate ut notarum gratia aspicientes retardet; et quia reptando pigrior est, quos adsequi non valet, miraculo sui stupentes capit. Tanti autem fervoris est ut etiam hiemis tempore exuvias corporis ferventis exponat.* De quo Lucanus: Et scytale sparsis *etiam nunc sola pruinis / exuvias positura suas.*
>
> The *scytale* serpent is so named *because it gleams with so much variety on its back that thanks to its markings it slows down those looking at it. And because it is rather slow at slithering, it captures those it cannot chase because they are stunned by its amazing appearance. It is a creature of such heat that even in wintertime it sheds the skin of its hot body.* Lucan says this about it [*Bellum civile* 9.717–18]: "And the *scytale, even now with scattered frosts, alone is going to shed its skin.*"

47.1 Note the hiatus in *aspera orbiculis*.

47.3 Note the extraordinary alliteration on *q-/c-* here.

47.4 False quantity: *hiemĕque* is the normal usage. It is tempting to emend to *spersis* or *sparsis*, following Lucan, as quoted by Isidore. It seems plausible, however, that Eusebius had in front of him a variant text of Isidore.

47.5 Compare Lucan, *Bellum civile* 9.717 *(exuvias positura suas),* quoted by Isidore above.

47.6 False quantity: *nŏtis* is the normal usage.

EUS 48

MANUSCRIPTS: L, fol. 119r; G, fol. 373r.

EARLIER EDITIONS AND TRANSLATIONS: Gl, 258; Wl, 228. (SK 10497)

SOLUTION: *DIES ET NOX* (day and night). See further Salvador-Bello, *Isidorean Perceptions,* 244–45.

This is the only aenigma within the last group of 20 (EUS 41–60) that is not largely or wholly reliant on Isidore, and both its length (four lines) and subject matter match more closely the first group of 40 (EUS 1–40). The deliberate contrast and double solution here match such earlier aenigmata in the sequence as EUS 24 (*MORS ET VITA,* "life and death"). Here, such balance is underlined by the monosyllabic leonine rhymes in EUS 48.1 and EUS 48.3 *(aequales . . . sorores; requiem . . . laborem;* compare EUS 48.2, *una . . . pulchra),* as well as by the characteristic love of contrast *(tetrica una . . . altera pulchra; horrida requiem . . . grata laborem).* See further Virgil, *Aeneid* 4.181 (quoted in ALD 97.13).

48.1 Compare SYM 77.1 *(aequales . . . sorores)* and ALD 66.1 *(sumus aequales . . . sorores).*

48.4 Note the emphatic alliteration here *(simul . . . semper sumus . . . secernimur).*

EUS 49

MANUSCRIPTS: L, fol. 119r–v; G, fol. 373r.

EARLIER EDITIONS AND TRANSLATIONS: Gl, 259; Wl, 229–30. See further ES, 236–37. (SK 5202)

SOLUTION: *AMPHISBAENA* (two-headed serpent); the given solution is *DE ANFIBINA SERPENTE* (on the serpent *amphisbaena*).

The given solution, generally emended to *AMPHISBAENA* on the model of the evident source, Isidore, may derive from a manuscript variant *anfivena,* so producing *Anfibana* L, *Anfivina* G. This aenigma links back to EUS 47 (*SCITALE,* "piebald serpent"), and is not only derived from the source passage from Isidore that immediately follows, but even includes a quotation from the next line in Lucan; once again, the supposition that EUS 48 (*DIES ET NOX,* "day and night") has been displaced would reestablish the sequence. The source is clearly Isidore, *Etym.* 12.4.20 (the specific parallels are in italics, following Wl):

> Amphisbaena dicta, *eo quod duo capita habeat,* unum in loco suo, *alterum in cauda, currens ex utroque capite,* tractu corporis circulato. *Haec sola serpentium frigori se committit,* prima omnium procedens. De qua idem Lucanus:
>
> > Et gravis *in geminum* vergens *caput* amphisbaena.
> >
> > *Cuius oculi lucent veluti lucernae.*
>
> The amphisbaena is so called *because it has two heads,* one in its proper place and *the other in the tail, and it travels with both heads in front* and its body in a loop dragged behind. *This is the only one of the serpents that entrusts itself to the cold,* and is the first of all to emerge. Lucan says this about it: "And the heavy amphisbaena, twisting *its heads in two / And its eyes shine like lamps.*"

49.1 Compare Lucan, *Bellum civile* 9.719 *(in geminum . . . caput),* quoted by Isidore above.

49.3 Reading *oculos* for *animos* LG. Despite the readings of both manuscripts, it seems preferable, given that both Isidore and the *Liber monstrorum* refer to the creature's "fiery eyes," to emend to *oculos.*

EUS 50

MANUSCRIPTS: L, fol. 119v; G, fol. 373r.
EARLIER EDITIONS AND TRANSLATIONS: Gl, 260; Wl, 231. (SK 12167)
SOLUTION: *SAURA* (lizard); the given solution is *DE SAURA LACERTO* (on the lizard called *saura*). See further ES, 213–14.

The source is clearly Isidore, *Etym.* 12.4.37 (the specific parallels are in italics, following Wl):

> *Saura lacertus qui quando senescit, caecantur oculi eius, et intrat in foramen parietis aspicientis contra Orientem, et orto sole* intendit, et *illuminatur.*
>
> *The saura is a lizard whose eyes go blind, as it grows old, and it goes into a hole in a wall facing east, and* looks towards *the rising sun,* and *is filled with light.*

50.1 For the ungrammatical *fugiens,* see the note to EUS 6.1 above. Compare ALD 27.3 (*COTICULA,* "whetstone": *senectutis . . . discrimina).* The opening *Porro,* which seems simply to serve to link aenigmata in the sequence, is found here and at EUS 52.1 and EUS 56.1; the word does not appear at all elsewhere in EUS.

EUS 51

MANUSCRIPTS: L, fol. 119v; G, fol. 373r.
EARLIER EDITIONS AND TRANSLATIONS: Gl, 261; Wl, 232. (SK 17124)
SOLUTION: *SCORPIO* (scorpion). See further ES, 210.

With the emphasis on double jeopardy, there seems to be a link here to EUS 49 (*AMPHISBAENA,* "two-headed serpent"). Note the alliteration of *f-/v-* and *s- (vermibus . . . vulnere virus diffundo . . . vocabar . . . vulnero; ascriptus . . . serpentibus . . . sociatus . . . solesco).* The source is clearly Isidore, *Etym.* 12.5.4:

Scorpio, vermis terrenus, qui potius vermibus ascribitur, non serpentibus: animal armatum aculeo, et ex eo Graece vocatum, quod cauda figat, et arcuato vulnere venena diffundat. Proprium autem est scorpioni, quod manus palmam non feriat.

The scorpion is an example of land-dwelling worm, and is reckoned rather among the worms than among the serpents: it is an animal armed with a sting, and was called from this in Greek, because it strikes with its tail and pours out venom in a bow-shaped wound. It is a feature of the scorpion that it does not attack the palm of the hand.

51.1 A gloss in L supplies *sum* after *ascriptus.*

51.4 Reading *vocabar* in place of the future *vocabor* of LG. For other examples, see the note at EUS 34.3. Isidore's unstated Greek etymology presumably derives from σκορπίζειν, "scatter, disperse," and matches Latin *diffundere* here.

51.5 Compare BER 37.5 *(Mordeo . . . nec vulnero dente);* BER 41.3 *(dente nec vulnero).*

EUS 52

MANUSCRIPTS: L, fol. 119v–20r; G, fol. 373r–v.
EARLIER EDITIONS AND TRANSLATIONS: Gl, 262; Wl, 233–34. (SK 12169)
SOLUTION: *CYMERA* (Chimera). See further ES, 238–40.

This aenigma links back to EUS 41 (*HYDRA,* "Hydra"), in that it too celebrates a famous classical monster-slayer, in that case Hercules and here Bellerophon. There is a clear contrast between TAT and EUS in their attitudes towards classical references. The source here is evidently Isidore, *Etym.* 11.3.36 and 1.40.4 (the specific parallels are in italics, following Wl):

Fingunt et Chimaeram triformem bestiam: ore leo, postremis partibus draco, media caprea. Quam quidam Physiologi non animal, sed Ciliciae montem esse aiunt, quibusdam locis leones et capreas nutrientem, quibusdam ardentem, *quibusdam plenum serpentibus. Hunc Bellorophontes habitabilem fecit, unde Chimeram dicitur occidisse.*

They also imagine the Chimera as a tripartite beast with the face of a lion, the hindquarters of a dragon, and a she-goat in the middle. Certain "scientists" say that the Chimera is not an animal, but rather a mountain in Cilicia that produces lions and she-goats in some areas, in others emits fire, *and is full of serpents in others. Bellerophon made this mountain habitable, and from that he is said to have killed the Chimera.*

Earlier on, in his section *De fabula* (On the fable), Isidore made further reference to the Chimera as a fictional beast conjured up in the classical and pagan past, citing Lucretius, *De rerum natura* 5.905 (Isidore, *Etym.* 1.40.4).

52.1 On *porro,* see the note at EUS 50.1.

52.2 and 4 Compare Lucretius, *De rerum natura* 5.903, quoted in Isidore, *Etym.* 1.11.4.

52.2 Compare ALD 69.7 *(rictibus oris).*

52.5 The form *considere* has been thought to mask either *considerare* or *consistere;* but compare LOR 5 (*CUPA VINARIA,* "wine cup"). The reference here to *filologi* (another false quantity: the usual form is *filolŏgi*) masks Isidore's *Physiologi,* which links back to the earlier acknowledgment of the *Physiologus* tradition in EUS 44 (*PANTER,* "panther"). The variant reading *philosophi* is indeed recorded at this point in the *Etymologiae.*

EUS 53

MANUSCRIPTS: L, fol. 120r; G, fol. 373v.

EARLIER EDITIONS AND TRANSLATIONS: Gl, 263; Wl, 235–36. (SK 10323)

SOLUTION: *HIPPOPOTAMUS* (hippopotamus); the given solution is *YPOTAMA* (note the absence here of *DE,* again suggesting that in other given solutions it is an addition). See further ES, 228–229.

The notion that the hippopotamus is a fish again suggests that the solution is a later addition, extrapolated from the two subsequent aenigmata; the categorization by Isidore himself may also have assisted the identification. Given the author's penchant for wordplay, the sequence *aeque . . . equo* seems deliberate. The source is clearly Isidore, *Etym.* 12.6.21 (the specific parallels are in italics, following Wl):

> *Hippopotamus vocatus, quod sit equo similis dorso, iuba et hinnitu, rostro resupinato, aprinis dentibus,* cauda tortuosa (ungulis bifidis). *Die in aquis commoratur; nocte segetes depascitur,* et hunc Nilus gignit.
>
> *The hippopotamus is so named because it is similar to the horse in its back, its mane, and its whinnying; its snout is curved back, and it has teeth like a boar,* a twisted tail, and split hooves. *By day, it lurks in the waters; by night, it grazes on crops,* and the Nile produces this creature.

53.1 Compare ALD 18.2 *(MYRMICOLEON,* "ant lion": *sermone Pelasgo),* ALD 35.6 *(NYCTICORAX,* "night-raven": *voce Pelasga),* ALD 60.10 *(MONOCERUS,* "unicorn": *lingua Pelasga);* ALF A.2 *(voce Pelasga).*

53.2 False quantity: *hinnītus* is the normal usage.

53.4 Compare ALD 39.1 *(dentibus apros).*

53.5 A gloss in G supplies *per* before *cunctos;* another in the same manuscript explains *phoebos* as *dies.* The use of *phoebos* to mean "days" is unusual; compare *phoebis* at EUS 60.3.

EUS 54

MANUSCRIPTS: L, fol. 120r; G, fol. 373v.
EARLIER EDITIONS AND TRANSLATIONS: Gl, 264; Wl, 237–38. (SK 5274)
SOLUTION: *ECHENEIS* (remora); the given solution is *DE OCEANO PISCE* (about an ocean fish). See further ES, 99.

The solution given in both manuscripts is garbled, and masks the true solution. The source is clearly Isidore, *Etym.* 12.6.34 (the specific parallels are in italics, following Wl):

> *Echeneis, parvus et semipedalis pisciculus nomen sumpsit, quod navem adhaerendo retineat. Ruant licet venti, et saeviant procellae, navis tamen, quasi radicata in mari stare videtur,* nec moveri, non retinendo, *sed tantummodo adhaerendo. Hunc Latini remoram appellaverunt,* eo quod cogat stare navigia.
>
> *The remora, a tiny little fish six inches long, took its name because it holds back a ship by sticking to it. Even though the winds howl and the storms rage, the ship nonetheless seems to stand as if rooted in the sea,* and is not moved, not because of being held back, *but just by being stuck to. Latin speakers have called this creature the remora (literally "delay")* because it makes ships stand still.

54.2 Compare ALD 92.7 *(et tamen immensis).*
54.3 Reading *tantum* for *tamen* LG.
54.6 Compare ALD 37.1 *(nomen dixere Latini)* and 60.11 *(dixerunt voce Latini).*

EUS 55

MANUSCRIPTS: L, fol. 120r–v; G, fol. 373v.
EARLIER EDITIONS AND TRANSLATIONS: Gl, 265; Wl, 239–40. (SK 2791)
SOLUTION: *TORPEDO* (electric ray); the given solution is *DE TURPEDO PISCE* (note the incorrect grammar, so again undermining the originality of the "*DE X*" form). See further ES, 199–200.

The source is clearly Isidore, *Etym.* 12.6.45 (the specific parallels are in italics, following Wl):

> Torpedo vocata, *eo quod corpus torpescere faciat, si eam quisquam viventem tangat.* Narrat Plinius Secundus, *"ex Indico mari torpedo etiam procul, et e longinquo, vel si hasta virgaque attingatur, quamvis praevalidos lacertos torpescere, quamlibet ad cursum veloces pedes alligari." Tanta enim vis eius est, ut etiam aura corporis sui afficiat membra.*
>
> The electric ray is so named *because it makes the body grow numb if anyone touches it while it is alive.* Pliny describes it as follows [*Nat. Hist.* 32.7]: *"From the Indian Ocean the electric ray, even from afar or some distance away, or if it is touched with a spear or stick, makes even very strong muscles grow numb, and fetters feet, however fast at running." Its force is such that even the aura of its body affects limbs.*

55.2 Another lengthening by position before *h,* as in EUS 38.2, 39.4, and 58.3. One wonders whether that explains the spelling *astis* in EUS 55.5. Compare ALD 58.1 *(mihi nomen adhaesit).* It is ambiguous whether *infandum* refers to *nomen* or *opus,* and so whether it is the "name" or the "deed" which is "wicked."

55.3 Compare ALD 35.4 and 82.6 *(quin magis).* The word *etsi* emphasizes the otherwise exotic and positive reputation of the Indian Ocean.

55.6 Reading *torpuerint* for *torpescerent* LG. Given *attingerint* in the preceding line, the emendation to *torpuerint* seems a safe one, and better in terms of meter.

55.8 A gloss in G explains *quo* as *ut.* Compare ALD 99.7 *(corporis artus);* Juvencus, *Evangelia* I.620 *(corporis artus).*

EUS 56

MANUSCRIPTS: L, fol. 120v; G, fol. 373v–74r.

EARLIER EDITIONS AND TRANSLATIONS: Gl, 266–67; Wl, 241–43. (SK 12168)

SOLUTION: *CICONIA* (stork); the given solution is *de ciconia avi*. See further ES, 186–89; Murphy, *Unriddling the Exeter Riddles,* 83.

After the previous set of aenigmata dealing with creatures whose main domain is in the water (EUS 53–55), this aenigma opens the closing sequence (EUS 56–60), where all the creatures concerned are birds of one sort or another; for a similar sequence of bird riddles, compare EXE 5–8. The switch in subject matter may explain the evident gloss *AVI,* "bird," attached to the given solution. This aenigma shows careful patterning in its placement of words, and exhibits embellishment in the form of both leonine rhyme in lines 3–5, 7–9, and 11 and considerable alliteration, notably on *c-*, *f-/v-*, *n-*, *p-*, and *s-*, generally in clusters. The particular focus on feeding and rearing is emphasized through repetition *(pascentur . . . cibabit . . . alentes . . . nutrimus . . . alemur),* and the strong emphasis is on the sociable and family-minded qualities of the stork, as well as its essential enmity toward snakes; hence it is another of the creatures perhaps best to be understood within the *Physiologus* tradition. Compare ALD 31 (*CICONIA,* "stork"), with which it shares many similarities. The source is clearly Isidore, *Etym.* 12.7.16–17 (the specific parallels are underlined, following Wl):

> *Ciconiae vocatae a sono quo crepitant,* quasi cicaniae: quem sonum oris potius esse quam vocis, *quia eum quatiente rostro faciunt. Hae veris nuntiae, societatis comites, serpentium hostes, maria transvolant, in Asiam collecto agmine pergunt. Cornices duces eas praecedunt, et ipsae quasi exercitus prosequuntur. Eximia illis circa filios pietas; nam adeo nidos inpensius fovent ut assiduo incubitu plumas exuant. Quantum autem tempus inpenderint in fetibus educandis, tantum et ipsae invicem a pullis suis aluntur.*

Storks are so named from the cracking sound they make, as if they were *cicaniae.* This sound is made with the mouth rather than the voice, *since they make it by shaking their beaks. They are harbingers of spring, members of a group, enemies of serpents; they fly across the seas, and reach Asia in a collected flock. Crows go ahead of them as leaders, and they follow like an army. They have an amazing concern for their offspring, for they guard their nests so carefully that they tear out their own feathers for the best bedding. Whatever time they spend rearing their chicks, they are in turn looked after for the same amount of time by their own chicks.*

56.1 On *porro,* see the note on EUS 50.1. A gloss in G explains *soni crepitus* as *sonus.*

56.2 Compare ALD 31.3 *(crepacula rostro).*

56.3 Compare SYM 2.3 *(nuntia sum);* SYM 13.2 *(stipata catervis).*

56.4 Preferring *chelidrorum* L to *chelidri* G. Eusebius seems to be assuming that the *ch-* of *chelydrorum* acts like an *h-,* and that therefore the final syllable of *hostis* does not make position. Compare Sedulius, *Carmen paschale* 3.190 *(Ille chelydrus adest, nigri qui felle veneni).*

56.5–7 The three future tenses *pascentur . . . ducet . . . cibabit* (as well as EUS 56.13 *alemur*) might just as easily be translated in the present, and may reflect Old English vernacular usage.

56.9 Note the archaic genitive form *iteris,* found elsewhere in Juvencus, *Evangelia* 1.243, 1.290, 1.318, 1.557, 2.184, 3.585, 4.767; and Bede, *Vita S. Cudbercti* 1.544.

EUS 57

MANUSCRIPTS: L, fol. 120v–21r; G, fol. 374r.

EARLIER EDITIONS AND TRANSLATIONS: Gl, 268; Wl, 244. (SK 8055)

SOLUTION: *STRUTIO* (ostrich). See further ES, 195–97.

Just as the previous aenigma uses repetition to stress the role of feeding, so here the emphasis is on nurturing *(foetum . . . fovere . . . fotu*

. . . *foventur).* Plentiful enjambment links this aenigma to several of the previous ones in the collection. Compare ALD 42 (*STRUTIO,* "ostrich"), although there are very few direct parallels. The source is clearly Isidore, *Etym.* 12.7.20, which is followed very closely here:

> Struthio Graeco nomine dicitur, quod animal in similitudine avis pinnas habere videtur; tamen de terra altius non elevatur. Ova sua fovere neglegit; sed proiecta tantummodo fotu pulveris animantur.

> The ostrich is called by a Greek name; and this animal seems to have feathers like a bird, but it does not rise higher than the ground. It does not bother to look after its eggs, but after being laid they are brought to life by the dust's nurturing alone.

57.1 A gloss in L, which reads *velocer,* offers *volucer* as an equivalent. For the notion of "having a name," see the note at ALD 50.3. Again, the future form *habebo* might just as well be translated by a present tense; see the note on 56.5–7 above. Glosses in both manuscripts explain *Pelasgum* as *Graecum.*

57.4 Reading *fotu* for *foetu* LG.

57.5 False quantity: the normal usage is *potiŭs* (here lengthened by position?); compare EUS 58.5 *(potius aliunde).*

EUS 58

MANUSCRIPTS: L, fol. 121r; G, fol. 374r.
EARLIER EDITIONS AND TRANSLATIONS: Gl, 269; Wl, 245–46. (SK 5484)
SOLUTION: *NOCTUA* (owlet). See further ES, 190–92.

This aenigma is linked to the previous one through the theme of its voice, and carefully alternates in its first four lines references to darkness (EUS 58.1 and EUS 58.3) and light (EUS 58.2 and EUS 58.4); it is connected also to EUS 60 (*BUBO,* "horned owl"), another kind of owl, the description of which precedes immediately in Isidore. Compare

ALD 35 (*NYCTICORAX*, "night-raven"). The source is clearly Isidore, *Etym.* 12.7.40 (the specific parallels are in italics, following Wl):

> Noctua dicitur pro eo quod nocte circumvolat et *per diem non possit videre; nam exorto splendore solis, visus illius hebetatur. Hanc autem insula Cretensis non habet; et si veniat aliunde, statim moritur.* Noctua autem non est bubo; nam bubo maior est.
>
> The night owl is so called because it flies around at night and *is unable to see during the day, for when the sun's splendor appears, its sight grows dull. The island of Crete does not contain this bird, and if it comes there from elsewhere, it immediately dies.* The night owl is not the same as the horned owl, for the horned owl is bigger.

58.2 Compare ALD 26.1–2 (*Garrula in tenebris . . . lucis radios et lumina Phoebi*) and 57.8 (*lumine Phoebi*); EUS 11.1 (*lumine Phoebi*). Note that ALD 26.1–2 also alternates between darkness and light, as here, and that both of the parallels noted here with ALD are to bird-aenigmata.

58.3 Note the dangling nominative here, as at BER 24.3; TAT 22.3; EUS 40.2, EUS 42.3, EUS 50.1, EUS 58.3 (the preponderance of these toward the end of the collection is striking). For the notion of "having a name," see the note at ALD 50.3. On the lengthening by position before *h-* here, see the note at EUS 28.4. Compare Virgil, *Aeneid* 2.605 (*Mortalis hebetat visus tibi et umida circum*).

58.6 It is unclear why the wind should come from the south. Compare Virgil, *Aeneid* 10.511 (*discrimine leti*); ALD 49.4 (*patior discrimine*), ALD 82.7 (*patitur discrimina*), ALD 87.2 (*patiens discrimina*).

58.7 Given the light/dark imagery here, it is tempting to see in *sola* a pun on *sol*, "sun"; compare in similar circumstances Aldhelm's use of *solebam* (albeit with *ŏ* rather than *ō*) in ALD 26.1, as noted at ALD 58.2 above.

EUS 59

MANUSCRIPTS: L, fol. 121r; G, fol. 374r.
EARLIER EDITIONS AND TRANSLATIONS: Gl, 270; Wl, 247–48. (SK 8036)
SOLUTION: *PSITTACUS* (parrot). See further ES, 197–98.

This aenigma, with its obvious focus on the garrulous nature of the bird in question, harks back both to the previous one, EUS 58 (*NOCTUA*, "owlet"), and to EUS 56 (*CICONIA*, "stork"). In this case, the poet's customary wordplay focuses on the key features of a parrot, namely its coloring and its ability to speak *(collum . . . colore; lingua loquax . . . loquelae)*. The observation that a parrot naturally makes sounds that mimic greetings in both Latin and Greek derives from Isidore, *Etym.* 12.7.24 (the specific parallels are in italics, following Wl):

> *Psittacus Indiae litoribus gignitur, colore viridi, torque puniceo, grandi lingua et ceteris avibus latiore. Unde et articulata verba exprimit, ita ut si eam non videris, hominem loqui putes. Ex natura autem salutat dicens: "have," vel "χαῖρε!" Cetera nomina institutione discit.* Hinc est illud:
>
> Psittacus a vobis aliorum nomina discam;
> hoc didici per me dicere: "Caesar have."
>
> *The parrot is produced on the shores of India, green in color, with a scarlet collar, and a big tongue which is broader than that of other birds. From there it produces fully formed words so that if you did not see it you would think a person was speaking. It gives a greeting naturally, saying, "Have!" or "χαῖρε!" Other words it learns through instruction.* Hence it is spoken of [Martial, *Epigramma* 14.73]: I am a parrot, will learn from you the names of others, / but on my own I have learnt to say this: "Hail *(Have)*, Caesar!"

Eusebius, or a scribe either of his works or of Isidore's, seems to have misunderstood the Greek, and may have deliberately substituted a

Latin vocative of the adjective *carus,* as if to say "(greetings), dear man." The use of the feminine form *amoenam* in EUS 59.1 in LG is at odds with the masculine gender of *psittacus,* but can be explained either as understanding *avem* or *volucrem,* "bird," or (appropriately enough) mimicking the genders of the other birds in this sequence (EUS 56–60).

59.1 The reading *amoenam* LG is contradicted by the masculine gender of *psitaccus,* unless Eusebius assumed *avem;* it seems safer to emend to *amoenum.*

59.4 Compare ALD 95.2 *(SCILLA,* "Scylla": *lingua loquelis);* TAT 10.3 *(RECITABULUM,* "lectern": *lingua loquendi);* EUS 12.4 *(BOS,* "bull": *verba sonabam).*

59.3 For the use of *tam* as a simple intensifier, see the note above on EUS 26.2.

59.6 A gloss in G explains *ave* as *salve.* The double elision in this line is unusually clumsy, even for Euesbius, though it seems farfetched to attribute it to an attempt to render "parrot-speak," even if the happy coincidence of the greeting *(ave)* and species *(avis)* is pleasing.

59.6–7 Compare Martial, *Epigramma* 14.71.1–2 (quoted in Isidore, *Etym.* 12.7.24).

EUS 60

MANUSCRIPTS: L, fol. 121r–v; G, fol. 374r–v.

EARLIER EDITIONS AND TRANSLATIONS: Gl, 271; Wl, 249. (SK 7675) See further ES, 190; Murphy, *Unriddling the Exeter Riddles,* 83.

SOLUTION: *BUBO* (horned owl); the given solution is *DE BUBALO,* "about a buffalo."

The fact that both manuscripts give the misleading solution suggests a high degree of confusion and ignorance, apparently emanating from *-b-* for *-f-* spellings of the kind discussed in the headnote on LEI below. Even the emended solution is not entirely without its problems, since *bubo* is usually masculine, and the creature in question is clearly feminine. However, *bubo* is apparently feminine in Virgil, *Aeneid* 4.462, which may have suggested the grammatical gender given here. Compare Isidore, *Etym.* 12.7.39 and 42 (the specific parallels are in italics, following Wl):

> *Bubo a sono vocis conpositum nomen habet, avis feralis, onusta quidem plumis, sed gravi semper detenta pigritia: in sepulcris die noctuque versatur, et semper commorans in cavernis.* De qua Ovidius:
>
> > Foedaque fit *volucris venturi nuntia luctus,*
> > *ignavus* bubo dirum mortalibus omen.
>
> Denique apud augures *malum portendere fertur:* nam cum in urbe visa fuerit, solitudinem significare dicunt. . . . Strix *nocturna avis, habens nomen de sono vocis*; quando enim clamat stridet. De qua Lucanus:
>
> > Quod trepidus bubo, quod strix nocturna queruntur.
>
> Haec avis vulgo amma dicitur, ab amando parvulos; unde et lac praebere fertur nascentibus.
>
> *The horned owl (bubo) has a name created from the sound of its call; it is a wild bird, certainly decked with feathers, but always held back by heavy laziness; it spends its time among tombs day and night, and always lurks about in caverns.* Ovid said this about it [*Metamorphoses* 5.549]:
>
> > He has become a dreadful *bird, a messenger of coming sorrow,* / the *lazy* horned owl, a dreadful omen for mortals.
>
> Finally, according to augurs, *it is said to signify evil,* for when it has been seen in a city, they say that it denotes desolation. . . . The screech owl is a *nocturnal bird, taking its name from the*

sound of its call, for when it calls it screeches. Lucan says this about it (*Bellum civile* 6.689):

> What the fearful horned owl and the nocturnal screech owl mourn.

This bird is commonly called *amma,* from loving *(amando)* its young, since it is also said to offer milk to its newly hatched chicks.

This aenigma is connected to EUS 56 and EUS 58–59 by reference to the creature's voice (emphasized through wordplay in the final line on *vocis . . . vocandum*), as well as to EUS 56–57 in the implied emphasis on the rearing of young, if Eusebius really does have Isidore's description of the *strix* in mind. Like the object of EUS 58 (*NOCTUA,* "owlet"), the description of which in Isidore immediately follows that of the *bubo,* this final creature has a dark quality about it, and indeed the darkness of both night and death, much like the closing subjects of Symphosius's final aenigmata (SYM 97–100: *UMBRA,* "shadow," *ECHO,* "echo," *SOMNIUM,* "dream," and *MONUMENTUM,* "tombstone"); see too OER 29 (*EAR,* "grave," the final riddle in the sequence). Note the extensive alliteration on *f-/p-/ph-/v-* throughout *(volucris venturi . . . vertor . . . phoebis . . . foeda . . . furva . . . umbriferas . . . vocis . . . vocandum),* with a local focus on *p* at EUS 60.2 *(pigraque perseverans . . . prae pondere plumae).*

60.1 Compare Ovid, *Metamorphoses* 5.549–50 (quoted in Isidore, *Etym.* 12.7.39). In quoting so freely from Ovid, the author introduces a false quantity: the normal form in the nominative (as here) is *ignavă.* For another example of borrowing from the classical poets cited by Isidore, see the note on EUS 47.5 (*SCITALE,* "piebald serpent") above. Very similar kinds of borrowing from the works of previous poets are also found in the Exeter Book riddles; compare EXE 36.6–7, and the note there.

60.3 A gloss in G explains *phoebis* as *diebus.*

60.5 Compare EXE 55.6b *(STAFAS,* "letters": *nemnað hi sylfe).*

BONIFACE

Authorship and Date

Boniface (b. ca. 675, d. 754) is perhaps best known as the Apostle to the Germans, a mission that was entrusted to him by Pope Gregory II in 716–17, when the pope also gave him the name by which he is now best known; he was born, certainly in Wessex, perhaps in Crediton, with the name Wynfrith.

Manuscript Context(s)

For a discussion of the rather convoluted continental manuscript transmission, see DüB, 1–3. The only manuscript of BON from Anglo-Saxon England (albeit written in France, likely at Limoges) is A[1], which lacks BON PR but follows the order used here, and was not collated by either DüB or Gl.

Subject Matter and Solutions

Unlike others in the Anglo-Saxon riddle tradition, Boniface sets out from the start both to focus on a conscious collection of connected abstract themes, in this case ten vices and virtues, and, while he is primarily in thrall to Aldhelm, to go beyond Tatwine in his use of an acrostic as a structuring principle, using the form to embed the solutions instead of securing the sequence. The dedication to an unnamed "sister" squares perfectly with what we know from his frequent correspondence with a variety of well-born Anglo-Saxon women who either supported his mission from home, or more intrepidly risked their lives and virtue in following him to the Continent. The suggestion by Gl that BON is dedicated to Leoba/Leofgyth (ca. 710–782), who corresponded with Boniface several times, including on the topic of verse composition, is attractive but cannot be proven.

Style

Boniface's style is among the roughest and least elegant of all those exhibited in the aenigmata. Like Aldhelm, his primary model, Boniface is very fond of compound adjectives, together with those formed from the (mostly poetic) suffixes *-abilis*, *-alis*, *-eus*, *-fer*, *-ficus*, *-genus*, *-ger*, and

-osus, albeit with many repetitions; there are seventy-nine of them in the collection, but such a high number masks the fact that the overwhelming majority of them are commonplace, banal, or simple repetitions (nine are forms of *aureus* and eight of *igneus*).

Sources and Parallels

Boniface's primary model is Aldhelm, as the sheer number of verbal parallels (even extending to metrical bloopers, as for example the hiatus in BON P1) makes plain in the notes to almost every single aenigma in BON, and indeed elsewhere in Boniface's letters and other poems. See further Orchard, *Poetic Art of Aldhelm.*

This Text and Translation

Here I rely heavily on DüB; several individual debts are acknowledged in the notes.

Further Reading

Dümmler, Ernst, ed. *Aenigmata Bonifatii*; Finch, "The Text of the *Aenigmata* of Boniface in Codex Reg. Lat. 1553."

BON PR

MANUSCRIPTS: Not in A[1]; G, fol. 382r–v; L[2], fol. 204r.
EARLIER EDITIONS AND TRANSLATIONS: DüB, 3–4; Gl, 278–81. (SK 1448)

Aside from the fundamental problem regarding the addressee, an issue compounded by the fact that there are several "sisters" who figure in Boniface's extensive extant letter collection, on whom see in particular Fell, "Some Implications of the Boniface Correspondence," the verse preface is a relatively straightforward piece of poetry: the twenty lines of verse break easily into two groups of ten, each dealing with the groups of ten virtues and ten vices that follow. The parallel and repeated references to coming joyful rewards on high that are either promoted or prevented by the apples growing on the trees in question, in BON PR.1–2 and 9–10 on the one hand and 11–12 and 19–20 on the other (compare *poma . . . in ligno vitae . . . cum quibus*

... malis ... regna futura ... gaudia caeli and *mala ... in ligno mortis ... talibus ... malis ... foedera sancta ... superi ... praemia regni*), set out the basic bipartite schema, with a certain amount of wordplay on *nardi/nares* in the first half and *maligna/malis* in the second. The first ten lines, dealing with the virtues, are characterized by a close parallelism of structure, with most of them featuring medial finite verbs of precisely the same metrical *molossus*-structure, consisting of three long syllables *(transmisi ... crescebant ... pendebant ... pendebat ... conprendas ... conpares)*; the second ten lines employ this template only twice *(franguntur ... perdantur)*. Such a pattern is a hallmark of Aldhelm's metrical works, and it is no surprise that he should be the single most imitated author throughout these aenigmata, as the notes clearly show. Within the ten lines referring to the virtues, moreover, the first four lines are likewise distinguished by referring to the past; the remaining six invoke the future through both the subjunctive and the future tense itself. A clearly parallel pattern emerges in the ten lines referring to the vices, with the first five focusing on these apples as still very much present, despite their historical harm, and the second five again expressing hopes for the future. Boniface implicitly contrasts the fatal action of Adam in "chewing" *(manducans)* the wrong kind of apples in the past with what he hopes for his addressee "chewing" *(manducans)* the right kind of apples in future.

Presumably the chewing in question also equates to the practice of *ruminatio,* which the essentially didactic and hectoring tone of Boniface's verses seems to admit. Such rigid parallelism is characteristic of Boniface's work, and presumably accounts for the oddities of BON PR.6, which as it stands is difficult both to scan and to construe. The unique form *complearis* cannot be accommodated to hexameter verse at all, unless by an odd kind of synizesis that would consider it yet another metrical *molossus,* although such a solution still leaves the line too long by a syllable. I have preferred to take *complearis* as masking an original *plena,* and the whole line as simply an extension of the description of joys both now and later. But such an editorial conjecture is hazardous, given Boniface's proven track record of verses that include both false quantities and other infelicities.

PR.1 A false quantity: *dĕcem* is the normal usage, unless Boniface has been misled by apparent hiatus of *decem* in ALD 30.1 (hiatus is assumed, since in his other three uses of the word, Aldhelm follows the norm). The scribe of G attempts to correct the fault by using *iure*.

PR.2 Compare BON PR.4 *(lignum vitae)*; BON PR.12 *(quae in ligno mortis)*; BON 10.1 *(floribus almis)*.

PR.3 Compare Aldhelm, *Carmen de virginitate* 342 *(dulcia de ramis)*.

PR.5 Compare Aldhelm, *Carmen ecclesiasticum* 3.63 *(gaudia mentis)*.

PR.6 The form *complearis* is an oddity, and would not scan in normal usage, while the line as a whole has too many syllables, a feature recognized in several manuscripts, which omit *tibi*. Perhaps the form *plearis* is intended, if Boniface considered it a disyllabic form through synizesis; compare BON 15.12, where an original form *misceantur*, regarded as trisyllabic, seems intended (on synizesis, see the headnote to BED 9). A gloss in G offers the alternative *repletus* for *complearis*.

PR.7 Compare ALD 100.31 *(nectaris haustus)*; BON 13.55 *(mulsum . . . nectaris haustum)*, BON 17.2 *(nectaris haustus)*; Aldhelm, *Carmen de virginitate* 239 *(nectaris et mellis mulsos)*; Aldhelm, *Carmen de virginitate* 2541 *(nectaris . . . mulsa)*.

PR.8 A gloss in G explains that *saeve* is an adverb. Compare ALD 100.16 *(spirantis nardi . . . plena)*.

PR.9 A false quantity: *conpăres* is the normal usage.

PR.10 A gloss in G explains *quondam* as *quandoque*.

PR.11 A false quantity: *ăcervissima* (for *ăcerbissima*) is the normal usage, giving the line a second elision. On such *-b-* for *-v-* or *-f-* spellings, see EXE 21.1 and the headnote on LEI below.

PR.12 Compare BON PR.12 *(quae in ligno mortis)*.

PR.13 Compare BON 13.21 *(morte peremi)*.

PR.14 Note the insistent alliteration here. The line contains both elision (twice), in *antiqui infecta* and *infecta et*, and hiatus, in *flatu et*.

PR.15 A gloss in G offers the alternative *repletus* for *complearis*. A false quantity: *perlĭta* is the normal usage, but compare Aldhelm, *Carmen de virginitate* 2575 *(lita veneno)*.

PR.16 A gloss in G supplies *mala* after *haec,* and explains *virgo* as *Æva.*

PR.18 A false quantity: *strīdeant* is the normal usage, but compare Aldhelm, *Carmen de virginitate* 2795 *(aut dentes stridant).*

PR.20 Compare BON 2.12 and 5.4 *(praemia regni);* Aldhelm, *Carmen de virginitate* 2005 *(praemia regni).*

BON 1

MANUSCRIPTS: A[1], fol. 1r1; G, fol. 383r–v (no. 5); L[2], fol. 204v–5r (no. 5).
EARLIER EDITIONS AND TRANSLATIONS: DüB, 6; Gl, 282–83. (SK 17248)
SOLUTION: *VERITAS* (truth); the acrostic reads *VERITAS AIT* (truth speaks).

This aenigma, like BON PR, splits easily into two halves, and demonstrates the tidy mind that Boniface exhibits throughout.

1.1 Compare SYM 58.1 *(Findere me nulli possunt);* ALD 2.1 *(Cernere me nulli possunt).* A gloss in G supplies *possunt* after *perdere multi.*

1.2 Compare BON 7.11 *(Christi quia sedibus adsto).*

1.4 Compare ALD 2.4; LOR 2.6 *(rura peragro).*

1.5 Compare ALD 8.1 *(stolidi dixere);* Aldhelm, *Carmen de virginitate* 1000 *(stolidi dicunt)* and 1332 *(stolidi dixerunt);* BON 6.3 *(terras liquisse nefandas).*

1.6 Compare BON 13.57 *(amplius in sceptris mundi).* A gloss in G gives an alternative to its reading, *degener erro,* as *degere nolo.*

1.8 Compare ALD PR.34 *(cecinit quod carmine David).*

1.9 Compare Aldhelm, *Carmen de virginitate* 1811 *(pro virgine adempta).* See too Psalms 5:10: *non est enim in ore eorum rectum interiora eorum insidiae,* "For there is no truth in their mouth: their heart is vain."

1.10 Compare ALD 37.5 *(sidere scando);* Aldhelm, *Carmen de virginitate* 2273 *(sidera scandunt).* There is tmesis of *trans . . . fugiens,* on which metrical license see the note at TAT 8.6 above.

BON 2

MANUSCRIPTS: A[1], fol. 1r1; G, fol. 382v–83r; L[2], fol. 204r–v.
EARLIER EDITIONS AND TRANSLATIONS: DüB, 4–5; Gl, 284–85. (SK 4977)
SOLUTION: *FIDES* (faith); the acrostic reads *FIDES CATHOLICA* (Catholic faith).

2.6 A gloss in G explains *Clamor* as *vocor.*

2.10 Compare BON 13.15 *(finibus orbis).*

2.11 Compare ALD PR.24 *(lumina saeclis).* The intended scansion *lucifluā* seems to occur through an odd lengthening at ictus or (again oddly) because of the following consonant cluster of a mute and liquid, here *pr-*. Compare BON 5.11, 9.20, 12.7, 13.18, and 14.2.

2.12 Compare ALD 91.5; BON 20.6 *(praemia vitae);* BON PR.20, BON 5.4 *(praemia regni);* Aldhelm, *Carmen de virginitate* 2005 *(praemia regni).* A false quantity: *rēlicta* is the normal usage; G corrects this by reading *nullusque.*

2.13 Compare Aldhelm, *Carmen de virginitate* 555 *(gratia fulgens).*

2.14 Compare BIB 8.11 *(scandere regna);* BON 8.17 *(heu miseris),* BON 17.11 *(heu miseri);* Aldhelm, *Carmen ecclesiasticum* 3.31, *Carmen de virginitate* 755 and 2160 *(regna polorum).* A gloss in G supplies *mihi* after *miserae.*

BON 3

MANUSCRIPTS: A[1], fol. 1r1; G, fol. 383r; L[2], fol. 204v.
EARLIER EDITIONS AND TRANSLATIONS: DüB, 5; Gl, 286–87. (SK 14596)
SOLUTION: *SPES* (hope); the acrostic reads *SPES FATUR* (hope declares).

3.3 Compare ALD 59.8, 86.4, and 100.3; TAT 40.4; BON 4.12, 8.8, 14.1, 16.12, and 17.7 *(caeli culmina, culmina caelorum, culmina caeli* or *culmine caeli).*

3.4 Reading *fata* for *facta,* which appears in many manuscripts: "fates," especially in the transfigurative sense of "death," seems to fit better with *fortunata* in the following line.

3.5 A gloss in G gives an alternative reading *et* for *si*.

3.6 A gloss in G explains *starent* as *desinerent*.

3.7 The term *Terrigenae*, "earth-dwellers," is evidently something of a favorite of Boniface's; compare BON 6.4, 9.21, 13.7, and 20.17.

3.8 The translation assumes a rather awkward hyperbaton *ad . . . poenas*, but seems the best way to construe the line.

BON 4

MANUSCRIPTS: A[1], fol. 1r1–2; G, fol. 383v (no. 6); L[2], fol. 205r (no. 6).
EARLIER EDITIONS AND TRANSLATIONS: DüB, 6; Gl, 288–89. (SK 9784)
SOLUTION: *MISERICORDIA* (mercy); the acrostic reads *MISERICORDIA AIT* (mercy speaks).

This aenigma is clearly a companion piece to BON 6 (*IUSTITIA*, "justice"), and Justice is the sister in question. If BON 5 is misplaced, then these aenigmata are contiguous, as they indeed appear in several manuscripts.

4.1 Compare ALD 23.1 *(geminas . . . sorores)*; BIB 9.1 *(geminae sorores)*; ALD 49.4 *(geminas vario)*. A gloss in G explains its reading, *vire*, as *vigore*.

4.4 Reading *luerent* for the otherwise baffling *lustrent*; I am grateful to Rob Getz for the suggestion.

4.5 Compare BON 8.2 *(sola per orbem)*.

4.9 Compare ALD 91.3 *(Nomine nempe meo)*; EUS 39.2 *(nempe mearum)*, EUS 43.4 *(Nomine nempe meo)*; BON 19.2 *(Germine nempe meo)*.

4.10 Reading *superi* for the manuscript *superis*, which makes little sense: why would those already in heaven require the light of mercy?

4.11 A gloss in G explains its reading, *Ingenti*, as a dative, *mundi* as a genitive, and its reading, *arvo*, as *telluri*. Compare Aldhelm, *Carmen de virginitate* 1669 *(floribus arva)*.

4.12 Compare ALD 59.8, 86.4, and 100.3; TAT 40.4; BON 3.3 *(caeli culmina, culmina caelorum, culmina caeli* or *culmine caeli),* BON 6.8 *(Aurea gens hominum),* BON 8.8, 14.1, 16.12, and 17.7 *(culmina caeli* or *culmine caeli).* The word *aurea* can agree with either *culmina* or *gens;* the parallel at BON 6.8 supports the latter reading. A gloss in G explains its reading, *qua,* as *per me.*

4.14 The second syllable of *impetrans* must be read as lengthened before *-tr-*. Compare ALD 23.4 and BON 8.1 *(fieret mortalibus aevum).*

4.15 Reading *ministra,* as in L[2]; other manuscripts prefer *ministro.* The verb *trano* is evidently another of Boniface's favorites: compare BON 9.23, 17.7, and 19.8.

BON 5

MANUSCRIPTS: A[1], fol. 1r2; G, fol. 382v (no. 1); L[2], fol. 204r (no. 1).
EARLIER EDITIONS AND TRANSLATIONS: DüB, 4; Gl, 290–91. (SK 2108)
SOLUTION: *CARITAS* (love, charity).

The double acrostic reads *CARITAS AIT* (love speaks), with *CARITAS* spelled out twice, both forwards at the beginning of the odd-numbered hexameters and in reverse in the corresponding even-numbered hexameters. This poem follows on immediately from BON PR in several manuscripts, including the Anglo-Saxon GL[2]. Note the double parallel to the connected sequence ALD 63–64 (*CORBUS,* "raven," and *COLUMBA,* "dove").

5.1 Compare ALD 54.1 *(credere quis poterit)* and ALD 73.4 *(quis numerus capiat vel quis laterculus aequet);* Aldhelm, *Carmen de virginitate* 855 *(quis modus aut numerus vel certe calculus index);* Aldhelm, *Carmen rhythmicum* 117–18 *(Quae nullus nequit numero / conputare in calculo);* BON 13.20 *(numerus aut calculus aequat).* This line contains both elision *(numero aut)* and hiatus *(calculo aequat,* presumably with shortening in *calculŏ),* although several manuscripts and editions, including G and DüB, read *calculus* to get around the latter.

5.2 Compare ALD PR.24 *(splendida . . . saeclis).* Note the nonclassical nonce form *praestavi,* where *praestitui* is preferred.

5.3 Compare Aldhelm, *Carmen de virginitate* 308 *(praesentis . . . vitae).*

5.4 Compare BON PR.20 and 2.12 *(praemia regni);* Aldhelm, *Carmen de virginitate* 271 *(atque futurorum),* 595 *(atque futurarum),* and 2005 *(praemia regni).*

5.5 Compare ALD 64.3 *(complevi iussa parentis);* BON 7.10 *(conplentur iussa superna).*

5.6 Compare Aldhelm, *Carmen de virginitate* 2876 *(miserescat in aevum).* A gloss in G explains *in* as *per.*

5.7 Compare BON 17.9 *(mortale genus).* The nonce form *iuvavi* is also nonclassical, where *iuvi* is preferred.

5.8 Compare Aldhelm, *Carmen de virginitate* 759 and 2072 *(famularier alto).*

5.9 Compare Aldhelm, *Carmen de virginitate* 99 *(mundani luxus calcans ludibria falsa),* 806 *(calcans ludicra severus),* and 1713 *(ludicra luxus);* BON 10.7 *(ludicra luxus).* Echoing Aldhelm closely may have led Boniface to produce a line that is too short by a syllable; the reading *calcent ut* in G and in DüB seems to be the result of conscious correction. A gloss in G explains *ludicra* as *fomenta.*

5.10 Compare Aldhelm, *Carmen ecclesiasticum* 3.2 *(filia regis);* BON 6.5 *(caelorum . . . filia regis).*

5.11 Compare Aldhelm, *Carmen de virginitate* 31 *(pulsare tonantem)* and 2811 *(ad requiem tendens).* The intended scansion *reginā* must be either through lengthening at ictus or because of the following consonant cluster of a mute and liquid, here *cl-*. Compare BON 2.11, 9.20, 12.7, 13.18, and 14.2.

5.12 Compare Aldhelm, *Carmen de virginitate* 2826 *(actibus aut dictis seu . . . sensu)* and 2871 *(ut . . . vincla resoluant).*

5.13 Compare Aldhelm, *Carmen de virginitate* 2745 *(sedibus et superis).*

5.14 Compare Aldhelm, *Carmen de virginitate* 2885 *(restaurat . . . saecla redemptor).*

5.15 Compare ALD PR.1 *(arbiter aethereo);* Aldhelm, *Carmen de virginitate* 615 *(calceque carebit)* and 2874 *(calce carens).*

5.16 Compare Virgil, *Aeneid* 1.278 *(nec metas . . . nec tempora).*

BON 6

MANUSCRIPTS: A[1], fol. 1r2; G, fol. 383r (no. 4); L[2], fol. 204v (no. 4).
EARLIER EDITIONS AND TRANSLATIONS: DüB, 5; Gl, 292–93. (SK 7682)
SOLUTION: *IUSTITIA* (justice); the acrostic reads *IUSTITIA DIXIT* (justice has said).

This aenigma is clearly a companion piece to BON 4 (*MISERICORDIA AIT,* "mercy speaks"). For the theme of kissing here, see the headnote to ALD 80.

6.3 Compare BON 1.5 *(Terras . . . liquisse nefandas);* compare too Virgil, *Georgics* 2.473–74 *(extrema per illos / iustitia excedens terris vestigia fecit).* A gloss in G supplies *dicor* after *liquisse.*

6.4 Compare BON 19.11 *(cernitur usquam);* the term *Terrigenae,* "earth-dwellers," is a favorite of Boniface's; compare BON 3.7, 9.21, 13.7, and BON 20.17. A gloss in G explains *Terrigenis* as ablative.

6.5 Compare BON 5.10 *(caelorum filia regis).*

6.6 A gloss in G explains its reading, *genitus,* as *filius.*

6.8 Compare BON 4.12 *(Aurea gens hominum).*

6.9 Compare ALD 23.5 *(normam si servent).*

6.9 Compare Aldhelm, *Carmen de virginitate* 2163 *(virginis almus).*

6.12 Compare ALD 79.11 *(Erebi . . . Tartara nigri);* BON 14.4 *(trudens in Tartara nigra).* A gloss in G supplies *loca* after *tristia.*

BON 7

MANUSCRIPTS: A[1], fol. 1r2–v1; G, fol. 383v–84r; L[2], fol. 205r.
EARLIER EDITIONS AND TRANSLATIONS: DüB, 6–7; Gl, 294–95. (SK 11847)
SOLUTION: *PATIENTIA* (patience); the acrostic reads *PATIENTIA AIT* (patience speaks).

7.2 A gloss in G supplies *sunt* after *expulsi.*

7.3 Compare BON 20.10 *(perdunt . . . pia facta).*

7.4 Reading *reorum;* G and other manuscripts (and DüB) read *meorum.*

7.5 The rather rare word *scaevus,* found here and at BON 8.15 and 12.3, has evidently been taken from Aldhelm, who uses it no fewer than fourteen times in his *Carmen de virginitate,* as well as once in his *Carmina ecclesiastica,* but never in ALD.

7.8 Compare ALD 100.30 *(torrentibus ardens).*

7.9 For the future form *vocabor* used in place of the present tense, see the note at ALD 33.6.

7.10 Compare ALD 20.3, BON 15.11, and 20.10 *(Arte mea);* ALD 64.3 *(complevi iussa parentis);* BON 5.5 *(conplentur iussa superna).*

7.11 Compare BON 1.2 *(Christi quod sedibus adsto).*

BON 8

MANUSCRIPTS: A[1], fol. 1v1; G, fol. 384r; L[2], fol. 205r–v.
EARLIER EDITIONS AND TRANSLATIONS: DüB, 7; Gl, 296–99. (SK 11522)
SOLUTION: *PAX* (peace); the acrostic reads *PAX VERA CRISTIANA* (true Christian peace), followed by five further and more enigmatic letters *HQCQQ.*

8.1 Compare ALD 23.4 *(fieret mortalibus aevum)* and BON 4.14 *(mortalibus aevi).*

8.2 Compare BON 4.5 *(sola per orbem).*

8.3 A reference to the angelic *Gloria in excelsis* in Luke 2:14.

8.4 Compare Aldhelm, *Carmen de virginitate* 247 *(saecla beavit)* and 394 *(saecula cuncta beavit).*

8.5 A gloss in G offers the alternative *ditor* for *dicor.*

8.6 Note the polyptoton in *vernacula vernans.*

8.8 Compare ALD 59.8, 86.4, and ALD 100.3; TAT 40.4; BON 3.3, 4.12, 14.1, 16.12, and 17.7; Aldhelm, *Carmen de virginitate* 2, 1445, and 2816 *(caeli culmina, culmina caelorum, culmina caeli* or *culmine caeli).*

8.9 The word *inlustro* carries the same dual sense of "wander through" and "illuminate" here as elsewhere; see the note at ALD 5.4 (*IRIS*, "rainbow") above.

8.10 A false quantity: *rŏgor* is the normal usage; G corrects to *poscor.*

8.14 Compare Aldhelm, *Carmen de virginitate* 1555 *(mente maligna).* It seems necessary to translate active *habere* as if *haberi;* all the manuscripts have *habere.*

8.16 A gloss in G explains *parta* as *parata.* Compare BON 2.14 *(heu miserae)* and 17.11 *(heu miseri).*

8.17 A gloss in G explains *quis* as *quibus,* so acknowledging the form *metri gratia.*

BON 9

MANUSCRIPTS: A[1], fol. 1v1–2; G, fol. 384r–v; L[2], fol. 205v.
EARLIER EDITIONS AND TRANSLATIONS: DüB, 7–8; Gl, 300–303. (SK 6495)
SOLUTION: *HUMILITAS* (humility); the acrostic reads *HUMILITAS CRISTIANA FATETUR* (Christian humility confesses), although in G the acrostic is spoiled.

9.1 A gloss in G supplies *sum* after *vix.*

9.2 Compare ALD 44.8 *(nigrior exsto).*

9.4 Compare BON 10.15 *(non est pulchrior ulla),* BON 11.1 *(Non est in terris me virgo stultior ulla),* BON 14.8 *(in terris non est crudelior ulla).*

9.8 Compare Aldhelm, *Carmen de virginitate* 873 *(scandens caelorum culmina).*

9.9 A gloss in G gives an alternative to its reading, *iure,* as *sorte.* Reading *sororum,* although compare ALD 66.1 *(sorte sorores).*

9.10 Reading *sim,* though GL[2] read *sit* and other manuscripts read *sint.*

9.12 Note the hiatus at *Innumeri heroes.*

9.13 A false quantity: *martyrum* with a short *y* is the normal usage, as in BON 10.9 *(Almae martyrii).*

9.14 Compare BON 13.12 *(viros . . . cum matribus).*

9.15 Compare ALD 93.2; Aldhelm, *Carmen de virginitate* 2740 *(viribus audax).*

9.19 Reading *monarchus,* for metrical reasons; the manuscripts mostly read *monachus,* which will not scan.

9.20 The intended scansion *meā* must be through an odd lengthening at ictus or (again oddly) because of the following consonant cluster of a mute and liquid, here *pr-*. Compare BON 2.11, 5.11, 12.7, 13.18, and 14.2

9.21 The term *Terrigenae,* "earth-dwellers," is a favorite of Boniface's; compare BON 3.7, 6.4, 13.7, and BON 20.17.

9.22 Compare Aldhelm, *Carmen de virginitate* 2158 *(lectissima virgo).*

9.24 There is a pun on *viribus* and *virago;* in using the form *virago* in preference to *virgo,* Boniface is echoing Aldhem's usage (see the note on ALD 95.6 above, as well as BON 10.13 and 16.2).

BON 10

MANUSCRIPTS: A[1], fol. 1v2; G, fol. 384v–85r; L[2], fol. 205v (only BON 10.1–5).

EARLIER EDITIONS AND TRANSLATIONS: DüB, 8–9; Gl, 304–7. (SK 17424)

SOLUTION: *VIRGINITAS* (virginity); the acrostic reads *VIRGINITAS AIT HUMILIUM* (the virginity of the humble speaks), although in G the acrostic is spoiled.

10.1 Compare BON PR.2 *(floribus almis).*

10.4 The theme of mothers giving birth to their own parents is common throughout the tradition as a whole, beginning with ps-SYM, which Aldhelm quotes as his inspiration; see too the note at ALD 33.1.

10.5 Compare Aldhelm, *Carmen ecclesiasticum* 5.9 *(sanguine saecla).*

10.7 Compare BON 5.9 *(ludicra luxus);* Aldhelm, *Carmen de virginitate* 1713 *(contemnens ludicra luxus).*

10.9 Compare Aldhelm, *Carmen ecclesiasticum* 4.9.12; Aldhelm, *Carmen de virginitate* 1121, 1444, 1766, 2341 *(martirii . . . serta).*

10.11 Compare Aldhelm, *Carmen de virginitate* 188 *(aurea flammigeris).*

10.12 Reading *splendentia* in place of *splendentes,* which does not work in terms of grammar. Compare BON 19.8 *(sidera supra);* Aldhelm, *Carmen de virginitate* 2902 *(sidera supra).*

10.14 Compare ALD 96.11 *(bratea . . . metallis);* Aldhelm, *Carmen de virginitate* 157 *(auri . . . metallum).*

10.15 Compare BON 9.4 *(In terris nusquam . . . vilior ulla),* BON 11.1 *(Non est in terris me virgo stultior ulla),* BON 14.8 *(in terris non est crudelior ulla).*

10.16 Note the extensive alliteration on *c-* in this line.

10.18 Compare ALD 91.5; BON 20.6 *(praemia vitae);* Aldhelm, *Carmen de virginitate* 1226 *(lucida perpetuae . . . praemia vitae).* Reading *te* produces a hiatus; compare BON PR.14, BON 9.18, BON 13.2, 13.6, 13.18, 13.66; BON 14.8. Note the hiatus at *exspectant;* this is a rare golden line.

10.19 The emendation to *aeternusque* (as G has it) is very tempting, but the notion of an inner light forms a likely parallel with the preceding line.

10.20 Compare ALD 63.4 *(foedera iuris).* The intended scansion *meā* must be through lengthening at ictus or because of the following consonant cluster of mute plus liquid (here *pr-*). See too BON 2.11 *(Luciflua promunt)* and 5.10 *(Regina clamor).*

BON EP

MANUSCRIPTS: A[1], fol. 1v2; G, fol. 385r (in both cases, it follows directly from BON 10).

EARLIER EDITIONS AND TRANSLATIONS: DüB, 9; Gl, 308–9. (SK 477)

In the manuscripts, this epilogue is attached to BON 10, but it seems reasonable to consider it a separate piece, describing as it does the special status of the virtues even among the elect in heaven, and their special song.

EP.2 A gloss in G explains its reading, *carmen hoc,* as *tale.*

BON 11

MANUSCRIPTS: A[1], fol. 2r1; G, fol. 388r (no. 19).
EARLIER EDITIONS AND TRANSLATIONS: DüB, 14; Gl, 310–11. (SK 10405)
SOLUTION: *NEGLEGENTIA* (negligence); the acrostic reads *NEGLEGENTIA AIT* (negligence speaks).

11.1 Compare BON 9.4 *(In terris nusquam . . . vilior ulla),* BON 10.15 *(non est pulchrior ulla),* BON 14.8 *(in terris non est crudelior ulla).*

11.4 Compare Aldhelm, *Carmen ecclesiasticum* 3.68 and 4.8.9 *(limpida . . . lumina);* Aldhelm, *Carmen de virginitate* 181 *(lustrat dum terras),* 775 *(lustrant lumina),* and 959 and 1404 *(limpida . . . lumina).* A gloss in G explains *quoque modo* as *quali cursu* and *lumina terras* as *luminaria sol et luna.* The double sense of *lustro* as "illuminate"and "traverse" seems likely here, as elsewhere, even if the use of *perlustro* in that context is not classical; see the note at ALD 5.4, and compare ALD PR.12 above.

11.5 The future form *depingent* seems to stand for a present, as elsewhere; see the note at ALD 33.6 above.

11.7 Note the extraordinary alliteration in *varias voluisset fingere formas.*

11.8 Compare Virgil, *Aeneid* 1.630 *(non ignara mali).*

11.11 Compare ALD 76.6; BON 13.66 *(arbiter orbis).*

11.12 Compare TAT 1.3; BON 16.13 *(ima profundi).*

11.14 Compare BON 13.60 *(dicor dulcissima virgo).*

BON 12

MANUSCRIPTS: A[1], fol. 2r1; G, fol. 388r–v (no. 20).
EARLIER EDITIONS AND TRANSLATIONS: DüB, 14–15; Gl, 312–15. (SK 7680)
SOLUTION: *IRACUNDIA* (anger); the acrostic reads *IRACUNDIA LOQUITUR* (anger declares).

12.2 Compare Aldhelm, *Carmen de virginitate* 1328 and 1545 *(corda venenis).*

12.3 For the use of the adverb *scaeve* here, see the note at BON 7.5.

12.4 A gloss in G explains its reading, *disseco,* as *dissiungo.*

12.5 Compare ALD 2.3 *(viribus . . . valeo confringere quercus);* BON 18.3; BER 63.3 *(Viribus atque meis).* A gloss in G offers an alternative for *sensus* in *mentes.*

12.6 A false quantity: *rătum* is the normal usage. A gloss in G supplies *valeo depellere* after its reading, *utque ratum* (which does scan).

12.7 The intended scansion *meā* must be through lengthening at ictus or because of the following consonant cluster of a mute and liquid, here *tr-*. Compare BON 2.11, 5.11, 9.20, 13.18, and 14.2.

12.10 Compare Aldhelm, *Carmen de virginitate* 1327 *(semina spargit).*

12.14 Compare ALD 41.1 *(irrita dicta).*

12.15 Compare ALD 37.2–3 *(spatior . . . retrograda).*

12.17 It is tempting to read *retibus;* compare Aldhelm, *Carmen de virginitate* 537 *(retibus angelicis raptos ex aequore mundi).* Retaining *ritibus,* which is found in both manuscripts, however, requires the word to be understood in the sense "offices, services, practices," as it appears to be at BON 5.5.

BON 13

MANUSCRIPTS: A[1], fol. 2r1–2 (up to 13.1–12); G, fol. 385r–86r (no. 11).
EARLIER EDITIONS AND TRANSLATIONS: DüB, 9–11; Gl, 316–23. (SK 2101)
SOLUTION: *CUPIDITAS* (greed); the acrostic reads *CUPIDITAS AIT* (greed speaks), in BON 13.1–12, with a further fifty-five lines of explanation. This extensive coda, however, is composed in the same heavily Aldhelmian style, and there seems no good reason to regard it as an interpolation.

13.1 Note that the opening word *Cernebam* aligns this aenigma with a whole range of riddles, mostly in Old English, that begin with some form of "I saw" (see Orchard, "Enigma Variations," 289–95). Compare ALD 97.13 *(NOX,* "night": *monstrum horrendum, ingens, cui quot sunt corpora plumae)* (= Virgil, *Aeneid* 4.181); BON 16.15 *(EBRIETAS,* "drunkenness": *per saecula monstrum).* The syntax is ambiguous: the present participle *lustrans* could refer to either the speaker or the *monstrum;* here, I opt for the latter.

13.2 Compare ALD 69.4 *(viribus horrendis).* Note both elision and hiatus in *dictu effabili ulli;* compare Virgil, *Aeneid* 3.621 *(Nec visu facilis nec dictu affabilis ulli).* Boniface is the first Latin poet to use the word *effabilis.*

13.3 Compare Aldhelm, *Carmen de virginitate* 2726 *(sanguine purpureo).* The subjunctive *maculet* (if that is the intention) is unusual: the scribe of the C manuscript corrects to the indicative *maculat.*

13.4 A gloss in G supplies *et* after *pectora.*

13.5 Compare ALD 96.6 *(murmura Martis).*

13.6 Compare Aldhelm, *Carmen de virginitate* 849 *(ad inferni . . . tartara).* Note double hiatus in *ignea inferni animabus.* The form *animabus* is unusual, though it is found in Aldhelm, *Carmen de virginitate* 2641, as well as twice in Prudentius.

13.7 The term *Terrigenae,* "earth-dwellers," is a favorite of Boniface's; compare BON 3.7, 6.4, 9.21, and 20.17.

13.8 Compare ALD 21.2–3 *(metallum / Auri materias);* ALD 55.5 *(Aurea . . . fulvis . . . metallis),* ALD 96.11 *(auri fulvis . . . metallis);* Aldhelm, *Carmen de virginitate* 157 *(auri materiem fulvi . . . metallum).*

13.9 Compare ALD 11.1 *(fratre gemello).*

13.10 For the spelling *gnatus,* compare BON 19.6 and Boniface, *Carmen* 2.30. Two false quantities: the normal usages are *gnātus* and *bĭbat.*

13.12 Compare BON 9.14 *(viri . . . cum matribus);* BER 50.1 *(DE VINO,* "on wine": *de matribus unum).* For *matres* ("mothers") used apparently to mean no more than "women," compare BON 9.14 and 17.12.

13.13 Compare ALD 67.7 *(limina Ditis).* A gloss in G explains *Ditis* as *Orci.*

13.14 Compare BON 13.24 *(haud secus).* A gloss in G supplies *quam sic* after its reading, *Haud secus.*

13.15 Compare BON 2.10 *(finibus orbis).* Beyond this example, the only others of *pinnipotens* in Latin poetry are in Lucretius,

De rerum natura 2.878 and 5.789 (where it is spelled *pennipotens*). A gloss in G explains its reading, *bestia pennipotens,* as *cupido dicit.*

13.16 Compare ALD 5.1 *(famine fingor).*

13.17 Compare ALD 70.3 *(carior et multo);* Aldhelm, *Carmen ecclesiasticum* 4.1.17 *(lumina vitae);* Aldhelm, *Carmen de virginitate* 308 *(lumina vitae).*

13.18 Note hiatus at *ego.* The intended scansion *infestā* must be through lengthening at ictus or because of the following consonant cluster of a mute and liquid, here *cr-*. Compare BON 5.11, 9.20, 12.7, and 14.2.

13.19 A gloss in G explains its reading, *stropha,* as *fraude.* Compare BON 14.16 *(prosternere nitor).*

13.20–65 This whole passage of demonic bragging about human conquests has several general parallels with a similar one in Cynewulf's *Juliana* (351–417a); it is noteworthy that the Old English version lacks a specific match in the putative Latin source.

13.20 Compare ALD 73.4 *(quis numerus . . . vel quis laterculus aequet)* and BON 5.1 *(numero aut quis calculo aequat);* Aldhelm, *Carmen de virginitate* 855 *(aut numerus . . . calculus index);* 5.1 *(quis . . . numero aut quis calculo aequat).*

13.21 A gloss in G explains its reading, *strophosa,* as *dolosa.* Compare BON PR.13 *(morte peremptus).*

13.22 A gloss in G explains *temerare* as *violare.*

13.23 Reading *at leges* for *atque.* Note that the hiatus *foedera at* here is matched by *candida ut* at 13.26.

13.24 Compare BON 13.14 *(haud secus).*

13.28 A gloss in G explains *degentes* as *perfruentes vel potientes.*

13.29 Reading *monarchos* for *monachos* (compare BON 9.19).

13.26 Compare LOR 9.3 *(atria caeli).*

13.31–33 The general sense of these lines echoes Matthew 13:30: *Sinite utraque crescere usque ad messem, et in tempore messis dicam messoribus: Colligite primum zizania, et alligate ea in fasciculos ad comburendum: triticum autem congregate in horreum meum,* "Suffer both to grow until the harvest, and in the time of the harvest I will say to the reapers: Gather up first the cockle, and bind it into bundles to burn, but the wheat gather ye into my barn."

13.33 Compare ALD 19.3 *(torrida dum calidos patior tormenta per ignes).*

13.36 Reading *nequiquam* for *nequicquam*. Compare ALD 100.52 *(CREATURA,* "Creation": *dapibus . . . opimis).*

13.40 Reading *dispergitur* ("is scattered") for *disperditur* ("is ruined") or *dispertitur* ("is divided").

13.44 Compare ALD PR.17 *(carmina vatem),* ALD 57.2 *(carmine vates),* ALD 79.2 *(carmina vatum),* ALD 97.3 *(carmine vates),* BIB 5.7 *(carmina vatum).*

13.45 Compare ALD 100.12 *(summus qui regnat in arce);* Aldhelm, *Carmen ecclesiasticum* 4.5.9 *(caeli qui regnat in arce);* Aldhelm, *Carmen de virginitate* 1393 *(quatenus altithronum lauta qui regnat in arce),* 1587 *(caeli qui regnat in arce),* and 2287 *(caeli qui regnat in arce).*

13.46 A gloss in G explains its reading, *devisas,* as *invisas.*

13.48 A gloss in G explains its reading, *hos ago,* as *instingo vel facio.*

13.50 Compare ALD 91.1 *(omnipotens auctor nutu qui cuncta creavit)* and 100.1 *(conditor aeternis fulcit qui saecla columnis);* Aldhelm, *Carmen de virginitate* PR.3 *(trinus in arce deus qui pollens saecla creavit).*

13.51 Compare ALD 66.7, BON 14.9 and 17.1 *(fraude maligna* or *fraude malignum).*

13.52 A gloss in G explains *natrix* as *serpens.*

13.53 A gloss in G supplies *me* after *edidit.* Compare ALD 66.7; Aldhelm, *Carmen de virginitate* 316, 585, 1007, 1639, and 2247 *(fraude maligna);* ALD 100.31 *(nectaris haustus);* BON PR.7 *(mulso . . . nectaris haustu),* BON 17.2 *(nectaris haustus).*

13.54 A gloss in G explains *Inlicio* as *suadeo.*

13.55 Compare ALD 100.31 *(dulcior . . . quam lenti nectaris haustus);* Aldhelm, *Carmen de virginitate* 239 *(nectaris et . . . mulsos) and 2541 (nectaris . . . mulsa);* BON 1.6 *(Amplius in sceptris mundi).*

13.56 Understanding *quique* as "whoever"; compare BON 10.20.

13.57 A gloss in G explains its reading, *vitatur,* as *cogitur.*

13.58 Compare BON 11.14 *(dicor stultissima virgo).* For the plural form *mentibus* for *mente* here *metri gratia,* compare BON 16.14.

13.60 Compare LOR 12.6 *(tartara trusum).*

13.61 Compare ALD 8.1 *(dixere priores).*

13.62 Compare Aldhelm, *Carmen de virginitate* 2552 *(haec bellona ferox sub tristia tartara trusit).*

13.64 Compare ALD 76.6; BON 11.11 *(arbiter orbis).*

13.65 A gloss in G supplies *et* for its reading, *stirpem cunctorum causamque.* The correct biblical attribution is to 1 Timothy 6:10. Compare Aldhelm, *Carmen de virginitate* 2585 *(cunctorum causam . . . esse malorum).*

13.66 Compare ALD 76.6 *(arbiter orbis).* Note hiatus at *prendere hunc* and false quantity: *tradĕret* is the normal usage.

13.67 Glosses in G supply *meis* after *dentibus* and *illius* after *artus.*

BON 14

MANUSCRIPTS: A[1], fol. 2r2; G, fol. 386r–v (no. 12).

EARLIER EDITIONS AND TRANSLATIONS: DüB, 11; Gl, 324–27. (SK 14940)

SOLUTION: *SUPERBIA* (pride); the acrostic reads *SUPERBIA LOQUITUR* (pride speaks).

14.1 Glosses in a later hand in N explain *Serpens* as *daemon, angleicis* (the reading in N) as *inter angelos,* and *in culmine caeli* as *in sidera caeli.* Compare ALD 59.8, 86.4, and 100.3; TAT 40.4; BON 3.3, 4.12, 8.8, 16.12, and 17.7 *(caeli culmina, culmina caelorum, culmina caeli* or *culmine caeli);* SYM 7.3 *(me genuit);* ps-SYM 1 *(Mater me genuit);* ALD 33.1 *(me genuit),* 59.1 *(Me . . . genuit),* and 97.1 *(me genuit);* TAT 11.1 *(me genuit);* BIB 1.1 *(me . . . genuit)* and BIB 2.1 *(me . . . genuit).*

14.2 A gloss in a later hand in N explains *noxia* as *culpabilis.* The intended scansion *vipereā* must be through lengthening at ictus or because of the following consonant cluster, here *sp-.* Compare BON 5.11, 9.20, 12.7, and 13.18.

14.3 A gloss in a later hand in N explains *Pellexi* as *decepi*. Compare SYM 95.2 *(milia multa)*.

14.4 A gloss in a later hand in N explains *trudens* as *cadens, tartara* as *inferna*, and *pigra* as *mala*. Compare ALD 79.11 *(Erebi . . . Tartara nigri)*; BON 6.12 *(Erebi . . . nigri / Tartara)*, 13.62 *(sub Tartara trusi)*, and 14.4 *(trudens in Tartara nigra)*; Aldhelm, *Carmen de virginitate* 849 *(trusit . . . tartara nigra)*.

14.5 A gloss in a later hand in N explains *praevia* as *perversa* and *dicor* as *vocor*.

14.6 A gloss in a later hand in N explains *Cella* as *bona* and *malunt* as *volunt*.

14.8 A gloss in a later hand in N explains *crudelior* as *impior* and *ulla* as *nulla*. Compare BON 9.4 *(In terris nusquam . . . vilior ulla)*, 10.15 *(non est pulchrior ulla)*, and 11.1 *(Non est in terris me virgo stultior ulla)*. Note hiatus at *altera in terris*.

14.9 A gloss in a later hand in N explains *Luciferum* as *primum angelicum* and *dudum* as *postea*. Compare ALD 66.7; BON 13.51 and 17.1 (all *fraude maligna* or *fraude malignum*); Aldhelm, *Carmen de virginitate* 316, 585, 1007, 1639, and 2247 *(fraude maligna)*.

14.10 Compare BON 17.12 *(disperdere temptat)*.

14.11 False quantity: *sĭnu* is the normal usage. A gloss in a later hand in N explains *gestant* as *portant* and *sternere* as *iacere;* a gloss in G renders *sternere* as *humiliare*. The close repetition *tempto . . . temptant* seems clumsy; here I emend to *tendent,* following a suggestion by Bob Babcock.

14.13 Compare SYM 57.2 *(Vertice tango)*.

14.15 False quantity: *perĭmo* is the normal usage (but compare the variant *perunco* in G, glossed *perimo vel obtrunco,* and the parallel case in TAT 23.5). There seems to be a double sense for *viribus invisis:* both "hateful strength" and "unseen strength" seem possible.

14.16 A gloss in a later hand in N explains *nitor* as *volo*. Compare BON 13.19 *(sternere nitor)*.

BON 15

MANUSCRIPTS: A[1], fol. 2r2; G, fol. 386v (no. 13).
EARLIER EDITIONS AND TRANSLATIONS: DüB, 11; Gl, 324–27. (SK 2336)
SOLUTION: *CRAPULA* (overindulgence); the acrostic reads *CRAPULA GULAE* (overindulgence of the gullet).

Another sense of *crapula* is "hangover, intoxication," so leading smoothly on to the next aenigma.

15.4 A gloss in G explains *Praevia* as *ductrix* and its reading, *foenore,* as *quasi foedere.*
15.5 A gloss in G explains *sorori* as *ebrietati.*
15.8 A gloss in G explains *mordax* as *manducans.*
15.9 Compare ALD 81.7 *(mente superbus);* BON 20.24 *(mente superba).*
15.11 Compare ALD 20.3; BON 7.10 and 20.10 *(Arte mea).*
15.12 A gloss in G explains its reading, *torrentibus,* as *ardentibus.* Reading *misceantur,* which can only be metrical if we assume some synizesis; see too the note on BON PR.6 above.

BON 16

MANUSCRIPTS: A[1], fol. 2r2; G, fol. 386v–87r (no. 14).
EARLIER EDITIONS AND TRANSLATIONS: DüB, 12; Gl, 330–31. (SK 4738)
SOLUTION: *EBRIETAS* (drunkenness); the acrostic reads *EBRIETAS DICEBAT* (drunkenness used to utter).

In the arrangement of this and the previous aenigma, with which it is evidently thematically connected, Boniface appears to have been influenced by Aldhelm's description of the wicked throngs that follow gluttony of the belly *(ingluviem ventris),* and which Aldhelm says are signified by the Egyptians drowned in the Red Sea. As Aldhelm notes (*Carmen de virginitate* 2487–89): *Quam sequitur scelerata falanx luxusque ciborum / Ebrietasque simul necnon et crapula cordis, / Ingluuiem dapibus quae semper pascit opimis,* "A damned horde follows [gluttony of the belly], an excess of food, drunkenness likewise and overindulgence of the heart, which always stuffs gluttony with sumptuous feasts."

16.1 Compare ALD 43.3; TAT 4.2; LOR 5.5 *(bibulis . . . buccis)*.

16.4 The rare verb *trico* (in the sense "trip up, cause to stumble, cause to fail") also appears in ALD 48.9, as well as in a letter from Ecgburg to Boniface dated 716/719 (*Ep 13*, ed. Tangl, 19, line 26: *si tarda mors non tricaverit*). A gloss in G explains *trico* as *corrumpo*.

16.5 A gloss in G explains *faxo* as *facio*. The manuscript reading *semina dira* seems nonsensical, perhaps influenced in part by the form *famine* in the previous line; *somnia dira* seems preferable.

16.11 A gloss in G gives *os* as an alternative to *animas*. It seems better to assume that Drunkenness herself is "cruel," rather than the souls she torments, and that therefore the reading *crudelis* is the correct one, rather than *crudeles*, despite the false quantity implied by the former (*crudelĭs* is the normal usage before a following vowel, but Boniface may be assuming lengthening in arsis). I am grateful to Rob Getz for the suggestion. Compare ALD 27.5; Aldhelm, *Carmen de virginitate* 1753 and 1991 *(torribus atris)*.

16.12 A gloss in G explains *Edita* as *celsa*. Compare ALD 59.8, ALD 86.4, ALD 100.3; TAT 40.4; BON 3.3, BON 4.12, BON 8.8, BON 14.1, BON 17.7 *(caeli culmina, culmina caelorum, culmina caeli* or *culmine caeli)*; LOR 9.3 *(stelligeri . . . caeli)*.

16.13 Compare TAT 1.3 *(ima profundi)*. False quantity: the normal usage is *bărătri* or *bărātri*; here again the G scribe seems to have cleaned up the text.

16.14 Both *(h)ydrus* and *(h)ydra* are attested in Anglo-Latin sources; see further EUS 41 (*HYDRA*, "Hydra"). A gloss in G explains its reading, *ydram*, as *serpentem*.

16.15 Compare BON 13.1 *(per saecula monstrum)*.

BON 17

MANUSCRIPTS: A[1], fol. 2r2–v1; G, fol. 387r (no. 15).
EARLIER EDITIONS AND TRANSLATIONS: DüB, 12; Gl, 332–35. (SK 8930)
SOLUTION: *LUXORIA* (lust); the acrostic reads *LUXORIA AIT* (lust speaks).

17.1 Compare ALD 100.53 *(limpida sum fateor);* Aldhelm, *Carmen de virginitate* 1007, 2247, and ALD 66.7; BON 13.53 and (by emendation) 14.9 *(fraude maligna).* Presumably it is only Boniface's slavish devotion to Aldhelm's phraseology that leads him to describe Luxoria as *limpida,* "bright." Glosses in a later hand in N explain its reading, *lipidarum,* as *aquarum; fateor* as *dicor;* and *saeva* as *mala.*

17.2 Glosses in a later hand in N explain *ceu* as *semper* and *nectaris haustus* as *desideras.* Compare ALD 100.31 *(nectaris haustus);* BON PR.7 *(mulso . . . nectaris haustu),* BON 13.55 *(mulsum . . . nectaris haustum);* Aldhelm, *Carmen de virginitate* 2691 *(usibus humanis).*

17.3 A gloss in a later hand in N explains *Xristicolas* as *qui Xristum colunt.* Compare Aldhelm, *Carmen de virginitate* 1093 *(ut tetra venena).*

17.4 A gloss in a later hand in N explains *viscera* as *membra.*

17.5 The form *ruricola* here seems to signify not so much "country-dweller" as "earth-dweller"; the word is used in the former sense in Aldhelm, *Carmen de virginitate* 23, 83, and 2495; compare Boniface, *Carmen* 2.31. Boniface uses the form *rurigena* likewise in BON 20.8 and Boniface, *Carmen* 2.31.

17.6 Glosses in a later hand in N explain *internis* as *in visceribus* and *Tartara* as *inferna.*

17.7 Compare ALD 59.8, ALD 86.4, ALD 100.3; TAT 40.4; BON 3.3, BON 4.12, BON 8.8, BON 14.1, BON 16.12 *(caeli culmina, culmina caelorum, culmina caeli* or *culmine caeli).*

17.8 Compare ALD 11.3 *(ars mea).* Glosses in a later hand in N explain its reading, *caenarum,* as *aescarum* and *vini* as *potus.*

17.9 Compare BON 5.7 *(mortale genus);* ALC 1.8 *(bestia talis).*

17.10 Compare Aldhelm, *Carmen ecclesiasticum* 4.2.14; Aldhelm, *Carmen de virginitate* 699 *(tartara mortis).*

17.11 Compare BON 2.14 *(heu miserae),* 8.16 *(heu miseris).*

17.12 Compare BON 14.10 *(perdere tempto).*

17.13 Either there is a false quantity here (*sumptuōsos* is the normal usage) or Boniface is scanning the word as trisyllabic through synizesis.

17.15 The best solution seems to be that Boniface has elided the required past tense of the verb "to be" (here the form *fuit* appears in several witnesses, but produces a line that contains too many syllables). A gloss in G supplies *Sodomae* after *regna.*

17.16 Compare ALD 58.6 *(ab aethra).*

BON 18

MANUSCRIPTS: A[1], fol. 2v1; G, fol. 387r (no. 16).
EARLIER EDITIONS AND TRANSLATIONS: DüB, 13; Gl, 336–37. (SK 7801)
SOLUTION: *INVIDIA* (envy); the acrostic reads *INVIDIA AIT* (envy speaks).

This aenigma is notable not only for its many metrical curiosities, but also for the sustained alliteration on *v-/f-,* and to a lesser extent *s-.*

18.2 A false quantity: *sătoris* is the normal usage.

18.3 Compare BON 12.5; ps-BER 1.3 *(Viribus atque meis).*

18.5 The reading *facta sanctorum* in Gl is metrically indefensible: the inversion is far preferable.

18.6 Compare ALD 89.4 *(infelix fato fraudabor);* Aldhelm, *Carmen de virginitate* 579 and 928 *(fraude fefellit).*

18.9 A false quantity: *martyria* with a short *y* is the normal usage, but compare BON 9.13 (with a long *y*) and BON 10.9 (with a short *y*).

18.10 A false quantity: *mācerans* is the normal usage, but compare Juvencus, *Evangelia* 2.385 *(măcerans)* and Aldhelm, *Carmen de virginitate* 2474 *(măcerare).* See too Aldhelm, *Carmen de virginitate* 1328 and 1545 *(corda venenis).*

BON 19

MANUSCRIPTS: A[1], fol. 2v1; G, fol. 387r–v (no. 17).
EARLIER EDITIONS AND TRANSLATIONS: DüB, 13; Gl, 338–39. (SK 7484)
SOLUTION: *IGNORANTIA* (ignorance); the acrostic reads *IGNORANTIA AIT* (ignorance says).

19.1 For the future form *vocabor* used in place of the present tense, see the note at BON 7.9 above; it is also tempting to emend to the imperfect *vocabar.*

19.2 Compare ALD 91.3 *(Nomine nempe meo);* EUS 39.2 *(nempe mearum),* EUS 43.4 *(Nomine nempe meo);* BON 4.9 *(Regmine nempe meo).* A gloss in G gives the alternative *pondera* for *pignora.*

19.4 Compare XMS P1.8 *(Horridum hoc animal genuit Germanica tellus),* and the note at ALD 18.5 above, where a further parallel is found in the final-line challenge of XMS P1.9 *(scrutetur sapiens lector quo nomine fungit);* see further Sims-Williams, *Milred of Worcester,* 32, n. 66, who highlights the Anglo-Saxon associations of manuscript P[5], which contains the series XMS P1–3.

19.6 A gloss in G explains *gnato* as *filio.*

19.7 Compare ALD 3.1 *(caelum terramque),* ALD 49.2 *(caelum . . . terramve),* ALD 97.16 *(caeli . . . terraeque);* ps-ALC 1.2 *(caeli terraeque).*

19.8 A gloss in G explains *Tranantem* as *currentem.* Compare BON 10.12 *(sidera supra);* Aldhelm, *Carmen de virginitate* 2902 *(sidera supra).*

19.10 A gloss in G supplies *ipse auctor* after *quid sit.*

19.11 Compare BON 6.4 *(cernitur usquam).*

19.12 The form *invisam* may stand for both “unseen, unperceived” and “hated, envied.”

BON 20

MANUSCRIPTS: A[1], fol. 2v1; G, fol. 387v–88r (no. 18).

EARLIER EDITIONS AND TRANSLATIONS: DüB, 13–14; Gl, 340–43. (SK 17144)

SOLUTION: *IACTANTIA* (boastfulness); the acrostic reads *VANA GLORIA IACTANTIA* (vainglory boastfulness).

20.1 For *versicolor,* compare ALD 3.1, TAT 9.1, and SYM 58.2.

20.3 A gloss in G supplies *a* before *specie.* Compare ALD 31.2 *(varia . . . imagine).*

20.4 Compare Aldhelm, *Carmen de virginitate* 160 *(auri flauentis).*

20.5 A gloss in G explains *apto* as *suadeo.*

20.6 Compare ALD 91.5; BON 10.18 *(praemia vitae);* Aldhelm, *Carmen de virginitate* 1226 *(lucida perpetuae visuros praemia vitae)* and 2275 *(tramite dissimili tendens ad praemia vitae).*

20.8 Compare ALD 60.5 *(vulnere sterno).* On the form *rurigenas,* see the notes on BON 17.5 above, and on 20.17 below.

20.10 Compare ALD 20.3, BON 7.10, and BON 15.11 *(Arte mea);* BON 7.3 *(perdunt . . . pia facta).*

20.11 A gloss in G supplies *et* before *pariter.*

20.13 A gloss in G supplies *o* before its reading, *si non es factor.*

20.14 A gloss in G supplies *perfecti* before *vocitant.*

20.15 Compare ALD 96.8 *(vitae);* Aldhelm, *Carmen de virginitate* 752 *(lucida perpetuae mercantes munera vitae)* and 2688 *(munera vitae).*

20.17 Reading *pererrans* after one witness; others read variously *pervertens* and *pervernas.* The term *Terrigenae,* "earth-dwellers," is a favorite of Boniface's; see the note at BON 3.7 above.

20.19 Compare Aldhelm, *Carmen de virginitate* 777 *(tendit ad aeterna felix habitacula miles).*

20.20 A gloss in G explains *texunt* as *induunt.*

20.20–21 Compare ALD 33.4 *(Seres texunt lanugine vermes).*

20.21 A gloss in G explains its reading, *ut propriae,* as *acsi essent meae.*

20.22 Glosses in G supply *dico* before its reading, *Omniaque,* and *esse* after *necessaria.*

20.24 Presumably *serviunt* is scanned as disyllabic, through synizesis. Compare too ALD 81.7 *(mente superbus);* BON 15.9 *(mente superba).*

ALCUIN

Authorship and Date

Alcuin (b. ca. 735, d. 804) is again one of the most prolific and erudite Anglo-Saxons whose name we know, a man who stepped out of the shadow of his Northumbrian model, Bede, and indeed out of Northumbria altogether, to make a massive mark on the international stage. Alcuin composed a vast number of works in an astonishing variety of fields, including orthography, grammar, rhetoric, dialectic, astronomy, and mathematics; as well as biblical exegesis, theology, and saints' lives in both prose and verse. There are also more than 270 extant letters from the correspondence of Alcuin, as well as more than 120 poems, so offering a further set of perspectives. The same didactic impulse that is so evident in the successive collections of ALD, BED, TAT, EUS, and BON is again apparent here.

Manuscript Context(s)

For the manuscript context of ALC, see DüA, 162–69. For ALC D, see DS, 134–37, where the ten manuscripts of that edition (which is followed closely here) are discussed; the manuscripts in question date from the ninth/tenth century to the fourteenth.

Subject Matter and Solutions

ALC is compiled here from scattered poems in various contexts; it was evidently never intended to circulate as a collection of aenigmata, and demonstrates Alcuin's command of a variety of different genres in both his longer poems and his many examples of occasional verse, to which these aenigmata belong. Nonetheless, there are three clear divisions within ALC. After ALC 1 (*PECTEN,* "comb"), there follow five aenigmata that are all logogriphs (ALC 2–6), while the final three aenigmata (which circulate together) all have the same solution (*FORNAX,* "furnace"). A final aenigma on a quite different theme that is found alongside genuine Alcuin material, ps-ALC 1 (*IHS,* "Christ"?), looks very like the work of another author altogether. In sharp contrast to this somewhat scattergun collection, ALC D has a clear chain of association linking many of its themes in different ways, and an envelope structure that appears to play on the twin meanings of *littera* as "letter of the alphabet" (ALC D1) and, more generally in the plural *litterae,* "epistle" (ALC D89 [*EPISTOLA,* "letter"]). In following "letter" with "word" (ALC D2), Alcuin may gesture towards the first book of Isidore's *Etymologiae, De grammatica* (On grammar). But even if the succeeding interchanges skip around in subject matter, they are securely linked not only by the universal experience of parents and teachers across the ages, but by the linguistic device whereby a young questioner repeats the last word of the respondent, and continues the interrogation; such is certainly the case in ALC D2–8 and ALC D10–11. The latter pair of interchanges also begins a sequence dealing with body parts (ALC D10–37), many of them the same and in the same order as those considered in Isidore, *Etym.* 1.1, *De homine et partibus eius* (On human beings and their body parts). There follows a further sequence (ALC D38–59) dealing with celestial and calendrical subjects, partly paralleled in Isidore, *Etym.* 13, *De mundo et partibus* (The world and its parts), and easily broken down into subsections, for example dealing with the four seasons (ALC D55–58), which leads naturally into the concluding discussion of the year (ALC D59). Once again, there follows a group of ten interchanges somewhat hard to fathom as a connected sequence (ALC D60–69), but with mini-sequences containing verbal and thematic associations of the kind already witnessed. ALC D61–62 are linked by the word "sand," ALC D62–63 by the word "earth," ALC D80–81 by the word "hope"; likewise, ALC D64–65 are linked by the concepts of food and hunger, and ALC D66–67 by those of tiredness and sleep. The final three interchanges in this sequence, ALC D68–70, deal with the familiar triad of faith, hope, and charity, given here as hope, friendship, and faith. The whole arrangement is introduced by the notion of *curiositas* ("curiosity"; ALC D60), and the connection with the previous sequence dealing with celestial themes is elegantly made through the ambiguity of the word *altum,* which can mean both "high" and "deep." Pippin sparks off the sequence at ALC D60 by making the intellectual leap toward thinking of the deep itself, essentially asking the question "What is a boat?" The notion of *curiositas,* "curiosity," seems to be invoked again in ALC D71, where Pippin asks "What is a wonder?" and is given a concrete example. This begins a further sequence of sixteen rather more conventionally framed riddles (ALC D71–85), where the role of questioner has been reversed, and it is now the youthful Pippin who takes up the challenge of supplying answers, which he does in a playfully cryptic fashion which in general merely hints at the solution. The switching of the roles of questioner and respondent seems to gesture toward the didactic tradition, and turns on the linguistic coincidence that while the Latin letters *M* and *D* stand for "master" *(MAGISTER)* and "student" *(DISCIPULUS),* the equivalent Greek letters *M* and *Δ* stand by contrast for "student" (ΜΑΘΗΤΗΣ) and "master" (ΔΙΔΑΣΚΟΛΟΣ) instead. Likewise, in the Old Norse eddic poem *Vafþrúðnismál,* the two protagonists, in this case the giant Vafþrúðnir and the god Óðinn, take turns asking a series of questions: in stanzas 11–18 the giant asks the questions, and the god supplies the answers; while in stanzas 20–55 the roles are reversed.

Style

Alcuin writes verse in a fluent, confident style that is well summarized by Godman and in far greater technical detail by Solana Pujalte ("Poesía de Alcuino de York"); it is technically proficient, and highly consistent, but also marked with a degree of formulaic phrasing that is characteristic of all of Alcuin's verse.

Sources and Parallels

Two kinds of sources and parallels need to be distinguished: on the one hand, for the verse aenigmata (ALC), and on the other hand for ALC D. The former occasionally use phrasing found elsewhere in the Latin poetry of the Anglo-Saxon riddle tradition, whereas the latter frequently deals with topics that can be widely paralleled in the tradition as a whole, and indeed in several cases appear to be prose renderings of specific verse aenigmata, mostly from SYM. Indeed, the whole central sequence of nine enigmata at ALC D75–83 seems drawn from earlier models, of which seven are from SYM and the other two from ps-BED and ALD respectively; the aenigmata in question are SYM 76 and 76a (*SILEX,* "flint"), ps-BED 10 (*LEBES,* "cauldron"), SYM 30 (*PEDICULI,* "lice"), SYM 14 (*PULLUS IN OVO,* "chick embryo"), SYM 98 (*ECHO,* "echo"), SYM 12 (*FLUMEN ET PISCIS,* "river and fish"), SYM 99 (*SOMNUS,* "sleep"), SYM 96 (*FLEXUS DIGITORUM,* "finger-counting"), and ALD 41 (*PILUILLUS,* "pillow"). ALC D85 has the same solution as SYM 65 (*SAGITTA,* "arrow"), but the whole treatment is quite different. In the case of ALC D, there is also the clear precedent of the anonymous and undated (but undoubtedly earlier) *Altercatio Hadriani Augusti et Epicteti philosophi* (Discussion between the Emperor Hadrian and the philosopher Epictetus), noted as AHE below (for the edition, see DS, 70–81), to which Alcuin alludes directly in one of his letters, and which supplies close and often verbatim parallels for a significant number of the questions that make up the text. By contrast, the later *Disputatio Hadriani cum Secundo Philosopho* (Conversation between Hadrian and the philosopher Secundus), noted as DHS below (for the edition, see DS, 38–70), borrows, always verbatim, from ALC D, notably from that part of the work which seems to be the most original.

This Text and Translation

Here I rely heavily on DüA, as well as the unpublished work of Rob Getz (for ALC); I have also relied in detail on DS and By (for ALC D), although I have renumbered the individual questions and riddles, the better to highlight the various sequences and repetitions within the text as whole. Several individual debts are acknowledged in the notes.

Further Reading

Reuschel, "Kenningar bei Alcuin"; Wilmanns, "Disputatio regalis et nobilissimi iuvenis Pippini cum Albino scholastico"; Suchier,

"Disputatio Pippini cum Albino"; Solana Pujalte, "Poesía de Alcuino de York"; Folkerts, "Die Alcuin zugeschriebenen 'Propositiones ad acuendos iuvenes'"; Hadley and Singmaster, "Problems to Sharpen the Young"; Sorrell, "Alcuin's 'Comb' Riddle"; Orchard, "Wish You Were Here"; Singmaster, "Alcuin's Propositions"; Gropp, "*Propositio de lupo et caprai*"; Garrison, "An Aspect of Alcuin"; Bitterli, "Alkuin von York und die angelsächsische Rätseldichtung"; Orchard, "Alcuin's Educational Dispute."

ALC 1

EARLIER EDITIONS AND TRANSLATIONS: DüA no. 5 (223). (SK 1684)

SOLUTION: *PECTEN* (comb). See further Sorrell, "Alcuin's 'Comb' Riddle"; Orchard, "Wish You Were Here"; Riddler and Trzaska-Nartowski, "Chanting upon a Dunghill." See too Leahy, *Anglo-Saxon Crafts*, 55–58.

The circumstances behind this aenigma, which was sent along with a letter of thanks to Archbishop Riculf of Mainz (787–813), are known with some precision, and are discussed by Sorrell and Orchard in the articles noted above.

1.8 Compare BON 17.9 *(bestia talis)*. Damoetas, who appears alongside Menalcas as a shepherd in Virgil, *Eclogue* 3, is the nickname that Alcuin gives elsewhere to Riculf, his addressee here. In this context, it is important to note that both Damoetas and Menalcas trade riddles (at *Eclogue* 3, lines 104–5 and 106–7 respectively), both beginning with a challenge, *Dic* ("say"; see too, for example, ps-BED 1, 4, and 5; ALC D84), and neither of which has found a universally acceptable solution. Note the final challenge here, as commonly in EXE, where twenty of the ninety-one end with one or other version of the challenge "Say what I am called" *(Saga hwæt ic hatte)* or "Find out what I am called" *(Frige hwæt ic hatte)*; see the headnote at EXE.

ALC 2

EARLIER EDITIONS AND TRANSLATIONS: DüA no. 63.1 (281). (SK 2106)
SOLUTION: *MALUM* (evil; apple) → *MULAM* (mule).

This aenigma begins a sequence of logogriphs (ALC 2–6) which might easily be considered part of one long poem; the sequence ends (ALC 6.7) with a challenge of the type found at ALC 1.8 (see note there). On logogriphs in general, see the note at ALD 63; it is important to stress that, unlike others within the tradition, Alcuin indulges here in sequences of multiple logogriphs, as does his great predecessor Bede (see, for example, BED 3–6). For an alternative interpretation of the same theme, see TAT 21 *(MALUM)*.

2.1–2 A reference to the eating of the fateful apple in Eden (Genesis 2:16–17), but also to the fact that the word *malum* (with a short "a") means "evil."

2.3 When reversed, the Latin homographs *malum,* "evil," and *malum* "apple," both produce *mulam,* "mule."

ALC 3

EARLIER EDITIONS AND TRANSLATIONS: DüA no. 63.2 (281–82). (SK 14972)
SOLUTION: *VIRTUS* (power) → *TUS* (incense) → *VIR* (man) → *VIRUS* (venom).

3.4 Compare ALD 63.10; ALC 5.2; TAT 4.5 *(Littera tollatur);* EUS 34.6 *(Littera subtrahitur).*

ALC 4

EARLIER EDITIONS AND TRANSLATIONS: DüA no. 63.3 (282). (SK 4633)
SOLUTION: *CANUS* (white-haired man) → *ANUS* (old woman) → *SUS* (swine).

Earlier editors have *SANUS* as the first element of the solution, but this seems unlikely, given that the word appears unhidden in the opening line, unlike those riddles where the solution is obscured or hinted at in the opening line, as described in the introduction to *OEALRT*, under "Use of Titles." Note that the logogriph rings the changes between male and female in the human world, and an animal. I am grateful to Bob Babcock for the suggestion that if the numeration in the riddle is progressive, and entails the removal of first one letter, then two, then three, there may also be a bilingual pun here on the Greek word ὗς, "pig, wild boar," which is grammatically both masculine and feminine.

4.3 Compare Virgil, *Georgics* 4.407 *(sus horridus).*

ALC 5

EARLIER EDITIONS AND TRANSLATIONS: DüA no. 63.4 (282). (SK 12470)
SOLUTION: *MAGNUS* (mighty) → *AGNUS* (lamb) → *MANUS* (hand) → *MAGUS* (magician) → *MUS* (mouse) → *ANUS* (old woman).

5.1 The fact that the line denoting *MAGNUS* contains the word *sacerdos* is presumably a reference to the antiphon and responsory from the common of confessors *(Ecce sacerdos magnus).*

5.2 Compare ALD 63.10; TAT 4.5 *(Littera tollatur);* EUS 34.6 *(Littera subtrahitur).*

5.7 The rare word *dolabra* usually means "pickax," but here uniquely seems to be used in the sense "old woman." Given that the word *abra,* "handmaid" (Greek *ἄβρα*), appears in the Vulgate Judith (at 8:2 and elsewhere), and is regularly glossed *ancilla,* "nurse; serving-woman," in Anglo-Saxon sources, it is tempting to assume that the *dol-* element derives from *dol-us,* "trick, trickery," rather than Greek δούλ-η or δοῦλ-ος, "slave-woman, slave," where the vowel would likely be long. A bilingual form relying on Old English *dol,* "foolish, folly," would bring this aenigma into line with (for example) EXE 10.9 *(dol drunc-mennen)* and 25.18 *(dole æfter dyntum),* both of which deal with the problems of booze, but that is likely too imaginative.

ALC 6

EARLIER EDITIONS AND TRANSLATIONS: DüA no. 63.5 (282). (SK 16549)
SOLUTION: *SIC ET NON* (yes and no) → *MEUM ET TUUM* (mine and yours) → *EGO ET TU* (I and you) → *NOS ET VOS* (we and you [?]). The first solution could also be *EST ET NON,* with essentially the same meaning.

6.2 Note the obvious repetition here at ALC 6.2–4.
6.4–5 These two lines circulate as a separate aenigma in M, and as the beginning of a hermeneutic poem of medical terms from Canterbury (see Lapidge, "Hermeneutic Style," 84 and 103–4).
6.5–6 The lines move through the constituent parts of grammar (word, syllable, and letter), and refer to the ways in which dead letters produce living meaning.
6.7 Reading *aurum* for manuscript *taurum*. For the closing challenge, see the note on ALC 1.8 above.

ALC 7

EARLIER EDITIONS AND TRANSLATIONS: DüA no. 64.1 (282). (SK 15057)
SOLUTION: *FORNAX* (furnace).

This aenigma opens a sequence of three (ALC 7–9) which all share the same solution; a similar strategy is found in several of the collections: see SYM 76 and 76a (both *SILEX,* "flint"); BER 55–59 (all *SOL,* "sun," *LUNA,* "moon," or *SOL ET LUNA,* "sun and moon"); GES 21–23a (all "waves," with different formulations).

7.1 Alcuin uses precisely the same line at DüA no. 101.3.3.

ALC 8

EARLIER EDITIONS AND TRANSLATIONS: DüA no. 64.2/1–2 (283). (SK 4414)
SOLUTION: *FORNAX* (furnace).

Although previous editors understand this as part of the aenigma that follows, it is taken here as a separate two-line text, because it is in hexameters, rather than the elegiac couplets of the aenigmata that precede and follow. For similar examples of riddles that are joined or separated in the manuscripts, see the headnotes to EXE 1, EXE 73, and EXE 76.

ALC 9

EARLIER EDITIONS AND TRANSLATIONS: DüA no. 64.2/3–6 (283). (SK 1562)

SOLUTION: *FORNAX* (furnace).

9.1 Compare ALD 1.4 *(aestate . . . tempore brumae).*

PS-ALC 1

EARLIER EDITIONS AND TRANSLATIONS: DüA, in footnote to no. 63.5 (282). (SK 5659)

SOLUTION: *IHS* (Christ)?

This aenigma follows ALC 6 in two manuscripts, but in style and general Latinity it is obviously defective (as it stands in both manuscripts, the fourth line does not scan, and the opening line is problematic), and seems highly unlikely to be by Alcuin. The solution offered here is little more than a guess.

1.2 Compare ALD 3.1 *(caelum terramque),* ALD 49.2 *(caelum . . . terramve),* ALD 97.16 *(caeli . . . terraeque);* BON 19.7 *(caelum terramve).*

1.4 I have supplied *necnon* to complete the meter; it is not in either manuscript.

ALC D1

EARLIER EDITIONS AND TRANSLATIONS: DS no. 1 (137); Or, 179.
SOLUTION: *LITTERA* (letter).

ALC D1–4 are echoed in DHS 22–26. For different interpretations of the same theme, compare BER 25 *(LITTERAE)*; EUS 7 *(LITTERAE)*; TAT 4 *(APICES)*; EXE 55 *(STAFAS)*; and Isidore, *Etym.* 1.15.

The word *historia* covers both "story" and "history"; both seem appropriate here.

ALC D2

EARLIER EDITIONS AND TRANSLATIONS: DS nos. 2–3 (138); Or, 179.
SOLUTION: *VERBUM* (word).

For an alternative interpretation of the same theme, compare Isidore, *Etym.* 1.11.1.

ALC D3

EARLIER EDITIONS AND TRANSLATIONS: DS no. 4 (138); Or, 179.
SOLUTION: *LINGUA* (tongue).

Compare Isidore, *Etym.* 11.1. 50.

ALC D4

EARLIER EDITIONS AND TRANSLATIONS: DS no. 5 (138); Or, 179.
SOLUTION: *AER* (air, breath).

For an alternative interpretation of the same theme, compare Isidore, *Etym.* 13.7.1.

ALC D5

EARLIER EDITIONS AND TRANSLATIONS: DS no. 6 (138); Or, 179.
SOLUTION: *VITA* (life).

The phrasing here draws on AHE 21, and is echoed in DHS 20.

For different interpretations of the same theme, compare EUS 24 *(MORS ET VITA)*; Isidore, *Etym.* 11.1.4.

ALC D6

EARLIER EDITIONS AND TRANSLATIONS: DS no. 7 (138); Or, 180.
SOLUTION: *MORS* (death).

The phrasing here draws on AHE 23, and is echoed in DHS 21.

For different interpretations of the same theme, compare EUS 24 *(MORS ET VITA)*; Isidore, *Etym.* 11.2.31.

ALC D7

EARLIER EDITIONS AND TRANSLATIONS: DS nos. 8–16 (138); Or, 180.
SOLUTION: *HOMO* (mankind).

The phrasing here draws on AHE 33–35, and is echoed in DHS 8.

For different interpretations of the same theme, compare EUS 4 *(HOMO)*; LOR 1 *(HOMO)*; Isidore, *Etym.* 11.1.4.

See further By, 167.

ALC D8

EARLIER EDITIONS AND TRANSLATIONS: DS no. 17 (138); Or, 180.
SOLUTION: *SOMNUS* (sleep).

The phrasing here draws on AHE 53, and is echoed in DHS 19.

For an alternative interpretation of the same theme, compare SYM 99 *(SOMNUS)*, and see too ALC D67 below. Compare Isidore, *Etym.* 7.8.34 (on *somnium*).

ALC D9

EARLIER EDITIONS AND TRANSLATIONS: DS no. 18 (138); Or, 180.
SOLUTION: *INNOCENTIA* (innocence).

The phrasing here draws on AHE 17, and is echoed in DHS 27.

ALC D10

EARLIER EDITIONS AND TRANSLATIONS: DS no. 19 (138); Or, 181.
SOLUTION: *CAPUT* (head).

The phrasing here is echoed in DHS 28–39.

For an alternative interpretation of the same theme, compare Isidore, *Etym.* 11.1.25. This aenigma opens a sequence on body parts (ALC D10–37).

ALC D11

EARLIER EDITIONS AND TRANSLATIONS: DS no. 20 (138); Or, 181.
SOLUTION: *CORPUS* (body).

For an alternative interpretation of the same theme, compare Isidore, *Etym.* 11.1.14.

ALC D12

EARLIER EDITIONS AND TRANSLATIONS: DS no. 21 (138); Or, 181.
SOLUTION: *COMAE* (hair).

For different interpretations of the same theme, compare SYM 58 *(CAPILLUS)*; Isidore, *Etym.* 11.1.30.

ALC D13

EARLIER EDITIONS AND TRANSLATIONS: DS no. 22 (138); Or, 181.
SOLUTION: *BARBA* (beard).

For an alternative interpretation of the same theme, compare Isidore, *Etym.* 11.1.45.

ALC D14

EARLIER EDITIONS AND TRANSLATIONS: DS no. 23 (138); Or, 181.
SOLUTION: *CEREBRUM* (brain).

Compare Isidore, *Etym.* 11.1.61 and 125.

ALC D15

EARLIER EDITIONS AND TRANSLATIONS: DS no. 24 (138); Or, 181.
SOLUTION: *OCULI* (eyes).

For different interpretations of the same theme, compare TAT 18 *(OCULI);* Isidore, *Etym.* 11.1.31.

ALC D16

EARLIER EDITIONS AND TRANSLATIONS: DS no. 25 (138); Or, 182.
SOLUTION: *NARES* (nostrils).

For an alternative interpretation of the same theme, compare Isidore, *Etym.* 11.1.47.

ALC D17

EARLIER EDITIONS AND TRANSLATIONS: DS no. 26 (138); Or, 182.
SOLUTION: *AURES* (ears).

For an alternative interpretation of the same theme, compare Isidore, *Etym.* 11.1.46.

ALC D18

EARLIER EDITIONS AND TRANSLATIONS: DS no. 27 (139); Or, 182.
SOLUTION: *FRONS* (face).

Compare Isidore, *Etym.* 11.1.35 *(Haec imago . . . animi).*

ALC D19

EARLIER EDITIONS AND TRANSLATIONS: DS no. 28 (139); Or, 182.
SOLUTION: *OS* (mouth).

For different interpretations of the same theme, compare BED 3 *(OS);* RUN 4 *(OS);* Isidore, *Etym.* 11.1.49.

ALC D20

EARLIER EDITIONS AND TRANSLATIONS: DS no. 29 (139); Or, 182.
SOLUTION: *DENTES* (teeth).

Reading *molae* (MSS *mola*; *moles*).

For an alternative interpretation of the same theme, compare Isidore, *Etym.* 11.1.52.

ALC D21

EARLIER EDITIONS AND TRANSLATIONS: DS no. 30 (139); Or, 182.
SOLUTION: *LABIA* (lips).

For an alternative interpretation of the same theme, compare Isidore, *Etym.* 11.1.50.

ALC D22

EARLIER EDITIONS AND TRANSLATIONS: DS no. 31 (139); Or, 182.
SOLUTION: *GULA* (throat).

Compare Isidore, *Etym.* 11.1.58 and 60.

ALC D23

EARLIER EDITIONS AND TRANSLATIONS: DS no. 32 (139); Or, 183.
SOLUTION: *MANUS* (hands).

The phrasing here is echoed in DHS 40–47.

Compare Isidore, Etym. 11.1.66 *(manus . . . totius corporis munus . . . ipsa operatur).*

ALC D24

EARLIER EDITIONS AND TRANSLATIONS: DS no. 33 (139); Or, 183.
SOLUTION: *DIGITI* (fingers).

For an alternative interpretation of the same theme, compare Isidore, *Etym.* 11.1.70.

ALC D25

EARLIER EDITIONS AND TRANSLATIONS: DS no. 34 (139); Or, 183.
SOLUTION: *PULMO* (lung).

For an alternative interpretation of the same theme, compare Isidore, *Etym.* 11.1.124.

ALC D26

EARLIER EDITIONS AND TRANSLATIONS: DS no. 35 (139); Or, 183.
SOLUTION: *COR* (heart).

For different interpretations of the same theme, compare LOR 2 *(ANIMA);* Isidore, *Etym.* 11.1.118.

ALC D27

EARLIER EDITIONS AND TRANSLATIONS: DS no. 36 (139); Or, 183.
SOLUTION: *IECUR* (liver).

For an alternative interpretation of the same theme, compare Isidore, *Etym.* 11.1.125.

ALC D28

EARLIER EDITIONS AND TRANSLATIONS: DS no. 37 (139); Or, 183.
SOLUTION: *FEL* (gall bladder).

Compare Isidore, *Etym.* 11.1.128 *(felle irascimur).*

ALC D29

EARLIER EDITIONS AND TRANSLATIONS: DS no. 38 (139); Or, 183.
SOLUTION: *SPLEN* (spleen).

Compare Isidore, Etym. 11.1.127 *(risus causa . . . splene ridemus).*

ALC D30

EARLIER EDITIONS AND TRANSLATIONS: DS no. 39 (139); Or, 184.
SOLUTION: *STOMACHUS* (stomach).

Reading *coctor* (manuscript *coquator*). Compare Isidore, *Etym.* 11.1.128.

ALC D31

EARLIER EDITIONS AND TRANSLATIONS: DS no. 40 (139); Or, 184.
SOLUTION: *VENTER* (belly).

Compare Isidore, *Etym.* 11.1.132.

ALC D32

EARLIER EDITIONS AND TRANSLATIONS: DS no. 41 (139); Or, 184.
SOLUTION: *OSSA* (bones).

The phrasing here is echoed in DHS 48.

Compare Isidore, *Etym.* 11.1.86 *(corporis solidamenta);* BED 3 (*OS,* "mouth; bone").

ALC D33

EARLIER EDITIONS AND TRANSLATIONS: DS no. 42 (139); Or, 184.
SOLUTION: *COXAE* (hips).

The phrasing here is echoed in DHS 51.

For an alternative interpretation of the same theme, compare Isidore, *Etym.* 11.1.107.

ALC D34

EARLIER EDITIONS AND TRANSLATIONS: DS no. 43 (139); Or, 184.
SOLUTION: *CRURA* (shins).

The phrasing here is echoed in DHS 50.

For an alternative interpretation of the same theme, compare Isidore, *Etym.* 11.1.110.

ALC D35

EARLIER EDITIONS AND TRANSLATIONS: DS no. 44 (139); Or, 184.
SOLUTION: *PEDES* (feet).

For an alternative interpretation of the same theme, compare Isidore, *Etym.* 11.1.112.

ALC D36

EARLIER EDITIONS AND TRANSLATIONS: DS no. 45 (139); Or, 185.
SOLUTION: *SANGUIS* (blood).

The phrasing here is echoed in DHS 52–53.

For an alternative interpretation of the same theme, compare Isidore, *Etym.* 11.1.122.

ALC D37

EARLIER EDITIONS AND TRANSLATIONS: DS no. 46 (139); Or, 185.
SOLUTION: *VENAE* (veins).

For an alternative interpretation of the same theme, compare Isidore, *Etym.* 11.1.121.

ALC D38

EARLIER EDITIONS AND TRANSLATIONS: DS no. 47 (139); Or, 185.
SOLUTION: *CAELUM* (sky).

The phrasing here draws on AHE 42, and is echoed in DHS 9.

For different interpretations of the same theme, compare EUS 5 *(CAELUM);* Isidore, *Etym.* 13.4.1. This aenigma opens a sequence on celestial bodies and calendrical features (ALC D38–43).

ALC D39

EARLIER EDITIONS AND TRANSLATIONS: DS no. 48 (139); Or, 185.
SOLUTION: *LUX* (light).

The phrasing here is echoed in DHS 54.

For an alternative interpretation of the same theme, compare Isidore, *Etym.* 13.10.14.

ALC D40

EARLIER EDITIONS AND TRANSLATIONS: DS no. 49 (139); Or, 185.
SOLUTION: *DIES* (day).

For different interpretations of the same theme, compare EUS 48 *(DIES ET NOX);* RUN 24 *(DÆG);* Isidore, *Etym.* 5.30.1.

ALC D41

EARLIER EDITIONS AND TRANSLATIONS: DS no. 50 (139); Or, 185.
SOLUTION: *SOL* (sun).

The phrasing here draws on AHE 40–41, and is echoed in DHS 5–6.

For different interpretations of the same theme, compare ALD 79 *(SOL ET LUNA);* BER 55 *(SOL);* BER 56 *(SOL);* BER 57 *(SOL);* EUS 10 *(SOL);* EXE 4 *(SUNNE);* EXE 27 *(MONA OND SUNNE);* GES 15 *(SÓL);* Isidore, *Etym.* 3.71.1; see too *Etym.* 3.47–52.

ALC D42

EARLIER EDITIONS AND TRANSLATIONS: DS no. 51 (139); Or, 186.
SOLUTION: *LUNA* (moon).

For different interpretations of the same theme, compare ALD 6 *(LUNA);* ALD 79 *(SOL ET LUNA);* BER 58 *(LUNA);* BER 59 *(LUNA);* EUS 11 *(LUNA);* EXE 27 *(MONA OND SUNNE);* Isidore, *Etym.* 3.71.1; see too *Etym.* 3.53–57.

ALC D43

EARLIER EDITIONS AND TRANSLATIONS: DS no. 52 (139); Or, 186.
SOLUTION: *STELLAE* (stars).

The phrasing here is echoed in DHS 55–58.

See too Isidore, *Etym.* 3.60–71.

ALC D44

EARLIER EDITIONS AND TRANSLATIONS: DS no. 53 (139); Or, 186.
SOLUTION: *PLUVIA* (rain).

For different interpretations of the same theme, compare SYM 9 *(PLUVIA);* BER 49 *(PLUVIA);* GES 10 *(HAGL OK REGN);* Isidore, *Etym.* 13.10.2. This aenigma opens a sequence on natural phenomena (ALC D44–54).

ALC D45

EARLIER EDITIONS AND TRANSLATIONS: DS no. 54 (139); Or, 186.
SOLUTION: *NEBULA* (cloud).

For different interpretations of the same theme, compare SYM 8 *(NEBULA);* ALD 3 *(NUBES);* Isidore, *Etym.* 13.10.10.

ALC D46

EARLIER EDITIONS AND TRANSLATIONS: DS no. 55 (139); Or, 186.
SOLUTION: *VENTUS* (wind).

For different interpretations of the same theme, compare ALD 2; BER 41 (both *VENTUS); EUS 8 (VENTUS ET IGNIS);* EXE 1 *(GODES WIND);* Isidore, *Etym.* 13.11.1. There are some broad parallels in *Hisperica famina* A479–96 (*DE VENTO,* "on wind"; see further Herren, *Hisperica Famina: The A-Text;* Orchard, "*Hisperica famina* as Literature").

ALC D47

EARLIER EDITIONS AND TRANSLATIONS: DS no. 56 (140); Or, 186–87.
SOLUTION: *TERRA* (earth).

The phrasing here draws on AHE 47, and is echoed in DHS 7.

For different interpretations of the same theme, compare ALD 1; EUS 6; BER 45 (all *TERRA*); RUN 29 *(EAR);* Isidore, *Etym.* 14.1.1.

ALC D48

EARLIER EDITIONS AND TRANSLATIONS: DS no. 57 (140); Or, 187.
SOLUTION: *MARE* (sea).

The phrasing here draws on AHE 48.

For different interpretations of the same theme, compare BED 15 *(MARE);* Isidore, *Etym.* 13.14.1. There are some broad parallels in *Hisperica famina* A381–425 (*DE MARI,* "on the sea"; see further Herren, *Hisperica Famina: The A-Text;* Orchard, "*Hisperica famina* as Literature").

ALC D49

EARLIER EDITIONS AND TRANSLATIONS: DS no. 58 (140); Or, 187.
SOLUTION: *FLUMINA* (rivers).

The phrasing here is echoed in DHS 59–60.

For an alternative interpretation of the same theme, compare Isidore, *Etym.* 13.21.1. Compare too EUS 34 (*FLUMEN,* "river").

ALC D50

EARLIER EDITIONS AND TRANSLATIONS: DS no. 59 (140); Or, 187.
SOLUTION: *AQUA* (water).

For different interpretations of the same theme, compare ALD 29 *(AQUA)*; LOR 3 *(AQUA)*; EXE 39 *(WÆTER),* EXE 80 *(WÆTER)*; RUN 21 *(LAGU)*; Isidore, *Etym.* 13.12.1.

ALC D51

EARLIER EDITIONS AND TRANSLATIONS: DS no. 60 (140); Or, 187.
SOLUTION: *IGNIS* (fire).

For different interpretations of the same theme, compare ALD 44; TAT 33; ALC D73 (and *IGNIS*); EXE 48 *(FYR)*; GES 29 *(ELDR)*; Isidore, *Etym.* 19.6.5. There are some broad parallels in *Hisperica famina* A426–51 (*DE IGNE,* "on fire"; see further Herren, *Hisperica Famina: The A-Text;* Orchard, "*Hisperica famina* as Literature").

ALC D52

EARLIER EDITIONS AND TRANSLATIONS: DS no. 61 (140); Or, 187.
SOLUTION: *FRIGUS* (cold).

ALC D53

EARLIER EDITIONS AND TRANSLATIONS: DS no. 62 (140); Or, 188.
SOLUTION: *GELU* (ice).

The phrasing here is echoed in DHS 61–65.

For different interpretations of the same theme, compare SYM 10 *(GLACIES);* LOR 4 *(GELU);* BER 38 *(GLACIES),* BER 42 *(GLACIES);* ps-BED 6 *(GLACIES);* EXE 31 *(IS),* EXE 66 *(IS);* RUN 11 *(IS);* Isidore, *Etym.* 13.10.7.

The variants *fons,* "spring, stream," and *pons,* "bridge," seem equally feasible: one links back to the customary "ice" riddles, and how ice both produces and is produced from water; the other to the notion of ice binding the waves.

ALC D54

EARLIER EDITIONS AND TRANSLATIONS: DS no. 63 (140); Or, 188.
SOLUTION: *NIX* (snow).

For different interpretations of the same theme, compare LOR 6 *(NIX);* SYM 11 *(NIX);* Isidore, *Etym.* 13.10.6.

ALC D55

EARLIER EDITIONS AND TRANSLATIONS: DS no. 64 (140); Or, 188.
SOLUTION: *HIEMS* (winter).

For an alternative interpretation of the same theme, compare Isidore, *Etym.* 5.35.6. This aenigma opens a sequence on the seasons, culminating with the year itself (ALC D55–59).

ALC D56

EARLIER EDITIONS AND TRANSLATIONS: DS no. 65 (140); Or, 188.
SOLUTION: *VER* (spring).

For an alternative interpretation of the same theme, compare Isidore, *Etym.* 5.35.3.

ALC D57

EARLIER EDITIONS AND TRANSLATIONS: DS no. 66 (140); Or, 188.
SOLUTION: *AESTAS* (summer).

For an alternative interpretation of the same theme, compare Isidore, *Etym.* 5.35.4.

ALC D58

EARLIER EDITIONS AND TRANSLATIONS: DS no. 67 (140); Or, 188.
SOLUTION: *AUTUMNUS* (autumn).

For an alternative interpretation of the same theme, compare Isidore, *Etym.* 5.35.5.

ALC D59

EARLIER EDITIONS AND TRANSLATIONS: DS no. 68–73 (140); Or, 189.
SOLUTION: *ANNUS* (year).

For an alternative interpretation of the same theme, compare Isidore, *Etym.* 5.36.1 and 3.71.23–32. The twelve palaces of the year are evidently the astrological houses of the relevant signs.

ALC D60

EARLIER EDITIONS AND TRANSLATIONS: DS no. 74–75 (140); Or, 189.
SOLUTION: *CURIOSITAS* (curiosity).

ALC D61

EARLIER EDITIONS AND TRANSLATIONS: DS no. 76 (140); Or, 189.
SOLUTION: *NAVIS* (ship).

The phrasing here draws on AHE 49–50.

For different interpretations of the same theme, compare SYM 13 *(NAVIS)*; BED 12 *(NAVIS)*; BER 11 *(NAVIS)*. Compare Isidore, *Etym.* 19.1.5 (on *nauta*).

ALC D62

EARLIER EDITIONS AND TRANSLATIONS: DS no. 77 (141); Or, 190.
SOLUTION: *HARENA* (sand).

For an alternative interpretation of the same theme, compare Isidore, *Etym.* 16.3.11.

ALC D63

EARLIER EDITIONS AND TRANSLATIONS: DS no. 78 (141); Or, 190.
SOLUTION: *HERBA* (grass).

Compare Isidore, *Etym.* 17.9.104 (on *gramen*).

ALC D64

EARLIER EDITIONS AND TRANSLATIONS: DS no. 79 (141); Or, 190.
SOLUTION: *OLERA* (herbs).

Compare Isidore, *Etym.* 17.9.10 *(De oleribus)*.

ALC D65

EARLIER EDITIONS AND TRANSLATIONS: DS no. 80 (141); Or, 190.
SOLUTION: *FAMES* (hunger).

The phrasing here is echoed in DHS 66.

ALC D66

EARLIER EDITIONS AND TRANSLATIONS: DS no. 81 (141); Or, 190.
SOLUTION: *LUCRUM* (wealth).

The phrasing here draws on AHE 11, and is echoed in DHS 67.

For an alternative interpretation of the same theme, compare RUN 1 (*FEOH*, "wealth").

ALC D67

EARLIER EDITIONS AND TRANSLATIONS: DS no. 82 (141); Or, 190.
SOLUTION: *SOMNUS* (sleep).

The phrasing here is echoed in DHS 68.

For an alternative interpretation of the same theme, compare SYM 99 *(SOMNUS)*, and see too ALC D8 above. Compare Isidore, *Etym.* 7.8.34 (on *somnium*).

ALC D68

EARLIER EDITIONS AND TRANSLATIONS: DS no. 83 (141); Or, 190.
SOLUTION: *SPES* (hope).

The phrasing here draws on AHE 14, and is echoed in DHS 69.

For different interpretations of the same theme, compare BON 3 *(SPES)*; TAT 2 *(SPES, FIDES, CARITAS)*. Compare Isidore, *Etym.* 8.2.5.

ALC D69

EARLIER EDITIONS AND TRANSLATIONS: DS no. 84 (141); Or, 191.
SOLUTION: *AMICITIA* (friendship). Should it be *CARITAS* to fit better with the preceding and following questions, and so provide the familiar triad of hope, faith, and charity?

The phrasing here draws on AHE 12, and is echoed in DHS 70.

For an alternative interpretation of the same theme, compare Isidore, *Etym.* 7.3.18 and 8.2.6.

ALC D70

EARLIER EDITIONS AND TRANSLATIONS: DS no. 85 (141); Or, 191.
SOLUTION: *FIDES* (faith).

The phrasing here is echoed in DHS 71.

For an alternative interpretation of the same theme, compare Isidore, *Etym.* 7.2.4. For a discussion linking this aenigma to the next, see Lockhart, "Everyday Wonders and Enigmatic Structures," 70–72.

ALC D71

EARLIER EDITIONS AND TRANSLATIONS: DS no. 86–89 (141); By, 174–77; Or, 191.
SOLUTION: *IMAGO IN AQUA* (reflection in water).

For a discussion linking this aenigma to the previous one, see Lockhart, "Everyday Wonders and Enigmatic Structures," 70–72.

ALC D72

EARLIER EDITIONS AND TRANSLATIONS: DS no. 90 (141); By, 175–77; Or, 191.
SOLUTION: *SOMNIUM* (dream); perhaps a better solution would be *HOMO IN SOMNIO VISUS* (man seen in a dream).

Compare Isidore, *Etym.* 7.8.34.

ALC D73

EARLIER EDITIONS AND TRANSLATIONS: DS no. 91 (141); By, 175–77.
SOLUTION: *IGNIS* (fire).

For different interpretations of the same theme, compare ALD 44; TAT 33; ALC D51 (all *IGNIS*); EXE 48 *(FYR)*; GES 29 *(ELDR)*; Isidore, *Etym.* 19.6.5. There are some broad parallels in *Hisperica famina* A426–51 (*DE IGNE,* "on fire"; see further Herren, *Hisperica Famina: The A-Text;* Orchard, "*Hisperica famina* as Literature").

None of these parallels employs quite the same imagery and diction as this somewhat quirky interpretation of this common theme, which in terms of language has most in common with ALC D76 (*LEBES,* "cauldron"), with which it seems to form a natural pair: compare the sequence *Vidi mortuos . . . vivum et in ira vivi . . . mortui* here with the sequence *Vidi mortuum . . . vivum et in risu mortui . . . vivus.* This link is part of a wider set of connections involving fire and water. The whole sequence ALC D72–79 is also notable for the carefully patterned responses by Alcuin, who effectively just says "yes" eight times in answer to Pippin's questions, each time in a different way.

ALC D74

EARLIER EDITIONS AND TRANSLATIONS: DS no. 92 (141); By, 175–77; Or, 192.
SOLUTION: *TINTINNABULA* (bells).

For different interpretations of the same theme, compare SYM 81 *(TINTINNABULUM)*; TAT 7 *(TINTINNUM)*; EXE 2 *(BELLE)*; EXE 67 *(BELLE)*, although none of these deals with the theme in the same way.

Compare Isidore, *Etym.* 3.21.13 (on *somnium*).

ALC D75

EARLIER EDITIONS AND TRANSLATIONS: DS no. 93 (141); By, 175–77; Or, 192.

SOLUTION: *SILEX* (flint).

See too SYM 76 and SYM 76a (*SILEX*, "flint"), especially SYM 76.3 *(nec lignis ut vivat eget, nec ut occidat undis)*, on which this aenigma seems to depend.

Compare Isidore, *Etym.* 16.3.1 (on *somnium*).

ALC D76

EARLIER EDITIONS AND TRANSLATIONS: DS no. 94 (141); By, 175–77; Or, 193.

SOLUTION: *LEBES* (cauldron).

Compare ALD 49 and ps-BED 10, which have the same solution. Here, as in the case of ps-BED 10, one wonders whether the reference to "laughter" is supposed to provide a clue to the solution, with the related verb *cachinno*, "laugh," perhaps suggesting *cacabus*, "cooking-pot," a synonym for *lebes*.

Compare Isidore, *Etym.* 20.8.4.

For a discussion on the sequence ALC D76–83, see Lockhart, "Everyday Wonders and Enigmatic Structures," 73–75.

ALC D77

EARLIER EDITIONS AND TRANSLATIONS: DS no. 95 (142); By, 175–77; Or, 193.
SOLUTION: *PEDICULI* (lice).

Compare SYM 30 (*PEDICULI,* "lice"), which may well be the source.

Compare Isidore, *Etym.* 12.7.5 (on *pullus*) and 12.7.80 (on *ovum*).

For a discussion on the sequence ALC D76–83, see the note at ALC D76.

ALC D78

EARLIER EDITIONS AND TRANSLATIONS: DS no. 96 (142); By, 175–77; Or, 194.
SOLUTION: *PULLUS IN OVO* (chick in egg).

Compare SYM 14 (*PULLUS IN OVO,* "chick in egg"), which may well be the source; see too BER 8 (*DE OVO,* "on an egg").

Compare Isidore, *Etym.* 7.8.34 (on *somnium*).

For a discussion on the sequence ALC D76–83, see the note at ALC D76.

ALC D79

EARLIER EDITIONS AND TRANSLATIONS: DS no. 97 (142); By, 175–77; Or, 194.
SOLUTION: *ECHO* (echo).

Compare SYM 98 (*ECHO,* "echo"), which may well be the source.

For a discussion on the sequence ALC D76–83, see the note at ALC D76.

ALC D80

PREVIOUS EDITION AND TRANSLATION: DS no. 98 (142); By, 175–77; Or, 194–95.
SOLUTION: *PISCIS ET FLUMEN* (fish and river).

The source is SYM 12 (*FLUMEN ET PISCIS,* "river and fish"); there is a further parallel at EXE 81 (*FISC OND EA,* "fish and river").

See further Bitterli, *Say What I Am Called,* 13–14. For a discussion on the sequence ALC D76–83, see the note at ALC D76.

ALC D81

EARLIER EDITIONS AND TRANSLATIONS: DS no. 99 (142); By, 175–77; Or, 195.
SOLUTION: *HOMO QUI SOMNIT* (a dreamer).

Compare SYM 99 (*SOMNUS,* "sleep"), especially SYM 99.3 *(sed me nemo videt, nisi qui sua lumina claudit),* which seems to have inspired the whole aenigma here. For a discussion on the sequence ALC D76–83, see the note at ALC D76.

ALC D82

EARLIER EDITIONS AND TRANSLATIONS: DS no. 100 (142); By, 175–77; Or, 195.
SOLUTION: *FLEXUS DIGITORUM* (finger-counting).

There is a parallel at SYM 96 (*FLEXUS DIGITORUM,* "finger-counting"), which seems the likely source; for details of the technique, see the headnote there.

For a discussion on the sequence ALC D76–83, see the note at ALC D76.

ALC D83

EARLIER EDITIONS AND TRANSLATIONS: DS no. 101 (142); By, 175 and 177–78; Or, 196.

SOLUTION: *PULUILLUS* (pillow).

There is a parallel at ALD 41 (*PULUILLUS,* "pillow"), although the treatment there is somewhat different.

Compare Isidore, *Etym.* 19.20.3 (on *somnium*).

For a discussion on the sequence ALC D76–83, see the note at ALC D76.

ALC D84

EARLIER EDITIONS AND TRANSLATIONS: DS no. 102–3 (142); By, 175 and 177–78; Or, 197.

SOLUTION: *ADAM, ENOCH/ELIAS, LAZARUS* (Adam, Enoch/Elijah, Lazarus).

The numbers at the end of this aenigma must be understood as equating to the Greek system, where letters represent numbers, in these cases α (I), ε (V), and λ (XXX), which are indeed (whether understood in Greek or in Latin) the first letters of the solutions. The Hebrew meaning of Adam is indeed "earth," as was widely understood in the Latin Middle Ages; both Enoch and Elijah are identified as types of Christ, since they were assumed into heaven without dying; Lazarus was indeed a poor man. For a quite different take on Adam, compare TAT 22 (*ADAM,* "Adam").

ALC D85

EARLIER EDITIONS AND TRANSLATIONS: DS no. 104 (142); By, 175 and 177–78; Or, 197.

SOLUTION: *SAGITTA* (arrow). See further Bitterli, *Say What I Am Called,* 110–13.

For different interpretations of the same theme, compare SYM 65 *(SAGITTA)*; BED 14 *(SAGITTA)*; TAT 32 *(SAGITTA)*; GES 13 *(ÖR)*. Compare Isidore, *Etym.* 18.8.

ALC D86

EARLIER EDITIONS AND TRANSLATIONS: DS no. 105 (142); Or, 197.
SOLUTION: *MILES* (soldier).

The phrasing here draws on AHE 66.

Compare Isidore, *Etym.* 9.3.32.

ALC D87

EARLIER EDITIONS AND TRANSLATIONS: DS no. 106 (142); Or, 197–98.
SOLUTION: *NIHIL* (nothing).

ALC D88

EARLIER EDITIONS AND TRANSLATIONS: DS no. 108–10 (143); Or, 198.
SOLUTION: *EPISTOLA* (letter).

The phrasing here draws on AHE 1–2.

Compare Isidore, *Etym.* 6.8.17.

See further Lockhart, "Everyday Wonders and Enigmatic Structures," 75–76.

THE LORSCH RIDDLES

Authorship and Date

This small collection of a dozen aenigmata, all in hexameters, survives in only a single manuscript, U, which has clear and close ties to the Anglo-Saxon riddle tradition and can be dated to the beginning of the ninth century, and is located at Lorsch Abbey. Important to the question of date is the role of an epitaph, inserted between LOR 4 (*GELU*, "ice") and LOR 5 (*CUPA VINARIA*, "wine cup"), for the Anglo-Saxon priest Domberht, who was part of Boniface's mission, and was apparently taught by him. Indeed, fourteen of the thirty-six lines of the epitaph focus on Boniface, rather than Domberht, stressing the extent to which Boniface (now dead, so dating the epitaph to after 754) "taught and nurtured and loved [Domberht] with great zeal." More interesting in the context of the composition of LOR is the fact that Domberht himself is "a bright lantern in the world, skilled in the study of grammar and the laws of meter" (lines 10–11: *mundi clara lucerna fuit / grammaticae studio, metrorum legibus aptus*), raising the question as to whether the insertion of the epitaph in the midst of LOR might be intended to signal authorship, or shared authorship with the epitaph, or is merely a coincidence, but there seems no way of verifying any of these possibilities. That the author of the epitaph was an Anglo-Saxon seems at least plausible given the pervasive use of light imagery to celebrate the dead Domberht, whose name means "bright judgment" in Old English; it is perhaps worth pointing out in this context that the most likely solution for LOR 10 also matches the theme (*LUCERNA*, "a lamp").

Manuscript Context

The single Lorsch manuscript U also contains both SYM and ALD, the latter in the context of the metrical treatises *De metris* and *De pedum regulis*. LOR, which DüL edited under the title *Aenigmata Anglica* (English aenigmata), appears on folios 115 and 117 of U, with the epitaph appearing in between. The seven first-person aenigmata are distributed in two groups (LOR 1–4 and 10–12), separated by three that are impersonal (LOR 5, 7, and 9), intertwined with two third-person aenigmata (LOR 6 and 8).

Subject Matter and Solutions

LOR has no titles/solutions in U, but the aenigmata are relatively simple to solve, and can be matched fairly frequently elsewhere in the tradition, as the notes to individual aenigmata demonstrate. There are a number of pairs within LOR, sometimes in sequence, sometimes not, notably LOR 1 (*HOMO,* "mankind") and 2 (*ANIMA,* "soul"), LOR 3 (*AQUA,* "water") and 4 (*GELU,* "ice") (with 6 [*NIX,* "snow"] also perhaps part of the pattern), LOR 9 (*PENNA,* "quill pen") and 12 (*ATRAMENTUM,* "ink"). Several of these aenigmata, as well as practically all of the others in the collection, have close connections and parallels elsewhere in the Anglo-Saxon riddle tradition; see especially the notes to LOR 5 (*CUPA VINARIA,* "a wine cup") and 11 (*IUVENCUS,* "bullock").

Style

In its use of compound adjectives, together with those formed from the (mostly poetic) suffixes *-abilis, -alis, -eus, -fer, -ficus, -genus, -ger,* and *-osus,* LOR reveals a certain fondness for these forms that is relatively unusual for collections of aenigmata within the tradition. There are sixteen such adjectives in the twelve aenigmata that make up LOR, although few of them are particularly notable or rare. LOR also demonstrates a fondness for alliterative effects: see further the notes on LOR 2.1, 2.4, 4.6, 5.2, 8.2, and 12.6 below.

Sources and Parallels

As has already been noted, almost all of the individual aenigmata in LOR have parallels with others in the tradition, including a significant number of notable verbal echoes of ALD in particular, as the notes below make clear. Such a set of verbal parallels with ALD is reminiscent of the heavy reliance of BON on ALD; on the other hand, however, the direct verbal overlap between LOR and BON seems slight, and there are often further and better parallels for each collection with ALD, suggesting that LOR and BON are independently reliant on ALD.

This Text and Translation

Here I have revised and updated the edition given by Gl (in turn based on the sometimes superior DüL); several individual debts are acknowledged in the notes.

Further Reading

In general, see Dümmler, "Lörscher Rätsel"; Dümmler, *Aenigmata Anglica;* Bieler, "Some Remarks on the *Aenigmata Laureshamensia*"; Lendinara, "Gli *Aenigmata Laureshamensia*"; Salvador-Bello, *Isidorean Perceptions,* 264–74 and 468.

LOR 1

MANUSCRIPT: U, fol. 115r.
EARLIER EDITIONS AND TRANSLATIONS: DüL, 20–21; Gl, 347. (SK 15863)
SOLUTION: *HOMO* (mankind).

This aenigma breaks easily into two parts: the first four lines deal with the double birth of mankind, with *deus,* "God," as the father and *terra,* "earth," as the mother, while the final eight form a long and complex single sentence bewailing what happens next. The whole aenigma is structured around an envelope pattern, on which see the introduction to *OEALRT,* under "Style." The connection of this aenigma to the one that follows—LOR 2 (*ANIMUS VEL ANIMA,* "mind or soul")—is clear.

1.1 Compare ALD 22.1 *(mea diversis variatur);* LOR 11.8 *(mea diversis variantur fata sub annis).*

1.2 Compare ALD 44.1 *(Me pater . . . gelido);* LOR 4.1 *(Me pater . . . gelido);* BER 3.1 *(Me pater).*

1.3 Reading *consatus,* as in the manuscripts; Glorie substitutes *consistus.*

1.5 Reading *cum fine;* the reading *sine fine* seems inappropriate for a world that by definition *will* end, unless the phrase is to be interpreted more closely with *tremendo:* the world is endlessly to be feared. But compare LOR 1.12 *(sine fine manendus).*

1.9 Compare SYM 100.3 *(morti . . . tempora vitae).*

1.12 Compare TAT 24.4 *(sine fine manebit).*

LOR 2

MANUSCRIPT: U, fol. 115r.

EARLIER EDITIONS AND TRANSLATIONS: DüL, 21; Gl, 348. (SK 4003)

SOLUTION: *ANIMUS VEL ANIMA* (mind or soul). Suggested solutions include *ANIMA/CORS* (soul/heart). See further Lockett, *Anglo-Saxon Psychologies,* 275–78.

This aenigma leads on naturally from the one that precedes. A likely partial source is Song of Songs 5:2 *Ego dormio et cor meum vigilat,* "I sleep and my heart watcheth"; see too Clemoes, *"Mens absentia cogitans,"* for the notion of the mind pondering absent things.

2.1 Note the alliteration on *Dum domus . . . dormit.*

2.4 Note the alliteration on *supernorum scrutans secreta.*

2.6 Compare ALD 2.4; BON 1.4 *(rura peragro).* Note the verbs of traversing, with a pun on *peragro,* a word also found (for example) in LOR 2.10, as well as ALD 2.4; EUS 40.4; SYM 35.2.

2.9 The reading *perpetuae* is unusual, making *Dis* feminine; given the grammatically feminine form *gehennae* in the previous line, however, the analogy with the feminine noun *lis, litis,* "lawsuit, dispute," and the fact that in the Germanic languages Hell is feminine, *perpetuae* can perhaps be defended. But it seems simpler to consider the form as a misreading of adverbial *perpetue* (the usual form is *perpetuo*).

2.10 False quantity: the normal usage is *spēlēo.*

2.13 Reading *fit.* The manuscript reading *fio* (presumably read as a monosyllable: compare the note on BER 45.5) would be odd in the context of the solution "soul," but makes more sense if it is assumed here, as elsewhere in the riddles, that the solution alludes to both a container and what is contained: Lockett's suggested solution *BREOST-COFA* is particularly attractive in this context.

2.13 Compare ALD 14.4 *(pulpa putrescit).*

LOR 3

MANUSCRIPT: U, fol. 115v.
EARLIER EDITIONS AND TRANSLATIONS: DüL, 21; Gl, 349. (SK 3367)
SOLUTION: *NIMBUS* (storm cloud); other suggestions include *AQUA* (water). See further Klein, "Of Water and the Spirit."

Given the possibility that the previous aenigma refers to both the body and the soul that it contains, it is tempting here too to prefer a similar kind of solution: both "storm cloud" and the rain it contains; compare BER 49 on a similar theme. This aenigma is notable for the large number of compound adjectives it contains *(velivolo . . . luciflui . . . horrifera . . . imbrifero),* and has broad parallels with EXE 1.

3.1 Reading *aethera* (manuscripts *aera*); compare ALD 42.3 *(trano per aethera),* ALD 48.6 *(aethera tranet).* The unusual adjective *velivolo* may derive directly from Virgil, *Aeneid* 1.224 *(mare velivolum)* or from Juvencus, *Evangelia* 2.11 *(mare velivolum).*

3.2 A golden line; the pronoun *cui* seems to refer to the speaker.

3.3 The form *resolvens* is usually transitive; here it seems intransitive ("becoming liquid").

LOR 4

MANUSCRIPT: U, fol. 115v.
EARLIER EDITIONS AND TRANSLATIONS: DüL, 21; Gl, 350. (SK 9492)
SOLUTION: *GELU* (ice).

This aenigma continues the theme of the previous sequence of discussing both a container and what it contains; the same theme continues in the aenigma that follows. The father here is presumably *ventus,* "wind," the mother *aqua,* "water." The final lines of the aenigma repeat the common riddling theme of the daughter who gives birth to her own mother, on which see the introduction to *OEALRT,* under "Shared Themes across the Collections."

4.1 Compare ALD 44.1 *(Me pater . . . gelido);* LOR 1.2; BER 3.1 *(Me pater);* ALD 27.1 *(ex gelido . . . viscere),* ALD 33.1 *(me genuit gelido de viscere);* TAT 31.2 *(nasci gelido natum de viscera matris),* TAT 39.1 *(Natam me gelido terrae de viscere).*
4.2 Compare Virgil, *Aeneid* 8.369 *(fuscis tellurem amplectitur alis).*
4.4 Compare ALD 22.4 *(fato terrente).*
4.6 Note the alliteration on *propriam progigno parentem.*

LOR 5

MANUSCRIPT: U, fol. 117r.
EARLIER EDITIONS AND TRANSLATIONS: DüL, 22; Gl, 351. (SK 9031)
SOLUTION: *CUPA VINARIA* (a wine cup).

This charming aenigma again describes both a container and what it contains. The "five branches" are the fingers that caress the bowl of the glass, and the quasi-erotic imagery is continued with some lines that seem directly related to ones from ALD 80 (*CALIX VITREUS,* "glass cup"); for the theme of kissing here, see the headnote there. There is a further close parallel in XMS X4.

5.2 Note the alliteration on *saepe solent pariter splendentes.*
5.5 This is a golden line; compare ALD 43.3 *(bibulis . . . buccis),* ALD 80.8 *(Dulcia . . . basia buccis),* TAT 4.2 and BON 16.1 *(bibulis . . . buccis).* Note the golden line structure, also found in several of the parallel lines noted, and their general suitability, although ALD 80.8 seems the likeliest direct source.
5.6 It is tempting to retain the otherwise unattested manuscript reading *mulcifer* (as from *mulceo,* and presumably meaning "soothing"), but emendation to the rare form *multifer* ("manifold, abundant"), which also appears at TAT 29.1, seems preferable.

LOR 6

MANUSCRIPT: U, fol. 115r.
EARLIER EDITIONS AND TRANSLATIONS: DüL, 22; Gl, 352. (SK 10642)
SOLUTION: *NIX* (snow).

This is an "I saw" aenigma, of the kind found frequently in the Old English riddles; see in general the note at EXE 11.1.

6.1 Reading *quandam,* to agree with the feminine gender of *nix,* picked up in *ipsa* in the next line; *dilabere* stands for the more usual deponent infinitive *dilabi.* Compare ps-SYM 4.1 *(dilabor nubibus).*

6.4 Note the oxymoron *leniter asprum.* Here I retain the manuscript reading *iosumque;* Dümmler conjectures *deorsumque* as an underlying form, but see *DMLBS* at *iosum.* The verb given in the manuscript, *cavavit,* "hollowed out," requires a direct object which is far from clear; it seems better to emend to an intransitive form such as *manavit,* "poured," even with false quantity: the usual scansion is *mānavit* (but see *mănavit* in Caelius Sedulius, *Carmen paschale* 1.156; Arator, *Ad Parthenium* 47; Aldhelm, *Carmen de virginitate* 1833; also *mănantes* at BIB 1.10).

6.5 The masculine accusative adjective form *asprum* in the manuscript at 6.4 (where one would in any case expect *asperum*) is without a referent, unless manuscript *terram* in the following line is emended to *torum,* "bed," accepting the false quantity: the usual scansion is *tŏrum* (but see *tōrum* at BER 30.6). The falling snow is then described forming a hard ridge on the harsh bed of the earth. Note the soundplay on *torum . . . terga . . . terrae.*

LOR 7

MANUSCRIPT: U, fol. 117r.
EARLIER EDITIONS AND TRANSLATIONS: DüL, 22; Gl, 353. (SK 14791)
SOLUTION: *CASTANEA* (chestnut).

This aenigma is an example of the kind of logogriph so favored in other collections; see the note at ALD 63 (*CORBUS,* "raven"). When the last three letters are taken away, what is left (*casta,* "a chaste girl") is declared a rarity. Such a sexist comment is all the more pointed when it is realized that Isidore (*Etym.* 17.8.25) takes the form *castanea* instead to be related to the verb *castro,* "castrate." The notion that the three letters taken away equate to the Greek word *νέα,* "a fresh girl, a new girl," is interesting in the context of a possible connection with the aenigma that follows, LOR 8 (*FETUS,* "fetus"), but perhaps seems farfetched. Compare BER 48 (*CASTANEA,* "chestnut tree").

7.2 There seems to be a pun on the form *demens,* which can be derived from the adjective *demens,* "out of one's mind," or from the verb *demo,* "take away."

7.3 Compare ALD 8.2 *(vix cernitur una).*

LOR 8

MANUSCRIPT: U, fol. 117r.

EARLIER EDITIONS AND TRANSLATIONS: DüL, 22; Gl, 354. (SK 4470)

SOLUTION: *FETUS* (foetus), or *OVUM* (egg), or *PULLUS IN OVO* (chick in egg).

For other similar riddles, see ps-BED 2; SYM 14 (*PULLUS IN OVO,* "chick in egg"); EUS 38 (*PULLUS,* "chick").

8.2 Note the alliteration on *pellis in pariete pendet.* The line does not scan easily as it stands, even if we assume that *pariete* is scanned as trisyllabic, as it is in Bede, *Vita S. Cudbercti* 169, itself likely based on Virgil, *Aeneid* 2.492 *(ariete),* nor does any obvious emendation suggest itself. The skin hanging on the wall of a stall is the membrane left behind in the broken eggshell.

LOR 9

MANUSCRIPT: U, fol. 117v.
EARLIER EDITIONS AND TRANSLATIONS: DüL, 22–23; Gl, 355. (SK 1885)
SOLUTION: *PENNA* (quill pen). See further Murphy, *Unriddling the Exeter Riddles,* 86.

For other aenigmata connected with the classroom and scriptorium, see the headnote to ALD 30 (*ELEMENTUM,* "letter of the alphabet"), and note especially ALD 59 (*PENNA,* "quill pen"), TAT 6 (*PENNA,* "about a pen"), EUS 35 (*PENNA,* "quill pen"). There is an evident link between this aenigma and LOR 12 (*ATRAMENTUM,* "about ink"). The notion of the "bright-white virgin" of LOR 9.1, ultimately derived from a bird, connects this aenigma back to both of those that precede it in the collection.

9.1–3 Compare EUS 35.3–4 *(aethera celsa . . . candida . . . vestigia tetra relinquens).*
9.2 Compare ALD 59.3 *(per albentes . . . campos).*
9.3 Compare BON 13.26 *(atria caeli),* BON 16.12 *(stelligeri . . . caeli).*

LOR 10

MANUSCRIPT: U, fol. 117v.
EARLIER EDITIONS AND TRANSLATIONS: DüL, 23; Gl, 356. (SK 14521)
SOLUTION: *LUCERNA* (lamp).

This aenigma is connected to the previous one by the contrast between light and darkness.

10.4 Compare ALD 100.42 *(viscere flammas),* TAT 11.1 *(viscere flammae),* TAT 14.3 *(mea viscera flammis),* TAT 34.1 *(mea viscera flammae).*

LOR 11

MANUSCRIPT: U, fol. 117v.
EARLIER EDITIONS AND TRANSLATIONS: DüL, 23; Gl, 357. (SK 13063)
SOLUTION: *IUVENCUS* (bullock); other suggestions include *TAURUS* (bull), *VITULUS* (bullock), or *BOS* (bull). See further Cavell, *Weaving Words,* 160.

There seems to be a potential connection between this aenigma and the one preceding, in terms of the cruel binding of limbs. The use of the word *iuvenis,* "young," in the opening line offers a clue to the solution. For aenigmata on similar themes, see ALD 83 (*IUVENCUS,* "bullock"), EUS 12 (*BOS,* "bull"), ps-BED 7 (*IUVENCUS,* "bullock").

11.1 Compare ALD 83.2 *(bis binis . . . fontibus hausi).*
11.3 Compare ALD 44.6 *(naturae iura resolvam).*
11.5 Gl prints *lucertos.*
11.8 Compare ALD 22.1 *(mea diversis variatur);* LOR 1.1 *(mihi diverso varia sub tempore fata).*

LOR 12

MANUSCRIPT: U, fol. 117v.
EARLIER EDITIONS AND TRANSLATIONS: DüL, 23; Gl, 358. (SK 15367)
SOLUTION: *ATRAMENTUM* (ink).

For other aenigmata connected with the classroom and scriptorium, see the headnote to ALD 30 (*ELEMENTUM,* "letter of the alphabet"). There is an evident link between this aenigma and LOR 9 (*PENNA,* "quill pen").

12.1–2 Compare ALD 19.1 *(dudum limpha fui).*
12.3 Compare ALD 29.6 *(Tertia pars . . . mihi).*
12.4 The last syllable of *Lucifica* is lengthened, due to *productio in arsi.*
12.4–5 For the "black on white" theme in the context of writing, see the note at ALD 59.3–5 (*PENNA,* "pen") above.

12.5 The use of the word *agellos,* literally "little fields," is unusual here. See too EXE 55 (*STAFAS,* "letters," likely "neumes").

12.6 The last syllable of *horrifera* is lengthened, due to *productio ob caesuram*. Note the alliteration on *tunc tartara trusum*. Reading *trusum,* as opposed to other suggestions such as *taetra* or *tristi,* and *relatu*. Compare BON 13.62 *(Tartara trusi).*

THE ABINGDON RIDDLE

Date and Authorship

This isolated aenigma is found on the flyleaf of Q, an eleventh-century manuscript, associated with two poems, one of which laments the death of Archbishop Ælfric of Canterbury (d. 1005) and the other likely addressing Abbot Wulfgar of Abingdon (d. 1016). Porter ("Æthelwold's Bowl") has identified the general subject as Æthelwold's bowl, a measure introduced by Abbot Æthelwold as the official measure for the amount of beer to be drunk daily in the monastery. The text's enigmatic nature turns partly on the double meaning of *caritas* in ABI, which either retains its usual sense "love, Christian charity," or the more specific monastic sense of a special measure of food or drink allowed to monks on particular high days and holidays; and partly on the rare term *fiala* in the same line. In the same manuscript the latter is glossed (AntGl 2 675: *fiala vel scale bledu*), where the Latin gloss *scalae,* "bowls, scales," appears to offer the double solution, and the Old English *bledu,* "cup, drinking-vessel, bowl," to focus on its bibulous aspect. At all events, this aenigma seems remarkably precise in its focus and intended audience, though it is notable that it shares with the general tradition a distinct focus on booze.

Style

The aenigma is woven out of a tissue of verbal echoes, with first-person plural references to "we" and "us" in every line *(nos . . . nosque . . . nobis . . . nos),* passive verb forms in three out of four *(vocitamur . . . dicimur . . . videmur),* an emphasis on duality three times in the first two lines *(Bis binae . . . due),* and a "greater"/"lesser" or "better"/"worse" dichotomy in the final three lines *(maiores . . . maiores . . . peiores).* The quadrisyllabic ending *vocitamur* links this aenigma to others in the tradition (see the notes at ALD PR.26 and TAT 1.10)

Sources and Parallels

Porter quotes a portion of the thirteenth-century *Abingdon Chronicle (Historia ecclesie Abbendonensis),* which (in the edition of Hudson, 342) notes that:

> Ad mensuram potus monachorum vir venerabilis Aþelwoldus quandam assisam, non ultra rationabilem sufficientiam progredientam, nec citra deficientem, constituendam perutile fore diiudicavit. Constituit itaque cifum quendam magnum, flasconem et dimidium, scilicet duas caritates, et eo amplius, in se plenarie continentem; quem cifum antiqui "bollam Aþelwoldi" vocabant. Hac vero mensura bis in die obbae monachorum implebantur, scilicet ad prandium et ad cenam.

> With regard to the measure of the monks' drink, the venerable man Æthelwold decreed that it would be extremely useful to establish a certain fixed allowance, neither exceeding nor falling short of a reasonable measure. So he established a certain great vessel, holding fully a gallon and a half (twelve pints), two "special measures" *(caritates)* and more. Men of old used to call it "Æthelwold's bowl." Indeed, twice a day, namely for dinner and supper, the monks' drinking-vessels were filled with this measure.

The connections between this passage and the aenigma are striking indeed, and support the double solution of Po.

Further Reading

Förster, "Die altenglische Glossenhandschrift Platinus 32 (Antwerpen) und Additional 32246 (London)," 155; Porter, "Æthelwold's Bowl"; Salvador-Bello, *Isidorean Perceptions*, 44–45.

ABI

MANUSCRIPT: Q, fol.1r.

EARLIER EDITIONS AND TRANSLATIONS: Po; I have also consulted Förster, "Die altenglische Glossenhandschrift Platinus 32 (Antwerpen) und Additional 32246 (London)," 155; Porter, "Æthelwold's Bowl."

SOLUTION: *SCALAE* (bowls, scales).

For other aenigmata with similar solutions, see both ALD 23 *(TRUTINA)*, BED 1 *(LIBRA)*, BER 53 *(TRUTINA)* and ALD 78 *(CUPA VINARIA)*, LOR 5 and XMS X4 (both *COPA VINARIA)*, EXE 9 *(WIN-FÆT)*. The double solution, Po argues, is entirely deliberate.

THE HIGH-MINDED LIBRARY

Authorship and Date

This collection, which survives only in G, has in its focus on educational and classroom subjects, as well as its obvious derivation from Isidore's *Etymologiae*, a self-evident connection to others within the Anglo-Saxon riddle tradition, especially ALD and EUS. Note that it begins with an aenigma on "wisdom" that repeatedly gestures towards the motifs of parent as child and virgin mother, and has parallels with TAT 1–3 in particular.

Manuscript Context(s)

BIB is preserved uniquely in G, fols. 423v–25r; for the wider context of G, see the introduction to *OEALRT*, under "Manuscript Contexts."

Subject Matter and Solutions

The solutions, all abstract classroom topics that derive directly and in order from their arrangement in Isidore's *Etymologiae*, are given explicitly in G, always in the ablative and preceded by the preposition *de*, "about, concerning," which marks the more bookish collections. Indeed, few collections that make up the Anglo-Saxon riddle tradition have such clear coherence in the intertwined connectedness of their individual riddles; perhaps only BON, OER, ALF, and OIR are as self-contained.

Style

By far the most notable stylistic feature of BIB is its resolutely formulaic and repetitive diction, which focuses in almost all cases on aspects of unorthodox parentage, so once again tracing a line through the Anglo-Saxon riddle tradition back to ps-SYM 1, which is cited as a model in the prose introduction to ALD 7 and 9. The meter is also distinctive: BIB is composed in elegiac couplets, whereas the other collections of aenigmata are almost exclusively in hexameters; notable exceptions are BON 5 (*CARITAS,* "love," where the subject matter may have dictated the change of meter), ALC, and BER (which follows a pattern of its own).

Sources and Parallels

BIB emphasizes the importance of both Isidore and the didactic impetus that underlies the Anglo-Saxon riddle tradition, especially in Latin. The consistently abstract subject matter is matched in BON, but otherwise is paralleled only sporadically.

This Text and Translation

Gi is flawed in many respects; this edition is founded on a fresh transcription, and takes account of several parallels with Isidore of which Gi was not aware.

Further Reading

BIB is the least studied and least annotated of the collections that make up the Anglo-Saxon riddle tradition; for the general context, see Rigg and Wieland, "A Canterbury Classbook" and Irvine, *The Making of Textual Culture,* 358–64.

BIB 1

MANUSCRIPT: G, fol. 423v–24r.
PREVIOUS EDITION: Gi, 50. (SK 9505)
SOLUTION: *SAPIENTIA* (wisdom).

The Trinitarian and Christological context here is clear, and clearer still when compared with the comments of Isidore, *Etym.* 7.2.25–26, where the context is designations of Christ:

> Sapientia, pro eo quod ipse revelet mysteria scientiae et arcana sapientiae. Sed tamen cum sit Pater et Spiritus sanctus sapientia et virtus et lumen et lux, proprie tamen his nominibus Filius nuncupatur. Splendor autem appellatur propter quod manifestat. Lumen, quia inluminat. Lux, quia ad veritatem contemplandam cordis oculos reserat. Sol, quia inlustrator.
>
> [He is called] Wisdom, because he himself reveals the mysteries of knowledge, and the secrets of wisdom. But although the Father and the Holy Spirit may be "Wisdom" and "Power" and "Illumination" and "Light," nevertheless it is properly the Son who is designated by these names. Again, he is called "Splendor" because of what he reveals. "Illumination," because he illuminates. "Light," because he unlocks the eyes of the heart for gazing at the truth. "Sun," because he is the illuminator.

1.1 Compare SYM 7.3 *(me genuit)*; ps-SYM 1 *(Mater me genuit)*; ALD 33.1 *(me genuit)*, 59.1 *(Me . . . genuit)*, and 97.1 *(me genuit)*; TAT 11.1 *(me genuit)*; BON 14.1 *(me genuit)*; BIB 2.1 *(me . . . genuit)*.

1.2 Reading *genita* (G *genito*).

1.4 Reading *nullo* (G *ullo*). Compare BIB 2.2 *(matris honor)*.

1.5 Compare ALD 20.1 *(sine semine creta)*; BER 19.2 *(nullo virili creta de semine)* and 55.1 *(Semine nec ullo patris creatus)*; BIB 3.1 *(patrio sine semine)* and 8.1 *(Sunt mihi . . . patrio sine semine ternae)*.

1.6 Compare BIB 3.2 *(in aeva manens)* and 8.2 *(virgo per aeva manet)*.

1.7 Compare BIB 2.7 *(Sunt mihi bis binae species),* 3.5 *(sub fronte tot ora),* 3.7 *(Una mihi species),* 4.1, 5.3 *(Sunt mihi tres mirae species),* 7.7 *(Sunt mihi bis binae),* 9.3 *(Tres mihi sunt species . . . tot fronte sub una).*

1.8 Reading *pectore* (G *pectora*). Compare BIB 2.9 *(niveo tot pectore),* 3.6 *(ubera tot niveo pectora sacra tument),* 5.4 *(ubera tot niveo pectora sacra tument).*

BIB 2

MANUSCRIPT: G, fol. 424r.
PREVIOUS EDITION: Gi, 50. (SK 8121)
SOLUTION: *PHYSICA* (physics).

The ultimate source is Isidore, *Etym.* 2.24.3–4:

> Ipsud autem nomen Latine interpretatum amorem sapientiae profitetur. Nam Graeci φιλ- amorem, σοφιαν sapientiam dicunt. Philosophiae species tripertita est: una naturalis, quae Graece Physica appellatur, in qua de naturae inquisitione disseritur: altera moralis, quae Graece Ethica dicitur, in qua de moribus agitur: tertia rationalis, quae Graeco vocabulo Logica appellatur, in qua disputatur quemadmodum in rerum causis vel vitae moribus veritas ipsa quaeratur. In Physica igitur causa quaerendi, in Ethica ordo vivendi, in Logica ratio intellegendi versatur. Physicam apud Graecos primus perscrutatus est Thales Milesius, unus ex septem illis sapientibus. Hic enim ante alios caeli causas atque vim rerum naturalium contemplata ratione suspexit, quam postmodum Plato in quattuor definitiones distribuit, id est Arithmeticam, Geometricam, Musicam, Astronomiam.

> The name itself ["philosophy"] when translated into Latin signifies the "love of wisdom," *(amor sapientiae),* for the Greek φιλ- means "love," and σοφιαν means "wisdom." There are three kinds of philosophy: one natural *(naturalis),* which is

called "physics" *(φυσικά)* in Greek, in which the investigation of nature is considered; the second moral *(moralis),* which is called "ethics" *(ἠθικά)* in Greek, in which moral behavior is treated; a third rational *(rationalis),* which is named with the Greek term "logic" *(λογικά),* in which there is discussion about how in the causes of things and in moral behavior the truth itself may be discerned. So physics involves the cause of inquiring, ethics, the order of living, and logic, the rationale of knowing. Among the Greeks then first who studied physics deeply was Thales of Miletus, one of the Seven Sages. Indeed, he before anyone else considered the first principles of the sky and the power of natural things with studied reason. Afterwards, Plato divided physics into four categories: arithmetic, geometry, music, and astronomy.

2.1 See the note on BIB 1.1 above.

2.2 Reading *patris amor,* and assuming lengthening of the final syllable of *amor* in arsis. Compare BIB 1.4 *(matris honor).*

2.7 Compare TAT 12.3 *(tot... lumina lucent);* BIB 1.7 *(Terna mihi est species),* BIB 3.7 *(Una mihi species),* BIB 4.1, 5.3 *(Sunt mihi tres mirae species),* BIB 7.7 *(Sunt mihi bis binae),* BIB 9.3 *(Tres mihi sunt species... tot fronte sub una).*

2.8 Compare BIB 7.8 *(pignora tot genui virgo sed ipsa manens),* BIB 9.4 *(tot genui pignora virgo manens).*

2.9 Compare BIB 1.8, 3.6, and 5.4 *(ubera tot niveo pectore sacra tument).*

BIB 3

MANUSCRIPT: G, fol. 424r.
PREVIOUS EDITION: Gi, 50–51. (SK 9507)
SOLUTION: *ARITHMETICA* (arithmetic).

Although one might compare in general Isidore, *Etym.* 3 *(mathematica: arithmetica, musica, geometria, astronomia),* the ultimate source seems to be Isidore, *Etym.* 2.24.14–15:

Doctrinalis dicitur scientia, quae abstractam considerat quantitatem. Abstracta enim quantitas dicitur, quam intellectu a materia separantes, vel ab aliis accidentibus, ut est par, inpar, vel ab huiuscemodi, in sola ratiocinatione tractamus. Cuius species sunt quattuor: Arithmetica, Geometrica, Musica, Astronomia. Arithmetica est disciplina quantitatis numerabilis secundum se. Geometrica est disciplina magnitudinis inmobilis et formarum. Musica est disciplina quae de numeris loquitur qui ad aliquid sunt, his qui inveniuntur in sonis. Astronomia est disciplina, quae cursus caelestium siderumque figuras contemplatur omnes, et habitudines stellarum circa se et circa terram indagabili ratione percurrit.

[Philosophy] is called doctrinal when it studies abstract quantity, for that quantity is called abstract which we separate through the intellect from matter or from other accidental qualities—as are even and odd—or from such things, and treat with pure reason. There are four kinds: arithmetic, geometry, music, astronomy. Arithmetic is the discipline of quantity that can be counted in itself. Geometry is the discipline of unchanging size and of shapes. Music is the discipline that speaks of numbers that are specific to something, namely those that are found in sounds. Astronomy is the discipline that contemplates all the courses of the heavenly bodies and the figures of the constellations, and with careful reason considers the customary movements of the stars around one another and around the earth.

3.1 Compare SYM 7.3 *(me genuit)*; ps-SYM 1 *(Mater me genuit)*; ALD 33.1 *(me genuit)*, 59.1 *(Me . . . genuit)*, and 97.1 *(me genuit)*; TAT 11.1 *(me genuit)*; BON 14.1 *(me genuit)*; BIB 2.1 *(me . . . genuit)*; ALD 20.1 *(sine semine creta)*; BER 19.2 *(nullo virili creta de semine)* and 55.1 *(Semine nec ullo patris creatus)*; BIB 1.5 *(ternae patrio sine semine)* and 8.1 *(Sunt mihi . . . patrio sine semine ternae)*.

3.2 Compare BIB 1.6 *(virginitas . . . in aeva manet)* and BIB 8.2 *(virgo per aeva manet).*

3.3 Compare BIB 7.1 *(Sunt mihi germanae genitae de virgine binae),* BIB 8.1 *(Sunt mihi germanae),* BIB 12.1 *(Sunt mihi germanae genitae de virgine binae).*

3.4 Reading *numina* for G *nomina*. Compare BIB 11.4 *(dum sine me nequeunt).*

3.5 Compare BIB 1.7 *(tot fronte sub una),* BIB 9.3 *(tot fronte sub una).*

3.6 Compare BIB 2.9 *(turgent niveo tot pectore),* BIB 1.8 and 5.4 *(ubera tot niveo pectore sacra tument).*

3.7 Compare BIB 1.7 *(Terna mihi est species),* 2.7 *(Sunt mihi bis binae species),* BIB 4.1 *(Sunt mihi tres mirae species),* 5.3 *(Sunt mihi tres mirae species . . . lumina trina),* 7.7 *(Sunt mihi bis binae),* and 9.3 *(Tres mihi sunt species . . . tot fronte sub una).*

3.8 Reading *lucis* instead of G *locis,* which does not scan.

BIB 4

MANUSCRIPT: G, fol. 424r–v.
PREVIOUS EDITION: Gi, 51. (SK 15871)
SOLUTION: *GEOMETRIA* (geometry); G has *DE GEOMETRICA.*

For the likely ultimate source, see Isidore, *Etym.* 2.24.15 above.

4.1 Compare BIB 1.7 *(Terna mihi est species),* 2.7 *(Sunt mihi bis binae species),* 3.7 *(Una mihi species),* 5.3 *(Sunt mihi tres mirae species),* 7.7 *(Sunt mihi bis binae),* and 9.3 *(Tres mihi sunt species . . . tot fronte sub una).*

4.2 Compare BIB 7.7 *(species bis lumina bina).*

4.3 Compare SYM 94.2 *(unus . . . oculus).*

4.6 Note that *-que* is lengthened here at the caesura, a license that Bede approves in his *De arte metrica.*

4.7 Reading *metior at* for G *meteoras.*

4.7–8 An allusion to the traditional etymology of *geometria.*

BIB 5

MANUSCRIPT: G, fol. 424v.
PREVIOUS EDITION: Gi, 51. (SK 17532)
SOLUTION: *MUSICA* (music).

For the likely ultimate source, see Isidore, *Etym.* 2.24.15 above.

5.2 Reading *canora* for G *corona.*

5.3 Compare BIB 3.7 *(lumine trino),* 1.7 *(Terna mihi est species),* 2.7 *(Sunt mihi bis binae species),* 3.7 *(Una mihi species),* 4.1 *(Sunt mihi tres mirae species),* 7.7 *(Sunt mihi bis binae),* and 9.3 *(Tres mihi sunt species . . . tot fronte sub una).*

5.4 Compare BIB 2.9 (*turgent niveo tot pectore*), BIB 1.8 and 3.6 *(ubera tot niveo pectore sacra tument).*

5.7 Reading *fuerit* for G *sunt* (otherwise the line is half a foot short), as well as *cum* for G *quid,* as in BIB 10.2 *(nescio sed quid sit littera quidve potest).* Compare ALF F.2 *(Nescio quid);* ALD PR.17 *(carmina vatem),* 57.2 *(carmine vates),* 79.2 *(carmina vatum),* and 97.3 (*NOX,* "night": *carmine vates);* BON 13.44 *(carmina vatum).*

5.8 For the motif of an object that contains or encompasses, but cannot comprehend, cf. ALD 89 (*ARCA LIBRARIA,* "book chest").

BIB 6

MANUSCRIPT: G, fol. 424v.
PREVIOUS EDITION: Gi, 51–52. (SK 7934)
SOLUTION: *ASTRONOMIA* (astronomy).

For the likely ultimate source, see Isidore, *Etym.* 2.24.15 above.

6.3 Reading *sese dum tempora volvunt* (G *se dudum tempora volutant*).

BIB 7

MANUSCRIPT: G, fol. 424v.
PREVIOUS EDITION: Gi, 52. (SK 15866)
SOLUTION: *ETHICA* (ethics).

For the likely ultimate source, see Isidore, *Etym.* 2.24.5:

> Ethicam Socrates primus ad corrigendos conponendosque mores instituit, atque omne studium eius ad bene vivendi disputationem perduxit, dividens eam in quattuor virtutibus animae, id est prudentiam, iustitiam, fortitudinem, temperantiam.
>
> As for ethics, Socrates first established it as a way of correcting and establishing the way we live, and put all his effort toward a discussion of living well, splitting it into the four virtues of the soul: prudence, justice, fortitude, and temperance.

7.1 Compare BIB 3.3 *(Sunt mihi germanae genitae de virgine trinae),* BIB 8.1 *(Sunt mihi germanae),* BIB 12.1 *(Sunt mihi germanae genitae de virgine binae).*

7.7 Compare BIB 1.7 *(Terna mihi est species),* 2.7 *(Sunt mihi bis binae species),* 3.7 *(Una mihi species),* 4.1, 5.3 *(Sunt mihi tres mirae species),* and 9.3 *(Tres mihi sunt species . . . tot fronte sub una).*

7.8 Compare BIB 2.8 *(pignora tot genui virgo sed ipsa manens)* and 9.4 *(tot genui pignora virgo manens).*

BIB 8

MANUSCRIPT: G, fol. 424v–25r.
PREVIOUS EDITION: Gi, 52. (SK 15866)
SOLUTION: *QUATUOR VIRTUTES* (the four virtues).

The four virtues are temperance, justice, prudence, and fortitude; for the likely ultimate source, see Isidore, *Etym.* 2.24.5 above.

8.1 Compare BIB 1.5 *(Sunt mihi . . . ternae patrio sine semine),* BIB 3.6 *(patrio sine semine);* BIB 3.3 *(Sunt mihi germanae genitae de virgine trinae),* BIB 7.1 *(Sunt mihi germanae genitae de virgine binae),* BIB 12.1 *(Sunt mihi germanae genitae de virgine binae);* ALD 20.1 (*APIS,* "bee": *sine semine creta);* BER 19.2 *(nullo virili creta de semine),* BER 55.1 *(Semine nec ullo patris creatus).*

8.2 Compare BIB 1.6 *(virginitas . . . in aeva manet)* and BIB 3.2 *(in aeva manens).*

8.11 Compare BON 2.14 *(scando regna).*

BIB 9

MANUSCRIPT: G, fol. 425r.
PREVIOUS EDITION: Gi, 52–53. (SK 4613)
SOLUTION: *LOGICA* (logic).

For the likely ultimate source, see Isidore, *Etym.* 2.24.7:

> Logicam, quae rationalis vocatur, Plato subiunxit, per quam, discussis rerum morumque causis, vim earum rationabiliter perscrutatus est, dividens eam in Dialecticam et Rhetoricam. Dicta autem Logica, id est rationalis. λόγος enim apud Graecos et sermonem significat et rationem.

> Plato added logic, which is called rational [philosophy], and through that, when the causes of things and their conduct had been analysed, he thought through carefully the reason for those causes, while dividing it into rhetoric and dialectic. This [philosophy] is called logic, that is, rational *(rationalis),* for λόγος in Greek means both "speech" *(sermo)* and "reason" *(ratio).*

9.1 Compare ALD 23.1 *(geminas . . . sorores);* BON 4.1 *(geminae . . . sorores).*

9.3 Compare BIB 1.7 *(Terna mihi est species . . . tot fronte sub una),* BIB 3.5 *(sub fronte tot ora).*

BIB 10

MANUSCRIPT: G, fol. 425r.
PREVIOUS EDITION: Gi, 53. (SK 8959)
SOLUTION: *GRAMMATICA* (grammar).

For the likely ultimate source, see Isidore, *Etym.* 1.2.1–3:

> Disciplinae liberalium artium septem sunt. Prima grammatica, id est loquendi peritia. Secunda rhetorica, quae propter nitorem et copiam eloquentiae suae maxime in civibibus quaestionibus necessaria existimatur. Tertia dialectica cognomento logica, quae disputationibus subtilissimis vera secernit a falsis. Quarta arithmetica, quae continet numerorum causas et divisiones. Quinta musica, quae in carminibus cantibusque consistit. Sexta geometrica, quae mensuras terrae dimensionesque conplectitur. Septima astronomia, quae continet legem astrorum.

> There are seven disciplines within the liberal arts. The first is grammar, that is, skill in speaking. The second is rhetoric, which, on account of the brilliance and fluency of its eloquence, is reckoned most necessary in public debates. The third is dialectic, otherwise known as logic, which separates the true from the false by highly subtle argumentation. The fourth is arithmetic, which contains the properties and types of numbers. The fifth is music, which consists of poems and songs. The sixth is geometry, which comprises the measures and dimensions of the earth. The seventh is astronomy, which covers the rules of the stars.

10.1 The distinction between Greek *gramma* and Latin *littera* lies at the core of this aenigma, which like many others in the Anglo-Saxon riddle tradition contains a clue in the opening line.

BIB 11

MANUSCRIPT: G, fol. 425r.
PREVIOUS EDITION: Gi, 53. (SK 1187)
SOLUTION: *RHETORICA* (rhetoric).

For the likely ultimate source, see Isidore, *Etym.* 2.23, *De differentia dialecticae et rhetoricae artis* (The difference between the arts of rhetoric and dialectic).

11.1 Some pun on *foecunda,* "fertile," and *facunda,* "eloquent," seems clear here.
11.4 Compare BIB 3.4 *(quae sine me nequeunt).*

BIB 12

MANUSCRIPT: G, fol. 425r.
PREVIOUS EDITION: Gi, 53. (SK 15864)
SOLUTION: *DIALECTICA* (dialectic); G has *DE DIALECTICA.*

For the likely ultimate source, see Isidore, *Etym.* 2.22, which, like the prose introduction to ALD, also mentions Aristotle.

12.1 Compare BIB 3.3 *(Sunt mihi germanae genitae de virgine trinae),* BIB 7.1 *(Sunt mihi germanae genitae de virgine binae),* BIB 8.1 *(Sunt mihi germanae).*

The Old English Tradition

THE FRANKS CASKET RIDDLE

Authorship and Date

The so-called Franks or Auzon Casket, most of which is in the British Museum, seems to have been carved around 700 in northern England, in a rare case where the linguistic, art historical, and runic evidence all converge. It is an extraordinarily intricate object, carved from whalebone, and containing a number of inscriptions, with Old English and runic script predominating (there are more than 260 runes, some of them, all on the right side, cryptic), but also including a number in Latin and in Roman script. The riddle proper consists of only two long alliterative lines, followed by the solution, the very "whale's bone" *(HWÆLES BAN)* from which the casket was carved.

Context

FRA is found written in runes on the front panel of the casket, clockwise from the top left, along the front, down the right side, across the bottom (with the runes running backwards), and up the left side. The inscription frames a double scene depicting the Adoration of the Magi on the right and the vengeance of the legendary Germanic smith Weland on the left; the gifts of the three kings to Christ (gold, frankincense, and myrrh) seem contrasted with the gifts that the vindictive Weland offers to Beaduhild, the daughter of his captor, King Nidhad: a cup of drugged drink, and jewelry made from the skulls of her murdered brothers.

Subject Matter and Solution

Since FRA not only supplies its own solution, but is carved on an object made from the material mentioned, it might be said to be perhaps the least enigmatic of all the riddles. Yet it is not entirely without mystery and interest, as seen in the notes below.

Style

Even though FRA is only two lines long, it nonetheless contains two unique compounds. The first, *fergen-berig* (1b), belongs to a family of seven surviving *fyrgen-* compounds that are mostly attested only in verse (where three of the others are also unique); two of these unique compounds (*fyrgen-beam,* "mountain tree," and *fyrgen-holt,* "mountain forest"), together with a third (*fyrgen-stream,* "mountain stream") which is more widely attested (for example in EXE 8.1), occur in *Beowulf,* always in relation to the monster-mere, and such a sense of awe also fits the context of *fergen-berig* in FRA. The other unique compound, *gas-ric* (2a), is harder to construe: the first element seems related to Gothic *gaisjan,* "to terrify," and the second to Gothic *reiks,* "king"; the alternative suggestion is that the form should be read as a metathesis of *gar-sic,* in the sense "king of the ocean," "king of piercing cold." Elsewhere on the casket we find *afitatores* for *habitatores,* "inhabitants," carved in the Roman alphabet, reflecting a *-b-* for *-f-* spelling that is found elsewhere in the Anglo-Saxon riddle tradition; see further the headnote on LEI below.

Sources and Parallels

Although the solution to FRA is embodied in the object on which it is found, it is important to note that it is couched in the third person, as opposed to the many first-person examples of speaking objects, especially the late ninth-century Alfred Jewel, with its inscription *Aelfred mec heht gevvyrcan,* "Alfred had me made," or the late tenth-century Brussels Reliquary Cross, which proclaims that *Drahmal me worhte,* "Drahmal made me"; in the context of the latter, the late seventh-century Ruthwell Cross, with its runic inscription apparently drawing on an earlier version of the *Dream of the Rood,* may be more pertinent to a discussion of FRA, since the object celebrating and commemorating its previous life as Christ's Cross *(rod)* is indeed itself a cross (see further Orchard, "*Dream of the Rood*"). Still more relevant in terms of an object describing the material of its manufacture is the ninth-century runic inscription on the Brandon antler, spelling out *wohs wildum deoræ an,* which is interpreted as "I grew on a wild animal" (see further Bammesberger, "Brandon Antler").

This Text and Translation

Here I rely heavily on the readings of Page, *Introduction to English Runes,* 174–77, supplemented by the interpretations below.

Further Reading

Parsons, *Recasting the Runes;* Webster, *The Franks Casket.*

FRA

1 My translation assumes that *flodu* is the subject and *fisc* the object, but in fact the terms could be reversed: "The fish raised up the sea onto the towering cliff" also works both grammatically and conceptually.

THE LEIDEN RIDDLE

Authorship and Date

The date of the manuscript, D, is variously given as "earlier ninth century" or "s. ix/x," while the language of LEI is described as "probably an eighth-century variety of Northumbrian"; the foreign scribe has transmitted a number of early Old English spellings, especially as compared with the updated version of LEI 1–12 found at EXE 33.1–12 (*BYRNE,* "mail-coat"), notably *ae* for *æ*, *b* for *f*, *th* for *þ*, and *u* for *w* (really ᚹ), as well as dialectal distinctions between the predominantly West-Saxon spellings of EXE 33 and the Anglian LEI. The fact that EXE 33 seems to preserve several Anglian spellings (notably *ærist* and *hafu,* EXE 33.2b and 33.5b) is of interest here, and given that ALD, including ALD 33 (*LORICA,* "mailcoat"), the direct source of LEI, was sent by Aldhelm along with the so-called *Epistola ad Acircium* to King Aldfrith of Northumbria (686–705), it is tempting to suggest that the Anglian version is original. This would place the translation of LEI in the context of Aldfrith's Northumbria, so aligning LEI with other early reflexes of the Anglo-Saxon riddle tradition, notably ALD and FRA. Indeed, all three of these texts share the *-b-* for *-f-* or *-v-* spelling that is found widely throughout the tradition, as for example at ALD PR.4 *(Vehemoth* for *Behemoth),* 27.4 *(mulcifer* for *mulciber),* and 63.10 *(CORBUS* for *CORVUS);* TAT 34.2 *(acervis* for *acerbis);* EUS 37.2 *(bibere* for *vivere)* and 60 *(BUBALO* as a variant of *BUFALO);* BON PR.11 *(acervissima* for *acerbissima);* SYM 33.1 *(videntes* as a variant of *bidentes).*

Manuscript Context

The manuscript, D, was at Fleury in the second half of the ninth century, and LEI was added alongside a series of pen-trials and neumes on fol. 25v; SYM appears on fols. 2v–8v, immediately followed by a list of solutions to ALD on fols. 8v–10r and then the collection of ALD proper on fols. 10v–25v.

Subject Matter and Solution

The solution is scarcely in doubt, given the manuscript context, the derivation from ALD 33 (*LORICA*, "mail-coat"), and the close relationship of LEI 1–12 with EXE 33.1–12 (*BYRNE*, "mail-coat").

Style

The strategy here of translating one Latin hexameter by two long lines of Old English verse is widely witnessed in Anglo-Saxon England (see Steen, *Verse and Virtuosity,* 35–110), and emphasized in LEI by capitalization of the opening word of every other line of the fourteen in the poem, corresponding to the seven Latin hexameters of ALD 33. So close is the correspondence that, since lines 7–8 of the Old English coincide with line 5 of the Latin and lines 9–10 of the Old English with line 4 of the Latin, the translator was likely working from a version of the Latin text with those lines transposed. An updated version of LEI 1–12 is found as EXE 33.1–12 (*BYRNE*, "mail-coat").

Sources and Parallels

LEI has a direct source in ALD 33, with the transposition discussed above. Although such transpositions are found with regard to other *aenigmata* of ALD, there has to date been no manuscript identified with the switching of lines 4 and 5 of ALD 33 suggested here; certainly D, which contains both LEI and a version of ALD 33, has the usual arrangement of lines, and so cannot itself be the source.

This Text and Translation

LEI has been edited and discussed many times; here I rely on the edition and notes of Sm, especially as supplemented by Dance, "The Old English Language and the Alliterative Tradition," 40–42.

Further Reading

Bremmer and Dekker, "Leiden, Universiteitsbibliotheek, Vossianus Lat. Q. 106"; Orchard, "Old English and Latin Poetic Traditions"; Leahy, *Anglo-Saxon Crafts,* 131–33; Cavell, *Weaving Words,* 54–67.

LEI

MANUSCRIPT: D, fol. 25v.

EARLIER EDITIONS AND TRANSLATIONS: Sm, 44–47.

SOLUTION: *BYRNE* (mailcoat), as in the closely related EXE 33 and ALD 33 (*LORICA,* "mailcoat").

1–2 Compare ALD 33.1 *(Roscida me genuit gelido de viscere tellus);* EXE 33.1–2 *(Mec se wæta wong, wundrum freorig, / of his innaþe ærist cende).*

2 An updated form of this line is found as *Paris Psalter* 126.4.4 *(of innaðe ærest cende).* LEI 2 derives very directly from ALD 33.1, while the various Latin equivalents available for Psalm 124.4 have only the general "children" *(filii)* at this same point. The final lines of LEI and ALD 33 speak of both "arrows" (*sagittae*) and (in some versions) "a quiver" or "quivers" (*faretram;* Old English *cocrum*), so it may be that the poet of *The Paris Psalter* is deliberately alluding to LEI.

2b None of *cændæ* is visible; the missing word is supplied from EXE 33.2b; see further Parkes, "Leiden Riddle," 208–9.

3–4 Compare ALD 33.2 *(non sum setigero lanarum vellere facta);* EXE 33.3–4 *(ne wat ic mec beworhtne wulle flysum, / hærum þurh heah-cræft, hyge-þoncum min).*

4–8 Noteworthy here is the sevenfold anaphora on *ne.*

4b Only *hygi-ðonc* is visible; the missing text is supplied from EXE 33.4b.

5–6 Compare ALD 33.3 *(licia nulla trahunt nec garrula fila resultant);* EXE 33.5–6 *(Wundene me ne beoð wefle, ne ic wearp hafu, / ne þurh þreata geþræcu þræd me ne hlimmeð).*

7–8 Compare ALD 33.5 *(nec radiis carpor duro nec pectine pulsor);* EXE 33.7–8 *(ne æt me hrutende hrisil scriþeð, / ne mec ohwonan sceal am cnyssan).*

7b Note the later substitution of *scriþeð,* "slides," for *scelfath,* "shake," and the change from plural to singular.

8b Note the later reversed word order in EXE 33.8b *sceal am* (E reads *amas*).

9–10 Compare ALD 33.4 *(nec crocea Seres texunt lanugine vermes);* EXE 33.9–10 *(Wyrmas mec ne awæfan wyrda cræftum, / þa þe geolo god-webb geatwum frætwað).*

11–12 Compare ALD 33.6 *(et tamen en vestis vulgi sermone vocabor);* EXE 33.11–12 *(wile mec mon hwæþre seþeah wide ofer eorþan / hatan for hæleþum hyhtlic gewæde).*

11a Note the later addition of *mon* in EXE 33.11a.

11b Compare EXE 38.21a *(ænig ofer eorþan),* 80.42b *(weras ofer eorþan),* 84.18a *(anga ofer eorþan),* and 91.10a *(ænig ofer eorðan);* note that there is no equivalent in the Latin source.

12a For the notion of the creature's speaking *for hæleþum,* compare EXE 18.12a *(mine for mengo);* 46.1a *(Ic gefrægn for hæleþum);* 46.4a *(sinc for secgum);* 53.8a *(eaþe for eorlum).*

13–14 EXE 33.13–14 is quite different *(Saga soð-cwidum, searo-þoncum gleaw, / wordum wis-fæst, hwæt þis gewæde sy),* a variant of the closing formulaic challenge *Saga hwæt ic hatte,* on which see the note at EXE 1.14b–15 above.

THE EXETER BOOK RIDDLES

Authorship and Date

Almost all of the collection that makes up EXE is found uniquely in three groups within the so-called Exeter Book (E). The manuscript itself can be fairly closely dated to the last quarter of the tenth century, and its provenance a century later is securely documented: the Exeter Book has been in the Library of Exeter Cathedral continuously and with only minor breaks since the bequest of Leofric in 1072, if we accept (as most do) that the reference in Leofric's will to "a large book in English about various things, written in verse" *(.i. mycel englisc boc be gehwilcum þingum on leoð-wisan geworht)* does indeed describe the Exeter Book. Older scholarship, long since discredited, both extended the number of the riddles to be considered part of the collection, and boldly attributed authorship to Cynewulf, one of the few Anglo-Saxon poets whose name we know, largely on the doubtful basis of mysterious references to wolves, in Old English on the one hand (*Wulf and Eadwacer,* considered the first poem in the collection) and in Latin (EXE 86) on the other. More recent scholarship has detected many different voices in EXE, as well as clear connections between individual riddles, sometimes suggesting a series of conscious attempts to emulate, improve, or otherwise echo earlier riddles not only from EXE itself, but from the wider Anglo-Saxon riddle tradition as a whole.

Manuscript Context

Of all the major Old English poetic codices, E has the most varied content, including not only riddles but also elegies, gnomic and heroic verse, and a number of longer religious and hagiographical poems. Only the near-contemporary Anglo-Saxon Latin manuscript G, the overarching educational purpose of which is widely acknowledged, contains a similar range and variety of verse (on which see the introduction to *OEALRT,* under "Manuscript Contexts"), including no fewer than seven of the fourteen collections of riddles considered here (specifically SYM, ALD, TAT, EUS, BED, BIB, and ALF). According to current editorial practice, there are three distinct groupings within the Exeter Book: EXE 1–57; EXE 28b and 58; and EXE 59–91. The first of these groupings is immediately preceded and followed by two undoubtedly enigmatic poems, *Wulf and Eadwacer* and *The Wife's Lament,* both voiced by lone female protagonists. It is notable that both the final line of the former and the opening line of the latter contain the Old English word *giedd,* which has a variety of meanings, including "poem," "song," "proverb," and "story," but also "riddle"; within EXE, the word appears at EXE 45.3b and 53.14b. It is the final grouping of EXE 59–91 that has been most affected by physical damage; the concluding folios of E have suffered extensive everyday damage over the years, perhaps from a poker and a beer mug, as well as having been used as a chopping board. Somewhat pleasingly, all three elements are enshrined in the Anglo-Saxon riddle tradition—for example, ps-BED 13 (*COPA,* "beer mug"), EXE 60 (for which one suggested solution is *BOR,* "poker," "borer"), and EXE 3 (*BORD,* "chopping board")—while missing leaves also echo the damaged and imperfect texts.

Subject Matter and Solutions

Like every other collection making up the Anglo-Saxon riddle tradition, EXE contains several readily identifiable sequences and groupings, whether considered by solution, or theme, or structure, or diction. The run of bird-solutions ("swan," "nightingale," "cuckoo," and "barnacle goose") in EXE 5–8 is only the most obvious; other suggested pairings and sequences are indicated in the notes to (for example) EXE 10–13, EXE 19–20, EXE 24–26, EXE 29–31, EXE 42–44, EXE 45–47, EXE 71–72, and EXE 73–75. There are also an unspecified number of so-called double-entendre riddles, although not all scholars are agreed on which ones fit the bill (see further the headnote at EXE 23). The fact that, as the index below makes clear, the solution "penis" has been suggested at one time or another for twenty-two of the ninety-one riddles of EXE perhaps says more about Anglo-Saxonists than Anglo-Saxons, although recent work by Salvador-Bello demonstrates that salacious solutions and double-entendre aenigmata are also found in the Latin collections of the Anglo-Saxon riddle tradition. The various elements of salacious suggestion in the double-entendre riddles have further parallels with the outlandish monstrosity shared between EXE and Anglo-Saxon accounts of the outside world, as generally accessed through Latin or ultimately Greek accounts, and can be considered under three main headings, as follows:

Miscegenation
Bodily deformity
Unusual enumeration of body parts

Several of the riddles speak of the creature in question as somehow exotic, and useful parallels might be drawn between the descriptions of exotic creatures in *The Letter of Alexander to Aristotle* or *The Wonders of the East* and several of those depicted in EXE; see particularly the notes to EXE 29–30 below (and see further Orchard, "Riddles of Lewdness and Learning").

There are half a dozen drinking-formulas within the collection that have been held to argue for its origins in the mead-hall, although given the explicit setting of the aenigmata of Symphosius at a drinking-party, such an assumption may seem rash; the formulas in question are found at EXE 12.12b *(OXA,* "ox": *þær weras drincað);* EXE 18.12b *(SECG,* "sword," "man": *þær hy meodu drincað);* EXE 53.1b *(*WÆPEN-HENGEN,* "weapon rack": *þær hæleð druncon);* EXE 54.11b *(*RID-ROD,* "pole-lathe": *þær hæleð druncon);* EXE 61.3b *(GLÆS-FÆT,* "glass beaker": *þær guman drincað);* EXE 65.14b *(CRISTES BOC,* "Gospel book": *þær guman druncon);* and perhaps EXE 82.1b *(AN-EAGEDE GAR-LEAC-MONGER,* "one-eyed garlic-seller": *þær weras sæton).* A further five riddles have solutions implicitly connected to drinking or drink: EXE 9 (*WIN-FÆT,* "cup of wine"); EXE 25 (*MEDU,* "mead" or *BEOR,* "beer"); EXE 26 (*EALU,* "ale"); EXE 57 (*CALIC,* "chalice"); EXE 61 (*GLÆS-FÆT,* "glass beaker").

Other themes have been detected that link EXE more broadly with other texts in the Anglo-Saxon riddle tradition; for example, several of the riddles in EXE have been suggested to be more or less clearly associated with biblical themes, and the Old Testament in particular: see the notes to EXE 1, 15, 23, 43, 44, and 79. Likewise, a good deal of battle imagery, as well as several riddles with mock-heroic themes, are found in EXE, notably EXE 13 (*IGIL*, "hedgehog," "porcupine"), EXE 15 (*COCER*, "quiver"), EXE 31 (*IS*, "ice, ice floe"), and EXE 80 (*WÆTER*, "water"), as the notes below demonstrate. See further in general the introduction to *OEALRT*, under "Shared Themes across the Collections."

Style

More than three quarters of the riddles that make up EXE begin with one or other of a dozen or more opening formulas so far identified (see in general the notes to EXE 2.1a, 3.1a, 8.1a, 11.1a, 12.1a, 16.1a, 29.1–2, 31.1a, 32.1a, 41.1a, 43.1a, 48.1, and 67.1a), occasionally in combination, of which the most common are of the "I am" or "I saw" kind (on which see the notes to EXE 3.1a and 11.1a). In a similar vein, just under a third of the riddles in EXE conclude with one or more of four formulaic challenges, demands, or appeals (see the notes to EXE 1.14b–15, 12.19b, 26.12b–13, and 33.13–14). Nearly a quarter of the riddles in EXE have both opening and closing formulas, and the fact that the overwhelming majority of these formulas are shared by the two major clusters of riddles (EXE 1–57 and 59–91), while both of the riddles in the other, smaller cluster (EXE 28b and 58) likewise share formulas with both of the larger clusters, attests to the extent to which the riddles of EXE can be considered as a distinct generic grouping within the manuscript.

Some structural and stylistic patterns can be matched in Latin, notably anaphora, on the wide distribution of which throughout EXE, see the note to EXE 1.16a. Several other shared patterns are considered in the introduction to *OEALRT*, under "Style." With regard to features generally regarded as native to Old English, it is notable that there are eighteen kennings in EXE, and their distribution is distinctly uneven: EXE 1.20b (*GODES WIND*, "Wind of God": *hwæl-mere)*, EXE 1.25b *(sund-helm)*, EXE 1.67a *(wæg-fatu)*, EXE 1.68a *(lagu-stream)*, and EXE 1.88b *(ryne-giest)*; EXE 3.7b *(BORD*, "shield," "chopping board": *homera laf)*; EXE 8.11a *(BYRNETE*, "barnacle goose": *seolh-baþo)*; EXE 11.6b *(TEN CICCENU*, "ten chickens":

mere-hengest); EXE 18.4a *(SECG,* "man," "sword": *wæl-gim);* EXE 19.3a *(SULH,* "plough": *holtes feond);* EXE 21.13a *(BOGA,* "bow": *man-drinc);* EXE 24.7b *(CRISTES BOC,* "Gospel book": *fugles wyn)* and EXE 24.14a *(wrætlic weorc smiþa);* EXE 71.19b *(ÆSC,* "spear made of ash": *heaþo-sigel);* EXE 74.1b *(OSTRE,* "oyster": *sund-helm);* EXE 83.5a *(BLÆST-BELG,* "bellows": *heofenes toþ);* EXE 89.28b *(BLÆC-HORN,* "inkhorn": *hiþende feond)* and EXE 89.32b *(dæg-condel).* The fact that five of the eighteen are found in EXE 1 (*GODES WIND,* "Wind of God") again attests to the highly wrought language of that riddle; the only others in the collection that contain more than one kenning are the equally ornate EXE 24 (*CRISTES BOC,* "Gospel book") and EXE 89 (*BLÆC-HORN,* "inkhorn"), both dealing with different aspects of manuscript production. Kennings, of course, are in a sense mini-riddles in their own right, and it is likewise of interest in this context that other riddles within riddles (on which see further the note to EXE 1.12–14a) are especially prevalent in the final quarter of the collection where by contrast true kennings are sparse.

Sources and Parallels

The Old English riddles of EXE lie at the very heart of the Anglo-Saxon riddle tradition, looking back toward Latin (specifically Anglo-Latin) texts, sideways insofar as several of the riddles in EXE deal with similar themes in similar ways, and forward to the extent that some individual riddles in EXE seem very clearly to have spawned and inspired others.

To be sure, there is a direct relationship between EXE 33 and ALD 33 on the one hand and EXE 38 and ALD 100 on the other, and several others of the riddles in EXE seem either to quote all or part of parallel Latin aenigmata (see, for example, the notes on EXE 31 and 36) or to develop the basic themes and structures of a Latin text in such a way as to make the connection between the texts very clear (see, for example, the notes on EXE 45, 63, and 82). It is also evident from the notes below, however, that many of the same themes, techniques, and topics link many of the individual riddles of EXE to a greater or lesser extent with many of the major Anglo-Latin collections of aenigmata (specifically ALD, ps-BED, TAT, EUS, ALC, and

BON), as well as the more important of their sources and analogues (particularly SYM, BER, and GES).

With regard to other Old English texts, there seems to be a specific link between *Andreas* and several riddles, including both EXE 1 (*GODES WIND*, "Wind of God": see the notes at 1.17b, 1.19b, 1.20, 1.21a, 1.38b, 1.71, and 1.74a) and EXE 20 (*CARLES WÆN*, "Charles's Wain": see the notes at 20.7a and 20.11a). Likewise, there seem to be close verbal parallels between the *Phoenix* and several riddles, including the two consecutive pairs EXE 5 (*SWAN*, "swan": see the notes at 5.6–9 and 5.7b–8a) and EXE 6 (*NIHTE-GALE*, "nightingale": see the note at 6.2) on the one hand, and EXE 40 (*HANA OND HÆN*, "cock and hen": see the notes at 40.4a and 40.17a) and EXE 41 (*GÆST OND LICHAMA*, "soul and body": see the notes at 41.2b–4a), on the other. It is worth emphasizing that there are other reasons to connect these pairs, as their headnotes also make clear.

This Text and Translation

There has been more discussion, spread over more editions and translations, of EXE than of all of the rest of the Anglo-Saxon riddle tradition put together. Here I have consulted all of the editions and translations listed in the headnotes to individual riddles, and have sought in the translations not to force the meanings to fit supposed solutions, however tempting that has sometimes seemed. In particular, differences from what might be considered the canonical texts of KD and Mu are highlighted in the notes, although of the other dedicated editions and translations I have made most use of Po and PZ.

Further Reading

Excellent and highly specific commentary is to be found in the various editions and translations of EXE given in the List of Abbreviations of Previous Editions, Translations, and Commentaries, above, especially Wi and PZ, and notably Ni, while of the various monographs and broader studies consulted, the most useful are Gleissner, *Die "zweideutigen" altenglischen Rätsel des "Exeter Book"*; Göbel, *Studien zu den altenglischen Schriftwesenratseln;* Rügamer, *Die Poetizität der altenglischen Rätsel;* Bitterli, *Say What I Am Called;* and Murphy, *Unriddling the Exeter Riddles.* For earlier general studies, see Schneider, *Satzbau und Wortschatz;* Thorpe, *Codex Exoniensis;* Chambers, Förster, and Flower, *Exeter Book of Old English Poetry;* Mackie, *The Exeter Book;* Carmody, "*Physiologus Latinus versio Y*"; Stewart, "Kenning and Riddle in Old English"; Barley, "Structural Aspects of the Anglo-Saxon Riddle"; Hacikyan, "Literary and Social Aspects"; Conlee, "Artistry"; Nelson, "Rhetoric"; Nelson, "Time in the Exeter Book Riddles"; Fry, "Solutions"; Lendinara, "Aspetti della società germanica"; Lendinara, "Gli enigmi del Codice Exoniense"; Tigges, "Signs and Solutions"; Tigges, "Snakes and Ladders"; Green, "Semiotics of Compounds"; Conner, "Structure of the Exeter Book Codex"; Kries, "*Fela í rúnum eða í skáldskap*"; Riedinger, "Formulaic Style"; Conner, *Anglo-Saxon Exeter*; Gameson, "Origin of the Exeter Book"; Lindow, "Riddles, Kennings"; Marino, "Literariness"; Pope, "Palaeography and Poetry"; Orton, "Technique of Object-Personification"; Oda, *A Concordance to the Riddles of the Exeter Book;* Rissanen, "*Nathwæt* in the *Exeter Book Riddles*"; Poole, *Old English Wisdom Poetry;* Zimmermann, *Four Poetic Manuscripts;* Salvador-Bello, "Patterns of Compilation"; Salvador-Bello, "Sexual Riddle Type in Aldhelm's *Enigmata*"; Salvador-Bello, *Isidorean Perceptions,* 291–344 and 473–74. Special mention might also be made of the dedicated website by Cavell, Symons, and Ammon, "The Riddle Ages."

EXE PART 1

EXE 1

MANUSCRIPT: E, fol. 101r–2v.

EARLIER EDITIONS AND TRANSLATIONS: Gr 2–4; Tr 1; Tu 2–4; Wy 1–3; Ma 1–3; KD 1–3; Ba 1–2, 3–7; Ab 1–3; WiR 1; WiF1 59–61; Wh 1–3, 161–65; PZ 1; CH 1–3, 3–7; Mu 1–3; WiC 1, 526–28 and 1151.

SOLUTION: *GODES WIND* (wind of God); other suggested solutions include: "storm" (Dietrich, "Würdigung, Lösung und Herstellung"), "wind" (Wy; Wi), "atmosphere" (Erhardt-Siebold, "Old

English Storm Riddles"), "power of Nature" (J. J. Campbell, "A Certain Power"), "apocalyptic storm" (Foley, "'Riddle I' of the *Exeter Book*"), "the Stoic cosmological concept of *pneuma*" (Lapidge, "Stoic Cosmology"). For EXE 1.1–15 (edited as a separate riddle), suggested solutions include: "fire" (Shook, "Old English Riddle I"), "raiding party" (Jember, *Old English Riddles*), "army" (Mitchell, "Ambiguity and Germanic Imagery"), "storm" (Ni). For EXE 1.16–30 (taken as a separate riddle), suggested solutions include: "anchor" (Gr; Jember, *Old English Riddles*), "submarine earthquake" (Tu); for EXE 1.16–104 (taken as a separate riddle), suggested solutions include: "sun" (Conybeare, *Illustrations of Anglo-Saxon Poetry*); for EXE 1.31–104 (taken as a separate riddle), suggested solutions include: "hurricane" (Gr); "revenant" (Jember, *Old English Riddles*); *god,* "god" (Ni). See further Pinsker, "Bemerkungen zum ae. Sturmrätsel"; E. Williams, "Pagan Survivals and Diction"; Salvador-Bello, "Compilation of the Old English Riddles," 76–103; E. Williams, "*Hwa mec rære?*"; Teele, "Heroic Tradition," 123–29; McFadden, "Raiding, Reform, and Reaction"; Salvador-Bello, *Isidorean Perceptions,* 291–98; Cavell, *Weaving Words,* 187–90; Dale, *Natural World,* 182–96; Lockhart, "Everyday Wonders and Enigmatic Structures," 99–100 and 118–19.

That the first riddle of the Exeter Book is a complex poem makes it a fittingly puzzling opening to the collection, and there is still debate as to whether what is given here as EXE 1 is in fact one poem, or two (as the scribe of the Exeter Book seems to indicate by his layout), or even three (as most modern editors have presented it). The problem is complicated by the fact that all of the collections contain sequences of riddles connected to the neighboring texts, or even consecutive riddles on the same theme; see the introduction to *OEALRT,* under "Shared Themes across the Collections," and the headnotes to SYM and TAT in particular. In other editions, EXE 1 is often read as a connected sequence of three, and some aspect of "storm" or "wind" has become a generally accepted solution. In fact, however, the three parts of the sequence, marked off as divisions within the manuscript in rather different ways, all focus on different aspects of a much larger issue: in a Christian context, the repeated question *hwa,* "who?," that runs through all three sections perceived separately can only be answered by "God," although the destructive nature of the being described has caused problems for some (compare, however, *Wan* 85–87 and EUS 1 [*DE DEO,* "about God"], both of which deal with a destructive God). For non-Christians, without such scruples, the figure in question might even be "Thor," especially given his supposed role as the primary wind-raiser (see Perkins, *Thor the Wind-Raiser*), or even Aeolus of classical literature, whose key role as storm-raiser and storm-appeaser appears in the opening book of Virgil's *Aeneid* (see the note at EXE 1.31–36b). Likewise, it is possible to see parallels with the account of Christ's calming of the storm at Matthew 8:24–27. In effect, this opening riddle poses the most fundamental questions about the collection as a whole, and the potential range of its sources and influences (imported vs. native, Christian vs. secular, learned vs. lay) reflects that of Anglo-Saxon literature in general.

A similarly fundamental question is also raised here that affects several of the other riddles in EXE (see, for example, the headnotes to EXE 73 and EXE 76), and indeed several of the other texts in the manuscript as a whole, since the manuscript layout clearly suggests two separate riddles (EXE 1.1–15 is marked off from EXE 1.16–104 [= 1b.1–15 and 1c.1–74]), while most editors present the material as either three separate texts (EXE 1.1–15, EXE 1.16–104 [= 1b.1–15], and EXE 1.31–104 [= 1c.1–74]), or one, with three distinct sections. Trautmann (*Die altenglische Rätsel,* 65) was the first to argue for the unity of this, perhaps the most sophisticated of all the riddles from Anglo-Saxon England, which, however, he carefully divided into no fewer than six sections, characterized and solved as follows:

1.1–15	storm on land
1.16–30 (1b.1–15)	earthquake under the sea
1.31–46 (1c.1–16)	earthquake on land
1.47–65 (1c.17–35)	storm at sea
1.66–96 (1c.36–66)	storm and thunderstorm in the sky
1.97–104 (1c.67–74)	summary and concluding challenge

The earth/sea/sky comparison is a commonplace in the riddle tradition elsewhere, notably in ALD 100 (*CREATURA*, "creation"), and the general theme of storms in all three regions is clear. But there are other ways to divide the text. There are, for example, eight separate explicit challenges scattered throughout this riddle, which combine in a clearly patterned fashion to ask both the nature of the creature in question and the identity of the individual who controls it by alternately unleashing and confining it, with an extensive central gap at 1.30–65a:

1.2b–6a	who unleashes?
1.14b	who confines?
1.15	what?
1.27b–29 (1b.12–14)	who unleashes?
. . .	
1.65b (1c.35b)	who confines?
1.102b (1c.72b)	what?
1.103	who unleashes?
1.104	who confines?

Such an intertwined variety of patterning of both who/what (AABAABAA) and unleashing/confining (CDCDCD) suggests a twin solution, with the storm-causing *GODES WIND* as raiser and calmer of storms as perhaps the most likely combination, as if the author were deliberately mingling elements found at the beginning of two other collections, since the closest analogues are ALD 2 (*VENTUS*, "wind") and EUS 1 (*DEUS*, "god").

However one chooses to divide it, this riddle stands out in Anglo-Saxon literature as an extraordinary piece of storm-poetry. It is intriguing to note that one of the few similarly extended descriptions is found in Aldhelm's *Carmen rhythmicum (CR)*, which relates to a violent storm that he witnessed himself while traveling through Cornwall toward Devon, and which has several parallels with EXE 1; overall, Aldhelm explicitly connects the mighty power of the wind-driven storm to the unknowable power of God: "What shall I say of the mighty works of the high-throned one, which no one can reckon in number on a counting-board?" (*Quid dicam de ingentibus / altithroni operibus, / quae nullus nequit numero / conputare in calculo?*). Specific parallels are noted at the relevant places below relating to imagery of the confinement of the winds (EXE 1.31–36b); the smashing of buildings (EXE 36b–39a); the crashing of waves on the shore (EXE 1.47–58a); the generation of thunder and lightning (EXE 1.69b–78a); and the depiction of a storm as a raging and marauding army (EXE 1.78b–82).

There are other analogues to EXE 1 both in the Anglo-Saxon riddle tradition and beyond. Note that Aldhelm begins his own aenigmata (ALD 1–2) with the sequence *TERRA,* "land" and *VENTUS,* "wind." Lapidge seeks to bring these aspects together in the Stoic conception of *pneuma* ("wind," "soul," "mind," "god"), as a combined solution to this riddle, while Lockett points to a "hydraulic" conception of mind/soul in Anglo-Saxon England that also seems to be echoed here. A particularly interesting link can be found in the extraordinary set of apparently seventh-century Hiberno-Latin texts known as the *Hisperica famina,* at least some version of which seems to have been known to Aldhelm (see the introduction to *OEALRT,* under "Sources and Analogues"; Herren, *Hisperica Famina: The A-Text;* Orchard, "*Hisperica famina* as Literature"). Several sections of the *Hisperica famina* closely resemble riddles, being essentially rhetorical exercises describing a number of topics matched elsewhere in the Anglo-Saxon riddle tradition, and often including formulaic beginnings and endings of a sort paralleled especially in EXE. *Hisperica famina* A479–96 (*DE VENTO,* "on the wind"), like EXE 1, focuses on the destructive power of the wind to uproot trees and tear the roofs off houses; to gust from the heights of the sky to the bottom of the pit; to be an instrument of a wrathful God; to be unseen, but to scream loud; and to be associated with the biblical Flood (*Hisperica famina* A477–82; 488–90; 493–96):

Hic sonoreus alma mactat sepherus robora,
aniosas terrestribus plicat ilices sulcis,
turrita robustis spoliat tugoria flabris,
superna cacuminum frictat laquearia,
tithica flectit telluri cerula,
ac marinas exaltat in astra spumas.

❦

mundanum vasto aethere proflant in follum;
trina mormoreus pastricat trophea nothus:
quod spumaticum rapuit tollo diluvium.

❦

nec sibilans intueri queat procella
Altusque poli rector
mormorantibus degesti de pennis euri
gibrosum reamine censebit lochum.

This booming breeze smashes the sacred oaks,
it flattens the ancient holm-oaks in their earthen furrows,
destroys the towering cottages with strong blasts,
beats down the lofty roof-tops,
bends the blue seas toward the shore,
and raises the watery spray up to the stars.

❦

[The winds] blow forth from the empty sky into the depths
 of the world
The roaring blast builds a triple victory
because it snatched away the foaming deluge in the Flood.

❦

nor can that whistling storm be seen;
and the lofty Ruler of the World,
from the roaring wings of aforementioned gust
will accuse the human race of guilt.

Such potential Hiberno-Latin connections are all the more intriguing given suggestions that another Hiberno-Latin text, ALF, may have influenced Anglo-Saxon texts in both Latin and Old English, notably ALD and OER (on which see the relevant headnotes below).

There is also a broad parallel to EXE 1 (including an allusion to the Flood) in one of the few medieval riddles in Welsh, the "Song of the

Wind" *(Kanu y gwynt)* found in the early fourteenth-century Book of Taliesin (see further Haycock, *Legendary Poems,* 328–47), which features the wind as a kind of juvenile delinquent, beginning with the challenge *Dechymic pwy yw / creat kyn Dilyw* ("Guess who it is, created before the Flood?"), and giving a catalogue of missing body parts that is widely paralleled throughout the Anglo-Saxon riddle tradition (lines 3–6: *creadur kadarn / heb gic, heb ascwrn, / heb wytheu, heb waet, / heb pen, a heb traet,* "a mighty creature / without flesh, without bone, / without veins, without blood, / without head, without feet"), as well as an assertion about the creature's ubiquity and invisibility (lines 17, 25–26, 28–29: *Ef ymaes, ef yg koet. . . . Ac ef yn gyflet / ac wyneb tytwet . . . ac ef ny welet. / Ef ar vor, ef ar tir,* "He's on the plain, / he's in the wood. . . . And he's as wide / as the face of the earth. . . . And he couldn't be seen. / He's on the sea, he's on the land"). Part of the poet's strategy seems to be to suggest through indirection that the "real" answer is God, who is revealed, as in EXE 1, as in fact the controller of the wind. As the opening lines of another poem in the same manuscript, the "Song of Ale" (*Kanu y cwrwf*) have it (Haycock, *Legendary Poems,* 361): *Teithi etmygynt / Gwr a gatwy gwynt,* "Would that they had honored the qualities / of the One who guards the wind!" The difficulty of assessing the significance of such parallels is compounded by the problem of dating these Welsh texts; several commentators have indeed assumed that it is precisely the Anglo-Saxon riddle tradition that inspired them.

Returning to the Old English text of EXE 1 itself, it is noteworthy that a number of verbal parallels link the constituent parts of this riddle together, as well as with other Old English poems. Particularly striking are those that appear to connect this poem with *Andreas,* a poem which has elsewhere been shown to rely on recycled phrasing from presumably remembered reading (and which also contains a storm scene at *Andreas* 369b–85), and what looks like a particularly close parallel in the opening line of EXE 1 to *Christ A,* currently the first text in the Exeter Book. There, the phrase in question occurs in the broader context of the "true mysteries" of Christ (*ChristA* 196a and 247a *ryht-geryno*: the compound is unique to the poem), and their essential unknowability by any mortal, however wise. In an initial passage, Christ is addressed directly (*ChristA* 219–23):

Nis ænig nu eorl under lyfte,
secg searo-þoncol, to þæs swiðe gleaw
þe þæt asecgan mæge sund-buendum,
areccan mid ryhte, hu þe rodera weard
æt frymðe genom him to freo-bearne.

There is now no noble under the sky, a man wise in cunning, sufficiently wise that he can say to those who live surrounded by sea, reckon rightly how in the beginning the ruler of the heavens took you as as his beloved son.

In what is evidently a parallel passage that follows soon afterwards (and completes what is, in effect, an envelope pattern within this part of the poem), the address to Christ continues: "Therefore there is none so brisk and crafty in mind as to be able to show clearly to the children of men whence you came" *(ChristA* 247–9a: *Forþon nis ænig þæs horsc, ne þæs hyge-cræftig, / þe þin from-cyn mæge fira bearnum / sweotule geseþan).* The latter passage obviously begins with a very close parallel to the opening line of EXE 1 (for a further parallel to the former passage, compare EXE 1.27b–30: *Saga, þoncol mon, / hwa mec brægde of brimes fæþmum, / þonne streamas eft stille weorþað, / yþa geþwære, þe mec ær wrugon*). A further potential parallel is found in Cynewulf, *Elene* 1270b–76a, in an apocalyptic passage toward the end of the poem that has no direct link to the putative Latin source. The relevant lines speak of the raging power of the wind when released from its confinement, and how at Doomsday the earth will vanish:

landes frætwe
gewitaþ under wolcnum winde geliccost,
þonne he for hæleðum hlud astigeð,
wæðeð be wolcnum, wedende fæeð
ond eft semninga swige gewyrðeð,
in ned-cleofan nearwe geheaðrod,
þream forþrycced.

> The trappings of the land disappear under the clouds, most like the wind when it rises up loud before men, wanders around the skies, travels raging, and suddenly again falls still, narrowly constrained in needful enclosure, forcibly repressed.

Such links between EXE 1 and a whole range of texts both within and beyond Anglo-Saxon England, in a variety of languages, only emphasize its literary qualities and appeal, as well as its central position within the Anglo-Saxon riddle tradition.

There are no fewer than thirty-five compounds in the combined 104 lines of EXE 1, of which sixteen are unique in extant Old English verse: *folc-sæl* (1.6b), *wæl-cwealm* (1.9a), *bled-hwæt* (1.9b), *holm-mægen* (1.24a), *hwyrft-weg* (1.36b), *flint-græg* (1.49a), *brim-giest* (1.55a), *stream-gewinn* (1.56b), *hop-gehnast* (1.57a), *stið-weg* (1.65a), *wæg-fæt* (1.67a), *eored-þreat* (1.79a), *deað-spere* (1.83b), *ryne-giest* (1.88b), *wolcen-gehnast* (1.90b), and *hloð-gecrod* (1.93a). In addition, the compound *sund-helm* (1.25b) is found only here and at EXE 74.1b (*OSTRE*, "oyster").

1.1 Compare *ChristA* 241 *(Forþon nis ænig þæs horsc, ne þæs hyge-cræftig)*. The opening *hwylc* is taken here as a question, though other editors have assumed that it is an exclamation.

1.2b Note the repeated *hwa*, found also at EXE 1.14b, 1.28a, 1.65b, 1.103a, and 1.104a, so binding the text together. Compare EXE 79.6b–8a *(Ic ful gearwe gemon / hwa min from-cynn fruman agette / eall of earde)*.

1.3a–6a Note the string of finite verbs in successive a-lines *(stige . . . þunie . . . fere . . . reafige)*, all emphasizing movement and power.

1.4b Reading *wræcca*, after Herzfeld, *Die Räthsel des Exeterbuches* (E reads *wræce*); compare EXE 27.10a ("moon": *wreccan*) and 37.8b (*wreccan*). Several editors, wishing to retain the manuscript form, read *wræce* as present subjunctive (as at EXE 18.18a), even though the form is usually *wrece;* otherwise, it must be perfect subjunctive.

1.7b Reading *hlyn* (altered in E from *hlin*).

1.8b Compare EXE 77.7b *(se þe wudu hrereð),* and see the note there.

1.10b Reading *heahum,* after Mu (E reads *heanū*). Compare EXE 1.24a *(holm-mægne biþeaht).*

1.11a Reading *wrecen* (E reads *wrecan*).

1.12–14a This is the first example in EXE of what might best be termed a riddle within a riddle; for other examples, see EXE 9.9b *(horda deorast);* 48.2b *(of dumbum twam);* 69.3b *(wraþra laf);* 76.7b *(þæt on bearwe geweox);* 77.7b *(se þe wudu hrereð);* 79.4b–6a *(Nu me fah warað / eorþan broþor, se me ærest wearð / gumena to gyrne);* 91.4a *(me fremdes ær).*

1.13b Compare *ChristB* 597b (*flæsc ond gæst*).

1.14b–15 A parallel closing formulaic challenge occurs at EXE 1.27–28 (in the form *Saga . . . / hwa mec bregde*); the more usual *Saga hwæt ic hatte* occurs at 1.102b, 6.8b, 8.11b, 10.13b, 17.9b (emended here to *Saga hwæt hio hatte*), 21.16b, 33.13–14 (in the form *Saga . . . hwæt þis gewæde sy*), 34.8b (in the form *Saga hwæt hio wære*), 37.29b (in the form *saga hwæt hio hatte*), 60.9b, 64.10b, 71.29b, 76.12b, 79.14b, and 82.7b (emended here to *Saga hwæt hio hatte*); the related formula *Ræd hwæt ic mæne* appears at EXE 59.9b. For the further variants *Frige hwæt ic hatte* and *Ræd hwæt ic mæne,* see the note on EXE 12.19b and 59.9b below.

1.16a The use of *Hwilum* here introduces a whole sequence throughout the riddle, where such anaphora occurs nine times in all (also at EXE 1.31a, 36a, 66a, 68b, 98a, 98b, 99b, and 100b). Extensive anaphora on *hwilum* also occurs in EXE 10 (five times), 12 (ten times), 22 (seven times), and 89 (six times). Other anaphora occurs on *oft* in EXE 18 (three times); on *ne* (as an adverb) in EXE 18 (five times), 33 (four times), 37 (five times), 38 (five times), and 56 (four times); and on *ne* (as a conjunction) in EXE 20 (seven times), 33 (four times), 37 (nine times), and 56 (four times). The extent to which anaphora is largely restricted to just eleven riddles (EXE 1, 10, 12, 18, 20, 22, 33, 37, 38, 56, and 89), all but one within the first group of riddles (EXE 1–57) and overwhelmingly in the subgroup EXE 1–38, is striking, as is the fact that only two of the riddles (EXE 33 and 38) derive directly from Latin originals (ALD 33 and 100), where anaphora is also found.

1.17b Compare EXE 20.7a *(atol yþa geþræc).* The same phrase also occurs at *Andreas* 823a *(ofer yþa geþræc).*

1.18a For the sequence *gar-secges grund,* compare EXE 38.93 *(se þe gar-secges grund bihealdeð);* the phrase there has a parallel in the Latin of ALD 100, its ultimate source.

1.19b Reading *famge wealcan* after Cosijn, "Anglosaxonica IV" (E reads *fam gewealcen*); compare *Andreas* 1524b *(famige walcan).* The parallel suggests that it is the a-line that is missing, and it is tempting to conjecture some form of *flod(-)* to fill the gap (compare *Elene* 1269a *flodas gefysde; ChristC* 985a *flodas afysde*).

1.20 Compare *Andreas* 370a *(onhrered hwæl-mere)* and *Andreas* 392b *(gar-secg hlymmeð).* The rhyme here *(hlimmeð . . . grimmeð)* is unusual; compare EXE 13.13 *(fergan . . . nergan);* 26.2 *(heardestan . . . scearpestan),* 26.4–6a *(corfen sworfen cyrred þyrred / bunden wunden blæced wæced / frætwed geatwed),* 26.8b *(clengeð lengeð);* 39.3–4a *(selestan . . . sweartestan . . . deorestan).*

1.21a Compare EXE 77.8b *(WEDER-COC,* "weathercock": *streamas beatað);* also *Andreas* 239a *(beoton brim-streamas), Andreas* 441b–42a *(eagor-streames / beoton bord-stæðu), Andreas* 495b–96a *(stream-welm hwileð / beateþ brim-stæðo).*

1.22a Compare EXE 1.56a *(stealc stan-hleoþu),* 89.9a *(stealc hliþo).*

1.24a For the concept, compare EXE 14.3a *(eorðe yðum þeaht),* and note the further parallel at EXE 1.29b.

1.25b For the compound *sund-helm,* compare EXE 74.1b.

1.27–28 This is a variant of the closing formulaic challenge *Saga hwæt ic hatte,* on which see the note at 1.14b–15 above.

1.28b Compare EXE 8.6b–7a *(of fæðmum cwom / brimes ond beames).*

1.29b Compare EXE 14.4b *(stille weorþe).*

1.30 Compare EXE 74.2a *(ond mec yþa wrugon);* see too the note on EXE 1.24a above.

1.31a For the sequence *mec min frea,* compare EXE 4.5a; see too EXE 69.4b *(fæste genearwad).*

1.31–36b For parallel imagery relating to the confinement of the winds, compare the successive ablative absolutes at Aldhelm, *Carmen rhythmicum* 23 (*fracto venti federe,* "with the wind's pact broken"), 25 (*rupto retinaculo,* "with the bond shattered"), and 26–27 (*libertate poplita / et servitute sopita,* "with freedom gained and slavery laid to rest"). The notion derives ultimately from the Roman idea of Aeolus as keeper and unleasher of the winds, for which compare Virgil, *Aeneid* 1.71–75.

1.32b Reading *sal-wonges,* after Wy (E reads *sal wonge*). For the compound *sæl-wong* (E reads *sal wonge*), compare EXE 17.3a.

1.33a Supplying *þone,* after Tu (not in the manuscript), for metrical reasons.

1.34b Translating *sumne* as "prince," in the sense "a certain significant one."

1.35a Reading *hæste,* after Cosijn, "Anglosaxonica IV" (E reads *hætst*), and *siteð* (altered in E from *sited*).

1.35b Reading *heard* (E reads *heord*).

1.36b–39a For parallel imagery relating to the smashing of buildings, compare Aldhelm, *Carmen rhythmicum* 131–36: *En, statim fulcra flamine / nutabant a fundamine; / tigna tota cum trabibus / tremibunda ingentibus / vacillabant ab omnibus/ aulae pulsata partibus,* "Look, straightaway from the blast the pillars began to bow down from their foundations, all the trembling timbers and the huge beams began to shake, blasted in every part of the hall."

1.37a Reading *aglace,* after Mu (E reads *aglaca*).

1.38a Reading *hrere* (E reads *hrera*). The emendation to the earlier form *hreru* from manuscript *hrera* is tempting, although *hrere* is attested at EXE 1.8, and would also need the same emendation.

1.38b The compound *horn-salu* appears only here and at *Andreas* 1158b.

1.42b Reading *aþringe* (altered in E from *þringe*).

1.43b Understanding *wræde* as a form of *wræðe.*

1.43b–45 For the phrase *mec . . . on . . . legde bende,* compare EXE 18.29b–30a *(mec . . . on bende legde).*

1.46b Reading *tæcneð* (altered in E from *tacnað*). Compare EXE 49.6b *(wægas tæcneþ).*

1.47–58a For parallel imagery relating to the crashing of waves on the shore, compare Aldhelm, *Carmen rhythmicum* 99–114, esp. 111–14: *Sic turgescebat trucibus / pontus ventorum flatibus / infligendo flaminibus / scopulosis marginibus,* "in this way the sea began to swell from the fierce gusts of the winds, pounding with its blasts on the rocky shores."

1.48a Supplying *streamas* after Th (not in the manuscript: compare EXE 1.100a, *streamas styrge*); and reading *þywan* (E reads *þyran*).

1.49b Reading *winneð* (altered in E from *winned*).

1.49b–50 Compare *Met28* 58–59a *(yð wið lande ealneg winneð / wind wið wæge).*

1.51a Reading *dun* (altered in E from *dum*).

1.54b Reading *wada* (E reads *wudu*); note similar confusion of *wudu* for *wadu* in *Beowulf* 581a and *Andreas* 1545b.

1.56a Compare EXE 1.22a *(on stealc hleoþa)* and EXE 89.9a *(hwilum stealc hliþo).*

1.60a Compare *ChristC* 1080a and 1333a *(on þa grimman tid).*

1.61a Reading *rince,* following Tr (E reads *rice*).

1.62a Reading *fere,* following Klaeber, "Emendations" (E reads *feore*), and *bifohten* (altered in E from *bifonten*). The spelling *fere* is here taken as a form of *fær;* the same apparent confusion of manuscript *feore* for *fere* is found earlier in E at *ChristC* 952a. Other editors retain *feore* here, and understand the phrase *feore bifohten* as "bereft of life"; *DOE* has "injured mortally."

1.64b Reading *þær þe ic yrnan,* partly following Wi *(þar þar ic hyran;* E *þara þe ic hyran).*

1.65b Reading *gestilleð* (altered in E from *gestilled*).

1.66b Similarly deferred alliteration occurs at EXE 2.8b *(hwilum bersteð),* 53.14b *(Nu me þisses gieddes),* 57.12b *(Ne mæg þære bene),* 70.12b *(moras pæðde),* 87.6b *(þæt mines frean).*

1.68b Compare EXE 18.13b *(hwilum læteð eft).* Other translations prefer to read *lagu-streama full* as adjectival, "full of liquid streams," although the parallel kenning *yþa full* ("cup of the waves," signifying the sea) is found at *Beowulf* 1208b.

1.69b Compare *Phoenix* 618b *(swega mæste).*

1.69b–78a For parallel imagery relating to the generation of lightning, compare Aldhelm, *Carmen rhythmicum* 93–98: *Attamen flagrant fulmina / late per caeli culmina / quando pallentem pendula / flammam vomunt fastigia / quorum natura nubibus / procedit conlidentibus,* "But bolts of lightning blaze widely throughout the heights of the sky, as their points dropping down spew pale flame; their nature arises from clashing clouds."

1.71 Compare *Andreas* 512b *(þonne sceor cymeð).*

1.72b Reading *eorpan* (E reads *earpan*).

1.74a Compare *Andreas* 1541b *(blacan lige).*

1.75a Reading *dreorgum,* after Wi (E reads *dreontum*).

1.77a Reading *swinsendu,* after Grein-Köhler (E reads *sumsendu*); the manuscript reading perhaps reflects an earlier *suinsendu.* Other editors retain the manuscript reading, and point to Modern German *summen,* "to buzz, hum," with variant forms in *sumsen.* The usual objection is that *swinsian* usually relates to harmonious sounds, but a gloss on the biblical *sonitus maris* in Luke 21:25 (of the roaring of the sea at the end of times) as *swinsunge sæs* suggests that *swinsian* might well be used here of stormy weather.

1.77b Compare EXE 10.6a *(beorne of bosme)* and 21.3b *(ond me of bosme fareð).*

1.78a Several of the riddles focus on the "belly" *(womb)* of the creature in question: compare EXE 15.10a *(womb-hord wlitig),* 16.3a *(wide wombe),* 34.3b *(fet under wombe),* 35.1b *(womb wæs on hindan),* 60.3a *(wade under wambe),* 82.5a *(hrycg ond wombe),* 83.1b *(wombe hæfde micle),* 84.30a *(wyrdaþ mec be wombe),* 85.2b *(wombe hæfde),* 89.30a *(oft me of wombe).* There is a still more pronounced focus on the "innards" *(viscera)* of the creature in question in ALD, on which see the note at ALD 12.2.

1.78b–82 For parallel imagery depicting a storm as a raging and marauding army (and one with a very clear general), compare Aldhelm, *Carmen rhythmicum* 29–30 and 33–36: *spissa statim spiramina / duelli ducunt agmina . . . horum archon atrociter / fumam verrens ferociter / furibundus cum flamine / veniebat a cardine / unde Titanis torrida / labuntur luminaria,* "Immediately, the scattered gusts drew up their battle-lines. . . . Their ruler, in a terrible way, fiercely churning up the spray, enraged through puffing up, began to come from the direction from where the burning lamps of the sun slip down."

1.81a Reading *brogan* (altered in E from *bratan*).

1.85a Suggesting *on geryhtum ryne,* after Sedgfield (E reads *on geryhtu*).

1.86a Reading *læteð* (altered in E from *lætað*).

1.87a Reading *færende,* after Tu (who reads *ferende*; E *farende*). Some editors emend manuscript *flan* to *flanas* for reasons of meter, but the manuscript form may also mask disyllabic *fla-an,* in which case the line may simply refer to "traveling arrows."

1.92a Reading *brunra,* after PZ (E reads *byrnan*).

1.94a Compare EXE 80.31a *(þæs þe under lyfte).*

1.95a Supplying *on* (not in the manuscript).

1.96a Reading *gemagnad,* after Tr (E reads *ge manad*).

1.98a Compare EXE 38.40a *(eac ic under eorþan).*

1.99a Reading *hean,* after KD (E reads *heah*).

1.100a Compare EXE 1.48a *(streamas styrgan).*

1.102a Reading *swiþ-from,* after PZ (E reads *swiþ-feorm*).

1.102b–4 This is a variant of the closing formulaic challenge *Saga hwæt ic hatte,* on which see the note at 1.14b–15 above.

EXE 2

MANUSCRIPT: E, fol. 102v.

EARLIER EDITIONS AND TRANSLATIONS: Gr 5; Tr 2; Tu 5; Wy 4; Ma 4; KD 4; Ba 35, 30; Ab 4, 4; WiR 2; WiF 2, 62; Wh 4, 165–66; PZ 2; CH 4, 8; Mu 4; WiC 2, 528–29 and 1151–52.

SOLUTION: *BELLE* (bell); see in particular Wh and Murphy, *Unriddling the Exeter Riddles,* 71–77. Other suggested solutions include: "millstone" (Dietrich, "Würdigung, Lösung und Herstellung"; Dietrich, "Die Räthsel des Exeterbuchs"), "revenant" (Bradley, "Two Riddles of the Exeter Book"), "flail" (Tr; PZ), "lock" (Holthausen, "Zu den altenglischen Rätseln" [1917]), "handmill" (Erhardt-Siebold, "Old English Riddle No. 4"), "quill" (Shook, "Anglo-Saxon Scriptorium"), "penis" (Jember, *Old English Riddles*), "bucket of water" (Stewart, "Old English Riddle 4"), "bucket on chain" or "rope in cistern" or "well" (Doane, "Implement Riddles"), "watchdog" (Brown, "The Exeter Book's *Riddle* 2"), "a devil" (Heyworth, "The Devil's in the Detail"); "plough team" (Cochran, "The Plough's the Thing"; Digan, "Aspects of Vocabulary," 46–61), *wæter-stoppa,* "water-bucket" (Ni), "sword" (Dale, "New Solution").

See further Erhardt-Siebold, "History of the Bell"; Stewart, "Inference in Socio-Historical Linguistics"; Salvador-Bello, "Compilation of the Old English Riddles," 103–5; Cavell, *Weaving Words,* 79–83; Dale, *Natural World,* 80–84; Lockhart, "Everyday Wonders and Enigmatic Structures," 119–21. See too Leahy, *Anglo-Saxon Crafts,* 132.

The chief difficulty in the interpretation of this riddle stems from the significance of the "rings" in EXE 2.2a *(hringum)* and 2.8a *(bæg),* as well as the number of unique compounds. There are six compounds in this riddle, of which three are unique in extant Old English verse: *þrag-bysig* (2.1a), *hals-wriþa* (2.4a), and *slæp-werig* (2.5a).

2.1a The opening formula *Ic eom* ("I am") is well attested in EXE, as the note to EXE 3.1a explains, but here and with the beginning of the second verse-paragraph at EXE 2.5a *(Ic sceal . . . Oft)* there seems a gesture towards a rather rarer *Oft ic . . . sceal* ("Often I . . . must") opening formula that is found in EXE 14.1a *(Oft ic sceal)* and 61.1a *(Oft ic . . . sceal)*.

2.2a Reading *hringum*, after KD (E reads *hringan*).

2.7b The half-line *wearm lim* seems metrically deficient, but the general opaqueness of the text hampers useful conjecture.

2.8a Understanding *bæg* as a variant spelling for *beag*.

2.8b Reading *hwilum* (altered in E from *hwilcum*). For the unusual alliteration, compare the note at EXE 1.66b.

EXE 3

MANUSCRIPT: E, fol. 102v.

EARLIER EDITIONS AND TRANSLATIONS: Gr 6; Tr 3; Tu 6; Wy 5; Ma 5; KD 5; Ba 49, 40; Ab 5, 4; WiR 3; WiF 3, 63; Wh 5, 166–67; PZ 3; CH 5, 9; Mu 5; WiC 3, 529 and 1152.

SOLUTION: *BORD* (chopping board, shield); other suggested solutions include: "shield" (Müller, *Collectanea;* Dietrich, "Würdigung, Lösung und Herstellung"; Holthausen, "Zu den altenglischen Rätseln"), "chopping block" (Tr; PZ), "guilt" (Jember, *Old English Riddles*), "whetstone" (Sayers, "Exeter Book Riddle No. 5"), *scild*, "shield" (Ni).

See further Stanley, "Heroic Aspects"; Salvador-Bello, "Compilation of the Old English Riddles," 105–7; Teele, "Heroic Tradition," 74–81; Murphy, *Unriddling the Exeter Riddles*, 68–70; Dale, *Natural World*, 35.

See too Leahy, *Anglo-Saxon Crafts*, 128–29.

The runic ᛋ (*s*) which follows this riddle in the manuscript supports the generally held solution "shield," both in Old English

(*SCYLD*) and Latin (*SCUTUM*). Jember's solution turns on a perceived aural pun on *scild*, "shield," and *scyld*, "guilt," which he then connects further with EXE 4, for which he proposes the solution "guilt and conscience." A more conceptual link between EXE 4 and 5 (if the commonly suggested solutions "shield" and "sun" are accepted) might be supplied by the circular shape of Anglo-Saxon shields. See further the note on ALD 70 (*TORTELLA*, "loaf of bread"), and the shield imagery there. The "chopping block" suggestion works well too, especially in the mock-heroic context of others of the collection, such as EXE 13 (*IGIL*, "hedgehog," "porcupine"), and therefore here the solution *BORD* is preferred, since it might well cover both the martial and the mundane. For other riddles with a similar solution, compare ALD 87 (*CLIPEUS*, "shield") and GES 26 (*SKJÖLDR*, "shield"). There are nine compounds in this riddle, of which two are unique in extant Old English verse: *læce-cynn* (3.10b) and *deað-slege* (3.14a).

3.1a The opening formula *Ic eom* is found in various forms in EXE 15.1a (*Ic eom mund-bora*), 25.1a (*Ic eom weorð werum*), 28.1a (*Ic eom leg-bysig*), 60.1a (*Ic eom heard ond scearp*), 64.1a (*Ic eom mare*), 69.1a (*Ic eom rices æht*), 76.1a and 2a (*Ic eom æþelinges*), 77.1a (*Ic eom bylged-breost*), and 91.1a (*Ic eom indryhten*). Several riddles in the first batch, almost in perfect sequence, have the more elaborate form *Ic eom wundorlicu wiht*, such as 16.1a, 18.1a, 21.2a (as a further variant *ic eom wrætlic wiht*), 22.1a, and 23.1a. A similar formula is found at EXE 27.7a (*Ða cwom wundorlicu wiht*). By contrast, it is notable that only eleven of the aenigmata in SYM are *not* in the first person (the exceptions are SYM 12, 30, 62, 72, 76 and 76a, 79, 90, and 94–96: it is striking that only two of these are found in the first sixty aenigmata).

3.2b For the compound *beadu-weorc*, compare EXE 31.6a.

3.4a Compare *Andreas* 1350a (*frecne feohtan*); *GuthA* 508b (*frofre ne wenað*); *Beowulf* 185b (*frofre ne wenan*).

3.5b Reading *guð-gewinnes* (altered in E from *gudgewinnes*).

3.6b Reading *forwurðe*, after Gr (E reads *for wurde*).

3.7b–8a Another riddle within a riddle (in the form of a kenning), repeated elsewhere; compare *Beowulf* 2829 *(hearde heaðo-scearpe homera lafe), Brun* 6b *(hamora lafan).*

3.8b Reading *hond-weorc* (E reads ⁊ *weorc*). Compare EXE 18.7b *(hond-weorc smiþa)* and 24.14a *(wrætlic weorc smiþa).*

3.9b Some editors (Gr, Wy, and Wi) read *abidan* as *a bidan,* "always await."

EXE 4

MANUSCRIPT: E, fol. 102v–3r.

EARLIER EDITIONS AND TRANSLATIONS: Gr 7; Tr 4; Tu 7; Wy 6; Ma 6; KD 6; Ba 17, 19–20; Ab 6, 5; WiR 4; WiF 4, 64; Wh 6, 167; PZ 4; CH 6, 10; Mu 6; WiC 4, 529 and 1152.

SOLUTION: *SUNNE* (sun); see in particular Dietrich, "Würdigung, Lösung und Herstellung"; Ni. Other suggested solutions include: "guilt and conscience" (Jember, *Old English Riddles*).

See further Salvador-Bello, "Compilation of the Old English Riddles," 107–9; Teele, "Heroic Tradition," 129–32; Murphy, *Unriddling the Exeter Riddles,* 126–27; Dale, *Natural World,* 38 and 114.

The runic ᛋ (*s*) which follows this riddle in the manuscript supports the generally held solution *sigel, sunne,* "sun," although as with the previous riddle, a Latin solution *(sol)* would also fit. Just as EXE 3 and 4 may be connected by the circular shapes of their solutions ("shield" and "sun" respectively), so too EXE 4 and 5 may be connected through the idea of a swan, like the sun, moving through the sky. Other sun riddles include: ALD 79 (*SOL ET LUNA,* "sun and moon"), EUS 10 (*SOL,* "sun"), BER 55–57 (*SOL,* "sun"), TAT 40 (*RADII SOLIS,* "about the rays of the sun"). There are no compounds in this riddle.

4.3a Compare *Pan* 2a *(unrimu cynn).*

4.3b Compare EXE 5.8b–9a *(þonne ic getenge ne beom / flode ond foldan)* and 74.2b *(eorþan getenge).*

4.5a For the sequence *mec min frea,* compare EXE 1.31a.

4.7a Some editors emend to *willum,* after Tr (E reads *hwilum*), to bolster the necessary alliteration; but alliteration of *hw-* and *h-* is also found (for example) at EXE 33.11 *(Wile . . . hwæþre . . . wide).*

4.10b Reading *bete,* after KD (E reads *betan*).

ᚠ EXE 5 ᚠ

MANUSCRIPT: E, fol. 103r.

EARLIER EDITIONS AND TRANSLATIONS: Gr 8; Tr 5; Tu 8; Wy 7; Ma 7; KD 7; Ba 21, 22; Ab 7, 5; WiR 5; WiF 5, 65; Wh 7, 167–68; PZ 5; CH 7, 11; Mu 7; WiC 5, 529–30 and 1152.

SOLUTION: *SWAN* (swan); see in particular Dietrich, "Würdigung, Lösung und Herstellung"; Ni. Other suggested solutions include: either "swan" or "soul" (Gardner, *Christian Poetry*), "soul" (Jember, *Old English Riddles*), both "swan" and "soul" (Tripp, "Occult and Supernatural"), "mute swan" (Kitson, "Swans and Geese").

A poorly formed letter, likely written after the main text and variously read as Roman *n,* or runic ᚾ (*u*) or ᚳ (*c*) follows this riddle in the manuscript, and has been used to support the Latin solutions *cygnus,* "swan," or *ulula,* "owl," for this riddle, or Old English *nihtegale,* "nightingale," or *ule,* "owl." Most commentators accept the solution "swan," a creature that fulfills the necessary conditions of being at home on land and in the water and in the air; compare EXE 1 (*GODES WIND,* "God's wind"). Such an answer is all the more appealing if it is supposed that the riddle also refers to the whistling sounds made by both the swan's wings in flight while alive and its wing-bones in the form of flutes after death. Kitson specifies this creature as a mute swan, by contrast with his proposed suggestion of "whooper swan" for EXE 72 (*AC,* "ship made of oak"). The parallel phrasing from *The Phoenix,* which also appears in the Exeter Book, is particularly striking, and strengthens the connection with two of the so-called *Physiologus* poems *(The Panther* and *The Whale),* also found in the Exeter Book (see further the notes at EXE 4.3a, 38.93a, 74.4a, and 80.7b; also the headnote to EXE 62). This whole riddle turns on the paradox of silence on land and water, contrasted with sound in the sky, and emphasized with a series of verbs *(swigað . . . swogað . . . swinsiað . . . singað)* which offer aural clues to the solution, *SWAN.* There are no compounds in this riddle.

This is the opening riddle in a sequence (EXE 5–8) with bird-solutions, all connected in various ways; see further Salvador-Bello, "Compilation of the Old English Riddles," 109–11; Meaney, "Birds on the Stream of Consciousness"; Bitterli, *Say What I Am Called,* 38–46; Orchard, "Performing Writing and Singing Silence," 83–86; Stanley, "Exeter Book *Riddles,* II," 355–56.

5.2a Compare EXE 13.8b *(þær ic wic buge), GuthA* 298b *(þe þa wic bugað).*

5.4a Compare EXE 8.8b *(hyrste mine).*

5.4b Compare EXE 55.1a *(Ðeos lyft byreð).*

5.6–9 Compare *Phoenix* 134–37 *(Ne magon þam breahtme byman ne hornas / ne hearpan hlyn ne hæleþa stefn / ænges on eorþan ne organan / sweg-hleoþres geswin ne swanes feðre);* see further Orchard, "Performing Writing and Singing Silence," 84–85.

5.7b–8a Compare *Phoenix* 124a *(swinsað ond singeð), Phoenix* 140a *(Singeð swa ond swinsað); ChristC* 884a *(singað ond swinsiaþ).*

5.9b The phrase *ferende gæst,* "traveling spirit," seems to combine the folk notion that swans embodied dead souls with, as commonly in the riddles, a sense of the creature's usefulness to mankind after death. Given the hollow nature of bird bones in general, swan-bone flutes are well attested from Anglo-Saxon England (and elsewhere in the period: there is a splendid example from Viking-age York in the Jorvík Museum). The whole riddle turns on the contrast between sound and silence, enshrined through assonance in the verbs *swigað* ("is silent") and *swogað* ("whistles") in EXE 5.1a and 5.7a.

EXE 6

MANUSCRIPT: E, fol. 103r.

EARLIER EDITIONS AND TRANSLATIONS: Gr 9; Tr 6; Tu 9; Wy 8; Ma 8; KD 8; Ba 22, 22–23; Ab 8, 6; WiR 6; WiF 6, 66; Wh 8, 168; PZ 6; CH 8, 12; Mu 8; WiC 6, 530 and 1152–53.

SOLUTION: *NIHTE-GALE* (nightingale); see in particular Dietrich, "Würdigung, Lösung und Herstellung"; Erhardt-Siebold, *Die lateinischen Rätsel der Angelsachsen;* Lendinara, "L'Enigma n. 8 del Codice Exoniense"; Salvador-Bello, "Evening Singer"; Ni. Other suggested solutions include: "pipe" (Dietrich, "Würdigung, Lösung und Herstellung"), "jay" (Müller, *Die Rätsel des Exeterbuches;* Tu; Klaeber, "Das 9. altenglische Rätsel"), "reed pipe" (Padelford, "Old English Musical Terms"), "bell" (Trautmann, "Die Auflösungen der altenglischen Rätsel"), "*ceo,*" "chough" or "jackdaw" (Ma), impossible to decide (Swaen, "Riddle 9 (6, 8)"), "song thrush" or "blackbird" (Young, "Riddle 8 of the *Exeter Book*"), "nightingale" or "frog" (Cassidy and Ringler, *Bright's Old English Grammar*), "crying baby" (Jember, *Old English Riddles*), "devil as buffoon" (Jember, "Generative Method"), "owl" (Wi), "flute" (PZ), "robin" (Digan, "Aspects of Vocabulary," 30–45).

See further Salvador-Bello, "Compilation of the Old English Riddles," 111–14; Hill, "Riddle 8"; Meaney, "Birds on the Stream of Consciousness"; Teele, "Heroic Tradition," 231–35; Hayes, "Talking Dead"; Bitterli, "Survival of the Dead Cuckoo"; Bitterli, *Say What I Am Called,* 46–56; Digan, "Aspects of Vocabulary," 30–45; Orchard, "Performing Writing and Singing Silence," 86; Soper, "Count of Days," 217–21; Stanley, "Exeter Book *Riddles,* II," 356.

Given what seems a clear sequence of bird-solutions for EXE 5–8, it seems most reasonable to read this as some nocturnal bird or other, given the reference to an *eald æfen-scop* in EXE 6.5; "nightingale" or "owl" both seem feasible. In view of the potential reference to swan-bone flutes at the end of the preceding EXE 5 (*SWAN,* "swan"), however, the supplementary solution "flute" is also attractive. This riddle, like the preceding one, to which it is linked by also containing phrasing parallel to *The Phoenix* elsewhere in the Exeter Book, is again distinguished by the contrast between sound and silence, and by the extraordinary variety of words for the sounds made by the creature in question *(reordum . . . wrencum . . . heafod-woþe . . . hleoþre . . . stefne . . . woþe).* Similarly, there are many specific verbal parallels with EXE 22 (*HIGORA,* "jay, magpie"), on which see Bitterli, *Say What I Am Called,* 48: where EXE 6 has the sequence *(muþ . . . reordum . . . hleoþre . . . stefne . . . swa . . . onhyrge),* EXE 22 (*HIGORA,* "jay, magpie") has a parallel concatenation of terms *(stefne . . . swa . . . swa . . . swa . . . swa . . . onhyrge . . . hleoþor . . . reorde muþe).* There are four compounds in this riddle, of which three are unique in extant Old English verse: *heafod-woþ* (6.3a), *æfen-scop* (6.5a), and *sceawend-wise* (6.9b). It is particularly notable that one of these unique compounds, *æfen-scop* (6.5a), which occupies a central position in the text, offers a broad clue to the solution, being in effect a paraphrase of *nihte-gale.*

6.1b Compare *GuthB* 898b *(mongum reordum).*

6.2 Compare *Phoenix* 131b–33 *(Biþ þæs hleoðres sweg / eallum song-cræftum swetra ond wlitigra / ond wynsumra wrenca gehwylcum);* see further Orchard, "Performing Writing and Singing Silence," 83–85.

6.3 Compare EXE 46.2b–3a *(tila þeah þe he hlude / stefne ne cirmde)* and 55.4b *(hlude cirmað).*

6.8a Reading *sittað swigende,* after Tu (E reads *siteð nigende*).

6.8–11 This is a variant of the closing formulaic challenge *Saga hwæt ic hatte,* on which see the note at 1.14b–15 above.

6.9a Reading *þe,* after Mu (E reads *þa*), and *scernicge,* following a suggestion by Cosijn (E reads *scirenige*), who notes the form *scericge,* found once glossing Latin *mima,* and describing Pelagia of Antioch, a famous actress who became a nun; given that Old High German and Old Saxon *scern* gloss Latin *scurrilitas,* "coarseness, indecency," and *spectaculum,* "show, spectacle," and that in Old English *-icge* is attested as a feminine ending, it seems possible that what was intended in both cases was the otherwise unattested *scernicge.*

EXE 7

MANUSCRIPT: E, fol. 103r–v.

EARLIER EDITIONS AND TRANSLATIONS: Gr 10; Tr 7; Tu 10; Wy 9; Ma 9; KD 9; Ba 20, 21–22; Ab 9, 6; WiR 7; WiF 7, 67; Wh 9, 168–69; PZ 7; CH 9, 13; Mu 9; WiC 7, 530 and 1153.

SOLUTION: *GEAC* (cuckoo); see in particular Dietrich, "Würdigung, Lösung und Herstellung"; Wi; Ni. Other suggested solutions include: "conception and birth/revenant/soul" (Jember, *Old English Riddles*). Bitterli, *Say What I Am Called,* points out a good parallel in ps-BED 9. See further Klaeber, "Das 9. altenglische Rätsel"; Nelson, "Plus Animate"; Salvador-Bello, "Compilation of the Old English Riddles," 114–16; Meaney, "Birds on the Stream of Consciousness"; Bitterli, "Survival of the Dead Cuckoo"; Bitterli, "The 'Cuckoo' in the *Collectanea* of Pseudo-Bede"; Lockhart, "Everyday Wonders and Enigmatic Structures," 114–16; Soper, "Count of Days," 71–77; Soper, "Exeter Book Riddles as Life-Writing," 844–45.

Most commentators accept the solution "cuckoo," given the widespread bird lore surrounding cuckoos as unwelcome visitors fostered on unsuspecting others. There are three compounds in this riddle, all of which are unique in extant Old English verse: *wel-hold* (7.4a), *hleo-sceorpe* (7.5b), and *friþe-mæg* (7.9a).

7.1b Reading *ofgeafun,* after Tu (E reads *ofgeafum*).

7.1–3 For the notion that while incubating in the egg, the bird is "unliving," compare Lockett, *Anglo-Saxon Psychologies,* 44.

7.3b Supplying *an,* after Tu (not in the manuscript).

7.4b Reading *þeccan,* after Th (E reads *weccan*).

7.6a Reading *swa arlice,* after Cosijn, "Anglosaxonica IV" (E reads *snearlice*).

7.7a Compare EXE 42.2a (*frean under sceate*).

EXE 8

MANUSCRIPT: E, fol. 103v.

EARLIER EDITIONS AND TRANSLATIONS: Gr 11; Tr 8; Tu 11; Wy 10; Ma 10; KD 10; Ba 23, 23; Ab 10, 7; WiR 8; WiF 8, 68; Wh 10, 169; PZ 8; CH 10, 14; Mu 10; WiC 8, 530–31 and 1153.

SOLUTION: *BYRNETE* (barnacle goose); see in particular Brooke, *History of Early English Literature;* Swaen, "Riddle 9 (12)" and "Riddle 8 (10, 11)"; Ni. Other suggested solutions include: "ocean-furrow" (Dietrich, "Würdigung, Lösung und Herstellung"), "bubble" (Trautmann, "Die Auflösungen der altenglischen Rätsel"), "water lily" (Holthausen, "Zu den altenglischen Literatur"), "anchor" (Trautmann, "Alte und neue Antworten"), "alchemy/baptism" (Jember, *Old English Riddles*), *byrnete,* "barnacle goose" (Ni).

See further Salvador-Bello, "Compilation of the Old English Riddles," 117–21; Meaney, "Birds on the Stream of Consciousness"; Soper, "Count of Days," 96–100; Soper, "Exeter Book Riddles as Life-Writing," 850–51.

Another bird riddle: the notion that the barnacle goose was part fish, part bird was known in Anglo-Saxon England, as witnessed in the *Antwerp Glossary* (AntGl 7 1): *lolligo .i. piscis maritimi uno anno piscis alio avis hoc est byrnete,* "cuttlefish: a sea fish that is one year a fish and the next a bird, namely a *byrnete* or barnacle goose."

See too ALD 16 (*LULIGO,* "cuttlefish"), which likewise plays on the paradox of a wondrous creature that is at home in both sea and air. There are two compounds in this riddle, one of which is unique in extant Old English verse: *seolh-bæþ* (8.11a).

8.1a This is the first example of a series of opening lines in the form *wæs min* (EXE 79.1a) or *is min* (EXE 9.1a, 13.1a, 19.1a, 21.1a, 81.1a [in the form *Nis min*], and 87.1a [in the form *Min . . . is*]), in what is evidently a recognized formula.

8.4a Compare EXE 14.3a *(eorþan yþum þeaht).*

8.6a Compare EXE 11.3a *(hæfdon feorg cwico)* and 72.5b *(hæfde ferð cwicu).* For the Anglo-Saxon concept of the beginning of life, compare Lockett, *Anglo-Saxon Psychologies,* 44.

8.7b Reading *hrægle,* after Gr (E reads *hrægl*).

8.11b This is a variant of the closing formulaic challenge *Saga hwæt ic hatte,* on which see the note at 1.14b–15 above.

EXE 9

MANUSCRIPT: E, fol. 103v.

EARLIER EDITIONS AND TRANSLATIONS: Gr 12; Tr 9; Tu 12; Wy 11; Ma 11; KD 11; Ba 18, 20; Ab 11, 7; WiR 9; WiF 9, 69; Wh 11, 169–70; PZ 9; CH 11, 15; Mu 11; WiC 9, 531 and 1153.

SOLUTION: *WIN-FÆT* (cup of wine); other suggested solutions include: "night" (Dietrich, "Würdigung, Lösung und Herstellung"; Trautmann, "Alte und neue Antworten"; Swaen, "Riddle 9 (12)"), "gold" (Walz, "Notes on the Anglo-Saxon Riddles"), "wine" (Trautmann, "Alte und neue Antworten"; Trautmann, "Zu meiner Ausgabe der altenglischen Rätsel"), "penis" (Jember, *Old English Riddles*), *Win ond winfæt,* "beaker of wine" (Ni).

See further Clemoes, *Interactions of Thought and Language,* 182–84; Salvador-Bello, "Compilation of the Old English Riddles," 121–24; Teele, "The Heroic Tradition," 178–80; Taylor, "Enigma Variations," 86–94; Stanley, "Exeter Book *Riddle 11*"; Dale, *Natural World,* 145–46, 149–58, and 162–65.

Given other riddles (especially in SYM) on wine and its dangers, as well as problems associated with other kinds of drink (for example GES 1), a solution "cup of wine" seems feasible. The continuing references to *hrægl* and *hyrste* (EXE 9.1) may then function as a form of misdirection, connecting this riddle back to the bird riddles preceding it. So, for example, *hrægl* is at EXE 5.1a *(SWAN,* "swan": *Hrægl min swigað),* 8.7b *(GEAC,* "cuckoo": *on blacum hrægle),* and 11.9b *(TEN CICCENU,* "ten chickens": *hrægl bið geniwad);* also in the "rude riddles" EXE 42.4b *(CÆG,* "key": *his agen hrægl),* 43.4b *(DAG,* "dough": *hrægle þeaht),* 52.4a *(CYRN,* "churn": *hrægl hondum up),* and 60.6a *(BOR,* "borer": *hæleð mid hrægle),* so supporting Jember's solution; *hyrst* is at EXE 5.4a *(SWAN,* "swan": *hyrste mine),* 8.8b *(BYRNETE,* "barnacle goose": *hyrste mine),*

12.11b *(HORN,* "horn": *hyrstum frætwed),* 29.20b *(*BLÆST-PIPE,* "bagpipes": *frætwed hyrstum),* 51.7b *(GEALGA,* "gallows," "cross": *wonnum hyrstum),* and 84.12a *(BLÆC-HORN,* "inkhorn": *hyrstum þy hyrra).* Other verbal parallels noted below seem strongly to connect this riddle to EXE 25 (*MEDU,* "mead"). There are two compounds in this riddle, both of which are unique in extant Old English verse: *haso-fag* (9.1a) and *unræd-siþ* (9.4a).

9.2b Supplying *hafu,* after Wy (not in the manuscript); other editors supply *minum.*

9.6b Compare EXE 25.13a *(strengo bistolen).*

9.6–7 These lines, containing a rhyme *(mode bestolene / dæde gedwolene),* seem to gesture toward the thought-word-deed triad that is found widely elsewhere in Anglo-Saxon literature; if wine befuddles the mind and trips up action, it tends (at first at least) to encourage speech.

9.7a Compare *GenA* 1936a and *Jul* 13a *(dædum gedwolene);* in *Jul,* the context relates to a condemnation of the folly of the followers of the wicked pagan Emperor Maximian.

9.9a Reading *bringað,* after Wi (E reads *bringeð*). Stanley, "Exeter Book *Riddle 11,*" argues in favor of retaining the manuscript reading, and translates "the most valued of stores brings on a high" (albeit he notes the "doubtful status" of the words).

9.9b Another riddle within a riddle, which could be solved as "soul." On such riddles within riddles, see the note at EXE 1.12–14a above.

9.10 The line is repeated almost verbatim at EXE 25.12 *(gif he unrædes ær ne geswiceð).* Compare too *Jul* 120 *(gif þu unrædes ær ne geswicest,* "If you do not already cease from foolishness"); *Elene* 516 *(ond þæs unrihtes eft geswiceð,* "and cease again from that foolishness").

EXE 10

MANUSCRIPT: E, fol. 103v–4r.

EARLIER EDITIONS AND TRANSLATIONS: Gr 13; Tr 10; Tu 13; Wy 12; Ma 12; KD 12; Ba 24, 24; Ab 12, 8; WiR 10; WiF 10, 70; Wh 12, 170–71; PZ 10; CH 12, 16; Mu 12; WiC 10, 531 and 1153.

SOLUTION: *OXA* (ox); other suggested solutions include: "leather" (Dietrich, "Würdigung, Lösung und Herstellung"), "oxhide" (Tu), "hide or skin" (Wy), "ox, and female masturbation with a leather dildo" (Rulon-Miller, "Sexual Humor and Fettered Desire"), *oxa ond oxanhyd,* "an ox and its hide" (Ni).

See further Williams, "What's So New about the Sexual Revolution?"; Tanke, "*Wonfeax wale*"; Salvador-Bello, "Compilation of the Old English Riddles," 124–26; Lendinara, "Aspetti della società germanica"; Rulon-Miller, "Sexual Humor and Fettered Desire"; Higley, "Wanton Hand"; Robson, "Feorran Broht"; Girsch, "Metaphorical Usage, Sexual Exploitation"; Fiocco, "Gli animali negli enigmi anglosassoni"; Digan, "Aspects of Vocabulary," 62–89; Bitterli, *Say What I Am Called,* 26–34; Murphy, *Unriddling the Exeter Riddles,* 176–77 and 195–98; Neville, "Speaking the Unspeakable"; Cavell, *Weaving Words,* 159–72; Dale, *Natural World,* 76–77. For the range of materials made from leather in Anglo-Saxon England, see Cameron, "Leather-work"; Cameron and Mould, "Devil's Crafts and Dragon's Skins?"

This is the first of no fewer than four Exeter Book ox riddles (EXE 10, 12, 36, and 70); similar aenigmata are produced by Aldhelm and Eusebius: ALD 83 (*IUVENCUS,* "bullock") and EUS 37 (*VITULUS,* "bullock"); less clearly related is another by Symphosius: SYM 56 (*CALIGA,* "boot"). The aenigmata all play on the paradox of a creature that "living, breaks up the soil; dead, binds men." The connection with the preceding EXE 9 here may lie in the notion of drink binding the unwary or unworthy; the "foolish drunken slave-girl" *(dol drunc-mennen)* is certainly bound in several senses. The picture painted here connects oxen and slaves in a fashion that may be proverbial: compare the headnote to EXE 20 (*CARLES WÆN,* Charles's Wain). There is also something clearly lascivious about the description (EXE 10.7b–13a) of the creature's dealings with the "dark-haired Welsh girl" *(wonfeax Wale);* many of the terms used there recur in several of the so-called rude riddles that employ double entendre as a matter of course. As elsewhere there appears to be a marginal rune at the end of this riddle too, one that looks rather like a reversed form of ᛖ *(eoh* or *ih).* It has been held to stand for the solution *IUVENCUS.* Note too the *hwilum . . . hwilum* sequence, repeated in EXE 12 (*HORN,* "horn").

There are four compounds in this riddle, all of which are unique in extant Old English verse: *fela-wlonc* (10.7a), *won-feax* (10.8a), *drunc-mennen* (10.9a), and *hyge-gal* (10.12a); note how they all focus on the proud dark-haired drunken Welsh slave girl, who is thereby depicted as a rather vivid and exotic creature.

10.2a Compare EXE 64.5a *(grene wongas); GenA* 1657b *(grene wongas).*

10.4b With regard to the notion of "binding better men," compare *Deor* 6b *(on syllan monn);* it is notable that *Deor,* and its apparent companion piece *Wulf and Eadwacer,* immediately precede the second group of riddles in the Exeter Book. On the fourfold anaphora on *hwilum* that begins here, see the note on EXE 1.16a above.

10.5 Compare EXE 70.9b *(Ic þæh on lust).*

10.6a Reading *beorne,* after Gr (E reads *beorn*). Compare EXE 1.77b *(seaw of bosme)* and 21.3b *(ond me of bosme fareð).*

10.8a On the unique compound *won-feax,* see the note on the equally unique *hwit-loc* at EXE 40.3b, and compare further EXE 50.6a.

10.10a Compare EXE 24.2b–3a *(wætte siþþan / dyfde on wætre).*

10.13 This is a variant of the closing formulaic challenge *Saga hwæt ic hatte,* on which see the note at 1.14b–15 above.

10.14–15 Note the parallelism of these lines, emphasized through end rhyme *(reafige . . . þeowige),* and effectively restating the premise of the opening lines (EXE 10.1–4), so forming an envelope pattern to the poem as a whole.

EXE 11

MANUSCRIPT: E, fol. 104r.

EARLIER EDITIONS AND TRANSLATIONS: Gr 14; Tr 11; Tu 14; Wy 13; Ma 13; KD 13; Ba 28, 25–26; Ab 13, 8; WiR 11; WiF 11, 71; Wh 13, 171; PZ 11; CH 13, 17; Mu 13; WiC 11, 531–32 and 1153–54.

SOLUTION: *TEN CICCENU* (ten chickens), on which see in particular Erhardt-Siebold, "Old English Riddle 13"; Ni. Other suggested solutions include: "aurelia of the butterfly, and its transformations" (Wright, *Biographia Britannica Literaria*), "letters of the alphabet" (Dietrich, "Würdigung, Lösung und Herstellung"), "looper caterpillar" (Grein, "Kleine Mitteilungen"), "ten fingers (with gloves)" (Tupper, "Originals and Analogues" and "Comparative Study of Riddles"; Wh), "ten chickens or pheasants" (Wy), "twelve chickens" (PZ), "hatchling chicks" (Murphy).

See further Salvador-Bello, "Compilation of the Old English Riddles," 127–31; Fiocco, "Gli animali negli enigmi anglo-sassoni"; Bitterli, *Say What I Am Called,* 115–21; Murphy, *Unriddling the Exeter Riddles,* 53–60 and 91–95.

There is an analogue in EUS 38 (*PULLUS,* "chicken"); a still better parallel is found in ps-BED 2, where the motif of skins hanging on the walls is particularly clear. EXE 11 links back to EXE 10 with the shared motifs of treading the earth, scouring the ground, and plundered skins. Particularly notable here is the envelope pattern that, as with the preceding EXE 10, structures the whole riddle, in this case from EXE 11.1a *(turf tredan)* to EXE 11.11b *(lond tredan),* as well as the multiplicity of terms for the various cloaks that cover the creatures in question *(fell . . . reafe . . . hrægl . . . frætwe),* several of which are matched in EXE 9. Erhardt-Siebold, pointing to the spelling *cicceno* in the Lindisfarne Gospels, suggests that the numbers ten, four, and six refer to the mixture of vowels and consonants in the solution, and so comes up with *ten ciccenu,* "ten chickens."

See further ALD 30 (*ELEMENTUM,* "alphabet"), which also discusses different kinds of letters, although in that case the "six bastards" are the combined and Greek-derived ones. There is only one compound in this riddle.

11.1a The phrase *Ic seah* is a standard formulaic opening: compare EXE 17.1a *(Ic on siþe seah)*, 29.3a *(Ic seah sellic þing)*, 30.3 *(Siþum sellic ic seah searo hweorfan)*, 40.1 *(Ic seah wyhte wrætlice twa)*, 49.1 *(Ic seah wrætlice wuhte feower)*, 50.1a *(Ic seah ræpingas)*, 51.1a *(Ic seah on bearwe)*, 53.1a *(Ic seah in healle)*, 57.1a *(Ic seah in healle)*, 62.1a *(Ic seah ᚹ ond ᛁ)*, 83.1a *(Ic seah wundorlice wiht)*. A parallel formula *(Ic geseah)* is found at EXE 27.1 *(Ic wiht geseah wundorlice)*, 32.1a *(Ic wiht geseah)*, 34.1a *(Ic wiht geseah)*, 35.1a *(Ic þa wihte geseah)*, 36.1a *(Ic þa wiht geseah)*, 54.1–2a *(Ic wæs þær inne þær ic ane geseah / winnende wiht)*, 66.1a *(Ic þa wiht geseah)*, 73.1a and 73.2a *(Ic swiftne geseah . . . Ic ane geseah)*. Where the phrase does not occur in the opening line itself, there is either an "extra" opening formula (as in EXE 29.3a and 30.3) or (as in EXE 73.2a) other issues at stake; see the relevant notes. Note too the Latin equivalent at EXE 86.1 *(Mirum mihi videtur)*, as well as Latin *(vidi: cernebam)* and Old Norse *(ek sá)* equivalents in other collections, for which see the notes at BON 13.1, ps-BED 2, and GES 2.

11.1b Note that the Roman numeral *X* (for *decem*, "ten") is a key part of the alliteration.

11.2a Note that the Roman numeral *VI* (for *sex*, "six") is a key part of the alliteration.

11.3a Compare EXE 8.6a *(Hæfde feorh cwico)* and 72.5b *(hæfde ferð cwicu)*.

11.4a Compare EXE 37.3a *(sweotol ond gesyne)*; the phrase is something of a commonplace.

11.4b Compare *Andreas* 714b *(on seles wage)*. The "wall" in question is the eggshell, as at ps-BED 2: see further the note there.

11.6a Reading *siðe* and *sarre*, after Gr (E reads *side* and *sarra*).

11.7a Compare *Hildebrandslied* 57a *(rauba birahanen)*; the fact that this early ninth-century Old High German heroic poem also has a version of the same phrase suggests either that it might be part of an inherited oral tradition, or even perhaps (as Trautmann thought) that *Hildebrandslied* is a translation of a lost Old English original.

11.11b Compare *Andreas* 801b–2a *(geweotan . . . mearc-land tredan)*.

EXE 12

MANUSCRIPT: E, fol. 104r.

EARLIER EDITIONS AND TRANSLATIONS: Gr 15; Tr 12; Tu 15; Wy 14; Ma 14; KD 14; Ba 53, 43; Ab 14, 9; WiR 12; WiF 12, 72; Wh 14, 171–72; PZ 12; CH 14, 18; Mu 14; WiC 12, 532 and 1154.

SOLUTION: *HORN* (horn); see in particular Dietrich, "Würdigung, Lösung und Herstellung"; Jember, *Old English Riddles.* Other suggested solutions include: *oxa ond oxhorn,* "an ox and its horns" (Ni).

See further Stanley, "Heroic Aspects of the Exeter Book Riddles"; Lendinara, "Aspetti della società germanica"; Salvador-Bello, "Compilation of the Old English Riddles," 131–34; Teele, "Heroic Tradition," 50–54; Bitterli, *Say What I Am Called,* 124–31 and 166–67; Cavell, "Sounding the Horn"; Dale, *Natural World,* 114; Stanley, "Exeter Book *Riddles,* II," 356.

This riddle seems closely connected both verbally and conceptually with EXE 10, notably in the focus at the beginning on the living creature, and then a series of *hwilum*-clauses describing the experiences of the finished object. A later hand seems to have added a capital *H* (or perhaps a variant form of runic ᚺ, *h*), so suggesting the solution "horn" that is so widely favored by most commentators; another horn riddle occurs at EXE 76. Aldhelm has an *aenigma* on *SALPIX* (trumpet) (ALD 68), which shares some of the same features as this one: see the notes at EXE 12.4–5a and 12.14b–15 below. Elsewhere in the Exeter Book, other horn riddles refer to inkhorns, such as EXE 84 (*BLÆC-HORN,* "inkhorn") and EXE 89 (*BLÆC-HORN,* "inkhorn"), a topic also covered by Eusebius (EUS 30.1–2: *ATRAMENTORIUM,* "inkhorn"). This poem can be connected to the preceding EXE 11 by the motif of hanging on the wall. For the theme of kissing here, see the headnote to ALD 80. There are ten compounds in this riddle, of which four are unique in extant Old English verse: *wir-boga* (12.3a), *wil-gehleþa* (12.5a), *fyrd-sceorp* (12.13a), and *folc-wiga* (12.13b).

12.1a Reading *wigan,* after Wi (E reads *wiga*); compare Bitterli, *Say What I Am Called,* 166–67. The fact that the following word *(nu)* begins with an *n-* may have led to haplography.

Also compare EUS 30.1–2 (*Armorum fueram vice meque tenebat in armis / fortis, et armigeri gestabar vertice tauri)*; see the headnote there for other riddles that focus on the close connection with arms and armor of the creature in question. The *Ic wæs* opening formula, also found at EXE 58.1a, 63.1a (in the variant form *wæs ic*), 70.1a, 72.1a, and 88.1a, is a variant on the more frequent *Ic eom,* "I am," on which see the note at EXE 3.1a above; it is notable that EXE 16 employs both, to signal different stages in the life of the creature in question: EXE 16.1a *(Ic eom)* and 16.4a *(Ic wæs)*.

12.2a For the compound *hagosteald-mon,* compare EXE 52.3a.

12.3b Compare EXE 28.6 *(þæt mec weras ond wif wlonce cyssað)* and 61.4–5a *(Hwilum mec on cofan cysseð muþe / tillic esne).* The initial *hwilum* here opens an extraordinary example of anaphora, with no fewer than ten in the sequence, describing the multifaceted nature of the creature in question. For other examples of anaphora, see the note on EXE 1.16a above.

12.4–5a Compare ALD 68.1–2 (*SALPIX,* "trumpet": *Sum cava, bellantum crepitu quae corda ciebo, / vocibus horrendis stimulans in bella cohortes).*

12.6b The kenning-compound *mere-hengest,* "sea-horse," here introduces a theme that is widespread within the tradition: see further (for example) ALC D61 and EXE 34, although the treatment there is quite different, as well as Rügamer, *Die Poetizität der altenglischen Rätsel,* 301–12.

12.9b Supplying *on,* after Tu (not in the manuscript).

12.10b Retaining *behlyþed* (as in E), and, after Tu, understanding this unique form as related to the root *hloþ,* "booty, plunder." Others (notably Tr and KD) emend to the equally unattested *behlywed,* understood as deriving from *hleow,* "protection"; these editors retain the simple *bordum* of 12.9b, and understand a pun on the fact that the creature in question is "protected" by the "boards" or "shields" of the table (on such a double sense, see too EXE 3 above).

12.11b Compare EXE 29.20b *(frætwed hyrstum)* and 51.7b–8a *(wonnum hyrstum / foran gefrætwed).*

12.12a Compare *Beowulf* 1662 *(þæt ic on wage geseah wlitig hangian); Andreas* 732a *(wlitig of wage).*

12.12b For similar drinking formulas, compare EXE 18.12b *(þær hy meodu drincað),* 53.1b *(þær hæleð druncon),* 54.11b *(þær hæleð druncon),* 61.3b *(þær guman drincað),* 65.14b *(þær guman druncon),* and perhaps 82.1b *(þær weras sæton).*

12.14a Supplying *on,* after KD (not in the manuscript).

12.14b–15 Compare ALD 68.5 *(SALPIX,* "trumpet": *spiritus in toto sed regnant corpore flabra).*

12.17b Reading *wraþum,* after Gr (E reads *wraþþum*). See further the notes at EXE 13.6a and 13.15b.

12.19b This is a variant of the closing formulaic challenge *Saga hwæt ic hatte,* on which see the note at 1.14b–15 above. *Frige hwæt ic hatte* also occurs at 14.10b, 24.26b, and 25.15b. A further variant of the formula is found at EXE 59.9b *(Ræd hwæt ic mæne).*

EXE 13

MANUSCRIPT: E, fol. 104v.

EARLIER EDITIONS AND TRANSLATIONS: Gr 16; Tr 13; Tu 16; Wy 15; Ma 15; KD 15; Ba 29, 26–27; Ab 15, 10; WiR 13; WiF 13, 73; Wh 15, 172–73; PZ 13; CH 15, 19; Mu 15; WiC 13, 532–33 and 1154.

SOLUTION: *IGIL* (hedgehog, porcupine); other suggested solutions include: "hedgehog" (Holthausen, "Zur Textkritik altenglischer Dichtungen"), "porcupine" (Holthausen, "Zur Textkritik altenglischer Dichtungen"; Walz, "Notes on the Anglo-Saxon Riddles"; Bitterli, "Exeter Book Riddle 15"), "weasel" (Young, "Riddle 15 of the *Exeter Book*"), "badger" (Dietrich, "Würdigung, Lösung und Herstellung"; MacLean, *Old and Middle English Reader;* Swaen, "Riddle XIII [XVI]"; Nelson, "Old English Riddle No. 15"), "fox" (Brett, "Notes on Old and Middle English"; PZ), "man" (Jember, *Old English Riddles*); *fox ond hund,* "fox and hound" (Ni). See further Lendinara, "Aspetti della società germanica"; Salvador-Bello, "Compilation of the Old English Riddles," 134–39; Fiocco, "Gli animali negli enigmi anglo-sassoni"; Teele, "The Heroic Tradition," 149–58; Cavell, "The *igil* and Exeter Book *Riddle 15*"; Dale, *Natural World,* 40–45.

The precise identity of this creature remains a source of conjecture: "fox" and "badger" are the usual choices. Here, although "weasel" (*WESLE*) is attractive, I prefer "hedgehog," based partly on the description in Isidore, *Etym.* 12.3.7:

> Ericium animal spinis coopertum, quod exinde dicitur nominatum, eo quod subrigit se quando spinis suis clauditur, quibus undique protectus est contra insidias. Nam statim ut aliquid praesenserit, primum se subrigit, atque in globum conversus in sua se arma recolligit. Huius prudentia quaedam est; nam dum absciderit uvam de vite, supinus sese volutat super eam, et sic eam exhibet natis suis.
>
> The hedgehog is an animal covered with spines, which is said to have been named for the following reason, that when it stiffens its spines it is closed about, and is protected by them from attacks on all sides. For as soon as it has sensed something, it first stiffens itself, and, turning into a ball, it gathers together its own weapons. This is a mark of its care: when it has sliced off a grape from the vine, it rolls itself backwards on it, and so offers it to its offspring.

Still more relevant is *Physiologus,* which describes how the hedgehog has a burrow with two separate entrances, in case of danger; for an aenigma with the same solution (albeit with a different treatment), see SYM 29. This riddle is linked to the preceding one, EXE 12 (*HORN,* "horn"), by the reference to the creature's weapons (compare EXE 12.1 and 13.3). There are thirteen compounds in this riddle, of which six are unique in extant Old English verse: *geoguð-cnosl*

(13.10a), *forht-mod* (13.13a), *feþe-mund* (13.17b), *dun-þyrel* (13.21b); *wæl-hwelp* (13.23a), and *gegn-pæþ* (13.26a), and *laþ-gewinna* (13.29a); presumably the density of the language adds to the difficulty of the interpretation. This riddle is notable for the extent to which it overlaps in diction with others in EXE: see the notes at EXE 13.3a, 13.6b, 13.8b, 13.20a, 13.22a, 13.25b, and 13.28b.

13.2b Reading *swift* (altered in E from *swist*). The *Ic eom* opening formula is found in various forms; see the note at 3.1a above.

13.3a The compound *beado-wæpen* is found only here and at EXE 15.8a.

13.4a Reading *hleorum,* after Gr (E reads *leorum*).

13.6a Reading *grene,* after Gr (E reads *grenne*). See further the notes at EXE 12.17b and 13.15b.

13.6b Compare EXE 13.11b *(him biþ deað witod)* and 18.24a *(me bið forð witod),* and EXE 81.7b *(me bið deað witod).*

13.8b Compare EXE 5.2a *(oþþe þa wic buge).*

13.9a Reading *bold,* after Tu (E reads *blod*).

13.11b See the note at EXE 13.6b above.

13.13b Compare *GenA* 2000b *(fleame nergan);* note the rhyme in the line as a whole.

13.14a Reading *æfterweard* (altered in E from *æfterwearð).*

13.15a Reading *breost berað,* after Herzfeld, *Die Räthsel des Exeterbuches* (E reads *berað breost*); the unemended order is retained by (for example) KD, but is metrically irregular.

13.15b Reading *bidan,* after Gr (E reads *biddan*).

13.16b Reading *ne ic,* after Wi (E reads *nele*).

13.20a For the compound *mæg-burg,* compare EXE 18.20a.

13.21a The scribe has corrected *weg* from *wig,* presumably having been initially influenced by the correct form *wig* found in EXE 13.23a.

13.21b Reading *dun-þyrel,* after Wi (E reads *dumþyrel*).

13.22a Compare EXE 24.22a *(swæsra ond gesibbra).*

13.24a Reading *gif se,* after Tr (E reads *gifre*).

13.24b Compare *Beowulf* 1409b *(stige nearwe).*

13.25b The verb *tosælan* is found only here and at EXE 14.5a.

13.28b The compound *hilde-pil* is found only here and at EXE 15.6b.

13.29a Reading *lað-gewinnan* and *fleah,* after Wi (E reads *laðgewinnum;* altered in E from *flean*).

EXE 14

MANUSCRIPT: E, fol. 104v–5r.

EARLIER EDITIONS AND TRANSLATIONS: Gr 17; Tr 14; Tu 17; Wy 16; Ma 16; KD 16; Ba 57, 47; Ab 16, 11; WiR 14; WiF 14, 74; Wh 16, 174; PZ 14; CH 16, 20; Mu 16; WiC 14, 533 and 1154.

SOLUTION: *ANCOR, ANCRA* (anchor; anchorite); other suggested solutions include: "anchor" (Dietrich, "Würdigung, Lösung und Herstellung"; Ni). See further Clemoes, *Interactions of Thought and Language,* 98–99; Salvador-Bello, "Compilation of the Old English Riddles," 139–40; Teele, "Heroic Tradition," 52–55; Bardowell, "Art and Emotion," 144–48; Dale, *Natural World,* 42.

This is one of the very few riddles for which the answer is universally accepted, based on Dietrich's initial comparison of the motifs here with SYM 61 (*ANCHORA,* "anchor"), although the parallels are not particularly striking. If the addition of *fremman* in EXE 14.2a is accepted, in order to preserve *sæcce* as a noun, the first four lines of this riddle are hypermetric, and to a Christian audience might just as easily suggest the secondary sense "anchorite." The anchor described here may have only one fluke (its *steort,* "tail"). There are no compounds in this riddle.

14.1–2 Compare SYM 61.1–2 *(ANCORA,* "anchor": *Mucro mihi geminus ferro coniungitur uno / cum vento luctor, cum gurgite pugno profundo).*

14.2a Supplying *fremman* (not in the manuscript), to preserve the hypermetric lines, and avoid the necessity of taking *sæcce* as an otherwise unattested form of *sacan,* "to fight, contend." Compare *Beowulf* 2499a *(sæcce fremman),* EXE 84.26b *(sæcce to fremmanne).* Note too the sound-play on *sæcce . . . secan.*

14.3a Compare EXE 1.24a *(holm-mægne beþeaht)* and 8.4a *(ufan yþum þeaht).*

14.4b Compare EXE 1.29b *(stille weorþað).*

14.5a The verb *tosælan* is attested only here and at EXE 13.25b.

14.10b This is a variant of the closing formulaic challenge *Saga hwæt ic hatte,* on which see the note at 1.14b–15 above; for *Frige hwæt ic hatte,* see the note on EXE 12.19b.

EXE 15

MANUSCRIPT: E, fol. 105r.

EARLIER EDITIONS AND TRANSLATIONS: Gr 18; Tr 15; Tu 18; Wy 17; Ma 17; KD 17; Ba 52, 42; Ab 17, 11; WiR 15; WiF 15, 75; Wh 17, 174–75; PZ 15; CH 17, 21; Mu 17; WiC 15, 533 and 1154.

SOLUTION: *COCER* (quiver); see in particular Dietrich, "Würdigung, Lösung und Herstellung." Other suggested solutions include: "ballista" (Dietrich, "Die Räthsel des Exeterbuchs"), "forge" (Pinsker, "Neue Deutungen"), "inkwell" (Shook, "Riddling Relating to the Anglo-Saxon Scriptorium"), "fortress" and "soul" (Lendinara, "E se B stesse per *bana?*"), "oven" (Trautmann, "Die Auflösungen der altenglischen Rätsel"; Trautmann, "Alte und neue Antworten"), "town" (Baum, *Anglo-Saxon Riddles*), "penis" (Jember, *Old English Riddles*), "plaited beehive" (Bierbaumer and Wannagat, "Ein neuer Lösungsvorschlag"; PZ), "fortress" (Wh), "quiver" (Wilcox, "New Solutions"), "bee-skep" (Osborn, "'Skep'"), *cocer,* "quiver," or **beoleap,* "bee-skep" (Ni), **lester* (Sayers, "*Exeter Book* Riddle 17"), "Samson's lion and bees" (Murphy, *Unriddling the Exeter Riddles,* 153–73). See further Stanley, "Heroic Aspects of the Exeter Book Riddles"; Salvador-Bello, "Compilation of the Old English Riddles," 140–42; Teele, "Heroic Tradition," 201–6; Sorrell, "A Bee in My Bonnet"; Osborn, "Anglo-Saxon Tame Bees"; Dale, *Natural World,* 157; Stanley, "Exeter Book *Riddles,* I."

The sheer number of solutions proposed for this riddle suggests something of its complexity; the two most compelling seem to be "quiver" and "beehive." The former suggestion turns on some neat verbal parallels with EXE 21 (*BOGA,* "bow"), universally accepted as having the solution "bow"; the latter on recognizing that Anglo-Saxons kept bees in skeps of upturned wickerwork or plaited straw. So for example EXE 15 and 21, uniquely in the Exeter Book, speak of spitting out deadly weapons the creature has previously swallowed (EXE 15.4 and 21.8). Alternatively, in his prose *De virginitate,* Aldhelm speaks of bees living in "little huts woven from the finest withies or sewn together from hollow bark" (Eh, 107: *exigua . . . tuguria gracillimis contexta viminibus seu cavatis consuta corticibus*). However, Aldhelm's own ALD 20 (*APIS,* "bee"), while it certainly refers to the "sharp spear-points of cruel battle" (ALD 20.4: *acuta . . . crudelis specula belli*), does not mention the hive. Yet the notion of weapon-bearing creatures links this riddle back to several of the preceding ones, such as EXE 12.1a *(HORN,* "horn": *Ic wæs wæpen wigan)* and 13.3 *(IGIL,* "hedgehog, porcupine": *beado-wæpen bere),* while the chaste nature of bees which Aldhelm certainly celebrates may connect this riddle to the one it immediately follows, if some preserved sense "anchorite" is accepted. Those who favor the "beehive" solution also focus on two runes that appear in the upper margin in the space between EXE 14 and 15, and appear to read ᛚ (l) and ᛒ (b); the latter rune is then taken to stand for some form of *beo,* "bee," and the former either for a *leap,* "basket" (so the unattested **beo-leap* or *leap beona*), or the equally unattested **lester,* "hive" (?) (formed on analogy with Celtic forms such as Irish *lestar,* Welsh *llestr,* Cornish *lester,* and Breton *lestr*). Immediately following this riddle is a peculiar sign, Ↄ, which looks like a reversed C, perhaps signifying the first letter of the solution to this riddle (if *COCER*) or the next (if *CROG*). There are eight compounds in this riddle, of which four are unique in extant Old English verse: *dryht-gestreon* (15.3a), *spere-broga* (15.4a), *attor-spere* (15.9a), and *womb-hord* (15.10a). The figures rise to nine and five if *eodor-wir* (15.2) is indeed a compound; see too the notes on 15.6b and 15.8a, which highlight two further compounds with only a single parallel elsewhere in the corpus.

15.1a The opening formula *Ic eom* is found in various forms; see the note at 3.1a above.

15.2b It is possible to take the phrase *eodor wirum fæst* either as "a lord ('protector') secure in wires" (taking *eodor* in apposition to 15.1 *mund-bora*) or as "secure in lordly ('protecting') wires" (taking *eodor-wir* in apposition to 15.3 *dryht-gestreon*). The latter course assumes an otherwise unattested compound *eodor-wir,* but is perhaps equally attractive, bearing in mind not only the sheer number of compounds in this riddle, but their unusual nature (note that *dryht-gestreon* is itself unique to this riddle).

15.5b Understanding manuscript *freo* as an antique form of *frea.* The "lord" in question would presumably be Samson, if the solution suggested by Murphy is preferred.

15.6b The compound *hilde-pil* is found only here and at EXE 13.28b. Compare EXE 21.12b *(þæt me of hrife fleogeð).*

15.8a The compound *beado-wæpen* is found only here and at EXE 13.3a.

15.10a Several of the riddles focus on the "belly" *(womb)* of the creature in question; compare the note at EXE 1.78a above.

EXE 16

MANUSCRIPT: E, fol. 105r.

EARLIER EDITIONS AND TRANSLATIONS: Gr 19; Tr 16; Tu 19; Wy 18; Ma 18; KD 18; Ba 82, 61; Ab 18, 12; WiR 16; WiF 16, 76; Wh 18, 175; PZ 16a–b; Mu 18; WiC 16, 533–34 and 1154.

SOLUTION: *CROG* (amphora, vessel); other suggested solutions include: "leather bottle" (Dietrich, "Würdigung, Lösung und Herstellung"), "cask" (Tr), "inkwell" (Shook, "Riddling Relating to the Anglo-Saxon Scriptorium"), "jug, amphora" (Wi), "penis" (Jember, *Old English Riddles*), *crog, wincrog, winsester,* "jug of wine" (Ni). See further Lendinara, "Aspetti della società germanica"; Salvador-Bello, "Compilation of the Old English Riddles," 142–44; Dale, *Natural World,* 42.

Physical damage to the manuscript prevents a clear solution to this riddle; the notion that many such items are carried in the hold of a ship supports the idea of amphorae or jugs, and helps connect this riddle to the next. There are no compounds in this riddle.

16.1a Reading *wundorlicu* (altered in E to *wunderlicu*). The *Ic eom* opening formula is found in various forms; see the note at 3.1a above. The similar formula found at EXE 27.7a *(Ða cwom wundorlicu wiht)* seems to be a deliberate conflation of this one and another *(Wiht cwom)*; see the note on EXE 31.1a.

16.1b Compare EXE 91.9b *(no þær word sprecan)*.

16.2a For the notion of the creature's speaking *for monnum*, compare EXE 18.12a *(for mengo)*, 33.12a and 46.1a *(for hæleþum)*, 46.4a *(for secgum)*, 53.8a *(for eorlum)*.

16.3a Several of the riddles focus on the "belly" *(womb)* of the creature in question; compare the note at EXE 1.78a above. The b-line is evidently missing in E.

EXE 17

MANUSCRIPT: E, fol. 105r.

EARLIER EDITIONS AND TRANSLATIONS: Gr 20; Tr 17; Tu 20; Wy 19; Ma 19; KD 19; Ba 70, 54; Ab 19, 12; WiR 17; WiF 17, 77; Wh 19, 175; PZ 17; Mu 19; WiC 17, 534 and 1154–55.

SOLUTION: *SNAC* (light warship); see in particular Griffith, "Riddle 19 of the Exeter Book"; Ni. Other suggested solutions include: "horse, man, wagon, and hawk" (Klipstein, *Analecta Anglo-Saxonica*), "sun" (Schneider, "Zu vier ae. Rätseln"), "falconry" (Hicketier, "Fünf Rätsel des Exeterbuches"; Erhardt-Siebold, "The Old English Hunt Riddles"), "man upon horseback with a hawk on his fist" (Tu; Wh; Brodeur and Taylor, "The Man, the Horse, and the Canary"), "horseman, servant, and hawk" (Tr), "writing" (Eliason, "Four Old English Cryptographic Riddles"), "hand writing on manuscript sheet with pen" (Lendinara, "Ags. *wlanc:* Alcune annotazioni"), "ship" (Wi). On this riddle in particular, see further Hacikyan, "The Exeter Manuscript: Riddle 19"; Wilcox, "Mock-Riddles"; Salvador-Bello, "Compilation of the Old English Riddles," 144–46; Teele, "Heroic Tradition," 59–61;

Bitterli, *Say What I Am Called,* 86–91; Simms, "Exeter Book *Riddle 19*"; Stanley, "Exeter Book *Riddles,* II," 356–57.

Most of the earlier attempts to solve this riddle have focused on the rather obvious collections of runes that spelled out backward the words HORS, "horse," MON, "man," WEGA, "ways" or "waves" (or perhaps "warrior," if *wiga* is intended), and HAOFOC, "hawk." Williamson went further, pointing out that much of the riddle plays on the common Old English kenning of a ship as a horse of the sea, and suggested that the proper solution was "ship." Other kennings are found at EXE 3.7b *(homera lafe)* and EXE 71.19b *(heaþo-sigel).* Griffith took the argument still a stage further, and offered a completely convincing solution which also explained why the runes spell out these words backward, by taking the final runes of each group to produce *SNAC,* the name of a swift, light kind of warship mentioned in the *Anglo-Saxon Chronicle* for 1052. This is the first of five runic riddles, which (like the runic signatures of Cynewulf) use a range of strategies to reveal (and conceal) their meaning. Here, seventeen runes spell backward in groups four nouns that are more or less straightforward in meaning, but which themselves mask deeper levels of understanding. EXE 22 (*HIGORA,* "jay, magpie") employs six runes singly to spell out the solution in anagram form, while EXE 62 (*BRIM-HENGEST,* "sea-steed") combines thirteen runes both singly and in pairs (one of the runes represents two letters in the Roman alphabet) to offer clues to seven nouns which, taken together, point the way to the ultimate solution. While the individual tactics for masking the constituent elements with runes are different, the strategy for indicating the overall answer (and indeed the broad answer itself) is identical in EXE 17 and EXE 62, which are likely related. Two further riddles, namely EXE 40 (*HANA OND HÆN,* "cock and hen") and EXE 56 (**RAD-ROD,* "well sweep"), employ the Roman alphabet to spell out the names of runes that gesture towards the solution. In the case of EXE 40, this results in a kind of anagram (in a manner like that of EXE 17), albeit that the intertwined elements of cock and hen are roughly presented in reverse, or, in the case of EXE 56, by specifying that the solution is composed of three runes, with RAD as the first. It seems likely that earlier versions of both EXE 40 and EXE 56 employed runes in the text, much as is found in EXE 17, EXE 22, and EXE 62, but that the runes were themselves subsequently "solved" and incorporated into the text; however, one might equally argue that in performance the rune-names would necessarily have been spelled out (as it were). It is at all events notable that in all five of these riddles the runes are (more or less) integrated into the wider alliterative and rhythmical scheme. This suggests that the four further runes (ᛞ ᚾ ᛚ ᚻ) found between the two lines of EXE 73 (*AC*, "oak"), each of which is presented as if it were a single-line riddle in the manuscript, are not integral to the riddle (since they do not fit the broader structural requirements of Old English verse), and are perhaps best interpreted as an interpolated attempt at a solution, similar to that found in a garbled and encoded form in the Roman alphabet in the middle of the line at EXE 34.5 (*BAT*, "boat"). In this context, one might also consider several riddles where the solution itself may be a rune, such as EXE 71 (*ÆSC*, "spear made of ash") and EXE 72 (*AC*, "ship made of oak"); less clearly to be included here are EXE 66 (*IS*, "ice") and EXE 73 (*AC*, "oak"). On the use of runes in the riddles, see Derolez, *Runica Manuscripta;* Derolez, "*Runica Manuscripta* Revisited"; Gleason, "*Per speculum in enigmate*"; Fell, "Runes and Riddles in Anglo-Saxon England"; Dewa, "The Runic Riddles of the Exeter Book"; DiNapoli, "Odd Characters"; Symons, *Runes and Roman Letters;* Birkett, *Reading the Runes.* There are seven compounds in this riddle, but none of them is unique in extant Old English verse.

17.1a Supplying *on siþe* (not in the manuscript). A standard formulaic opening; see the note at EXE 11.1a above.

17.2a The compound *hyge-wlonc* is found only here and at EXE 43.4a (*DAG*, "dough").

17.3a Reading *swiftne,* after Tu (E reads *swist ne*).

17.5b The word *rad* may conceal the further rune-name RAD, so leading some commentators to suppose that what is carried by the creature in question is a riveted WEGAR (for WIGGAR, "war spear").

17.9b Reading *hit,* after Gr (E reads *ic*). This is a variant of the closing formulaic challenge *Saga hwæt ic hatte,* on which see the note at 1.14b–15 above. See, however, Wilcox, "Mock-Riddles," who regards the apparently incorrect pronominal forms here and at 82.7b as deliberate bits of misdirection.

EXE 18

MANUSCRIPT: E, fol. 105r–v.

EARLIER EDITIONS AND TRANSLATIONS: Gr 21; Tr 18; Tu 21; Wy 20; Ma 20; KD 20; Ba 51, 41–42; Ab 20, 13; WiR 18; WiF 18, 78; Wh 20, 175–76; PZ 18; CH 20, 22–23; Mu 20; WiC 18, 534–35 and 1155.

SOLUTION: *SECG* (sword; man); other suggested solutions include: "hawk" and "sword" (Davidson, *The Sword in Anglo-Saxon England*), *heoru-swealwe* (a uniquely attested compound, meaning "fierce swallow," "taloned swallow," signifying some bird of prey, presumably a hawk or falcon; Shook, "Old English Riddle No. 20"; Nelson, "Old English Riddle 18 (20)"), "sword" (Dietrich, "Würdigung, Lösung und Herstellung"; Swaen, "Het 18e Oudengelsche Raadsel"), "hawk, falcon" (Tr), "penis" (Kay, "Riddle 20: A Revaluation"; Jember, *Old English Riddles*), "falcon" (PZ), *"sweord,"* "sword," with wordplay on *wæpen*, "weapon" (Ni). See further Stanley, "Heroic Aspects of the Exeter Book Riddles"; Lendinara, "Aspetti della società germanica"; Salvador-Bello, "Compilation of the Old English Riddles," 146–50; Tanke, "Bachelor-Warrior"; Teele, "Heroic Tradition," 58–62; Heyworth, "Perceptions of Marriage"; Bitterli, *Say What I Am Called*, 124–31; Murphy, *Unriddling the Exeter Riddles*, 206–15; Owen-Crocker, "'Seldom . . . does the deadly spear rest for long'"; Cavell, *Weaving Words*, 174–79; Dale, *Natural World*, 39, 114, and 177; Bardowell, "Art and Emotion," 148–52; Soper, "Exeter Book Riddles as Life-Writing," 859–60.

This is a problematic riddle, with two main schools of thought: those who would solve it as some kind of bird of prey promote some rather strained readings, but equally those who believe that the solution is "sword" cannot easily account for what looks like obviously sexual overtones toward the end of the text. Combining the basic "sword" solutions with suggestions of phallic aggression, Niles (137–39) offers his compromise: *sweord,* "sword," with wordplay on *wæpen,* "weapon," since males could be designated as *wæpned-men*. A preferable solution in such a context is more likely to be *SECG,* denoting both "sword" and "man." Both the martial and avian solutions link back to the previous riddle, depending on whether one focuses on the third or fourth of the runic groups. The final lines of the riddle as it survives offer a charming vignette of a henpecked victim, verbally and physically assailed with a slew of verbs in EXE 19.33–35 *(spreceð floceð . . . firenað . . . gæleð).* The end of the riddle is curtailed through physical damage; there is at least one leaf missing. There are twelve compounds in this riddle, of which seven are unique in extant Old English verse: *wæl-gim* (18.4a), *comp-wæpen* (18.9a), *word-lof* (18.11a), *rad-werig* (18.14a), *orleg-from* (18.15a), *bearn-gestreon* (18.27a), and *hago-steald* (18.31a).

18.1 Compare EXE 21.2 *(ic eom wrætlic wiht on gewin sceapen).* The *Ic eom* opening formula is found in various forms; see the note at 3.1a above, as well as the one at 27.7a *(Ða cwom wundorlicu wiht).*

18.2a Compare EXE 76.3b *(frean minum leof).*

18.2b Compare EXE 26.1b *(fægre gegierwed).*

18.3b Reading *seomað* (altered in E from *seomad*).

18.7b Reading *smiþa* (altered in E from *smiþe*). Compare EXE 3.8b *(hond-weorc smiþa)* and 24.14a *(wrætlic weorc smiþa).*

18.8a Reading *geardas* (altered in E from *geardus*). Compare EXE 88.4a *(gold on geardum).*

18.10a Compare EXE 65.15a *(since ond seolfre).*

18.12a For the notion of the creature speaking *for mengo,* see the note at EXE 16.2a above.

18.12b For similar drinking formulas, see the note at EXE 12.12b above.

18.13a Compare EXE 63.3a *(hafað mec on headre).*

18.13b Compare EXE 1.68 *(hwilum læte eft).*

18.15b–16a Compare *GenA* 1597b *(frecne scodon).*

18.24a See the note at EXE 13.6b *(me biþ gyrn witod)* above.
18.25a Compare *Andreas* 1354b *(guþe fremme)*.
18.29b Reading *geara,* after Tu (E reads *gearo*).
18.34b Reading *firenaþ,* after Wi (altered in E from *firenuw*).
18.35b A leaf is missing in E after *compes,* which some editors move to the beginning of the next line for metrical reasons, though that seems unnecessary.

EXE 19

MANUSCRIPT: E, fol. 106r.

EARLIER EDITIONS AND TRANSLATIONS: Gr 22; Tr 19; Tu 22; Wy 21; Ma 21; KD 21; Ba 32, 28–29; Ab 21, 14; WiR 19; WiF 19, 79; Wh 21, 177–78; PZ 19; CH 21, 24; Mu 21; WiC 19, 535 and 1155.

SOLUTION: *SULH* (plow); see in particular Dietrich, "Würdigung, Lösung und Herstellung"; Ni. Other suggested solutions include: "penis" (Jember, *Old English Riddles*). See further Schlutter, "Afog 'peruersus'"; Colgrave, "Some Notes on Riddle 21"; Salvador-Bello, "Compilation of the Old English Riddles," 150–52; Murphy, *Unriddling the Exeter Riddles,* 175–76; Cavell, *Weaving Words,* 82–83; Dale, *Natural World,* 34–35.

The solution "plow," first suggested by Dietrich, is generally accepted, though the secondary sense "penis" is by no means unlikely, given both the common sexual associations of the activity of plowing and the verbal parallels with several of the so-called double-entendre riddles, with which this riddle also shares the concept of a "lord" or "master" bringing up the rear. While the secondary sense connects this riddle to the one preceding, the primary sense also connects it to the one following. It is notable that several of the implement riddles have sexual overtones, often barely concealed; compare EXE 35 (*BLÆST-BELG,* "bellows"), EXE 50 (*ÞERSCEL,* "flail"), EXE 52 (*CYRN,* "churn"), and EXE 60 (*SPURA,* "spur"). The whole riddle is structured by an envelope pattern *(niþerweard . . . hlaford min . . . hinde-weardre . . . hlaford min)*. The single compound *orþonc-pil* (19.12a) is unique to this riddle. Note too the directional designations *niþerweard* (19.1a), *forðweard* (19.13a), and *hindeweard* (19.15a).

19.1a Compare EXE 29.6a *(Niþerweard . . . wæs neb hyre)* and 32.3b *(nebb biþ hyre . . . niþerweard gongeð).*

19.5a Reading *wrigaþ,* after Mu (E reads *wriguþ*). Compare EXE 10.8b *(wegeð ond þyð)* and 77.7a *(þær mec wegeð).*

19.7a Reading *bearwe,* after Gr (E reads *bearme*). Compare EXE 25.2a *(brungen of bearwum).*

19.8b Compare EXE 79.10b *(Hæbbe ic wunda fela).*

EXE 20

MANUSCRIPT: E, fol. 106r–v.

EARLIER EDITIONS AND TRANSLATIONS: Gr 23; Tr 20; Tu 23; Wy 22; Ma 22; KD 22; Ba 63, 50–51; Ab 22, 14–15; WiR 20; WiF 20, 80; Wh 22, 178–79; PZ 20; CH 22, 25; Mu 22; WiC 20, 535–36 and 1155.

SOLUTION: *CARLES WÆN* (Charles's Wain, Ursa Major); see in particular Ni. Other suggested solutions include: "days of the month" (Dietrich, "Würdigung, Lösung und Herstellung"; Wh), "bridge" (Tr), "rite of passage" (Jember, *Old English Riddles*), "ice bridge" (PZ). See further Blakeley, "Riddles 22 and 58 of the Exeter Book"; Osborn, "Old English Ing and His *Wain*"; Salvador-Bello, "Compilation of the Old English Riddles," 152–56; Teele, "Heroic Tradition," 54–59; Murphy, "Riders of the Celestial Wain"; Murphy, *Unriddling the Exeter Riddles,* 111–23; Salvador-Bello, *Isidorean Perceptions,* 327–35.

This riddle fits an astronomical solution best, and several commentators point to the constellation variously known as the Plough or the Great Bear (Ursa Major). Bitterli, *Say What I Am Called,* 59–68, in the course of an illuminating discussion, points out the extraordinary number of synonyms here for the key concepts of men *(monna . . . eored-mæcgas . . . mago-rincas . . . weras . . . eorlas . . . gestum . . . beornas . . . ellen-rofe weras),* horses *(wicgum . . . frid-hengestas . . . sceamas . . . wicg . . . hors . . . eh . . . fæt-hengest . . . bloncan . . . wicg),* water *(mere*

. . . flod . . . yþa geþræc . . . streamas . . . wætres byht . . . flode . . . lagu . . . burnan . . . wæge), and land *(wæg-stæþe . . . ofras . . . lande . . . grunde . . . stæðe).* A strikingly similar kind of strategy is found in several of the aenigmata of ALD, notably ALD 38 (*TIPPULA,* "water-strider"), which also describes crossing water without getting wet, and from the point of view of poetic composition again employs a useful variety of different terms for the key concepts. Whereas in the Latin it is the variety of metrical forms offered by the synonyms, here there is instead a range of alliterative options offered, so reflecting the different kinds of poetry addressed. Note too that ALD 38 is immediately preceded in the collection by an aenigma on yet another astrological animal that is found on land and in the sea and sky, namely *CANCER* (ALD 37, "crab"); it seems plausible that the author of EXE 20 was influenced conceptually by ALD 37–38. The closing lines of two aenigmata on astronomical signs stress that they function both on the land and in the sky (SYM 32.3 [*TAURUS,* "bull"]: *et vehor in caelis, et in ipsis ambulo terris*) and in the sea and sky (ALD 71.5–6 [*PISCIS,* "fish"]: *Quamvis in caelis convexa cacumina cernam, / non tamen undosi contemno marmora ponti*) respectively. This riddle seems to play with the same conceit, invoking the land/sea/sky triad also found (for example) in EXE 1 as part of an eightfold anaphora on *ne* which includes a monosyllabic verb form for each of the three relevant areas *(ne on flode swom / ne be grunde wod . . . / ne on lyfte fleag);* note that parallels for precisely these phrases are found elsewhere in the collection, as the notes on EXE 20.14b and 16b below indicate. In the same context, and given that many of the Exeter Book riddles also appear in pairs and sequences, it may seem significant that EXE 20 is itself preceded by one universally solved as "plow," so perhaps suggesting at least to the compiler of the collection a connection with the very specific kind of wagon described here.

For the use of the term *Carles wæn,* compare (for example) the description by Ælfric, *De temporibus anni* 9.6 (Henel, 68; the same text is referred to in the headnote to EXE 27 below), itself based on Isidore, *De rerum natura* 26.3, the source of ALD 53 (*ARCTURUS,* "Arcturus"), which likewise shares a number of features with EXE 20. There are six compounds in this riddle, of which four are unique in extant Old English verse: *wæg-stæþ* (20.2a), *eored-mæcg* (20.3b), *frid-hengest* (20.4a), and *fæt-hengest* (20.14a); note that three of these refer to the horses in question. Likewise unique are the words *sceamu* (20.4b, again referring to the horses) and *hrung* (20.10a).

20.1a It is tempting to connect the simple use of *cwom* here to what looks like an opening formula *Wiht cwom,* on which see the note at EXE 31.1a.

20.1b Note that the Roman numeral LX (for *sixtig*) is a key part of the alliteration. On the use of the number sixty here, see further Tucker, "'Sixty' as an Indefinite Number."

20.2b Compare EXE 76.8b *(wicge ride).*

20.3a Note that the Roman numeral XI (for *endleofan*) is a key part of the alliteration.

20.4a The hapax *frid-hengestas* is of uncertain meaning, though the second element clearly means "stallions"; here the simplest rendering seems to be "fine steeds."

20.4b Note that the Roman numeral IV (for *feower*) is a key part of the alliteration.

20.7a Compare EXE 1.17a *(under yþa geþræc)* and *Andreas* 823a *(ofer yþa geþræc).*

20.9 Compare EXE 20.21 below *(weras . . . ond hyra wicg), Beowulf* 2175b *(wicg somod).*

20.11a Compare *Andreas* 1094b–97a *(Beornas comon, / wiggendra þreat, wicgum gengan, / on mearum modige, mæðel-hegende, / æscum dealle).* Note that this passage, apart from the uniquely shared half-line *æscum dealle,* also shares with this riddle a propensity for varied designations of men and horses.

20.13b It is tempting to emend to *assena,* "asses," here, since the pairing of oxen and asses is biblical, and the riddle as a whole has a focus on equine creatures, while it is unclear whether "slaves" *(esna)* pulled carts in Anglo-Saxon England.

20.13–17a Notable here is the eight-part anaphora on *ne;* for anaphora elsewhere in EXE, see the note on EXE 1.16a above.

20.14b Compare EXE 72.3b *(on flode swom).*

20.16b Retaining the reading of E, following Wi, where most editors emend to *on*. Compare, however, EXE 49.4b (*fleag on lyfte*) and 20.14b above; compare too *Husb* 21b (*lagu drefde*).

20.17a Reading *ne under,* after Gr (E reads *neon der*). Compare EXE 87.8 (*Hwilum ic under bæc*).

20.21 Compare EXE 20.9 above (*weras ond hyra wicg*).

EXE 21

MANUSCRIPT: E, fol. 106v.

EARLIER EDITIONS AND TRANSLATIONS: Gr 24; Tr 21; Tu 24; Wy 23; Ma 23; KD 23; Ba 46, 39; Ab 23, 15; WiR 21; WiF 21, 21; Wh 23, 179; PZ 21; CH 23, 26; Mu 23; WiC 21, 536 and 1155.

SOLUTION: *BOGA* (bow); see in particular Dietrich, "Würdigung, Lösung und Herstellung"; Ni. Other suggested solutions include: "crossbow" (Hoops, "Die Armbrust im Frühmittelalter"; Tr), "penis" (Jember, *Old English Riddles*). See further Schlutter, "Afog 'peruersus'"; Erhardt-Siebold, "Old English Riddle 23"; Lendinara, "*Poculum mortis:* una nota"; Lendinara, "Aspetti della società germanica"; Salvador-Bello, "Compilation of the Old English Riddles," 156–58; Teele, "The Heroic Tradition," 98–106; Afros, "Linguistic Ambiguities"; Murphy, *Unriddling the Exeter Riddles,* 158–59; Owen-Crocker, "'Seldom . . . does the deadly spear rest for long'"; Rudolf, "Riddling and Reading," 505–8; Cavell, *Weaving Words,* 179–84; Stanley, "Exeter Book *Riddles,* II," 357; Dale, *Natural World,* 106.

The opening line offers the solution *boga,* "bow," backwards, with the substitution of *f* for *h,* a phonological and orthographical variant that may point to an early date of composition (see the headnote to the eighth-century FRA). More significant, perhaps, is the fact that EXE 21.2 is almost identical to EXE 18.1 (*SECG,* "sword," "man": *Ic eom wunderlicu wiht, on gewin sceapen*), as well as to the opening lines of several other riddles: EXE 16.1a (*CROG,* "amphora, vessel": *Ic eom wundorlicu wiht*), EXE 22.1a (*HIGORA,* "jay, magpie": *Ic eom wunderlicu wiht*), and

EXE 23.1a *(CIPE,* "onion": *Ic eom wunderlicu wiht).* This suggests that the first line here is a later interpolation of a coded solution to what is in any case a rather obvious riddle. There are five compounds in this riddle, of which three are unique in extant Old English verse: *man-drinc* (21.13a), *full-wered* (21.14a), and *searo-sæled* (21.16a).

21.1 Reading *onhwyrfed* (altered in E from *onhwyrfeð*). For the opening word of the translation, "UUOB," I am indebted to Ba.

21.2 For a very similar line, compare EXE 18.1 *(Ic eom wunderlicu wiht, on gewin sceapen).* The *Ic eom* opening formula is found in various forms; see the note at EXE 3.1a above, as well as the one at 27.7a *(Ða cwom wundorlicu wiht).*

21.3b See the note at EXE 1.77b above.

21.9a Compare *Andreas* 770a *(attor æl-fæle).*

21.9b Reading *æror,* after Tu (E reads *ær*), for metrical reasons; a similar emendation is proposed at 80.19b.

21.11b Compare EXE 41.16b *(þe ic her ymb sprice).*

21.12b Compare EXE 15.6a *(hu me of hrife fleogað).*

21.13a The notion of the "cup of death" *(poculum mortis)* or "drink of death" is expanded in *GuthB* 980b–91a.

21.14a Reading *full-wered,* after KD (E reads *full wer*).

21.16b This is a variant of the closing formulaic challenge *Saga hwæt ic hatte,* on which see the note at 1.14b–15 above.

EXE 22

MANUSCRIPT: E, fol. 106v.

EARLIER EDITIONS AND TRANSLATIONS: Gr 25; Tr 22; Tu 25; Wy 24; Ma 24; KD 24; Ba 68, 53; Ab 24, 16; WiR 22; WiF 22, 82; Wh 24, 180; PZ 22; CH 24, 27; Mu 24; WiC 22, 536 and 1155.

SOLUTION: *HIGORA* (jay, magpie); see in particular Dietrich, "Würdigung, Lösung und Herstellung." Other suggested solutions include: "jay" (Dietrich, "Würdigung, Lösung und Herstellung"), "magpie" (Dietrich, "Würdigung, Lösung und Herstellung"), "woodpecker" (GW), "actor specializing in animal and bird noises" (Sonke, "Zu dem 25. Rätsel des Exeterbuches"), "jay" or "green woodpecker" (Wells, "Ornithological Content"), *higoræ (higere),* "magpie" (Ni). See further Stanley, "Heroic Aspects of the Exeter Book Riddles"; Salvador-Bello, "Compilation of the Old English Riddles," 158–59; Hayes, "The Talking Dead"; McFadden, "Raiding, Reform, and Reaction"; Bitterli, *Say What I Am Called,* 91–97; Salvador-Bello, *Isidorean Perceptions,* 327–35.

This riddle carries its solution (*higora,* "jay, magpie") embedded in runes and in the form of an anagram (*garohi*); the kind of dislocation of syllables that resembles the "breaking of words" *(scinderatio fonorum)* that is described by the idiosyncratic seventh-century Hiberno-Latin author Virgilius Maro Grammaticus in the context of Latin grammar (see further Doležalová, "On Mistake and Meaning"). The unusual form of the G-rune suggests a scribe unused to copying runes, or an exemplar that was similarly problematic, or both. (It looks more like an *X* in the Roman alphabet, although the use of *X* to denote an unknown name is only attested much later, so making sadly anachronistic the otherwise attractive notion that EXE 22.7b could mean "They call me X.") For more on the use of runes in EXE, see the headnote to EXE 17 (*SNAC,* "light warship") above. As for the notion that the jay or magpie (Latin *pica*) has a distinctive and unbirdlike voice, capable of imitating human speech, see Isidore, *Etym.* 12.7.46. In this context, it is intriguing that the riddle splits into two parts, the first of which, EXE 22.1–7a, describes the noises the bird makes using seven different verbs highlighted by sevenfold anaphora on *hwilum (wræsne . . . beorce . . . blæte . . . græde . . . gielle . . . onhyrge . . . gemæne),* while the second, EXE 22.7b–10, sounds out the bird's names using six different runes. On anaphora elsewhere in EXE, see the note on EXE 1.16a above. For a similarly bipartite structure in another of the runic riddles, see the headnote to EXE 40 (*HANA OND HÆN,* "cock and hen") below. The only compound, *guð-fugol* (22.5a), is unique to this riddle, and again emphasizes the avian solution.

22.1a The *Ic eom* opening formula is found in various forms; see the note at 3.1 above.

EXE 23

MANUSCRIPT: E, fol. 106v–7r.

EARLIER EDITIONS AND TRANSLATIONS: Gr 26; Tr 23; Tu 26; Wy 25; Ma 25; KD 25; Ba 74, 57; Ab 25, 16; WiR 23; WiF 23, 83; Wh 25, 180–81; PZ; CH 25, 28; Mu 25; WiC 23, 536–37 and 1156.

SOLUTION: *CIPE-LEAC* (onion); see in particular Dietrich, "Würdigung, Lösung und Herstellung"; Ni. Other suggested solutions include: "hemp" (Bouterwek, *Cædmon's des Angelsachsen biblische Dichtungen*; Dietrich, "Die Räthsel des Exeterbuchs"), "mustard" (Walz, "Notes on the Anglo-Saxon Riddles"), "leek" (Dietrich, "Würdigung, Lösung und Herstellung"), "rosehip" (Trautmann, "Die Auflösungen der altenglische Rätsel"), "penis" (Jember, *Old English Riddles*). See further Stewart, "Diachronic Study"; Williams, "What's So New about the Sexual Revolution?"; Salvador-Bello, "Compilation of the Old English Riddles," 160–62; Shaw, "Hair and Heathens"; Orchard, "Enigma Variations," 295–97; Murphy, *Unriddling the Exeter Riddles,* 176–77 and 221–34; Cavell, *Weaving Words,* 35.

Following hard on two somewhat self-evident riddles, this one employs a form of misdirection through double entendre, with what seems an obvious solution, "penis," masking the "true" one, *cipe-leac,* "onion." This is the first of two "onion" riddles (the other is EXE 63), and while they both share many of the same motifs, this is the more highly sexualized. Both ultimately derive from an aenigma of Symphosius (SYM 44, *CEPA,* "onion"), but while EXE 63 clearly relies directly on the Latin text, EXE 23 seems to be based on EXE 63. The sexual aspects of EXE 23 may have been suggested by the fact that the Latin word *cepa* appears to equate to a number of vernacular terms, including *cipe-leac, gar-leac,* and *secg-leac* (compare *crop-leac*), several of which (with their notions of "spear," "sword/man") might have prompted a fallacious response. This is the first of the undoubted so-called double-entendre riddles (on which see further Gleissner, *Die "zweideutigen" altenglischen Rätsel des "Exeter Book"*; Stewart, "Double-entendre in the Old English Riddles"; Davis, "Sexual Idiom"; Bueno Alonso, "Actitudes anglosajonas hacia el humor"; Coleman, "Sexual Euphemism in Old English";

Frank, "Sex in the *Dictionary of Old English*"; Salvador-Bello, "Sexual Riddle Type"). The list certainly includes EXE 23 (*CIPE,* "onion"), EXE 40 (*HANA OND HÆN,* "cock and hen"), EXE 42 (*CÆG,* "key"), EXE 43 (*DAG,* "dough"), EXE 44 (*LOTH OND BEARN,* "Lot and his children"), EXE 52 (*CYRN,* "churn"), EXE 59 (*CYRTEL,* "shirt, garment"), and EXE 60 (*SPURA,* "spur"), while less overt sexual imagery is also found in others in the collection, such as EXE 9 (*WIN-FÆT,* "cup of wine"), EXE 10 (*OXA,* "ox"), EXE 18 (*SECG,* "sword," "man"), EXE 35 (*BLÆST-BELG,* "bellows"), EXE 61 (*GLÆS-FÆT,* "glass beaker"), EXE 63 (*CIPE,* "onion"), EXE 83 (*BLÆST-BELG,* "bellows"), and EXE 87 (*CÆG,* "key"). There are six compounds in this riddle, of which two are unique in extant Old English verse: *neah-buend* (23.2) and *steap-heah* (23.4).

23.1a The *Ic eom* opening formula is found in various forms; see the note at 3.1 above.

23.4a Reading *stapol,* after Tr (E reads *staþol*). Other editors retain the reading of the manuscript, and understand *staþol* in the sense "base, foundation," but compare *Beowulf* 927a *stapole* (where the manuscript again reads *staþole*).

23.7 Compare EXE 43.3b–4a *(bryd grapode / hyge-wlonc hondum);* note that the parallel comes from another of the so-called double-entendre riddles.

23.7b–10 Note the number of finite verbs in *-að* or *-eð* in these lines: there are six, four of them in conjunction with *mec* or *mec on;* compare 63.2b–4, which contains five finite verbs in *-að* or *-eð,* three of them in conjunction with *mec* or *mec on.*

23.8b Compare EXE 63.2b–3 *(æghwa mec reafað / hafað mec on headre ond min heafod scireþ);* note that the parallel comes from another of the so-called double-entendre riddles.

23.9a–10a Compare EXE 59.6b *(on nearo fegde);* note that the parallel comes from another of the so-called double-entendre riddles.

23.10b Reading *seo,* after Gr (E reads *se*).

EXE 24

MANUSCRIPT: E, fol. 107r–v.

EARLIER EDITIONS AND TRANSLATIONS: Gr 27; Tr 24; Tu 27; Wy 26; Ma 26; KD 26; Ba 43, 35; Ab 26, 17; WiR 24; WiF 24, 84; Wh 26, 181–82; PZ 23; CH 26, 29; Mu 26; WiC 24, 537 and 1156.

SOLUTION: *CRISTES BOC* (Gospel book); see in particular Ni. Other suggested solutions include: "book" (Müller, *Die Rätsel des Exeterbuches*; Dietrich, "Würdigung, Lösung und Herstellung"), "hide" (Tr), "*halig gewritu*," "holy scripture" (Shook, "Riddling Relating to the Anglo-Saxon Scriptorium"). See further Lester, "*Sindrum begrunden* in Exeter Riddle No. 26"; Lendinara, "Aspetti della società germanica"; Neville, *Representations of the Natural World*, 113–14; Salvador-Bello, "Compilation of the Old English Riddles," 162–65; Teele, "Heroic Tradition," 110–20; Afros, "*Sindrum Begrunden* in Exeter Book *Riddle 26*"; Marsden, "'Ask What I Am Called'"; Hayes, "Talking Dead"; Bitterli, *Say What I Am Called*, 171–78; Murphy, *Unriddling the Exeter Riddles*, 90–91; Bardowell, "Art and Emotion," 154–57; Dale, *Natural World*, 65–66, 87–102, 113–16, 158–59, and 161–65.

See too Leahy, *Anglo-Saxon Crafts*, 89–93.

This violent and graphic riddle offers the most comprehensive description of the whole process of book-making, from the death of the unwitting donor of the raw material through to its ultimate adornment; there is a likely source (at least for EXE 24.1–6) in TAT 5 (*MEMBRANUM*, "parchment"). The connection of this to both the preceding and following riddles is striking, although later riddles also exploit the juxtaposition between the sacred and the profane. This is the first of a scattered series of riddles relating to writing, also comprising EXE 45 (**BOC-MOÐÐE*, "book moth"), EXE 49 (*FEÐER OND FINGRAS*, "quill pen and fingers"), EXE 55 (*STAFAS*, "letters"), EXE 58 (*HREOD*, "reed"), EXE 65 (*CRISTES BOC*, "Gospel book"), EXE 88 (*BOC*, "book," "beech"), EXE 89 (*BLÆCHORN*, "inkhorn"), EXE 91 (*BOC*, "book"); for aenigmata relating to the scriptorium, see the headnote to ALD 30 (*ELEMENTUM*, "alphabet"). Many of these riddles are discussed in detail by Göbel,

Studien zu den altenglischen Schriftwesenrätseln; this one is considered at 182–224. There are ten compounds in this riddle, of which five are unique in extant Old English verse: *woruld-streng* (24.2a), *sped-drop* (24.8a), *beam-telg* (24.9b), *sweart-last* (24.11a), and *hleo-bord* (24.12a); note that all of these are found in the first half of the riddle.

24.1b Compare *Beowulf* 2925b *(ealdre besnyðede)*; *Andreas* 1324b *(ealdre besnyðede)*.

24.3a Reading *dyfde* (altered in E from *difde*).

24.6a Reading *ecg* (E reads *ecge*). Compare *ChristC* 1140b *(swylce ic seaxes ecg)*.

24.7b Another riddle within a riddle. On such riddles within riddles, see the note at EXE 1.12–14a above.

24.8a Reading *geondsprengde* (E reads *geond*); some editors (including KD) retain the manuscript reading, but if *geond* bears primary stress, one would expect it to alliterate; some emendation seems preferable.

24.11a The compound *sweart-last* is unique to this riddle; but compare EXE 49.2b *(swearte wæran lastas)*.

24.12b Reading *hyde*, after Gr (E reads *hyþe*).

24.13a Compare EXE 65.14a *(golde gegierwed)*.

24.13b Reading *glisedon*, after Tr (E reads *gliwedon*). Other editors retain the manuscript reading, but then have to assume an otherwise unattested sense "adorn" for *gliwian*, which normally means "play on a musical instrument," "sing"; the verb *glisian* preferred here is rare, but the sense "glow-worm" for the phrase *se glisienda wibba* supports the reading here.

24.14a Compare EXE 3.8b *(hond-weorc smiþa)*.

24.16b Understanding *mære* as an alternative form of *mæren*, the third-person plural present subjunctive form of *mæran*; for a parallel, see EXE 80.32b *(sawe* for *sawen)*. Tr and Wy emend to *mæren*.

24.22a Compare EXE 13.22 *(swæse ond gesibbe)*, *GenA* 1612a *(swæsum ond gesibbum)*.

24.26b–28 This is a variant of the closing formulaic challenge *Saga hwæt ic hatte,* on which see the note at 1.14b–15 above.

24.27a For the phrase *to nytte,* compare EXE 47.9b *(þe him to nytte swa),* 48.2a *(dryhtum to nytte),* and 68.2b *(hæleþum to nytte).*

24.28a The form *gifre* in the sense "useful" is found only here and at EXE 47.3b.

EXE 25

MANUSCRIPT: E, fol. 107v.

EARLIER EDITIONS AND TRANSLATIONS: Gr 28; Tr 25; Tu 28; Wy 27; Ma 27; KD 27; Ba 59, 48; Ab 27, 18; WiR 25; WiF 25, 85; Wh 27, 182–83; PZ 24; CH 27, 30; Mu 27; WiC 25, 538 and 1156.

SOLUTION: *MEDU* (mead); see in particular Dietrich, "Die Räthsel des Exeterbuchs." Other suggested solutions include: "whip" (Dietrich, "Würdigung, Lösung und Herstellung"), "sleep"? (Jember, *Old English Riddles*), *mele-deaw ond medu,* "mead (and its source)" (Ni). See further Neville, *Representations of the Natural World,* 200–1; Salvador-Bello, "Compilation of the Old English Riddles," 166–68; Teele, "Heroic Tradition," 181–87; Murphy, *Unriddling the Exeter Riddles,* 164–65; Biggam, "True Staff of Life," 30–32; Cavell, *Weaving Words,* 221–23; Price, "Hive of Activity"; Dale, *Natural World,* 144–49, 154–65, and 198.

This riddle offers a full account of the making and the power of mead (or perhaps beer, which in Anglo-Saxon England was often made with fruit and honey), from the production of honey by bees to the binding and punishing effects of the mead when made. The closing formula here is very close in length and structure to that of the preceding riddle, by contrast with the simple *Frige hwæt ic hatte* formula of EXE 12.19 and EXE 14.10, and underlines that association. The close verbal parallels linking this riddle with EXE 9 (*WIN-FÆT,* "cup of wine") seem especially appropriate. There are two compounds in this riddle, of which *mægen-þise* (25.10a) is unique in extant Old English verse, although some editors have emended to a form of *mægen-wisa,* "army-leader."

25.1a The *Ic eom* opening formula is found in various forms; see the note at 3.1a above.

25.2a Compare EXE 19.7a *(brungen of bearwe).*

25.7b Reading *weorpe,* after Tu (E reads *weorpere*).

25.8a Reading *esne,* after Tu (E reads *efne*).

25.9a Reading *onfindeð* (altered in E from *onfindet*).

25.12 The line is repeated almost verbatim at EXE 9.10 *(WIN-FÆT,* "cup of wine": *gif hi unrædes ær ne geswicaþ).* Compare too *Jul* 120 (*gif þu unrædes ær ne geswicest,* "if you do not already cease from foolishness"), *Elene* 516 (*ond þæs unrihtes eft gesviceð,* "and cease again from that foolishness").

25.15b–17 This is a variant of the closing formulaic challenge *Saga hwæt ic hatte,* on which see the note at 1.14b–15 above.

EXE 26

MANUSCRIPT: E, fol. 107v.

EARLIER EDITIONS AND TRANSLATIONS: Gr 29; Tr 26; Tu 29; Wy 28; Ma 28; KD 28; Ba 60, 48–49; Ab 28, 18; Wi 26; WiF 26, 86; Wh 28, 183; PZ 25; CH 28, 31; Mu 28; WiC 26, 538 and 1156–57.

SOLUTION: *BOC-FELL* (parchment); see in particular Ziegler, "Ein neuer Lösungsversuch"; Bitterli, *Say What I Am Called.* Other suggested solutions include: "harp" (Padelford, "Old English Musical Terms"; Tr), "John Barleycorn" (Wright, *Biographia Britannica Literaria I;* Wh), "stringed instrument" (Ma), "wine cask" (Dietrich, "Würdigung, Lösung und Herstellung"), "beer" (Tu), "tortoise" (Shook, "Old English Riddle 28"), "malt liquor" (Baum, *Anglo-Saxon Riddles*), "trial of the soul," "barrow" (Jember, *Old English Riddles*), "yew-horn"? (Wi), "pattern-welded sword" (Göbel and Göbel, "Solution of an Old English Riddle"), "woman" (Stewart, "Diachronic Study"), "mead" (PZ), *bere ond ealu,* "ale (and its source)" (Ni). See further Bitterli, *Say What I Am Called,* 178–90; Cavell, *Weaving Words,* 167–71; Ooi, "Speaking Objects," 59–61; Dale, *Natural World,* 19.

This is a somewhat perplexing riddle, though perhaps those suggested solutions which point to associations with brewing, such as "beer" or "ale," come closest to catching the flavor of the elongated process by which the end product is made. The juxtaposition with the preceding EXE 24 *(CRISTES BOC)* and EXE 25 (*MEDU,* "mead") is striking; all three seem to make use of the "suffering servant" motif discussed in the introduction to *OEALRT,* under "Shared Themes across the Collections." There is only a single compound in this riddle.

26.1 The line looks like a variant of an opening formula found at EXE 29.1–2 and 30.1–2 *(Is þes middan-geard missenlicum wisum gewlitegad, wrættum gefrætwad).*

26.2 As it stands, the line lacks alliteration, though perhaps the end rhyme compensates; other editors emend, for example reading *sceardestan* (E reads *heardestan*), and presumably understanding "the most carved up."

26.6b Compare EXE 10.7b *(hwilum feorran broht).*

26.9a Reading *þær þær* (E reads *þara þær*).

26.10b Reading *wiht,* after Tr (E reads *wið*).

26.12b Compare EXE 29.23b *(Micel is to hycgenne).*

26.12b–13 This is part of an elaborate closing challenge formula, essentially an appeal to the cleverness of the potential solver, found in slightly variant forms at EXE 29.23b–24 *(Micel is to hycgenne / wisum woð-boran, hwæt sio wiht sie),* 30.13b–14 *(Rece, gif þu cunne / wis worda gleaw, hwæt sio wiht sie),* 33.13–14 *(Saga soð-cwidum, searo-þoncum gleaw, / wordum wis-fæst, hwæt þis gewæde sy),* 39.8–9 *(Þæt is to geþencanne þeoda gehwylcum, / wis-fæstum werum, hwæt seo wiht sy),* and 65.15b–16 *(Secge se þe cunne, / wis-fæstra hwylc, hwæt seo wiht sy).* The formula is inverted as the opening line of EXE 37 *(Gewritu secgað þæt seo wiht sy),* and seems to have inspired the unusual challenge of EXE 41.14b–16 *(Mon se þe wille, / cyþe cyne-wordum hu se cuma hatte, / eðþa se esne, þe ic her ymb sprice).*

EXE 27

MANUSCRIPT: E, fol. 107v–8r.

EARLIER EDITIONS AND TRANSLATIONS: Gr 30; Tr 27; Tu 30; Wy 29; Ma 29; KD 29; Ba3, 7; Ab 29, 19; WiR 27; WiF 27, 87; Wh 29, 183–84; PZ 27; CH29, 32; Mu 29; WiC 27, 538–39 and 1157.

SOLUTION: *MONA OND SUNNE* (moon and sun); see in particular Dietrich, "Würdigung, Lösung und Herstellung"; Ni. Other suggested solutions include: "bird and wind," "swallow and sparrow" (Trautmann, "Die Auflösungen der altenglischen Rätsel"), "cloud and wind" (Walz, "Notes on the Anglo-Saxon Riddles"; Trautmann, "Alte und neue Antworten"), "abduction of Venus" (PZ). See further Joyce, "Natural Process in *Exeter Book* Riddle #29"; Clemoes, *Interactions of Thought and Language,* 187–88; Salvador-Bello, "Compilation of the Old English Riddles," 139–40, 172–75; Teele, "Heroic Tradition," 52–55 and 132–36; Wright, "Persecuted Church"; Murphy, *Unriddling the Exeter Riddles,* 123–39; Salvador-Bello, *Isidorean Perceptions,* 327–35.

Dietrich's early solution was based on the perceived parallel between the opening lines of this riddle and *Met4* 10–11a *hwilum eac þa sunnan sines bereafað / beorhtan leohtes,* "sometimes [the moon] also robs the sun of its bright light"; other suggested solutions are more or less fanciful. The notion that the moon takes its light from the sun is also repeated by Ælfric, *De temporibus anni* 1.31–32; the same text is referred to above in the headnote to EXE 20 (*CARLES WÆN,* "Charles's Wain"). There are three compounds in this riddle, of which one, *lyft-fæt* (27.3a), is unique in extant Old English verse.

27.1a For the opening formula *Ic (þa) wiht(e) geseah,* see the note at EXE 11.1a. Compare especially EXE 83.1a *(Ic seah wundorlice wiht).*

27.2a Reading *hornum bitweonum,* after Gr (E reads *horna abitweonū*).

27.4 Compare EXE 27.9 *(ahredde þa þa huþe ond to ham bedraf)* and 32.4 *(hiþeð holdlice ond to ham tyhð);* the repetition within this riddle of the concept of "booty" *(huþe)* links the two halves together.

27.5b Reading *atimbran,* after Gr (E reads *atimbram*).

27.7a The phrase *Ða cwom wundorlicu wiht* here looks like a conflation of the elaborate opening *Ic eom wunderlicu wiht* found in EXE 16.1a, 18.1a, 21.2a (as a variant, *ic eom wrætlic wiht*), 22.1a, 23.1a, on which see further the note at EXE 3.1a above, and the less spectacular opening formula *Wiht cwom,* on which see the note at EXE 31a below. In any case, the use of a second such opening formula gives a broad hint about the double nature of the solution, since this is the beginning of the description of the second half of the solution.

27.9a See the note on EXE 27.4. Compare *GenA* 2113a *(huðe ahreddan).*

27.9b Reading *bedraf,* after Tu (E reads *bedræf*).

27.11b Reading *onette,* after Gr (E reads *o netteð*).

EXE 28A AND 28B

MANUSCRIPT: E, fol. 108r, 122v.

EARLIER EDITIONS AND TRANSLATIONS: Gr 31; Tr 28; T 31; Wy 30; Ma 30; KD 30; Ba 14, 17–18; Ab 30, 19; WiR 28; WiF 28, 88; Wh 30, 184–85; PZ 28; CH 30a, 33; Mu 30; WiC 28a, 539, 577, 1157, and 1163.

SOLUTION: *BEAM* (beam, tree, wood, beam of light, cross, gallows); other suggested solutions include: "rain-water" (Dietrich, "Würdigung, Lösung und Herstellung"), "cornfield" (Trautmann, "Die Auflösungen der altenglischen Rätsel"), "tree" and "cross" (Trautmann, "Alte und neue Antworten"), "cross" or "wood" (Tr), "wooden cross" (Trautmann, "Zu meiner Ausgabe der altenglische Rätsel"), "penis" (Jember, *Old English Riddles*), "cross/sun" (Ritzke-Rutherford, *Light and Darkness*), "birch" (Schneider, "Zu vier ae. Rätseln"), "cross as vehicle of salvation" (Talentino, "Riddle 30: The Vehicle of the Cross"), "snow" (Pinsker, "Neue Deutungen"; PZ), "fire," "Easter fire" (Anderson, *Two Literary Riddles*), *treow,* "a tree/grove/firewood/wooden objects" (Ni). See further Fiocco, "Cinque enigmi dall'Exeter Book"; Liuzza, "Old

English *Riddle 30*"; Morgan and McAllister, "Reading *Riddles 30A* and *30B* as Two Poems." Salvador-Bello, "Compilation of the Old English Riddles," 175–80 and 263–66; Doane, "Spacing, Placing and Effacing"; Afros, "Linguistic Ambiguities"; Afros, "Syntactic Variation in *Riddles 30A* and *30B*"; Salvador-Bello, *Isidorean Perceptions,* 328–29; Bardowell, "Art and Emotion," 157–60; Stanley, "Exeter Book *Riddles,* II," 357.

This riddle appears in slightly different forms on fols. 108r and 122v of E, and is generally solved either as "wood" (or some kind of wooden object) or "fire," with the former preferred by the majority. A solution such as *BEAM,* covering all of the possibilities "beam," "tree," "wood," "beam of light," "gallows," especially with the supplementary sense "cross" witnessed in the *Dream of the Rood,* might cover all objections, and at the same time emphasize the necessity of thinking in terms of potential wordplay. Note too that in *Exodus,* the term *beam* is used twice to signify the pillars of fire and cloud (*Exodus* 94b and 568a). In the right-hand margin of fol. 108r at this point a later hand has written an *r,* enclosed by points, perhaps a guess at the solution *ROD,* "cross." For the theme of kissing here, see the headnote to ALD 80. There are three compounds in this riddle, of which one, *leg-bysig/lig-bysig* (28a.1b; 28b.1), is unique in extant Old English verse.

28.1a The *Ic eom* opening formula is found in various forms; see the note at 3.1 above.

28a.3a Compare the formula *fus on forð-weg,* "eager to depart," "eager to die," which is found in variant forms in *Exodus* 129a and 248a; *GuthA* 801a; *GuthB* 945a; *Men* 218a; *Dream* 125a.

28a.4a Compare *Andreas* 1448 (*geseah he geblowene bearwas standan,* "he saw blossoming groves standing"), describing the saint's ecstatic vision.

28a.7b Reading *onhnigaþ,* after Tr (E reads *on hin gaþ*).

28b.2 The manuscript is damaged, but the text can be recovered by reference to EXE 28a.2.

28b.3a The manuscript is damaged, but the text can be recovered by reference to EXE 28a.3a.

28b.3b Compare *Elene* 1311–12a, describing the purging of souls that are not damned on Judgment Day (*þurh ofnes fyr eall geclænsod / amered ond gemylted,* "cleansed, refined, and smelted through the fire of the furnace").

EXE 29

MANUSCRIPT: E, fol. 108r–v.

EARLIER EDITIONS AND TRANSLATIONS: Gr 32; Tr 29; Tu 32; Wy 31; Ma 31; KD 31; Ba 44, 36–37; Ab 31, 20; WiR 29; WiF 29, 89; Wh 31, 185–86; PZ 29; CH 31, 34; Mu 31; WiC 29, 539–40 and 1157.

SOLUTION: *SALTERE* (psaltery). Other suggested solutions include: "bagpipe" (Dietrich, "Würdigung, Lösung und Herstellung"; Padelford, "Old English Musical Terms"), "fiddle" (Trautmann, "Die Auflösungen der altenglischen Rätsel"), "musical instrument" (Tr), "portable organ" (Holthausen, "Nochmals die altenglische Rätsel"), "organistrum" (Holthausen, "Zu den altenglischen Rätseln"), "harp" (Jember, *Old English Riddles*), "feather-pen" (Fry, "Exeter Riddle 31"), "cithara" (Musgrave, "Cithara as the Solution"), **blæst-pipe,* "bagpipes" (Ni). See further Lendinara, "Aspetti della società germanica"; Salvador-Bello, "Compilation of the Old English Riddles," 139–40, 180–81; Teele, "Heroic Tradition," 52–55; Orchard, "Performing Writing and Singing Silence," 88–89; Dale, *Natural World,* 187 and 193; Lockhart, "Everyday Wonders," 129–30.

The opening lines of this and the following riddle are very close, and suggest a link. The creature in question in EXE 29 is generally taken to be some kind of musical instrument, and taking the various parts described to refer to spread drones and a downward-pointing chanter, most commentators have accepted the solution "bagpipe," despite the rather obvious difficulty that no bagpipes from the period are attested. Given the various parallels to other riddles dealing with writing, however (detailed most fully by Fry, "Exeter Riddle 31"), the solution *FEÐER OND FINGRAS* (quill pen and fingers) is certainly in play. An elegant way to deal with the tension between a solution involving a musical instrument and the practice of writing may be a psaltery, a stringed instrument shaped like an inverted delta and plucked with a quill rather than strummed with the fingers; I am grateful to Chris Laprade for this inventive suggestion, which has the added advantage of linking this riddle to the next (with which it is in any case verbally connected): the inverted delta shape of a psaltery also fits the most plausible suggested solutions there, namely "wheelbarrow," "cart," and "ship." There are three compounds in this riddle, of which two are unique in extant Old English verse: *feþe-georn* (29.9a) and *woð-giefu* (29.18a).

29.1–2 The lines are repeated verbatim at EXE 30.1–2, and seem to be a kind of "extra" formulaic opening, of which a variant is found at EXE 26.1 *(Biþ foldan dæl fægere gegierwed).*

29.3a A standard formulaic opening; see the note at EXE 11.1a above.

29.4a Reading *nower,* after Herzfeld, *Die Räthsel des Exeterbuches* (E reads *on*).

29.4b Compare EXE 29.11b *(eorlum on gemonge)* and 29.14a *(werum on gemonge).*

29.6a Reading *niþerweard* (E reads *niþerwearð*), and supplying *onhwyrfed* (not in E), after Herzfeld, *Die Räthsel des Exeterbuches.* Alternatively, one might take the whole manuscript line as the a-line: compare EXE 19.1a *(Neb is min niþerweard)* and 32.3 *(nebb biþ hyre æt nytte niþerweard gongeð).*

29.7–9 The continued alliteration on *f-* in these lines is striking: could it be (or have been) interpreted as a gesture toward the (possible) solution?

29.7a Compare EXE 25.15a *(fota ne folma),* 37.10a *(fot ne folme),* and 65.7a *(fot ne folme),* and *Beowulf* 745a *(fet ond folma).*

29.8 Compare EXE 56.3 *(ne fela rideð, ne fleogan mæg).*

29.11b Compare EXE 29.4b and 29.14a *(werum on gemonge).*

29.14b Reading *gemonge,* after PZ (E reads *wonge*); compare EXE 29.4b *(werum on gemonge)* and 29.11b *(eorlum on gemonge).*

29.15b Reading *habbað,* after Gr (E reads *habbad*).

29.16b The word *deor* here can be interpreted in several different ways: "brave" or "dear" if an adjective; "animal" if a noun.

29.18a Reading *woð-giefu* (altered in E from *wodgiefu*).

29.20b Compare EXE 12.11b *(hyrstum frætwed)* and 51.7b–8a *(gealga,* "gallows," "cross": *hyrstum . . . gefrætwed).*

29.21b Compare EXE 89.28a *(Nu min hord warað).*

29.22a Reading *baru,* after Wi (E reads *bær*), to give the correct feminine nominative singular form.

29.23a Reading *mæge* (E reads has *mægne*), as in *Beowulf* 1978a *(mæg wið mæge).*

29.23b Compare EXE 26.12b *(Micel is to hycganne).*

29.23b–24 This is part of an elaborate closing challenge formula, essentially an appeal to the cleverness of the potential solver, found in slightly variant forms, on which see the note at EXE 26.12b–13 above.

29.24b Supplying *sio* (not in E), on the model of EXE 30.14b *(hwæt sio wiht sie).*

EXE 30

MANUSCRIPT: E, fol. 108v.

EARLIER EDITIONS AND TRANSLATIONS*:* Gr 33; Tr 30; Tu 33; Wy 32; Ma 32; KD 32; Ba 58, 47–48; Ab 32, 20–21; WiR 30; WiF 30, 90; Wh 32, 186; PZ 30; CH 32, 35; Mu 32; WiC 30, 540 and 1157–58.

SOLUTION: *CEAP-SCIP* (merchant ship); see in particular Ni. Other suggested solutions include: "wagon" (Conybeare, *Illustrations of Anglo-Saxon Poetry*), "millstone" (Bouterwek, *Cædmon's des Angelsachsen biblische Dichtungen*), "ship" (Dietrich, "Würdigung, Lösung und Herstellung"; Wh), "wheel" (Wy), "wheelbarrow" (PZ). See further Fiocco, "Il viaggio della nave nell'enigma 32"; Salvador-Bello, "Compilation of the Old English Riddles," 181–82; Thier, "Steep Vessel, High Horn-ship"; Lockhart, "Everyday Wonders," 129–30; Dale, *Natural World,* 150, 187, and 192.

Like the preceding riddle, with which it shares both opening and closing formulas, EXE 30 describes a one-footed open-mouthed creature, in this case capable of carrying food across a distance. The solutions "wheelbarrow," "cart," and "ship" all seem feasible, with the last perhaps the most likely. There are three compounds in this riddle, of which two are unique in extant Old English verse: *searo-ceap* (30.7a) and *foddur-wela* (30.10a); likewise, the word *folc-scipe* (30.10b) is unique to this riddle.

30.1–2	The lines are repeated verbatim at EXE 29.1–2.
30.2b	Reading *wrættum* (altered in E from *wrætum*).
30.3a	A standard formulaic opening; see the note at EXE 11.1 above.
32.4a	Compare *GuthB* 1335a *(grond wið greote).*
30.6a	Compare EXE 82.6a *(earmas ond eaxle)* and *Beowulf* 835a and 972a *(earm ond eaxle).*
30.8b	Reading *fela,* after Tu (E reads *fella*).
30.10a	Reading *fereð,* after Tr (E reads *fere*).
30.13a	Compare EXE 91.2b *(ricum ond heanum), GuthB* 995b *(ricra ne heanra).*
30.13b	Compare *Elene* 856b *(Saga gif ðu cunne).*
30.13b–14	This is part of an elaborate closing challenge formula, essentially an appeal to the cleverness of the potential solver, found in slightly variant forms, on which see the note at EXE 26.12b–13 above.

EXE 31

MANUSCRIPT: E, fol. 108v–9r.

EARLIER EDITIONS AND TRANSLATIONS: Gr 34; Tr 31; Tu 34; Wy 33; Ma 33; KD 33; Ba 6, 10; Ab 33, 21; WiR 31; WiF 31, 91; Wh 33, 186–87; PZ 31; CH 33, 36; Mu 33; WiC 31, 540 and 1158.

SOLUTION: *IS* (ice, ice floe); see in particular Dietrich, "Würdigung, Lösung und Herstellung"; PZ; Ni. Other suggested solutions include: "archetypal feminine" (Jember, *Old English Riddles*), "iceberg" and "hatred" (Nelson, "Four Social Functions"). See further

Clemoes, *Interactions of Thought and Language,* 184–85; Salvador-Bello, "Compilation of the Old English Riddles," 139–40; Teele, "Heroic Tradition," 52–55; Afros, "Linguistic Ambiguities"; Orchard, *Elder Edda;* Salvador-Bello, *Isidorean Perceptions,* 327–35; Cavell, *Weaving Words,* 256–57; Soper, "Count of Days," 115–17.

If the solution "ship" is accepted for the preceding EXE 30, then that of "iceberg" here makes a likely connection. Certainly, the reference to mothers and daughters by the female creature in EXE 31.9–10 seems to recollect ps-SYM, which is quoted by Aldhelm as an inspiration for ALD, the solution to which is the Latin feminine noun *glacies,* "ice": *Mater me genuit, eadem mox gignitur a me,* "a mother bore me, and the same is soon born from me." The same notion is enshrined in *Met28* 59b–64a:

Hwa wundrað þæs
oððe oþres eft, hwi þæt is mæge
weorðan of wætere; wlite-torh scineð
sunna swegle hat; soma gecerreð
is-mere ænlic on his agen gecynd,
weorðeð to wætre.

Who wonders about that, or something else again, how ice can come from water; the beautifully bright sun shines hot in the sky, the splendid sheet of ice comes to water through its own nature.

See too OER 11 (*IS,* "ice"). If the impressive references to the sounds in EXE 31.2–3 do indeed refer to the awe-inspiring sounds of an iceberg being calved, then the riddle may owe something to ear- or eyewitness accounts from mainland Scandinavia; Iceland is likewise a possible source: the written record is certainly somewhat sparse. The riddle breaks down easily into three sections (for similar structural divisions, see for example the headnotes to EXE 52 and 58): EXE 31.1–4 offer a fairly straightforward opening, while there are a striking number of compounds in the second section, EXE 31.5–8, with no fewer than six in the space of only four lines; the final section, EXE 31.9–13, effectively recasts in Old English the familiar *GLACIES* (ice) aenigma (see the headnote to ps-SYM 1 below). The heroic language of martial valor in this riddle is underscored by the number of verbal parallels to both *Beowulf* and *Andreas,* as the notes to EXE 31.2a, 5a, 7b, and 11b make clear. The particular parallels to EXE 80 (*WÆTER,* "water") are also evident.

There seem too to be shades here of several supernatural creatures who appear in Norse eddic poetry and turn to stone, often as coastal markers, especially the suitably named Hrímgerd, "frost goddess," in *Helgakviða Hjǫrvarðssonar* 30, who is mocked by the warrior Atli:

Dagr er nú, Hrímgerðr, en þik dvalða hefr
 Atli til aldrlaga,
hafnarmark þykkir hlœgligt vera,
 þars þú í steins líki stendr.

Day's here now, Hrímgerd, Atli's delayed you
until you have laid down your life;
as a harbor marker you'll seem quite a joke,
as you stand in the likeness of stone.

A similar conceit seems to underlie the structure of *Alvíssmál* elsewhere in the Poetic Edda, where we are given to understand that the wise dwarf Alvíss, "all-wise," having engaged in a contest of wits with the otherwise unwise god Thor, is tricked into staying past daybreak, with dire consequences; see too the note on GES 8 below. There are six compounds in this riddle, of which two are unique in extant Old English verse: *heard-hiþende* (31.7a) and *hete-run* (31.7b).

31.1a Compare EXE 52.1a *(Hyse cwom gangan)* and 82.1a *(Wiht cwom gongan),* as well as 27.7a *(Da cwom wundorlicu wiht);* the last of these is in effect an opening line to the second part of the solution to that riddle. See too the note at EXE 20.1a.

31.2a There may be deliberate confusion here between *ceol,* "ship, seagoing vessel," and *ceole,* "throat, gorge." Compare (for the former) *Andreas* 361 *(þon cymlicor ceol gehladenne),*

Beowulf 38 *(ne hyrde ic cymlicor ceol gegyrwan).* It is tempting to emend to *ceolan,* after Wi, which could only signify "throat." EXE 16 deals with a seaborne creature with a mouth but no voice, and again employs the same term *ceole* (EXE 16.4a) in a manner that may be intended similarly to confuse.

31.3b Reading *hleahtor,* after Gr (E reads *leahtor*).

31.5a The compound *hete-grim* is found only here and at *Andreas* 1395a and 1562a.

31.7b Compare *Beowulf* 501a *(onband beadu-rune).*

31.9b Reading *mægða,* after Tr (E reads *mæg da*).

31.9–10 Compare EXE 39.2–4 *(WÆTER,* "water": *þæt is moddor monigra cynna, / þæs selestan, þæs sweartestan, / þæs deorestan þæs þe dryhta bearn / ofer foldan sceat to gefean agen)* and EXE 80.4 *(WÆTER,* "water": *modor is monigra mærra wihta).*

31.9–13 For the use of a quotation alluding to another riddle, in this case ps-SYM 1 (*GLACIES,* "ice"), compare EXE 36.6–7, and the note there. For the use of direct quotations within riddles and aenigmata, see the note at ALD 7.2 above.

31.11a Reading *uploden,* after Wi (E reads *upliden*), and assuming a past participle form of *leodan* or *liodan,* "to spring, grow"; other editors (including KD), retain the manuscript reading, taken as a past participle of *liðan,* "to travel, sail." Support for the reading here is found at EXE 80.31.b *(WÆTER,* "water": *aloden wurde),* and likewise, for the description of the daughter as "pregnant" *(eacen),* compare 80.21 *(Biþ sio moddor mægene eacen)* and 80.27b *(cræfte eacen).*

31.11b Compare *Beowulf* 705b *(þæt wæs yldum cuþ).*

EXE 32

MANUSCRIPT: E, fol. 109r.

EARLIER EDITIONS AND TRANSLATIONS: Gr 35; Tr 32; Tu 35; Wy 34; Ma 34; KD 34; Ba 31, 28; Ab 34, 21; WiR 32; WiF 32, 92; Wh 34, 187; PZ 32; CH 34, 37; Mu 34; WiC 32, 540–41 and 1158.

SOLUTION: *RACA* (rake); see in particular Dietrich, "Würdigung, Lösung und Herstellung"; PZ; Ni. Other suggested solutions include: "bee" (Trautmann, "Die Auflösungen der altenglischen Rätsel"), "harrowing of Hell" or "penis" (Jember, *Old English Riddles*). See further Salvador-Bello, "Compilation of the Old English Riddles," 185–86; Soper, "Count of Days," 104–5; Stanley, "Exeter Book *Riddles*, II," 357–58; Dale, *Natural World,* 77.

See too Riley, *Anglo-Saxon Tools,* 126.

The painful and fearsome marine scraping of the "iceberg" connects the previous EXE 31 to the strictly earthbound EXE 32; the early suggested solution "rake" is generally accepted. This riddle contains many verbal parallels with the wider corpus of Old English poetry, as the notes show. There is only one compound in this riddle.

32.1a For the opening formula *Ic (þa) wiht geseah,* see the note at EXE 29.1a.

32.3 Compare EXE 19.1a *(Neb is min niþerweard),* 29.6 *(Niþerweard . . . wæs neb hyre).*

32.4 See notes on EXE 27.4 *(huþ to þam ham of þam here-siþe)* and 27.9 *(ahredde þa þa huþe ond to ham bedraf).*

32.7b Compare *Beowulf* 1364a *(wudu wyrtum fæst), Dan* 498 *(wudubeam wlitig, se wæs wyrtum fæst).*

32.9a Compare *GenA* 1822a *(beorhte blican), Andreas* 789a *(beorhte blican), ChristB* 701a *(beorhte bliceð), ChristB* 903a *(beorhte blican), Phoenix* 599a *(beorhte bliceð).*

32.9b Compare *Met20* 90b *(bloweð ond groweð), PPs* 64.11 4b *(blowað ond growað).*

EXE 33

MANUSCRIPT: E, fol. 109r–v.

EARLIER EDITIONS AND TRANSLATIONS: Gr 36; Tr 33; Tu 36; Wy 35; Ma 35; KD 35; Ba 50, 40–41; Ab 35, 22; WiR 33; WiF 33, 93; Wh 35, 188; PZ; CH 35, 38; Mu 35; WiC 33, 541 and 1158.

SOLUTION: *BYRNE* (mailcoat); see in particular Dietrich, "Würdigung, Lösung und Herstellung"; Ni. See further Erhardt-Siebold, "Old English Loom Riddles"; Gerritsen, "*þurh þreata geþræcu*"; Parkes,

> "Manuscript of the Leiden Riddle"; Gerritsen, "Leiden Revisited"; Gleissner, "*Leiden Riddle* 3a"; Klein, "Aldhelm's Riddle *Lorica*"; Stanley, "Heroic Aspects"; Salvador-Bello, "Compilation of the Old English Riddles," 187–89; Laszlo, *Köcherfliege und Seidenraupe in den altenglischen Rätseln;* Salvador-Bello, "Editorial Hypercorrection"; Bremmer and Dekker, "Leiden, Universiteitsbibliotheek, Vossianus Lat. Q. 106"; Steen, *Verse and Virtuosity,* 91–98; Murphy, *Unriddling the Exeter Riddles,* 3–4; Hyer and Owen-Crocker, "Woven Works"; Owen-Crocker, "'Seldom . . . does the deadly spear rest for long'"; Weber, "Isidorian Context"; Soper, "Count of Days," 78–82; Cavell, *Weaving Words,* 54–67; Taylor, "Enigma Variations," 74–77; Dale, *Natural World,* 6 and 192.

See too Leahy, *Anglo-Saxon Crafts,* 131–33.

It was noticed long ago that EXE 33 (largely an updated version of LEI) translates closely ALD 33 (*LORICA,* "mailcoat"), with each of Aldhelm's hexameters being translated into two long lines of Old English verse, albeit that a change in word order suggests that the original Latin text that the Old English translator was working from had lines 4 and 5 transposed. The final line of ALD 33 is not translated in EXE 33, which instead substitutes a pair of lines that constitute a form of the standard concluding challenge. LEI, by contrast, translates the whole of ALD 33, including the final line, and the two long lines of Old English so produced appear in place of those that conclude EXE 33. There are six compounds in this riddle, of which one, *heah-cræft* (33.4a), is unique in extant Old English verse.

33.1–2 Compare ALD 33.1 *(Roscida me genuit gelido de viscere tellus),* LEI 1–2 *(Mec se ueta uong, uundrum freorig, / ob his innaðae aerest cændæ).*

33.3–4 Compare ALD 33.2 *(non sum setigero lanarum vellere facta),* LEI 3–4 *(Ni uaat ic mec biuorthæ uullan fliusum, / herum ðerh heh-craeft, hygi-ðoncum min).*

33.4–8 Noteworthy here is the sevenfold anaphora on *ne,* including an extra one apparent added to the equivalent LEI 6b.

On anaphora elsewhere in EXE, see the note on EXE 1.16a above.

33.5–6 Compare ALD 33.3 *(licia nulla trahunt nec garrula fila resultant),* LEI 5–6 *(Uundnae me ni biað ueflæ, ni ic uarp hafæ, / ni ðerih ðreatun giðraec ðret me hlimmith).*

33.7–8 Compare ALD 33.5 *(nec radiis carpor duro nec pectine pulsor),* LEI 7–8 *(Ne me hrutendo hrisil scelfath, / ne mec ouana aam sceal cnyssa).*

33.7b Note that the equivalent line in LEI has *hrisil* in the plural, and a different verb *(scelfath).*

33.8b Reading *am* (E reads *amas*), following the parallel text of LEI; the alternative is to take *amas* as plural, and so emend singular *sceal.*

33.9–10 Compare ALD 33.4 *(nec crocea Seres texunt lanugine vermes),* LEI 9–10 *(Uyrmas mec ni auefun uyrdi craeftum, / ða ði geolu godueb geatum fraetuath).*

33.11–12 Compare ALD 33.6 *(et tamen en vestis vulgi sermone vocabor),* LEI 11–12 *(Uil mec huethrae suae ðeh uidæ ofaer eorðu / hatan mith hęliðum hyhtlic giuæde).*

33.11b Compare EXE 38.21a *(ænig ofer eorþan),* 80.42b *(weras ofer eorþan),* 84.18a *(anga ofer eorþan),* and 91.10a *(ænig ofer eorðan).*

33.12a For the notion of the creature speaking *for hæleþum,* compare EXE 18.12a *(mine for mengo),* 46.1a *(Ic gefrægn for hæleþum),* 46.4a *(sinc for secgum),* 53.8a *(eaþe for eorlum).*

33.13–14 This is part of an elaborate closing challenge formula, essentially an appeal to the cleverness of the potential solver, found in slightly variant forms, on which see the note at EXE 26.12b–13 above. What distinguishes this version of the formula is the demand for true words, a demand that goes on to become a formula of its own at EXE 34.12b–14 *(Þu wast, gif þu const, / to gesecganne, þæt we soð witan: / hu þære wihte wise gonge)* and 37.28–29 *(Gif þu mæge reselan recene gesecgan soþum wordum, saga hwæt hio hatte).* LEI 13–14 *(Ni anoegun ic me aerig-faerae egsan brogum, / ðeh ði numen siæ niudlicae ob cocrum)* is quite different, and much closer to the Latin of ALD 33.7. See further Orchard, "Old English and Latin Poetic Traditions."

33.14b Reading *gewæde,* after Gr (E reads *ge wædu*).

EXE 34

MANUSCRIPT: E, fol. 109v.

EARLIER EDITIONS AND TRANSLATIONS: Gr 37; Tr 34; Tu 37; Wy 36; Ma 36; KD 36; Ba 72, 55–56; Ab 36, 22; WiR 34; WiF 34, 94; Wh 36, 188–89; PZ 34a–b; Mu 36; WiC 34, 541 and 1158–59.

SOLUTION: *BAT* (boat); other suggested solutions include: "two men, woman, horses, dog, bird on ship" (Ma), "pregnant sow" (Dietrich, "Würdigung, Lösung und Herstellung"), "ship" or "man, woman, and horse" (Trautmann, "Die Auflösungen der altenglischen Rätsel"), "waterfowl hunt" (Erhardt-Siebold, "Old English Hunt Riddles"), "pregnant horse with two pregnant women on its back" (lines 1–8 only) and "ship" (Eliason, "Four Old English Cryptographic Riddles"), monster (Wh). See further Clemoes, *Interactions of Thought and Language,* 239–40; Orchard, "Oral Tradition"; Salvador-Bello, "Compilation of the Old English Riddles," 139–40 and 189–93; Ni, 85–89; Teele, "Heroic Tradition," 52–55; Bitterli, *Say What I Am Called,* 68–74.

This riddle looks to be a composite text, with an interpolated "solution" (printed as line 5 in most editions), and six further lines later added. The "solution" appears as *monn·h·w·M·wiif·m·x·l·kf·wf·hors·qxxs·,* likely the product of a series of misreadings. The Old English words *monn,* "man," *wiif,* "woman," and *hors,* "horse," are relatively transparent, and their Latin equivalents *homo, mulier,* and *equus* can be derived from the remaining jumble of letters, if we assume the common Latin substitution cipher that replaces vowels with the consonants that follow them in the Roman alphabet (see further Levison, *England and the Continent in the Eighth Century,* 290–94). In that case, the encoded Latin would originally have read *·hpmp·mxlkfr·fqxxs·,* and such was presumably the original "solution," itself glossed in the vernacular by an enterprising Anglo-Saxon, and with conflation of the two sets of answers further confounded by visual confusion of Latin *p* and vernacular ƿ (runic *wynn,* standing for Modern English *w*), as well as scribal ƿ (for *w*) and *r* (for *r*), with haplography of ƿ for ƿƿ. Such a process implies at least three stages, which can be represented in the Roman alphabet as follows:

1. *·hpmp·mxlkfr·fqxxs·*
2. *·monn·hpmp·wiif·mxlkfr·hors·fqxxs·*
3. *monn·h·w·M·wiif·m·x·l·kf·wf·hors·qxxs·*

The detached *f* from *fqxxs* that occurs between stages 2 and 3 may suggest that the Old English "glosses" were originally written above their Latin lemmata. Alas, the putative solution "man, woman, and horse" does not fit EXE 34, which appears in its original form to have comprised only the first six lines; the final six lines look like a later attempt at elucidation that, like the interpolated erroneous "solution," should be treated with caution. The augmented portion of the riddle clearly envisions a water traveler, though it is hard to come up with a solution that fits all the clues. The first six lines might also be solved as "boat" or "ship," if we assume a four-oared rowing boat with a man at each oar (so accounting for the four "feet" beneath the creature's belly and the eight on the back); just such a tenth-century Viking boat, known as "Skuldelev 3," was excavated in 1962, and there may have been similar vessels in Anglo-Saxon England. The six heads and two wings and twelve eyes can only be accounted for by supposing ship's figureheads fore and aft, and perhaps also sails. It is worth noting that the substitution cipher employed in the erroneous interpolated solution is found elsewhere in a number of late tenth- and early eleventh-century manuscripts of SYM and ALD (including G), as well as of Alcuin's *Propositiones* and the so-called *Reichenau Riddles,* which follow the *propositiones* in the tenth-century manuscript Z. There is only a single compound in this riddle.

34.1a For the opening formula *Ic (þa) wiht geseah,* see the note at EXE 29.1a.

34.2 The line is repeated almost verbatim at EXE 66.2 *(heo wæs wrætlice wundrum gegierwed).*

34.3–8a For another such enumerative riddle, see EXE 82.3 *(hæfde an eage ond earan twa).*

34.3b Compare EXE 60.3a *(wade under wambe)*. Several of the riddles focus on the "belly" *(womb)* of the creature in question; compare the note at EXE 1.78 above.

34.8b This is a variant of the closing formulaic challenge *Saga hwæt ic hatte,* on which see the note at 1.14b–15 above.

34.9a Compare *Exodus* 106a *(foron flod-wege), Elene* 215a (*feran flod-wege;* the manuscript reads *foldwege*).

34.12b–13 This is part of a closing challenge formula, found in slightly variant forms, but essentially a demand for true words, on which see the note at EXE 33.13–14 above.

34.13 For the phrase *to gesecganne,* compare EXE 37.22b *(long is to secganne)* and 37.25 *(to gesecganne)*. Also compare *Daniel* 543a *(to gesecganne), Andreas* 1481b *(mycel is to secganne), Beowulf* 473a *(sorh is me to secganne)* and 1724b *(wundor is secganne)*. See too *Andreas* 603 *(miht ðu me secgan þæt ic soð wite), ChristB* 442b *(þæt þu soð wite).*

EXE 35

MANUSCRIPT: E, fol. 109v.

EARLIER EDITIONS AND TRANSLATIONS: Gr 38; Tr 35; Tu 38; Wy 37; Ma 37; KD 37; Ba 80, 59–60; Ab 37, 23; WiR 35; WiF 35, 95; Wh 37, 189; PZ 35; CH 37, 39; Mu 37; WiC 35, 541–42 and 1159.

SOLUTION: *BLÆST-BELG* (bellows); see in particular Dietrich, "Die Räthsel des Exeterbuchs"; Wh; Ni. Other suggested solutions include: "wagon" (Dietrich, "Würdigung, Lösung und Herstellung"), "penis" (Jember, *Old English Riddles*). See further Nelson, "Plus Animate"; Salvador-Bello, "Compilation of the Old English Riddles," 193–94; Hill, "Anglo-Saxon Mechanics"; Murphy, *Unriddling the Exeter Riddles,* 215–19.

Though this riddle, like EXE 23, uses the device of misdirection by giving what is crying out to be seen as a graphic description of sexual activity, the "true" solution is more mundane: "bellows" seems most plausible, though "wagon" would connect it better to the preceding riddle. The parallel opening of EXE 83 (*BLÆST-BELG,* "bellows") strongly implies a connection between the two texts, which again are from different clusters of riddles in the Exeter Book; see too EXE 85 (*BLÆST-BELG,* "bellows"). The last half of this riddle, EXE 35.5–9, with its focus on life and death and breath, appears to derive from SYM 73 (*UTER FOLLIS,* "bellows"), and while EXE 83 seems to echo EXE 35, there seems to be no link between EXE 83 and SYM 73; for another similar sequence, compare SYM 44 (*CAEPA,* "onion")—EXE 23 (*CIPE,* "onion")—EXE 63 (*CIPE,* "onion"). There is only a single compound in this riddle. The form *aþrunten* (35.2a) is unique to this riddle.

35.1a For the opening formula *Ic (þa) wiht geseah,* see the note at EXE 29.1a. Several of the riddles focus on the "belly" *(womb)* of the creature in question; compare the note at EXE 1.78 above.

35.2 Compare EXE 83.2 *(þryþum geþrungne. Þegn folgade).*

35.4a Reading *þæt,* after KD (E reads *þær*).

35.7b Compare *Beowulf* 1703b *(blæd is aræred);* note too the gloss *blæd-bylig* for *follis,* "bellows," at WW 241.33. The word *blæd* is ambiguous: elsewhere, according to *DOE,* it means variously "blade (of grass or an oar)," "breath," "pride," "glory."

35.8b Compare the mother–daughter motif in EXE 31.9–10 (*IS,* "ice, ice floe").

EXE 36

MANUSCRIPT: E, fol. 109v.

EARLIER EDITIONS AND TRANSLATIONS: Gr 39; Tr 36; Tu 39; Wy 38; Ma 38; KD 38; Ba 26, 25; Ab 38, 23; WiR 36; WiF 36, 96; Wh 38, 189–90; PZ 36; CH 38, 40; Mu 38; WiC 36, 542 and 1159.

SOLUTION: *HRYÐER* (bullock); other suggested solutions include: "young bull" (Dietrich, "Würdigung, Lösung und Herstellung"), "man" (Jember, *Old English Riddles*), *bulluc*, "bull calf (young ox)" (Ni). See further Clemoes, *Interactions of Thought and Language*, 97–98 and 104–5; Salvador-Bello, "Compilation of the Old English Riddles," 194–96; Fiocco, "Gli animali negli enigmi anglo-sassoni dell'*Exeter Book*"; Orchard, "Enigma Variations," 297–99; Stanley, "Riddling: A Serious Pursuit," 25–28; Bitterli, *Say What I Am Called*, 26–34; Murphy, *Unriddling the Exeter Riddles*, 186–87; Salvador-Bello, *Isidorean Perceptions*, 327–35; Cavell, *Weaving Words*, 159–72; Soper, "Count of Days," 115–17; Stanley, "Exeter Book *Riddles*, II," 358; Dale, *Natural World*, 26, 71, 79, and 83.

This riddle has parallels with several related Latin aenigmata: ALD 83 (*IUVENCUS*, "young bull") and EUS 37 (*VITULUS*, "young bull"); indeed, in its closing lines it seems to paraphrase Eusebius. Further parallels with EXE 10 mean that a solution signifying a young bull is not in doubt. There are three compounds in this riddle.

36.1a For the opening formula *Ic (þa) wiht geseah*, see the note at EXE 29.1a.

36.1b Compare EXE 12.1a *(Ic wæs wæpen wigan)*.

36.2a Reading *geoguð-myrþe*, after Tu (E reads *geoguð myrwe*).

36.3b Compare ALD 83.1–2 *(IUVENCUS*, "young bull": *Arida spumosis dissolvens faucibus ora / bis binis bibulus potum de fontibus hausi)* and EUS 37.1–2 *(VITULUS*, "young bull": *Post genitrix me quam peperit mea saepe solesco / inter ab uno fonte rivos bis bibere binos)*.

36.5–7 Note the change of gender here. For the use of a quotation alluding to another riddle, in this case EXE 10.14–15 (*OXA*, "ox"), ALD 83.3–6 (*IUVENCUS*, "young bull"), or most likely EUS 37.3–4 (*VITULUS*, "young bull"), compare EXE 31.9–13 (*IS*, "ice, ice floe"), and the note there. For the use of direct quotations within riddles and aenigmata, see the note at ALD 7.2 above.

EXE 37

MANUSCRIPT: E, fol. 109v–10r.

EARLIER EDITIONS AND TRANSLATIONS: Gr 40; Tr 37; Tu 40; Wy 39; Ma 39; KD 39; Ba 4, 7–8; Ab 39, 24; WiR 37; WiF 37, 97; Wh 39, 190–91; PZ 37; CH 39, 41; Mu 39; WiC 37, 542 and 1159.

SOLUTION: *DEAĐ* (death); other suggested solutions include: "day" (Dietrich, "Würdigung, Lösung und Herstellung"), "moon" (Tu; Wh), "time" (Löwenthal, *Studien zum germanischen Rätsel*), "Creature Death" (Erhardt-Siebold, "Old English Riddle No. 39"; Dennis, "Exeter Book Riddle 39"), "cloud" (Kennedy, "Old English Riddle No. 39"; Meyvaert, "Solution to Old English Riddle 39"), "revenant" (Jember, *Old English Riddles*), "speech" (Wi), "dream" (Greenfield, "Old English Riddle 39"; Stanley, "Stanley B. Greenfield's Solution of *Riddle* (ASPR) 39"), "dream" or "cloud" (PZ), "comet" (Wilson, "Old English Riddle No. 39"), *swefn,* "auspicious dream" (Ni). See further Kennedy, "Old English Riddle No. 39"; Salvador-Bello, "Compilation of the Old English Riddles," 196–200; Harbus, "Exeter Book Riddle 39 Reconsidered"; Salvador-Bello, *Isidorean Perceptions,* 327–35; Dale, *Natural World,* 77.

The evidently Christian tone and anaphoric style of this highly puzzling riddle connects it with EXE 38 (*GESCEAFT,* "creation"), which follows, and it may also share with that riddle a learned, literate, and Latinate motivation; some have even suggested shared authorship. From that perspective, Erhardt-Siebold's closely argued suggestion that the solution should be "Creature death" (building on a Platonic notion) is perhaps the most attractive, one that would tie it to Lapidge's suggestion of *PNEUMA,* "the breath of life," as the solution to EXE 1. There are also parallels to be drawn with ALD 3 (*NUBES,* "cloud"). There are ten compounds in this riddle, of which three are unique in extant Old English verse: *sundor-cræft* (37.3b), *wundor-woruld* (37.17a), and *ealdor-gesceaft* (37.23a).

37.1a This opening is elsewhere found as part of a closing challenge formula found in slightly variant forms, on which see the note on EXE 26.12b–13 above. Compare EXE 37.13b (*ac gewritu*

	secgað). See too *GenA* 1121b, 1630b, 2563b, 2611b *(ac gewritu secgað), Elene* 674b *(swa gewritu secgaþ), Phoenix* 313b *(þæs gewritu secgað)* and 655b *(swa us gewritu secgað), CEdg* 14b *(þæs þe gewritu secgað).*
37.2b	Reading *tidum* (altered in E from *tilum*).
37.3a	Compare EXE 11.4a *(sweotol ond gesyne).* Notions of what the creature has (or most often has not), recur throughout this poem; compare EXE 37.10, 37.12, 37.13, 37.16, 37.18, and 37.27.
37.4a	Reading *maran,* after Tu (E reads *maram*).
37.5	Compare *Elene* 407a *(sundor asecað)* and 1018a *(sundor asecean).*
37.7a	The fourteenfold anaphora on *ne* (as both conjunction and adverb) that begins here and focuses on (lack of) specific body parts is noteworthy. On anaphora in EXE, see the note on EXE 1.16a above.
37.8a	Compare EXE 37.21a *(ac hio sceal wide-ferh).*
37.10a	Reading *folme,* after KD (E reads *folm*).
37.11	Reading *eagena hafað ægþer,* after Gr (E reads *eage neægþer*), for metrical reasons and to preserve the parallelism of *ne . . . hafað . . . ne . . . hafaþ . . . ne . . . hafað* in the immediately preceding and following a-lines.
37.12a	Compare EXE 65.6b *(nænne muð hafað).*
37.13b	Compare EXE 37.1a *(Gewritu secgað),* and the note there.
37.21a	Compare EXE 37.8a *(ac hio sceal wide-ferh).*
37.21b	Reading *wuldor-cyninges,* after Gr (E reads *wuldorcyninge*).
37.22b	For the phrase *to (ge)secganne,* compare EXE 34.13, and the note there.
37.22b–35a	Note the envelope pattern *to secganne . . . to gesecganne.*
37.24b	Supplying *is,* after Tu (not in E).
37.24b–29a	Note the envelope pattern *Soð . . . wordum . . . soþum wordum.*
37.27a	Reading *heo ænig,* after Gr (E reads *hehænig*); in the manuscript, *he* has been crowded into the space preceding *hænig,* apparently by a different hand.

37.28–29 This is part of a closing challenge formula, found in slightly variant forms, but essentially a demand for true words, on which see the note at EXE 33.13–14 above. In this case, the final half-line (EXE 37.29b) is also a variant of the common closing formulaic challenge *Saga hwæt ic hatte,* on which see the note at 1.14b–15 above.

EXE 38

MANUSCRIPT: E, fol. 110r–11v (incomplete).

EARLIER EDITIONS AND TRANSLATIONS: Gr 41; Tr 38; Tu 41; Wy 40; Ma 40; KD 40; Ba 11, 12–16; Ab 40, 25–27; WiR 38; WiF 38, 98–100; Wh 40, 191–95; PZ 38; CH 40, 42–45; Mu 40; WiC 38, 543–44 and 1159.

SOLUTION: *GESCEAFT* (creation); see in particular Dietrich, "Würdigung, Lösung und Herstellung"; Ni. Other suggested solutions include: "nature" (Moorman, *Interpretation of Nature*), "primordial matter: water" (PZ). See further Konick, "Exeter Book Riddle 41 as a Continuation of Riddle 40"; O'Brien O'Keeffe, "Exeter Riddle 40"; Laszlo, *Die Sonne bringt es an den Tag;* O'Brien O'Keeffe, "Aldhelm's *Enigma* no. C"; Salvador-Bello, "Compilation of the Old English Riddles," 200–9; Steen, *Verse and Virtuosity,* 98–109; Afros, "Linguistic Ambiguities"; Murphy, *Unriddling the Exeter Riddles,* 154–56; Stanley, "Riddling: A Serious Pursuit," 20–23; Salvador-Bello, *Isidorean Perceptions,* 335–39; Soper, "Count of Days," 78–82; Cavell, *Weaving Words,* 253–56; Dale, *Natural World,* 114.

This riddle, the longest in the Exeter Book, has as its direct source Aldhelm's longest and final aenigma, ALD 100 (CREATURA, "creation"), and to that extent its solution is not in doubt. Even in the manuscript, EXE 38 is distinctive, with an extra blank line inserted before its opening, something that is unique in the formatting of the Exeter Book riddles. The technique of translation is very similar to that in EXE 33, namely that each of Aldhelm's hexameters is generally (but far from universally) rendered by two long lines of Old English, a feature that is found elsewhere in direct translations of

Latin hexameters into Old English verse. The importance of ALD 100 as a capstone aenigma seems to be recognized in Old English by the fact that there are two other creation riddles in the Exeter Book, specifically EXE 64 and 90. With regard to EXE 38, it is striking that several lines of ALD 100 are not rendered into Old English at all, notably lines 47, 51–58, and 67–83, although in the case of the final lines, physical damage to the manuscript resulting in loss of a leaf between fols. 111v and 112r is the cause, meaning that there is no Old English equivalent for the rare Latin challenge that concludes ALD 100. O'Brien O'Keeffe, "Aldhelm's *Enigma* no. C," has demonstrated that this riddle derives from a version of the text of ALD 100 found in Manuscript O. There are twenty-four compounds in this riddle, of which five are unique in extant Old English verse: *wreð-stuþu* (38.2a), *segn-berend* (38.20b), *wrað-scræf* (38.41a), *halsre-feþer* (38.80b), and *boc-wudu* (38.106b).

38.1–5	Compare ALD 100.2–3 *(rector regnorum, frenans et fulmina lege, / pendula dum patuli vertuntur culmina caeli).*
38.2	Compare EXE 38.5a *(healdeð ond wealdeð)* and 38.22b *(healdeþ ond wealdeþ).* See too *PPs* 75.9 2 *(wealdeð and healdeð)* and *PPs* 122.1 2 *(healdest and wealdest); Andreas* 225b *(healdend ond wealdend).*
38.2a	Supplying *wealdeð* (not in the manuscript).
38.3a	Reading *rice,* after Gr (E reads *ric*).
38.5a	See the note at EXE 38.2.
38.6–7	Compare ALD 100.4 *(me varium fecit, primo dum conderet orbem).*
38.8–9	Compare ALD 100.5 *(pervigil excubiis: numquam dormire iuvabit).*
38.10	Compare *Andreas* 464 and 820 *(oððæt hie semninga slæp ofereode).*
38.10–11	Compare ALD 100.6 *(sed tamen extemplo clauduntur lumina somno).*
38.11b	Reading *betyned* (altered in E from *betyneð*).
38.12–13	Compare ALD 100.7 *(nam Deus ut propria mundum dicione gubernat).*

38.14–15 Compare ALD 100.8 (*sic ego complector sub caeli cardine cuncta*).

38.16–17 Compare ALD 100.9 (*segnior est nullus, quoniam me larbula terret*).

38.18–19 Compare ALD 100.10 (*setigero rursus constans audacior apro*).

38.19b Compare *Jul* 388b (*bid-steal gifeð*, "he makes a firm stand"); the context is that of a devil describing the actions of a saint confronting his temptations.

38.20–21 Compare ALD 100.11 (*nullus me superat cupiens uexilla triumphi*).

38.21a See the note at EXE 33.11b.

38.21–22 Compare ALD 100.12 (*ni Deus, aethrali summus qui regnat in arce*).

38.22b See the note at EXE 38.2 (*wealdeð ond . . . healdeð*).

38.23b Supplying *micle*, after Gr (not in the manuscript).

38.23–32 Compare ALD 100.13–17 (*prorsus odorato ture flagrantior halans / olfactum ambrosiae, necnon crescentia glebae / lilia purpureis possum conexa rosetis / vincere spirantis nardi dulcedine plena / nunc olida caeni squalentis sorde putresco*).

38.33–37 Compare ALD 100.18–20 (*omnia, quaeque polo sunt subter et axe reguntur, / dum pater arcitenens concessit, iure guberno / grossas et graciles rerum comprenso figuras*).

38.38–39 Compare ALD 100.21 (*altior, en, caelo rimor secreta Tonantis*).

38.40a See the note at EXE 1.98 above.

38.40–41 Compare ALD 100.22 (*et tamen inferior terris tetra Tartara cerno*).

38.42–43 Compare ALD 100.23 (*nam senior mundo praecessi tempora prisca*).

38.42b Reading *þes*, after Tu (E reads *þæs*).

38.44–45 Compare ALD 100.24 (*ecce, tamen matris horno generabar ab alvo*).

38.46–47 Compare ALD 100.25 (*pulchrior auratis, dum fulget fibula, bullis*).

38.48–49 Compare ALD 100.26 *(horridior ramnis et spretis vilior algis).*

38.49a Reading *waroð* (altered in E from *warod*).

38.50b–51 The same lines are repeated almost verbatim at EXE 38.82b–83 *(æghwær brædre / ond widgelra þonne þes wong grena).*

38.50–52 Compare ALD 100.27 *(latior, en, patulis terrarum finibus exto).*

38.52–53 Compare ALD 100.28 *(et tamen in media concludor parte pugilli).*

38.54–55 Compare ALD 100.29 *(frigidior brumis necnon candente pruina).*

38.56–57 Compare ALD 100.30 *(cum sim Vulcani flammis torrentibus ardens).*

38.56a Supplying *Ic eom,* after Gr (not in the manuscript).

38.58–59 Compare ALD 100.31 *(dulcior in palato quam lenti nectaris haustus).* For the combination *beo-bred . . . mid hunige* (EXE 38.59), Murphy, *Unriddling the Exeter Riddles,* 155–56, points to parallels with Old English renderings of Psalm 18:11 *(hi synt swetran ðonne hunig odðe beebread).*

38.60–61 Compare ALD 100.32 *(dirior et rursus quam glauca absinthia campi).*

38.61a Supplying *þe,* after Gr (not in the manuscript).

38.62–63 Compare ALD 100.33 *(mando dapes mordax lurconum more Ciclopum).*

38.63b Reading *þyrse,* after Gr (E reads *þyrre*).

38.64–65 Compare ALD 100.34 *(cum possim iugiter sine victu vivere felix).*

38.66b The poet has misconstrued *pernix,* "swift, agile," as *perdix,* "partridge"; oddly enough, the mistake is matched by Chaucer, *House of Fame* 1392.

38.66–69 Compare ALD 100.35–36 *(plus pernix aquilis, Zephiri velocior alis / necnon accipitre properantior, et tamen horrens).*

38.70b Reading *snelra,* after Gr (E reads *snel ro þonne*).

38.71 The poet has substituted a frog for the original tortoise.

38.70–73 Compare ALD 100.37–39 *(lumbricus et limax et tarda testudo palustris / atque, fimi soboles sordentis, cantarus ater / me dicto citius vincunt certamine cursus).*

38.72a Reading *is,* after Tu (E reads *ic*).

38.74b Compare *Beowulf* 887b, 2553b, and 2744b *(under harne stan); Beowulf* 1415a *(ofer harne stan); Andreas* 841b *(ymbe harne stan).*

38.74–75 Compare ALD 100.40 *(sum gravior plumbo: scopulorum pondera vergo).*

38.76–77 Compare ALD 100.41 *(sum levior pluma, cedit cui tippula limphae).*

38.77a Reading *on flode,* after Gr (E reads *onflonde*).

38.78a Reading *heardre,* after Tu (altered in E from *heardra*).

38.78b Reading *fyr* (E reads followed by an erased letter).

38.78–79 Compare ALD 100.42 *(nam silici, densas quae fudit viscere flammas).*

38.79–80 Compare ALD 100.43 *(durior aut ferro, tostis sed mollior extis).*

38.81–83 Compare ALD 100.61–62 *(senis, ecce, plagis, latus qua panditur orbis, / ulterior multo tendor, mirabile fatu).*

38.82b–83 The same lines are repeated almost verbatim at EXE 38.50b–51 *(æghwær brædre / ond wid-gielra þonne þes wong grena).*

38.84a Supplying *eaþe,* after Tu (not in the manuscript).

38.84–85 Compare ALD 100.59–60 *(et versa vice protendor ceu Serica pensa / in gracilem porrecta panum seu stamina pepli).*

38.86–88 Compare ALD 100.63 *(infra me suprave nihil per saecula constat).*

38.88b Supplying *þonne* (not in the manuscript).

38.89–92 Compare ALD 100.64 *(ni rerum genitor mundum sermone coercens).*

38.91b Reading *onþunian* (E reads *on rinnan*).

38.92a Compare EXE 38.105a *(Mara ic eom ond fættra).*

38.92–94 Compare ALD 100.65 *(grandior in glaucis ballena fluctibus atra).*

38.93a For the sequence *gar-secges grund,* compare EXE 2.3. See too *Whale* 29 *(gar-secges gæst grund geseceð).*

38.95–97 Compare ALD 100.66 *(et minor exiguo, sulcat qui corpora, verme).*

38.96a For the *hond-wyrm,* compare EXE 64.2 (*GESCEAFT,* "creation").

38.97a Compare *ChristA* 220a *(secg searo-þoncol),* quoted in the headnote to EXE 1.

38.98–99 Compare ALD 100.44–45 *(cincinnos capitis nam gesto cacumine nullos, / ornent qui frontem pompis et tempora setis).*

38.100b Reading *brucan* (altered in E from *brucam*).

38.102–3 Compare ALD 100.46–47 *(cum mihi caesaries volitent de vertice crispae, / plus calamistratis se comunt quae calamistro).*

38.105a Compare EXE 38.92a *(Mara ic eom ond strengra).*

38.105–7 Compare ALD 100.48–49 *(pinguior, en, multo scrofarum axungia glesco, / glandiferis iterum referunt dum corpora fagis).*

38.106a Reading *bearg* (altered in E from *bear*).

38.106b Supplying *þe,* after Tu (not in the manuscript).

38.107–08 Compare ALD 100.50 *(atque saginata laetantur carne subulci).*

38.108a A leaf is missing after *he;* the text resumes at EXE 39.1b.

EXE 39

MANUSCRIPT: E, fol. 112r (incomplete).

EARLIER EDITIONS AND TRANSLATIONS: Gr 42; Tr 39; Tu 42; Wy 41; Ma 41; KD 41; Ba 83, 61; Ab 41, 28; WiR 39; WiF 39, 101; Wh 41, 195–96; PZ 41; Mu 41; WiC 39, 545 and 1159.

SOLUTION: *WÆTER* (water); see in particular Tupper, "Solutions of the Exeter Book Riddles"; Ni. Other suggested solutions include: "earth" (Dietrich, "Würdigung, Lösung und Herstellung"), "fire"

(Trautmann, "Die Auflösungen der altenglischen Rätsel"), "wisdom" (Tupper, "Originals and Analogues" and "Comparative Study of Riddles"), "water," "barm, dough-starter" (Moser, "New Solution to Riddle 41"). See further Konick, "Exeter Book Riddle 41 as a Continuation of Riddle 40"; Salvador-Bello, "Compilation of the Old English Riddles," 210–11; Dale, *Natural World,* 193.

The beginning of this riddle is missing, through the loss of a leaf between fols. 111v and 112r, and so several of the suggested solutions seem feasible; "water" is perhaps the likeliest, since many of the motifs here are matched in EXE 31 (*IS,* "ice, ice floe"), as well as, for example, ALD 29 (*AQUA,* "water") and ALD 73 (*MELARIUS,* "apple tree"). It is hard to imagine how one would test the suggestion that this riddle in fact represents the ending of EXE 38. There is only one compound in this riddle.

39.1–2 See the note at EXE 31.9–10 (*IS,* "ice, ice floe") above; compare ALD 29.4–5 *(AQUA,* "water": *Nam volucres caeli nantesque per aequora pisces / olim sumpserunt ex me primordia vitae),* ALD 73.4–5 *(quis numerus capiat vel quis laterculus aequet / vita viventum generem quot milia partu?).*

39.4a Compare EXE 31.10a *(þæs deorestan).*

39.5a Compare *ChristA* 72 *(ofer ealne foldan sceat).*

39.8–9 This is part of an elaborate closing challenge formula, essentially an appeal to the cleverness of the potential solver, found in slightly variant forms, on which see the note at EXE 26.12b–13 above.

EXE 40

MANUSCRIPT: E, fol. 112r.

EARLIER EDITIONS AND TRANSLATIONS: Gr 43; Tr 40; Tu 43; Wy 42; Ma 42; KD 42; Ba 69, 53–54; Ab 42, 28; WiR 40; WiF 40, 102; Wh 42, 196–97; PZ 40; CH 42, 46; Mu 42; WiC 40, 545 and 1159–60.

SOLUTION: *HANA OND HÆN* (cock and hen); see in particular Dietrich, "Würdigung, Lösung und Herstellung"; Ni. See further

Lerer, "The Riddle and the Book"; Salvador-Bello, "Compilation of the Old English Riddles," 211–16; Anderson, "Two Spliced Riddles"; Fiocco, "Gli animali negli enigmi anglo-sassoni dell'*Exeter Book*"; McFadden, "Raiding, Reform, and Reaction"; Salvador-Bello, "Key to the Body," 63–72; Orchard, "Enigma Variations," 287–88; Bitterli, *Say What I Am Called,* 121–24; Murphy, *Unriddling the Exeter Riddles,* 40–41.

EXE 40 and 41 appear in the manuscript as if they were one, but while both have double solutions, the tone of each is quite different. EXE 40 is unabashedly sexual, a celebration of the "sex play" *(hæmed-lac)* of two creatures who are identified as a cock and hen by the rearrangement of the runic letters presented, which spell out HANA, "cock," and HÆN, "hen."

The riddle divides into two parts, of which the first is a description (EXE 40.1–5a) and the second a runic exposition (EXE 40.5b–17); for a similarly bipartite structure in another of the runic riddles, see the headnote to EXE 22 (*HIGORA,* "jay, magpie") above. There are eight compounds in this riddle, of which four are unique in extant Old English verse: *hæmed-lac* (40.3a), *hwit-loc* (40.3b), *hord-geat* (40.11b), *ryne-monn* (40.13b), and *orþonc-bend* (40.15a).

40.1a A standard formulaic opening; see the note at EXE 11.1 above.

40.3b The compound *hwit-loc* is unique to this riddle, but compare EXE 76.5a *(hwit-loccedu);* in both cases, there is the same implied context of well-born women, presumably contrasted with the dark-haired Welsh woman of EXE 10.8a.

40.4a Compare *Phoenix* 100a *(fugel feþrum wlonc).*

40.4b Reading *speow,* after Tu (E reads *speop*).

40.11b Reading *swa ic* and *þæs,* after Wi (E reads *Hwylc* and *wæs*).

40.12 Compare Ælfric's preface to his *Grammar* (Zupitza, *Ælfrics Grammatik und Glossar,* 2): *Stæf-cræft is seo cæg ðe ðæra boca and-git unlicþ,* "Grammar is the key that unlocks the understanding of those books."

40.16a Compare EXE 44.1a *(Wer sæt æt wine).*

40.17a Reading *heah-mode* (E reads *hean-mode*); editors are split as to whether to retain the reading of the manuscript or emend, as here. The compound *hean-mod* appears only in *GuthB* 1379a and *Jul* 390a (*Ic sceal . . . hean-mod hweorfan,* "I must depart, sad-minded" in both), where the sense "dejected" seems required; by contrast, the compound *heah-mod* also appears in *Phoenix* 112a (in the context *æfter sund-plegan / heah-mod hefeð,* "rises up, haughty-minded") and *Vain* 54a in the sense "haughty, proud," and that seems more appropriate here (compare EXE 40.4a: *wlanc under wædum*).

EXE 41

MANUSCRIPT: E, fol. 112r–v.

EARLIER EDITIONS AND TRANSLATIONS: Gr 44; Tr 41; Tu 44; Wy 43; Ma 43; KD 43; Ba 10, 12; Ab 43, 29; WiR 41; WiF 41, 103; Wh 43, 197; PZ 41; CH 43, 47; Mu 43; WiC 41, 545–46 and 1160.

SOLUTION: *GÆST OND LIC-HAMA* (soul and body); see in particular Dietrich, "Würdigung, Lösung und Herstellung"; Müller, *Die Rätsel des Exeterbuches;* Dietrich, "Die Räthsel des Exeterbuchs"; Ni. Other suggested solutions include: "mind and body" (Wy). See further Williams, "What's So New about the Sexual Revolution?"; Salvador-Bello, "Compilation of the Old English Riddles," 216–20; Anderson, "Two Spliced Riddles"; Salvador-Bello, "Key to the Body," 72–76; Lockett, *Anglo-Saxon Psychologies,* 28–30.

This riddle clearly depicts life as a journey in a way that makes the solution "soul and body" almost universally accepted. It is evidently presented in the manuscript as a spiritual contrast to the rather earthy EXE 40 that precedes it, although in fact they are copied as if coupled. There are three compounds in this riddle, of which one, *cyne-word* (41.15a), is unique in extant Old English verse.

41.1a This is the first of three riddles to begin with the formula *Ic wat* (the others are EXE 47.1a and 56.1a). Compare EXE 91.1 (*Ic eom indryhten ond eorlum cuð*).

41.2b–4a Compare *Phoenix* 613–14 (*[ne] hungor se hata ne se hearde þurst / yrmþu ne yldo*) and *ChristC* 1660b (*Nis þær hungor ne þurst*).

41.7a Compare *GuthB* 918a (*witude fundon*).

41.14b–16 This closing formula seems a development of the more usual appeal to the cleverness of the solver found elsewhere, on which see the note at 26.12b–13.

41.16b Compare EXE 21.11b (*þæt ic þær ymb sprice*).

EXE 42

MANUSCRIPT: E, fol. 112v.

EARLIER EDITIONS AND TRANSLATIONS: Gr 45; Tr 42; Tu 45; Wy 44; Ma 44; KD 44; Ba 75, 57–58; Ab 44, 29; WiR 42; WiF 42, 104; Wh 44, 197–98; PZ 42; CH 44, 48; Mu 44; WiC 42, 546 and 1160.

SOLUTION: *CÆG* (key); see in particular Dietrich, "Würdigung, Lösung und Herstellung." Other suggested solutions include: "dagger-sheath" (Dietrich, "Würdigung, Lösung und Herstellung"), "penis" (Jember, *Old English Riddles*), *cæg ond loca,* "key and lock" (Ni). See further Salvador-Bello, "Compilation of the Old English Riddles," 220–21; Digan, "Aspects of Vocabulary," 62–89; Smith, "Humor in Hiding," 88–94; Salvador-Bello, "The Key to the Body," 76–82; Murphy, *Unriddling the Exeter Riddles,* 176–81; Stanley, "Exeter Book *Riddles,* II," 358.

See too Leahy, *Anglo-Saxon Crafts,* 130–31.

This riddle introduces a sequence of three with more or less overt sexual elements (EXE 42–44). The generally accepted solution is "key," although given the clearly phallic language it is worth pointing out that the Old English word *cæg(e)* is usually feminine (unlike Latin *clavis*). A rather milder and somewhat less sexualized "key" riddle is found at EXE 87. There is only one compound; the word *hangelle* (42.6a) is unique to this riddle.

42.2a Compare EXE 7.7a (*oþþæt ic under sceate*). Some Anglo-Saxon keys are indeed pierced at their front end: see Wilson,

Anglo-Saxon Ornamental Metalwork, items 40 and 140; compare too EXE 87.5b *(hindan þyrel).*

42.7a Reading *efenlang,* after Tr (E reads *efe lang*).

EXE 43

MANUSCRIPT: E, fol. 112v.

EARLIER EDITIONS AND TRANSLATIONS: Gr 46; Tr 43; Tu 46; Wy 45; Ma 45; KD 45; Ba 76, 58; Ab 45, 29; WiR 43; WiF 43, 105; Wh 45, 198; PZ 43; CH 45, 49; Mu 45; WiC 43, 546 and 1160.

SOLUTION: *DAG* (dough); see in particular Herzfeld, *Die Räthsel des Exeterbuches;* Ni. Other suggested solutions include: "bee" (Dietrich, "Würdigung, Lösung und Herstellung"), "penis" (Jember, *Old English Riddles*). See further Salvador-Bello, "Compilation of the Old English Riddles," 222–23; Hill, "Old English Dough Riddle"; Digan, "Aspects of Vocabulary," 62–89; Smith, "Humor in Hiding," 97–98; Salvador-Bello, "Key to the Body," 82–86; Salvador-Bello, "Sexual Riddle Type in Aldhelm's *Enigmata,*" 358; Rudolf, "Riddling and Reading," 508–23; Cavell, *Weaving Words,* 35; Stanley, "Exeter Book *Riddles,* II," 358.

Like the preceding EXE 41, this one too is evidently intended as employing misdirection through double entendre, although "dough" (*dag, dah:* the noun is grammatically either masculine or neuter) is generally accepted as the solution. Compare PZ on the sexually aggressive woman at EXE 23 (*CIPE,* "onion"), EXE 40 (*HANA OND HÆN,* "cock and hen"), EXE 59 (*CYRTEL,* "shirt, garment"), and EXE 76 (*HORN,* "horn"). There are only two compounds in this riddle.

43.1a This is the first of the riddles in EXE to employ the *Ic . . . gefrægn* opening formula; the others are EXE 46.1a *(Ic gefrægn)* and 65.1a *(Ic . . . gefrægn).* Compare EXE 52.2 *(stondan in wincle),* another riddle relying on double entendre. See too *nat-hwæt* at 52.5 and 59.9, as well as *nat-hwær* at 23.5 and 60.8 (all with similar double entendre).

43.1b Reading *weaxan,* after Gr (E reads *weax*).

43.4a The compound *hyge-wlonc* is found only here and at EXE 17.2a.
43.5b Compare EXE 23.6b *(ceorles dohtor).*

EXE 44

MANUSCRIPT: E, fol. 112v.

EARLIER EDITIONS AND TRANSLATIONS: Gr 47; Tr 44; Tu 47; Wy 46; Ma 46; KD 46; Ba 64, 51; Ab 46, 30; WiR 44; WiF 44, 106; Wh 46, 198–99; PZ 44; CH 46, 50; Mu 46; WiC 44, 546 and 1160.

SOLUTION: *LOTH OND HIS BEARN* (Lot and his children); see in particular Wright, *Biographia Britannica Literaria I;* Dietrich, "Würdigung, Lösung und Herstellung"; Ni. Other suggested solutions include: "Adam and Eve with two sons and a daughter" (Conybeare, *Illustrations of Anglo-Saxon Poetry*). See further Salvador-Bello, "Compilation of the Old English Riddles," 223–27; Salvador-Bello, "The Key to the Body," 86–93; Bitterli, *Say What I Am Called,* 58–59; Murphy, *Unriddling the Exeter Riddles,* 143–44; Stanley, "Exeter Book *Riddles,* II," 358–59.

The generally accepted solution is "Lot and his daughters," based on the account in Genesis 19:32–38, in which Lot's daughters have sex with him after getting him drunk, and each has a son. The riddle plays on the conflation and confusion of kinship relationships shared by the five key players. Somewhat like the conjunction of the sexual and spiritual motifs in the conjoined EXE 40–41, here we find a clever combination of the learned and (as it were) the lay. On incest riddles in general, see the headnote to SYM below. There is only one compound in this riddle.

44.1a Reading *wer,* after Gr (E reads *wær*).
44.3b Reading *hyra,* after Tu (E reads *hyre*).
44.4a Compare *GenA* 968 *(freolicu twa frum-bearn cenned),* 1189a *(freolic frum-bearn),* 1618 *(ful freolice feorh, frum-bearn Chames).* The biblical overtone of the phrase seems clear, although none of these usages is found in connection with Lot.

EXE 45

MANUSCRIPT: E, fol. 112v–13r.

EARLIER EDITIONS AND TRANSLATIONS: Gr 48; Tr 45; Tu 48; Wy 47; Ma 47; KD 47; Ba 42, 34–35; Ab 47, 30; WiR 45; WiF 45, 107; Wh 47, 197; PZ 45; CH 47, 51; Mu 47; WiC 45, 546 and 1160–61.

SOLUTION: **BOC-MOÐÐE* (book moth); see in particular Gr; Dietrich, "Würdigung, Lösung und Herstellung." Other suggested solutions include: "demon" (Jember, *Old English Riddles*), "writing on vellum" (Jacobs, "Old English 'Book-moth' Riddle Reconsidered"), *maþa ond sealm-boc,* "maggot and psalter" (Ni). See further Russom, "Exeter Riddle 47"; Sutherland, "Paradoxes in the Riddles of the Anglo-Saxons," 161–63; Stewart, "Old English Riddle 47"; Stewart, "Diachronic Study"; Salvador-Bello, "Compilation of the Old English Riddles," 227–31; Anderson, "Two Spliced Riddles"; Scattergood, "Eating the Book"; Fiocco, "Gli animali negli enigmi anglo-sassoni dell'*Exeter Book*"; Defour, "Use of Memory"; Göbel, *Studien zu den altenglischen Schriftwesenrätseln,* 226–55; Bitterli, *Say What I Am Called,* 191–93; Zweck, "Silence in the Exeter Book Riddles," 326–31; Ramey, "Crafting Strangeness," 210–11; Orchard, "Performing Writing and Singing Silence," 80–81; Lockhart, "Everyday Wonders and Enigmatic Structures," 133–35; Ooi, "Speaking Objects," 67–69; Stanley, "Exeter Book *Riddles,* II," 358–59; Foys, "The Undoing of Exeter Book Riddle 47"; Dale, *Natural World,* 77 and 100.

The solution "bookworm" or "book moth" has been widely accepted ever since Dietrich pointed out the parallel SYM 16 (*TINEA,* "bookworm"), although the differences in treatment are striking. Robinson, "Artful Ambiguities," skillfully points out the artful use of ambiguity on the part of the Old English poet. The whole riddle is structured around an envelope pattern *(word fræt . . . wordum swealg),* and it is notable that four out of the six lines alliterate on *w-*. The repeated use of the term *tinea* in the Vulgate (for example, Job 4:19 and 13:28, Isaiah 50:9 and 51:18, Baruch 6:11, Matthew 6:19–20, Luke 12:33) as a symbol of decay, as well as the reference to poetry *(gied),* leads Ni to suggest that it is specifically a Bible that is being consumed;

compare EXE 58 (*HREOD,* "reed") and ALD 89 (*ARCA LIBRARIA,* "bookcase") for the parallel notion of a creature ignorantly containing book-learning. There are only two compounds in this riddle, of which one, *stæl-giest* (45.5b), is unique in extant Old English verse, and given the strict Anglo-Saxon laws covering hospitality the very notion would have seemed a shocking oxymoron: guests should neither steal nor be stolen from.

45.2a Note an apparent play on words between *wyrd,* "fate," and *gewyrd,* "speech," "sentence"), especially since *wyrd* here is back-linked alliteratively to *word,* "words," in the previous line.

45.4a The *þystro,* "darkness," may also of course be metaphorical, and denote ignorance; likewise, some pun on *cwide,* "speech," "sentence," and *cwidu,* "cud, what is chewed," seems likely, especially given the prominence of the latter term in phrases such as *cwudu ceowan,* "to chew the cud," so emphasizing the notion of *ruminatio,* "rumination."

45.5a The *staþol,* "support," may likewise signify both a physical and an intellectual foundation.

45.6b The verb *swelgan,* "to swallow," again covers both corporeal and mental consumption.

EXE 46

MANUSCRIPT: E, fol. 113r.

EARLIER EDITIONS AND TRANSLATIONS: Gr 49; Tr 46; Tu 49; Wy 48; Ma 48; KD 48; Ba 15, 18; Ab 48, 30; WiR 46; WiF 46, 108; Wh 48, 199; PZ 46; CH 48, 52; Mu 48; WiC 46, 546–47 and 1161.

SOLUTION: *HUSEL-DISC* (paten); see in particular Tu and Ni. Other suggested solutions include: "chrismal" (Dietrich, "Würdigung, Lösung und Herstellung"), "chalice" (Wy), "bell/sacramental vessel" (Jember, *Old English Riddles*), "gospel book or book of offices"? (Anderson, "Two Spliced Riddles"), "inscription ring on a chalice" (PZ). See further Nelson, "The Paradox of Silent Speech"; Jember, "Proposed Restoration in *Riddle 48*"; Okasha, "Old English *hring* in Riddles 48 and 59"; Okasha and O'Reilly,

"Anglo-Saxon Portable Altar"; Salvador-Bello, "Compilation of the Old English Riddles," 231–33; Teele, "Heroic Tradition," 162–65; Hayes, "Talking Dead"; Ramey, "Writing Speaks," 344–45; Cavell, "Powerful Patens"; Bardowell, "Art and Emotion," 160–64; Orchard, "Performing Writing and Singing Silence," 78–79; Ooi, "Speaking Objects," 63–64; Dale, *Natural World,* 68.

If the words that are so unprofitably consumed by the subject of the preceding EXE 45 are taken to be the edifying words of scripture or sacred study, the evidently Christian tone of EXE 46 may well maintain or indeed reclaim the pious tone and feel of the sequence. The most likely solution is some item of church furnishings, probably "chalice," given the specification here that the object in question be made of "red gold" (EXE 46.6); one might compare Aldhelm's description of an altar-chalice (*Carmen ecclesiasticum* 3.72–73: *Aureus atque calix gemmis fulgescit opertus, / ut caelum rutilat stellis ardentibus aptum,* "And the golden broad-mouthed chalice shines with gems, as the heaven sparkles, set with burning stars"). It is also possible that "paten" is intended. In either case, EXE 46.5 looks very like an inscription around the mouth of the chalice or the edge of the paten (compare EXE 57: *CALIC,* "chalice"). The whole riddle is again structured around an envelope pattern, perhaps with a pun on the words of the inscription *(hæleþum hring . . . hælo . . . hring).* The only compound in this riddle, *galdor-cwide* (46.7a), is unique in extant Old English verse.

46.1a Reading *for* (E reads *fer*). On the *Ic . . . gefrægn* formula, see the note at EXE 43.1a above. For the notion of the creature speaking *for hæleþum,* see the note at EXE 18.12 above.

46.1b Reading *hring gyddian,* after Wi (E reads *hringende an*). Other editors (including KD) consider that the manuscript reading conceals a form of *ærendian,* "to act as a messenger," with loss of *r* (*DOE* offers three other examples of the related *geærendian,* all from the *Metrical Charms,* where a similar loss has been argued). Some verb of speaking is undoubtedly required.

46.2a The notion of dumbly or silently containing words of wisdom may link this riddle with both the preceding and following *Riddles;* compare EXE 57.8b *(dumba).*

46.4a With regard to *for secgum,* see the note on 46.1a above.

46.4b Reading *swigende* (altered in E from *swigend*).

46.4–5 For other uses of quotations with riddles, see the notes on EXE 31.9–13 (*IS,* "ice, ice floe") and 36.5–7 (*HRYÐER,* "bullock") above.

46.6b The manuscript reading *wægas* is a Northumbrian spelling of *wegas;* many editors normalize, but compare 51.8b.

46.7b Reading *beþencan,* after Th (E reads *beþuncan*).

EXE 47

MANUSCRIPT: E, fol. 113r.

EARLIER EDITIONS AND TRANSLATIONS: Gr 50; Tr 47; Tu 50; Wy 49; Ma 49; KD 49; Ba 38, 32; Ab 49, 31; WiR 47; WiF 47, 109; Wh 49, 200; PZ 47; CH 49, 53; Mu 49; WiC 47, 547–47 and 1161.

SOLUTION: *BÆC-OFEN* (baking oven); other suggested solutions include: "falcon cage" (Dietrich, "Würdigung, Lösung und Herstellung"), "bookcase" (Dietrich, "Die Räthsel des Exeterbuchs"), "oven" (Trautmann, "Alte und neue Antworten"), "books" (Swaen, "Notes on Anglo-Saxon Riddles"), "barrow, sacrificial altar" (Jember, *Old English Riddles*), "altar" (Tripp, "Occult and Supernatural"), "millpond and its sluice" (Doane, "Three Old English Implement Riddles"), *hlaf ond ofen,* "bread and oven" (Ni). See further Davis, "*Agon* and *Gnomon*"; Breeze, "Old English *gop* "servant" in Riddle 49"; Salvador-Bello, "Compilation of the Old English Riddles," 234–36; Hough, "Place-Names and the Provenance of Riddle 49"; Zweck, "Silence in the Exeter Book Riddles," 325–26; Dale, *Natural World,* 48. For the notion that this is one of the riddles that focus on the scriptorium and the process of writing, see in particular Göbel, *Studien zu den altenglischen Schriftwesenrätseln,* 256–83.

This riddle continues to resist interpretation, partly due to some obscure vocabulary: *gop* is unique, though some sense of "slave" or "servant" seems highly likely; *DOE* suggests possible connections to words meaning "bent" *(geap)* on the one hand or "swallow" (*geopan*) on the other. The motif of "swallowing" here may align EXE 47 with EXE 45, in which case the solution "bookcase" may be the most promising: certainly, Aldhelm's aenigma on the topic (ALD 89: *ARCA LIBRARIA*, "bookcase") has several elements in common with all three of EXE 45–47. The whole riddle, like the previous two, is structured around an envelope pattern *(dumban . . . swilgeð . . . dumba . . . forswilgeð)*. There are two compounds in this riddle, of which one, *salo-neb* (47.5b), is unique in extant Old English verse.

47.1a On the *Ic wat* formula, see the note at EXE 41.1a.

47.3b The word *gifre* in the sense "useful" is found only here and at EXE 24.28a. There may also be a play on the homograph *gifre*, "greedy," here, coming so close after the word *swilgeð*, "swallows," in the previous line.

47.4a Reading *hwilum on þam*, after Gr (E reads *hwilū monþā*).

47.7–8a For the similar theme of how royalty values the products of the creature in question, see the note at BER 22 (*OVIS*, "sheep") below.

47.9b For the phrase *to nytte*, see the note at EXE 24.27a above.

47.11b Reading *forswilgeð* (E reads *fer swilgeð*).

EXE 48

MANUSCRIPT: E, fol. 113r.

EARLIER EDITIONS AND TRANSLATIONS: Gr 51; Tr 48; Tu 51; Wy 50; Ma 50; KD 50; Ba 8, 11; Ab 50, 31; WiR 48; WiF 48, 110; Wh 50, 200–201; PZ 48; CH 50, 54; Mu 50; WiC 48, 547 and 1161.

SOLUTION: *FYR* (fire); see in particular Herzfeld, *Die Räthsel des Exeterbuches;* Schneider, "Zu vier ae. Rätseln"; Ni. Other suggested solutions include: "dog" (Dietrich, "Würdigung, Lösung und Herstellung"); "penis" (Jember, *Old English Riddles*); "fire" and "anger" (Nelson, "Four Social Functions"). See further Hill,

"Anglo-Saxon Mechanics"; Salvador-Bello, "Compilation of the Old English Riddles," 236–39; Soper, "Count of Days," 78–82; Neville, "Unexpected Treasure"; Stanley, "Exeter Book *Riddles,* II," 359; Dale, *Natural World,* 21 and 177.

There are some broad parallels in *Hisperica famina* A426–51 (*DE IGNE,* "on fire"; see further Herren, *Hisperica Famina: The A-Text;* Orchard, "*Hisperica famina* as Literature").

The solution "fire" seems to fit best all the requirements of this riddle, being produced from two dumb creatures, namely flint and steel. Note too how this same theme of dumbness found at EXE 48.2 also appears in 47.2, 47.10, and 57.8. There are no compounds in this riddle.

48.1 Compare the opening of EXE 80.1 *(WÆTER,* "water": *An wiht is on eorþan wundrum acenned),* so forming a verbal parallel between the two major blocks of riddles in the Exeter Book for riddles dealing with the conceptual opposites "fire" and "water."

48.2a For the phrase *to nytte,* see the note at EXE 24.27a (*CRISTES BOC,* "Gospel book") above.

48.2b On the "two dumb ones" *(of dumbum twam),* which constitute a riddle within a riddle to be solved as "flint" and "steel," compare the two Latin aenigmata ALD 44.1 *(IGNIS,* "fire": *Me pater et mater gelido genuere rigore*) and BER 23.1–2 *(IGNIS SCINTILLA,* "spark of flame": *Durus mihi pater, dura me generat mater / verbere nam multo huius de viscere fundor*). On such riddles within riddles, see the note at EXE 1.12–14a above.

48.4b Reading *forstrangne,* after Wi (E reads *fer strangne*).

48.6 Compare *Met29* 75a *(þenað and ðiowað).*

48.7a Compare *GuthB* 861a *(mægð ond mæcgas).*

48.8a Compare EXE 51.4a *(feddon fægre)* and 70.6a *(fedde me[c fægre]).*

48.10a Supplying *þam,* after Tr (not in the manuscript).

EXE 49

MANUSCRIPT: E, fol. 113r–v.

EARLIER EDITIONS AND TRANSLATIONS: Gr 52; Tr 49; Tu 52; Wy 51; Ma 51; KD 51; Ba 40, 33; Ab 51, 31; WiR 49; WiF 49, 111; Wh 51, 201; PZ 49; CH 51, 55; Mu 51; WiC 49, 547 and 1161.

SOLUTION: *FEÐER OND FINGRAS* (quill pen and fingers); see in particular Ni. Other suggested solutions include: "dragon" (Dietrich, "Würdigung, Lösung und Herstellung"), "alchemy" (Jember, *Old English Riddles*), "horse and wagon" (Trautmann, "Die Auflösungen der altenglischen Rätsel"), "quill pen" or "pen and three fingers" (Trautmann, "Alte und neue Antworten"; PZ). See further Salvador-Bello, "Compilation of the Old English Riddles," 239–40; Gwara and Bolt, "A 'Double Solution' for Exeter Book Riddle 51"; Bitterli, *Say What I Am Called,* 145–50; Murphy, *Unriddling the Exeter Riddles,* 85–86; Dale, *Natural World,* 35 and 150.

This riddle is widely agreed to depict the act of writing, a combined effort of three fingers and (in this case at least) a quill pen. There are many parallels to aspects of this text in the Exeter Book, including EXE 24 (*CRISTES BOC,* "Gospel book"), 29 (*FEÐER OND FINGRAS,* "quill pen and fingers"), 58 (*HREOD,* "reed"), 65 (*CRISTES BOC,* "Gospel book"), 84 (*BLÆC-HORN,* "inkhorn"), 89 (*BLÆC-HORN,* "ink horn"), and 91 (*BOC,* "book"), as well as several aenigmata: ALD 30 (*ELEMENTUM,* "alphabet"), ALD 59 (*PENNA,* "pen"), TAT 6 (*DE PENNA,* "about a pen"). See in particular Göbel, *Studien zu den altenglischen Schriftwesenrätseln,* 284–305. A common scribal colophon, dating from the seventh century, reads "Three fingers write, and the whole body labors" (*Tres digiti scribunt totum corpusque laborat*). There are no compounds in this riddle.

49.1a A standard formulaic opening; see the note at EXE 9.1 above.

49.2b The notion of "dark tracks" *(swearte wæran lastas)* repeats that of EXE 24.11a *(CRISTES BOC,* "Gospel book": *siþade sweart-last);* compare ALD 59.3–5 *(PENNA,* "pen": *Pergo per albentes directo tramite campos / candentique viae vestigia caerula linquo / lucida nigratis fuscans anfractibus arva)* and EUS 35.4 *(DE PENNA,* "about a quill pen": *candida conspicior vestigia tetra relinquens).*

49.3 The sudden shift from plural to singular again offers a clue to the collective solution: the individual fingers and the pen are urged on by the writing scribe. For the "black on white" theme in the context of writing, see the note at ALD 59.3–5 (*PENNA,* "pen") above.

49.4b Reading *fleag on,* after Cosijn, "Anglosaxonica IV" (E reads *fleotgan*).

49.4–5 Compare EXE 72.3a and 4a *(AC,* "ship made of oak": *fleah mid fuglum . . . deaf under yþe).*

49.6b The reading *wægas* in E is Northumbrian, as is *wæg* at EXE 51.8. Compare EXE 1.46b *(þe me wegas tæcneð).*

49.7 Gilded vellum also features in EXE 24.13a *(CRISTES BOC,* "Gospel book": *gierede mec mid golde).*

EXE 50

MANUSCRIPT: E, fol. 113v.

EARLIER EDITIONS AND TRANSLATIONS: Gr 53; Tr 50; Tu 53; Wy 52; Ma 52; KD 52; Ba 65, 51; Ab 52, 32; WiR 50; WiF 50, 112; Wh 52, 201; PZ 50; CH 52, 56; Mu 52; WiC 50, 547–48 and 1161.

SOLUTION: *ÞERSCEL* (flail); see in particular Trautmann, "Zu den altenglischen Rätseln"; PZ; Ni. Other suggested solutions include: "two buckets" (Dietrich, "Würdigung, Lösung und Herstellung"), "well-buckets" (Grein, "Kleine Mitteilungen"), "broom" (Trautmann, "Die Auflösungen der altenglischen Rätsel"), "yoke of oxen led into barn or house by female slave" (Walz, "Notes on the Anglo-Saxon Riddles"). See further Lendinara, "Aspetti della società germanica"; Salvador-Bello, "Compilation of the Old English Riddles," 241; Murphy, *Unriddling the Exeter Riddles,* 198–200; Hill, "Agriculture Through the Year," 17–22; Cavell, *Weaving Words,* 164–66; Brady, "The 'Dark Welsh,'" 248–50; Stanley, "Exeter Book *Riddles,* II," 359–60.

This riddle, like the one that precedes it, speaks of collaborative work, and the solution "flail" is generally accepted. The reference to a Welsh slave at EXE 50.6 connects this riddle to EXE 10 (*OXA*, "ox"), with the added frisson that of course the slave who controls these poor captive creatures is herself bound. There is only one compound in this riddle, *won-fah* (EXE 50.6a), which is unique in extant Old English poetry; but see the note below.

50.3a Reading *genumne,* after Th (E reads *genamne*).
50.6a It is tempting to emend to *won-feax Wale,* as in EXE 10.8a.

EXE 51

MANUSCRIPT: E, fol. 113v.

EARLIER EDITIONS AND TRANSLATIONS: Gr 54; Tr 51; Tu 54; Wy 53; Ma 53; KD 53; Ba 47, 39; Ab 53, 32; WiR 51; WiF 51, 113; Wh 53, 201–2; PZ 51; CH 53, 57; Mu 53; WiC 51, 548 and 1161–62.

SOLUTION: *GEALGA* (gallows, cross). Other suggested solutions include: "spear" (Trautmann, "Die Auflösungen der altenglischen Rätsel"), "battering ram" (Dietrich, "Würdigung, Lösung und Herstellung"), "penis" (Jember, *Old English Riddles*), "cross" (Whitman, "Significant Motifs in Riddle 53"; PZ), "gallows" (Wilcox, "New Solutions"), *gealg-treow,* "gallows/cross" (Ni). See further Foley, "Riddles 53, 54, and 55"; Fiocco, "Cinque enigmi dall'Exeter Book"; Stanley, "Heroic Aspects of the Exeter Book Riddles"; Lendinara, "Aspetti della società germanica"; Salvador-Bello, "Compilation of the Old English Riddles," 241–43; Teele, "Heroic Tradition," 85–90; Dale, *Natural World,* 103–6 and 110–15; Stanley, "Exeter Book *Riddles,* II," 360; Soper, "Count of Days," 113–15.

There is a certain amount of misdirection here through double entendre, so linking this riddle to the one that follows. Foley, "Riddles 53, 54, and 55," argues that EXE 51 opens a sequence of three closely connected riddles that echo in structure the three *Christ*-poems that open the Exeter Book, or the three parts of EXE 1 (which he solves as "apocalyptic storm"), and which he interprets as a repeated reference to an archetypal pattern of Christian spiritual fertilization. There are only two compounds in this riddle, of which one, *hilde-giest* (51.9b), is unique in extant Old English poetry.

51.1a A standard formulaic opening; see the note at EXE 9.1 (*WIN-FÆT,* "cup of wine") above.

51.1b The appearance of the word *beam* here may again be a clue to the solution; the challenge is to work out which of the many meanings of the word ("tree," "timber," "beam," "beam of light," "cross," "gallows") is appropriate. See further EXE 28a and 28b.

51.4a Compare EXE 48.8a *(fedað hine fægre)* and 70.6a *(fedde mec [fægre]).*

51.7b–8a Compare EXE 12.11b *(hyrstum frætwed)* and 29.20b *(frætwed hyrstum).*

51.8b For the Northumbian form *wæg,* compare *wægas* at EXE 49.6b. Note also the Northern form *weo* at EXE 54.6a.

51.9a Reading *mægen,* after Tu (E reads *mæg*).

51.10b The manuscript reading *yst* must be accusative, marking manner after *on* (here *an*), as Wi notes; other editors emend to the dative *yste.*

EXE 52

MANUSCRIPT: E, fol. 113v–14r.

EARLIER EDITIONS AND TRANSLATIONS: Gr 55; Tr 52; Tu 55; Wy 54; Ma 54; KD 54; Ba 77, 58; Ab 54, 33; WiR 52; WiF 52, 114; Wh 54, 202–3; PZ 52; CH 54, 58; Mu 54; WiC 52, 548 and 1162.

SOLUTION: *CYRN* (churn); other suggested solutions include: "baker's boy and oven" (Dietrich, "Würdigung, Lösung und Herstellung"), "churn" (Trautmann, "Die Auflösungen der altenglischen Rätsel"), "penis/intercourse" (Jember, *Old English Riddles*), "butter-churning servant" (PZ), *cyrn ond butere,* "churn and butter" (Ni), "male masturbation" (Murphy, *Unriddling the Exeter Riddles,* 184–95). See further Foley, "Riddles 53, 54, and 55"; Digan, "Aspects of Vocabulary,"

62–89; Salvador-Bello, "Compilation of the Old English Riddles," 243–44; Smith, "Humor in Hiding," 94–97; Hill, "*Cyrn*"; Rudolf, "Riddling and Reading"; Stanley, "Exeter Book *Riddles,* II," 360.

In this riddle, the stratagem of misdirection through double entendre is so overt that scholars have sometimes struggled to identify alternatives: if the activity described is not simply sexual, then the churning of butter or cheese seems the most likely solution; verbal parallels with other riddles employing double entendre only strengthen the supposition that the author of this riddle feels part of a wider tradition. More specific verbal echoes, noted below at EXE 52.6b and 52.8a, connect this riddle with EXE 61 (*GLÆS-FÆT,* "glass beaker"). This twelve-line riddle breaks easily into two halves, linked partly through diction (*under gyrdels[e]* at EXE 52.4b and 52.11a), and partly through alliterative patterning; note that the first half is made up of a consistent set of sounds *h-/(-)st-/w-* highlighted by both structural and ornamental alliteration, two of which *(st-/w-)* are echoed at EXE 52.9 and 52.10; for similar structural divisions, see for example the headnotes to EXE 31 and 58. There are three compounds in this riddle, though none is particularly noteworthy.

52.1 See the note at EXE 31.1 (*IS,* "ice, ice floe") above.

52.2a Reading *in wincle,* after Tu (E reads *Inwinc sele*); KD retain the manuscript reading, noting, however, that a churn would hardly be likely to stand in the main hall.

52.3a For the compound *hægsteald-mon,* compare EXE 12.2a (*HORN,* "horn": *geong hago-steald-mon).*

52.4b Reading *hrand,* after Gr (E reads *rand*); Murphy, *Unriddling the Exeter Riddles,* 189–90, suggests emending to *hran,* "touched," instead. Compare EXE 52.11a *(under gyrdelse).*

52.5b Compare EXE 59.9a *(ruwes nat-hwæt)* and 89.27a *(eorpes nat-hwæt).*

52.6b Compare EXE 61.7a *(wyrceð his willan).*

52.8a Compare EXE 61.5a *(tillic esne).*

52.9b Reading *þon hio,* after Wy (E reads *þon hie o*), and understanding *þon* as a variant of *þonne* (as do KD).

52.11a Compare EXE 52.4b *(hrand under gyrdels).*

52.12b The notion of purchase once again links this riddle with others emphasizing the sexual quality of slaves, such as EXE 10, 50, and 70. See further Girsch, "Metaphorical Usage, Sexual Exploitation."

EXE 53

MANUSCRIPT: E, fol. 114r.

EARLIER EDITIONS AND TRANSLATIONS: Gr 56; Tr 53; Tu 56; Wy 55; Ma 55; KD 55; Ba 13, 17; Ab 55, 33; WiR 53; WiF 53, 115; Wh 55, 203; PZ 53; CH 55, 59; Mu 55; WiC 53, 548–49 and 1162.

SOLUTION: **WÆPEN-HENGEN* (weapon rack); see further Ni. Other suggested solutions include: "shield" (Dietrich, "Würdigung, Lösung und Herstellung"), "scabbard" (Dietrich, "Die Räthsel des Exeterbuchs"), "harp" (Trautmann, "Die Auflösungen der altenglischen Rätsel"; Padelford, "Old English Musical Terms"), "swordstand" (Liebermann, "Das ags Rätsel 56"), "cross" (Erhardt-Siebold, *Die lateinischen Rätsel der Angelsachsen;* Patch, "Anglo-Saxon Riddle 56"; PZ; Cherniss, "The Cross as Christ's Weapon"), "tetractys" (Jember, *Old English Riddles*), "reliquary (containing a splinter of the True Cross)" (Fanger, "A Suggestion"), "wooden liturgical cross" (Tristram, "In Support of Tupper's Solution"), "cross reliquary" (Machan and Peterson, "Crux of Riddle 53"), "mead-barrel and drinking-bowl" (Taylor, "Mazers, Mead, and the Wolf's-head Tree"). See further Foley, "Riddles 53, 54, and 55"; Fiocco, "Cinque enigmi dall'Exeter Book"; Lerer, *Literacy and Power,* 113. Stanley, "Heroic Aspects of the Exeter Book Riddles"; Clemoes, *Interactions of Thought and Language,* 189–90; Salvador-Bello, "Compilation of the Old English Riddles," 245–51; Teele, "Heroic Tradition," 147–57; Ni, 61–84; Bitterli, *Say What I Am Called,* 124–31; Murphy, *Unriddling the Exeter Riddles,* 61–67; Dale, *Natural World,* 40–42 and 192.

This riddle is one of the most perplexing in the Exeter Book, with suggested solutions varying between the martial, the mundane, and the marvelous. It is tempting to associate the four kinds of wood specified in EXE 53.9–10 with the idea that four kinds of wood went into the making of Christ's Cross (compare BL, no. 172). Specific verbal parallels connect this riddle to EXE 54, which follows. There are six compounds in this riddle, of which three are unique in extant Old English verse: *searo-bunden* (53.4a), *wulf-heafed-treo* (53.12a), and *gold-hilted* (53.14a).

53.1a Reading *healle,* after Th (E reads *heall*). A standard formulaic opening; see the note at EXE 11.1 above. Compare EXE 53.13b *(maðm in healle),* 57.1 *(Ic seah in healle hring gyldenne),* and 57.17 *(hringes to hæleþum þa he in healle).* For similar drinking formulas, compare EXE 18.12, 54.11, 61.3, 65.14, and 82.1.

53.2a Compare EXE 54.12b *(on flet beran).*

53.4a The compound *searo-bunden* is unique to this riddle; compare EXE 54.5b–6a *(ond se wudu searwum / fæste gebunden)* and *Andreas* 1396b *(searwum gebunden).*

53.5 Outside this riddle, the wordplay on *rode* and *rodorum* is found in poetry only in poems signed by Cynewulf (*ChristB* 727; *Elene* 147, 206, 482, 624, 631, 855, 886, 918, 1022, 1066, 1074, 1234; *Jul* 305 and 447).

53.5b–6a Compare *GenA* 1675 *(and to heofnum up hlædræ rærdon).*

53.8a For the notion of the creature's speaking *for eorlum,* see the note at EXE 18.12a above.

53.9a The form *hlin* is unique to this riddle; compare manuscript *hlyn* in EXE 1.7b, corrected from *hlin.*

53.11b–12a These half-lines seem to give away the solution, or at least offer a broad clue; for other examples, see the headnote to EXE above.

53.13b See the note at EXE 53.1a above.

EXE 54

MANUSCRIPT: E, fol. 114r.

EARLIER EDITIONS AND TRANSLATIONS: Gr 57; Tr 54; Tu 57; Wy 56; Ma 56; KD 56; Ba 37, 31; Ab 56, 34; WiR 54; WiF 54, 116; Wh 56, 203–4; PZ 54; CH 56, 60; Mu 56; WiC 54, 549 and 1162–63.

SOLUTION: **RID-ROD* (pole lathe); other suggested solutions include: "lathe" (Dietrich, "Die Räthsel des Exeterbuchs"), "loom" (Dietrich, "Würdigung, Lösung und Herstellung"), "flail" (Wy), "web in the loom" (Erhardt-Siebold, "Old English Riddle No. 57"), "execution" (Jember, *Old English Riddles*), "lathe" (PZ), *webb ond web-beam,* "tapestry and loom" (Ni). See further Erhardt-Siebold, "Old English Loom Riddles"; Lendinara, "Aspetti della società germanica"; Salvador-Bello, "Compilation of the Old English Riddles," 251–55; Teele, "Heroic Tradition," 157–61; Cavell, *Weaving Words,* 27–45; Dale, *Natural World,* 40–42.

See too Leahy, *Anglo-Saxon Crafts,* 30–35; Riley, *Anglo-Saxon Tools,* 80–82.

This riddle also seems to focus on the domestic, and some solution involving weaving has been suggested, especially given the similarly martial and violent imagery of such weaving songs as the Old Norse *Darraðarljóð* (found in chapter 157 of the fourteenth-century Icelandic *Njáls saga*). Here I prefer the suggestion of PZ, building on a second thought of Dietrich, namely that what is at issue here is a wood-turning lathe, also known as a pole lathe, whereby a sappy branch is drawn up and down by a treadle, rotating a piece of wood that can be carved both outside and in by one or more metal points or blades (the "arrows" mentioned at 54.12a). A reconstruction of such a tool is found at http://www.regia.org/woodwork.htm, and a common product of such a lathe would be wooden beakers or drinking vessels, which would indeed be borne high in a hall. The Old English word for such a wood-turning lathe is unrecorded or unknown, so here I have adopted the "riding-rod" or "riding-beam" that Ni suggests as the solution for the equally mysterious EXE 56 (though his intended sense there is "well sweep"). Given the idea that in both cases the creature in question facilitates the raising of liquids, it seems possible that "lathe" is a likely answer there too (see the headnote). There are two compounds in this riddle, of which one, *heaþo-glemm* (54.3b), is unique in extant Old English verse; the other, *bid-fæst* (54.7a), is found only here and at *ChristC* 1597b.

54.1a For the opening formula *Ic (þa) wiht geseah,* compare EXE 27.1, 32.1, 34.1, 35.1, 37.1, 66.1. Related sequences occur at 73.1–2 *(ic ane geseah).* For a parallel formula *Ic seah,* see the note at 11.1.

54.2b The Northern form *wido* (for West Saxon *wudu*) may point to the origin of the riddle.

54.4a Compare EXE 51.6a *(deope gedolgod)* and *Andreas* 1244a *(deopum dolg-slegum).*

54.5a The Northern form *weo* (for West Saxon *wea*) may point to the origin of the riddle.

54.5b–6a Compare EXE 53.4a *(CYRN,* "churn": *sinc searo-bunden)* and *Andreas* 1396b *(searwum gebunden).*

54.7a Reading *biid-fæst,* after Gr (E reads *biid fæſt*).

54.7b Reading *dreag* (altered in E from *dretg*).

54.8a Compare *GenA* 448a *(leolcon lyſte).*

54.9b Reading *torhtan* (altered in E from *torhtun*).

54.11b For similar drinking formulas, see the note at EXE 12.12b above.

54.12a Reading *flana,* after Tu (E reads *flan*).

54.12b Compare EXE 53.2a *(on flet beran).*

EXE 55

MANUSCRIPT: E, fol. 114r–v.

EARLIER EDITIONS AND TRANSLATIONS: Gr 58; Tr 55; Tu 58; Wy 57; Ma 57; KD 57; Ba 19, 21; Ab 57, 34; WiR 55; WiF 55, 117; Wh 57, 204; PZ 55; CH 57, 61; Mu 57; WiC 55, 549 and 1163.

SOLUTION: *STAFAS* (letters, likely "neumes," though the Old English is in the latter case unclear); see in particular Shook, "Riddling Relating to the Anglo-Saxon Scriptorium"; Murphy, *Unriddling the Exeter Riddles,* 79–107. Other suggested solutions include:

"martins" (Brooke, *History of Early English Literature*), "gnats" (Dietrich, "Würdigung, Lösung und Herstellung"), "swallows" (Dietrich, "Würdigung, Lösung und Herstellung"; Welsh, "Swallows Name Themselves"), "starlings" (Dietrich, "Die Räthsel des Exeterbuchs"; GW), "storm clouds" (Prehn, "Komposition und Quellen"; Trautmann, "Alte und neue Antworten"), "a somewhat mysterious brown bird" (Burton, "Nature in Old English Poetry"), "hailstones" (Trautmann, "Zu den altenglischen Rätseln"), "raindrops" (Trautmann, "Die Auflösungen der altenglischen Rätsel"), "rooks" or "crows" (Holthausen, "Ein ae. Rätsel"), "midges" (Wy; Swaen, "Het Angelsaksische Raadsel 58"), "swifts" (Tr), "swifts" or "jackdaws" (Brett, "Notes on Old and Middle English"), **ca,* "jackdaw" (Erhardt-Siebold, "Old English Riddle No. 57"), "bees" (Garvin, *"Nemnað hy sylfe";* Wh), "damned souls" (Jember, *Old English Riddles;* Pulsiano and Wolf, "*Exeter Book* Riddle 57"), "blackbirds" (Wells, "Ornithological Content"), "crows" (PZ), *crawan,* "crows" (Ni). See further Garvin, *"Nemnað hy sylfe";* Jember, *"Riddle 57";* Pulsiano and Wolf, "*Exeter Book* Riddle 57"; Meaney, "Exeter Book Riddle 57 (55)"; Salvador-Bello, "Compilation of the Old English Riddles," 255–58; Lendinara, "'In a Grove'"; Orchard, "Performing Writing and Singing Silence," 81–83.

This riddle seems at first sight somewhat out of place in the sequence, which otherwise appears to be concerned with man-made objects and processes; few of the solutions proposed so far move beyond the natural world, and the notion that the solution may be a kind of bird is supported by the verbal parallel to EXE 5.4b (*SWAN,* "swan") and 6.3b (*NIHTE-GALE,* "nightingale") at EXE 55.1a and 55.4b (see notes below). But this may be a form of misdirection: the much closer conceptual parallels with aenigmata such as TAT 4 (*APICES,* "letters") and EUS 7 (*LITTERAE,* "letters") support the solution (*STAFAS,* "letters"), with the proviso that musical notes or "neumes" would also fit well, and maintain the link with the singing birds. A very similar kind of misdirection seems to be involved in the equally musical EXE 29 (*SALTERE,* "psaltery"), where a musical instrument is also figured as a form of writing. The final line has been seen as ambiguous: "name them yourselves" or "they name themselves" *(Nemnað hy selfe),* but since the overwhelming majority of the attested challenges, whether in Latin or Old English, are directed towards a singular audience, the latter possibility seems the likeliest. Unfortunately, we have little idea of what animal noises Anglo-Saxons recognized, although a perhaps surprising number of texts do survive. Earlier scholars therefore opted for suggested solutions such as the unattested **ca,* "jackdaw," or *beon,* "bees," or *crawan,* "crows." It seems notable that several of the names of neumes in the early medieval period, namely *virga,* "rod," "branch," *clivis,* "slope," *podatus,* "footed," *scandicus,* "ascending," and *climacus,* "descending," also fit the general themes of EXE 55, so if the correct solution really is "neumes," they do indeed seem to "name themselves." The idea of writing on "little fields" is also found at LOR 12.5 (*agellos*). For the same "black on white" theme in the context of writing, see the note at ALD 59 (*PENNA,* "pen"). Given the conceptual connection between bulls and parchment enshrined in EXE 26, it is intriguing that ALD 36 (*SCNIFES,* "midge") describes (like EXE 55) small black creatures that (if the solution *STAFAS,* "letters," for the latter is correct) infest the flesh of cattle; it seems possible that the author of the Old English riddle has Aldhelm's aenigma in mind, and is echoing it as a form of misdirection. There are four compounds in this riddle, of which two are unique in extant Old English verse: *salo-pad* (55.3a) and *bearo-næs* (55.5a).

55.1a The opening word "this" *(Ðeos)* gives a broad clue to the solution; if the riddle is intended to be read, then "this air" that carries these flying creatures is indeed in the reader's gaze. Compare ALC D88 (*EPISTOLA,* "letter"), where the letter in the hand provides the answer. Indeed, if the final riddle in the extant Exeter Book, EXE 91 (*BOC,* "book"), really was the final riddle of the collection, then its preferred solution is equally apposite. Compare EXE 5.4b *(SWAN,* "swan": *ond þeos hea lyft).*

55.2–3 For the "black on white" theme in the context of writing, see the note at ALD 59.3–5 (*PENNA,* "pen") above.

55.2b Reading *blăce;* other editors (notably Ba) translate as "They are very bright," but *blāce* would disrupt the meter.

55.4b Compare EXE 6.3b (*NIHTE-GALE,* "nightingale": *hlude cirme).*

55.6b The final half-line could also be translated "Name them yourselves."

EXE 56

MANUSCRIPT: E, fol. 114v.

EARLIER EDITIONS AND TRANSLATIONS: Gr 59; Tr 56; Tu 59; Wy 58; Ma 58; KD 58; Ba 34, 21–22; Ab 58, 35; WiR 56; WiF 56, 118; Wh 58, 204–5; PZ 56; CH 58, 62; Mu 58; WiC 56, 549–50 and 1163.

SOLUTION: **RAD-ROD* (well sweep). Other suggested solutions include: "well sweep" (Holthausen, "Zu den altenglischen Rätseln"; Blakeley, "Riddles 22 and 58 of the Exeter Book"), "well" (Dietrich, "Würdigung, Lösung und Herstellung"; Grein, "Kleine Mitteilungen"), "penis" (Jember, *Old English Riddles*), **ridrod,* "moving pole" (Schneider, "Zu vier ae. Rätseln"), "drawing-well"? (PZ), ᚱ-ᚱᚩᛞ, **rad-rod,* "well sweep" (Ni). See further Blakeley, "Riddles 22 and 58 of the Exeter Book"; Lendinara, "Aspetti della società germanica"; Salvador-Bello, "Compilation of the Old English Riddles," 258–60; Ni, 89–92; Bitterli, *Say What I Am Called,* 98–105; Dale, *Natural World,* 150; Stanley, "Exeter Book *Riddles,* II," 360–61.

See too Leahy, *Anglo-Saxon Crafts,* 30–35; Riley, *Anglo-Saxon Tools,* 80–82.

The notion of naming connects this riddle with the one preceding, EXE 55, although it also seems very concerned with defining the creature in question in relation to a whole slew of characteristics, both positive (being earth-bound, being one-footed, being useful, having particular body parts) and negative (it needs neither food nor drink), that effectively characterize so many of the previous riddles. The notion that this is a summary text from a knowing poet seems strengthened by the paradox of an earthbound item bearing water into the air, the runic solution to which can be summarized as signifying something beginning with *r* (or at least ᚱ, *"r,"* or maybe just *rad*). Both **rid-rod,* "moving pole, pole lathe" and **rad-rod,* "well sweep," have been suggested, and both seem possible, with the latter more likely as being able to be written with three runes. Here, I adopt the (unattested) Old English solution of Ni, but wonder whether this is a twin riddle to EXE 54 (see the headnote there), and whether the solution here is the same as there, namely "pole lathe." For more on the use of runes in EXE, see the headnote to EXE 17 (*SNAC,* "light warship") above. The sheer effort required in premodern times for drawing water is emphasized in SYM 71 *(PUTEUS,* "well": *et trahor ad superos alieno ducta labore).* The riddle is structured around two sets of anaphora on *ne* (as both conjunction and adverb), at EXE 56.2–4 (where the focus is on the immobility of the creature in question) and 56.10–12 (where the focus is on its lack of food and drink); the passage in between includes an enumeration of body parts of the kind found elsewhere at EXE 77 (*WEDER-COC,* "weathercock") and 82 (*AN-EAGEDE GAR-LEAC-MONGER,* "one-eyed garlic-seller"). On anaphora elsewhere in EXE, see the note at EXE 1.16a. There are six compounds in this riddle, of which two are unique in extant Old English verse: *an-fete* (56.1a) and *eorð-græf* (56.9b).

56.1a On the *Ic wat* formula, see the note at EXE 41.1a. The compound *an-fete* is unique to this riddle, but for the concept of one-footedness (or one-leggedness), compare EXE 30.6b *(CEAP-SCIP,* "merchant ship": *sceal on anum fet),* 77.3b *(WEDER-COC,* "weathercock": *ond ænne foot),* and 89.27b *(BLÆC-HORN,* "inkhorn": *hæbbe anne fot).*

56.3 Compare EXE 29.8 *(no hwæþre fleogan mæg ne fela gongan).*

56.6a Reading *mon-dryhtne,* after Tu (E reads *dryht ne*); it is tempting to suggest that the original reading incorporated the M-rune (ᛗ), in a manner not dissimilar to that found at EXE 87.7a *(mod·ᚹ·)* and, elsewhere in the Exeter Book, at *Ruin* 23b *(·ᛗ·dreama).*

56.7 Compare EXE 77.2 *(heafod hæbbe ond heane steort).*

56.15b Reading *foran,* after KD (E reads *furum*).

EXE 57

MANUSCRIPT: E, fol. 114v–15r.

EARLIER EDITIONS AND TRANSLATIONS: Gr 60; Tr 57; Tu 60; Wy 59; Ma 59; KD 59; Ba 16, 18–19; Ab 59, 35; WiR 57; WiF 57, 119; Wh 59, 205–6; PZ 57; CH 59, 63; Mu 59; WiC 57, 550 and 1163.

SOLUTION: *CALIC* (chalice); see in particular Dietrich, "Würdigung, Lösung und Herstellung"; Ni. Other suggested solutions include: "inscription ring on a chalice" (PZ), *husel-fæt,* "chalice" (Ni). See further Okasha, "Old English *hring* in Riddles 48 and 59"; Salvador-Bello, "Compilation of the Old English Riddles," 260–62; Teele, "Heroic Tradition," 166–70; Hayes, "Talking Dead"; Ramey, "Writing Speaks," 345–46; Orchard, "Performing Writing and Singing Silence," 79–80; Ooi, "Speaking Objects," 64–66; Dale, *Natural World,* 35, 39, 66, and 158.

This is one of the few riddles for which there exists a generally accepted solution, in this case "chalice." Certainly, the emphasis on both wounding and visual signs *(gesihð . . . tacen . . . dolg . . . benne)* combines nicely with the idea of an engraved chalice that symbolizes the suffering of Christ. As such, this riddle provides a useful point of comparison for others where the solution remains more controversial, notably EXE 46, with which there are also certain verbal parallels. The whole riddle is again structured around an envelope pattern *(in healle hring . . . hringes . . . in healle),* intertwined with words for "wounds" *(dolg . . . benne . . . wunda).* There are three compounds in this riddle, of which one, *till-fremmend* (57.7a), is unique in extant Old English verse.

57.1a A standard formulaic opening; see the note at EXE 11.1 above. Compare EXE 53.1 *(in healle),* 53.13 *(in healle),* and 57.17 *(hringes . . . in healle).*

57.1b Reading *gyldenne,* after Gr (E reads *gylddene*).

57.3b Reading *friþo-spede,* after Tu (E reads *friþo spe*). For the compound *friþo-spede,* compare *GenA* 1198a (*freoðo-sped folces wisa).*

57.9b Reading *æþelestan,* after Tu (E reads *æþelan*) for metrical reasons. Compare for example *Elene* 732a *(ofer þam æðelestan),* 1024a *(mid þam æþelestum),* 1106b *(þær þa æþelestan),* and 133a *(þam æðelestan).*

57.11a Supplying *ond* (not in the manuscript) and reading *dryhtnes* (E reads *dryht*), after Tr.

57.13b Reading *ungefullodre,* after Tu (E reads *ungaful lodre*).

57.17b Reading *þa* (altered in E from *þe*). Compare EXE 53.1 *(in healle),* 53.13 *(in healle),* and 57.1 *(in healle hring).*

EXE PART 2

EXE 58

MANUSCRIPT: E, fol. 122v–23r.

EARLIER EDITIONS AND TRANSLATIONS: Gr 61; Tr 58; Tu 61; Wy 60; Ma 60; KD 60; Ba 41, 33–34; Ab 60, 36; WiR 58; WiF 58, 120; Wh 60, 206–7; PZ 58 "introduction piece to the *Husband's Message*"; CH 60, 64; Mu 60; WiC 58, 577–78 and 1163–64.

SOLUTION: *HREOD* (reed); see in particular Brooke, *History of Early English Literature*; Whitman, "Riddle 60 and Its Source"; Göbel, *Studien zu den altenglischen Schriftwesenrätseln,* 306–68; Ni. Other suggested solutions include: "letter beam cut from stump of old jetty" (Morley, *English Writers*), "reed pen" (Greenfield, *Interpretation of Old English Poems;* Tu), "yew-tree" (Elliott, "Runic Mythology"), "reed flute" (Dietrich, "Würdigung, Lösung und Herstellung"), "reed pipe" (Padelford, "Old English Musical Terms"), "kelp-weed" (Colgrave and Griffiths, "A Suggested Solution"), "revenant" (Jember, *Old English Riddles*). See further Leslie, "Integrity of Riddle 60"; Kaske, "A Poem of the Cross in the Exeter Book"; Greenfield, *Interpretation of Old English Poems,* 150–53; Whitman, "Riddle 60 and Its Source"; Bragg, "Runes and Readers"; Nelson, "Paradox of Silent Speech"; Jember, "Generative Method"; Clemoes, *Interactions of Thought and Language,* 177–78;

Neville, *Representations of the Natural World,* 114–15; Salvador-Bello, "Compilation of the Old English Riddles," 266–69; Afros, "Linguistic Ambiguities"; Kirby, "The Exeter Book, *Riddle 60*"; Bitterli, *Say What I Am Called,* 137–45; Murphy, *Unriddling the Exeter Riddles,* 140–41; Ramey, "Writing Speaks," 338–39; Orchard, "Performing Writing and Singing Silence," 89–90; Lockhart, "Everyday Wonders and Enigmatic Structures," 132–33; Dale, *Natural World,* 38, 40–41, and 44–47; Soper, "Count of Days," 94–96; Soper, "Exeter Book Riddles as Life-Writing," 851–52; Stanley, "Exeter Book *Riddles,* I"; Ooi, "Speaking Objects," 70–76.

This riddle, which appears on fols. 122v–23r, follows EXE 28b, the solution to which seems to be *BEAM,* "beam," "tree," "wood," "beam of light," "cross," "gallows." Likewise, it is not at all clear that this poem is not part of *The Husband's Message,* which certainly contains enigmatic runes, nor that the text that follows *The Husband's Message* in the Exeter Book, namely *The Ruin* (which also contains a not very enigmatic rune), was not perceived as part of a wider pattern. Just as the first batch of *Riddles* in the Exeter Book is bracketed by two enigmatic texts, namely *Wulf and Eadwacer* and *The Wife's Lament,* so too the second batch, which ends at a damaged section of the manuscript, is introduced by two others, namely *The Husband's Message* and *The Ruin,* that the compiler may have thought were simply part of the whole sequence, preceded as they are by EXE 28b and 58. This riddle divides easily into two parts (for similar structural divisions, see for example the headnotes to EXE 31 and 52), dealing with the past (60.1–7a) and present (60.7b–17) of the creature in question; the immediacy, indeed intimacy, of the present situation is emphasized through the use of second-person singular and first-person dual pronouns and pronominal adjectives *(þe . . . unc . . . uncre).* Compare SYM 2 (*HARUNDO,* "reed"), on the supposed connection of which with EXE 58 see Whitman, "Riddle 60 and Its Source"; Bitterli, *Say What I Am Called,* 137–40. There are eight compounds in this riddle, of which two are unique in extant Old English verse: *frum-staþol* (58.3a) and *lagu-fæðm* (58.7a).

58.1a Reading *sonde* (altered in E from *sunde*). For the *Ic wæs* opening formula, see the note at EXE 12.1a above.

58.1b Compare *Beowulf* 1924b *(sæ-wealle neah).*

58.3a The compound *frum-staþol* is unique to this riddle, but compare *GuthB* 1274b *(staþelum fæste).*

58.9a Reading *meodu-bence,* after Gr (E reads *meodu*).

58.9b–10a Compare EXE 65.6b *(CRISTES BOC,* "Gospel book": *nænne muð hafað)* and 91.9b–10a *(BOC,* "book": *no þær word sprecan / ænig ofer eorðan),* and more broadly EUS 7.2 *(DE LITTERA,* "about letters": *una loqui nequit),* EUS 32.1–2 *(DE MEMBRANO,* "about parchment": *Antea per nos vox resonabat verba nequaquam / distincta sine nunc voce edere verba solemus).*

58.12a Reading *seaxes,* after Gr (E reads *seaxeð*). Compare EXE 74.6b *(seaxes orde).*

58.15a Reading *twam,* after Gr (E reads *twan*).

58.16a Compare *Res* 174a *(Abead þa bealdlice).*

EXE PART 3

EXE 59

MANUSCRIPT: E, fol. 124v.

EARLIER EDITIONS AND TRANSLATIONS: Gr 62; Tr 59; Tu 62; Wy 61; Ma 61; KD 61; Ba 78, 59; Ab 61, 36; WiR 59; WiF 59, 121; Wh 61, 207; PZ 59; CH 61, 65; Mu 61; WiC 59, 584 and 1164.

SOLUTION: *CYRTEL* (shirt, garment); see in particular Dietrich, "Würdigung, Lösung und Herstellung"; Swaen, "Notes on Anglo-Saxon Riddles"; Ni. Other suggested solutions include: "kirtle" (Tu), "helmet" (Wy), "mailshirt" (Tr), "vagina" (Jember, *Old English Riddles*), "hood" (PZ). See further Williams, "What's So New about the Sexual Revolution?"; Salvador-Bello, "Compilation of the Old English Riddles," 269–71; Heyworth, "Perceptions of Marriage"; Higley, "Wanton Hand," 48–58; Murphy, *Unriddling the Exeter Riddles,* 178–79 and 197–98; Stanley, "Exeter Book *Riddles,* II," 361.

Perhaps the marital difficulties regaled in *The Husband's Message* and the internal seething implied in *The Ruin,* both of which precede this group (see further the note on EXE 58 above), have informed the more or less overtly sexual impetus that opens what is generally seen as the third set of riddles in the Exeter Book. Certainly, EXE 59–60 are both firmly in the double-entendre camp, as may also be the fragmentary EXE 61, and all three have many similarities with the several of those in the first batch in a similar vein. EXE 59 is customarily solved simply as "shirt," a gendered item that, if we trust the analogous Norse sources, was made by a woman for her man; to the extent that both sexes were involved, it only seems reasonable that both are represented here. There is only one compound in this riddle.

59.6b Compare EXE 23.9a *(CIPE,* "onion": *fegeð mec on fæsten)* and 60.8b *(BOR,* "borer": *on nearo nat-hwær).*

59.8a Reading *mec,* after Tu (E reads *þemec*).

59.9a Compare EXE 23.5a *(CIPE,* "onion": *neoþan ruh nat-hwær)* and 52.5b *(CYRN,* "churn": *stiþes nat-hwæt).*

59.9b This is a further variant of the closing formulaic challenges *Saga hwæt ic hatte* and *Frige hwæt ic hatte,* on which see the notes at 1.14b–15 and 12.19b above.

EXE 60

MANUSCRIPT: E, fol. 124v–25r.

EARLIER EDITIONS AND TRANSLATIONS: Gr 63; Tr 60; Tu 63; Wy 62; Ma 62; KD 62; Ba 79, 59; Ab 62, 37; WiR 60; WiF 60, 122; Wh 62, 207–8; PZ 60; CH 62, 66; Mu 62; WiC 60, 584–85 and 1164.

SOLUTION: *SPURA* (spur); other suggested solutions include: "gimlet" (Dietrich, "Würdigung, Lösung und Herstellung"), "poker" (Tu), "borer" (Wy), "burning arrow" (Tr), "oven rake" (Swaen, "Riddle 63 (60, 62)"), "penis" (Jember, *Old English Riddles*), *nafugar,* "auger" (Ni), "spear, lance" (Stanley, "Exeter Book *Riddles,* II,"

361). See further Salvador-Bello, "Compilation of the Old English Riddles," 271–72; Murphy, *Unriddling the Exeter Riddles,* 202–4; Bitterli, "Spur, a New Solution."

See too Riley, *Anglo-Saxon Tools,* 68–70 and 78.

The frankly phallic language here limits the range of possible solutions, of which "auger," "borer," and "poker" are the most commonly proposed, though "spur," as suggested by Bitterli, is preferred here. This riddle shares many words and contains language similar to that of several of the others that employ double entendre. There are three compounds in this riddle.

60.1 For the use of the terms *heard,* "hard," and *strong,* "strong," in the context of double entendre, compare EXE 42.3a *(bið stiþ ond heard)* and 52.9 *(strong ær þon hio).*

60.1a The *Ic eom* opening formula is found in various forms; see the note at 3.1 above.

60.1b Reading *hin-gonges* for the alliteration, after Gr (E reads *ingonges*), though it is tempting to retain the manuscript reading and understand "(strong) going in."

60.3a Compare EXE 34.3b *(fet under wombe).* Several of the riddles focus on the "belly" *(womb)* of the creature in question; compare the note at EXE 1.78 above.

60.3b–4a Compare *Dream* 88b–89a *(ær þan ic him lifes weg / rihtne gerymde).*

60.5a For the use of the term *þyð,* "presses," in the context of double entendre, compare EXE 10.8 *(wegeð ond þyð),* 19.5 *(wegeð mec ond þyð),* and (perhaps) 61.6 *(fingrum þyð).*

60.7b Reading *fereð,* after Ma (E reads *fareð*); other editors emend to *fegeð* (in the sense "fits [me] in again"); both notions play up the sense of double entendre, and the second has parallels with other double-entendre riddles, notably EXE 23.9a *(fegeð mec on fæsten)* and 59.6b *(on nearo fegde).* It seems difficult to retain the manuscript reading, though KD do.

60.8a For the use of the terms *nearo,* "narrowness," and *nathwær,* "somewhere," in the context of double entendre, compare EXE 23.5a *(neoþan ruh nat-hwær),* 23.9a *(fegeð mec on fæsten),* 52.5b *(stiþes nat-hwæt),* and 59.6b *(on nearo fegde).*

60.9a The use of the term *suþerne,* "southern," here seems at first glance obscure, perhaps, as some have suggested, simply denoting the direction of the thrust in a winking fashion, although such an explanation has to deal with the fact that medieval maps do not in general place the south at the bottom. Given, however, that the adjective modifies *secg* (EXE 60.10a), a word which has multiple meanings including both "man" and "sword," and what looks like a parallel usage *suþerne gar,* "southern spear," in *Mald* 134b, the term "southern" may simply denote an element of exoticism.

60.9b Reading *hatte* (altered in E from *natte*). This is a variant of the closing formulaic challenge *Saga hwæt ic hatte,* on which see the note at 1.14b–15 above.

EXE 61

MANUSCRIPT: E, fol. 125r.

EARLIER EDITIONS AND TRANSLATIONS: Gr 64; Tr 61; Tu 64; Wy 63; Ma 63; KD 63; Ba 84, 62; Ab 63, 37; WiR 61; WiF 61, 123; Wh 63, 208; PZ 61; Mu 63; WiC 61, 585 and 1164.

SOLUTION: *GLÆS-FÆT* (glass beaker); see in particular PZ, Ni. Other suggested solutions include: "beaker" (Dietrich, "Würdigung, Lösung und Herstellung"), "flute" (Trautmann, "Die Auflösungen der altenglischen Rätsel"), "can or flask" (Tr). See further Salvador-Bello, "Compilation of the Old English Riddles," 272–75; Bitterli, *Say What I Am Called,* 124–31; Murphy, *Unriddling the Exeter Riddles,* 204–6; Stephens, "The Bright Cup"; Stanley, "Exeter Book Riddles, II," 362; Dale, *Natural World,* 40–42 and 163.

See too Leahy, *Anglo-Saxon Crafts,* 106–7.

This badly damaged riddle supplies enough tantalizing information to make it worth hazarding a guess, especially since it follows two riddles relying on double entendre, and there is a close parallel for the central lines of a creature whose body is pressed with fingers and kissed on the mouth (EXE 61.4–6) in Aldhelm's aenigma on *CALIX VITREUS* (ALD 80.5–9). Note too the parallels with several others of the double-entendre riddles, such as (especially) EXE 52 (*CYRN,* "churn"), EXE 12 (*OXA,* "ox"), EXE 23 (*SULH,* "plow"), EXE 59 (*CYRTEL,* "shirt, garment"), and EXE 60 (*SPURA,* "spur"). There is only one compound in this riddle.

61.1a Reading *secga,* after Th (E reads *secgan,* altered from *secgun*). Compare *Andreas* 1656a *(secga sele-dream).*

61.3b For similar drinking formulas, see the note at 12.12b above.

61.5a Compare EXE 52.8a *(CYRN,* "churn": *tillic esne).*

61.6b For the use of the term *þyð,* "presses," in the context of double entendre, compare EXE 10.8b, EXE 19.5b, and EXE 60.5a.

61.7a Reading *willan* (E is damaged). Compare EXE 52.6a *(worhte his willan).*

61.7b There have been various attempts to supply the missing words in the damaged manuscript; perhaps the most likely are *wealdeð lustum,* "has power over passions," and *weneð lustes,* "hopes for passion."

61.14a Reading *torhte getacnad* (E is damaged).

61.14b Supplying *sohte* (E is damaged).

61.15a Reading *receleas rinc* (E is damaged).

EXE 62

MANUSCRIPT: E, fol. 125r.

EARLIER EDITIONS AND TRANSLATIONS: Gr 65; Tr 62; Tu 65; Wy 64; Ma 64; KD 64; Ba 71, 54–55; Ab 64, 37; WiR 62; WiF 62, 124; Wh 64, 208–9; PZ 62; Mu 64; WiC 62, 585 and 1164.

SOLUTION: *BRIM-HENGEST* (sea-steed); see in particular Wi, PZ, Ni. Other suggested solutions include: "ring-tailed peacock" (Dietrich, "Würdigung, Lösung und Herstellung"), "snake-eating bird of prey and ring-shaped adder" (Grein, "Kleine Mitteilungen"), "horseman and hawk" (Hicketier, "Fünf Rätsel des Exeterbuches";

Wh), "horseman, hawk, and servant" (Tr), "falconry" (Erhardt-Siebold, "Old English Hunt Riddles"; Brodeur and Taylor, "The Man, the Horse, and the Canary"), "writing" (Eliason, "Four Old English Cryptographic Riddles"). See further Salvador-Bello, "Compilation of the Old English Riddles," 275–77; Teele, "Heroic Tradition," 59–61; Olsen, "Animated Ships"; Bitterli, *Say What I Am Called,* 86–91.

This riddle is unique in containing runes in every line, and several commentators have compared it to EXE 17, which also appears to offer a description of a kind of horse bearing both a man and a bird on a journey. Many of the suggested solutions rely on the assumption that the groups of runes spell out the initial letters of other elements of the solution. Typical is Wi, 325, who takes the runes to indicate wi*cg,* "horse," be*orn,* "warrior," ha*foc,* "hawk," þe*gn,* "servant," fæ*lca,* "falcon," and *ea-sp*or,* "water-track." Williamson's solution seems as plausible as any other, although one wonders why he suggests the unattested **ea-spor* rather than (say) *ea-spring,* "water-spring," which is relatively common. At all events, and again relying on the perceived parallel with EXE 17, this would seem to be another ship riddle, playing on the many ship-kennings based on some term for "horse," such as *brim-hengest* (*Andreas* 513b; *MRun* 47a and 66a), *lagu-mearh* (*GuthB* 1332b), *mere-hengest* (EXE 12.6 (*HORN,* "horn"); *Met*26 25a), *sæ-mearh* (*Andreas* 267a; *Elene* 228a and 245b; *Whale* 15a), *sund-hengest* (*ChristB* 852b and 862b), *wæg-hengest* (*Elene* 236b; *GuthB* 1329a), *yð-mearh* (*ChristB* 863a; *Whale* 49a), all of which roughly mean "sea-stallion." It is striking that of these sixteen occurrences, six occur in two closely related passages in two of the signed poems of Cynewulf (*Elene* 228–45 and *ChristB* 852–63), and six more in three poems closely associated with Cynewulf's style (*Andreas, GuthB,* and *Whale*). In the right-hand margin of the manuscript at this point, five dry-point runes have been identified, usually transcribed as ᛒ ᚢᚾᚱᚦ *(b unrþ).* Wi reports a personal communication from R. I. Page that these runes represent the phrase *beo unreþe,* "don't be cruel," and such a suggestion is as good as any other for this frustrating riddle. (In a conversation with me on the subject of his previous personal communication to Williamson, Page simply smiled enigmatically: even to the most skeptical of runologists, the runes had apparently seemed tantalizingly both legible and unreadable.) There are no compounds in this riddle.

62.1a A standard formulaic opening; see the note at EXE 11.1 above.

62.1b Reading *faran* (altered in E from *fanan*).

62.3a The manuscript reading *hæbbendes* could be interpreted as a form of *habban,* "to have," or *hebban,* "to lift"; in either case, the "one having" or the "one lifting" would seem to be the creature controlling the notional "hawk" that follows.

62.5–6 These lines seem to gesture toward the familiar earth/sea/sky triad that is found elsewhere; see further the headnotes at EXE 1 and ALD 100.

62.5b The rune ᛠ generally signifies *ea,* "grave," "earth," but is here held to represent the first two letters of *eard,* "land," "dwelling"; the broad clue of a creature who travels over water as if it were land is of course implicit in the solution.

EXE 63

MANUSCRIPT: E, fol. 125r.

EARLIER EDITIONS AND TRANSLATIONS: Gr 66; Tr 63; Tu 66; Wy 65; Ma 65; KD 65; Ba 39, 32; Ab 65, 38; WiR 63; WiF 63, 125; Wh 65, 209; PZ 63; CH 65, 67; Mu 65; WiC 63, 585 and 1164.

SOLUTION: *CIPE* (onion); see in particular Dietrich, "Würdigung, Lösung und Herstellung"; Ni. Other suggested solutions include: "chive, leek" (Tr), "revenant, spirit" (Jember, *Old English Riddles*). See further Whitman, "The Origin of Old English 'Riddle LXV'"; Kries, "*Fela í rúnum eða í skáldskap*"; Salvador-Bello, "Compilation of the Old English Riddles," 277–78; Orchard, "Enigma Variations," 295–97; Murphy, *Unriddling the Exeter Riddles,* 223–24; Stanley, "Exeter Book *Riddles,* II," 362.

This is the second of two "onion" riddles in the Exeter Book (the other is EXE 23), both of which derive ultimately from an aenigma of Symphosius, SYM 44 *(CEPA)*. A number of verbal parallels link this riddle closely with EXE 23. There are no compounds in this riddle.

63.1–2 The meter of these lines is unusual, but this seems the cleanest division of the text; it is also possible to read these lines as exemplifying the kind of meter called *ljóðaháttr* in Norse (on which in general see the headnote to GES), Old English examples of which are considered by Bliss, "Single Half-lines in Old English Poetry."

63.1a For the *Ic wæs* opening formula, of which this seems a variant, see the note at EXE 12.1a above.

63.2b–3b Compare EXE 23.8b *(CIPE,* "onion": *reafað min heafod).*

63.2b–4 Note the number of finite verbs in *-að* or *-eð* in these lines: there are five, three of them in conjunction with *mec* or *mec on;* compare EXE 23.7–10, which contains six finite verbs in *-að* or *-eð,* three of them in conjunction with *mec* or *mec on.*

63.3a Reading manuscript *headre* as a form of *heað(o)re,* after KD; compare EXE 18.13a *(healdeð mec on heaþore);* this is of course another of the so-called double-entendre riddles, on which see the headnote to EXE 23.

63.5–6 These lines effectively recast SYM 44.1–2 *(CAEPA,* "onion": *Mordeo mordentes, ultro non mordeo quemquam / sed sunt mordentem multi mordere parati)* in Old English; for a similar situation where an Old English riddle essentially quotes from a Latin aenigma in its closing lines, see the note on EXE 31.9–13 and 36.5–7 above.

EXE 64

MANUSCRIPT: E, fol. 125r–v.

EARLIER EDITIONS AND TRANSLATIONS: Gr 67; Tr 64; Tu 67; Wy 66; Ma 66; KD 66; Ba 16, 16; Ab 66, 38; WiR 64; WiF 64, 126; Wh 66, 209–10; PZ 64; CH 66, 68; Mu 66; WiC64, 586 and 1165.

SOLUTION: *GESCEAFT* (creation); Dietrich, "Würdigung, Lösung und Herstellung." Other suggested solutions include: "divine power" (Conybeare, *Illustrations of Anglo-Saxon Poetry*), "nature" (Ma), "water" (PZ), *gesceaft,* "Creation; God" (Ni). See further Salvador-Bello, "Compilation of the Old English Riddles," 278–81.

This riddle, like the one preceding it, has links with both a Latin aenigma (in this case ALD 100) and an earlier riddle in the Exeter Book (EXE 38). Most commentators consider this an abbreviation of EXE 38, which is itself a close translation of most of ALD 100. Another editor, Tu, considers this a "very free reshaping of some of the material" in EXE 38.82–97. There are four compounds in this riddle.

64.1a The *Ic eom* opening formula is found in various forms; see the note at 3.1 above.

64.1b Reading *middan-geard,* after Gr (E reads *mindan geard*).

64.2a For the *hond-wyrm,* compare EXE 38.96a. Beyond these two texts, the word only appears elsewhere in Old English poetry in *MCharm*12 12 *(alswa anes hand-wurmes hupe-ban).*

64.4b Reading *þes,* after Gr (E reads *þas*). Compare *Beowulf* 1137a *(fæger foldan bearm), GenA* 1664a (*geond foldan bearm* [E *bearn*]).

64.5a Compare EXE 10.2 *(grene wongas), GenA* 1657b *(grene wongas).*

64.7a Compare *GenA* 83a *(wuldres eðel).*

64.8a The phrase *engla eard* is found in extant Old English poetry only here and in *ChristB* 646a *(hwilum engla eard)* and *Vain* 74a *(on engla eard).*

64.9a Reading *ealne,* after Mu (E reads *ealdne*); the scribe makes the same error at *GuthA* 817b and *Jul* 286a.

64.10a The final *-c* of *mec* has been partially erased; compare EXE 70.5a.

64.10b This is a variant of the closing formulaic challenge *Saga hwæt ic hatte,* on which see the note at 1.14b–15 above.

EXE 65

MANUSCRIPT: E, fol. 125v.

EARLIER EDITIONS AND TRANSLATIONS: GW 68; Tr 65; Tu 68; Wy 67; Ma 67; KD 67; Ba 85, 62; Ab 67, 38; WiR 65; WiF 65, 127; Wh 67, 210; PZ 65; Mu 67; WiC 65, 586 and 1165.

SOLUTION: *CRISTES BOC* (Gospel book). Other suggested solutions include: "bible" (Tr), "bible" or "cross" (Ma), "holy book" (PZ).

See further Fiocco, "Cinque enigmi dall'Exeter Book"; Göbel, *Studien zu den altenglischen Schriftwesenrätseln,* 284–305; Salvador-Bello, "Compilation of the Old English Riddles," 282–83; Marsden, "'Ask What I Am Called'"; Hayes, "Talking Dead"; Bitterli, *Say What I Am Called,* 124–31; Salvador-Bello, *Isidorean Perceptions,* 392–97; Ooi, "Speaking Objects," 61–62; Dale, *Natural World,* 40 and 100.

Another fragmentary riddle, which in its celebration of a mouthless creature who nonetheless dispenses wisdom has parallels in two of the aenigmata of Eusebius (EUS 7 [*LITTERAE,* "letters"] and EUS 33 [*MEMBRANUM,* "parchment"]), as well as many other features in common with EXE 24 (*CRISTES BOC,* "Gospel book"). For both these reasons, the likely solution seems to be "Gospel book." There are three compounds in this riddle, of which one, *word-galdor* (65.2b), is unique in extant Old English verse; but compare EXE 46.7a *(HUSEL-DISC,* "paten": *galdor-cwide),* another riddle wrapped up in issues of writing and inscription.

65.1a On the *Ic . . . gefrægn* opening formula, see the note at EXE 43.1a above.

65.6b Compare EXE 37.12a *(ne muð hafaþ).*

65.7a Supplying *folme* (E is damaged), on the model of EXE 25.15a *(fota ne folma),* 29.7a *(fet ond folme),* and 37.10a *(fot ne folme),* and *Beowulf* 745a *(fet ond folma).*

65.8 PZ conjecture *wis-fæstra worda* for the a-verse, and emend *sacaþ* to *sagaþ* in the b-verse.

65.11a Supplying *awa to* (E is damaged) on the model of *Exodus* 425a, *XSt* 361a, *XSt* 618a, *JDayI* 29a, *ChristB* 479a,

ChristC 1645a, *GuthA* 786a, *Sea* 79a, *OrW* 32a, *Beowulf* 955a, *Jud* 120a.

65.13a Compare EXE 84.24a *(eorþan sceata).*

65.14a For the phrase *golde gegierwed,* compare EXE 24.13a *(CRISTES BOC,* "Gospel book": *gierede mec mid golde).*

65.14b For similar drinking-formulas, compare EXE 18.12, 53.1, 55.11, 61.3, and 82.1.

65.15a Compare EXE 18.10a *(since ond seolfre).*

65.15b–16 This is part of an elaborate closing challenge formula, essentially an appeal to the cleverness of the potential solver, found in slightly variant forms, on which see the note at EXE 26.12b–13 above.

EXE 66

MANUSCRIPT: E, fol. 125v.

EARLIER EDITIONS AND TRANSLATIONS: Gr 68; GW 69; Tr 66–67; Tu 69; Wy 68; Ma 68; KD 68–69; Ba 7, 10; Ab 68, 39; WiR 66; WiF 66, 128; Wh 68, 210; PZ 66; CH 69, 69; Mu 68; WiC 66, 586 and 1165.

SOLUTION: *IS* (ice); see in particular Dietrich, "Würdigung, Lösung und Herstellung." Other suggested solutions include: "winter" (Gr), "petrifaction" (Wy), "Christ walking on the sea" (Eliason, "Riddle 68 of the Exeter Book"), "running water" (Ba), "iceberg" (Wi), *is,* "ice," or *ismere* "frozen pond" (Ni). See further Salvador-Bello, "Compilation of the Old English Riddles," 283–84; Davis, "*Agon* and *Gnomon*"; Orchard, "Enigma Variations," 290–91; Salvador-Bello, *Isidorean Perceptions,* 398–402; Dale, *Natural World,* 133; Stanley, "Exeter Book *Riddles,* II," 362.

In the manuscript, this riddle is presented as if it were two, comprising lines 1–2 and line 3 respectively. There are several other apparently single-line riddles in this part of the Exeter Book (see the headnotes to EXE 73 and 76), but they too can be explained as parts of longer structures, and here too it seems simplest to consider this a three-line riddle, with "iceberg" as the most feasible solution. Part of the rationale for considering these lines together is that EXE 67.1–2 are matched closely in EXE 34.1–2, where they seem to be simply an introductory formula for a riddle that depicts another waterborne creature. All three lines alliterate on *w-*, including copious nonstructural alliteration, and other verbal connections (1–3, *on weg . . . on wege*; 2–3, *wundrum . . . Wundor*) link the last line with the first two. The first of these parallels holds part of the key to the solution, playing as it does on the similarity between the two phrases *on weg*, "on the way," and *on wege*, "on the water," reading *wēge* or *wǣge*. In the final line of the riddle, which in its concluding half-line expresses the essence of the "wonder," it is notable that both halves have precisely the same metrical and syntactical structure. There are no compounds in this riddle.

66.1a For the opening formula *Ic (þa) wiht geseah*, compare EXE 27.1, 32.1, 34.1, 35.1, 36.1. Related sequences occur at 73.1–2 *(Ic swiftne geseah on swaþe feran / Ic ane geseah)*. For a parallel formula *Ic seah*, see the note at 13.1. Compare in particular the opening lines of EXE 34 and 73.

66.2 The line is repeated almost verbatim at EXE 34.2 *(seo wæs wrætlice wundrum gegierwed)*.

EXE 67

MANUSCRIPT: E, fol. 125v–26r.

EARLIER EDITIONS AND TRANSLATIONS: Gr 69.1–4; GW 70.1–4; Tr 68.1–4; Tu 70.1–4; Wy 69.1–4; Ma 69.1–4; KD 70.1–4; Ba 45, 37; Ab 69.1–4, 39; WiR 67; WiF 67, 129; Wh 69, 210–11; PZ 67; CH 70.1–4, 70; Mu 69; WiC 67, 586 and 1165.

SOLUTION: *BELLE* (bell); other suggested solutions include: "harp" (Tr; Schneider, "Zu vier ae. Rätseln"; Wrenn, "Two Anglo-Saxon Harps"), "shawm, shepherd's pipe" (Dietrich, "Würdigung, Lösung und Herstellung"), "rye flute" (Trautmann, "Die Auflösungen der altenglischen Rätsel"), "shawm" (Padelford, "Old English Musical Terms"), "organistrum" (Holthausen, "Zu den altenglischen Rätseln"), "shuttle" (Erhardt-Siebold, "Old English Loom Riddles"), "harp" (Pope, "Unsuspected Lacuna"; Schneider, "Zu vier ae. Rätseln"), "bell" (PZ), *cyricean belle,* "church bell" (Ni), "double flute" (Moser, "New Solution to Riddle 70"). See further Salvador-Bello, "Compilation of the Old English Riddles," 285–88; Ni, 92–96; Salvador-Bello, *Isidorean Perceptions,* 392–97; Stanley, "Exeter Book *Riddles,* II," 362.

See too Leahy, *Anglo-Saxon Crafts,* 132.

Pope, "Unsuspected Lacuna," argued persuasively that a folio is missing between fols. 125 and 126, so rendering what previous editors had thought to be one riddle as most likely fragments of two. The first fragmentary riddle seems to depict some kind of musical instrument that "sings through its sides" (EXE 67.2); either "harp" or "bell" seems plausible. Given the preferred solution for EXE 68 (*BEACEN-FYR,* "lighthouse"), it is tempting to consider this as a similarly lofty construction: perhaps **BELLE-TORR,* "bell tower," is more fitting. There are no compounds in this riddle.

67.1a It looks as if this is a further example of an opening formula; compare EXE 78.1 *(Wiht is),* 80.1 *(An wiht is),* and perhaps EXE 85.1 *(se wiht).*

67.1b Reading *hyre,* after Tu (E reads *hyra*).

67.4a Reading *scearpan gescyldru,* after KD (E reads *scearp on gescyldrum*). For the suggestion that *scearp,* "sharp," is a miswriting or misunderstanding of *sceorp,* "dress, ornament," see Pope, "Unsuspected Lacuna," who cites numerous parallel forms.

67.4b Supplying *dreogeð* (E is damaged), on the model of *Phoenix* 210b *(gesceapu dreogeð)* and *HomFrII* 7b *(gesceap dreogeð).*

EXE 68

MANUSCRIPT: E, fol. 126r (incomplete).

EARLIER EDITIONS AND TRANSLATIONS: Gr 69.5–6; GW 70.5–6; Tr 68.5–6; Tu 70.5–6; Wy 69.5–6; Ma 69.5–6; KD 70.5–6; Ba 45, 37; Ab 69.5–6, 39; WiR 68; WiF 68, 130; Wh 69, 211; PZ 68; CH 70.1–4, 70; Mu 70; WiC 68, 587 and 1165.

SOLUTION: *BEACEN-FYR* or *BEACEN-STAN* (lighthouse, literally "beacon-fire" or "beacon-stone": both terms gloss Latin *farus* lighthouse); see in particular Pope, "Unsuspected Lacuna," PZ. Other suggested solutions include: "nose" (Stévanovitch, "Exeter Book Riddle 70a"), *candel,* "candle" (Ni). See further Salvador-Bello, *Isidorean Perceptions,* 392–97.

This fragmentary two-line riddle depicts a towering and bright-cheeked creature that stands either "at the water's edge" (reading *wēge*) or simply "on the way" (reading *wǣge*), and is useful for men; on the model of EXE 6 (*NIHTE-GALE,* "nightingale") and EXE 25 (*MEDU,* "mead"), it is likely that these final two lines followed immediately on a phrase *Saga hwæt ic hatte* or *Frige hwæt ic hatte.* Of the two suggested solutions made so far, that of "lighthouse" at least has a parallel in ALD 92 (*FARUS EDITISSIMA*: see the headnote there), while "candle" seems less convincing. It should also be noted that lighthouses are not the only objects that stand towering at the sea's edge, shining brightly as landmarks for passing men: very similar language is used of the vast barrow built for Beowulf after his death at his own command (*Beowulf* 2802–08):

Hatað heaðo-mære   hlæw gewyrcean
beorhtne æfter bæle   æt brimes nosan;
se scel to gemyndum   minum leodum
heah hlifian   on Hronesnæsse,
þæt hit sæ-liðend   syððan hatan
Biowulfes biorh,   ða ðe brentingas
ofer floda genipu   feorran drifað.

Order those famed in battle to make a mound, bright after the pyre, at the edge of the flood, so that it shall tower high on Hronesness as a memorial to my people, so that seafarers afterwards will call it Beowulf's barrow, as they drive their steep ships over the depths of the flood.

There is only one compound in this riddle, *hleor-torht* (68.2), and it is unique in extant Old English verse.

68.1b The phrase *be wege* can be translated both as "by the way" and "by the water"; the preferred solution fits both.

68.2b For the phrase *to nytte,* see the note at EXE 24.27a.

EXE 69

MANUSCRIPT: E, fol. 126r.

EARLIER EDITIONS AND TRANSLATIONS: Gr 70; GW 71; Tr 69; Tu 71; Wy 70; Ma 70; KD 71; Ba 86, 62; Ab 70, 39; WiR 69; WiF 69, 131; Wh 70, 211; PZ 69; Mu 71; WiC 69, 587 and 1165.

SOLUTION: *SECG* (sword, man). Other suggested solutions include: "cuppingglass" (Dietrich, "Würdigung, Lösung und Herstellung"), "iron helmet" (Trautmann, "Die Auflösungen der altenglischen Rätsel"), "sword, dagger" (Tu; Wh), "iron weapon or ore" (Wy), "iron shield" (Tr), "revenant" (Jember, *Old English Riddles*), *sweord,* "sword" (Ni). See further Stanley, "Heroic Aspects of the Exeter Book Riddles"; Salvador-Bello, "Compilation of the Old English Riddles," 288–90; Teele, "Heroic Tradition," 84–85.

This riddle has several parallels with EXE 18, which is generally solved as "sword," the solution that most commentators have accepted here too. The problematic lines EXE 69.2–3 introduce the notion of a *staþol . . . wyrta wlite-torhtra,* "set up among beautiful plants," which seems to run contrary to the usual answer. If, however, we contemplate the solution *secg,* "sword," "man," "sedge," that part of the answer that pertains to plants may be satisfied. In the context of the three riddles that immediately follow this in the Exeter Book, at least two of which seem to permit runic solutions, it may be worth noting the stanza in the *Rune Poem* on ᛉ EO "eolhx" (OER 15), although other runic poems give the equivalent "mon" *(secg)*. There are two compounds in this riddle, of which one, *steap-wong* (69.2a), is unique in extant Old English verse; the figures rise to three and two if the emendation *gold-dryhtne* (69.9a) is accepted.

69.1a The *Ic eom* opening formula is found in various forms; see the note at 3.1 above.

69.3b–4a Compare EXE 3.7b *(homera lafe) and Beowulf* 1032a *(þæt him fe[o]la laf),* both signifying blades. On such riddles within riddles, see the note at EXE 1.12–14a above.

69.4b Compare EXE 1.31b *(fæste genearwað).*

69.9a Reading *gold-dryhtne* (E reads *go[. .]dryhtne*).

EXE 70

MANUSCRIPT: E, fol. 126r.

EARLIER EDITIONS AND TRANSLATIONS: Gr 71; GW 72; Tr 70; Tu 72; Wy 71; Ma 71; KD 72; Ba 25, 24–25; Ab 71, 40; WiR 70; WiF 70, 132; Wh 71, 211–12; PZ 70; CH 72, 71; Mu 72; WiC 70, 587 and 1166.

SOLUTION: *OXA* (ox); see in particular Brooke, *History of Early English Literature,* PZ, Ni. Other suggested solutions include: "axle and wheel" (Dietrich, "Würdigung, Lösung und Herstellung"), "slave"? (Jember, *Old English Riddles*). See further Lendinara, "Aspetti della società germanica"; Salvador-Bello, "Compilation of the Old English Riddles," 290–91; Bitterli, *Say What I Am Called,* 26–34; Cavell, *Weaving Words,* 159–72; Brady, "The 'Dark Welsh,'" 244–48; Zweck, "Silence in the Exeter Book Riddles," 324–25; Dale, *Natural World,* 6–7, 70–85, and 158–59; Soper, "Count of Days," 105–7; Soper, "Exeter Book Riddles as Life-Writing," 854–55.

Just as the previous riddle has a parallel in the first batch of riddles in the Exeter Book, so does this match two in the same group (EXE 10 and EXE 36). In particular, the motif of being fed from four fountains is found in EXE 36.3–4, as well as in two Latin aenigmata (ALD 83 and EUS 37). The form *mearc-paþ* is found elsewhere only in *Andreas* 788a and 1061b and *Elene* 233a. Bearing in mind the fact that the next two *Riddles* appear to have the runic solutions ᚫ (Æ, *ÆSC,* "ash") and ᚪ (A, *AC,* "oak, oak tree, oak boat"), it is tempting to solve this riddle also in a runic fashion, namely as ᚢ (U, *UR,* "aurochs"). Likewise the "iceberg" *Riddles* might be solved simply as ᛁ (I, *IS,* "ice"). There are three compounds in this riddle, of which one, *ord-stapu/ord-stæpe* (70.18a), is unique in extant Old English verse.

70.1a For the *Ic wæs* opening formula, see the note at EXE 12.1a above.

70.5a The final *-c* of *mec* has been partially erased; compare EXE 64.10a. For the conjecture *fægre,* see the note at 48.8a.

70.7b Compare EXE 10.5b *(drincan selle).*

70.8b Understanding *þæh* as the past tense of *þicgan,* "to consume."

70.12a The manuscript reading *mearc-paþas walas træd* is problematic in terms of meter; it seems likely that *walas* is an interpolated explanatory gloss. The Welsh were certainly "march-dwellers," and the appearance of Welsh slaves elsewhere in EXE, in 10.4a *(OXA,* "ox": *swearte Wealas),* 10.8a *(won-feax Wale),* and 50.6 *(ÞERSCEL,* "flail": *won-fah Wale),* may have encouraged the identification; it is notable in this regard that the notion of "treading" is also found in EXE 10.6b *(OXA,* "ox": *hwilum mec bryd triedeð).*

70.13b Compare *Beowulf* 1721b *(weorc þrowade), Fates* 80b *(weorc þrowigan).*

70.14a Compare *GenA* 180a *(earfoða dæl), Deor* 30b *(earfoða dæl).*

EXE 71

MANUSCRIPT: E, fol. 126r–v.

EARLIER EDITIONS AND TRANSLATIONS: Gr 72; GW 73; Tr 71; Tu 73; Wy 72; Ma 72; KD 73; Ba 48, 39–40; Ab 72, 40; WiR 71; WiF 71, 133; Wh 72, 212–13; PZ 71; Mu 73; WiC 71, 587–88 and 1166.

SOLUTION: *ÆSC* (spear made of ash); see in particular Griffith, "Exeter Book Riddle 74," Ni. Other suggested solutions include: "lance" (Dietrich, "Würdigung, Lösung und Herstellung"), "spear" (Wy), "battering ram" (Tr), "revenant, spirit" (Jember, *Old English Riddles*), "cross" (Whitman, "Significant Motifs in Riddle 53"), "writing"/"pen" (Wh), "lance" or "javelin" (Fiocco, "Cinque enigmi dall'Exeter Book"), "bow and incendiary arrow" (PZ), "bow" (Doane, "Three Old English Implement Riddles"). See further Stanley, "Heroic Aspects of the Exeter Book Riddles"; Lendinara, "Aspetti della società germanica"; Salvador-Bello, "Compilation of the Old English Riddles," 291–93; Teele, "Heroic

Tradition," 90–97; Owen-Crocker, "'Seldom . . . does the deadly spear rest for long'"; Soper, "Count of Days," 113–15; Dale, *Natural World,* 5–6, 42–43, and 105–6.

See too Leahy, *Anglo-Saxon Crafts,* 125–28.

Among the many solutions for what seems clearly a weapon made of wood, that of "spear" held the day until Niles, with his argument significantly augmented by Griffith, pointed out that the solution *æsc,* "ash, ash spear," covered all the options. Griffith went still further, connecting this riddle with the one that follows it, and suggesting instead the runic solution ᚨ (Æ, *æsc,* "ash"), as in OER 26. For *stiþ on staþule* in OER 26.2, compare EXE 69.2 *(SECG,* "sword," "man": *stið on steap-wong staþol wæs iu þa).* There are five compounds in this riddle, of which four are unique in extant Old English verse: *wroht-stæp* (71.15a), *heaþo-sigel* (71.19b), *brægn-loca* (71.24a), and *eþel-fæsten* (71.25b).

71.1b Reading *wunode,* after Gr (E reads *wonode*).

71.2a Reading *heofon-wolcn,* after Gr (E reads *heofon wlonc*).

71.5b Compare EXE 79.8a *(eall of earde)* and 89.16b *(ond mec of eared adraf).*

71.9b Compare *Andreas* 458–60 (*Forþan ic eow to soðe secgan wille, / þæt næfre forlæteð lifgende god / eorl on eorðan, gif his ellen deah,* "Therefore I want to tell you the truth, that the living God never abandons any man on earth, if his courage endures") and *Beowulf* 572b–73 (*Wyrd oft nereð / unfægne eorl, þonne his ellen deah,* "fate often spares an undoomed man, if his courage endures").

71.11b Compare *Beowulf* 2134a *(mærðo fremede),* 2514a *(mærðu fremman),* 2645b *(mærða fremede), Sea* 84b *(mærþa gefremedon).*

71.19b The "sun of battle," signified by a compound unique to this riddle *(heaþo-sigel),* is a kenning for "shield" which offers yet another riddle within a riddle. On such riddles within riddles, see the note at EXE 1.12–14a above.

71.23a Reading *þristra* (E reads *þista*).

71.24a Reading *brægn-locan,* after Gr (E reads *hrægn locan*).
71.29a Reading *siþas,* after Tr (E reads *wisan*), to make the line alliterate.
71.29b For the closing formulaic challenge *Saga hwæt ic hatte,* see the note at EXE 1.14–15.

EXE 72

MANUSCRIPT: E, fol. 126v.

EARLIER EDITIONS AND TRANSLATIONS: Gr 73; GW 74; Tr 72; Tu 74; Wy 73; Ma 73; KD 74; Ba 66, 51–52; Ab 73, 41; WiR 72; WiF 72, 134; Wh 73, 213; PZ 72; CH 74, 72; Mu 74; WiC 72, 588 and 1166.

SOLUTION: *AC* (ship made of oak); see in particular *ac,* "ship (made of oak wood)" (Griffith, "Exeter Book Riddle 74"; Niles, "Exeter Book Riddle 74.") Other suggested solutions include: "swan" (Holthausen, "Ein ae. Rätsel"; Salvador-Bello, "Direct and Indirect Clues: Exeter Riddle No. 74 Reconsidered"), "nature" or "life" (Alexander, *Earliest English Poems*), "cuttlefish" (Dietrich, "Würdigung, Lösung und Herstellung"; Walz, "Notes on the Anglo-Saxon Riddles"), "siren" (Tupper, "Originals and Analogues" and "Comparative Study of Riddles"; "Solutions of the Exeter Book Riddles"), "water" (Trautmann, "Alte und neue Antworten"; Klein, "Of Water and the Spirit"), "hyena" (Löwenthal, *Studien zum germanischen Rätsel*), "rain" (Baum, *Anglo-Saxon Riddles*), "pen" (Whitman, "Old English Riddle 74"), "diving bird" (Kiernan, "Mysteries of the Sea-eagle"), "ship's figurehead" (Wi), "sun" (McCarthy, "A Solution to Riddle 72"), "whooper swan" (Kitson, "Swans and Geese"), "barnacle goose" (Donoghue, "An *anser* for Exeter Book Riddle 74"). For the notion that this is one of the riddles that deal with the scriptorium and the act of writing, see Göbel, *Studien zu den altenglischen Schriftwesenrätseln,* 390–420. See further Erhardt-Siebold, "Anglo-Saxon Riddle 74"; Erhardt-Siebold, "Note on Anglo-Saxon Riddle 74"; Sutherland, "Paradoxes in the Riddles of the Anglo-Saxons," 153–55; Davis, "*Agon* and *Gnomon*"; Salvador-Bello, "Compilation of the Old English Riddles,"

293–97; Sorrell, "Oaks, Ships, Riddles"; Salvador-Bello, "Direct and Indirect Clues"; Fiocco, "Gli animali negli enigmi anglosassoni dell'*Exeter Book*"; Ni, 11–54; Murphy, *Unriddling the Exeter Riddles,* 13–18; Stanley, "Exeter Book *Riddles,* II," 362–63.

This has long been considered one of the most frustrating and perplexing of all the riddles, as the great range of suggested solutions makes clear. The latest solution, that by Griffith, seems entirely the most satisfying, building as it does on an earlier suggestion (Ni). What is intended is a creature that is both masculine and feminine, a condition filled by the word *ac,* which in its feminine form signifies a tree, but in its masculine form equates to the rune ᚪ (*ac,* "oak"), specifically in its role as an oaken ship, as outlined rather precisely in OER 25. The phrase *ganotes bæþ* appears only here, at *Beowulf* 1861b, and at *DEdg* 26a; the stanza seems also to play on the double senses of both *gar-secg,* "ocean" and "spear-man," and *treow,* "faith" and "tree." Note too that *ac* and *æsc* appear (in that order) as stanzas 25 and 26 of the Old English *Rune Poem.* The notion of solving a riddle with a rune-name seems to play on previous riddles on letters from the Latin alphabet, such as EUS 14 (*X LITTERA,* "the letter *X*"), EUS 19 (*V LITTERA,* "the letter *V*"), and EUS 39 (*I LITTERA,* "the letter *I*"). The only compound, *feax-har* (72.1b), is unique in extant Old English verse.

72.1a For the *Ic wæs* opening formula, see the note at EXE 12.1a above.

72.3b Compare EXE 20.14b *(ne on flode swom).*

72.3–4a Compare EXE 49.4–5a *(fuglum framra / fleag on lyfte deaf under yþe).*

72.5b Reading *ferð,* after Tu (E reads *forð*). For the phrase *hæfde ferð cwicu,* compare EXE 8.6a *(Hæfde feorh cwico)* and 11.3a *(hæfdon feorg cwico).*

EXE 73

MANUSCRIPT: E, fol. 127r.

EARLIER EDITIONS AND TRANSLATIONS: Gr 74–75; GW 75–76; Tr 73–74; Tu 75–76; Wy 74–75; Ma 74–75; KD 75–76; Ba 73 and 27, 56 and 25; Ab 74–75, 41; WiR 73; WiF 73, 135; Wh 74–75, 213–14; PZ 73; CH 76, 73; Mu 75; WiC 73, 588 and 1166.

SOLUTION: *AC* (oak). Other suggested solutions include: "piss" (Wi), "cock and hen" (Anderson, "Two Spliced Riddles"), *hund ond hind*, "hound and hind" (Ni). Suggested solutions for EXE 73.1 (taken as a separate riddle) include: "dog" (Gr; Wh), *hælend*, "savior" (Ma), "elk hunter" (Eliason, "Four Old English Cryptographic Riddles"); a suggested solution for EXE 73.3 (taken as a separate riddle) is "hen" (Wy). See further Salvador-Bello, "Compilation of the Old English Riddles," 297–300; Davis, "*Agon* and *Gnomon*"; Ni, 96–100; Bitterli, *Say What I Am Called*, 105–10; Salvador-Bello, *Isidorean Perceptions*, 398–402.

Here again there is debate about whether one riddle or two is intended, as well as about the precise status (not to mention meaning) of the runes ᛞ ᚾ ᛚ ᚻ (D N L H) which, if one considers two riddles to be involved, come as the second line of the first, or as the middle line of a single combined riddle. Elsewhere, however, any runes that appear as an integral part of the text also partake of the structural alliteration (see further Luo, "Prosody and Literary Play," 28–32); it seems safest to take these runes as an interpolated attempt at a solution, and such is the route taken by those who also assume that the solution is given in some sort of code. Unfortunately, such a strategy in effect makes the runes yet another kind of riddle, and has duly exercised the ingenuity of commentators who, having come up with a more or less ingenious answer to the problem of the runes, have then to make the rest of the riddle(s) fit such a solution. The simplest approach to these enigmatic runes has been to read them backwards, supplying vowels as required or imagined, and so reading HUND, "dog" (this reading requires the further assumption that the third rune, normally considered ᛚ [*L*], is an ill-formed, incomplete, or misconstrued ᚢ *[U]*), H*æ*L*e*ND, "savior," or HL*a*ND, "piss." Niles takes the runes to stand for both lines in different ways, and so comes up with *hund ond hind,* "hound and hind." The more complicated suggestion that the first two runes (and only the first two runes) stand for the vowels that follow them in the Roman alphabet allows the interpretation *eolh,* "elk," but there the solution founders. Note that if we take the two lines (excluding the runes) to be a single riddle, there are again several examples of nonstructural alliteration which both bind the lines together and ornament the second and final line. Given the runic solutions that immediately precede, one is tempted to suggest *eolhx* or *ior,* in view of the relevant stanza OER 28 (ᛡ *ior,* "otter," "beaver"), or even OER 25 (ᚪ *ac,* "oak"), as at the immediately preceding EXE 72. There may also in that context be a connection with the "fish and river" solution of EXE 81. If one or other of the runic solutions offered here is accepted, then there is a further link with the riddle that follows; alternatively, one might make the still more dramatic suggestion that the two lines of this riddle are a set of clues to the one that follows, with two "I saw" perspectives on the "I am" riddle that follows, and that the solution "oyster," generally accepted for EXE 74, fits this combined one too. Or perhaps this is another AC-riddle, playing on the fact that the creature in question is both male and female, and both moves (when a boat) and stands still (when a tree or rune). There are no compounds in this riddle.

73.1a For the opening formula *Ic (þa) wiht geseah,* compare EXE 27.1, 32.1, 34.1, 35.1, 36.1, 66.1. Related sequences occur at 54.1 and 73.2. For a parallel formula *Ic seah,* see the note at 11.1. Compare in particular the opening lines of EXE 36 and EXE 66.

73.2a For the opening formula *Ic (þa) wiht geseah,* compare EXE 27.1, 32.1, 34.1, 35.1, 36.1, 66.1. Related sequences occur at 54.1 and 73.1. For a parallel formula *Ic seah,* see the note at 11.1. Compare in particular EXE 54.1b *(þær ic ane geseah).*

EXE 74

MANUSCRIPT: E, fol. 127r.

EARLIER EDITIONS AND TRANSLATIONS: Gr 76; GW 77; Tr 75; Tu 77; Wy 76; Ma 76; KD 77; Ba 30, 27; Ab 76, 41; WiR 74; WiF 74, 136; Wh 76, 214; PZ 74; CH 77, 74; Mu 76; WiC 74, 588 and 1167.

SOLUTION: *OSTRE* (oyster); see in particular Dietrich, "Würdigung, Lösung und Herstellung"; Ni. other suggested solutions include: "female genitalia" (Jember, *Old English Riddles*), *facg* or *floc,* "flatfish" (Preston, "Alternative Solution"). See further Salvador-Bello, "Compilation of the Old English Riddles," 300–302; Fiocco, "Gli animali negli enigmi anglo-sassoni dell'*Exeter Book*"; Salvador-Bello, "The Oyster and the Crab"; Salvador-Bello, *Isidorean Perceptions,* 402–13; Dale, *Natural World,* 130–31; Stanley, "Exeter Book *Riddles,* II," 363; Soper, "Count of Days," 113–15.

Like the preceding, this riddle too seems to speak of a stationary female creature matched with a moving male, in this case a creature that is brutally skinned at knifepoint and eaten raw. The preferred solution "oyster" (Old English *ostre* is feminine) is accepted by most commentators, although Preston argues further that a secondary solution "flatfish" is intended, offering a form of misdirection. Various elements of vocabulary link this riddle to the one that follows. The only compound, *sund-helm* (74.1b), appears only here and at EXE 1.25.

74.1a Reading *Sæ,* after Gr (E reads *Se*).

74.1b–2b Compare EXE 8.3b–4 *(ond on sunde awox / ufan yþum þeaht anum getenge).*

74.2a Compare EXE 1.30 *(yþa geþwære þe mec ær wrugon)* and 75.8b *(CRABBA,* "crab": *yþum bewrigene).*

74.2b Compare EXE 4.3b *(eorþan getenge).*

74.3b Compare EXE 75.1a *(CRABBA,* "crab": *Oft ic flodas).*

74.4a Compare *Whale* 53b *(muð ontyneð).*

74.5 Compare EXE 78.4a *(CRABBA,* "crab": *fell ne flæsc).*

74.6b Compare EXE 58.12a *(seaxes orde).*

74.7b Reading *ond mec hraþe siþþan,* after Mu (E reads *[. . . . .]ec hr[.]þe siþþan).*

EXE 75

MANUSCRIPT: E, fol. 127r.

EARLIER EDITIONS AND TRANSLATIONS: GW 78; Tr 76; Tu 78; Wy 77; Ma 77; KD 78; Ba 87, 62; WiR 75; WiF 75, 137; Wh 77, 214; PZ 75; Mu 77; WiC 75, 589 and 1167.

SOLUTION: *CRABBA* (crab); see in particular Ni. Other suggested solutions include: "water-dwelling creature" (Holthausen, "Nochmals die ae. Rätsel"), "oyster" (Tu), "lamprey" (Wi). See further Salvador-Bello, "Compilation of the Old English Riddles," 302–5; Salvador-Bello, "The Oyster and the Crab"; Salvador-Bello, *Isidorean Perceptions,* 402–13; Dale, *Natural World,* 162–65.

This is another riddle which damage to the manuscript has rendered more or less unintelligible. The repetition of the words *flodas* (EXE 75.1a) and *yþum* (EXE 75.8b) with similar forms in the preceding EXE 74 (74.3b *flode* and 74.2a *yþa*) have led some to suggest that this is another "oyster" riddle, but Salvador-Bello in particular has noted the association between crab and oyster in such authors as Isidore and Aldhelm, not to mention Ælfric. See further the headnote to ALD 37 (*CANCER,* "crab"). There are no compounds in this riddle.

75.4a The emendation *dyde me to mose* can perhaps be made by comparison with *Andreas* 27a (*dydan him to mose,* "they made them into food"), where the phrase describes the cannibalistic customs of the Mermedonians.

75.8b Compare EXE 74.2a *(OSTRE,* "oyster": *yþa wrugon).*

EXE 76

MANUSCRIPT: E, fol. 127r.

EARLIER EDITIONS AND TRANSLATIONS: Gr 77–78; GW 79–80; Tr 77–78; Tu 79–80; Wy 78–79; Ma 178–79; KD 79–80; Ba 54–55, 43–44; Ab 78–79, 41–42; WiR 76; WiF 76, 138; Wh 78–79, 214–15; PZ 76a–b; CH 80, 75; Mu 78–79; WiC 76, 589 and 1167.

SOLUTION: *HORN* (horn); see in particular Müller, *Die Rätsel des Exeterbuches;* Trautmann, "Alte und neue Antworten"; Swaen,

"Anglo-Saxon Horn Riddles"; Wi; Ni. Other suggested solutions include: "spear" (Trautmann, "Die Auflösungen der altenglischen Rätsel"), "sword" (Walz, "Notes on the Anglo-Saxon Riddles"), "penis" (Jember, *Old English Riddles*). Suggested solutions for EXE 76.1, considered as a separate riddle: "falcon" (Dietrich, "Würdigung, Lösung und Herstellung"), "hawk" (Dietrich, "Würdigung, Lösung und Herstellung"), "sword in its scabbard" (Davidson, *The Sword in Anglo-Saxon England*), "horn" (Wi), *horn*, "horn" (Ni). See further Sutherland, "Paradoxes in the Riddles of the Anglo-Saxons," 157–60; Stanley, "Heroic Aspects of the Exeter Book Riddles"; Salvador-Bello, "Compilation of the Old English Riddles," 305–7; Davis, "*Agon* and *Gnomon*"; Bitterli, *Say What I Am Called*, 167–69; Salvador-Bello, *Isidorean Perceptions*, 398–402; Stanley, "Exeter Book *Riddles*, II," 363.

Like EXE 73.2, EXE 76.1 appears as a single stray short line in the manuscript, and here again a single riddle seems to have been split into two; what several earlier editors, based on manuscript layout, have considered another one-line riddle by analogy with the equally pithy and puzzling EXE 73 (again, following the manuscript). Given the similar structure and close sound-patterning, it seems safer to assume that lines 1 and 2 are in fact variants (perhaps produced by oral/aural confusion?), and that the combined riddle is not only a noble's "comrade in arms" *(eaxl-gestealla)*, but his "property and pride" *(æht ond gewilla)*. The solution "horn" seems to fit best. This combined riddle, like the next, carries a riddle within it, since one first has to solve "what grew in the grove" (EXE 76.7). The first clue is that this is a creature borne by a "bright-locked lady," a description of the horn carried by well-born women at feasts, and therefore it is striking that the mead/ale/beer of EXE 25 should be described as *brungen of bearwum*, "brought from groves" (EXE 25.2), so apparently answering the enigmatic EXE 76.7b. This riddle, like so many in the second batch in the Exeter Book, has a parallel in the first group, namely EXE 12 (*HORN*, "horn"). In the context of the apparent connection of several riddles in EXE to runes in general, and to OER 2 (ᚢ *ur*, "aurochs") and OER 27 (ᚣ *yr*, "horn," "bow") in particular, it is interesting to compare the following verses. There are five compounds in this riddle, of which two are unique in extant Old English verse: *hwit-locced* (76.5a) and *word-lean* (76.10b).

76.1 Compare EXE 69.1a *(ic eom rices æht).*

76.2a The *Ic eom* opening formula is found in various forms; see the note at 3.1a above.

76.3b Compare EXE 18.2a *(frean minum leof).*

76.7b For a similar riddle within a riddle, compare EXE 1.12 *(hæbbe me on hrycge þæt ær hadas wreah).* On such riddles within riddles, see the note at EXE 1.12–14a above. The solution here would seem to be "beer" or "mead"; compare EXE 25.1–3a *(Ic eom weorð werum, wide funden, / brungen of bearwum ond of burg-hleoþum, / of denum ond of dunum).*

76.8b Cf. EXE 20.2b *(wicgum ridan), Mald* 240a *(on wlancan þam wicge).*

76.8b–9a Compare EXE 12.5b–6a *(hwilum wycg byreþ / mec ofer mearce).*

76.10–11a The not-so-subtle reference to drink being offered as a reward to someone singing a riddle again emphasizes the drinking connection found elsewhere in the collection, where several drinking formulas are found; see further the note at EXE 12.12b above.

76.12b For the closing formulaic challenge *Saga hwæt ic hatte,* see the note at EXE 1.14–15.

EXE 77

MANUSCRIPT: E, fol. 127v.

EARLIER EDITIONS AND TRANSLATIONS: Gr 79; GW 81; Tr 79; Tu 81; Wy 80; Ma 80; KD 81; Ba 36, 30–31; Ab 80, 42; WiR 77; WiF 77, 139; Wh 80, 215–16; PZ 77; CH 81, 76; Mu 80; WiC 77, 589–90 and 1167.

SOLUTION: *WEDER-COC* (weathercock); see in particular Trautmann, "Die Auflösungen der altenglische Rätsel"; Ni. Other suggested solutions include: "ship" (Dietrich, "Würdigung, Lösung und Herstellung"), "helmet with visor" (Dietrich, "Die Räthsel des Exeterbuchs"), "man" (Jember, *Old English Riddles*). See further Salvador-Bello, "Compilation of the Old English Riddles," 307–9; Salvador-Bello, *Isidorean Perceptions,* 413–22; Dale, *Natural World,* 36–38 and 48; Stanley, "Exeter Book *Riddles,* II," 363–64.

This riddle, like the preceding one, carries a riddle within a riddle: any solution must also be able to explain "what shakes the woods" (EXE 77.7b *se þe wudu hrereð*); on such riddles within riddles, see the note at EXE 1.12–14a above. In this case, the answer occurs earlier in the same manuscript, when the creature of EXE 1 (*GODES WIND,* "Wind of God") claims that "I shake the woods" (EXE 1.8 *ic wudu hrere*), an association that might seem tenuous, except that fully three consecutive lines of this riddle have parallels with what some earlier commentators considered three separate texts, but which on this evidence seems to be a single coherent whole. The author of this riddle evidently considers the correct solution to EXE 1 to be "wind," since the ultimate and generally accepted solution to this riddle of a one-footed masculine creature that is pierced is "weathervane" or "weathercock," an example of which is described by Wulfstan Cantor of Winchester as sitting atop the tower of the Old Minster, Winchester as follows (lines 193–94 and 201–4; ed. Lapidge, 388–89):

Additur ad specimen stat ei quod vertice gallus
 aureus ornatu, grandis et intuitu.

❦

Impiger imbriferos qui suscipit undique ventos
 seque rotando suam prebet eis faciem;
turbinis horrisonos suffertque viriliter ictus
 intrepidus perstans, flabra nives tolerans.

As an addition to [the lightning-rod's] appearance, a cock stands at its top, golden in decoration and mighty to see. . . . Briskly it withstands rainy winds, and by turning it presents

> them its face; bravely it bears the screaming buffets of the storm, standing unabashed, facing gales and snow.

See too the illustration in Prescott, *The Benedictional of St. Æthelwold,* fol. 118v, which depicts a bishop (presumably Æthelwold himself) consecrating a church with a prominent bell tower and a weather-cock whose belly is indeed pierced right through. There are five compounds in this riddle, of which four, namely *bylged-breost* (77.1a), *belced-sweora* (77.1b), *heard-nebb* (77.4a), and *þyrel-womb* (77.11a), are unique in extant Old English verse; it is notable that each refers to a different body part of the creature in question, just as the catalogue of no fewer than eleven different body parts in 77.1–5 *(bylged-breost, belced-sweora, heafod . . . steort eagan earan . . . foot hrycg . . . heard-nebb hneccan . . . sidan)* gestures toward the enumerative body-part riddles, on which see the headnote to ALD 84, while only specifying numbers for two of the features *(ænne . . . twa).*

77.1a Reading *bylged-breost,* after Tu (E reads *by led breost*); other editors (including KD) retain the manuscript reading. The *Ic eom* opening formula is found in various forms; see the note at 3.1a above.

77.4b Reading *hneccan* (altered in E from *n-*).

77.5b Reading *sagol,* after Tu (E reads *sag*).

77.6b–8b Compare EXE 1.8b *(þonne ic wudu hrere),* 1.21a *(streamas staþu beatað),* 1.37–38a *(of þam aglace ac ic eþel-stol / hæleþa hreru).* Note that these parallels come from all three of the subsections of what has often been seen as a discrete sequence.

77.7a Compare EXE 10.8b *(wegeð ond þyð)* and 19.5b *(wegeð mec ond þyð);* the association with these two riddles highlights this as another associated with the "suffering servant" motif, as well as linking it through the use of the word *þyð* with several of the double-entendre riddles; see further the note to EXE 19.5b above.

77.11a Supplying *on,* after Gr (not in the manuscript).

EXE 78

MANUSCRIPT: E, fol. 127v.

EARLIER EDITIONS AND TRANSLATIONS: GW 82; Tr 80; Tu 82; Wy 81; Ma 81; KD 82; Ba 88, 63; WiR 78; WiF 78, 140; Wh 81, 216; PZ 78; Mu 81; WiC 78, 590 and 1167.

SOLUTION: *CRABBA* (crab); see in particular Holthausen, "Zu den altenglischen Rätseln." Other suggested solutions include: "harrow" (Wi). See further Salvador-Bello, "Compilation of the Old English Riddles," 309–10.

This is another badly damaged riddle for which most commentators have effectively despaired of offering a solution. The creature travels on feet and consumes greatly, but it is unclear whether the reference to neither "skin nor flesh" *(fell ne flæsc)* refers to the creature itself or to what it consumes. There are no compounds in this riddle.

78.1a It looks as if this is a further example of an opening formula; compare EXE 67.1a *(Wiht is)*, 80.1a *(An wiht is)*, and perhaps 85.2 *(se wiht)*.

78.4a Reading *fell* (E is damaged). Elsewhere in extant Old English poetry, the alliterative combination *fell/flæsc* occurs only in EXE 74.5 *(OSTRE*, "oyster": *min flæsc fretan felles ne recceð)* and *MCharm4* 20 *(Gif ðu wære on fell scoten oððe wære on flæsc scoten)*.

EXE 79

Manuscript: E, fol. 127v.

EARLIER EDITIONS AND TRANSLATIONS: Gr 80; GW 83; Tr 81; Tu 83; Wy 82; Ma 82; KD 83; Ba9, 11; Ab 82, 43; WiR 79; WiF 79, 141; Wh 82, 216–17; PZ 79; CH 83, 77; Mu 82; WiC 79, 590 and 1167–68.

SOLUTION: *GOLD* (gold); see in particular Ma. Other suggested solutions include: "ore" (Dietrich, "Würdigung, Lösung und Herstellung"), "metal or money" (Wy), "revenant, spirit" (Jember, *Old English Riddles*), *ora*, "ore/metal/coins" (Ni). See further Lendinara, "Aspetti della società germanica"; Salvador-Bello, "Compilation of the Old English Riddles," 310–12; Teele, "Heroic Tradition," 197–200; Murphy, *Unriddling the Exeter Riddles,* 139–51; Soper, "Exeter Book Riddles as Life-Writing," 861–62; Dale, *Natural World,* 27–28, 123–44, and 147–48.

This riddle describes a creature born of earth, purified by fire, and capable of bestowing power; the language is not particularly spiritual, and so most commentators have opted for concrete solutions along the lines of "ore" or "gold" or even specifically "coinage," which in Anglo-Saxon England would have been predominantly silver. The riddle shares certain themes with SYM 92 (*PECUNIA,* "money"). There are four compounds in this riddle.

79.1a Reading *from-cynn,* after Gr (E reads *from cym*).

79.3b Reading *lige,* after Tu (E reads *life*). The emendation *lige* from manuscript *life* seems warranted by the parallel *fyre gefælsad* in the very next half-line, but is not accepted by all editors and commentators.

79.4a Reading *gefælsad,* after Gr (altered in E from *gefælsað*).

79.4b–6a Again, a riddle within a riddle, with the crux occurring with respect to *eorþan broþor.* On such riddles within riddles, see the note at EXE 1.12–14a above. Murphy, *Unriddling the Exeter Riddles,* 141–43, following an original suggestion by Dietrich, believes that there is a reference here to Tubal-Cain as the first metalworker (compare Genesis 4:22).

79.7a See note at EXE 1.2 above.

79.8a Compare EXE 71.5b *(wegedon mec of earde)* and 89.16b *(BLÆC-HORN,* "inkhorn": *ond mec of earde adraf).*

79.9a Reading *hæft-nyd,* after Gr (E reads *onhæft nyd*).

79.10b Several editors and commentators emend manuscript *wunda* to *wundra,* perhaps after the model of EXE 19.8b *(hæbbe wundra fela),* but for the concept of speaking wounds, compare 57.16b *(wunda cweden);* the reading of E is retained here.

79.12 Compare EXE 91.13 *(bemiþe monna gehwylcum).*

79.13a The compound *degol-ful* is unique to this riddle, but compare *PPs* 147.9 2 (*þæt he him his domas digle gecydde).*

79.13b It is tempting to emend to *dyrnan,* to match *degol-fulne* in the same line.

79.14b This is a variant of the closing formulaic challenge *Saga hwæt ic hatte,* on which see the note at 1.14b–15 above.

EXE 80

MANUSCRIPT: E, fol. 127v–28v.

EARLIER EDITIONS AND TRANSLATIONS: Gr 81; GW 84; Tr 82; Tu 84; Wy 83; Ma 83; KD 84; Ba 5, 8–9; Ab 83, 43–44; WiR 80; WiF 80, 142–43; Wh 83, 217–19; PZ 80; CH 84, 78–79; Mu 83; WiC 80, 590–91 and 1168.

SOLUTION: *WÆTER* (water); see in particular Dietrich, "Würdigung, Lösung und Herstellung"; PZ; Ni. See further Williams, "The Relation between Pagan Survivals and Diction"; Salvador-Bello, "Compilation of the Old English Riddles," 312–13; McFadden, "Raiding, Reform, and Reaction"; Salvador-Bello, *Isidorean Perceptions,* 422–32; Stanley, "Exeter Book *Riddles,* II," 364; Dale, *Natural World,* 132–33, 167–69, and 177–82.

Most commentators have accepted the solution "water," based on the parallel between EXE 80.4, where the creature is described as "mother of many famous creatures" *(Modor . . . monigra mærra wihta),* and EXE 39.2 (also generally solved as "water"), where the creature in question is described as "mother of many species" *(moddor monigra cynna).* The general situation is also addressed in several Latin aenigmata by Aldhelm (ALD 29 *AQUA,* "water," and ALD 73 *FONS,* "spring"), and a particular parallel has been detected between the opening of this riddle and the first line of an aenigma by Eusebius (EUS 23 *AEQUOR,* "ocean"). There are eight compounds in this riddle, of which five are unique in extant Old English verse: *nearo-grap* (80.6a), *wuldor-nyttung* (80.25b), *wuldor-gimm* (80.26a), *world-bearn* (80.30b), and *hord-word* (80.54a).

80.1a Supplying *on eorþan,* after Tu (not in E). It looks as if this is a further example of an opening formula; compare EXE 67.1 *(Wiht is),* 78.1 *(Wiht is),* and perhaps 85.1 *(se wiht).* The whole line is perhaps deliberately close to the opening line of EXE 48 *(Wiga is on eorþan wundrum acenned),* so forming a verbal parallel between the two major blocks of riddles in the Exeter Book for riddles dealing with the conceptual opposites "fire" and "water."

80.1b Reading *acenned,* after Gr (E reads *acenneð*).

80.2b Compare EXE 17.6a *(ryne-strong).*

80.3b Reading *fareð* (altered in E from *farað*).

80.7b Compare *Whale* 2b *(wordum cyþan).*

80.8 This line is repeated almost verbatim at EXE 80.56 *(hu mislic sy mægen þara cynna).*

80.11b Supplying *meahta sped* (E is damaged, and only *-ed* is visible), after the model of *GenA* 1696a; *Dan* 334b; *Elene* 366b; *ChristA* 296b; *ChristB* 488b; *ChristC* 1383b; *Phoenix* 640b; *Met4* 9b, 32b; *Met20* 258b.

80.12 Supplying *mægen halges gæstes* (E is damaged, and only *mæ*[. . . . .]*es gæ*[. . . .] is visible).

80.19b Reading *æror* (E reads *ær*), for metrical reasons; a similar emendation is proposed at 21.9b.

80.26b Reading *wolcnum,* after PZ (E reads *wloncum*).

80.31a Compare EXE 1.94a *(under lyfte helm).*

80.32a The phrase *ælda bearn* is a commonplace; compare EXE 91.10b *(BOC,* "book": *þeah nu ælda bearn).*

80.32b Understanding *sawe* as an alternative form of *sawen,* the third-person plural present subjunctive form of *seon;* for a parallel, see EXE 24.16b (there *mære* for *mæren*). Gr emends to *sawen.*

80.33b Reading *mægen,* after Gr (E reads *mæge*).

80.35a Compare EXE 82.2b *(mode snottre)* and *Prec* 87b *(modes snottor).*

80.38a–41b Compare *Andreas* 543 *(wuldre gewlitegad ofer werþeoda).*

80.42b Compare EXE 33.11b *(wide ofer eorþan),* 38.21a *(ænig ofer eorþan),* 84.18a *(anga ofer eorþan),* and 91.10a *(ænig ofer eorðan).*

80.43b It is tempting to read *to metod-sceafte,* given that the same half-line is found at *ChristC* 887b, *Beowulf* 2815b, and *Men* 172b, but it is difficult to make such a reading make sense.

80.54a The rhyming compound *hord-word* is uniquely attested here, and seems to be a deliberate coinage on the more common compound *word-hord,* which only occurs in verse, seven times in all, at *Andreas* 316b and 601b, *Vain* 3a, *Widsith* 1b, *OrW* 19b, *Beowulf* 259b, and *Met6* 1b. In every case but one (*OrW* 19b), the compound is part of an evidently formulaic half-line: in five cases *word-hord onleac,* in the sixth (*Vain* 3a) a variant, *word-hord onwreah.* In the last of these instances, the scribe, who may have been confused, in fact wrote the nonsensical *onwearh,* but the emendation to *onwreah* may help shed light on the perhaps fragmentary *wreoh* at 80.55a (note *wordum geopena* at 80.55b).

80.56 This line is repeated almost verbatim at EXE 80.8 *(hu mislic biþ mægen þara cynna).*

EXE 81

MANUSCRIPT: E, fol. 128v.

EARLIER EDITIONS AND TRANSLATIONS: Gr 82; GW 85; Tr 83; Tu 85; Wy 84; Ma 84; KD 85; Ba 62, 49–50; Ab 84, 44; WiR 81; WiF 81, 144; Wh 84, 219; PZ 91; CH 85, 80; Mu 84; WiC 81, 591 and 1168.

SOLUTION: Both *FISC OND EA* (fish and river) and *GÆST OND LICHAMA* (soul and body). Other suggested solutions include: "fish and river" (Dietrich, "Würdigung, Lösung und Herstellung"), "body and soul" (Jember, *Old English Riddles*), *fisc ond flod,* "fish and river" (Ni). See further Nelson, "The Paradox of Silent Speech"; Salvador-Bello, "Compilation of the Old English Riddles," 313–15; Fiocco, "Gli animali negli enigmi anglo-sassoni dell'*Exeter Book*";

Orchard, "Enigma Variations," 293–94; Bitterli, *Say What I Am Called,* 14–18; Dale, *Natural World,* 68.

Ever since the similarities between this riddle and the aenigma by Symphosius on "fish and river" (SYM 12) were first noted, it has become conventional simply to adopt the Latin solution for the Old English riddle too. But EXE 81.3b–7 introduce a number of elements that are entirely original, and draw the vernacular riddle into a whole new area of interpretation, where indeed there are several useful parallels to be drawn with the widespread "soul and body" literature of Anglo-Saxon England, a point first made in unpublished comments by Irina Dumitrescu, to whom I am grateful for pointing it out. There are no compounds in this riddle.

81.2a Something has clearly been lost here; it is tempting to suspect eye-skip through homoeoteleuton, as did Tu, and read *ymb unc domas dyde.*

81.2b Reading *dryhten* (E reads *dryht*); compare EXE 84.14b *(unc gescop meotud).*

81.3b Reading *swiftre* (E reads *swistre*). The *Ic eom* opening formula is found in various forms; see the note at 3.1 above. Compare EXE 38.94b *(ic eom swiþre þonne he).*

81.4b The form *þreohtigra* is unique to this riddle.

81.5b Reading *rinnan,* after Tr (E reads *yrnan*); the scribe seems to have substituted the usual later form, so spoiling the required alliteration. The emendation of manuscript *yrnan* to *rinnan* is required by structural alliteration.

81.7b Compare EXE 13.6b *(me biþ gyrn witod),* 13.11b *(him biþ deað witod),* and 18.24a *(me bið forð witod).*

EXE 82

MANUSCRIPT: E, fol. 128v–29r.

EARLIER EDITIONS AND TRANSLATIONS: Gr 83; GW 86; Tr 84; Tu 86; Wy 85; Ma 85; KD 86; Ba 61, 49; Ab 85, 44; WiR 82; WiF 82, 145; Wh 85, 219; PZ 82; CH 86, 81; Mu 85; WiC 82, 592 and 1168.

SOLUTION: *AN-EAGEDA GAR-LEAC-MONGER* (one-eyed garlic-seller); see in particular Dietrich, "Die Räthsel des Exeterbuchs"; Ni. Other suggested solutions include: "organ" (Dietrich, "Würdigung, Lösung und Herstellung"; Padelford, "Old English Musical Terms"). See further Pinsker, "Ein verschollenes altenglisches Rätsel?"; Wilcox, "Mock-Riddles"; Salvador-Bello, "Compilation of the Old English Riddles," 315–17; DiNapoli, "In the Kingdom of the Blind"; Bitterli, *Say What I Am Called,* 68–74 and 124–31; Taylor, "Enigma Variations," 78–85; Murphy, *Unriddling the Exeter Riddles,* 42–43; Stanley, "Exeter Book *Riddles,* II," 364.

Like the preceding riddle, this one has been conventionally associated with an aenigma by Symphosius (SYM 95), which also describes a creature with many heads but only one eye. The solution given in the Latin manuscripts is "one-eyed garlic seller" *(Luscus alium vendens),* without which this riddle would surely seem obscure indeed. But in fact the differences that separate the two riddles are at least as great as their similarities: the Old English says nothing about selling, while the Latin does not specify any body parts except for the heads and the eye. Moreover, given that the Latin term *alium* is used to signify both "garlic" and "onion," there is nothing to connect this riddle with either of the others usually solved "onion." There are no compounds in this riddle.

82.1a Compare EXE 31.1 *(Wiht cwom æfter wege wrætlicu liþan)* and 52.1a *(Hyse cwom gongan);* for similar drinking-formulas, compare EXE 18.12, 53.1, 55.11, and 61.3.

82.2a Compare *Andreas* 1626a *(manige on mæðle).*

82.2b Compare EXE 80.35a *(mon mode snottor).*

82.3 Other such enumerative riddles include EXE 29, 30, 34, 56, and 77. See in particular EXE 34.3 *(Hæfde feowere fet under wombe)* and 34.7 *(hæfde tu fiþru ond twelf eagan).*

82.4 Note that the Roman numerals II (for *twegen*) and XII (for *twelf*) together form the alliteration.

82.5a Reading *hrycg,* after Gr (E reads *hryc*). Several of the riddles focus on the "belly" *(womb)* of the creature in question; compare the note at EXE 1.78 above.

82.7a Compare EXE 77.5a *(ond sidan twa).*

82.7b Reading *hio,* after Wi (E reads *ic*). This is a variant of the closing formulaic challenge *Saga hwæt ic hatte,* on which see the note at 1.14b–15 above. See further the note on 17.9b above.

EXE 83

MANUSCRIPT: E, fol. 129r.

EARLIER EDITIONS AND TRANSLATIONS: Gr 84; GW 87; Tr 85; Tu 87; Wy 86; Ma 86; KD 87; Ba 81, 60; Ab 87, 45; WiR 83; WiF 83, 146; Wh 86, 219–20; PZ 83; Mu 86; WiC 83, 592 and 1168.

SOLUTION: *BLÆST-BELG* (bellows); see in particular Müller, *Die Rätsel des Exeterbuches;* PZ; Ni. Other suggested solutions include: "cask and cooper" (Gr; Dietrich, "Würdigung, Lösung und Herstellung"), "penis" (Jember, *Old English Riddles*). See further Salvador-Bello, "Compilation of the Old English Riddles," 317–19; Hill, "Anglo-Saxon Mechanics"; Davis, "*Agon* and *Gnomon*"; Murphy, *Unriddling the Exeter Riddles,* 216–17; Salvador-Bello, *Isidorean Perceptions,* 422–32; Stanley, "Exeter Book *Riddles,* II," 364.

This is one of the more obviously sexualized of the double-entendre riddles, and again, like several in this batch of the Exeter Book, contains a riddle within a riddle: the phrase "heaven's tooth" *(heofenes toþe)* in EXE 83.5 presumably refers to the wind, at least to judge by the perceived parallels to BER 41 (*VENTUS,* "wind"). The generally accepted solution is "bellows," especially given the close verbal relationship between this and EXE 35, but there are also obvious parallels to others of the so-called double-entendre riddles, on which see the headnote to EXE 21 above. In that case, the two problematic verbs *boncade* (EXE 83.6) and *wancode* (EXE 83.7) look disturbingly close to Modern English "bonked" and "wanked," two sexual terms of unknown etymology; reading the manuscript as *borcade* may not be much better from a prudish perspective, if the sense "barked" is accepted. There are three compounds in this riddle, of which one, *mund-rof* (83.3a), is unique in extant Old English verse.

83.1a For this standard formulaic opening, see the note at EXE 11.1; compare especially 27.1 *(Ic wiht geseah wundorlice).* See too the damaged EXE 85.2b *(BLÆST-BELG,* "bellows": *wombe hæfde).*

83.1b Several of the riddles focus on the "belly" *(womb)* of the creature in question; compare the note at EXE 1.78a above.

83.2 Compare EXE 35.2 *(BLÆST-BELG,* "bellows": *þriþum aþrunten. þegn folgade).*

83.3a Reading *mægen-strong,* after Gr (E reads *męgenstrong*).

83.4b Compare EXE 23.7b *(þæt heo on mec gripeð).*

83.5a Another riddle within a riddle; compare BER 41.3–4 *(VENTUS,* "wind": *Os est mihi nullum, dente nec vulnero quemquam / mordeo sed cunctos silvis campisque morantes).*

83.5b A half-line has been lost.

83.6a For the phrase *bleowe on eage,* compare EXE 35.4b *(BLÆST-BELG,* "bellows": *fleah þurh his eage).*

83.6b The manuscript is unclear at this point: the reading may be *boncade,* "stamped," or *borcade;* those who prefer the latter generally translate it as "barked."

83.7a Several editors emend E's *wancode* to *þancode* (in the sense "was glad"; "gave thanks"), but there seems to be a cognate in Old High German *wankōn,* "to waver, vacillate." Compare EXE 85.8b *(BLÆST-BELG,* "bellows": *him þoncade).*

EXE 84

MANUSCRIPT: E, fol. 129r–v.

EARLIER EDITIONS AND TRANSLATIONS: Gr 85; GW 88; Tr 86; Tu 88; Wy 87; Ma 87; KD 88; Ba 55, 44–45; WiR 84; WiF 84, 147; Wh 87, 220–21; PZ 84; Mu 87; WiC 84, 592–93 and 1168–69.

SOLUTION: *BLÆC-HORN* (inkhorn); Tu; PZ; Swaen, "Anglo-Saxon Horn Riddles"; Ni. Other suggested solutions include: "horn" (Ma), "antler" (Dietrich, "Würdigung, Lösung und Herstellung"), "staghorn" (Dietrich, "Würdigung, Lösung und Herstellung"), "body and soul" (Jember, *Old English Riddles*). See in particular Göbel, *Studien zu den altenglischen Schriftwesenrätseln,* 422–59. See further Lendinara, "Aspetti della società germanica"; Salvador-Bello, "Compilation of the Old English Riddles," 319–21; Teele, "Heroic Tradition," 106–9; Bitterli, *Say What I Am Called,* 152–57; Trzaska-Nartowski, "Chanting upon a Dunghill"; Salvador-Bello, *Isidorean Perceptions,* 422–32; Bardowell, "Art and Emotion," 152–54; Dale, *Natural World,* 23–24, 35–36, and 42–52; Stanley, "Exeter Book *Riddles,* II," 364; Soper, "Count of Days," 110–12.

Most commentators agree that the solution here should be "inkhorn," as at EXE 89, as the riddle contains (as do so many of the riddles) a description of both the "former life" of the object in question, as well as its current manifestation. Although there is also an aenigma by Eusebius on the same subject (*ATRAMENTORIUM,* "inkhorn"), it bears little relationship to this one, which provides instead an alternative Anglo-Saxon perspective on the item. There are only two compounds in this riddle.

84.1a Supplying *stod* (E is damaged, and only *s-* is visible), on the model of EXE 84.5a (itself an emendation) and 84.9a. For notes on the growth of the creatures involved, compare EXE 7.1, 8.3, 51.3, 70.1, and 71.1.

84.5a Reading *stod ic on staðole,* after Tr (E is damaged), on the model of *Dream* 71a *(stodon on staþole); Beowulf* 927a (*stodon on stapole* [E reads *staþole*]).

84.9a Compare *Exodus* 303a *(uplang gestod)* and *Beowulf* 759b *(uplang astod).*

84.9b Supplying *ær aweox,* after Tr (E is damaged).

84.10a Reading *min,* after Gr (E reads *mine*).

84.14b Compare EXE 81.2b *(unc dryhten scop).*

84.16b–17a Compare EXE 89.15b–16 (*gingra broþor / min agnade ond mec of earde adraf*).

84.18a For the phrase *anga ofer eorþan*, see the note at EXE 33.11b above.

84.18b Supplying *innaþ* and reading *blæc*, after Tr (E reads *bæc*).

84.19–20 The close and chiastic repetition of the elements *bordes on ende* . . . *broþor* . . . *broþorleas bordes on ende* is striking indeed, and hard to parallel in extant Old English poetry. The close pairing echoes the twin attachments and shared fates of the brother-antlers in question.

84.22b Reading *stondan*, after Gr (E reads *stodan*).

84.24a Compare EXE 65.13a (*eorþan sceatas*).

84.26b Compare *Beowulf* 2499a (*sæcce fremman*), EXE 14.2a (*sæcce fremman*).

84.27b Compare *Beowulf* 2695b (*ellen cyðan*).

84.29a Reading *nu*, after Gr (E reads *hu*). Presumably, these *unsceafta* (the form is unique to this riddle) are as monstrous as the *untydras* of *Beowulf* 111a, and refer to the "weapons" that penetrate and wound the belly of the inkhorn, namely quill pens.

84.30a Several of the riddles focus on the "belly" (*womb*) of the creature in question; compare the note at EXE 1.78 above.

84.31b Compare *Met31* 9b (*saula rædes*) and *HomFr* 1 42b (*sawle rædes*).

EXE 85

MANUSCRIPT: E, fol. 129v.

EARLIER EDITIONS AND TRANSLATIONS: GW 89; Tr 87; Tu 89; Wy 88; Ma 88; KD 89; Ba 89, 63; WiR 85; WiF 85, 148; Wh 88, 221; PZ 85; Mu 88; WiC 85, 593 and 1169.

SOLUTION: *BLÆST-BELG* (bellows). Other suggested solutions include: "bellows or leather bottle" (Tu), "penis" (Jember, *Old English Riddles*). See further Salvador-Bello, "Compilation of the Old English Riddles," 321–22; Teele, "Heroic Tradition," 50–54; Stanley, "Exeter Book *Riddles*, II," 364.

This is another riddle so fragmentary as not easily to permit of a solution. The suggested solutions of "leather bottle" or "bellows" both seem feasible, though it is also true, as Jember notes, that almost the only words that survive also have sexual connotations in the double-entendre riddles. There are no compounds in this riddle.

85.2a It looks as if this may be a further example of an opening formula, or at least a variant on it, notably confined to the third of the three groupings in EXE; compare EXE 67.1a *(Wiht is),* 78.1a *(Wiht is),* and 80.1a *(An wiht is).*

85.2b Compare EXE 83.1b *(BLÆST-BELG,* "bellows": *wombe hæfde micle).* Several of the riddles focus on the "belly" *(womb)* of the creature in question; compare the note at EXE 1.78 above.

85.8b It is tempting to emend manuscript *þoncade* to *woncade;* compare the note at EXE 83.7a *(BLÆST-BELG,* "bellows": *wancode willum).*

EXE 86

MANUSCRIPT: E, fol. 129v.

EARLIER EDITIONS AND TRANSLATIONS: Gr 86; GW 90; Tr 88; Tu 90; Ma 89; KD 90; WiR 86; WiF 86, 149; PZ 86; Mu 89; WiC 86, 593 and 1169.

SOLUTION: *AGNUS DEI* (Lamb of God); see further Morley, *English Writers.* Other suggested solutions include: "lupus" (Dietrich, "Würdigung, Lösung und Herstellung"), "Cynewulf" (Dietrich, "Die Räthsel des Exeterbuchs"; Wülker, "Die Bedeutung einer neuen Entdeckung"; Bradley, "Two Riddles of the Exeter Book"), "pike" (Hicketier, "Fünf Rätsel des Exeterbuches"), an allusion to some person whose name contained the element *wulf* (Trautmann, "Zu den altenglischen Rätseln"), "Cynwulf" [*sic*] (Edmund Erlemann, "Zu den altenglischen Rätseln"; Fritz Erlemann, "Zum 90. angelsächsischen Rätseln"), "web and loom" (Wi), "Augustine and Tertullian" (Davis and Schlueter, "The Latin Riddle of the Exeter Book"). See further Whitbread, "The Latin Riddle in the

Exeter Book" (1946); WiF, 149; Whitbread, "The Latin Riddle in the Exeter Book" (1949); Stanley, "Heroic Aspects of the Exeter Book Riddles"; Salvador-Bello, "Compilation of the Old English Riddles," 322–27; Anderson, "Exeter Latin Riddle 90"; Davis, "*Agon* and *Gnomon*"; Bitterli, *Say What I Am Called,* 74–79; Salvador-Bello, "Exeter Book Riddle 90."

This is the only Latin aenigma in the Exeter Book, and it is enigmatic indeed. Even the form of the text is problematic, and the lines can be viewed as rhythmic hexameters somewhat similar to those found in BER, but only by emending several lines. If some form of medial rhyme is assumed, five long lines of between fourteen and seventeen syllables can be produced; the usual number in BER is six, and it is possible that a line has been omitted altogether. The scribe is on the one hand careful to use the slightly different form of Caroline script appropriate to Latin, most notably in the forms of *d* and *s,* as well as in the use of an ampersand instead of the tironian nota. In its description of a four-footed creature with seven eyes, and its detailing of several beasts (in this case, three wolves and at least one lamb), the riddle has many conceptual parallels with other enumerative riddles, on which see the note at EXE 82.3. A solution involving a loom and loom weights seems likely, on which see in general Erhardt-Siebold, "Old English Loom Riddles." However, there is an intriguing parallel in Apc 5:6: *Et vidi: et ecce in medio throni et quatuor animalium, et in medio seniorum, Agnum stantem tamquam occisum, habentem cornua septem, et oculos septem: qui sunt septem spiritus Dei, missi in omnem terram,* "And I saw: and behold in the midst of the throne and of the four living creatures, and in the midst of the ancients, a Lamb standing as it were slain, having seven horns and seven eyes: which are the seven Spirits of God, sent forth into all the earth." Recently, Salvador-Bello ("Exeter Book Riddle 90") has argued that EXE 86 is not a riddle at all, but a school drill of the kind that aligns itself with Æthelwold and his school at Winchester.

86.1 Reading *mihi videtur,* after KD (E reads *uidetur mihi*), for the sake of preserving the medial rhyme. For the continental *d* in *videtur,* compare EXE 37.2b (*tidum*). The use of the verb *video,* "I see," in lines 1, 3, and 5 may connect this aenigma with the many "I saw" formulas noted at EXE 11.1 and EXE 27.1a.

86.2 Supplying *rupi* (not in the manuscript); other editors supply *morti.*

86.3 Reading *mirarem,* after KD (E reads *misarē*) and *parem* (E reads *magnan*), the latter to preserve the rhyme (other editors prefer *magnam*).

86.4 Reading *duo* and *tribulantes,* after KD (E reads *dui* and *tribul*).

EXE 87

MANUSCRIPT: E, fol. 129v–30r.

EARLIER EDITIONS AND TRANSLATIONS: Gr 87; GW 91; Tr 89; Tu 91; Wy 89; Ma 90; KD 91; Ba 33, 29; Ab 89, 46; WiR 87; WiF 87, 150; Wh 89, 221–22; PZ 87; CH 91, 82; Mu 90; WiC 87, 593 and 1169–70.

SOLUTION: *CÆG* (key); see in particular Dietrich, "Würdigung, Lösung und Herstellung." Other suggested solutions include: "sickle" (Trautmann, "Die Auflösungen der altenglischen Rätsel"), "keyhole" (Williams, "What's So New about the Sexual Revolution?"), "penis" (Jember, *Old English Riddles*). See further Salvador-Bello, "Compilation of the Old English Riddles," 327–28; Digan, "Aspects of Vocabulary," 62–89; Teele, "Heroic Tradition," 193–97; Stanley, "Exeter Book *Riddles,* II," 364.

See too Leahy, *Anglo-Saxon Crafts,* 130–31.

This is another riddle from the second group in the Exeter Book that matches one in the first. In this case, while EXE 42 (*CÆG,* "key") is a highly sexualized text making much use of double entendre, the language is at least slightly more subtle, although still pretty saucy; the further resemblances between both Old English riddles and SYM 4 (*CLAVIS,* "key") are relatively slight. The arguments put forward by Williams ("What's So New about the Sexual Revolution?") that the solution here should be "keyhole," rather than "key," and that the creature in question is the feminine counterpart to the masculine "key," with the corresponding sexual switch, are very tempting.

There are four compounds in this riddle, of which three are unique in extant Old English verse: *searo-pil* (87.2a), *mod-wynn* (87.7a), and *wæl-cræft* (87.11a).

87.1b Reading *geþruen,* after Gr (E reads *geþuren*). Several editors emend the manuscript *geþruen* to *geþūren,* for the sake of meter; the same emendation is assumed at *Beowulf* 1285b (also *hamere geþuren*) and *Met20* 134a (where the manuscript actually reads *geþruen,* corrected by dot and superscript *u* to *geþuren*). When three different texts all require emendation to supply the same supposed reading, however, one might well question the conjecture; the general meaning "beaten," "made" seems broadly accepted.

87.7a It has been suggested that the unique term *mod-wynn,* literally "mind-joy," signifies "treasure." The use here of runic ᚹ for *wyn(n),* "joy," is matched elsewhere in Old English verse in the runic signatures of Cynewulf (*Fates* 100b, *Elene* 1262b, *ChristB* 804b, *Jul* 706a), as well as in the *Rune Poem* (*Run* 22a); the form appears as Roman *w* (apparently standing for ᚹ [*wyn(n)*]) in *Elene* 788a and 1089a.

87.8a Compare EXE 20.17a *(ne under bæc cyrde).*

87.9a Compare *Beowulf* 887a *(hordes hyrde).*

87.11b Compare EXE 89.2b *(willum sinum).*

EXE 88

MANUSCRIPT: E, fol. 130r.

EARLIER EDITIONS AND TRANSLATIONS: Gr 88; GW 92; Tr 90; Tu 92; Wy 90; Ma 91; KD 92; Ba 90, 63; Ab 90, 46; WiR 88; WiF 88, 151; Wh 90, 220; PZ 88; Mu 91; WiC 88, 593–94 and 1170.

SOLUTION: *BOC* (book, beech); see, in particular, Göbel, *Studien zu den altenglischen Schriftwesenrätseln,* 460–85; Ni. Other suggested solutions include: "ash tree" (Holthausen, "Nochmals die ae. Rätsel"), "beech" (Trautmann, "Die Auflösungen der altenglischen Rätsel"), "book" (Wy), "beechwood shield" (Tr), "beechwood battering ram" (Trautmann, "Weiteres zu den altenglischen

Rätseln"), "yew (Yggdrasill)" (Schneider, "Zu vier altenglischen Rätseln"). See further Salvador-Bello, "Compilation of the Old English Riddles," 328–30; Davis, "*Agon* and *Gnomon*"; Stanley, "Exeter Book *Riddles*, II," 364; Dale, *Natural World*, 43.

The badly damaged ending of this poem has not prevented commentators from attempting to solve this riddle. The suggestion that the solution may turn on Old English *boc,* meaning both "book" and "beech-tree," as well as (less certainly on the evidence beyond this riddle) "beechnuts" (though compare below), is an intriguing one, made still more attractive by the similarly homonymic tree-based solutions *ac* and *æsc* for EXE 71 and 72. In both those cases a rune is involved, however, whereas the ᛒ-rune, while it does indeed signify a tree, generally stands for "birch" *(berc* or *beorc)* rather than "beech" *(boc)*. Both of the main suggested meanings for *boc* connect this riddle to the one that follows. It is notable that all five of the lines that survive whole contain double alliteration. There are three compounds in this riddle, of which two are unique in extant Old English verse: *feorh-bora* (88.2a) and *wynn-staþol* (E reads *wym staþol*; 88.3a).

88.1a For the *Ic wæs* opening formula, see the note at EXE 12.1a above. The phrase "boast of brown ones" *(brunra beot),* if the solution *boc* is accepted, presumably refers to pigs fed on beechnuts, just as is described in EXE 38.105–8a above *(Mara ic eom ond fættra þonne amæsted swin / bearg bellende, þe on boc-wuda, / won wrotende wynnum lifde / þæt he)*. It should also be noted, however, in the context of the generally accepted solution "inkhorn" for EXE 89, that if there is indeed a connection between the two riddles, that deer too have a passion for eating beechnuts, and may indeed be better described as "brown" or "red-brown" *(brun)* than pigs.

88.3a Supplying *weres* (not in the manuscript) and reading *wynn-staþol* (E reads *wym staþol*). The phrase "man's joy-foundation" *(weres wynn-staþol),* which at first glance seems to have the potential for double entendre, more likely refers to the secondary sense "book" of *boc,* given the phrases *þæs strangan staþol,* "and its strong foundation," and *Bec sindon breme . . . ge strangað ond staþeliað staðolfæstne geðoht,* "Books are famous . . . they strengthen and support steadfast thought," at EXE 45.5a and SOL 1.9a and 1.11 respectively, both in clearly bookish contexts.

88.4a Compare EXE 18.8a *(gold ofer geardas).* In the context of an allusion to books, compare EXE 24.13a *(CRISTES BOC,* "Gospel book": *gierede mec mid golde)* and EXE 65.14a *(CRISTES BOC,* "Gospel book": *golde gegierwed).*

88.5a In the context of the preferred solution, Tupper cites the use of the term *boc-scyld* in a will dated 938 (S1503), but another manuscript witness has the spelling *boh-scyld,* and so it is not clear whether "beech-shield," "curved shield," or "bow-shield" is at issue; *DOE* narrows the choice to "curved shield" and "archer's shield." Beech is a hard white wood, and was certainly used to make bows, although it is unclear whether Anglo-Saxons would have used it alongside yew for the purpose. The suggestion by Schneider that "yew" is the answer here ("Zu vier ae. Rätseln") must be balanced against the fact that the seeds of its berries are toxic (if *brunra beot* necessarily refers to consumption).

EXE 89

MANUSCRIPT: E, fol. 130r–v.

EARLIER EDITIONS AND TRANSLATIONS: GW 93; Tr 91; Tu 93; Wy 91; Ma 92; KD 93; Ba 56, 45–46; Ab 91, 46–47; WiR 89; WiF 89, 152; Wh 91, 222–24; PZ 89; CH 93, 83; Mu 92; WiC 89, 594 and 1170.

SOLUTION: *BLÆC-HORN* (ink-horn); see in particular Dietrich, "Würdigung, Lösung und Herstellung"; Swaen, "Anglo-Saxon Horn Riddles"; PZ; Göbel, *Studien zu den altenglischen Schriftwesenrätseln,* 486–537; Ni. Other suggested solutions include: "antler or horn" (Wy). See further Stanley, "Heroic Aspects of the Exeter Book Riddles"; Lendinara, "Aspetti della società germanica"; Salvador-Bello, "Compilation of the Old English Riddles," 330–32; Teele, "Heroic Tradition," 106–9; Bitterli, *Say What I Am Called,*

157–63; Murphy, *Unriddling the Exeter Riddles,* 69–70; Riddler and Trzaska-Nartowski, "Chanting upon a Dunghill"; Salvador-Bello, *Isidorean Perceptions,* 422–32; Dale, *Natural World,* 43–45 and 48–50; Stanley, "Exeter Book *Riddles,* II," 364; Soper, "Count of Days," 110–12.

This riddle, like EXE 84, is generally solved "inkhorn," and indeed there are certain parallels to be drawn, more so than with the aenigma on the same topic by Eusebius (EUS 30, *ATRAMENTORIUM*). If the solutions *boc,* "beech," "book," for the previous riddle and "inkhorn" for this are accepted, the past and present lives of the current creature as a beechnuts-eating animal and object crucial for book production make a pleasing pair. There are eight compounds in this riddle, of which four are unique in extant Old English verse: *stan-wong* (89.12b), *hrimig-heard* (89.13a), *gleaw-stol* (89.15a), and *stið-ecg* (89.20a).

89.2a Compare EXE 87.11b *(willum sinum).*

89.4b The fact that the line requires alliteration on *h-* and the evident fivefold anaphora on *hwilum* in 89.5–10 encourages the emendation.

89.5a Supplying *scearpne* (E is damaged, and only *-rpne* is visible).

89.8a Compare EXE 1.22a *(on stealc hleoþa)* and 1.56a *(stealc stan-hleoþu).*

89.11b For the phrase *duguþe secan,* meaning both "to seek a group of tried and trusted warriors" and "seeking gain," see Wi.

89.14a Reading *feaxe,* after Gr (E reads *feax*).

89.14b Reading *on,* after Gr (E reads *of*).

89.15b–16b Compare 84.16b–17a *(eard oðþringan / gingran broþor).*

89.15b Reading *gingra,* after Gr (E reads *gingran*).

89.16b Compare EXE 71.5b *(wegedon mec of earde)* and 79.8a *(eall of earde).* For the compound *gleaw-stol,* unique to this riddle, both "seat of joy" and "seat of wisdom" are suggested as translations by *DOE.*

89.24a E is damaged, but the word *me* seems to appear before *bord.* It is hard to construe the sentence with *me* included, however, and so it is omitted here.

89.24b For the phrase *blace swelge,* compare EXE 24.9b *(CRISTES BOC,* "Gospel book": *beam-telge swelge).* See too the final lines of EUS 30.3–4 (*DE ATRAMENTORIO,* "about an inkhorn": *vas tamen intus habens sum nunc intestina amara / viscera sed ructans bonus ibit nitor odoris,* "But now, a vessel, I have inside me bitter gall as my innards, / but when I belch, a fine brilliance of scent will be sent forth."

89.25b Reading *wombe* (E is damaged).

89.28b The same notion of the pen plundering the inkhorn is found in the parallel EXE 84.29–30a (*BLÆC-HORN,* "inkhorn": *Nu mec unsceafta innan slitað / wyrdaþ mec be wombe,* "Now monstrous creatures tear at my insides, / injure me in the belly"). Compare too EXE 91.5a (*BOC,* "book": *hiþendra hyht*).

89.30a Compare EXE 1.78a *(wætan of wombe).* Several of the riddles focus on the "belly" *(womb)* of the creature in question; compare the note at EXE 1.78a above.

89.35a It is tempting to read the fragmentary *ond spe* . . . in the light of EXE 24.7b–8 *(CRISTES BOC,* "Gospel book": *ond mec fugles wyn / geondsprengde sped-dropum spyrede geneahhe).*

EXE 90

MANUSCRIPT: E, fol. 130v.

EARLIER EDITIONS AND TRANSLATIONS: GW 94; Tr 92; Tu 94; Wy 92; Ma 93; KD 94; Ba 91, 63; WiR 90; WiF 90, 153; Wh 92, 224; PZ 90; Mu 93; WiC 90, 594 and 1170.

SOLUTION: *GESCEAFT* (creation); see in particular Tu; Ni. Other suggested solutions include: "nature" (Ma). See further Salvador-Bello, "Compilation of the Old English Riddles," 333–34; Salvador-Bello, *Isidorean Perceptions,* 422–32.

Even in its badly damaged state, the fact that the six presumed lines of this riddle seem to contain six comparative adjectives has led most commentators to draw parallels with EXE 38 and EXE 64, both of which are generally solved as "creation." There are no compounds in this riddle.

90.2a Compare EXE 38.38a *(Hyrre ic eom heofene).*

90.4b Compare EXE 38.79b *(style heardan).*

90.6b It is tempting to supply *wyrm* on the model of EXE 38.76 *(leohtre ic eom micle þonne þes lytla wyrm).*

EXE 91

MANUSCRIPT: E, fol. 130v.

EARLIER EDITIONS AND TRANSLATIONS: Gr 89; GW 95; Tr 93; Tu 94; Wy 93; Ma 94; KD 95; Ba 67, 52; Ab 93, 47; WiR 91; WiF 91, 154; Wh 93, 224; PZ 91; CH 95, 84; Mu 94; WiC 91, 595 and 1170.

SOLUTION: *BOC* (book); see in particular Göbel, *Studien zu den altenglischen Schriftwesenrätseln,* 538–606; Murphy, *Unriddling the Exeter Riddles,* 41–42 and 86–91. Other suggested solutions include: "word of God" (Morley, *English Writers*), "thought" (Holthausen, "Zu den altenglischen Rätseln"), "wandering singer" (Dietrich, "Würdigung, Lösung und Herstellung"; Nuck, "Zu Trautmanns Deutung des ersten und neunundachtzigsten Rätsels"), "riddle" (Trautmann, "Cynewulf und die Rätsel"; Wülker, "Die Bedeutung einer neuen Entdeckung"), "moon" (Tupper, "Solutions of the Exeter Book Riddles"), "soul, spirit" (Tr), "quill pen" (Erhardt-Siebold, "Old English Riddle No. 95"; Wh), *halig gewrit,* "holy text" (Göbel, *Studien zu den altenglischen Schriftwesenrätseln,* 538–606), "prostitute" (Kiernan, "*Cwene:* The Old Profession of Exeter Riddle 95"), "book with gilding" (Wi), "riddle book" (PZ), "holy scriptures" (Korhammer, "Last of the Exeter Book Riddles"), *mona,* "moon" (Ni). See further Stanley, "Heroic Aspects of the Exeter Book Riddles"; Salvador-Bello, "Compilation of the Old English Riddles," 334–37; Davis, "*Agon* and *Gnomon*"; Taylor, "Enigma Variations," 94–105; Salvador-Bello, *Isidorean Perceptions,* 433–36; Dale, *Natural World,* 42 and 48.

The precise interpretation of this riddle is problematic, as the multiplicity and range of suggested solutions both make clear. The method employed by several commentators, namely looking for parallels with other riddles whose solutions are generally accepted, seems a plausible one, but alas leads to conflicting results. Tupper pointed out some perceived parallels with EXE 29 (*MONA OND SUNNE,* "moon and sun"), leading him to suggest "sun," while Erhardt-Siebold connected the notion of plundering in EXE 91.5 with a similar notion in EXE 84.29–30 (*BLÆC-HORN,* "inkhorn") and EXE 89.28 (*BLÆC-HORN,* "inkhorn"), so suggesting "pen," "quill." Williamson also notes these connections with the whole writing process, adding further perceived parallels with EXE 24.13 (*CRISTES BOC,* "Gospel book") and EXE 65.14 (*CRISTES BOC,* "Gospel book"), as well as with EUS 7 (*DE LITTERA,* "about letters") and EUS 32 (*DE MEMBRANO,* "about parchment"), so concluding that the proper solution should be "book." There are only two compounds in this riddle.

91.1a The *Ic eom* opening formula is found in various forms; see the note at 3.1 above.

91.3a Compare *Beowulf* 55a; *Men* 54a; *GuthB* 820a (*folcum gefræge).*

91.4a Following Korhammer, "Last of the Exeter Book Riddles," 73, I interpret the half-line *me fremdes ær* as a riddle within a riddle, and so translate as "me, who was formerly a stranger's."

91.5a For the phrase "pleasure of plunderers" *(hiþendra hyht),* which looks like another riddle within a riddle, compare EXE 27.4 *(huþe to þam ham of þam here-siþe).* On such riddles within riddles, see the note at EXE 1.12–14a above. The idea of a pen plundering ink is also found in EXE 89.28 *(BLÆC-HORN,* "inkhorn": *Nu min hord warað hiþende feond)* and 84.29–30a *(BLÆC-HORN,* "inkhorn": *Nu mec unsceafta innan slitað / wyrdaþ mec be wombe).*

91.6b Reading *beorhte* (E reads *beorhtne*). Commentators are split as to whether to read *beorhtne gŏd,* "bright god," as in the manuscript, or emend to *beorhte gōd,* "bright wealth"; here, I prefer the latter.

91.8b–10a For the idea of an object that imparts wisdom without speaking, see the note at EXE 46.2a above.

91.9b Reading *sprecan,* after Wi (E reads *sprecað*). Compare EXE 16.1b *(ne mæg word sprecan).*

91.10a See the note at EXE 33.11b above.

91.10b The phrase *ælda bearn* is a commonplace; compare EXE 80.32a *(ond ælda bearn).*

91.13 Compare EXE 79.12 *(ac ic miþan sceal monna gehwylcum).*

THE OLD ENGLISH RUNE POEM

Authorship and Date

The circumstances surrounding the survival of the sole manuscript witness to OER make any pronouncements about the likely antiquity of the text particularly precarious; compare the headnote to OIR, which offers similar difficulties. Linguistic evidence suggests a tenth-century date for the poem as a whole, although the material may well be older: the earliest English list of rune names has been dated to the late eighth or early ninth century. What is clear is that OER is not only the earliest of the three rune poems (the others being OIR and ONR, which is given in the notes to OIR), but also the longest, with twenty-nine stanzas, as opposed to the sixteen each in the other two. OER uses a specifically Anglo-Saxon reworking of the so-called older *futhark* of twenty-four runes found in earlier continental and Scandinavian inscriptions; this Anglo-Saxon development toward the *futhorc* reflected in the poem took place over the course of the seventh and eighth centuries, and shows direct influence from innovations in manuscript-writing of the Roman alphabet (see especially Parsons, *Recasting the Runes*). Particular changes to rune-names and rune-meanings reflect divergences and developments within the various languages, and are discussed in detail in the notes below.

Manuscript Context

The original manuscript of OER (London, British Library, Cotton Otho B. 10) was destroyed in the fire of 1731, and the text that we have derives instead from the transcription by Humfrey Wanley which is printed in Hi, 135; the text in Hi combines material from another manuscript, Cotton Domitian A. 9, though it is unclear at what stage this conflation occurred.

Subject Matter and Solutions

Each rune has a name, which supplies the solution; many (but by no means all) of the names are shared with other runic alphabets from other Germanic languages, as comparison with OIR and other Scandinavian sources confirms. Further corroboration comes from an extraordinary list of supposedly "Gothic" letter-names in Vienna, Österreichische Nationalbibliothek 795, fol. 20v, which may suggest considerable antiquity and a shared Germanic heritage for the common names. It has recently been suggested that the Vienna manuscript was compiled by Candidus, a student of Alcuin's (Diesenberger and Wolfram, "Arn und Alkuin 790 bis 804," 102–3); at all events, the "Gothic" given there looks more like Old High German reflexes of what are reckoned to be Gothic forms (see further Zironi, "Reading and Writing Gothic in the Carolingian Age," at 109–10). Here, following Ha and especially Page, *Introduction to Old English Runes,* 73–85, I give the relevant Norse and "Gothic" forms, and focus in particular on disparities between the texts.

Style

Like the other runic and alphabetical poems considered here, namely ALF, OIR, and ONR (given in the notes to OIR), OER is highly repetitive and formulaic, with such a structure presumably a deliberately designed mnemonic aid.

Sources and Parallels

The general form of the text strikingly resembles that of ALF, since although unlike the regular length of individual three-line stanzas there, here they vary from two long lines to five; eighteen of the twenty-nine come in at three long lines. Close comparisons can likewise be made with the texts of both OIR and ONR, as the notes below demonstrate.

This Text and Translation

Here I have principally relied on Di for establishing the text, though I have also consulted closely Page, *Introduction to Old English Runes,* which is to be preferred over Ha.

Further Reading

Halsall, *The Old English Rune Poem;* Ross, "Anglo-Saxon and Norse *Rune Poems*"; Page, *Introduction to Old English Runes,* 73–85; Page, "Icelandic Rune Poem"; Parsons, *Recasting the Runes;* Findell, *Runes.*

OER 1

PREVIOUS EDITIONS AND TRANSLATIONS: Hi, 135; Di, 12–13; Ha, 86–87 and 96–103.

SOLUTION: *FEOH* (wealth). Compare OIR 1, OIR 1 (*FÉ,* "wealth"), "Gothic" *fe.*

The primary meaning "livestock, cattle" was extended early on to signify any kind of moveable wealth, and hence ultimately "money" (the same semantic trajectory is found in the movement from Latin *pecus,* "cattle," to *pecunia,* "money"). The link to the subject matter of the next stanza seems clear.

1.3 The phrase *for drihtne,* "in the presence of his lord," is ambiguous, since it might refer either to a secular lord or the Christian Lord.

OER 2

PREVIOUS EDITIONS AND TRANSLATIONS: Hi, 135; Di, 12–13; Ha, 86–87 and 104–7.

SOLUTION: *UR* (aurochs). Compare OIR 2, ONR 2 (*ÚR,* "shower"), "Gothic" *uraz.*

The difference in sense strongly suggests that OIR has updated an obsolete solution; the fact that OER has not is equally interesting in suggesting its traditional and perhaps ancient nature. The aurochs *(Bos primigenius)* was an enormous wild ox, native to Europe, Asia, and North Africa, standing as much as six feet high at the shoulder and with impressive and massive horns. In Europe the aurochs only became extinct in the seventeenth century, but in Britain it died out in the Bronze Age, so its survival here presumably reflects continuity from the continental tradition. Compare Caesar, *De bello Gallico,* 6.28, describing the different kinds of wild beast he has encountered, beginning with stags and elks:

> Tertium est genus eorum qui uri appellantur. Hi sunt magnitudine paulo infra elephantos, specie et colore et figura tauri. Magna vis eorum est et magna velocitas, neque homini neque ferae quam conspexerunt parcunt. Hos studiose foveis captos interficiunt. Hoc se labore durant adulescentes atque hoc genere venationis exercent, et qui plurimos ex his interfecerunt, relatis in publicum cornibus, quae sint testimonio, magnam ferunt laudem. Sed adsuescere ad homines et mansuefieri ne parvuli quidem excepti possunt. Amplitudo cornuum et figura et species multum a nostrorum boum cornibus differt. Haec studiose conquisita ab labris argento circumcludunt atque in amplissimis epulis pro poculis utuntur.

> There is a third kind, of those animals that are called *uri*. These are in size a little smaller than an elephant, with the appearance, color, and shape of a bull. They have strength and speed, and spare neither man nor wild beast, once they have spotted them. [The Germanic people] carefully capture them in pits and kill them. The young men harden themselves, and exercise themselves in this kind of hunting, and those who have slain the greatest number of them, after producing the horns in public as evidence, receive mighty praise. But even those that are captured very young cannot be made used to humans and tamed. The size, shape, and appearance of their horns are

very different from the horns of our oxen. These are carefully sought after, and they bind them at the lips with silver, and use them instead of goblets at their most lavish banquets.

2.3 The generally martial and heroic apects of this stanza are condensed here, with the phrase *mære mor-stapa* recalling the description of Grendel and his mother at *Beowulf* 103 and 1348 *(mære mearc-stapa se þe moras heold; micle mearc-stapan moras healdan)*; the second half-line here *(þæt is modig wuht)* likewise recalls the common formula repeated in *Beowulf* 11a, 863b, and 2390b *(þæt wæs god cyning)*.

OER 3

PREVIOUS EDITIONS AND TRANSLATIONS: Hi, 135; Di, 12–13; Ha, 86–87 and 107–9.

SOLUTION: *ÞORN* (thorn). Compare OIR 3, ONR 3 (*ÞURS*, "giant"), "Gothic" *thyth* (perhaps a form of Gothic *þiud*, "people").

As with the last stanza, the differences in sense between OER and OIR are striking: either OER has made mundane a figure of myth, or OIR has preserved or perhaps reinvented an ancient pagan tradition.

OER 4

PREVIOUS EDITIONS AND TRANSLATIONS: Hi, 135; Di, 12–13; Ha, 86–87 and 109–11.

SOLUTION: *OS* (god or mouth). Compare OIR 4 (*ÓSS*, "god"), ONR 4 (*ÓSS*, "river-mouth").

The ambiguity of the solution here is intriguing: either the poet is acknowledging the idea that letters (or in this case runes) and poetry are within the purview of the god Woden (figured elsewhere as Mercury, the inventor of letters), or a gesture towards the Latin word *os*, "mouth." The solution in ONR seems to reflect a conscious effort to sanitize an originally pagan text, through the deployment of an innocuous homograph. Germanic **ansuz,* "god" (compare Old Norse *áss,* plural *æsir)* developed naturally to Old English *ōs,* and the sound change seems to have necessitated some reevaluation or updating of the original solution.

ᚱ OER 5 ᚱ

PREVIOUS EDITIONS AND TRANSLATIONS: Hi, 135; Di, 14–15; Ha, 86–87 and 111–13.

SOLUTION: *RAD* (riding). Compare OIR 5, ONR 5 (*REIÐ*), "Gothic" *reda.*

5.3 The compound *mil-paþas* is found in Old English poetry only here and at *Exodus* 171a *(mæton mil-paðas)* and *Elene* 1262a *(mil-paðas mæt);* both times, intriguingly, in the context of racing horses: some connection between the texts seems likely.

ᚳ OER 6 ᚳ

PREVIOUS EDITIONS AND TRANSLATIONS: Hi, 135; Di, 14–15; Ha, 86–87 and 113–14.

SOLUTION: *CEN* (torch). Compare OIR 6, ONR 6 (*KAUN,* "ulcer"), "Gothic" *chozma.*

The diversity of solutions across the poems makes determining the order and development of the rune-names problematic. The sense "torch" is evident in at least three of the four runic signatures of Cynewulf (*ChristB* 797a, *Elene* 1257b, *Fates* 103a; the exception is *Jul* 704a, where a different strategy is evidently being employed), but the distribution of the rune in general seems extremely limited.

ᚷ OER 7 ᚷ

PREVIOUS EDITIONS AND TRANSLATIONS: Hi, 135; Di, 14–15; Ha, 86–87 and 115–16.

SOLUTION: *GYFU* (gift). There is no parallel in OIR or ONR; compare "Gothic" *geuua.*

ᚹ OER 8 ᚹ

PREVIOUS EDITIONS AND TRANSLATIONS: Hi, 135; Di, 12–13; Ha, 86–87 and 116–19.
SOLUTION: *WYNN* (joy) or *WEN* (hope). Compare "Gothic" *uuinne.*

8.1 The addition of *-ne* after the rune (if *WYNN* is understood) is to provide the usual genitive inflection after *brucan,* as at OER 23 and 28. If *WEN* is understood, it can stand without further addition, since there are examples where *brucan* takes the accusative. See further Stanley, "Notes," 453–54.

ᚻ OER 9 ᚻ

PREVIOUS EDITIONS AND TRANSLATIONS: Hi, 135; Di, 14–15; Ha, 88–89 and 119–20.
SOLUTION: *HÆGL* (hail). Compare OIR 7, ONR 7 (*HAGALL*), "Gothic" *haal.*

9.1a The connection between hail and corn is echoed in OIR 7.1a *(kaldakorn)* and ONR 7.1a *(kaldastr korna),* and seems traditional: compare *Seafarer* 32b–33a *(hægl feol on eorþan, / corna caldast).*

ᚾ OER 10 ᚾ

PREVIOUS EDITIONS AND TRANSLATIONS: Hi, 135; Di, 14–15; Ha, 88–89 and 121–22.
SOLUTION: *NYD* (need, oppression, conflict). Compare OIR 8, ONR 8 (*NAUÐR,* "constraint"), "Gothic" *noicz.*

The range of possible solutions across the languages is broad but interconnected; the basic themes remain the same.

OER 11

PREVIOUS EDITIONS AND TRANSLATIONS: Hi, 135; Di, 14–15; Ha, 88–89 and 122–24.
SOLUTION: *IS* (ice). Compare OIR 9 *(ÍSS),* "Gothic" *iiz.*

For a putative connection with EXE, see the headnote to EXE 31 (*IS,* "ice, ice floe") above.

OER 12

PREVIOUS EDITIONS AND TRANSLATIONS: Hi, 135; Di, 16–17; Ha, 88–89 and 124–26.
SOLUTION: *GER* (year, specifically the start of the growing season). Compare OIR 10 *(ÁR),* "Gothic" *gaar.*

The manuscript form is ᛄ, while the equivalent epigraphical form is ᛡ; such variants are relatively uncommon, and Page, *English Runes,* 42–43, considers this a "pseudo-rune."

OER 13

PREVIOUS EDITIONS AND TRANSLATIONS: Hi, 135; Di, 16–17; Ha, 88–89 and 126–28.
SOLUTION: *EOH* (yew). Compare "Gothic" *ih.*

OER 14

PREVIOUS EDITIONS AND TRANSLATIONS: Hi, 135; Di, 16–17; Ha, 88–89 and 128–29.
SOLUTION: *PEORÐ* (gaming piece). Compare "Gothic" *pertra.*

14.2 Something is obviously missing in the transcription after *wlancum,* and there have been a number of suggestions, including *will-gesiðum,* "willing companions," *werum,* "men," *on win-gedrince,* "in wine-drinking," *on middum,* "in the midst of," *and wisum,* "and the wise." Here, I prefer *æt wine,* "at wine," on the model of *Daniel* 695a *(Sæton him æt wine),* as well as EXE 12.17a *(wlonce to wine),* 40.16a *(werum æt wine),* and 44.1a *(Wer sæt æt wine).*

ᚴ OER 15 ᚴ

PREVIOUS EDITIONS AND TRANSLATIONS: Hi, 135; Di, 16–17; Ha, 88–89 and 129–33.
SOLUTION: *EOLH-SECG* (elk-sedge).

For a putative connection with EXE, see the headnote to EXE 69 (*SECG,* "sword," "man") above, with which this stanza shares many similarities. The plant sedge grows best in wetlands, and the whole stanza plays on the fact that the Old English form *secg* can be used not only for the plant, but for the term for a "man" or "warrior," as well as a word for "sword" that is only found in verse.

ᚴ OER 16 ᚴ

PREVIOUS EDITIONS AND TRANSLATIONS: Hi, 135; Di, 16–17; Ha, 88–89 and 133–35.
SOLUTION: *SIGEL* (sun). Compare OIR 11 *(SÓL);* "Gothic" *sugil.*

16.2 The kenning *fisces beþ* is found in Old English poetry only here and at *Andreas* 293b; similar formulations are found elsewhere, notably *fisces eþel,* "fish's homeland" (*Judgement Day 1* 39b) and *ganotes bæþ,* "gannet's bath," which also appears at OER 25.3: see the note there.

16.3 The kenning *brim-hengest* is found in Old English poetry only here, at OER 21.4, and *Andreas* 513b.

OER 17

PREVIOUS EDITIONS AND TRANSLATIONS: Hi, 135; Di, 18–19; Ha, 90–91 and 135–37.

SOLUTION: *TIR* (Mars, Tiw, glory, honor). Compare OIR 12 *(TÝR),* "Gothic" *tyz.*

The sense here seems to be of some kind of star, and the cognates suggest that the original name was that of the Germanic god Tiw (**teiuaz*), a form of whose name is found in the earliest Corpus, Épinal, and Erfurt glosses for the Roman god of war *(mars martis tiig),* and it may be that the planet Mars is the star in question. The poetic noun *tir* signifies "glory" or "honor."

OER 18

PREVIOUS EDITIONS AND TRANSLATIONS: Hi, 135; Di, 18–19; Ha, 90–91 and 137–39.

SOLUTION: *BEORC* (birch, poplar). Compare OIR 13 *(BJARKAN),* "Gothic" *bercna.*

Although the cognate modern English word is "birch," the fact that the creature in question "bears twigs without seeds" and is of extraordinary height seems better to fit the poplar, specifically the gray poplar *(Populus canescens)* native to England and Western Europe.

18.4a Compare *Elene* 1227a *(geloden under leafum).*

OER 19

PREVIOUS EDITIONS AND TRANSLATIONS: Hi, 135; Di, 18–19; Ha, 90–91 and 139–41.

SOLUTION: *EH* (horse). Compare "Gothic" *eyz.*

The West Saxon equivalent is *eoh,* but the rune-name is routinely spelt *eh,* presumably through a form of Anglian smoothing.

OER 20

PREVIOUS EDITIONS AND TRANSLATIONS: Hi, 135; Di, 18–19; Ha, 90–91 and 141–43.

SOLUTION: *MANN* (man). Compare OIR 14 *(MAÐR),* "Gothic" *manna.*

OER 21

PREVIOUS EDITIONS AND TRANSLATIONS: Hi, 135; Di, 18–19; Ha, 90–91 and 143–45.

SOLUTION: *LAGU* (liquid). Compare OIR 15 *(LÖGR),* "Gothic" *laaz.*

21.4 On the kenning *brim-hengest* see the note at 16.3 above.

OER 22

PREVIOUS EDITIONS AND TRANSLATIONS: Hi, 135; Di, 20–21; Ha, 90–91 and 146–48.

SOLUTION: *ING* (Ing). Compare OIR 16 (*ÝR,* "yew"), "Gothic" *enguz.*

22.1b The specific reference to the East Danes has been taken to refer to the island of Zeeland, or the rising of the sun in the East.

22.4 Compare the use of the word *heardingas* in the sense "warriors" in *Elene* 25b and 130b.

OER 23

PREVIOUS EDITIONS AND TRANSLATIONS: Hi, 135; Di, 20–21; Ha, 90–91 and 148–50.

SOLUTION: *EÞEL* (homeland). Compare "Gothic" *utal.*

Note that the rune ᛟ appears in place of the word *eðel* three times in *Beowulf* (at 520b, 913a, and 1702a) and once in *Waldere* (at 31a).

OER 24

PREVIOUS EDITIONS AND TRANSLATIONS: Hi, 135; Di, 20–21; Ha, 92–93 and 150–52.
SOLUTION: *DÆG* (day). Compare "Gothic" *daaz.*

OER 25

PREVIOUS EDITIONS AND TRANSLATIONS: Hi, 135; Di, 20–21; Ha, 92–93 and 152–54.
SOLUTION: *AC* (oak).

This stanza, like the next (and less securely OER 27 and 28), has been linked to the sequence EXE 71–73 and 76; see the relevant headnotes above.

25.2a The phrase *flæsces fodor* refers to the feeding of acorns to pigs to fatten them up for meat.
25.3a The phrase *ofer ganotes bæþ* is also found at *Beowulf* 1861b, *Death of Edgar* 24a, and (as *ganetes beð*) in the *Anglo-Saxon Chronicle* D975 2a. A parallel kenning, *fisces beþ,* is found at OER 16.2; see the note there.

OER 26

PREVIOUS EDITIONS AND TRANSLATIONS: Hi, 135; Di, 22–23; Ha, 92–93 and 154–55.
SOLUTION: *ÆSC* (ash). Compare "Gothic" *aza.*

For a putative connection with EXE 71–73, see the headnote to the preceding stanza.

OER 27

PREVIOUS EDITIONS AND TRANSLATIONS: Hi, 135; Di, 22–23; Ha, 92–93 and 155–57.
SOLUTION: *YR* (horn, bow).

This stanza has several parallels with the "ox" riddles found widely elsewhere in the tradition: see especially the headnotes to EXE 12 and EXE 76 (both *HORN,* "horn"), as well as OER 2 above.

OER 28

PREVIOUS EDITIONS AND TRANSLATIONS: Hi, 135; Di, 22–23; Ha, 92–93 and 157–60.
SOLUTION: *IOR* (beaver?).

For a possible connection with EXE, see the headnotes at EXE 73 and OER 25 above.

OER 29

PREVIOUS EDITIONS AND TRANSLATIONS: Hi, 135; Di, 22–23; Ha, 92–93 and 160–63.
SOLUTION: *EAR* (grave).

The Old English word *ear* only appears in runic contexts, and the closest cognate seems to be the Old Norse word *aurr,* "clay," hence the interpretation as "grave"; compare SYM 100 (*MONUMENTUM,* "tombstone"), which concludes that collection, as well as EUS 60, again the final poem, which celebrates a sepulchral bird (*BUBO,* "horned owl").

THE RIDDLES OF SOLOMON AND SATURN II

Date and Authorship

The two riddles that comprise SOL are embedded within a much longer poem, *Solomon and Saturn II,* which is itself just one of several Old English texts in both prose and verse depicting a wisdom-contest between the biblical King Solomon, representing in this context the cream of the Judeo-Christian tradition, and the ancient pagan (which here is to say classical) lore personified by the figure of Saturn. The context and the language of the riddles themselves have close parallels to those of the Old Norse GES, where the embedded riddles form part of a wisdom-contest between the hapless King Heiðrekr and the pagan god Óðinn, disguised as the wanderer Gestumblindi. The scribal hand in the sole manuscript of SOL has been dated to the mid-tenth century, with a more precise focus on the 930s also suggested, and the general cultural background has been thoroughly addressed in the broader edition of An, who favors composition in the circle surrounding Dunstan at Glastonbury (where he was abbot 940–57, before becoming Archbishop of Canterbury 960–78). Such a link to a noted church figure ties SOL back to other collections in the Anglo-Saxon riddle tradition such as ALD, BED, TAT, EUS, BON, and ALC in Latin, all of which come from the earlier period, as well as in the later period to OEP in Old English.

Manuscript Context

The sole manuscript witness, C^1, contains on 1–26 various texts in both prose and verse relating to the Old English Solomon and Saturn materials, of which *Solomon and Saturn II* (and within that, SOL) play only a very small part. The other texts are edited by An as *Solomon and Saturn I, Solomon and Saturn Prose Pater Noster Dialogue,* and *Solomon and Saturn Poetic Fragment,* and several aspects of the relevant texts here have been shown to have Irish connections (see further Wright, *Irish Tradition,* especially 233–48 and 255–61). The relationships and relative chronology of these texts are a complex issue, discussed in detail by An, 41–49.

Subject Matter and Solutions

The two solutions are given explicitly in each case as the first word of Solomon's response: *BEC* (books) and *YLDO* (old age). There is some irony in the fact that the famously ancient pagan Saturn, a representative of the old order, should pose riddles that are so focused on the one hand on the tools of Judeo-Christian exegesis and learning, and on the other on the aging process that will see both his words and Solomon's refigured in a Christian context. The fact that the second of these riddles should also closely reflect aspects of one of the earliest of the sequence of Anglo-Latin aenigmata, namely ALD 2 (*VENTUS*, "wind"), lends further heft to the idea that the tradition was self-reflexive (see further Hill, "Saturn's Time Riddle").

Style

The riddles are fully integrated within *Solomon and Saturn II*, and are in general indistinguishable in style from the surrounding material, although like others within the Anglo-Saxon riddle tradition, their focused use of compounds is of particular interest. SOL 1 includes two compounds (*win-rod* and *ðrea-medlan*) otherwise unattested, and of interest in other ways, while SOL 2 employs not only another such unique compound (*wop-dropan*), but also and in sequence three rare or unique compounds (*grund-buendra, lyft-fleogendra, lagu-swemmendra*) to highlight the earth/sky/sea triad that is elsewhere such a feature of the tradition; see further the headnote to EXE 1.

Sources and Parallels

Both of the riddles given here seem very knowing in their form and function, and have many parallels in sense or style or solution with others within the tradition, notably EXE 24, 88, and 91 (*BOC*, "beech" or "book") on the one hand, and BED 16 and ps-BED 4 (*AETAS HOMINIS*, "the age of man"), ALD 2 (*VENTUS*, "wind") on the other. A particularly pertinent parallel is with GES, with which SOL shares several verbal parallels, and which also gives the solutions explicitly, and in the framing context of a wisdom contest; SOL is the best example of a genre better attested in Old Norse.

This Text and Translation

Here I have in general followed An, with differences noted below, but have normalized manuscript punctuation and in particular capitalization of the introductory statements *SATVRNVS CVÆÐ* and *SALOMON CVÆÐ*, in part to match the other texts edited here.

Further Reading

Anlezark, *Old English Dialogues of Solomon and Saturn*; Hill, "Saturn's Time Riddle"; Wright, *Irish Tradition*.

SOL 1

MANUSCRIPT: C[1], 16.
EARLIER EDITIONS AND TRANSLATIONS: An, 80–83 (lines 52–64).
SOLUTION: *BEC* (books).

The solution and general treatment tie this riddle closely to others in the Anglo-Saxon riddle tradition that deal with the classroom and the scriptorium; see further the headnote to ALD 30 (*ELEMENTUM*, "alphabet"). Saturn responds to Solomon's answer by noting that *Bald bið se ðe onbyrgeð boca cræftes, / symle bið ðe wisra ðe hira geweald hafað*, "Bold is the one who tastes the power of books: he is always the wiser who has control of them" (*Solomon and Saturn II*, lines 65–66), an opinion that rather contradicts the sentiments of EXE 45, which resembles SOL 1 in other respects. In discussing SOL 1, An notes its "eschatological flavour," 121, and highlights some general biblical parallels.

1.1 The formula *Ac hwæt is se . . . se ðe* is matched in the opening line of SOL 2 *(Ac hwæt is ðæt wundor ðe)*, but also has a number of remarkably close parallels in Old Norse in the opening lines of GES 3–6, 8–16, 18–23, 25–26, 29, 31, and 35, as the notes there make clear.

1.6 The phrase *gesiehst Hierusalem* masks the usual etymology of Jerusalem, here likely the New Jerusalem of Revelation *(visio pacis)*, as An argues.

1.7 The unique compound *win-rod* is often emended, and An argues for its meaning "chorus" here, while I prefer the more usual sense "cross," "rood"; for the second element, varied as it is by "banner of the righteous" in the following half-line, consider the first element an ambiguous form, signifying either the "joy" of the cross *(wyn)* or its element of trial or contention *(win)*.

1.8 For the formula *Saga hwæt ic mæne*, see the headnote to EXE on the parallel *Saga hwæt ic hatte;* the distinction between simple naming in most of the relevant riddles in EXE (the exception is

EXE 59.9b *Ræd hwæt ic mæne*) and meaning here seems to point to a conscious development within the tradition.

1.10 Here I follow An, and most previous editors, in reading *willan* (C[1] has *wilian*).

SOL 2

MANUSCRIPT: C[1], 17–18.
EARLIER EDITIONS AND TRANSLATIONS: An, 84–85 (lines 104–23).
SOLUTION: *YLDO* (old age). See further Hill, "Saturn's Time Riddle."

Although the solution is given explicitly, this riddle also has much in common with ALD 2 and especially its prose reflex in ps-BED 5, where the solution is generally accepted as *VENTUS* (wind). See further Lockhart, "Everyday Wonders and Enigmatic Structures," 105–8; Ooi, "Speaking Objects," 58–59; Soper, "Count of Days," 193–97.

2.1 For the formula, see the note on SOL 1.1 above.
2.7a Reading *micles ond mætes* (C[1] omits *ond*).
2.16a Reading *standendne* (C[1] has *stan dene*).

THE OLD ENGLISH PROSE RIDDLE

Date and Authorship

This is one of a number of incest riddles, of which the best known in Old English is EXE 44 (*LOTH OND BEARN,* "Lot and his children"), and the solution suggested by Förster ("Die Lösung des Prosarätsels") here, namely *EVA* (Eve), gives this prose riddle an equally Old Testament theme. This composite text appears on fol. 16v of manuscript C, introduced by a coded phrase using the same vowel-substitution cipher as in EXE 34 (*BAT,* "boat") above, and in several of the solutions to the Latin aenigmata, notably XMS Z1–5. OEP is immediately followed by a series of explanations and exercises employing various versions of the cipher, including phrases from the Psalms and the Pater Noster, all appropriately encoded; the page ends with a final cryptic line that, even when deciphered according to the principles laid out there, still gives the puzzling *Æluunfei euumart. deræ cðeðunnuun.* This line has been explained as a kind of anagram, and rearranged as *Ælfuuine me uurat. ræd nu ðu ðe cunne,* "Ælfwine wrote me: read me now, you who know how," identifying the writer as Abbot Ælfwine of Winchester, though whether as author of OEP or simply scribe is unclear; in either case an eleventh-century date is clear.

Manuscript Context

Manuscript C mainly contains an annotated Gallican Psalter, preceded by a series of shorter texts in both Latin and Old English, including a liturgical calendar, computus material, prognostics, charms, and veterinary recipes, along with OEP and its associated cryptographic material, which (assuming the solution is correct) sit well within the learned ecclesiastical setting.

Subject Matter and Solution

Förster ("Die Lösung des Prosarätsels") defends his suggested solution *EVA* (Eve) by making the pertinent point that, just as Adam can be figured as both a son of God and a son of Earth (as indeed the universal interpretation of his Hebrew name—Jerome gives the Latin equivalent *terra,* "earth"), so too Eve can be considered a daughter of both Adam and Earth (through his rib) and of God. On this reading, Adam and Eve are at once father and daughter, brother and sister, and husband and wife, and since Mary is effectively both the daughter of Eve and the mother of God, so too is Eve ultimately the mother of her father. Such an interpretation leaves the problem of how precisely to explain the two phrases *minre modor ceorl* and *min agen wif.* Eve's mother (via Adam) is Earth, and while *ceorl* can mean "husband," and that is the sense toward which the reader is being steered; it can also mean simply "man," "peasant," or "property holder," all senses where Earth's *ceorl* would be Adam. By the same logic, Eve's *agen wif* must signify Earth, who gave birth to Adam, so suggesting that the usual interpretation of the phrase as "wedded wife" is another piece of misdirection, and what is intended is an otherwise unattested compound *agen-wif,* meaning either "rightful lady-owner" or "serving woman," referring to Earth by this devious designation.

Style

The persistent stream of names for family relationships is a uniting theme of incest riddles and is generally intended, as here, to have a bewildering effect while the various permutations of the multiple designations are computed. As in EXE 44 and elsewhere, the simple style and plain words are effectively a smoke screen: at stake is the complexity of relationships implied, and how individuals might share multiple connections. There are no compounds in this riddle, unless the otherwise unattested *agen-wif* is accepted.

Sources and Parallels

For other riddles and aenigmata dealing with the theme of incest, see in general the material surrounding Apollonius of Tyre (on which see the headnote to SYM), SYM 48 (*MURRA,* "myrrh"), EXE 44 (*LOTH OND BEARN,* "Lot and his children"), and BER 56 (*SOL ET LUNA,* "sun and moon").

This Text and Translation

Here I have followed HoP closely, while also consulting the articles by Förster and Pulsiano listed below.

Further Reading

Förster, "Ein altenglisches Prosa-Rätsel"; Förster, "Die Lösung des Prosarätsels"; Pulsiano, "Abbot Ælfwine and the Date of the Vitellius Psalter."

Sources and Analogues of the Tradition

SYMPHOSIUS

Authorship and Date

The name Symphosius (or as Aldhelm has it, *Simfosius*) seems, on the model of the Greek *symposium,* to mean "[drinking-]party animal." Such an idea, which ties together the Latin and Greek traditions of *aenigmata* as drinking-party entertainments for the educated classes, makes the transition to the riddles of EXE, where drinking is frequently mentioned, seem seamless. More of a mystery is why the name is spelled *-ph-* (or, for Aldhelm, *-f-*) in the sources: there seems little reason to emend to the more etymologically correct *-p-,* though the notion that the aspirated form reflects drunken pronunciation is perhaps too cute. As to date, see Bergamin, *Aenigmata Symposii,* xiv–xvi, who favors the second half of the fifth century, based partly on an exhaustive (and occasionally overly imaginative) list of potential sources and other parallels on pages 205–44.

Manuscript Contexts

A large number of manuscripts contain all or part of SYM; in her edition, Be considers no fewer than thirty-one, many of them also containing other key collections in the Anglo-Saxon riddle tradition, as the table of manuscript sigla clearly demonstrates. The particular linkage between SYM and ALD in the manuscripts is of course especially significant in terms of the tradition as a whole, and is discussed above in the relevant section of the notes relating to ALD. Five of the aenigmata in SYM are also included in the so-called

Collectanea pseudo-Bedae, now preserved only in Herwagen's editio princeps of Bede of 1563, and likewise including five aenigmata from ALD: the aenigmata in question are SYM 1, 4, 7, 10, and 12; ALD 2–4, 9, and 90. In the case of two of these aenigmata (SYM 1 and 4), there are uniquely shared variants between the readings found in the *Collectanea* and in manuscript D, which contains SYM, ALD, and the Old English *Leiden Riddle,* so again underlining the integrity of the Anglo-Saxon riddle tradition. Likewise, Aldhelm includes thirteen citations from SYM (with some slight variants) in the two metrical treatises that sometimes circulated alongside his own ALD; the lines from SYM appear alongside others from such standard curriculum authors as Virgil, Sedulius, Lucan, and Prosper of Aquitaine, as follows: six in Aldhelm's *De metris* (SYM 17.2 [Eh, 95], 47.1 [Eh, 93], 72.1 [Eh, 95], 84.3 [Eh, 96], 91.3 [Eh, 96], and 98.2 [Eh, 94]), and seven in *De pedum regulis* (SYM 22.3 [Eh, 154], 24.3 [Eh, 167], 36.2 [Eh, 167], 52.2 [Eh, 197], 53.3 [Eh, 154], and 58.3 [twice: Eh, 154 and 160]). See further Lapidge, *Anglo-Saxon Library,* 187; Orchard, *Poetic Art,* 155–61.

Ten aenigmata by Symphosius are also found embedded in the extraordinary Latin romance *Historia Apollonii Regis Tyri* (The history of Apollonius, king of Tyre), chapters 42–44, as part of a battle of wits and wills between the shipwrecked Apollonius and his daughter Tarsia (see further Archibald, *Apollonius of Tyre,* 114–15). The aenigmata in question appear in the following order: SYM 12 (*FLUMEN ET PISCIS,* "river and fish"), 2 (*HARUNDO,* "reed"), 13 (*NAVIS,* "ship"), 90 (*BALNEUM,* "bathhouse"), 61 (*ANCORA,* "anchor"), 63 (*SPONGIA,* "sponge"), 59 (*PILA,* "ball"), 69 (*SPECULUM,* "mirror"), 79 (*ROTAE,* "wheels"), and 78 (*SCALAE,* "ladder"). It is notable that the solutions of these aenigmata fit more or less well into the wider narrative of shipwreck, recovery, and a trip to a bathhouse that involves gymnastics with a ball. Alas, this is the section of the text that is missing through physical damage in the Old English version found in Cambridge, Corpus Christi College 201, perhaps suggesting that someone made off with the relevant quire because they valued the riddles therein, although the surviving Old English text does contain a version of the earlier incest riddle, that of Antiochus

(*HA* 4; Archibald, *Apollonius of Tyre,* 114–15: *Scelere vehor, maternam carnem vescor, quaero fratrem meum, meae matris virum, uxoris meae filium: non invenio,* "I am carried off with wickedness; I feed upon my mother's flesh; I look for my brother, my mother's husband, the son of my wife: I do not find him"). OEP, contained in manuscript C, also deals with incest in a strikingly similar way, as does EXE 44 (*LOTH OND BEARN,* "Lot and his children").

Subject Matter and Solutions

The extent to which SYM sets the trend for the clustering of similar solutions in consecutive or proximate riddles cannot be stressed too highly. Notwithstanding the ongoing debate about the age and/or Christianity of the author (see in particular Se, 57–62), it seems unlikely in the extreme that an Anglo-Saxon reader of the collection would not have perceived both the clear clustering and progression of related topics as solutions, and then gone on to use similar associative techniques in formulating collections of his own (see in particular Le, 13–26, and Se, 179–81, who trace threads throughout the entire collection). Many sequences are evident in the course of the hundred aenigmata, such as (a) the weather- or water-based grouping of SYM 8 (*NEBULA,* "cloud"), 9 (*PLUVIA,* "rain"), 10 (*GLACIES,* "ice"), and 11 (*NIX,* "snow"), (b) the marine-based grouping of SYM 61 (*ANCORA,* "anchor"), 62 (*PONS,* "bridge"), 63 (*SPONGIA,* "sponge"), and 64 (*TRIDENS,* "trident"), (c) the light-based grouping of SYM 67 (*LANTERNA,* "lantern"), 68 (*VITREUM,* "windowpane"), and 69 (*SPECULUM,* "mirror"), and (d) the water-based grouping of SYM 70 (*CLEPSYDRA,* "water clock"), 71 (*PUTEUS,* "well"), and 72 (*TUBUS,* "pipe"). Other themes run through the collection: several aenigmata focus on a home or dwelling *(domus)* associated with the creature in question: SYM 4.2–3 (*CLAVIS,* "key"), 6.2 (*TEGULA,* "roof tile"), 12.1–3 (*FLUMEN ET PISCIS,* "river and fish"), 18.1 (*COCLEA,* "snail"), 25.1 (*MUS,* "mouse"), 29.1 (*ERICIUS,* "hedgehog"), and 89.3 (*STRIGILIS AENEA,* "bronze strigil"). There are also a significant number of classical references in the collection: the Muses are mentioned at SYM PR.17, 2.2, 16.3; the moon is called by her classical name, Cynthia, at 8.3; Pallas Athena at 17.1; Ceres at 24.3; the Consul

Publius Decius Mus at 25.3; Mars at 26.2; the *Manes* at 31.3; Jupiter at 35.1; Deucalion at 74.1; Prometheus at 81.1; Cato at 85.1. The collection contains other notably Mediterranean names and items: Taurus appears as both a constellation and a mountain in Cilicia at SYM 32, the River Tigris at 38.1, and ivory as an Eastern treasure in 49. There are also references to names in both Greek and Latin at SYM 42.1, and to Greek alone at 84.1. All of these would have seemed more or less exotic to Anglo-Saxon audiences, but ALD in particular appears most closely to emulate the classical focus, albeit with a much more explicitly Christian perspective.

Style

SYM overall exudes a polished elegance, albeit one based on closely patterned parallels and contrasts. In metrical terms, it is notable that elisions only take place with *est* (perhaps more properly to be seen as contractions: see Pezzini), and only in the following six places: SYM PR.16 *(necesse est)*, 53.2 *(propago est)*, 69.1 *(nulla est)*, 73.3 *(magna est)*, 85.3 *(nata est)*, 92.3 *(secuta est)*. Note that most occur in the second half of the collection, although otherwise there is little indication of the possibility of more than one author's being involved. In only one place is there lengthening at the caesura: SYM 58.2 *(versicolor)*. There are two examples of false or doubtful quantity, at SYM 16.3 *(profeci)* and 88.1 *(rubida)*, but in general the metre is as correct as one would hope for in a teaching text. Likewise, the language is relatively plain: in the 315 lines of SYM combined (allowing that the initial distich is a later interpolation) there are only thirteen complex adjectives of the type described in the introduction to *OEALRT*, under "Style": PR.8 *(verbosa)*, 13.1 *(formosae)*, 16.2 *(studiosior)*, 20.3 *(mortua)*, 26.2 *(cruenta)*, 33.1 *(bidentes)*, 33.2 *(sanguineas)*, 36.1 *(Setigerae)*, 58.2 *(versicolor)*, 60.2 *(frondicomam)*, 77.1 *(aequales)*; SYM 93.1 *(Bellipotens)*, 95.1 *(lucifluum)*. Many of these complex forms are commonplace, although the adjective *setiger* is comparatively rare, even if it is somewhat overrepresented in the aenigmata tradition, being found also at ALD 12.2, 17.2, 33.2, 36.5, 39.1, and 100.10; EUS 52.2. Such a distribution only highlights the propensity to such forms exhibited by, for example, ALD and (especially) BON.

Sources and Parallels

There is a lot of playfulness in many of the more or less clear Virgilian echoes, and one wonders how far Anglo-Saxon authors perceived the same striking juxtapositions (if we can assume that they did, given that Virgil seems to have been well known in early Anglo-Saxon England, at least). On the one hand, the verbal connection of SYM 13.2 *(NAVIS,* "ship": *Innumeris pariter comitum stipata catervis)* with Virgil, *Aeneid* 1.497 *(Incessit magna iuvenum comitata catervis),* where Dido is introduced, seems to point to a simple desire to replicate a felicitous verbal combination. On the other, the more obviously subversive pun on the Latin word *mundus* (as an adjective, "clean"; as a noun, "world") undercuts the connection of the literally mundane SYM 79.1 *(ROTAE,* "wheels": *Mundi magna parens)* with Virgil, *Georgics* 2.173 *(Salve, magna parens frugum Saturnia tellus),* which offers a touching hymn to the earth mother. Still more striking and apparently deliberately comic are the associations of SYM 95.1 *(FUNAMBULUS,* "tightrope walker": *Inter lucifluum caelum terrasque iacentes)* and a description of the god Jupiter in Virgil, *Aeneid* 1.223–4 *(Iuppiter aethere summo / despiciens mare velivolum terrasque iacentis),* or SYM 56.1 *(CALIGA,* "boot": *Maior eram longe quondam dum vita manebat)* with the dead Anchises, speaking with Aeneas in Virgil, *Aeneid* 5.724-5 *(Nate, mihi vita quondam, dum vita manebat / care magis;* Virgil, *Aeneid* 6.608 and 6.660 *[dum vita manebat]).* Nor is Virgil the only classical author apparently lampooned: SYM 42.3 *(BETA,* "beet": *In terris nascor, lympha lavor, unguor olivo)* has a close verbal parallel with Horace, *Satires* 1.6.123 *(unguor olivo),* which deals with wrestling!

A compelling case can be made that Symphosius, in addition to his debt to the common curriculum authors Virgil and Horace, has also been heavily influenced by more outré authors, especially Ausonius, whose *Griphus ternarii numeri* ("Riddle on the number three") was composed in 368, and Martial's *Xenia* and *Apophoreta* (Books 13–14, both collections of verses describing gifts given by hosts to their dinner guests during the Saturnalia); for details, see especially Le, 5–8 and 28–29. More than a quarter of the topics that Symphosius discusses in his aenigmata can be paralleled in the latter's two collections. More scattered parallels link Symphosius less clearly with the works of other authors, notably Ovid, Juvenal, and Lucretius, and perhaps even Manilius and Silius Italicus.

While the more obscure classical references made by Symphosius would have escaped an Anglo-Saxon audience, such a readership would likely have perceived some link between these aenigmata and Isidore's encyclopedic *Etymologiae* (Etymologies), although the latter certainly postdates Symphosius. The parallels between Isidore's *Etymologiae* and no fewer than twenty-three of the twenty-five aenigmata that make up the sequence SYM 15–39—the exceptions are SYM 16 (*TINEA*, "bookworm") and SYM 27 (*CORNIX*, "crow")—cover all eight chapters of Book 12 (Isidore, *Etym.* 12.1.15–8.17). It is notable that while there is no mention of the *cornix* in the *Etymologiae*, there is indeed an entry for *tinea* in *Etym.* 12.5.3, but it is quite clear there that it is the clothes moth, rather than the bookworm (as also in EXE 45, evidently drawing on SYM 16), which is in question.

This Text and Translation

Here I have relied heavily on the recent editions and translations of Be and Le, which, while they often disagree, nonetheless together offer a useful corrective to the occasional eccentricities of Gl; I have also consulted closely the edition and translation by Ohl.

Further Reading

In general, see Ohl, "Symphosius and the Latin Riddle"; Finch, "Codex Vat. Barb. Lat. 721 as a Source for the Riddles of Symphosius"; Finch, "Symphosius in Codices Pal. lat. 1719, 1753, and Reg. lat. 329, 2078"; Goolden, *The Old English "Apollonius of Tyre"*; Scott, "Rhetorical and Symbolic Ambiguity"; Salvador-Bello, "Compilation of the Old English Riddles," 17–19; Bergamin, *Aenigmata Symposii;* Salvador-Bello, *Isidorean Perceptions,* 141–62 and 457–59.

SYM PR

MANUSCRIPTS: D, fol. 2v; X, 374; L, fol. 104r; G, fol. 389r–v.

EARLIER EDITIONS AND TRANSLATIONS: DB, 16–17; Oh, 30–35; Gl, 621; Be, 2–5 and 73–79; Le, 39 and 53–64; Se, 51–53 and 151–52. (SK 5984 and 838)

See too Crane, "Describing the World," 56–59; Orchard, "Performing Writing and Singing Silence," 73–74; Salvador-Bello, *Isidorean Perceptions,* 118–20; Dale, *Natural World,* 160–61.

The Preface focuses on issues of sound and (less so) silence, using a large number of words for each concept *(loquaces . . . linguae . . . verbosa . . . sermonis . . . locuta . . . tacuisse . . . dicere . . . vocis),* scanned in a variety of ways.

PR.1–2 The opening pair of lines is only found in one class of manuscripts, including the Anglo-Saxon L; the explicit attribution to Symphosius here implies that he is also the author of other works unidentified. Sextus is too common a name to aid identification, but the allusion here to teaching attests to the classroom context in which Anglo-Saxons seem to have become well acquainted with Symphosius's aenigmata.

PR.3 Compare ALD 12.1 *(Annua . . . tempora).* The reference to the Saturnalia is clear; it was a festival that began on December 17, and eventually extended to a full-week celebration.

PR.4 Le prefers (but obelizes) *nec semper.* Compare Virgil, *Aeneid* 5.605 *(sollemnia ludis).*

PR.8 Reading *tentamine* after Le.

PR.9–10 Compare Horace, *Sermones* 1.9.2 *(nescio quid meditans nugarum).*

PR.10 The use of the term *frivola* here echoes the way that Ausonius (who died ca. 395) speaks of his own aenigmata (*Epist.* 14.67); compare too Ausonius's description in the introduction to his "Riddle on the number three" *(Griphus ternarii numerarii),* addressed to Symmachus:

> Ac ne me nescias gloriosum, coeptos inter prandendum versiculos ante cenae tempus absolve, hoc est, dum bibo et paulo ante quam biberem. Sit ergo examen pro materia et tempore. Sed tu quoque hoc ipsum paulo hilarior et dilutior lege; namque inurium est de poeta male sobrio lectorem abstemium iudicare.

> And just so that you don't deny that I am boastful: I began these little verses over lunch and finished before suppertime; that is to say, I began while drinking and then a bit before I was drinking again. Let that be your scale for the theme and the timing. Read them too while a bit merrier and more drenched; for it is unfair for a sober reader to pass judgement on a poet in his cups. (Combeaud, *Ausonius, Opuscula Omnia, Œuvres complètes,* 20, lines 14–17)

The emphasis here on drinking and the necessary forgiveness of a sober reader *(lector)* for the works of a drunk poet seem closely to echo the whole tenor of the verse preface to Symphosius's own collection, and the context here of an extended riddle on the number three by the leading teacher *(rhetor)* of the day makes it highly likely that Symphosius is here imitating a distinguished predecessor, perhaps even to the extent of making his own aenigmata three-line poems.

PR.11–12 The mention of an after-dinner riddle contest is found in Aulus Gellius 18.2–6. The whole frame-tale as described by Symphosius has intriguing parallels with the tale of the sudden inspiration of the tongue-tied Cædmon at a party of his own: Bede's Latin describes the setting as a "feast" *(convivium),* where the ninth-century Old English translation is still more specific (and closer to the account of Symphosius), describing the event in question as a "drinking party" *(gebeorscipe).*

PR.11 Le reads *non mediocre.*

PR.15 Reading *discrimine* (with Be) for *de carmine* LGW. It is certainly possible to construe *subito* both as an adverb, so denoting extemporized composition, or as an adjective agreeing with *discrimine vocis.* In the latter case, the poet is describing a process of working up written texts from the sudden poetry of the spoken word.

PR.16 Note the elision at *necesse est;* there are only six examples of elision in the whole collection, all involving prodelision or aphaeresis of *est:* SYM 53.2 *(propago est),* 69.1 *(nulla est),* 73.3 *(magna est),* 85.3 *(nata est),* 92.3 *(secuta est).* On this feature in Latin verse, see in general Pezzini, "Contraction of *est* in Latin."

PR.17 The reference to a *lector,* "reader," here again combines aspects of both oral and written material that run like a thread throughout the Anglo-Saxon riddle tradition. For a possible connection to Ausonius, see too the note at PR.10 above. The reference to an *ebria Musa* is particularly striking, given that the same phrase is used in *Anthologia Latina* 280/280a in a poem on "barbarian banquets" which immediately precedes SYM PR in the celebrated seventh- or eighth-century uncial manuscript known as the Codex Salmasianus (Paris, BNF, Pal. lat. 10318, 141–42).

SYM 1

MANUSCRIPTS: D, fol. 2v; X, 374; L, fol. 104r–v; G, fol. 389v.

EARLIER EDITIONS AND TRANSLATIONS: DB, 18–19; Oh, 34–35; Gl, 622; Be, 4–5 and 80–81; Le, 39 and 64–66; Se, 152. (SK 3391)

SOLUTION: *GRAPHIUM* (stylus), as in the majority of manuscripts. See further Orchard, "Performing Writing and Singing Silence," 91; Lockhart, "Everyday Wonders and Enigmatic Structures," 49–50.

Given the subject matter of the *Preface,* it seems especially fitting that the creature that is the subject of the first aenigma should be a writing instrument that can recall and correct false words, an attribute pointedly unavailable to speakers of the spoken word. This first aenigma also exemplifies in its opening and closing lines the extreme fondness for parallelism and paradox that is the hallmark of Symphosius's aenigmata. This aenigma is also found embedded in the pseudo-Bede *Collectanea* (BL §101, 132–33).

1.1 Note the chiasmus *summo planus . . . planus . . . imo.*

1.2 Note wordplay on *versor . . . diverso.* Be reads *utrimque manu diverso et munere.*

1.3 Note the chiasmus *altera pars . . . pars altera.*

SYM 2

MANUSCRIPTS: D, fol. 2v–3r; X, 376 (no. 13); L, fol. 104v; G, fol. 389v.

EARLIER EDITIONS AND TRANSLATIONS: DB, 18–19; Oh, 36–37; Gl, 623; Be, 4–5 and 81–84; Le, 39 and 66–69; Se, 152–53. (SK 3974)

SOLUTION: *HARUNDO* (reed), as in the majority of manuscripts. For the supposed connection of this aenigma with EXE 58, see Whitman, "Riddle 60 and Its Source"; Bitterli, *Say What I Am Called,* 137; Ramey, "Writing Speaks," 337–38; Orchard, "Performing Writing and Singing Silence," 90–91.

This aenigma, which is also found embedded in the *Historia Apollonii Regis Tyri* (see *Manuscript Contexts* above), can be linked to the preceding one by the similar shapes of the stylus and reed, as well as by the use of sharpened reeds in writing.

2.1 The god in question is Pan; see Ovid, *Metamorphoses* 1.689–712 for an account of his dealings with the nymph Syrinx, who is transformed into a reed.

2.2 Compare SYM 45.1 *(ROSA,* "rose": *perfusa colore).*

2.3 Compare EUS 56.3 *(nuntia sum).*

SYM 3

MANUSCRIPTS: D, fol. 3r; X, 376 (no. 14); L, fol. 104v; G, fol. 389v.
EARLIER EDITIONS AND TRANSLATIONS: DB, 18–19; Oh, 36–39; Gl, 624; Wi3, 153; Be, 6–7 and 84–85; Le, 39 and 69–71; Se, 153. (SK 2817)
SOLUTION: *ANULUS CUM GEMMA* (ring with gem), as in the majority of manuscripts.

Presumably it is the hollow reed of the preceding aenigma that prompts the association here with a finger ring; perhaps the gem gives off multiple reflections, as the final line describes, or it is a seal ring, producing many figures in wax. I am grateful to Bob Babcock for the latter suggestion.

3.1 Compare SYM 63.1 *(pondus inhaeret).*

SYM 4

MANUSCRIPTS: D, fol. 3r; X, 374–75 (no. 2); L, fol. 104v; G, fol. 389v.
EARLIER EDITIONS AND TRANSLATIONS: DB, 18–19; Oh, 38–39; Gl, 625; Wi3, 152; Be, 6–7 and 85–86; Le, 40 and 71–73; Se, 61–62 and 153. (SK 17370)
SOLUTION: *CLAVIS* (key).

This aenigma is also found embedded in the pseudo-Bede *Collectanea* (BL §239, 150–51). The connection between this aenigma and the preceding one may lie in the fact that unlike their modern counterparts, classical key-rings often combined both functions. This key-aenigma is itself also a metaphor for the riddle, and the whole aenigma also serves as an excellent example of Symphosius's style, since each line contains examples both of his love of contrast *(magnas . . . parvas; pando . . . claudo; servo . . . servor)* and of wordplay in the form of polyptoton *(virtutes . . . viribus; clausas . . . claudo; domo . . . domino).* Other examples of polyptoton are noted at SYM 5, 9, 20, 22, 56, 59, and 72; see too ALD 7; TAT 8 and 22; EUS 15, 42, and 44; BON 8. For a potential Christian echo here and in the aenigma that follows of the language of the Fourth Advent Antiphon, *O clavis David,* see Se, 61–62.

SYM 5

MANUSCRIPTS: D, fol. 3r; X, 376 (no. 15); L, fol. 104v; G, fol. 389v.
EARLIER EDITIONS AND TRANSLATIONS: DB, 20–21; Oh, 38–39; Gl, 626; Be, 6–7 and 86–87; Le, 40 and 73–74; Se, 62 and 153. (SK 10183)
SOLUTION: *CATENA* (chain). See further Murphy, *Unriddling the Exeter Riddles,* 40; Cavell, *Weaving Words,* 121.

Here again, the binding and loosing motif provides a connection between successive aenigmata, in this case linking back to the preceding one. The whole notion of a *catena* also underlies the collection as a whole, and seems to have inspired several Anglo-Saxon riddlers also to seek connecting themes to link consecutive texts.

5.2 Note the wordplay, here in the form of polyptoton, emphasized through alliteration: *vincior . . . vincio . . . vincta vicissim.*

SYM 6

MANUSCRIPTS: D, fol. 3r; X, 376 (no. 16); L, fol. 104v; G, fol. 389v.
EARLIER EDITIONS AND TRANSLATIONS: DB, 20–21; Oh, 40–41; Gl, 627; Be, 8–9 and 87–89; Le, 40 and 74–76; Se, 154. (SK 16265)
SOLUTION: *TEGULA* (roof tile).

The connection here with the preceding aenigma is presumably derived from the resemblance of interlinked curved terracotta tiles to a chain.

6.2 Here, I follow both Be and Le, against alternative readings (found in DGLX, for example), generally of the pattern *est domus in alto,* and which form the basis for the emendation to *est domus in imo* in Gl. See in particular the reasoning of Be, 88–89.

6.3 Compare Virgil, *Georgics* 1.70 *(deserat umor).*

SYM 7

MANUSCRIPTS: D, fol. 3r; X, 376 (no. 17); L, fol. 105r; G, fol. 389v.

EARLIER EDITIONS AND TRANSLATIONS: DB, 20–21; Oh, 40–41; Gl, 628; Wi2, 26; Be, 8–9 and 89–90; Le, 40 and 76–78; Se, 154. (SK 15870)

SOLUTION: *FUMUS* (smoke). See further Murphy, *Unriddling the Exeter Riddles,* 219.

This aenigma is also found embedded in the pseudo-Bede *Collectanea* (BL §102, 134–35). From the roof tile of the previous aenigma it is a short conceptual step to the smoke that rises from rooftops. Even the syntax is strikingly similar to what went before.

7.1 Be prefers the alternative reading *Nunc mihi sunt* (as she explains on 89–90). Compare Virgil, *Aeneid* 1.462 *(sunt lacrimae rerum).*

7.3 The theme of the child giving rise to the parent in turn is here introduced, and connects this riddle to a range of others, considered in the note to ps-SYM 1 (*GLACIES,* "ice") below. For the formula *me genuit,* see the note at ALD 33.1.

SYM 8

MANUSCRIPTS: D, fol. 3r; X, 376–77 (no. 18); L, fol. 105r; G, fol. 389v.

EARLIER EDITIONS AND TRANSLATIONS: DB, 20–21; Oh, 42–43; Gl, 629; Be, 8–9 and 90–91; Le, 40 and 78–79; Se, 154. (SK 10622)

SOLUTION: *NEBULA* (cloud).

This aenigma follows immediately on from the last, and in turn links neatly to the next.

8.3 The moon is here called by her classical name, Cynthia; for other classical references in SYM, see the main headnote above.

SYM 9

MANUSCRIPTS: D, fol. 3r; X, 377 (no. 19); L, fol. 105r; G, fol. 389v–90r.
EARLIER EDITIONS AND TRANSLATIONS: DB, 20–21; Oh, 42–43; Gl, 630; Be, 10–11 and 91–93; Le, 40 and 79–81; Se, 154. (SK 4737)
SOLUTION: *PLUVIA* (rain).

This aenigma follows smoothly on in thematic sequence.

9.3 Symphosius has a particular fondness for repeating elements of the same word form (polyptoton), especially in the final line, as here, often emphasized by medial rhyme *(excepit . . . recepit);* compare SYM 22.3 *(gero . . . congero),* 49.3 *(remanent . . . mansit),* 51.3 *(inmotus . . . moveri),* 56.3 *(dedita . . . condita),* 59.3 *(mittunt . . . remittor),* 70.3 *(fluuens . . . fluunt),* 71.3 *(labor . . . labore),* 72.3 *(ligno vehitur . . . ligna vehebat),* 97.3 *(movet . . . movetur),* 98.3 *(loqui . . . loquenti).* Here again the theme of being born and received back is reprised. Be and Le both prefer *remittit.*

SYM 10

MANUSCRIPTS: D, fol. 3r–v; X, 377 (no. 20); L, fol. 105r; G, fol. 390r.
EARLIER EDITIONS AND TRANSLATIONS: DB, 22–23; Oh, 42–43; Gl, 631; Be, 10–11 and 93–95; Le, 40 and 81–83; Se, 154–55. (SK 16741)
SOLUTION: *GLACIES* (ice).

This aenigma is also found embedded in the pseudo-Bede *Collectanea* (BL §241, 152–53); once again, there seems a clear connection between this aenigma and the one preceding.

10.1 An evident gesture towards the theme of the child begetting the parent. Compare SYM 58.3 *(ultima fata);* for variations on the formula *nomen habens,* see the note at ALD 50.3.

10.2 The image of the binding of ice follows on from SYM 5.1 *(nexa ligor),* but is a striking and original image in Latin literature. Compare in Old English *waþema gebind.*

10.3 Be prefers *et calcata . . . nec unda,* noting that ice (sometimes!) melts in water.

SYM 11

MANUSCRIPTS: D, fol. 3v (no. 12); X, 377 (no. 21); L, fol. 105r–v (no. 12); G, fol. 390r (no. 12).

EARLIER EDITIONS AND TRANSLATIONS: DB, 22–23; Oh, 44–45; Gl, 632; Be, 10–11 and 95; Le, 40 and 83–84; Se, 155. (SK 12779)

SOLUTION: *NIX* (snow).

The self-evident association of snow and ice connects this aenigma to the previous one.

11.2 Compare ALD 1.4 *(Prole virens aestate, tabescens),* ALD 100.73b–74a *(solis / Rore madens).*

11.3 Note the alliterative patterning on *f-* and *t-* in this line.

SYM 12

MANUSCRIPTS: D, fol. 3v (no. 11); X, 377 (no. 22); L, fol. 105r (no. 11); G, fol. 390r (no. 11).

EARLIER EDITIONS AND TRANSLATIONS: DB, 22–23; Oh, 44–47; Gl, 633; Be, 12–13 and 95–97; Le, 41 and 84–86; Se, 155. (SK 4576)

SOLUTION: *FLUMEN ET PISCIS* (river and fish). See further Orchard, "Enigma Variations," 293–94; Murphy, *Unriddling the Exeter Riddles,* 19–20; Lockhart, "Everyday Wonders and Enigmatic Structures," 50–51.

This aenigma, which appears in the *Historia Apollonii Regis Tyri* (see *Manuscript Contexts* above), is also found embedded in the pseudo-Bede *Collectanea* (BL §240, 150–51). Presumably the fact that the subject of the previous aenigma concludes with a reference to the rivers *(flumina)* that snow creates leads to the association here. Compare ALC D80 (*PISCIS ET FLUMEN,* "fish and river") and EXE 81 (*FISC OND EA,* "fish and river"); this aenigma is very close in spirit to EXE 81 in particular, for which it has often been adduced as a source.

12.1 Compare SYM 6.2 *(de terra nascor, sedes sed semper in alto).*

SYM 13

MANUSCRIPTS: D, fol. 3v; X, 375 (no. 3); L, fol. 105v; G, fol. 390r.
EARLIER EDITIONS AND TRANSLATIONS: DB, 22–23; Oh, 46–47; Gl, 634; Be, 12–13 and 97–99; Le, 41 and 87–88; Se, 155. (SK 8986)
SOLUTION: *NAVIS* (ship). See too Crane, "Describing the World," 119–20.

Following on from an aenigma with the given solution of *FLUMEN ET PISCIS* (river and fish), this aenigma, which is also found embedded in the *Historia Apollonii Regis Tyri* (see *Manuscript Contexts* above), focuses instead on a different water-dwelling creature. Note the alliterative patterning here *(feror velox formosae filia . . . vias . . . vestigia; comitum . . . catervis curro);* compare the four ship-riddles of EXE (17, 30, 34, and 62), as well as EXE 16 (*CROG*, "amphora, vessel").

13.2 Compare EUS 56.3 *(stipata catervis);* Virgil, *Aeneid* 1.497 *(incessit magna iuvenum stipante caterva)* and 4.136 *(tandem progreditur magna stipante caterva).*

13.2 The line presumably refers to packed cargo. Note that EXE 16 (*CROG*, "amphora, vessel") is followed by EXE 17 (*SNAC*, "light warship").

13.3 Compare BER 11.6 *(et onusta currens viam nec planta depingo),* BER 59.3 *(currens vias);* ALF O.2 *(Curro vias multas);* EUS 2.3; BER 55.4 *(vestigia nulla).*

SYM 14

MANUSCRIPTS: D, fol. 3v; X, 375 (no. 4); L, fol. 105v; G, fol. 390r.
EARLIER EDITIONS AND TRANSLATIONS: DB, 22–23; Oh, 46–47; Gl, 635; Be, 12–13 and 99–100; Le, 41 and 88–90; Se, 155. (SK 9660)

SOLUTION: *PULLUS IN OVO* (chick in egg). See further Murphy, *Unriddling the Exeter Riddles,* 39; Lockhart, "Everyday Wonders and Enigmatic Structures," 51–52.

The continuing chain of connections in the collection so far surely encourages something similar to be sought in this case, and it might be argued that a ship on the ocean, the subject of SYM 13 (*NAVIS,* "ship"), is conceptually similar to the given solution here, the more so since in the preceding aenigma the ship itself carries other creatures inside. The repetition *natus . . . natus . . . natum* emphasizes the prevailing theme of birth. Compare ALC D78 (*PULLUS IN OVO,* "chick in egg"); BER 8 (*OVUM,* "egg").

14.1 Compare ALD 29.5 *(AQUA,* "water": *primordia vitae).*

14.2 Be prefers *nondum natus eram nec eram iam matris in alvo.* Compare SYM 36.1 *(matris . . . natus in alvo);* ALD 93.10 *(genetrix . . . generaret ab alvo),* ALD 100.24 *(matris . . . generabar ab alvo);* TAT 15.5 *(matris . . . in alvum),* TAT 17.1 *(nascor . . . matris in alvo),* BER 34.1 *(mater concipit alvo).* Note also Horace, *Carmina* 4.6.20 and Ovid, *Metamorphoses* 1.420 *(matris in alvo).*

14.3 Compare SYM 21.3 *(nemo videbit),* SYM 99.3 *(nemo videt).*

SYM 15

MANUSCRIPTS: D, fol. 3v; X, 375 (no. 5); L, fol. 105v; G, fol. 390r.
EARLIER EDITIONS AND TRANSLATIONS: DB, 24–25; Oh, 48–49; Gl, 636; Be, 14–15 and 100–102; Le, 41 and 90–91; Se, 156. (SK 10460)
SOLUTION: *VIPERA* (viper).

The evident subject of this aenigma, the viper, is proverbially the most ungrateful child, a notion described by Isidore, *Etym.* 12.4.11:

> Vipera dicta, quod vi pariat. Nam et cum venter eius ad partum ingemuerit, catuli non expectantes maturam naturae solutionem conrosis eius lateribus vi erumpunt cum matris interitu.

> The viper is so called because it gives birth with violence. For when its womb is bursting to deliver, the little ones, not waiting for nature's proper solution, gnaw through their mother's sides and burst through, leading to her death.

The same notion is found in Pliny, *Nat. Hist.* 10.170.

SYM 16

MANUSCRIPTS: D, fol. 3v; X, 375 (no. 6); L, fol. 105v; G, fol. 390r.
EARLIER EDITIONS AND TRANSLATIONS: DB, 24–25; Oh, 48–49; Gl, 637; Wil, 1; Be, 14–15 and 102–3; Le, 41 and 92–93; Se, 156. (SK 8961)
SOLUTION: *TINEA* (bookworm). Compare Bitterli, *Say What I Am Called,* 191–93; Lockhart, "Everyday Wonders and Enigmatic Structures," 133–35; Ramey, "Crafting Strangeness," 210–11.

The violence and pointless consumption of the viper in the preceding aenigma seems to have prompted the more sedate and aimless munching of the bookworm, a metaphor for the kind of dull student who was presumably as much a feature of ancient and medieval classrooms as today's. It is widely accepted that this aenigma is the source and inspiration for EXE 45 (**BOC-MOÐÐE,* "book moth"). In Isidore, *Etym.* 12.5.11, while it is specified that *tinea* refers also to clothes-vermin, the word is also linked specifically to the term *pertinax,* denoting a creature who keeps on stubbornly at the same task. See further Pliny, *Nat. Hist.* 11.117.

16.3 False quantity: the usual form is *prōfeci.*

SYM 17

MANUSCRIPTS: D, fol. 3v; X, 375 (no. 7); L, fol. 105v; G, fol. 390r.
EARLIER EDITIONS AND TRANSLATIONS: DB, 24–25; Oh, 48–51; Gl, 638; Be, 14–15 and 103–4; Le, 41 and 93–95; Se, 156. (SK 11537)
SOLUTION: *ARANEA* (spider).

The connection of the goddess Pallas Athena with wisdom makes an implicit link to the preceding aenigma; her further association with weaving leads on to the main theme of this aenigma. Moreover, the spider is classified as *vermis* (meaning both "vermin" and "worm"; see for example Isidore, *Etym.* 12.5.1), so providing a still more specific bond to the previous aenigma. The story of Arachne's transformation into a spider is widely told, for example in Ovid, *Metamorphoses* 6.5–145. See further Pliny, *Nat. Hist.* 11.79–85.

17.2 The word *peplum* refers to a garment specifically associated with Pallas Athena, but which becomes generalized. Compare ALD 12.1 *(BOMBIX,* "silkworm": *texendi . . . telas).* Le prefers *telae* for *pepli* and *telam* for *telae.* Compare Virgil, *Georgics* 1.285 *(licia telae).*

17.3 Be prefers *fingo* for *fiunt* (as she explains on 104).

SYM 18

MANUSCRIPTS: D, fol. 3v–4r; X, 377 (no. 23); L, fol. 106r; L^2, fol. 199r; G, fol. 390r.

EARLIER EDITIONS AND TRANSLATIONS: DB, 24–25; Oh, 50–51; Gl, 639; Be, 15–17 and 104–6; Le, 41 and 95–99; Se, 156. (SK 12182)

SOLUTION: *COCLEA* (snail).

This aenigma is another riddle that concerns both a house and its inhabitant, itself a variant on the container-and-what-it-contains model. Arguments have been made that this is also a kind of soul-and-body riddle, which may help to explain the common manuscript form *concilium* at SYM 18.3, and would help link this aenigma to the one preceding it. There is a good deal of snail lore relevant to this aenigma in Isidore, *Etym.* 12.6.48–50.

18.2 Compare EUS 3.1 *(sim miserabilis exul).*

18.3 Reading *conchilium,* as in G. The manuscripts are split between forms of *concilium* and *consilium,* but there seems no special reason to suppose that snails of any kind are associated with wisdom, while *conchilium* or *conchylium* refers to precisely the kind of purple dye extracted from the snail *murex*. This is, however, to allow a false quantity: the usual form is *conquīlium*. It is interesting to note that ALD 98.2 contains the same word with the same false quantity. Be prefers *concilium* (as she explains on 106), as does Le (as he explains on 97–99).

SYM 19

MANUSCRIPTS: D, fol. 4r; X, 377 (no. 24); L, fol. 106r; L², fol. 199r; G, fol. 390r.

EARLIER EDITIONS AND TRANSLATIONS: DB, 24–25; Oh, 52–53; Gl, 640; Wi3, 153; Be, 15–17 and 106–8; Le, 41 and 99–101; Se, 157. (SK 14058)

SOLUTION: *RANA* (frog).

Compare Isidore, *Etym.* 12.6.58:

> Ranae a garrulitate vocatae, eo quod circa genitales strepunt paludes, et sonos vocis inportunis clamoribus reddunt.
>
> Frogs are so called from their garrulous nature, since they make sounds around the swamps of their birth, and render the sounds of their voices with insistent croaking.

See further Pliny, *Nat. Hist.* 11.173. Repetition underlines the major themes of sound, songs, and praise *(sonans . . . vocalis . . . vox . . . sonat; canam . . . carmina; laude . . . laudet . . . laudat).*

19.1 Reading *Rauca sonans;* compare Virgil, *Aeneid* 9.125 *(rauca sonans)* and Aldhelm, *Carmen de virginitate* 1549 *(rauca sonant);* Be and Le prefer *Raucisonans,* a unique formulation, where other poets use a form of the compound adjective *raucisonus* instead (including ALD 22.2 and 35.5).

19.2 Be prefers the alternative reading *quasi quae laudetur et ipsa* (as she explains on 107–8). Le transposes 19.2 and 3.

SYM 20

MANUSCRIPTS: D, fol. 4r; X, 375 (no. 8); L, fol. 106r; L^2, fol. 199r; G, fol. 390v.

EARLIER EDITIONS AND TRANSLATIONS: DB, 26–27; Oh, 52–55; Gl, 641; Be, 15–17 and 108–10; Le, 42 and 101–3; Se, 152. (SK 16028)

SOLUTION: *TESTUDO* (tortoise).

There is a clear contrast made between the raucous and unpleasant sounds made by the living frog of the previous aenigma and the silence of the living tortoise, when compared with the beautiful sounds it makes when dead as a musical stringed instrument (χέλυς in Greek; *testudo* in Latin) said to have been invented by the god Hermes; compare in that regard the contrast between sound and silence in EXE 5 (*SWAN*, "swan"); see further Orchard, "Performing Writing and Singing Silence," 83–86. Compare Isidore, *Etym.* 12.6.56 and Pliny, *Nat. Hist.* 9.35–39.

20.1–2 Note the polyptoton *praedita . . . prodita.*

20.2 Le prefers *tecta . . . subito,* which, while it certainly makes sense, is not a reading found in any of the manuscripts, all of which offer the reading given here. Quite how a tortoise can be said to be "well taught . . . by study" is a puzzle: the term would seem to fit more properly the player of the lyre made from the dead shell.

20.3 Most manuscripts read *mihi* rather than *nihil.*

SYM 21

MANUSCRIPTS: D, fol. 4r; X, 377 (no. 25); L, fol. 106r; L^2, fol. 199r; G, fol. 390v.

EARLIER EDITIONS AND TRANSLATIONS: DB, 26–27; Oh, 54–55; Gl, 642; Be, 18–19 and 110–11; Le, 42 and 103–4; Se, 157. (SK 1766)

SOLUTION: *TALPA* (mole).

The information given here is strikingly close to what is found in Isidore, *Etym.* 12.3.5:

Talpa dicta, quod sit damnata caecitate perpetua tenebris. Est enim absque oculis, semper terram fodit, et humum egerit, et radices subter frugibus comedit.

The mole is so called because it is condemned to perpetual blindness in the dark. For it is without eyes, and always digs in the earth, and has thrown out the soil, and eats the roots under the crops.

21.2 Both *ipse* and *ipsa* are found in the manuscripts; the common gender of *dies* admits both.

21.3 Compare SYM 14.3 *(nemo videbat),* SYM 99.3 *(nemo videt).*

SYM 22

MANUSCRIPTS: D, fol. 4r; X, 377–78 (no. 26); L, fol. 106r; L², fol. 199r; G, fol. 390v.

EARLIER EDITIONS AND TRANSLATIONS: DB, 26–27; Oh, 54–57; Gl, 643; Wi3, 154; Be, 18–19 and 111–13; Le, 42 and 104–6; Se, 157. (SK 12700)

SOLUTION: *FORMICA* (ant). See further Cesario, "Ant-lore in Anglo-Saxon England."

The information given here is again strikingly close to what is found in Isidore, *Etym.* 12.3.9:

Formica dicta, ab eo quod ferat micas farris. Cuius sollertia multa; providet enim in futurum, et praeparat aestate quod hieme comedat.

The ant is so called, because it carries small bits of grain. Its cleverness is great, since it plans for the future, and piles up in summer what it eats in winter.

22.3 On the polyptoton here *(gero . . . congero),* see the note on SYM 9.3 above.

SYM 23

MANUSCRIPTS: D, fol. 4r; X, 378 (no. 27); L, fol. 106r–v; G, fol. 390v.
EARLIER EDITIONS AND TRANSLATIONS: DB, 26–27; Oh, 56–57; Gl, 644; Wi3, 154; Be, 18–19 and 113–14; Le, 42 and 106–8; Se, 158. (SK 7814)
SOLUTION: *MUSCA* (fly).

After treating in the previous two aenigmata two creatures classified (by Isidore at least) as "small animals" *(De minutis animantibus),* Symphosius turns here to one defined as among the "small flying animals" *(De minutis volatibus),* with a particular description at Isidore, *Etym.* 12.8.11.

SYM 24

MANUSCRIPTS: D, fol. 4r; X, 378 (no. 28); L, fol. 106v; L[2], fol. 199r; G, fol. 390v.
EARLIER EDITIONS AND TRANSLATIONS: DB, 26–27; Oh, 56–57; Gl, 645; Be, 20–21 and 114–15; Le, 42 and 108–10; Se, 158. (SK 10371)
SOLUTION: *CURCULIO* (weevil).

This aenigma, like the last, deals with one of the "small flying animals" *(De minutis volatibus),* with a particular description at Isidore, *Etym.* 12.8.17. Isidore's etymology connects the name of the weevil with the Latin word for "gut" *(gula),* precisely the term used in SYM 23.1 (*MUSCA,* "fly") above. The fourfold negative repetition *(non . . . nec . . . nec . . . nec)* again demonstrates the poet's rhetorical sensitivity.

24.1 Compare ALD 34.1 *(LOCUSTA,* "locust": *agricolis non . . . laudabilis hospes).*

24.3 Reading *sed multa vivo sagina* with Le. Symphosius here introduces the term *sagina,* "stuffing, fattening," which will feature in several of the succeeding aenigmata, notably SYM 25.2 (*MUS,* "mouse"), 36.2 (*PORCUS,* "pig"), and 54.3 (*AMUS,* "hook"), with the phrase *vivo sagina* repeated verbatim in the aenigma that immediately follows (25.2).

SYM 25

MANUSCRIPTS: D, fol. 4r; X, 375 (no. 9); L, fol. 106v; L², fol. 199r; G, fol. 390v.

EARLIER EDITIONS AND TRANSLATIONS: DB, 28–29; Oh, 58–59; Gl, 646; Wi3, 153; Be, 20–21 and 115–16; Le, 42 and 110–11; Se, 158. (SK 11661)

SOLUTION: *MUS* (mouse).

Apart from the verbal parallel that links this aenigma to the last, there is also a perceived etymological connection with SYM 23 (*MUSCA*, "fly"). According to Isidore, *Etym.* 12.3.1, the mouse is the first of the "small animals" *(De minutis animantibus)*. In L and G, this aenigma is followed by the confected aenigma *DE PILACE*, on which see ALD 65 (*MUSIO*, "mouser").

25.1 Compare ALD 93.3 *(Parva mihi)*.

25.2 Compare SYM 24.3 *(vivo sagina)*.

25.3 The reference is likely to Publius Decius Mus, who was consul in 340 BCE, and whose brave self-sacrifice at the Battle of Vesuvius in the same year is celebrated in Livy, *Ab urbe condita* 8.9. Two later members of the same family (also named Publius Decius Mus, being the son and grandson of the first) likewise became consul (the first four times, 312 BCE, 308 BCE, 297 BCE, and 295 BCE; the second in 279 BCE), and they too died bravely in battle while consul, at Sentinum and Asculum respectively. The contrast between such a mighty and martial family and the proverbially timid mouse is surely deliberate.

SYM 26

MANUSCRIPTS: D, fol. 4r–v; X, 378 (no. 29); L, fol. 106v (no. 27); L², fol. 199r; G, fol. 390v (no. 27).

EARLIER EDITIONS AND TRANSLATIONS: DB, 28–29; Oh, 58–61; Gl, 647; Be, 20–21 and 116–17; Le, 42 and 111–13; Se, 158–59. (SK 8971)

SOLUTION: *GRUS* (crane). See further Murphy, *Unriddling the Exeter Riddles*, 95.

Compare Isidore, *Etym.* 12.7.15, which mentions cranes in connection with letterforms, based on their flight in a v-formation; see further Pliny, *Nat. Hist.* 10.58–60.

26.1 Be prefers the alternative *volanti* (as she explains on 88–89), but I am swayed by the echoes of *volantis* elsewhere. Compare ALF C.3 *(Littera sum terrae . . . perscripta),* ALF Z.1 *(Littera sum),* ALF Ya.1 *(Littera sum);* SYM 28.2 *(penna volantis);* ALD 30.4 *(ELEMENTUM,* "alphabet": *penna volitantis);* ALF X.2 *(penna volantis).* The phrase *penna . . . volantis* is itself ambiguous, meaning not only "by the feather (or 'pen') of a flying creature" but "with the wing of a bird."

26.2 Compare SYM 85.3 *(bella cruenta);* ALD 60.1; TAT 17.5 *(discrimina Martis).* The term *volucri* preserves the ambiguity, meaning both "swift" and "winged."

26.3 The final line alludes to the legendary hostility between cranes and the pygmies, mentioned by, for example, Ovid, *Metamorphoses* 6.90–93.

SYM 27

MANUSCRIPTS: D, fol. 4v; X, 378 (no. 30); L, fol. 106v (no. 28); L[2], fol. 199r; G, fol. 390v (no. 28).

EARLIER EDITIONS AND TRANSLATIONS: DB, 28–29; Oh, 60–61; Gl, 648; Be, 22–23 and 117–18; Le, 42 and 113–15; Se, 159. (SK 17474)

SOLUTION: *CORNIX* (crow).

This aenigma is linked to the last by the association of birds, and to the one that follows by blackness.

27.1 Be reads *retia fallunt,* presumably as a gesture toward the trapping of birds with nets. Most manuscripts read *Graecia fallit* (as here), a reference to Hesiod's assertion, as reported by Pliny, *Nat. Hist.* 7.153, that crows live nine human life spans, a notion that Pliny calls "fanciful" *(fabulose).*

27.2 Be prefers the alternative reading *atraque sum semper* (as she explains on 118), as does Le; I retain the more formulaic *nomen habens atrum,* found in the manuscripts listed above, for variations of which see the note at ALD 50.3.

27.3 The notion of insulting language turns on the fact that the crow's caw in Latin, *caca,* repeats the stem of the verb *caco,* "defecate."

SYM 28

MANUSCRIPTS: D, fol. 4v; X, 378 (no. 31); L, fol. 107r (no. 29); L^2, fol. 199r–v; G, fol. 390v (no. 29).

EARLIER EDITIONS AND TRANSLATIONS: DB, 28–29; Oh, 60–63; Gl, 649; Be, 22–23 and 118–19; Le, 43 and 115–17; Se, 159. (SK 10631)

SOLUTION: *VESPERTILIO* (bat).

Compare Isidore, *Etym.* 12.7.36.

28.1 Be prefers the alternative reading *Vox,* but compare ALD 58.1 *(tempore de primo noctis mihi nomen adhaesit).*

28.2 Compare SYM 26.1 *(penna . . . volantis);* ALD 30.4 *(penna volitantis);* ALF X.2 *(penna volantis).*

28.3 Be prefers the reading *sedeo,* but the majority of manuscripts (including all of the Anglo-Saxon $DXLL^2G$) have *redeo* (as here).

SYM 29

MANUSCRIPTS: D, fol. 4v; X, 378 (no. 32); L, fol. 107r (no. 33); L^2, fol. 199v; G, fol. 391r (no. 33).

EARLIER EDITIONS AND TRANSLATIONS: DB, 28–29; Oh, 62–63; Gl, 650; Wi3, 152; Be, 22–23 and 120–21; Le, 43 and 119–21 (no. 30); Se, 159–60. (SK 12056)

SOLUTION: *ERICIUS* (hedgehog).

Compare Isidore, *Etym.* 12.6.57; for a riddle with the same solution (albeit with a rather different treatment), see EXE 13.

29(30).1 Compare SYM 18.1 (*COCLEA,* "snail"), for a similar focus on the "house" *(domus)* of the creature in question.

29(30).2 Compare SYM 45.2 *(telis . . . acutis).*

29(30).2–3 Compare Virgil, *Aeneid* 345–46 *(hic confixum ferrea texit / telorum seges et iaculis increvit acutis).*

29(30).3 The word *sustinet* (translated here as "upholds") could also be translated as "withstands."

SYM 30

MANUSCRIPTS: D, fol. 4v; X, 378 (no. 33); L, fol. 107r–v (no. 34); L², fol. 199v; G, fol. 391r (no. 34).

EARLIER EDITIONS AND TRANSLATIONS: DB, 30–31; Oh, 62–65; Gl, 651; Wi3, 153; Be, 24–25 and 121–22; Le, 43 and 121–22 (no. 31); Se, 160. (SK 4618)

SOLUTION: *PEDICULI* (lice).

This is a version of the famous riddle that is supposed to have frustrated Homer to death, according to a legend cited by Hippolytus in his *Refutatio omnium haeresium* (9.9.5), and also has a parallel in ALC D77 (*PEDICULI,* "lice"), for which this aenigma is the likeliest source. Compare Isidore, *Etym.* 12.5.14.

30(31).1 Note the medial rhyme *nostrarum . . . ferarum.*

30(31).2 Be prefers the alternative reading *hoc tu* (as she explains on 122); Le prefers *id tu.*

30(31).2–3 Note the patterning *capias . . . recuses . . . capias . . . reportes.*

SYM 31

MANUSCRIPTS: D, fol. 4v; X, 375–76 (no. 10); L, fol. 107r (no. 30); L², fol. 199v; G, fol. 391r (no. 30).

EARLIER EDITIONS AND TRANSLATIONS: DB, 30–31; Oh, 64–65; Gl, 652; Wi1, 1; Be, 24–25 and 122–25; Le, 43 and 117–19 (no. 29); Se, 160. (SK 17416)

SOLUTION: *PHOENIX* (phoenix).

The basic elements of the story of the exotic phoenix, a bird that appears twice in a millennium, flying from the East to India and then immolating itself on a pyre of spice-woods, from which it emerges reborn, are found in many different sources. Compare Isidore, *Etym.* 12.7.24; Pliny, *Nat. Hist.* 10.3; Ovid, *Metamorphoses* 15.392–407; and the Old English poem *The Phoenix,* which is an elaboration on the *De ave phoenice* of Lactantius.

31(29).1 Compare ALD 11.2 *(Non est vita mihi);* BER 30.3 *(Vita mihi mors est),* BER 50.4 *(mihi mors est).*

31(29).3 The word *Manes,* "spirits of the dead," is used here metonymically for death itself.

SYM 32

MANUSCRIPTS: D, fol. 4v; X, 378–79 (no. 34); L, fol. 107v (no. 35); L^2, fol. 199v; G, fol. 391r (no. 35).

EARLIER EDITIONS AND TRANSLATIONS: DB, 30–31; Oh, 64–67; Gl, 653; Wi2, 25; Be, 24–25 and 125–26; Le, 43 and 122–24; Se, 67–68 and 160–61. (SK 9729)

SOLUTION: *TAURUS* (bull).

This aenigma relies on offering four different perspectives on the same creature, by focusing in turn on the story of Pasiphaë, wife of King Minos, who was impregnated by a bull and gave birth to the Minotaur; the Taurus mountain chain in Asia Minor; the sign of the zodiac; and the Roman general and twice consul Titus Statilius Taurus. Compare Isidore, *Etym.* 12.1.29.

32.2 Be and Le both prefer the variant reading *sed non sum nomine solo* (as she explains on 126, and he defends on 123–24; among the Anglo-Saxon manuscripts the reading is witnessed in L^2), though that seems to trivialize the enigmatic aspect somewhat. Here I prefer the reading witnessed in XLG.

SYM 33

MANUSCRIPTS: D, fol. 4v; X, 376 (no. 11); L, fol. 107r (no. 31); L^2, fol. 199v; G, fol. 391r (no. 31).

EARLIER EDITIONS AND TRANSLATIONS: DB, 30–31; Oh, 66–69; Gl, 654; Be, 26–27 and 126–28; Le, 43 and 124–26; Se, 161. (SK 3494)

SOLUTION: *LUPUS* (wolf).

Compare Isidore, *Etym.* 12.2.23, as well as Pliny, *Nat. Hist.* 8.80, which describes the belief that if a wolf saw a man before a man saw him, the man would be struck dumb. Also relevant here, given the reference to *bidentes,* is Isidore, *Etym.* 12.1.9, which explains that:

> Ovis molle pecus lanis, corpore inerme, animo placidum, ab oblatione dictum; eo quod apud veteres in initio non tauri, sed oves in sacrificio mactarentur. Ex his quasdam bidentes vocant, eas quae inter octo dentes duos altiores habent, quas maxime gentiles in sacrificium offerebant.

> A sheep *(ovis)* is a gentle wooly animal, with an unarmed body, and a peaceful temperament, and it is named after "sacrifice" *(oblatio),* because the ancients at first slaughtered in sacrifice not bulls, but sheep. They call some of them "two-toothed" *(bidentes),* those that have two of their eight teeth longer than the others; and these were the ones the pagans used to sacrifice most often.

33.1 The variant *videntes,* "those seeing," is an example of the *b* for *f* or *v* spellings, on which see the headnote on LEI above. Le prefers the more vivid *trunco,* "mutilates," to *vinco,* which he considers "tame" (p. 126). The pun on *dentibus . . . bidentes* is characteristic of the wordplay widespread in SYM.

33.2 Compare ALD 36.3 *(Sanguineas . . . praedas).*

33.3 Be prefers the alternative reading *multaque cum rapiam* (as she explains on 127–28).

SYM 34

MANUSCRIPTS: D, fol. 4v–5r; X, 376 (no. 12); L, fol. 107r (no. 32); L^2, fol. 199v.

EARLIER EDITIONS AND TRANSLATIONS: DB, 30–31; Oh, 68–69; Gl, 655; Be, 26–27 and 128–29; Le, 43 and 127–28; Se, 161. (SK 4802)

SOLUTION: *VULPES* (fox).

This aenigma plays on the proverbially cunning nature of the fox. Compare Isidore, *Etym.* 12.2.29.

34.1 Note the wordplay on *corpus . . . cor . . . corpore.*

34.3 The studied chiasmus *fera . . . sapiens sapiens fera* emphasizes the key characteristic of the fox as a "wise beast."

SYM 35

MANUSCRIPTS: D, fol. 5r; X, 379; L, fol. 107v (no. 36); L^2, fol. 199v; G, fol. 391r (no. 36)

EARLIER EDITIONS AND TRANSLATIONS: DB, 32–33; Oh, 68–69; Gl, 656; Be, 26–27 and 129–30; Le, 43 and 128–29; Se, 161. (SK 589)

SOLUTION: *CAPRA* (she-goat).

Compare Isidore, *Etym.* 12.1.15.

35.1 The she-goat in question is Amalthea, who according to classical myth nursed the young Zeus in Crete.

35.2 Be and Le both prefer *difficili,* and indeed the function of *de* here is hard to explain; but goats are notoriously sure-footed. Compare ALD 36.2 *(volitans super ardua pennis)* and ALD 74.8 *(versant super ardua corpus).*

35.3 Be prefers the alternative reading *voce* for *lingua,* although the sense remains the same.

SYM 36

MANUSCRIPTS: D, fol. 5r; X, 379; L, fol. 107v (no. 37); L², fol. 199v; G, fol. 391r (no. 37).

EARLIER EDITIONS AND TRANSLATIONS: DB, 32–33; Oh, 70–71; Gl, 657; Be, 28–29 and 130–31; Le, 44 and 129–31; Se, 161–62. (SK 14519)

SOLUTION: *PORCUS* (pig).

Compare Isidore, *Etym.* 12.1.25 *(sus).*

36.1 Note that *alvus,* though second declension, is grammatically feminine. Compare SYM 14.2 *(matris . . . natus in alvo);* ALD 93.10 *(genetrix . . . generaret ab alvo),* ALD 100.24 *(matris . . . generabar ab alvo);* TAT 15.5 *(matris . . . in alvum),* TAT 17.1 *(nascor . . . matris in alvo);* BER 34.1 *(mater concipit alvo).*

36.2 The "food from above" is mast or acorns.

36.3 Removing the *p* from *porcus* produces *orcus,* "death, the underworld." A similar kind of logogriph is found at SYM 74.3 (*LAPIS,* "stone," where *lapis* becomes *apis,* "bee"). The alliteration of *prima periret* presumably highlights the letter to be removed. Other logogriphs in the Anglo-Saxon riddle tradition are discussed in the headnote to ALD 63 (*CORBUS,* "raven") above.

36.3 Note the paronomasia at *nomine numen habens.* For variations on the formula *nomen habens,* see the note at ALD 50.3.

SYM 37

MANUSCRIPTS: D, fol. 5r; X, 379; L, fol. 107v (no. 38); L², fol. 199v; G, fol. 391r (no. 38).

EARLIER EDITIONS AND TRANSLATIONS: DB, 32–33; Oh, 70–71; Gl, 658; Wi2, 25; Be, 28–29 and 131–32; Le, 44 and 131–32; Se, 162. (SK 13806)

SOLUTION: *MULA* (mule).

Compare Isidore, *Etym.* 12.1.57.

37.1 Reading *patri matri* with Be. Compare Ovid, *Metamorphoses* 5.211 *(simulacra videt diversa figuris).*

37.3 Le reads *quicquam* (as he explains on 132).

SYM 38

MANUSCRIPTS: D, fol. 5r; X, 379; L, fol. 107v (no. 39); L², fol. 199v; G, fol. 391r (no. 33).

EARLIER EDITIONS AND TRANSLATIONS: DB, 32–33; Oh, 70–73; Gl, 659; Wi3, 152; Be, 28–29 and 132–33; Le, 44 and 133–34; Se, 162. (SK 7)

SOLUTION: *TIGRIS* (tigress).

Compare Isidore, *Etym.* 12.2.7.

38.1 The idea that the Persian word for "arrow" was *tigris,* and that both the river and the beast were named from there, is found in Pliny, *Nat. Hist.* 7.127.

38.2 The notion that swift creatures are impregnated by the wind is discussed by Pliny, *Nat. Hist.* 8.166.

SYM 39

MANUSCRIPTS: D, fol. 5r; X, 379; L, fol. 108r (no. 40); L², fol. 200r; G, fol. 391r–v (no. 40).

EARLIER EDITIONS AND TRANSLATIONS: DB, 32–33; Oh, 72–73; Gl, 660; Wi2, 25; Be, 30–31 and 133–34; Le, 44 and 64–66; Se, 162. (SK 13140)

SOLUTION: *CENTAURUS* (centaur).

Compare Isidore, *Etym.* 12.1.43.

39.1 Compare ALD 71.1 *(pedibus manibusque);* EUS 40.2 *(manibus pedibusque).*

SYM 40

MANUSCRIPTS: D, fol. 5r; X, 379; L, fol. 108r (no. 41); L², fol. 79r, 201r; G, fol. 391v (no. 41).

EARLIER EDITIONS AND TRANSLATIONS: DB, 34–35; Oh, 72–73; Gl, 661; Wi3, 153; Be, 30–31 and 134–35; Le, 44 and 136–37; Se, 163. (SK 5664)

SOLUTION: *PAPAVER* (poppy).

Compare Isidore, *Etym.* 17.9.31. For other one-footed creatures in the tradition, see the headnote to TAT 10 (*RECITABULUM*, "lectern").

40.1 Compare SYM 87.3 *(Grande mihi caput est);* TAT 28.1 *(Grande caput).*

40.2 Compare SYM 64.2 *(unus praeterea dens est et solus in imo).*

SYM 41

MANUSCRIPTS: D, fol. 5r; X, 379; L, fol. 108r (no. 42); L², fol. 79r, 201r; G, fol. 391v (no. 42).

EARLIER EDITIONS AND TRANSLATIONS: DB, 34–35; Oh, 72–75; Gl, 662; Be, 30–31 and 135; Le, 44 and 137–38; Se, 163. (SK 862)

SOLUTION: *MALVA* (mallow).

Compare Isidore, *Etym.* 12.5.5.

41.2–3 Compare Virgil, *Aeneid* 6.482 *(quos ille omnis longo ordine cernens).*

SYM 42

MANUSCRIPTS: D, fol. 5r; X, 379–80; L, fol. 108r (no. 43); L², fol. 79r, 201r; G, fol. 391v (no. 43).

EARLIER EDITIONS AND TRANSLATIONS: DB, 34–35; Oh, 74–75; Gl, 663; Be, 32–33 and 135–36; Le, 44 and 138–41; Se, 163. (SK 1685)

SOLUTION: *BETA* (beet).

Compare Isidore, *Etym.* 17.10.15. The conceit turns on the fact that the whole of *beta* is the name of a Greek letter, while half of it (*be*) is the name of the equivalent Latin letter.

42.2 There are widely divergent readings in the manuscripts here (see Le, 140); I take the one preferred here to mean that in the middle of the word *tabernam* we find *be*, preceded by *ta* (with *ta–be* being also obviously a reversal of *be–ta*). Compare ALD 78.4 *(nectare cauponis complens ex vite tabernam).*

42.3 Compare Horace, *Sermones* 1.6.123 *(unguor olivo).*

SYM 43

MANUSCRIPTS: D, fol. 5v; X, 380; L, fol. 108r (no. 44); L², fol. 79r, 201r; G, fol. 391v (no. 44).

EARLIER EDITIONS AND TRANSLATIONS: DB, 34–35; Oh, 74–77; Gl, 664; Be, 32–33 and 136–37; Le, 44 and 141–42; Se, 163. (SK 11829)

SOLUTION: *CUCURBITA* (gourd).

Compare Isidore, *Etym.* 17.10.16; Pliny, *Nat. Hist.* 19.69–74.

The whole aenigma is constructed around wordplay on *Pendeo . . . pendeo . . . pendens . . . Pendula.*

SYM 44

MANUSCRIPTS: D, fol. 5v; X, 380; L, fol. 108r–v (no. 45); L², fol. 79r, 201r; G, fol. 391v (no. 45).

EARLIER EDITIONS AND TRANSLATIONS: DB, 34–35; Oh, 76–77; Gl, 665; Be, 32–33 and 137–38; Howe (1985), 40–41; Le, 45 and 142–43; Se, 164. (SK 9777)

SOLUTION: *CAEPA* (onion). See further Orchard, "Enigma Variations," 295–97; Murphy, *Unriddling the Exeter Riddles,* 166 and 223–24.

Like the previous aenigma, this one is also constructed around wordplay, in this case *Mordeo mordentes . . . mordeo . . . mordentem . . . mordere . . . morsum.* This is the earliest example of the "biter bitten" motif, playing on the *dentes,* "teeth," element in *mordentes,* "biters." Compare Isidore, *Etym.* 17.10.12; Pliny, *Nat. Hist.* 19.101.

44.1 Compare ALD 46.1 *(torqueo torquentes sed nullum torqueo sponte);* TAT 7.6 *(Mordeo mordentem);* BER 37.5 *(Mordeo mordentem).*

SYM 45

MANUSCRIPTS: D, fol. 5v; X, 380; L, fol. 108v (no. 46); L², fol. 79r, 201r; G, fol. 391v (no. 46).

EARLIER EDITIONS AND TRANSLATIONS: DB, 36–37; Oh, 76–79; Gl, 666; Wi3, 152; Be, 34–35 and 138–43; Le, 45 and 143–45; Se, 164. (SK 12790)

SOLUTION: *ROSA* (rose).

Compare Isidore, Etym. 17.9.17. Note the insistent alliteration on *p-* and *f-/v- (Purpura . . . pulchro perfuse . . . violer . . . defendor . . . felix . . . vivere fato).*

45.1 Be prefers the alternative reading *rubore* (as she explains on 141), but compare SYM 2.2 *(perfusa colore).*

45.2 Compare SYM 29.2 *(telis . . . acutis).* The form *violer* is presumably a pun on *viola,* "violet," the subject of the aenigma that follows.

45.3 Compare ALD 81.6 *(O felix).*

SYM 46

MANUSCRIPTS: D, fol. 5v; X, 380; L, fol. 108v (no. 47); L², fol. 79r, 201r; G, fol. 391v (no. 47).

EARLIER EDITIONS AND TRANSLATIONS: DB, 36–37; Oh, 78–79; Gl, 667; Wi3, 152; Be, 34–35 and 143–44; Le, 45 and 145–46; Se, 164. (SK 9178)

SOLUTION: *VIOLA* (violet).

Compare Isidore, *Etym.* 17.9.19.

46.2 The violet's scent *(spiritus)* is indeed strong, and plays on the primary meaning of the Latin word as "spirit"; there is a clear contrast between body and spirit in this line.

46.3 The contrast is with the harmful thorns of the rose, the subject of the preceding aenigma.

SYM 47

MANUSCRIPTS: D, fol. 5v; X, 380; L, fol. 108v (no. 48); L^2, fol. 79r, 201r; G, fol. 391v (no. 48).

EARLIER EDITIONS AND TRANSLATIONS: DB, 36–37; Oh, 78–81; Gl, 668; Wi3, 153; Be, 34–35 and 144–45; Le, 45 and 147–49; Se, 147. (SK 3989)

SOLUTION: *TUS* (incense). See further Salvador-Bello, *Isidorean Perceptions,* 131–32.

There is an evident olfactory connection between the subjects of this and the preceding aenigma. Compare Isidore, *Etym.* 17.8.3.

47.1 Note the insistent alliteration of *flamma fumoque fatigor.*

47.3 Reading *nec mihi poena datur sed habetur gratia dandi* with Be.

SYM 48

MANUSCRIPTS: D, fol. 5v; X, 380; L, fol. 108v (no. 49); L^2, fol. 79r, 201r; G, fol. 391v (no. 49): *DE SUCINO.*

EARLIER EDITIONS AND TRANSLATIONS: DB, 36–37; Oh, 80–81; Gl, 669; Be, 36–37 and 145–46; Le, 45 and 149–50; Se, 68–69 and 165. (SK 3363)

SOLUTION: *MURRA* (myrrh).

Just as the rose and the violet of SYM 45–46 are traditionally linked, so too are incense and myrrh, as in Pliny, *Nat. Hist.* 10.66–71, so providing a further pair at SYM 47–48. The reference here is to the mythical origin of myrrh as the resinous teardrops of the metamorphosed Myrrha, the mother of Adonis, bewailing her incestuous relationship with her father, Cinyras. The tale is told with customary flair by Ovid, *Metamorphoses* 10.298–502. Compare Isidore, *Etym.* 17.8.4.

48.3 Reading *frondis* with Be.

SYM 49

MANUSCRIPTS: D, fol. 5v; X, 380; L, fol. 108v (no. 50); L^2, fol. 79v, 201r–v; G, fol. 391v (no. 50).

EARLIER EDITIONS AND TRANSLATIONS: DB, 36–37; Oh, 80–83; Gl, 670; Be, 36–37 and 146–47; Le, 45 and 151–52; Se, 165. (SK 3484)

SOLUTION: *EBUR* (ivory).

The exotic origins of both incense and myrrh in SYM 47–48 presumably provide a link to the subject of this aenigma. Compare Isidore, *Etym.* 16.5.19.

49.1 Le prefers *prognatus* (as he explains on 151).

SYM 50

MANUSCRIPTS: D, fol. 5v; X, 380–81; L, fol. 109r (no. 51); L^2, fol. 79v and 201v; G, fol. 392r (no. 51).

EARLIER EDITIONS AND TRANSLATIONS: DB, 38–39; Oh, 82–83; Gl, 671; Be, 36–37 and 147–48; Le, 45 and 152–54; Se, 165. (SK 6199)

SOLUTION: *FAENUM* (hay).

Compare Isidore, *Etym.* 17.9.106.

50.1 Compare Virgil, *Georgics* 2.219 *(viridi de gramine).*

50.2 Note the oxymoron *duro mollis,* and the paronomasia on *mollis . . . mole.*

50.3 The enclosure mentioned here is presumably the barn. Other riddles that focus on both the container and the contained include SYM 14.3 (*PULLUS IN OVO,* "chick in egg").

SYM 51

MANUSCRIPTS: Not in D; X, 381; L, fol. 109r (no. 52); L², fol. 79v, 201v; G, fol. 392r (no. 52).

EARLIER EDITIONS AND TRANSLATIONS: DB, 38–39; Oh, 82–83; Gl, 672; Be, 38–39 and 148–49; Le, 45 and 154–55; Se, 165. (SK 700)

SOLUTION: *MOLA* (millstone).

Compare Isidore, *Etym.* 20.8.6.

The connection to the preceding aenigma seems slight, although the forms *mollis,* "soft," and *mole,* "bulk," in successive lines (SYM 50.2–3) may have prompted thoughts of the bulky but not-so-soft *mola.*

51.2 Be prefers the alternative reading *tantum non est* (as she explains on 149).

SYM 52

MANUSCRIPTS: D, fol. 5v–6r (no. 51); X, 381; L, fol. 109r (no. 53); L², fol. 79v, 201v; G, fol. 392r (no. 53).

EARLIER EDITIONS AND TRANSLATIONS: DB, 38–39; Oh, 84–85; Gl, 673; Wi2, 26; Be, 38–39 and 149–51; Le, 46 and 155–57; Se, 166. (SK 8227)

SOLUTION: *FARINA* (flour).

The link between this aenigma and the previous one seems obvious. Compare Isidore, *Etym.* 20.2.18.

52.3 Compare ALD 80.4; TAT 8.1, TAT 9.1, TAT 12.5; ALF X.1 *(mihi . . . forma).*

SYM 53

MANUSCRIPTS: D, fol. 6r (no. 52); X, 381; L, fol. 109r (no. 54); L[2], fol. 79v, 201v; G, fol. 392r (no. 54).

EARLIER EDITIONS AND TRANSLATIONS: DB, 38–39; Oh, 84–85; Gl, 674; Wi2, 26; Be, 38–39 and 151–52; Le, 46 and 157–59; Se, 166. (SK 10308)

SOLUTION: *VITIS* (vine).

The anaphora on *Nolo* is striking. Compare Isidore, *Etym.* 17.5.2.

53.1 The grafting of a vine onto a tree was widely described as a form of marriage, and the metaphor is exploited here to the full. Note the number of aenigmata in this collection that concern wine and drinking in general, of which this is the first; the others are in a sequence SYM 82 (*LAGENA,* "earthenware jar"), 83 (*CONDITUM,* "spiced wine"), and SYM 84 (*VINUM IN ACETUM CONVERSUM,* "wine turned to vinegar"). Such a focus only emphasizes the etymological connection of Symphosius with drinking parties (*symposia*).

53.2 Note the elision at *propago est*; see further the note at SYM PR.16 above.

SYM 54

MANUSCRIPTS: D, fol. 6r (no. 53); X, 381; L, fol. 109r (no. 55); L[2], fol. 79v, 201v; G, fol. 392r (no. 55).

EARLIER EDITIONS AND TRANSLATIONS: DB, 38–39; Oh, 86–87; Gl, 675; Be, 40–41 and 152–53; Le, 46 and 159–64; Se, 166. (SK 4803)

SOLUTION: *HAMUS* (hook).

See too Riley, *Anglo-Saxon Tools,* 127–29.

54.1 Le prefers *corpus,* and notes the parallels with SYM 34.1 (*Exiguum corpus*). Compare Lucretius, *De rerum natura* 2.427 (*flexis mucronibus unca*).

SYM 55

MANUSCRIPTS: D, fol. 6r (no. 53); X, 381; L, fol. 109r–v (no. 56); L[2], fol. 79v, 201v; G, fol. 392r (no. 56).

EARLIER EDITIONS AND TRANSLATIONS: DB, 40–41; Oh, 86–87; Gl, 676; Be, 40–41 and 153–54; Le, 46 and 162–63; Se, 166. (SK 8989)

SOLUTION: *ACULA* (needle). See further Cavell, *Weaving Words,* 36.

Compare Isidore, *Etym.* 19.31.9.

SYM 56

MANUSCRIPTS: D, fol. 6r (no. 55); X, 381; L, fol. 109v (no. 57); L[2], fol. 79v, 201v; G, fol. 392r (no. 57): *DE FICONE.*

EARLIER EDITIONS AND TRANSLATIONS: DB, 40–41; Oh, 88–89; Gl, 677; Be, 40–41 and 154–55; Le, 46 and 163–65; Se, 167. (SK 9233)

SOLUTION: *CALIGA* (boot). See further Bitterli, *Say What I Am Called,* 32; Cavell, *Weaving Words,* 159.

Compare Isidore, *Etym.* 19.34.12.

56.1 The phrase *dum vita manebat* is a particular favorite of Virgil's (*Aeneid* 5.724, 6.608, and 661); here, the living creature from which the boot is formed is speaking, a contrast between the different fates and functions of the living and the dead that is a commonplace of the tradition. See further the headnote to EXE 10 above.

56.2–3 Each of the five successive adjectives (four of them past participles) signals a stage in the formation of the boot *(exanimis lacerata ligata revulsa dedita);* compare the same technique in EXE 26.4–6 (*EALU,* "ale").

56.3 For the polyptoton *dedita . . . condita* here, see the note on SYM 9.3 above.

SYM 57

MANUSCRIPTS: D, fol. 6r (no. 56); X, 381; L, fol. 109v (no. 58); L[2], fol. 79v, 201v; G, fol. 392r (no. 58).

EARLIER EDITIONS AND TRANSLATIONS: DB, 40–41; Oh, 88–89; Gl, 678; Be, 42–43 and 155–56; Le, 46 and 166–67; Se, 167. (SK 7828)

SOLUTION: *CLAVUS CALIGARIS* (hobnail).

The connection between this aenigma and the previous one is obvious.

57.1–2 Note the wordplay in the form of paronomasia on *solo*, "alone," and *solum* (which can mean both "ground" and "sole of the foot"). Compare Virgil, *Aeneid* 4.177 *(ingreditur . . . solo et caput inter nubila condit).*

57.2 Compare BON 14.13 *(vertice tango).*

SYM 58

MANUSCRIPTS: D, fol. 6r (no. 57); X, 381–82; L, fol. 109v (no. 59); L[2], fol. 80r; G, fol. 392r (no. 59).

EARLIER EDITIONS AND TRANSLATIONS: DB, 40–41; Oh, 88–91; Gl, 679; Wi2, 25; Be, 42–43 and 156–57; Le, 46 and 167–69; Se, 167. (SK 5136)

SOLUTION: *CAPILLUS* (hair).

The connection between this aenigma and the next is obvious. Note the insistent alliteration on *f-/v-* in *Findere . . . versicolor . . . futurus . . . fata verebor.*

58.1 Compare ALD 2.1 *(VENTUS,* "wind": *Cernere me nulli possunt),* BON 1.1 *(VERITAS AIT,* "truth speaks": *Vincere me nulli possunt).*

58.2 The final syllable of *versicolor* is lengthened at the caesura.

58.3 Compare SYM 10.1 *(GLACIES,* "ice": *ultima fata);* note the insistent alliteration.

SYM 59

MANUSCRIPTS: D, fol. 6r (no. 58); X, 382; L, fol. 109v (no. 60); L^2, fol. 80r; G, fol. 392r (no. 60).
EARLIER EDITIONS AND TRANSLATIONS: DB, 40–41; Oh, 90–91; Gl, 680; Be, 42–43 and 157–58; Le, 46 and 169–71; Se, 167. (SK 10493)
SOLUTION: *PILA* (ball).

The connection between this aenigma, which is also found embedded in the *Historia Apollonii Regis Tyri* (see *Manuscript Contexts* above), and the last is the hair with which the ball is stuffed. Compare Isidore, *Etym.* 18.69.2. The three words for "hair" here *(comis . . . capillis . . . crines)* are each scanned differently, a phenomenon observed widely within the Anglo-Latin tradition; see further the headnote to ALD PR.

59.1 Note the parallelism and insistent alliteration here *(cincta comis . . . compta capillis)*. Le prefers *compta comis . . . nuda capillis* (as he explains on 170–71).

59.3 For the polyptoton *mittunt . . . remittor* here, see the note on SYM 9.3 above. Note the impressive amount of alliteration in the first five words of this line too, this time on *m* (*Meque manus mittunt manibusque remittor)*.

SYM 60

MANUSCRIPTS: D, fol. 6r–v (no. 59); X, 382; L, fol. 109v (no. 61); L^2, fol. 80r; G, fol. 392r–v (no. 61).
EARLIER EDITIONS AND TRANSLATIONS: DB, 42–43; Oh, 92–93; Gl, 681; Be, 44–45 and 158–59; Le, 47 and 171–72; Se, 167–68. (SK 16265)
SOLUTION: *SERRA* (saw).

Once again, the link with the preceding aenigma is hair, in this case the metaphorical hair of trees (using the extremely rare compound *frondicomas*). The conceit offers a kind of riddle within a riddle, as commonly within the tradition (see further the note at EXE 1.12–14a). Such an implicit connection may have inspired ALC 1 (*PECTEN*, "comb"). Compare Isidore, *Etym.* 19.19.9.

60.2 Compare Virgil, *Aeneid* 2.215 *(morsu depascitur).*

60.3 The use of the word *praemia,* "booty," for what the creature in question produces is echoed in SYM 22.2 *(ipsa ferens umeris securae praemia brumae).*

SYM 61

MANUSCRIPTS: D, fol. 8v (no. 99); X, 382; L, fol. 113v (no. 101); L[2], fol. 80r; G, fol. 394r (no. 101).

EARLIER EDITIONS AND TRANSLATIONS: DB, 42–43; Oh, 92–93; Gl, 682; Be, 44–45 and 159–60; Le, 47 and 173–74; Se, 168. (SK 3493)

SOLUTION: *ANCORA* (anchor).

In this aenigma, which is also found embedded in the *Historia Apollonii Regis Tyri* (see *Manuscript Contexts* above), there seems to be a self-conscious attempt to cover earth, sea, and sky, a feature that is found widely elsewhere in the tradition. See further the headnote to EXE 1, and Lendinara, "Aspetti della società germanica"; Bardowell, "Art and Emotion," 144–48. Compare Isidore, *Etym.* 19.2.15.

61.1 The use of the word *mucro,* "blade," for what the creature in question wields is echoed in SYM 54.1 *(AMUS,* "hook": *Exiguum munus flexu mucronis adunci).*

SYM 62

MANUSCRIPTS: D, fol. 6v (no. 60); X, 382; L, fol. 110r; L[2], fol. 80r; G, fol. 392v.

EARLIER EDITIONS AND TRANSLATIONS: DB, 42–43; Oh, 92–93; Gl, 683; Be, 44–45 and 160–61; Le, 47 and 175–76; Se, 168. (SK 15661)

SOLUTION: *PONS* (bridge). Note the three different words for water *(lymphis . . . gurgite . . . undis),* each of which might fulfill a different function in a hexameter line.

62.3 The sense seems to be that just as the trees that supply the wood for the bridge come out of the ground, so too they give a good grounding for those traveling over the bridge. This is another riddle within a riddle.

SYM 63

MANUSCRIPTS: D, fol. 6v (no. 61); X, 382; L, fol. 110r; L², fol. 80r; G, fol. 392v.

EARLIER EDITIONS AND TRANSLATIONS: DB, 42–43; Oh, 94–95; Gl, 684; Be, 46–47 and 161–62; Le, 47 and 176–78; Se, 168. (SK 8342)

SOLUTION: *SPONGIA* (sponge).

The watery associations of the previous two aenigmata presumably prompt this one, which is also found embedded in the *Historia Apollonii Regis Tyri* (see *Manuscript Contexts* above); the sequence is maintained in the aenigma that follows.

63.1 Compare SYM 3.1 *(pondus inhaesi).*

SYM 64

MANUSCRIPTS: D, fol. 6v (no. 62); X, 382; L, fol. 110r; L², fol. 80r; G, fol. 392v.

EARLIER EDITIONS AND TRANSLATIONS: DB, 42–43; Oh, 94–95; Gl, 685; Wi2, 26; Be, 46–47 and 162–63; Le, 47 and 178–80; Se, 58–59 and 168. (SK 16460)

SOLUTION: *TRIDENS* (trident). See too Riley, *Anglo-Saxon Tools,* 127.

See the headnote to the previous aenigma; this is the fourth in a sequence of aenigmata linked with water. It also begins a sequence of three aenigmata on weapons of various kinds, associated with sea, sky, and earth. For the notion that there is a potential Christian Trinitarian–Unitarian perspective here, see Se, 58–59, and the note at SYM 82 (*CONDITUM,* "spiced wine") below.

64.1 The opening line offers a broad hint to the solution through etymological association *(tres . . . dentes).* For the phrase *unus quos continent ordo,* compare SYM 41.2 *(plures ordine cernis)* and 78.2 *(quas unus continet ordo).*

64.2 Presumably a spiked handle is being described.

64.3 The divinity in question is of course the trident-wielding Neptune.

SYM 65

MANUSCRIPTS: D, fol. 6v (no. 63); X, 382; L, fol. 110r; L², fol. 80r; G, fol. 392v.

EARLIER EDITIONS AND TRANSLATIONS: DB, 44–45; Oh, 96–97; Gl, 686; Be, 46–47 and 163–64; Le, 47 and 180–81; Se, 169. (SK 14516)

SOLUTION: *SAGITTA* (arrow).

See the headnote to the preceding aenigma. Compare ALC D85 (*SAGITTA,* "arrow"), which, however, deals rather differently with the creature in question.

65.1–2 Compare ALD 75.1 *(aera per sudum . . . pennis).*

SYM 66

MANUSCRIPTS: D, fol. 6v (no. 64); X, 382–83; L, fol. 110r; L², fol. 80r; G, fol. 392v.

EARLIER EDITIONS AND TRANSLATIONS: DB, 44–45; Oh, 96–97; Gl, 687; Be, 48–49 and 164–65; Le, 47 and 181–82; Se, 169. (SK 3374)

SOLUTION: *FLAGELLUM* (whip).

See the headnote to SYM 64 (*TRIDENS,* "trident"). Compare SYM 56 (*CALIGA,* "boot") for another aenigma that mentions both the leather product and the living creature from which it was made, a commonplace of the "bullock" riddles (on which see the note on ALD 83 (*IUVENCUS,* "bullock").

66.2 Be prefers the alternative reading *obsequio cogens moderati* (as she explains on 154–55; note that manuscript D has *moderate*); here I give *memorata,* following LL^2GX.

SYM 67

MANUSCRIPTS: D, fol. 6v (no. 65); X, 383; L, fol. 110r–v; L^2, fol. 80v; G, fol. 392v.

EARLIER EDITIONS AND TRANSLATIONS: DB, 44–45; Oh, 96–99; Gl, 688; Be, 48–49 and 165–66; Le, 47 and 183–84; Se, 44 and 169. (SK 2783)

SOLUTION: *LANTERNA* (lantern).

Ancient lanterns consisted of a frame made from any number of substances, such as wood, metal, or ceramic, to which were fitted "windows" made of some translucent material such as horn, glass, or stretched skin, usually bladder. This aenigma introduces a sequence of three dealing with light and vision. Compare Isidore, *Etym.* 20.10.7.

67.2 Compare ALD 44.7 *(sideris instar).*

SYM 68

MANUSCRIPTS: D, fol. 6v (no. 66); X, 383; L, fol. 110v; L^2, fol. 81r (after SYM 78); G, fol. 392v.

EARLIER EDITIONS AND TRANSLATIONS: DB, 44–45; Oh, 98–99; Gl, 689; Be, 48–49 and 166–67; Le, 48 and 184–87; Se, 169. (SK 11934)

SOLUTION: *VITREUM* (windowpane).

The second of three aenigmata dealing with the visual world; see the headnote to the preceding aenigma. The fact that so many of the alliterating elements begin with or simply comprise the first two letters of the Latin word *me,* "me," is presumably part of the clue, reflecting back the reader *(<u>me</u>a <u>me</u>mbra <u>me</u>antes . . . <u>me</u> . . . <u>me</u>).*

SYM 69

MANUSCRIPTS: D, fol. 6v (no. 67); X, 383; L, fol. 110v; L^2, fol. 80v; G, fol. 392v.

EARLIER EDITIONS AND TRANSLATIONS: DB, 44–45; Oh, 100–101; Gl, 690; Wi2, 25; Be, 50–51 and 167–68; Le, 48 and 187–89; Se, 169–70. (SK 10664)

SOLUTION: *SPECULUM* (mirror).

This aenigma, which is also found embedded in the *Historia Apollonii Regis Tyri* (see *Manuscript Contexts* above), is the third in a sequence that focuses on aspects of sight and vision; see the headnote to SYM 67 (*LANTERNA*, "lantern") above.

69.1 Note the elision at *nulla est;* see further the note at SYM PR.16 above.

SYM 70

MANUSCRIPTS: D, fol. 7r (no. 68); X, 383; L, fol. 110v; L^2, fol. 80v; G, fol. 392v.

EARLIER EDITIONS AND TRANSLATIONS: DB, 46–47; Oh, 100–103; Gl, 691; Be, 50–51 and 168–69; Le, 48 and 189–91; Se, 170. (SK 8877)

SOLUTION: *CLEPSYDRA* (water clock).

Note the insistent alliteration on *l-* and *f-*, as well as the contrast between silence and speech underlined by the gerunds in successive lines *(dicendi . . . tacendi . . . loquendi),* on which see further Orchard, "Performing Writing and Singing Silence," 84–85. This aenigma highlights the rhetorical concerns of the collection as a whole, since the use of water clocks in the ancient world was particularly prevalent for allotting the amount of time a speaker was allowed to make his case. This aenigma introduces a sequence of three aenigmata dealing with water.

SYM 71

MANUSCRIPTS: D, fol. 7r (no. 69); X, 383; L, fol. 110v; L², fol. 80v; G, fol. 392v–93r.

EARLIER EDITIONS AND TRANSLATIONS: DB, 46–47; Oh, 102–3; Gl, 692; Be, 50–51 and 169–70; Le, 48 and 191–93; Se, 170. (SK 9612)

SOLUTION: *PUTEUS* (well). See further Bitterli, *Say What I Am Called,* 103–5.

For the connection of this aenigma to both the preceding and following aenigmata, all with watery connections, see the headnote to SYM 70 (*CLEPSYDRA,* "water clock") above.

71.1 Compare SYM 72.1 *(terra . . . in cespite lymphae).*

71.3 Note the pun (a form of paronomasia) on the verb *labor* and the noun *labore.*

SYM 72

MANUSCRIPTS: D, fol. 7r (no. 70); X, 383; L, fol. 110v; L², fol. 80v; G, fol. 393r.

EARLIER EDITIONS AND TRANSLATIONS: DB, 46–47; Oh, 102–5; Gl, 693; Be, 52–53 and 170–71; Le, 48 and 193–94; Se, 170. (SK 16503)

SOLUTION: *TUBUS* (pipe).

What seems at issue here is a wooden water pipe, rather than those of lead or terracotta which were widely prevalent in the ancient world; Pliny, *Nat. Hist.* 16.224, considers what kind of wood is best suited to be made into pipes. This is the third in a sequence of three aenigmata that focus on aspects of water; see the headnote to SYM 70 (*CLEPSYDRA,* "water clock") above.

72.1 Be prefers *stipite* (as she explains on 170), but compare SYM 71.1 *(PUTEUS,* "well": *terris in cespite lympha).* Note the insistent alliteration on *t-* and *l-.*

72.3 Note the double polyptoton *ligno vehitur . . . ligna vehebat;* compare the note on SYM 9.3 (*PLUVIA,* "rain"). On the idea of water supporting wood, see, for example, ALD 29 (*AQUA*, "water") and EUS 23 (*AEQUOR*, "ocean").

SYM 73

MANUSCRIPTS: D, fol. 7r (no. 71); X, 383; L, fol. 111r; L^2, fol. 80v; G, fol. 393r.

EARLIER EDITIONS AND TRANSLATIONS: DB, 46–47; Oh, 104–5; Gl, 694; Wi2, 26; Be, 52–53 and 171–72; Le, 48 and 194–96; Se, 170–71. (SK 10387)

SOLUTION: *UTER FOLLIS* (bellows). See further Murphy, *Unriddling the Exeter Riddles*, 216.

Here we find yet another creature that is created from leather; the pipe at the tip of the bellows provides an obvious link back to the preceding aenigma. The anthropocentric tenor of the majority of the texts in the riddle tradition is particularly pronounced here. This aenigma appears to have inspired at least the second half of EXE 35 (*BLÆST-BELG*, "bellows"; see especially EXE 35.5–8).

73.3 Note the elision at *magna est;* see further the note at SYM PR.16 and 9.3 above.

SYM 74

MANUSCRIPTS: D, fol. 7r (no. 72); X, 383–84; L, fol. 111r; L^2, fol. 80v; G, fol. 393r.

EARLIER EDITIONS AND TRANSLATIONS: DB, 46–47; Oh, 104–5; Gl, 695; Wi2, 26; Be, 52–53 and 172–73; Le, 48 and 196–97; Se, 45, 63–65, and 171. (SK 3534)

SOLUTION: *LAPIS* (stone).

This aenigma opens a sequence of three (or four: see the headnote on SYM 76 below) that deal with the mineral world, and is one of several in SYM that make cunning use of classical allusion, on which see Se, 62–69.

74.3 Compare SYM 36.3 (*PORCUS*, "pig") for a similar logogriph; for variations on the formula *nomen habens*, see the note at ALD 50.3. Note that bees were classified alongside the birds in ancient texts, as in Isidore, *Etym.* 20.8.1, where bees appear first in the list of "small flying creatures" *(De minutis volatilibus)*, immediately after birds.

SYM 75

MANUSCRIPTS: D, fol. 7r (no. 73); X, 384; L, fol. 111r; L^2, fol. 80v; G, fol. 393r.

EARLIER EDITIONS AND TRANSLATIONS: DB, 48–49; Oh, 106–7; Gl, 696; Be, 54–55 and 173–74; Le, 48 and 198–99; Se, 171. (SK 4735)

SOLUTION: *CALX* (lime).

For the use of lime in the Roman world, mostly for building, see Pliny, *Nat. Hist.* 36.173–79.

75.1 Another example of chiasmus, bracketed by finite verbs.

75.2 Compare ALD 54.2 *(contraria fata)*. The sense is that lime is consumed by fire through the very substance that should naturally consume fire.

75.3 Compare ALD 100.76 *(gelidis . . . limphis)*. Le prefers *accendor* (as he explains on 198–99).

SYM 76 AND 76A

MANUSCRIPTS: D, fol. 7r (no. 74); X, 384 (no. 76); L, fol. 111r; L^2, fol. 80v; G, fol. 393r.

EARLIER EDITIONS AND TRANSLATIONS: DB, 48–49; Oh, 106–9; Gl, 697; Be, 54–55 and 174–75; Le, 49 and 198–201; Se, 171. (SK 14872 and 17362)

SOLUTION: *SILEX* (flint).

There are two aenigmata on the same subject that appear adjacent in one class of manuscripts and as alternatives in two others, apparently part of a sequence that deals with the mineral world; the link with the preceding aenigma focuses on the intimate association of both lime and flint with fire. Part of the difference between them lies in the fact that the former is couched in the third person, and the latter in the first. Note the wordplay in SYM 76a on *intus . . . intus, ignis . . . lignis, igne . . . ignis, intus inest in*. The existence of variant versions provides powerful testimony that the sequence of associations is a significant feature of the collection as a whole. For a similar aenigma, see ALC D75 (*SILEX*, "flint"). On flint in general, see Pliny, *Nat. Hist.* 36.168–69.

76.1 Compare SYM 76a.3 (*SILEX*, "flint": *Semper inest in me, sed raro cernitur ignis)*.

SYM 77

MANUSCRIPTS: D, fol. 7r (no. 75); X, 384 (no. 77); L, fol. 111r; L^2, fol. 81r; G, fol. 393r.

EARLIER EDITIONS AND TRANSLATIONS: DB, 48–49; Oh, 108–9; Gl, 700; Be, 56–57 and 175–76; Le, 49 and 201–2; Se, 172. (SK 13116)

SOLUTION: *ROTAE* (wheels).

The plural solution for this aenigma echoes that for the next, and the order of both is different in different manuscripts, again underlining the notion that the association of each (in either order) is a feature of the collection as a whole, with sequencing a central issue.

77.1 Compare ALD 66.1 *(aequales . . . sorores)* and EUS 48.1 *(aequales . . . sorores)*.

77.2 Compare Virgil, *Georgics* 4.184 *(omnibus una quies operum, labor omnibus unus)*.

77.3 Reading *prope sunt* after Le; Be prefers *properant*.

SYM 78

MANUSCRIPTS: D, fol. 7r–v (no. 76); X, 387 (no. 99); L, fol. 111r; L[2], fol. 81r; G, fol. 393r.

EARLIER EDITIONS AND TRANSLATIONS: DB, 48–49; Oh, 108–11; Gl, 699; Be, 56–57 and 176–77; Le, 49 and 203–4; Se, 172. (SK 10574)

SOLUTION: *SCALAE* (steps, ladder).

See the headnote to the previous aenigma. This aenigma, like the one that follows, is also found embedded in the *Historia Apollonii Regis Tyri* (see *Manuscript Contexts* above).

78.2 Compare SYM 64.1 *(unus quos continet ordo).*

78.3 Le prefers *comitemur* (as he explains on 204–5).

SYM 79

MANUSCRIPTS: D, fol. 7v (no. 77); X, 384 (no. 78); L, fol. 111v; L[2], fol. 81r; G, fol. 393r.

EARLIER EDITIONS AND TRANSLATIONS: DB, 50–51; Oh, 110–11; Gl, 701; Be, 56–57 and 177–78; Le, 49 and 204–5; Se, 172. (SK 9882)

SOLUTION: *SCOPA* (broom).

This aenigma is also found embedded in the *Historia Apollonii Regis Tyri* (see *Manuscript Contexts* above).

79.1 There is wordplay here on *mundus,* which as an adjective means “clean,” and as a noun “world.” Both are applicable here; the translation “great mother of the world” is also applicable.

79.2 Reading *iuncta* after Be and Le; Gl prefers *vincta.*

SYM 80

MANUSCRIPTS: D, fol. 7v (no. 78); X, 384 (no. 79); L, fol. 111v; L[2], fol. 81r; G, fol. 393r.

EARLIER EDITIONS AND TRANSLATIONS: DB, 50–51; Oh, 110–13; Gl, 702; Be, 58–59 and 178–79; Le, 49 and 205–7; Se, 172. (SK 389)

SOLUTION: *TINTINNABULUM* (bell). See further Murphy, *Unriddling the Exeter Riddles,* 72; Cavell, *Weaving Words,* 166.

80.3 Be reads *motus quam* for *motus quoque* (as she explains on 179).

SYM 81

MANUSCRIPTS: D, fol. 7v (no. 79); X, 384 (no. 80); L, fol. 112r–v (no. 89); L[2], fol. 81r; G, fol. 393v (no. 89): *DE OLLA* (on a pot).
EARLIER EDITIONS AND TRANSLATIONS: DB, 50–51; Oh, 112–15; Gl, 703; Be, 58–59 and 179–80; Le, 49 and 207–10; Se, 173. (SK 9414)
SOLUTION: *LAGENA* (earthenware jar).

The open mouth of the jar is what likely links this aenigma to the last; the creature in question might also be construed as the first in a sequence of wine-related items that would encompass the following two aenigmata as well.

81.1 The mention of Prometheus links this aenigma back to those that are connected by fire, such as SYM 73–77. On the classical reference employed here, see the headnote to SYM, under "Subject Matter and Solutions."
81.2 Reading *rigent* after Le (as he explains on 208–9); Be prefers *regunt* (as she explains on 179–80).
81.3 Reading *dum cecidi subito mater mea me laniavit* after Be. Note the insistent alliteration, as well as the quadrisyllabic ending, found elsewhere at SYM 96.3 (*remanebunt*). The whole notion that the mother is the destroyer here contrasts sharply with others in the tradition.

SYM 82

MANUSCRIPTS: D, fol. 7v (no. 80); X, 384 (no. 81); L, fol. 111v (no. 81); L[2], fol. 81r; G, fol. 393r (no. 81): *DE POTU CUM MELLE* (about a drink with honey).

EARLIER EDITIONS AND TRANSLATIONS: DB, 50–51; Oh, 114–15; Gl, 704; Be, 58–59 and 180–81; Le, 49 and 210–12; Se, 57–58, and 173. (SK 16462)
SOLUTION: *CONDITUM* (spiced wine).

The suggested solution in L, which directly contradicts the single-word answer apparently required in the opening line, seems to reflect a particularly northern European concern, where the honeyed drink mead is the staple, and wine a luxury. Nonetheless, ancient recipes for spiced wine commonly combine the three elements wine, pepper, and honey; from a Christian perspective, the Trinitarian–Unitarian potential concerns are powerful here (see especially Be, 180–81, and Se, 57–58). This is the most obvious of the three (appropriately enough) three-in-one aenigmata in SYM: the others are 92 (*MULIER QUAE GEMINOS PARIEBAT,* "mother of twins") and 64 (*TRIDENS,* "trident"). This aenigma is evidently connected to the one that follows, as well as to the one preceding.

SYM 83

MANUSCRIPTS: D, fol. 7v (no. 81); X, 384–85 (no. 82); L, fol. 111v (no. 82); L², fol. 81r; G, fol. 393v (no. 82).
EARLIER EDITIONS AND TRANSLATIONS: DB, 50–51; Oh, 114–15; Gl, 705; Be, 60–61 and 181–82; Le, 49 and 212–13; Se, 57–58 and 173. (SK 15722)
SOLUTION: *VINUM IN ACETUM CONVERSUM* (wine turned to vinegar).

The connection of this aenigma to the previous one seems obvious, with the bitterness of the vinegar contrasting with the sweetness of the spiced wine noted previously. See further Dale, *Natural World,* 139 and 144.

83.3 Reading *inveni* after Be; Le prefers *invenio,* and transposes 83.2 and 3.

SYM 84

MANUSCRIPTS: D, fol. 7v (no. 82); X, 385 (no. 83); L, fol. 111v–12r (no. 83); L², fol. 81v (after SYM 87); G, fol. 393v (no. 83).

EARLIER EDITIONS AND TRANSLATIONS: DB, 52–53; Oh, 116–17; Gl, 706; Wi2, 25; Be, 60–61 and 182–83; Le, 50 and 213–16; Se, 174. (SK 110325)

SOLUTION: *MALUM* (apple).

84.1 Greek *μῆλον* can signify both "apple" (in its Attic form) and "sheep" (in its Homeric form); the further reference is to the tale of the apple inscribed "to the fairest" that was the focus of dispute between the goddesses Hera, Athena, and Aphrodite (Juno, Minerva, and Venus in the Roman tradition). They asked Paris (presumably the "beautiful" youth, reading *pulchri;* the alternative *cincti,* "bound up, girt," is obscure), and his decision to award the apple to Aphrodite helps spark the Trojan War. Compare ALF IIn.1 *(contentio magna).*

84.2 Reading *pulchri* after Be; Le prefers *functi,* "dead," which is indeed the reading of the majority of the manuscripts, but makes no clear sense.

84.3 The pun on *mălum,* "evil," as contrasted with *mālum,* "apple," is commonplace; the line is cited by Aldhelm towards the end of his *De metris* (Eh, 96). Several manuscripts contain an extra line: *excidium Troiae, dum bella cruenta peregi,* "the fall of Troy, when I ended bloody battles," with which compare SYM 26.2 *(bella cruenta).*

SYM 85

MANUSCRIPTS: D, fol. 7v (no. 83); X, 385 (no. 84); L, fol. 112r (no. 84); L², fol. 81v (after SYM 87); G, fol. 393v (no. 84).

EARLIER EDITIONS AND TRANSLATIONS: DB, 52–53; Oh, 118–19; Gl, 707; Be, 60–61 and 183–85; Le, 50 and 216–18; Se, 174. (SK 10235)

SOLUTION: *PERNA* (ham).

85.1 The reference is presumably to Marcus Porcius Cato, though the name is shared by both Cato the Elder (also known as Cato the Censor; 234–149 BCE), who among other things composed the treatise *De agri cultura* (On agriculture), and his grandson Cato the Younger (95–46 BCE), the Stoic, who clashed famously with Julius Caesar.

85.2 The "sister" is of course the other ham from the other back leg, though one can imagine a butcher's shop hung with many. Compare BER 56.1 *(Una mihi soror).*

85.3 Note the elision at *nata est;* see further the note at SYM PR.16 above. The salting and smoking of ham was commonplace; note the chiastic arrangement. The use of the term *sapientia* in its primary sense "savor" or "flavor" recalls *sapor.* Compare Isidore, *Etym.* 10.S.240 *(sapiens dictus a sapore).* Glorie reads *de muria mihi sapor inhaesit.*

SYM 86

MANUSCRIPTS: D, fol. 7v (no. 84); X, 385 (no. 85); L, fol. 112r (no. 85); L[2], fol. 81r; G, fol. 393v (no. 85).

EARLIER EDITIONS AND TRANSLATIONS: DB, 52–53; Oh, 118–19; Gl, 708; Be, 62–63 and 185–86; Le, 50 and 218–19; Se, 174. (SK 10388)

SOLUTION: *MALLEUS* (hammer).

This aenigma is presumably linked to the previous one by the similar shapes of a ham and a hammer.

86.3 Compare SYM 40.1 *(Grande mihi caput est);* TAT 28.1 *(Grande caput).* Be reads *cetera corporis absunt.*

SYM 87

MANUSCRIPTS: D, fol. 7v–8r (no. 85); X, 385 (no. 86); L, fol. 112r (no. 86); L[2], fol. 81v; G, fol. 393v (no. 86).

EARLIER EDITIONS AND TRANSLATIONS: DB, 52–53; Oh, 120–21; Gl, 709; Wi3, 153; Be, 62–63 and 186; Le, 50 and 219–20; Se, 175. (SK 2694)

SOLUTION: *PISTILLUS* (pestle).

Some conceptual link between this aenigma and the preceding one seems likely.

87.2 Compare SYM 94.2 *(unus . . . oculus capitum sed)* and BER 46.1 *(una mihi . . . cervix)*.

87.3 Reading *cetera corporis absunt* with Be. The contrast between heads and feet is a commonplace observation, characteristic of Symphosius: see, for example, SYM 40 (*PAPAVER*, "poppy"), SYM 41 (*MALVA*, "mallow"), SYM 57 (*CLAVUS CALIGARIS*, "hobnail"), and SYM 86 (*MALLEUS*, "hammer").

SYM 88

MANUSCRIPTS: D, fol. 8r (no. 86); X, 385 (no. 87); L, fol. 112r (no. 87); L², fol. 81v; G, fol. 393v (no. 87).

EARLIER EDITIONS AND TRANSLATIONS: DB, 52–53; Oh, 120–23; Gl, 710; Be, 62–63 and 186–87; Le, 50 and 220–22; Se, 175. (SK 14341)

SOLUTION: *STRIGILIS AENEA* (bronze strigil).

This aenigma introduces a series that focuses on leisure, with two on athletic activities (SYM 89–90) and two on gambling (SYM 91–92).

88.1 False quantity: the usual form is *rŭbida,* although the word is rare. Compare ALD 49.1 *(Horrida, curva, capax)*, ALD 93.8 *(Truxque rapaxque capaxque feroxque)*.

88.2 Glorie reads *fluminibus falsis aurum metita metallo.*

88.3 Note the medial rhyme at *sudori . . . labori.*

SYM 89

MANUSCRIPTS: D, fol. 8r (no. 87); X, 385 (no. 88); L, fol. 112r (no. 88); L[2], fol. 81v; G, fol. 393v (no. 88).

EARLIER EDITIONS AND TRANSLATIONS: DB, 54–55; Oh, 122–23; Gl, 711; Be, 64–65 and 187–89; Le, 50 and 222–24; Se, 175. (SK 11861)

SOLUTION: *BALNEUM* (bathhouse).

The connection of this aenigma with the preceding one is obvious.

89.3 For the contrast between a house and its guest, compare SYM 12.3 (*FLUMEN ET PISCIS,* "river and fish": *ambo tamen currunt hospes simul et domus una).* The phrase *nudus convenit hospes* is ambiguous, meaning "a naked guest convenes there," but also "a naked guest is convenient."

SYM 90

MANUSCRIPTS: D, fol. 8r (no. 88); X, 385 (no. 89); L, fol. 112v; L[2], fol. 81v; G, fol. 393v.

EARLIER EDITIONS AND TRANSLATIONS: DB, 54–55; Oh, 122–25; Gl, 712; Be, 64–65 and 189–90; Le, 50 and 224–26; Se, 175. (SK 3430)

SOLUTION: *TESSERA* (die).

The late antique association of gambling and the bathhouse connects this aenigma, which is also found embedded in the *Historia Apollonii Regis Tyri* (see *Manuscript Contexts* above), to the previous one.

90.1 Reading *futuri* with Be.

SYM 91

MANUSCRIPTS: D, fol. 8r (no. 89); X, 385–86 (no. 90); L, fol. 112v; L[2], fol. 81v; G, fol. 393v.

EARLIER EDITIONS AND TRANSLATIONS: DB, 54–55; Oh, 124–25; Gl, 713; Be, 64–65 and 190–91; Le, 50 and 226–28; Se, 175–76. (SK 16262)

SOLUTION: *PECUNIA* (money).

The link between this aenigma and the last is presumably through the gambler's dream of winnings; the aenigma is notable for its fourfold repetition of *terra,* twice in the first line and twice in the last.

91.1 Reading *abscondita terrae* with Be.

91.3 For the unusual sense "bought" for *paretur,* compare SYM 94.3 *(parabit).* There is presumably a pun on the creature's having been born of earth, and earth's having been born of it (which would require the unmetrical form *parietur*).

SYM 92

MANUSCRIPTS: D, fol. 8r (no. 90); X, 386 (no. 91); L, fol. 112v; L², fol. 81v; G, fol. 394r.

EARLIER EDITIONS AND TRANSLATIONS: DB, 54–55; Oh, 126–27; Gl, 714; Be, 66–67 and 191–93; Le, 51 and 228–30; Se, 58 and 176. (SK 12086)

SOLUTION: *MULIER QUAE GEMINOS PARIEBAT* (mother of twins).

This aenigma begins a sequence of four dealing with "wonders" or "marvels," all in the human sphere. For the Trinitarian aspects of this aenigma, see the note at SYM 82 above, and Se, 58.

92.3 Reading *peregit* after Le; Be prefers *secuta est.*

SYM 93

MANUSCRIPTS: D, fol. 8r (no. 91); X, 386 (no. 92); L, fol. 112v; L², fol. 81v; G, fol. 394r.

EARLIER EDITIONS AND TRANSLATIONS: DB, 54–55; Oh, 126–27; Gl, 715; Be, 66–67 and 193–94; Le, 51 and 230–33; Se, 176. (SK 1650)

SOLUTION: *MILES PODAGRICUS* (gouty soldier).

93.1 The compound *bellipotens* (as found for example in Virgil, *Aeneid* 11.8) is used here in a mock-heroic fashion, a theme found commonly in the Anglo-Saxon riddle tradition; see further the headnote at ALD 26 (*GALLUS*, "cockerel").

93.2 Reading *quinque pedes* with Be, who suggests (194) that five feet was the minimum height requirement for the Roman army. For an alternative suggestion, see Sebo, "Symphosius 93.2," who notes that three feet was the allotted space for each infantryman, to be added to the two feet on which he once stood in line while a serving soldier. Now, with his crippling gout and retirement, this veteran has barely two feet left.

93.3 Compare Ovid, *Metamorphoses* 3.466 *(inopem me copia fecit)*, which puns on the name of Saturn's wife, Ops, "plenty," and so is fitting as we come toward the boozy end of SYM, which celebrates the Saturnalia.

SYM 94

MANUSCRIPTS: D, fol. 8r (no. 92); X, 386 (no. 93); L, fol. 112v–13r; L², fol. 82r; G, fol. 394r.

EARLIER EDITIONS AND TRANSLATIONS: DB, 56–57; Oh, 128–29; Gl, 716; Be, 66–67 and 194–95; Le, 51 and 233–35; Se, 176–77. (SK 2104)

SOLUTION: *LUSCUS ALIUM VENDENS* (one-eyed garlic-seller). See further DiNapoli, "In the Kingdom of the Blind"; Bitterli, *Say What I Am Called*, 68–69; Murphy, *Unriddling the Exeter Riddles*, 42–43; Taylor, "Enigma Variations," 78–85; Lockhart, "Everyday Wonders," 54–55.

This aenigma is evidently the source of EXE 82, and indeed without it (and its extraordinary subject) we would be unlikely to solve the latter.

94.2 Compare BIB 4.3 *(Unus . . . oculus)*; SYM 87.2 *(una mihi . . . capitum sed)* and BER 46.1 *(una mihi . . . cervix)*; BON 14.3 *(milia multa)*.

94.3 For the unusual sense "get" (signifying "buy") for *parabit*, compare SYM 91.3 *(paretur)*, and the note there.

SYM 95

MANUSCRIPTS: D, fol. 8r (no. 93); X, 386 (no. 94); L, fol. 113r; L², fol. 82r; G, fol. 394r.

EARLIER EDITIONS AND TRANSLATIONS: DB, 56–57; Oh, 128–29; Gl, 717; Wi3, 152; Be, 68–69 and 195–96; Le, 51 and 235–37; Se, 46 and 177. (SK 8212)

SOLUTION: *FUNAMBULUS* (tightrope walker).

95.1 Be prefers the alternative reading *luciferum* (as she explains on 195). Compare Virgil, *Aeneid* 1.224 *(despiciens mare velivolum terrasque iacentis).*

95.2 Compare SYM 65.2 *(aera per medium)* and ALD 75.1 *(aera per sudum . . . pennis).*

SYM 96

MANUSCRIPTS: D, fol. 8r–v (no. 94); L, fol. 113r; L², fol. 202v; G, fol. 394r.

EARLIER EDITIONS AND TRANSLATIONS: DB, 56–57; Oh, 128–29; Gl, 717; Be, 68–69 and 196; Le, 51 and 237–41; Se, 177. (SK 10755)

SOLUTION: *FLEXUS DIGITORUM* (finger-counting). See further: Sanford, "*De loquela digitorum*"; Turner, "Roman Elementary Mathematics"; Menninger, *Number Words and Number Symbols,* 201–8; Bayless, "Alcuin and the Early Medieval Riddle Tradition," 172–73; Lockhart, "Everyday Wonders and Enigmatic Structures," 54–55.

Note the close parallel at ALC D82 *(FLEXUS DIGITORUM)*, and compare Bede, *De temporum ratione, praefatio* (ed. Jones, *Bedae Venerabilis Opera,* 269):

> Cum ergo dicis unum, minimum in laeva digitum inflectens, in medium palmae artum infiges. Cum dicis duo, secundum a minimo flexum, ibidem impones. Cum dicis tria, tertium similiter adflectes. Cum dicis quattuor, itidem minimum levabis. Cum dicis quinque, secundum a minimo similiter

> eriges. Cum dicis sex, tertium nihilominus elevabis, medio dumtaxat solo, qui medicus appellatur, in medium palmae fixo. Cum dicis septem, minimum solum, ceteris interim levatis, super palmae radicem pones. Iuxta quem cum dicis octo, medium.
>
> If you want to say "one," you should bend the little finger of your left hand, and place its tip on the palm; for "two," place down the ring finger next to it; for "three," the middle finger as well; for "four," you must again raise the little finger; for "five," the ring finger as well; for "six," you must extend the middle finger, and then the ring finger, which is also called the "doctor," is the only one left bent down on the palm; for "seven," extend all the fingers, and bend only the little finger along the wrist; for "eight," place the ring finger down next to it.

Le offers the alternative solution *VERBA* (words), based on the fascinating observation that in this aenigma (as in no other in SYM) the number of words in each line is eight, then seven, then six. Note in this context the (apparently false) solution given in several manuscripts for the next aenigma, usually solved *UMBRA* (shadow) as *DE VERBO* (on a word).

SYM 97

MANUSCRIPTS: D, fol. 8v (no. 95); X, 386 (no. 95); L, fol. 113r; L², fol. 81v; G, fol. 394r: *DE VERBO* (on a word).

EARLIER EDITIONS AND TRANSLATIONS: DB, 56–57; Oh, 130–31; Gl, 718; Be, 68–69 and 197–98; Le, 51 and 241–43; Se, 178. (SK 8144)

SOLUTION: *UMBRA* (shadow).

This aenigma begins a sequence of three that deal with illusions of one sort or another. The solution offered in L again emphasizes the connection between this aenigma and the one that follows. Indeed, one wonders whether what is at issue here is not so much a shadow as a reflection, and whether what links this aenigma with the next is the legend of Echo and Narcissus, as outlined in Ovid, *Metamorphoses* 3.356–401. Compare BER 61 (*DE UMBRA,* "on shadow").

SYM 98

MANUSCRIPTS: D, fol. 8v (no. 96); X, 386 (no. 96); L, fol. 113r; L[2], fol. 81v; G, fol. 394r.

EARLIER EDITIONS AND TRANSLATIONS: DB, 56–57; Oh, 130–31; Gl, 719; Be, 70–71 and 198–99; Le, 51 and 243–44; Se, 51 and 178. (SK 17343)

SOLUTION: *ECHO* (Echo).

This aenigma follows on naturally from the preceding one, and is in turn linked conceptually to the next. The sad story of Echo and Narcissus is told by Ovid, *Metamorphoses* 3.339–510. Compare ALC D79 (*ECHO,* "echo").

SYM 99

MANUSCRIPTS: D, fol. 8v (no. 97); X, 386–87 (no. 97); L, fol. 113r; L[2], fol. 81v; G, fol. 394r.

EARLIER EDITIONS AND TRANSLATIONS: DB, 56–57; Oh, 132–33; Gl, 720; Wil, 1; Be, 70–71 and 199–200; Le, 51 and 244–45; Se, 178. (SK 15639)

SOLUTION: *SOMNIUM* (dream), although the majority of manuscripts suggest *SOMNUS* (sleep). The preferred solution makes a stronger connection between this aenigma and the two that precede, while the more generally accepted solution makes an arguably closer link with the aenigma that follows. Compare ALC D81 (*HOMO QUI SOMNIT,* "a dreamer").

99.1 Compare ALD 47.6 (*HIRUNDO,* "swallow"), ALD 51.1 (*ELIOTROPUS,* "heliotrope": *Sponte mea).*

99.3 Compare SYM 14.3 (*PULLUS IN OVO,* "chick in egg": *nemo videbat),* SYM 21.3 (*TALPA,* "mole": *nemo videbit).*

SYM 100

MANUSCRIPTS: D, fol. 8v (no. 98); X, 387 (no. 98); L, fol. 113r–v; L², fol. 81v; G, fol. 394r.

EARLIER EDITIONS AND TRANSLATIONS: DB, 58–59; Oh, 132–33; Gl, 721; Be, 70–71 and 200–202; Le, 52 and 245–47; Se, 48 and 178. (SK 10320)

SOLUTION: *MONUMENTUM* (tombstone).

The subject is a fitting one to conclude the collection; one might compare OER 29 (*EAR,* "grave"), the last stanza of the poem. See further Taylor, "Enigma Variations," 67–68.

PS-SYM 1

EARLIER EDITION: Le, 249. (SK 9418)

SOLUTION: *GLACIES* (ice).

Compare ps-BED 6, which is clearly a prose version of this aenigma; Aldhelm quotes ps-SYM 1 in the *De metris* (Eh, 77), describing it as *illud poeticum,* "that piece of poetry," and citing it as a model for the form of aenigmata.

1.1 For the formula *me genuit,* see the note at ALD 33.1.

PS-SYM 2

MANUSCRIPTS: L, fol. 106v (no. 26); G, fol. 390v (no. 26). (not in SK)

SOLUTION: *PILAX* (cat), as in the manuscripts.

This aenigma is found only in the Anglo-Saxon manuscripts LG, where it follows directly on from SYM 25 (*MUS,* "mouse"), through an obvious association of subject matter.

2.1 The line is taken verbatim from ALD 65.5 (*MURICEPS*, "mouser").

2.2–3 These spurious lines are defective in both syntax and meter.

PS-SYM 3

EARLIER EDITION: Le, 249. (SK 5387)
SOLUTION: *CUCULUS* (cuckoo).

This aenigma is itself something of a cuckoo, having been wished on SYM by earlier editors, on account of its form, when in fact it is not found in any manuscripts containing all or part of SYM.

3.3 The idea that the bird utters its own name can be matched in EXE 55.6 *(STAFAS,* "letter": *nemnað hy sylfe),* where, however, the poet seems to be using misdirection to suggest a bird-solution.

PS-SYM 4

MANUSCRIPT: L², fol. 202v.
EARLIER EDITION: Le, 249. (SK 1883)
SOLUTION: *NIX* (snow).

4.1 Compare LOR 6.1 *(DE NIVE,* "about snow": *nubibus . . . dilabere).*

THE BERN RIDDLES

Authorship and Date

This collection of aenigmata comprises sixty-two six-line poems of rhythmical hexameters, with fourteen syllables in each line, and each aenigma generally structured in terms of three distichs. As such, the collection bears obvious comparison with that of Symphosius, whose aenigmata appear to have influenced it at various points, and begins in a strikingly similar, seemingly mundane manner. Some scholars have suggested that this idiosyncratic collection originated in some insular center on the Continent, perhaps the Irish foundation of Bobbio in northwest Italy, and perhaps in the seventh century. The earliest witness, manuscript H, is of the early eighth century, and contains the collection on fols. 73r–80v. Another important witness, Manuscript N, intersperses on fols. 8v–21v some forty-five of BER with those of both ALD and SYM, grouped according to supposed solution, alongside BON. Tupper, *Riddles,* xlvii, notes that the aenigmata of this collection "belong to the same circle of thought as the Anglo-Latin problems," and indeed one might go further and note their resemblance to the Anglo-Saxon riddle tradition in general, both in Latin and Old English, as the various parallels noted both above and below amply demonstrate.

Manuscript Context(s)

There are no fewer than nine manuscripts of BER, of which the three most relevant in the immediate context are HIN, dating from the first quarter of the eighth century to the beginning of the ninth. H, the earliest, is typical, containing as it does a series of texts clearly aimed at the encyclopedic and wisdom tradition, with a heavy focus on Isidore, in much the same fashion as several of the manuscripts containing others of the major Anglo-Latin collections.

Subject Matter and Solutions

Many of the subjects of BER overlap with those found in the other collections, and while often several of the details are shared, BER also offers many unique perspectives. There are a number of pairs and sequences throughout the compilation, although the order of the aenigmata differs significantly from manuscript to manuscript of BER.

Style

The aenigmata in BER differ in style from all of the other collections considered part of the Anglo-Saxon riddle tradition. This is especially true with regard to the kinds of poetic language employed in the verse texts, notably the compound and poetic adjectives routinely and sometimes extremely frequently used by the Anglo-Latin poets; by contrast, there are only seven such adjectives here, none of them particularly rare, at BER 18.1 *(florigeras),* BER 20.6 *(aureamque),* BER 25.3 *(multmoda),* BER 39.1 *(lapidea),* BER 44.1 *(mirifica),* BER 50a.1 *(multimodo),* BER 55.6 *(aligeras).*

Sources and Parallels

A number of parallels with aenigmata and riddles are noted below, though they are relatively sparse compared with the other collections, and indicate the independence of mind (and indeed meter) that shines through BER. To the extent that the model seems to be SYM, the overlap there seems greatest, but it is very apparent that this collection above all, while having a number of parallels with the Anglo-Saxon riddle tradition as a whole, is largely anomalous.

This Text and Translation

Here I rely on the editions of St and Gl, as well as a series of unpublished notes by Rob Getz; I have introduced a number of conjectures of my own, and have acknowledged individual debts as called for.

Further Reading

In general, see Riese, "Bern Riddles"; Strecker, *Aenigmata hexasticha*; Finch, "The Bern Riddles in Codex Vat. Reg. Lat. 1553"; Finch, "The Riddles in Cod. Barb. Lat. 1717 and Newberry Case Mediaeval Studies f 11"; Salvador-Bello, *Isidorean Perceptions,* 250–64 and 466–67.

BER 1

MANUSCRIPT: N, fol. 73r.
EARLIER EDITIONS AND TRANSLATIONS: St, 737–38; Gl, 547. (SK 4300)
SOLUTION: *OLLA* (earthenware jar).

The two fathers are presumably *limus,* "clay, earth," and *ignis,* "fire," both of which are grammatically masculine; the former endures, while the latter is consumed as its fuel is used up. The "harsh mother" is presumably the grammatically feminine *manus,* "hand," that throws the clay on a potter's wheel, or perhaps the *rota,* "wheel," itself.

1.3 Reading *duram* (manuscripts *dura*).
1.4 For the spelling *giro* (rather than the usual *gyro*), see the note at ALD 53.3.

BER 2

MANUSCRIPT: N, fol. 73r.
EARLIER EDITIONS AND TRANSLATIONS: St, 738; Gl, 548. (SK 9485)
SOLUTION: *LUCERNA* (lamp); the solution given is *DE LUCERNA.*

This aenigma seems connected both to the previous one and to the next by fact that the fathers are in each case the same: *ignis,* "fire." The "aged mother" here may be *lux,* "light," whence, according to Isidore, *Etym.* 20.10.2, the word *lucerna* derives.

2.6 Reading *umbra* (manuscripts *umbras*; *umbris*).

BER 3

MANUSCRIPT: N, fol. 73r.
EARLIER EDITIONS AND TRANSLATIONS: St, 738; Gl, 549. (SK 9493)
SOLUTION: *SAL* (salt).

As with the previous two aenigmata, the "father" here is *ignis,* "fire"; the "mother" is presumably *aqua,* "water." For another aenigma on the same subject, see ALD 19 (*SAL,* "salt"). Compare Isidore, *Etym.* 16.2.3.

3.1 Compare ALD 44.1 *(Me pater . . . gelido);* LOR 1.2 *(me pater),* 4.1 *(Me pater . . . gelido).*
3.4 Compare ALD 100.11; TAT 8.2; BER 3.4 *(Nullus me).*

BER 4

MANUSCRIPT: N, fol. 73r.
EARLIER EDITIONS AND TRANSLATIONS: St, 739; Gl, 550. (SK 9746)
SOLUTION: *SCAMNUM* (bench).

The continued conceit that the object is metaphorically quite a different kind of quadruped, namely, a horse, is extremely well sustained.

4.1 Compare BER 61.1 *(semper consistere loco).*

4.4 Note that the word *libens* also features prominently in the two aenigmata that follow, at BER 5.2 and 6.1; the word is something of a favorite with this riddler, however, and also appears in BER 12.1, 32.6, 36.3, and 45.2.

4.5 Strecker conjectures *nulla* for manuscript *nolo,* and the suggestion seems a happy one, given the parallels to be observed in the two aenigmata that follow, with BER 5.5 *(nulli sicut mihi pro bonis mala redduntur)* and BER 6.1 *(Nullius ut meam lux solam penetrat umbram).*

BER 5

MANUSCRIPT: N, fol. 73v.
EARLIER EDITIONS AND TRANSLATIONS: St, 739; Gl, 551. (SK 12757)
SOLUTION: *MENSA* (table).

The connection between this aenigma and the previous one seems clear, even down to the use of a second solution heavily hinted at, but ultimately misleading, in this case *sapientia,* "wisdom," the mother who offers the fruits of her breasts, namely, the milk of wisdom, to any who asks it, as noted at ps-BED 1. Other kinds of double entendre are hinted at in the sexualized imagery, which also draws on the motif of the "suffering servant" (on which see the introduction to *OEALRT,* under "Shared Themes across the Collections"). Note too the connection to the aenigma that follows, through the equally anthropomorphized theme of kisses; compare BER 5.3 *(MENSA,* "table": *oscula nam mihi prius qui cara dederunt)* and BER 6.6 *(CALIX,* "cup": *et amica libens oscula porrego cunctis),* BER 35.5 *(LILIA,* "lilies": *Oscula si nobis causa figantur amoris),* BER 42.3 *(GLACIES,* "ice": *Cuncti me solutam cara per oscula gaudent),* BER 46.6 *(PISTILLUS,* "pestle": *vertice nitenti plures per oscula gaudent).* For the theme of kissing in general, see the headnote to ALD 80.

5.4 Compare BER 24.3 *(Vestibus exuta).*

5.5 See the note on BER 4.5 for examples of parallel phrasing.

5.6 The neuter form *angula* is extremely rare, but *angulos* will not scan.

BER 6

MANUSCRIPT: N, fol. 73v.

EARLIER EDITIONS AND TRANSLATIONS: St, 739; Gl, 552. (SK 10689)

SOLUTION: *CALIX VITREUS* (glass cup); the solution given is *DE CALICE.*

Given the references to light penetrating the object in question, it is tempting to see this as a companion aenigma to those on a glass chalice and a drinking cup in ALD 80 (*CALIX VITREUS,* "glass cup") and LOR 5 (*COPA VINARIA,* "wine cup"). This aenigma is evidently linked to the preceding one through the themes of shared kisses (compare BER 5.3 and 6.6), as well as to the one that follows through the theme of transparency.

6.1 Reading *nullius* (manuscripts *nulli*) and *solam* (manuscripts *sola*). See the note on BER 4.5, and compare the use of *umbra* in the sense "semblance" in the related BER 29.1 (*SPECULUM,* "mirror"), though the same word is used in its more usual meaning "shade" in BER 2.6 (*LUCERNA,* "lamp"), 36.1 (*CROCUS,* "crocus"), and 55.6 (*SOL,* "sun").

BER 7

MANUSCRIPT: N, fol. 73v.
EARLIER EDITIONS AND TRANSLATIONS: St, 740; Gl, 553. (SK 16232)
SOLUTION: *VESICA* (bubble).

In describing both a dwelling and its inhabitant, this aenigma seems to be developing the same theme as other riddles, such as SYM 12 (*FLUMEN ET PISCIS,* "river and fish"), SYM 14 (*PULLUS IN OVO,* "chick in egg"); EXE 81 (*FISC OND EA,* "fish and river"). Note that here, unlike the "river and fish" riddles, it is the inhabitant that is liquid. This aenigma is connected to the preceding one by the notion of transparency, and to the following one by the spherical shape.

7.4 Compare BER 24.6 *(nullo sub pondere).*

BER 8

MANUSCRIPT: N, fol. 73v.
EARLIER EDITIONS AND TRANSLATIONS: St, 740; Gl, 554. (SK 10015)
SOLUTION: *OVUM* (egg).

See the headnote to BER 7 (*VESICA,* "bubble"); once again, as in several of the preceding, the emphasis is on a container and what it contains. Here, there seems also to be a gesture toward the motif of "the daughter giving birth to the mother," in riddles usually solved as "ice." Note here how the presumed neuter solution *ovum,* "egg," is feminized, to produce a parallel mother/son motif. The further reference to intact virginity inevitably invites the suspicion of an allusion to the Virgin Mary, the more so when the explicit reference to Eve in the aenigma that follows is taken into account; for similar Christological misdirection, see BER 12 (*GRANUM,* "grain"). Compare SYM 14 (*PULLUS IN OVO,* "chick in egg"); ALC D78 (*PULLUS IN OVO,* "chick in egg").

BER 9

MANUSCRIPT: N, fol. 74r.
EARLIER EDITIONS AND TRANSLATIONS: St, 740; Gl, 555. (SK 14891)
SOLUTION: *MOLA* (millstone).

Presumably there is a connection between this aenigma and the one preceding: Isidore, *Etym.* 20.8.6, among others, focuses on the round shape of the stones, and the motif of a round object giving birth links both. The aenigma is linked to the one that follows by the fact that, just as the riddler distinguishes there between singular *scala* and plural *scalae,* so too here the mill cannot function with only one stone; the paradox of objects that combine both stability and motion supplies a further link.

9.1 Note the chiastic structure, and the wordplay on *aevo,* "age," and *Eva,* "Eve."
9.2 Reading *senecta* (the manuscripts have *senectam*).
9.5 Reading *satura nam victum;* the manuscripts have a selection of *satura(m) nam victu(m),* while Gl reads *saturamen victu.* Presumably the fire is produced by sparks when the grain is gone.
9.6 Reading *vagantes* (the manuscripts have variously *vacantes, cavantes,* and *cavantis*). These are presumably the draft animals who turn the quern-stones, or perhaps the stones themselves.

BER 10

MANUSCRIPT: N, fol. 74r.
EARLIER EDITIONS AND TRANSLATIONS: St, 741; Gl, 556. (SK 15394)
SOLUTION: *SCALA* (ladder).

This is another example where the given solution *(DE SCALA)* is in question, since the aenigma itself makes a distinction between the lack of usefulness of the creature in question when singular (despite the common Medieval Latin form, *scala,* and the fact that in the Vulgate Jacob's ladder is also singular), and its concomitant utility when plural; compare SYM 78 (*SCALAE,* "ladder"). For the connection to the preceding aenigma, see the headnote to BER 9.

10.1 Compare BER 39.5 *(consistere plantis)* and 50.3 *(firmis consistere plantis).*

BER 11

MANUSCRIPT: N, fol. 74r.
EARLIER EDITIONS AND TRANSLATIONS: St, 741; Gl, 557. (SK 9815)
SOLUTION: *NAVIS* (ship).

This aenigma is linked to the one preceding by their shared wooden substance, and by the fact that while a ladder is more use when vertical than horizontal, here the wood that constitutes a ship is far more useful when horizontal, as opposed to its original state. Note too the use of *vivens* in the opening line of each: both aenigmata speak of the difference between the living tree and the object created from the cut-down tree.

11.2 The phrase *multos servo* presumably refers to the ship's cargo.

11.6 Compare SYM 13.3 (*NAVIS,* "ship": *curro vias multas vestigia nulla relinquens); BER 59.3 (currens vias);* ALF O.2 *(Curro vias multas).* For the slightly odd sense of *depingit* here, compare BER 20.6.

BER 12

MANUSCRIPT: N, fol. 74r.
EARLIER EDITIONS AND TRANSLATIONS: St, 741; Gl, 558. (SK 9811)
SOLUTION: *GRANUM* (grain).

This aenigma links back in terms of its evident subject matter to BER 9 (*MOLA,* "millstone"), but is also tied to the immediately preceding aenigma, which opens with the portentous word "dead" (BER 11.1: *mortua*), by its own evident focus on death *(mortem . . .*

mortuum . . . mortem) and burial *(sepultum . . . tumulor)*. It is hard not to recognize here overtones from John 12:24–25: *amen amen dico vobis nisi granum frumenti cadens in terram mortuum fuerit ipsum solum manet si autem mortuum fuerit multum fructum adfert,* "Amen, amen I say to you, unless the grain of wheat falling into the ground die, itself remaineth alone. But if it die, it bringeth forth much fruit." A Christological reading naturally follows (compare BER 8 [*OVUM,* "egg"]), and it is striking that the immediately following aenigmata BER 13 (*VITIS,* "vine"), BER 14 (*OLIVA,* "olive tree"), BER 15 (*PALMA,* "palm tree"), and BER 16 (*CEDRIS,* "cedar tree") all have both vegetable and Christological connections.

12.1 Compare BER 28.4 *(adsumo libenter)*.

12.3 The form *parentes* presumably refers to humankind in general, who profit from the demise of the kernel of grain by feeding children of their own.

BER 13

MANUSCRIPT: N, fol. 74v.
EARLIER EDITIONS AND TRANSLATIONS: St, 742; Gl, 559. (SK 16788)
SOLUTION: *VITIS* (vine).

This aenigma is linked to the previous one, since just as crushed grains go to make food, as explained in BER 9 (*MOLA,* "millstone"), so too do crushed grapes make wine. The feminine gender of the speaker fits well the preferred *vitis,* "vine," but the masculine offspring fit less well: both *uva,* "grape," and *botrus,* "bunch of grapes," are grammatically feminine, although the *-us* ending of the latter might well confuse. It is, however, striking that Aldhelm, for one, believed that *botrus* was masculine (compare Aldhelm, *Carmen de virginitate* 178: *Pampinus immensos dum gignit palmite botros*), and it may be that the poet here thinks the same. Compare SYM 53 (*VITIS* ["vine"]). This aenigma plays into the motif of the "suffering servant," on which see the introduction to *OEALRT,* under "Shared Themes across the Collections." This aenigma opens a sequence of four on different types of tree.

13.4 Compare BER 14.2, 29.3, and 52.1 *(genero natos)*.

13.6 On the effects of intoxication, a common theme in the Anglo-Saxon riddle tradition, see the note at ALD 80.9 *(CALIX VITREUS*, "glass cup": *Atque pedum gressus titubantes . . . ruina)*.

BER 14

MANUSCRIPT: N, fol. 74v.
EARLIER EDITIONS AND TRANSLATIONS: St, 742; Gl, 559. (SK 10673)
SOLUTION: *OLIVA* (olive tree).

14.2 Compare BER 13.4, 29.3, and 52.1 *(genero natos)*.

14.5 Reading *fili* (manuscripts *filii*), to preserve the fourteen-syllable rhythm; compare BER 52.3 (*ROSA*, "rose").

14.6 Compare Isidore, *Etym*. 17.7.65, which describes the use of olive oil for lighting.

BER 15

MANUSCRIPT: N, fol. 74v.
EARLIER EDITIONS AND TRANSLATIONS: St, 742; Gl, 560. (SK 12761)
SOLUTION: *PALMA* (palm tree).

15.3 Reading *petenti* (Gl follows a handful of manuscripts in reading *patenti*).

BER 16

MANUSCRIPT: N, fol. 74v.
EARLIER EDITIONS AND TRANSLATIONS: St, 743; Gl, 561. (SK 9486)
SOLUTION: *CEDRUS* (cedar tree).

16.1 Reading *mater* (Gl reads *pater*, following a single manuscript, but trees are feminine). The reference to hostile thorns again links the subject to Christ.

BER 17

MANUSCRIPT: N, fol. 75r.
EARLIER EDITIONS AND TRANSLATIONS: St, 743; Gl, 562. (SK 11751)
SOLUTION: *CRIBRUS* (sieve); the solution given is *DE CRIBRO.*

BER 18

MANUSCRIPT: N, fol. 75r.
EARLIER EDITIONS AND TRANSLATIONS: St, 743; Gl, 563. (SK 5232)
SOLUTION: *SCOPA* (broom).

This aenigma seems to look back to the preceding sequence on trees, although it also gives an insight into the plight of serving girls, a focus of several of the Exeter Book riddles. This aenigma plays into the notion of the "suffering servant" motif, on which see the introduction to *OEALRT*, under "Shared Themes across the Collections." It is hard to recreate in English the sense that in Latin the terms *comas* and *capillos* in BER 18.1 and 18.3 can serve for both human hair and foliage. Compare SYM 80 (*SCOPA,* "broom").

BER 19

MANUSCRIPT: N, fol. 75r.
EARLIER EDITIONS AND TRANSLATIONS: St, 744; Gl, 564. (SK 3804)
SOLUTION: *LINEA CEREA* (candle wick); the solutions given are *DE CERA* (on wax) and *DE PICE* (on pitch).

The first two lines again seem to point to Christological narrative, while the third line points to cesarean section (with the added etymological clue of *caesa* at BER 19.3). The solutions "on wax" and "on pitch" given in the manuscripts can be made to fit the sequence of aenigmata, with the former pointing forward to BER 20 (*MEL,* "honey") and BER 21 (*APIS,* "bee"), and the latter pointing back to a sappy and resinous tree such as BER 16 (*CEDRUS,* "cedar tree"). If we reject both transmitted suggestions and go back to the aenigma itself, a better solution for BER 19, linking it both back and forward, might be "candle wick." The usual term *linum,* literally "linen," is grammatically neuter, but the feminine form *linea,* "linen thread," might suffice, and would seem to fit.

19.1 Compare BER 32.1 *(Dissimilem sibi . . . mater),* BER 34.1 *(me mater concipit).*

19.2 ALD 20.1 *(sine semine creta);* BER 55.1 *(Semine nec ullo patris creatus);* BIB 1.5 *(ternae patrio sine semine),* BIB 3.1 *(patrio sine semine),* BIB 8.1 *(Sunt mihi . . . patrio sine semine ternae).*

19.4 Understanding *nam* as *autem.*

BER 20

MANUSCRIPT: N, fol. 75r.

EARLIER EDITIONS AND TRANSLATIONS: St, 744; Gl, 566. (SK 9026)

SOLUTION: *MEL* (honey). See further Murphy, *Unriddling the Exeter Riddles,* 168–69.

20.6 For the slightly odd sense of *depingit* here, compare BER 11.6 (*NAVIS,* "ship").

BER 21

MANUSCRIPT: N, fol. 75v.

EARLIER EDITIONS AND TRANSLATIONS: St, 744; Gl, 567. (SK 9409)

SOLUTION: *APIS* (bee); the solution given is *DE APIBUS* (on bees) in most of the manuscripts, although the subject is certainly singular; one manuscript has *APIS*. See further Murphy, *Unriddling the Exeter Riddles,* 165.

Given the aenigma as a whole, the queen bee seems to be the specific subject.

21.4 Reading *nulla de venere sumpsi* (most manuscripts read *nullo de ventre resumpsi*). The virginal nature of bees is a byword: see Casiday, "St. Aldhelm's Bees."

BER 22

MANUSCRIPT: N, fol. 75v.
EARLIER EDITIONS AND TRANSLATIONS: St, 745; Gl, 568. (SK 4800)
SOLUTION: *OVIS* (sheep).

22.2 Compare BER 53.3 *(nulli quaero).*

22.6 Compare BER 24.5 *(manibus me postquam reges et visu mirantur),* BER 28.6 *(efferunt, et reges infra supraque mirantur).* For a further reference to the value attached by kings to the creatures in question, see EXE 47.7–8a *(þa æþelingas oft wilniað, / cyningas ond cwene)* and ALD 20.3.

BER 23

MANUSCRIPT: N, fol. 75v.
EARLIER EDITIONS AND TRANSLATIONS: St, 745; Gl, 569. (SK 4103)
SOLUTION: *IGNIS* (fire).

For aenigmata with similar themes, compare ALD 93 (*SCINTILLA,* "spark") and TAT 31 (*SCINTILLA,* "spark"). This is another of those riddles that focus on life and death; see further Soper, "Count of Days," 78–82.

23.1 Compare BER 39.1 *(mihi pater... mater).*

23.6 A riddle within a riddle: the answer is "water." For others of the same sort, see the introduction to *OEALRT,* under "Shared Themes across the Collections."

BER 24

MANUSCRIPT: N, fol. 75v.
EARLIER EDITIONS AND TRANSLATIONS: St, 745; Gl, 570. (SK 9051)
SOLUTION: *MEMBRANUM* (parchment). See further Bitterli, *Say What I Am Called,* 178–90; Cavell, *Weaving Words,* 169–71.

This aenigma seems to follow on more appropriately from BER 22 (*OVIS*, "sheep"), and evidently describes a chained-up book, whose contents, presumably of a sacred sort, are of benefit even to kings. For a similar riddle, compare EXE 24 (*CRISTES BOC*, "Gospel Book").

24.3 Compare BER 5.4 *(Vestibus exutam)*.

24.5 Compare BER 22.6 *(pauperaque multum ipsos nam munero reges)*, 28.6 *(efferunt, et reges infra supraque mirantur)*. The form *postquam* is used for *postea*, as at BER 32.4 and 52.5.

24.6 Compare BER 7.4 *(nullo sub pondere)*. The "many thousands" are letters, here described in another riddle within a riddle. For others of the same sort, see the introduction to *OEALRT*, under "Shared Themes across the Collections."

BER 25

MANUSCRIPT: N, fol. 76r.

EARLIER EDITIONS AND TRANSLATIONS: St, 746; Gl, 571. (SK 9990)

SOLUTION: *LITTERAE* (letters). See further Murphy, *Unriddling the Exeter Riddles*, 85.

The connection between this aenigma and the preceding one is obvious; it is also connected to the one following by the notion of small objects' having extraordinary power. See further TAT 4 (*APICES*, "letters"); EUS 7 (*LITTERAE*, "letters"); EXE 55 (*STAFAS*, "letters"). With its reference to the "house" (presumably parchment), there is a further connection to SYM 12 (*FLUMEN ET PISCIS*, "river and fish").

25.1 For the "black on white" theme in the context of writing, see the note at ALD 59.3–5 (*PENNA*, "pen") above.

25.2 Compare ALD 30.5 (*ELEMENTUM*, "alphabet": *terni nos fratres incerta matre crearunt)*.

BER 26

MANUSCRIPT: N, fol. 76r.
EARLIER EDITIONS AND TRANSLATIONS: St, 746; Gl, 572. (SK 9501)
SOLUTION: *SINAPIS* (mustard seed).

For aenigmata with similar themes, see ALD 40 (*PIPER,* "pepper") and BER 37 (*DE PIPERE,* "on pepper"). This aenigma plays into the notion of the "suffering servant" motif, on which see the introduction to *OEALRT,* under "Shared Themes across the Collections."

26.1 The positive form *parvus* seems to be used in place of a comparative; the same phenomenon can be observed in BER 57.3 *(mihi velox).*

26.5 For the spelling *giro* (rather than the usual *gyro*), see the note at ALD 53.3.

BER 27

MANUSCRIPT: N, fol. 76r.
EARLIER EDITIONS AND TRANSLATIONS: St, 746; Gl, 573. (SK 725)
SOLUTION: *PAPIRUS* (papyrus).

This aenigma would seem to follow on more easily from BER 24 (*MEMBRANUM,* "parchment") and BER 25 (*LITTERAE,* "letters"). For an aenigma that shares several of the same themes, compare SYM 2 (*HARUNDO,* "reed") and EXE 58 (*HREOD,* "reed").

27.2 The form *levi* could derive from *lĕvi,* "light," or *lēvi,* "smooth."

BER 28

MANUSCRIPT: N, fol. 76r.
EARLIER EDITIONS AND TRANSLATIONS: St, 747; Gl, 574. (SK 975)
SOLUTION: *BOMBIX* (silkworm); the solution given is *DE SERICO.*

Here again, the end product and the process are conflated; compare BER 43 (*BOMBICES,* "silkworms"). The close parallel between the last line of this aenigma and that of BER 24.5 (*MEMBRANUM,* "parchment") provides a connection that is also reflected in both SYM 16 (*TINEA,* "bookworm") and EXE 47 (**BOC-MOĐĐE,* "book moth").

28.4 Compare BER 12.1 (*libens adsumo).*

28.6 Compare BER 22.6 (*pauperaque multum ipsos nam munero reges),* BER 24.5 (*manibus me postquam reges et visu mirantur).* For the royal motif, see further the notes there.

BER 29

MANUSCRIPT: N, fol. 76v.
EARLIER EDITIONS AND TRANSLATIONS: St, 747; Gl, 575. (SK 16932)
SOLUTION: *SPECULUM* (mirror).

For the translation "likeness" for *umbra,* compare BER 6.1. The feminine gender of *devota* in BER 29.1 belies the given solution, but accords well with the further feminine forms *mater* and *mentita,* presumably prompted by the word *uterus* in the opening line. Compare SYM 69 (*SPECULUM,* "mirror").

29.3 Compare BER 13.4, 14.2, and 52.1 (*genero natos).*

BER 30

MANUSCRIPT: N, fol. 76v.
EARLIER EDITIONS AND TRANSLATIONS: St, 747; Gl, 576. (SK 10680)
SOLUTION: *PISCIS* (fish).

The connection here between the fish and its friendly "swirling home" links this aenigma with SYM 12 (*FLUMEN ET PISCIS,* "river and fish") and EXE 81 (*FISC OND EA,* "fish and river"). Compare ALD 71 (*PISCIS,* "fish"), EUS 40 (*PISCIS,* "fish").

30.3 Compare SYM 31.1 *(Vita mihi mors est);* ALD 11.2 *(Non est vita mihi);* BER 50.4 *(mihi mors est).* The line emphasizes the Christological identification of the symbol of a fish.

BER 31

MANUSCRIPT: N, fol. 76v.
EARLIER EDITIONS AND TRANSLATIONS: St, 748; Gl, 577. (SK 11444)
SOLUTION: *SIPHO* (siphon); the solution given is *DE NYMPHA* (on a siphon?). The masculine gender of *ebrius* in 31.2 suggests *SIPHO.*

This aenigma is linked to the next by the notion of sucking up water and then giving it back again. The same idea underlies the basic paradox of the mother/daughter ice/water riddles; see too the note at BER 32.1 (*SPONGIA,* "sponge") below.

31.4 Compare BER 58.4 *(ab ima).*

BER 32

MANUSCRIPT: N, fol. 76v.
EARLIER EDITIONS AND TRANSLATIONS: St, 740; Gl, 578. (SK 3803)
SOLUTION: *SPONGIA* (sponge).

32.1 The mother in question is presumably water *(aqua),* which is grammatically feminine. Compare BER 19.1 *(Dissimilem sibi . . . mater).*

32.2 The reading found in several manuscripts *(viscera vacua latebris)* may be original, but if so, *vacua* must be scanned as disyllabic through diaeresis (on which see the headnote to BED 9), to preserve the requisite syllable count. On *latebris,* compare BER 52.3 *(sed dum infra meis concrescunt filii latebris).*

32.4 The form *postquam* is used for *postea,* as at BER 24.5 and BER 52.5. The line alludes to the mother/daughter theme found also in ps-SYM 1; see the introduction to *OEALRT,* under "Shared Themes across the Collections."

BER 33

MANUSCRIPT: N, fol. 77r.
EARLIER EDITIONS AND TRANSLATIONS: St, 748; Gl, 579. (SK 11673)
SOLUTION: *VIOLA* (violet).

Note that the sequence BER 33–34 (*VIOLA,* "violet," and *ROSA,* "rose") is matched in reverse by SYM 45–46 (*ROSA,* "rose," and *VIOLA,* "violet").

33.5 Reading *spiritus de corpore parvo* (most manuscripts read *parvo de corpore sumptus*), with *reddet* understood as a future form standing for a present tense (on which see the note at ALD 33.6 above). Compare SYM 46.2 *(spiritus . . . quamvis sim corpore parvo).*

BER 34

MANUSCRIPT: N, fol. 77r.
EARLIER EDITIONS AND TRANSLATIONS: St, 749; Gl, 580. (SK 12762)
SOLUTION: *ROSA* (rose).

This aenigma follows naturally on from the last, and connects again to the one following. Compare SYM 45 (*ROSA,* "rose"), and see the headnote for BER 33 (*VIOLA,* "violet").

34.1 For more examples of the mother and womb motif, see the note at ALD 93.10.

34.2 For the notion of being cradled in five arms, see LOR 5 (*COPA VINARIA,* "about a wine cup").

BER 35

MANUSCRIPT: N, fol. 77r.
EARLIER EDITIONS AND TRANSLATIONS: St, 749; Gl, 581. (SK 10569)
SOLUTION: *LILIA* (lilies).

This aenigma follows naturally on in sequence from the previous one, especially since the connection of roses and lilies (the plural answer seems required here) is traditional.

35.2 The "spear" here is presumably the stalk, the tip of which is indeed packed *(onusta)* with bright orange pollen that is released easily on contact, leaving the stamen wilting.

35.5 For the motif of kisses here, see the headnote at BER 5.

BER 36

MANUSCRIPT: N, fol. 77r.
EARLIER EDITIONS AND TRANSLATIONS: St, 749; Gl, 582. (SK 11680)
SOLUTION: *CROCUS* (saffron crocus); the solution given is *DE CROCO.*

This aenigma continues the floral theme, and is specifically linked to the last by the rich golden-yellow color that saffron imparts.

36.6 Reading *modica* (most manuscripts read *modicus* or *modicos*).

BER 37

MANUSCRIPT: N, fol. 77v.
EARLIER EDITIONS AND TRANSLATIONS: St, 750; Gl, 583. (SK 11876)
SOLUTION: *PIPER* (pepper).

This aenigma leads on naturally from the previous one, which mentions spices in its closing line.

37.1 Compare BER 55.4 *(SOL,* "sun": *perambulo terras).*

37.1–2 Given the sexualized descriptions of slaves and other creatures in bondage in several of the Exeter Book riddles, it is hard not to see something of the same double entendre here. Note another reference to the "suffering servant" motif, as discussed in the introduction to *OEALRT,* under "Shared Themes across the Collections."

37.5 Reading *dente* (most manuscripts read *dentem*). For the "biter bitten" motif, see the note on SYM 44 (*CAEPA*, "onion"), and note how the sequence SYM 44–46 is therefore matched in reverse by BER 33–34 and 37, as outlined in the headnote to BER 33 above. See too EUS 51.5 *(SCORPIO*, "scorpion": *mordens . . . non vulnero)*; BER 37.5 *(Mordeo . . . nec vulnero dente)*, BER 41.3 *(VENTUS*, "wind": *dente nec vulnero quemquam)*.

37.6 The line presumably describes the grinding of peppercorns by wood or stone.

BER 38

MANUSCRIPT: N, fol. 77v.
EARLIER EDITIONS AND TRANSLATIONS: St, 750; Gl, 584. (SK 2797)
SOLUTION: *GLACIES* (ice).

The solution given makes no real sense; given the sequencing, one would expect some kind of plant or vegetable as the solution.

38.3 An allusion to the mother/daughter motif, on which see the introduction to *OEALRT*, under "Shared Themes across the Collections," here reconfigured as the father/son motif.

38.4 Reading *creata* (most manuscripts read *cretam*), for the sake of the syllable count.

BER 39

MANUSCRIPT: N, fol. 77v.
EARLIER EDITIONS AND TRANSLATIONS: St, 750; Gl, 585. (SK 971)
SOLUTION: *HEDERA* (ivy).

This aenigma is connected to one following by the notion of multiple grasping hands on many limbs.

39.1 Compare BER 23.1 *(mihi pater . . . mater).*

39.5 Compare BER 10.1 *(constitero plantis),* BER 50a.3 *(firmis consistere plantis).*

BER 40

MANUSCRIPT: N, fol. 77v.
EARLIER EDITIONS AND TRANSLATIONS: St, 751; Gl, 586. (SK 17254)
SOLUTION: *MUSCIPULA* (mousetrap).

This aenigma is connected to the previous one by the notion of gripping hands. There seems also to be a contrastive link to the various aenigmata such as SYM 77 (*SCALAE,* "ladder") and BER 10 (*SCALA,* "ladder"), which stress the creature's relative efficacy when upright and when prone. Here, I follow the solution given, though in the absence of any firm knowledge of early medieval mousetraps, some details are unclear.

40.3 Compare BER 53.1 *(Venter mihi nullus).*

BER 41

MANUSCRIPT: N, fol. 78r.
EARLIER EDITIONS AND TRANSLATIONS: St, 751; Gl, 587. (SK 17026)
SOLUTION: *VENTUS* (wind).

The connection with the previous aenigma (*MUSCIPULA,* "mousetrap") seems to derive from the notion of multiple biting mouths; the link to the aenigma that follows (*GLACIES,* "ice") derives from the fact that it is a cold and indeed biting wind that turns water into ice. Compare ALD 2 *(VENTUS),* which seems closely related. There are some broad parallels in *Hisperica famina* A479–96 (*DE VENTO,* "on wind"; see further Herren, *Hisperica Famina: The A-Text;* Orchard, "*Hisperica famina* as Literature").

41.3 Compare BER 45.1 *(Os est mihi).*

41.3–4 Compare EXE 83.5 (*BLÆST-BELG,* "bellows"), which apparently refers to a blast of air by the term *heofenes toþ,* "heaven's tooth."

41.4 Another example of the "biter bitten" motif, on which see the introduction to *OEALRT,* under "Shared Themes across the Collections"; compare especially EUS 51.5 *(SCORPIO,* "scorpion": *mordens . . . non vulnero);* BER 37.5 *(PIPER,* "pepper": *Mordeo . . . nec vulnero dente).*

41.5 For the notion of binding the wind, compare classical conceptions of Aeolus (as embodied in Virgil, *Aeneid 1),* as well as the headnote to EXE 1.

41.6 The heroic trio of Bacchus *(Liber),* Alexander, and Hercules comprises those popularly supposed to have conquered the known world.

BER 42

MANUSCRIPT: N, fol. 78r.
EARLIER EDITIONS AND TRANSLATIONS: St, 751; Gl, 588. (SK 1075)
SOLUTION: *GLACIES* (ice).

This aenigma follows on neatly from the preceding one. The final lines are perplexing as they stand, turning as they do on the contrast between forms of *turp-* in the sense "ugly," with an apparent pun on *torp-* (the same thing is found in BER 62.5). For other aenigmata sharing similar themes, see SYM 10 (*GLACIES,* "ice"); BER 38 (*GLACIES,* "ice"); TAT 15 (*NIX, GRANDO, ET GLACIES,* "snow, hail, and ice"); LOR 4 (*GELU,* "ice").

42.3 Compare BER 46.6 *(per oscula gaudent).* For the theme of kissing here, see the headnote to ALD 80.

BER 43

MANUSCRIPT: N, fol. 78r.
EARLIER EDITIONS AND TRANSLATIONS: St, 752; Gl, 589. (SK 8126)
SOLUTION: *BOMBYCES* (silkworms); the solution given is *DE VERMIBUS BOMBYCIBUS SERICAS VESTES FORMATIS* (on the insects called silkworms that create silk clothing).

The apparently ungrammatical use of the past participle form *FORMATIS* in a present and active participle sense (for *FORMANTIBUS?*) is in fact echoed in the text of the aenigma itself, and opens up the twin possibilities of authorial titles (something that seems unlikely given the discrepancies already noted) or a kind of idiolect. An alternative suggestion (for which I am grateful to Rob Getz) might be that the solution *ARANEA* (spider) better fits the revulsion apparently expressed in BER 43.5–6.

43.1 The form *concepta* seems best interpreted as active, a part of some putative deponent verb (nonetheless, the passive must be required in BER 44.3); other past participle forms that are more easily understood as present and active are found at BER 48.1 and 58.2.

BER 44

MANUSCRIPT: N, fol. 78r.
EARLIER EDITIONS AND TRANSLATIONS: St, 752; Gl, 590. (SK 2654)
SOLUTION: *MARGARITA* (pearl).

This aenigma is another that does not seem to fit the given solution; could the real solution be "oyster"?

44.2 An alternative is to read *nodis,* "knots," as Rob Getz suggests.

BER 45

MANUSCRIPT: N, fol. 78v.
EARLIER EDITIONS AND TRANSLATIONS: St, 752; Gl, 591. (SK 11480)
SOLUTION: *PILA* (mortar); the solution given is *DE TERRA* (on earth).

This aenigma is another that does not seem to fit the given solution. Since the one that follows has the given solution *DE PISTILLO* (on a pestle), which fits it well, this one would suit perfectly the solution *PILA* (mortar); compare Isidore, *Etym.* 4.11.4. For other aenigmata that share the theme of taking in sustenance and then giving it back, see BER 31 (*SIPHO*, "siphon") and BER 32 (*SPONGIA*, "sponge").

45.1 Compare BER 41.3 *(Os est mihi).*
45.5 The form *efficio* must be read as trisyllabic, through synizesis; compare BER 14.5 (*filii*, which must be disyllabic) and 57.2 (*fugiens*, which must be disyllabic).

BER 46

MANUSCRIPT: N, fol. 78v.
EARLIER EDITIONS AND TRANSLATIONS: St, 753; Gl, 592. (SK 16724)
SOLUTION: *PILUM* (pestle); the solution given is *DE PISTILLO* (on a pestle).

This aenigma leads on very naturally from the last, perhaps with the proviso that the alternative term *PILUM*, "pestle," may have been intended as a closer link to the preceding aenigma.

46.1 Compare SYM 87.2 *(una mihi cervix).*
46.3 Compare ALD 100.59 *(versa vice)*; BER 31.3 *(Versa mihi . . . vice).*
46.5 Compare BER 60.5 *(Nullus mihi).*
46.6 Compare BER 42.3 *(per oscula gaudent).* For more on the theme of kisses in this collection in particular, see the note at BER 5 (*MENSA*, "table") above.

BER 47

MANUSCRIPT: N, fol. 78v.
EARLIER EDITIONS AND TRANSLATIONS: St, 753; Gl, 593. (SK 1114)
SOLUTION: *CONCHA* (conch); the solution given is *DE COCHLEA* (on a snail).

Given that BER 47.3–4 appears to suggest that the creature in question is employed as some kind of horn (as in Virgil, *Aeneid* 6.171 and 10.209), it is tempting to suggest that the true solution here may be *CONCHA* (conch), especially if BER 47.5–6 is taken to refer to the deliciousness of shelled conch meat. If the reference is not to a horn, but instead describes how the sea sounds in seashells, any kind of shell could be at issue. Other aspects of this aenigma seem very similar to riddles on the oyster (such as EXE 74); compare Isidore, *Etym.* 12.6.48 and 51, where the crab, a common companion to the oyster, is described as a *concha*. Note too the double entendre in BER 47.5–6, which clearly seems to be a sexual reference, presumably predicated on the sensuous pleasures of eating shelled conch flesh.

47.1 Compare BER 51.1 *(ALIUM,* "garlic": *natus de matre producor).*

BER 48

MANUSCRIPT: N, fol. 78v.
EARLIER EDITIONS AND TRANSLATIONS: St, 753; Gl, 594. (SK 13130)
SOLUTION: *CASTANEA* (chestnut).

If the solution to the previous aenigma is accepted as *CONCHA* (conch), then what seems at issue here is not so much the tree as the chestnut itself, a delicacy enclosed in a rigid covering. It is also striking that the sea urchin *(echinus)* is described as having a spiny shell "like chestnuts" (Isidore, *Etym.* 12.6.57: *in modum castanearum*). The four contradictory aspects of the kernel, as opposed to the shell, described in the opening line are explained in the remainder of the aenigma: wet/dry, fat/thin, sweet/bitter, soft/hard. Compare the very different LOR 7 (*CASTANEA,* "chestnut").

BER 49

MANUSCRIPT: N, fol. 79r.
EARLIER EDITIONS AND TRANSLATIONS: St, 754; Gl, 595. (SK 9667)
SOLUTION: *NIMBUS* (storm cloud); the solution given is *DE PLUVIA* (rain).

The given solution, which appears in all manuscripts, has a feminine gender that is belied by the masculine form *improbus* (BER 49.5), which is presumably why Glorie suggests instead *IMBER* (storm). A more acceptable solution is perhaps *NIMBUS* (storm cloud), which may then connect this aenigma to both of those preceding in focusing both on the container and what is contained. Compare Isidore, *Etym.* 13.10.3 and 19.31.2.

BER 50

MANUSCRIPT: N, fol. 79r.
EARLIER EDITIONS AND TRANSLATIONS: St, 754; Gl, 596. (SK 8123)
SOLUTION: *VINUM* (wine).

This aenigma is conceptually linked to the previous one by the notion of drops of liquid produced from a larger container, in this case wine squeezed from grapes. Other riddles on alcoholic drinks make much of their ambivalent nature, just as BER 50.5–6 does here; see further the note at ALD 80 (*CALIX VITREUS,* "glass cup").

50.1 Reading *unum* (most manuscripts read *unus*), to match the gender of the solution. Compare BON 13.12 *(CUPIDITAS AIT,* "greed speaks": *cum matribus una).*

50.2 Reading *genitum* (manuscripts *genitus*), to match the gender of the solution.

50.3 Compare BER 10.1 *(firmis constitero plantis),* BER 39.5 *(consistere plantis).*

50.4 Compare SYM 31.1 *(Vita mihi mors est);* ALD 11.2 *(Non est vita mihi);* BER 30.3 *(Vita mihi mors est).*

BER 50A

EARLIER EDITIONS AND TRANSLATIONS: St, 754; Gl, 597. (SK 9859)
SOLUTION: *CALIX VITREUS* (glass cup); Gl suggests *DE CHARTA* (concerning paper).

This aenigma is only found in a single manuscript, I, hence its numbering both here and in Gl. Based on the suspected solution to the previous aenigma, one might at first wonder whether a possible solution here is *UTER* (wineskin). However, the solution "glass," and perhaps more specifically "wine glass," seems very feasible, especially given the parallel solutions for ALD 80 (*CALIX VITREUS,* "glass cup") and LOR 5 (*COPA VINARIA,* "a wine cup"); compare ALD 78 (*CUPA VINARIA,* "wine cask"). The somewhat convoluted description appears to chart the creation of glass from sand snatched from the earth (the "mother" of BER 50a.1) and the production of a glass beaker which can itself be re-formed, and which carries liquid.

50a.6 Reading *quo . . . credantur* (I reads *quae creduntur*).

BER 51

MANUSCRIPT: N, fol. 79r.
EARLIER EDITIONS AND TRANSLATIONS: St, 755; Gl, 598. (SK 9865)
SOLUTION: *BULBUS* (bulb, onion); one manuscript suggests *ALIUM* (garlic).

The gender of the creature described is masculine, according to the manuscripts, four of which have no solution, and the fifth of which nonetheless gives the neuter solution *ALIUM* (garlic), even if it requires emendation in half the lines. Others have suggested *CAEPA* (onion), which would require similar emendations, or *BULBUS* (bulb, onion), which seems to work the best, since it can also mean "onion" specifically, and links to the aenigma that follows.

51.1 Compare BER 47.1 *(nascor . . . producor a matre).*

51.3 There seems to be a reference here to the notion of a child giving birth to its parent, as commonly elsewhere: see the introduction to *OEALRT,* under "Shared Themes across the Collections."

BER 52

MANUSCRIPT: N, fol. 79r.

EARLIER EDITIONS AND TRANSLATIONS: St, 755; Gl, 599. (SK 9748)

SOLUTION: *ROSA* (rose).

52.1 Compare BER 13.4, 14.2, and 29.3 *(genero natos).*

52.3 Reading *filii,* rather than the *fili* of the manuscripts, but nonetheless assuming that it is counted as disyllabic through syncopation (on which see the headnote to BED 9); see further BER 14.5.

52.5 Understanding *postquam* as *postea;* compare the note at BER 24.5.

BER 53

MANUSCRIPT: N, fol. 79v.

EARLIER EDITIONS AND TRANSLATIONS: St, 755; Gl, 600. (SK 17064)

SOLUTION: *TRUTINA* (pair of scales).

The suggested solution seems reasonable enough, relying as it does on what looks very like a weighing process as described in BER 53.4–6. For an aenigma with a similar solution, see BED 1.

53.1 Compare BER 40.3 *(Venter mihi nullus).*

53.2 Reading *sicca* (manuscripts variously *siccus, sicco, siccum*) to agree with the gender of *trutina;* the sense seems to be "empty, unfilled."

53.3 Compare BER 22.2 *(nulli quaero).*

53.4 The sense "running" *(currens)* echoes that of *currens* and *cursum* in BER 17.2 and 17.4.

BER 54

MANUSCRIPT: N, fol. 79v.
EARLIER EDITIONS AND TRANSLATIONS: St, 756; Gl, 601. (SK 4090)
SOLUTION: *INSUBULUM* (weaver's heddle, treadle on a weaver's loom).

Compare Isidore, *Etym.* 19.29.1:

> Insubuli, quia infra et supra sunt, vel quia insubulantur.
>
> Heddles [are so called] because they are below and above, or because they make a swishing sound.

See further Cavell, *Weaving Words,* 37. Several themes from previous aenigmata coalesce here, namely, a twin form, also evident in the preceding BER 53 (*TRUTINA,* "pair of scales"), and a contrast between different powers when horizontal and vertical. Rob Getz suggests to me that the solution may be the paddles on a water mill.

54.4 The future form *requiret* seems more appropriately translated by the present tense, as elsewhere; see further the note on ALD 33.6.
54.6 Supplying *sed;* as it stands in the manuscripts, the line lacks a syllable.

BER 55

MANUSCRIPT: N, fol. 79v.
EARLIER EDITIONS AND TRANSLATIONS: St, 756; Gl, 602. (SK 14853)
SOLUTION: *SOL* (sun).

This aenigma begins a sequence that seems to focus on the twin heavenly bodies of the sun and the moon (BER 55–59); there are also parallels with EXE 91.

55.1 Compare ALD 20.1 *(sine semine creta)*; BER 19.2 *(nullo virili creta de semine)*; BIB 1.5 *(ternae patrio sine semine)*, BIB 3.1 *(patrio sine semine)*, BIB 8.1 *(Sunt mihi . . . patrio sine semine ternae)*.

55.2–3 The notion of suckling and nipples here recalls the various aenigmata on *SAPIENTIA* (wisdom) elsewhere in the Anglo-Saxon riddle tradition, on which see in particular ps-BED 1.

55.4 Compare SYM 13.3; EUS 2.3 *(vestigia nulla)*; BER 37.1 *(perambulo terras)*.

BER 56

MANUSCRIPT: N, fol. 79v.

EARLIER EDITIONS AND TRANSLATIONS: St, 756; Gl, 603. (SK 16723)

SOLUTION: *SOL ET LUNA* (sun and moon); the solution given is *DE SOLE* (on sun). Other suggestions include *CAELUM ET TERRA* (heaven and earth), *VERBUM* (word), *ANNUS* (year).

This aenigma seems to lead on easily from the one that precedes it, with the same suggested solution; the notion of "covering" in the final line suggests the Isidorian etymology (*caelum quod celat,* "a celestial thing, because it conceals"). The theme of incest here is explored more fully elsewhere in the Anglo-Saxon riddle tradition; see further the headnote to OEP.

56.1 Compare SYM 86.2 *(una mihi soror)*.

56.3 Compare TAT 16.4 *(coniungimur ambis)*; EUS 15.1 *(cum iungimur)*.

BER 57

MANUSCRIPT: N, fol. 80r.
EARLIER EDITIONS AND TRANSLATIONS: St, 757; Gl, 604. (SK 12657)
SOLUTION: *SOL* (sun).

This aenigma again seems suggested by the preceding ones, but offers a further different slant.

57.2 The form *fugiens* is evidently disyllabic: see the note on BER 45.5.

BER 58

MANUSCRIPT: N, fol. 80r.
EARLIER EDITIONS AND TRANSLATIONS: St, 757; Gl, 605. (SK 1172)
SOLUTION: *LUNA* (moon).

This aenigma follows on naturally from the preceding ones that seem to focus on the sun.

58.3 Compare ALD 100.59 *(versa vice);* BER 31.3 and 46.3 *(PILUM,* "pestle": *Versa mihi . . . vice).*
58.4 Compare BER 31.4 *(ab ima).*
58.6 The new moon and the old moon share the same crescent shape.

BER 59

MANUSCRIPT: N, fol. 80r.
EARLIER EDITIONS AND TRANSLATIONS: St, 758; Gl, 606. (SK 13850)
SOLUTION: *LUNA* (moon).

This aenigma follows smoothly on from the one preceding.

59.1 Reading *Quo movear gressum nullus cognoscere temptat* (the manuscripts have a variety of readings, none of them particularly coherent).

59.3 Compare SYM 13.3 *(Curro vias multas);* BER 11.6 *(currens viam);* ALF O.2 *(Curro vias multas).*

59.4 The twofold iteration seems to refer to the four main phases that follow the new moon: crescent, half, gibbous, and full.

59.5 The form *glacies* is evidently disyllabic: see the note on BER 45.5. This noun-rich line suggests the solutions to several of the riddles in the Anglo-Saxon riddle tradition.

BER 60

MANUSCRIPT: N, fol. 80r.
EARLIER EDITIONS AND TRANSLATIONS: St, 758; Gl, 607. (SK 12666)
SOLUTION: *CAELUM* (sky); the solution given is *DE CAELO.* There are some broad parallels in *Hisperica famina* A358–80 (*DE CAELO,* "on the sky"; see further Herren, *Hisperica Famina: The A-Text;* Orchard, "*Hisperica famina* as Literature").

If the suggested solution is correct, this aenigma follows on very suitably from those that precede.

60.5 Compare BER 46.5 *(Nullus mihi).*

BER 61

MANUSCRIPT: N, fol. 80v.
EARLIER EDITIONS AND TRANSLATIONS: St, 758; Gl, 608. (SK 7348)
SOLUTION: *UMBRA* (shadow).

Again, if the suggested solution is correct, the connection between this aenigma and those that directly precede seems clear.

61.1 Reading *humili . . . loco* (most manuscripts read *humidis . . . locis*). Compare BER 4.1 *(semper consistere locis).*

BER 62

MANUSCRIPT: N, fol. 80r.
EARLIER EDITIONS AND TRANSLATIONS: St, 758; Gl, 609. (SK 9627)
SOLUTION: *STELLAE* (stars). See further Murphy, *Unriddling the Exeter Riddles,* 115.

The sequence of suggested solutions in these last few aenigmata is evidently predicated on a series of associations that holds up well here, and culminates in a suitably cosmic conclusion, such as is found, for example, in TAT 40 (*RADII SOLIS,* "rays of the sun").

62.5 The present participle *turpentem* is unexampled elsewhere in Latin verse.
62.6 The form *odiunt* (rather than *oderunt*) again highlights the specific (and postclassical) idiolect of the author.

PS-BER 1

MANUSCRIPT: N, fol. 80v.
EARLIER EDITIONS AND TRANSLATIONS: St, 759; Gl, 610. (SK 12767)
SOLUTION: *VINUM* (wine).

This poem is of a very different pattern from those that precede, and is clearly not of the same fourteen-syllable rhythmical form; it is attached to the collection in only a single manuscript, but nonetheless in its evident subject matter speaks well to the Anglo-Saxon riddling tradition in general. The evident acrostic *PAULUS* presumably identifies the author (and it has been suggested that the "Paul" in question is the Carolingian poet Paul the Deacon), who cannot, however, be reckoned to have written the whole collection. On the seductive dangers of alcohol, see further the note at ALD 80 (*CALIX VITREUS,* "glass cup") above, as well as the headnotes to EXE 9 and GES 1.

1.3 Compare BON 12.5 and 18.3 (*Viribus atque meis*).

THE VERSES OF A CERTAIN IRISHMAN ON THE ALPHABET

Authorship and Date

These three-line aenigmata on individual letters of the Roman alphabet seem to mimic in their basic format the three-line aenigmata of Symphosius; the same three-line format is also found in OER, as well as ONR, if the three verses of a typical *ljóðaháttr* distich are considered in that way. The manuscripts vary in terms of the title (or lack of it): only three of the ten manuscripts specify that the author is an Irishman (including two Anglo-Saxon manuscripts G and L), but several linguistic features (discussed below in the notes to ALF B, E) support the attribution.

Manuscript Context(s)

There are ten medieval manuscripts, ranging in date from the ninth century to the twelfth, which in itself testifies to the importance and wide circulation of this collection; the fact that it is witnessed in no fewer than six manuscripts ($F^1F^2GLOP^3$) containing other relevant collections again bears witness to its close connection to the wider Anglo-Saxon riddle tradition. In three of these seven manuscripts (GOP^3), ALF is found alongside both ALD and SYM; in two others (F^1F^2), alongside ALD alone. L is badly damaged, and only witnesses ALF A–O, with eight of those stanzas having physical damage. In O, ALF is found between ALD 98 and ALD 99.

Subject Matter and Solutions

This is by its very nature one of the most coherent of the riddle collections, and yet it is also very well integrated into the riddle tradition as a whole, as the notes make clear. Several of the stanzas focus on issues of scansion, so again emphasizing the connection with the composition of poetry that is found elsewhere in the Anglo-Latin riddle tradition, as well as in the presumably mnemonic list of mostly poetic synonyms for "ruler" that travels alongside OIR. Part of the focus, as HoA observes, is on the so-called *tres linguae sacrae,* "three sacred languages," of the Bible, namely, Hebrew, Greek, and Latin;

much of the text itself, as well as the commentary to ALF A–S that accompanies the text in a single manuscript, Chartres, Bibliothèque Municipale, 75 (55), fols. 1–2 (s. ix/x = manuscript C in Gl), focuses on just this area (see further Howlett, "'Tres Linguae Sacrae' and Threefold Play in Insular Latin").

Style

The formulaic and repetitive nature of the individual stanzas belies the complexity of the text as a whole, a feature examined in great detail in Ho, to whose analysis I am greatly indebted. The utility of this text for teaching Latin in general, and Latin verse in particular, is highlighted by the comments of HoA, 136–37, who notes: "The poet's orthography is perfect. . . . The poet's prosody is competent." The latter comment, at least, is perhaps somewhat generous: see the notes to ALF B.3, C.2, D.2, M.1, P.3, R.3, S.1, and Z.3, which highlight some metrical infelicities and/or licenses. There is also fairly frequent elision here, at ALF A.1, A.3, D.1, D.3, E.3, F.2, I.2, L.3, M.3, S.1, S.3, T.1, Y.2, Y.3, and Z.3.

Sources and Parallels

Much of the material covered in ALF can be traced back to Isidore's *Etymologiae,* as the notes make clear. Although the primary focus is on Isidore, *Etym.* 1 (which deals with issues of language), as one would expect, it is evident that the author was fully familiar with the whole of the work. A number of parallels of phrasing link ALF to ALD in particular, though the direction of borrowing is unclear: see further the notes to ALF A.2, T.3, X.1, and X.2. The question of Aldhelm's potential use of Hiberno-Latin material in ALD is complex, and is also tied up with his relationship with the puzzling *Hisperica famina* (on which see the introduction to *OEALRT,* under "Sources and Analogues"), a text that also contains parallels to the Anglo-Saxon riddle tradition.

This Text and Translation

Gl provides the basis for the text, although he does not provide a translation; I have also consulted Ha and (especially) HoA.

Further Reading

Halsall, *The Old English Rune Poem,* 42–45; Ross, "The Anglo-Saxon and Norse *Rune Poems*"; Page, "The Icelandic Rune Poem."

ALF A

MANUSCRIPTS: L, fol. 137v; G, fol. 381r; O, fol. 13v.
PREVIOUS EDITION: Gl, 729. (SK 12594 [includes all of ALF])

The idea of A as the first letter may seem banal, since it is so obviously the first letter in the Latin, Greek, and Hebrew alphabets; the commentary offers considerably more detail.

A.1 Reading *prima* (F[1]LO have *mira*). As the commentary notes: *Principium vocis id est quia infans mox ut nascitur prima voce dicit A. Veterumque inventio prima, hoc est quia A littera prima litterarum inventa est, et ideo prima scribitur in alphabeto,* "The beginning of speech, that is, because as soon as it is born, a child says A with its first utterance. The first invention of the ancients, this is because A was first discovered of all the letters, and so is written first in the alphabet." A likely source is Isidore, *Etym.* 1.4.16.

A.2 For the notion of "having a name," see the note at ALD 50.3. As the commentary notes: *Nomen habens domini, id est quia apud pelasgos (hoc est graecos) ALPHA appellatur A; et in apocalypsi Iohannis dominus dicit: "Ego sum A et Ω,"* "Having the name of the Lord, that is, because among the Pelasgians, which is to say the Greeks, A is called ALPHA; and in the Apocalypse of John the Lord says: 'I am A and Ω.'" Compare Revelation 1:8, 21:6, 22:13. A likely source is Isidore, *Etym.* 1.3.4.

A.3 Reading *dira* (P[3] has *dura*). As the commentary notes: *Exsecrantis item, hoc est quia interdum A interiectio est exsecrantis, sicut habens in propheta: "Et dixi A, A, A, domine deus,"* "Again . . . by one cursing, this is because sometimes A is the exclamation of one imploring, just as the prophet mentions: 'and I said, A, A, A, Lord God.'"

ALF B

MANUSCRIPTS: L, fol. 137v; G, fol. 381r; O, fol. 13v.
PREVIOUS EDITION: Gl, 730.

The use of the word *tertia* here, where it must carry the sense "one of three" rather than the usual "third" (since *be* is the first syllable of *beatus* rather than the third), may point to an Irish author, since that sense is found in Hiberno-Latin. For a similar use of *altera* as "one of two," rather than "second," see ALF E, where *quinta* can mean either "fifth" or "one of five."

B.1 As the commentary notes: *Principium libri id est psalmorum: primus psalmus incipit a littera B; item prologus evangelii: beatissimo pape Damaso. Mutis caput, quia in ordine alphabeti secundum locum tenet,* "The beginning of 'The Book,' that is, of the psalms: the first psalm begins with the letter B; likewise the prologue to the Gospel: 'To the most blessed Pope Damasus.' The head of the mutes, because it is second in the sequence of the alphabet."

B.2 As the commentary notes: *Tercia felicis v. s. s. s. quia in trisyllabo nomine quod est BEATUS, prima sonum B habet,* "I am always one of three syllables of the blessed because in the three-syllable word *beatus,* the first has the sound *b.*"

B.3 Reading *Si me grece legas* (P[3] has *Littera greca manens*) and *horto* (G has *orto*). False quantity: the normal form is *Graecē*; see too ALF C.2 and L.1. Compare ALF C.2 *(legeres si Graece),* ALF L.1 *(Si me Graece legas).* As the commentary notes: *Si me graece legas v. t. n. i. h. quia B littera apud grecos appellatur BETA, quo nomine—hoc est BETA—vocatur quaedam herba quae in horto nascitur,* "If you read me in Greek, then I am born in a green garden because the letter *B* is called *beta* among the Greeks, and this word, which is to say *beta,* is the name of a vegetable that is in the garden." A likely source is Isidore, *Etym.* 1.3.10.

ALF C

MANUSCRIPTS: L, fol. 137v; G, fol. 381r; O, fol. 13v.
PREVIOUS EDITION: Gl, 730.

C.1 As the commentary notes: *Principium caeli quia C littera prima est in nomine CELI. Primis et luna figuris, quia nova luna, primis diebus vel noctibus similitudinem C litterae habet,* "The beginning of "celestial" because *C* is the first letter in the word *celi.* And the moon in its first phases, because the new moon, for the first days and nights looks like the letter *C.*"

C.2 L has *clarus,* corrected to *clerus* by means of a superscript. False quantity: the normal form is *Graecē;* compare ALF B.3 *(Si me Graece legas),* ALF L.1 *(Si me Graece legas).* As the commentary notes: *Et me clerus amat quia greci pro C habent K litteram, quae graece dicitur KAPPA: apud latinos vero CAPPA est quaedam vestis quam clerici induere solent, maxime pro pluvia,* "The Latin cleric loves me because the Greeks have the letter *K* for *C,* which is called *kappa* in Greek; among the Latins in fact *cappa* is a type of clothing that clerks are accustomed to wear, especially in the rain." A likely source is Isidore, *Etym.* 19.3.3.

C.3 Compare SYM 26.1 *(GRUS,* "crane": *Littera sum caeli . . . perscripta);* ALF Z.1 *(Littera sum).* As the commentary notes: *Littera sum terrae, quia vestigia pedum equi in terra similitudinem C litterae latinae exprimunt,* "I am the letter . . . on the ground, because the tracks of a horse's hoofs look like the Latin letter *C.*"

ALF D

MANUSCRIPTS: L, fol. 137v (damaged); G, fol. 381r; O, fol. 13v–14r.
PREVIOUS EDITION: Gl, 731.

D.1 Reading *vox* (F[1]O has *mox*). As the commentary notes: *Ablati casus vox sum et pars septima linguae, hoc est DE prepositio casus ablative sonum D littere habet, et ipsa prepositio septima pars est in ordine octo partium orationis; "orationem" vero "linguam" vocat, quia in illa constat omnis locutio humanae linguae,* "I am the sound of the ablative case and the seventh part of speech, that is, because the preposition *de,* which takes the ablative, has the sound of the letter *D,* and the preposition itself is the seventh of the eight parts of speech; [the poet] calls "speech" "language," since "speech" comprises the whole of the speaking of human language."

D.2 Reading *Omnipotentis habens nomen* (G and L have *Omnitenens nomen et habens*) and *iuncta* (F[1] has *vincta*). False quantity: the normal form is *nōmen,* and presumably *iuncta* is scanned as trisyllabic. For the phrase *nomen habens,* see the note at ALF A.2. As the commentary notes: *Omnipotens nomen habens, "us" bannita iuncta, hoc est cum nominaveris D litteram, si subiunxeris us syllabam, dixisti DEUS; "bannita" vero "syllaba,"* "Having the name of the almighty when the syllable "us" has been added, namely, when you say the name of the letter *D,* if you add the syllable 'us,' you have said *deus,* "god"; 'bannita' means 'syllable.'" The word *bannita* is generally associated with Celtic Latin texts (see further Bischoff, "Bannita: 1. Syllaba, 2. Littera").

D.3 As the commentary notes: *Sum medium mille quia D littera significat in numero "quingentos." Et veterum mala nota deorum hoc est apud antquos D littera sola scripta significabat DEMONEM sive DIABOLUM; aliquando propriis nominibus idolorum praeposita significabat DEUM,* "I am half a thousand because the letter *D* signifies the number 500. And a wicked sign of ancient gods, namely, among the ancients the letter *D* written on its own used to mean "demon" or "devil"; sometimes when placed before the proper names of idols it used to mean "divine."

ALF E

MANUSCRIPTS: L, fol. 137v (damaged); G, fol. 381r; O, fol. 14r.
PREVIOUS EDITION: Gl, 731.

E.1 Note the use of the future here, where one might expect the present; for other examples in the Anglo-Saxon riddle tradition, see the note at BON 7.9. Compare ALF K.1 (*vocalis habebar*). As the commentary notes: *Pars ego mutarum, quia mute litterae in sonum E desinunt, ut BE, CE, DE, GE, PE, TE, exceptis tribus "ha," "ka," "quu." Vere vocalis habebor, quia E littera vocalis est*, "I am part of the mutes, because the mute letters end in *E*, thus *BE, CE, DE, GE, PE, TE*, with three exceptions: *ha, ka, quu*. Really I shall be reckoned to be a vowel, because the letter E is a vowel." A likely source is Isidore, *Etym*. 1.4.4.

E.2 As the commentary notes: *Altera deceptae q. s. s. m, hoc est in nomine EVAE prima syllaba est*, "I am one of two syllables of a mother deceived long ago, namely, it is the first syllable in the name Eve."

E.3 The second *pars* is omitted by F[2]GLP[3]. As the commentary notes: *Pars quoque sum plena, quia E prepositio integra pars orationis est. Et vocis pars q.l., quia una est ex quinque vocalibus litteris latinis*, "I am also a full part, because the preposition *E* is a complete part of speech. And the fifth part of Latin speech, because among Latin letters it is one of the five vowels."

ALF F

MANUSCRIPTS: L, fol. 137v (damaged); G, fol. 381r–v; O, fol. 14r.
PREVIOUS EDITION: Gl, 732.

F For the logogriph, compare the headnote to ALD 63 (*CORBUS*, "raven").

F.1 As the commentary notes: *Semisonus dicor, quia semivocalis est. Liquidis ut m. m., hoc est sicut una ex mutis litteris, ita F semivocalis praeposita liquidis L, R, facit commune syllabam*, "I am pronounced half-sounded, because it is semivocalic. Whenever, unvoiced, I am of service to liquids, namely, just like one of the mutes, so the semivowel *F* when placed before the liquids *L* and *R* creates a common syllable." A likely source is Isidore, *Etym.* 1.4.4 and 1.4.9.

F.2 P^3 has *odit Hebraeus,* and G has the rather comic *ebrius odit* (as if drunks do not use *f*-words). Given the false quantities elsewhere, it seems likely that *Hebrĕus* is another one, the usual form is *Hebrǣus.* Compare BIB 5.7 (*Nescio quid*), Alcuin, *Carmen* 8.7 (*Nescio quid causae est*). As the commentary notes: *Nescio quid causae est c. m. s. e. o., quia apud ebreos F littera non est,* "I don't know why it is that the Hebrew hates me so, because there is no letter *F* in Hebrew."

F.3 As the commentary notes: *Nox perit e. t. s. m. d. f. t., hoc est si de nomine, quod est FLUMEN, F tuleris, LUMEN erit,* "Night disappears and darkness, if you remove me from 'river,' namely, if you take away the letter *F* from the word FLUMEN, 'river,' LUMEN, 'light,' will be left."

ALF G

MANUSCRIPTS: L, fol. 138r (damaged); G, fol. 381v; O, fol. 14r.
PREVIOUS EDITION: Gl, 732.

G.1 Reading *legeres*] (P^5 has *recites*).

G.1–2 B omits *tunc . . . legeres* by eye-skip. Note the use of the futures here, where one might expect the present tense; for other examples in the Anglo-Saxon riddle tradition, see the note at BON 7.9. As the commentary notes: *Si solam legeres t. c. c. h.; si duplicem legeres hoc est si unam litteram G scribitur, significant GAIUM cesarem; si vero duplex GG scribitur, significant GREGORIUM papam,* "If you were to read me once, I shall be reckoned a famous Caesar; If you were to read me twice, namely, if a single letter G is written, it signifies GAIUS Caesar; if a double G is written, it signifies Pope GREGORY."

G.2 Reading *Si, legeres,* and *habebor* (P^3 has *Si vero* and *honorus*).

G.3 As the commentary notes: *Post me quinta s. p. v. i. o., hoc est U post G scripta non habet plenum vocalis sonum, ut "lingua," "pinguis," "sanguis,"* "After me, the fifth vowel sounds only a little in the mouth, namely, *U* written after *G* does not have the full sound of a vowel, as in *lingua, pinguis, sanguis.*

ALF H

MANUSCRIPTS: L, fol. 138r; G, fol. 381v; O, fol. 14r.
PREVIOUS EDITION: Gl, 733.

H.1 For the phrase *nomen habens*, see the note at ALF A.2. As the commentary notes: *Nomen habens vacuum, hoc est quia non habet potestatem consonantis. Fragilem d. f., quia in duas figuras, id est dasian ⊢ et psilen ⊣, solvitur,* "Having an empty name, namely, that it does not have the force of a consonant. I sport a fragile figure, because it can be broken into two symbols, that is, dasian ⊢ and psilen ⊣." A likely source is Isidore, *Etym.* 1.4.11 and 1.19.9–11.

H.2 Reading *manet* (P[5] has *valet*). As the commentary notes: *Non nisi per versus in m. u. u. p., id est quia nisi communem syllabam fecerit, non servat vim consonantis,* "Nor does any force remain in me, except in verses, that is, unless it has formed a common syllable, it does not keep the force of a consonant."

H.3 As the commentary notes: *Hoc tantum valui l. s. f., id est aspirationem tantum facit vocalibus et quibusdam consonantibus,* "This is all I can do: carry aspirations in languages, that is, it only causes aspiration with vowels and certain consonants." A likely source is Isidore, *Etym.* 1.27.10.

ALF I

MANUSCRIPTS: L, fol. 138r; G, fol. 381v; O, fol. 14r.
PREVIOUS EDITION: Gl, 733.

I.1 Compare SYM 85.1 *(contentio magna).* As the commentary notes: *Sum numerus primus, quia in numero I littera significat, "unum." Iuvenum contentio magna, id est qui I littera similitudinem habet virgae; iuvenes autem ludentes solent uti virga pro gladio, scutumque tenentes duellum simulare,* "I am the first number, because as a number, the letter *I* signifies 'one.' A great contention of youngsters, that is, because the letter *I* looks like a stick; but youngsters, when playing, often use a stick in place of a sword, and while they hold a shield they pretend to fight." A likely source is Isidore, *Etym.* 1.4.15 and 17, and 1.27.11.

I.2 As the commentary notes: *Spreta mihi figura est etiam, id est quia omnibus littera minorem figuram habet. Sed mira potestas, quia et vocalis est et pro duplici consonante fungitur,* "Even my figure is slighted, that is, because the letter has a thinner shape than all of them. But my power is amazing, because it is also a vowel and functions in a double way as a consonant."

I.3 Reading *Me* (P^3 has *Ne*). As the commentary notes: *Me tamen haud dominus voluit d. l. p., hoc est quod dominus in evangelio secundum Mattheum dicit: "Iota unum aut unus apex non peribit a lege donec omnia fiant,"* "Yet the Lord did not want me to perish from the Law, namely, that the Lord says in the Gospel of Matthew: 'neither an iota nor a single letter shall perish from the Law until all shall come to pass'" (Matthew 5:18).

ALF K

MANUSCRIPTS: L, fol. 138r; G, fol. 381v; O, fol. 14r.
PREVIOUS EDITION: Gl, 734.

K.1 Reading *primos* with the manuscripts; some editors emend to *priscos*. Reading *habebar* (G has *habebor*). For the imperfect *habebar* here, compare the future tenses *(habebor)* at ALF E.1 and G.1–2. As the commentary notes: *Dux ego per primos p. v. h. hoc quia antiqui K scribebant ubicumque A sequebatur, ut "kaput," "karo," "kanis," et cetera,* "I used to be reckoned a leader of the first vowel among the first men, namely, because the ancients used to write *K* everywhere when it was followed by *A*, as in *kaput, karo, kanis,* etc." A likely source for this information is Isidore, *Etym.* 1.4.12 and 1.27.13.

K.2 Reading *Meque meo* (O has *Denique me;* F[1]F[2] has *Deque meo)* and *pellerunt* (L has *pellerunt*). As the commentary notes: *meque meo p. p. i. m. id est quod moderni C scribunt pro K,* "But modern folk have utterly expelled me from my rightful position, that is, that modern-day people write *C* instead of *K*."

K.3 As the commentary notes: *nunc caput affrorum m. v. m. h. hoc est quia KARTAGO et KALENDAE tantum nunc scribuntur per K; et KARTAGO est metropolis affricae, KALENDAE vero initium mensis,* "Now I have deserved to hold the headship of the Africans or of the month, namely, because only *Kartago* and *kalendae* are now written with *K;* and *Kartago* is the main city in Africa, but *kalendae* is the beginning of the month." A likely source is Isidore, *Etym.* 25.1.30.

ALF L

MANUSCRIPTS: L, fol. 138r (damaged); G, fol. 381v; O, fol. 14r.
PREVIOUS EDITION: Gl, 734.

L.1 False quantity: the normal form is *Graecē;* see too ALF B.3 and C.2. Compare ALF B.3 *(Si me Graece legas),* ALF C.2 *(legeres si Graece).* As the commentary notes: *Si me grece legas t. s. s. v., id est quia L littera LAUTA dicitur apud grecos,* "If you read me in Greek, you will see me completely spotless, that is, because the letter *L* is called *lauta,* 'washed,' among the Greeks." A likely source is Isidore, *Etym.* 10.L.163.

L.2 As the commentary notes: *nec frustra q. p. c. s. l., id est quia communem syllabam facit in metro,* "And not in vain, since I often make liquids in poems, that is, because it creates a common syllable in meter." A likely source is Isidore, *Etym.* 1.4.9.

L.3 As the commentary notes: *sed tamen agricola i. c. m. v. p., hoc est quia falx et alia quaedam rustica ferramenta similitudinem habent L litterae,* "But yet a farmer carries me on a curved neck, namely, because the sickle, like several other farm implements, looks like the letter *L*." A likely source is Isidore, *Etym.* 20.14.4–5.

ALF M

MANUSCRIPTS: L, fol. 138r (damaged); G, fol. 381v; O, fol. 14r.
PREVIOUS EDITION: Gl, 735.

M For the logogriph *MATER* → *ATER*, compare the headnote to ALD 63 (*CORBUS*, "raven").

M.1 False quantity: the normal form is *iūgiter*. As the commentary notes: *In metris iugiter c. s. v. e., id est in metris per synalipham sepe absumitur cum praecedente vocali*, "Although in poems I am continually a food for vowels, that is, it is often taken away with the preceding vowel in elision." A likely source is Isidore, *Etym*. 1.35.5.

M.2 Reading *tollas me non*, which violates the normal rules of syntax (P[3] has *ne tollas me genitrice* through what looks like a hypercorrection; G has *genitricis*).

M.3 Reading *Ne atra* (L has *Neutra*).

ALF N

MANUSCRIPTS: L, fol. 138r (damaged); G, fol. 381v; O, fol. 14r.
PREVIOUS EDITION: Gl, 735.

N For the logogriph *NOMEN* → *OMEN*, compare the headnote to ALD 63 (*CORBUS*, "raven").

N.1 As the commentary notes: *Vox sum sonans certa q. r. m. a., id est quia cum N littera sola nominatur tunc in voce sonat EN, quod est adverbium demonstrandi, ut: "En illum quem queris,"* "I am a sure-sounding noise, by which a thing is shown to be present, that is, because when the letter *N* is named on its own, it makes the sound *en*, which is an adverb that calls attention to something [in other words, an interjection], as in 'Look: there is the one you are looking for.'"

N.2 As the commentary notes: *tollere me m. q. d. n. f., id est NOMEN, si primam litteram sit OMEN; quod quaerentibus una res est,* "Many seek in vain to take me from a 'name,' that is, if you take away the first letter of *nomen,* it would make *omen,* which is the same thing for those who are seeking it."

N.3 Compare Alcuin, *Carmen* 7.20 *(pitheo . . . carmine).* As the commentary notes: *vim quoque sic solitam p. d. c. p., hoc est quia sepe liquescit in carminibus Apollonis qui Pithius dicitur; nam apud grecos sepe liquescit N littera, sicut apud latinos L et R,* "So also I am losing my accustomed force in Pythian song, namely, because it often becomes liquid in the songs of Apollo, who is called Pythian; for in Greek the letter *n* often becomes liquid, just as *L* and *R* do in Latin." Note the connection between Pythian meter and the Delphic oracles, as outlined in Isidore, *Etym.* 1.39.13, where of a certain meter it is said that: *Pythium autem vocatum volunt eo, quod hoc genere metri oracula Apollinis sint edita,* "They want to call it Pythian because Apollo's oracles used to be declared in this kind of meter."

ALF O

MANUSCRIPTS: L, fol. 138r (damaged); G, fol. 381v; O, fol. 14r.
PREVIOUS EDITION: Gl, 736.

O.1 Reading *choris en sum* (P^3 has *chori sensum;* G has *choris sensum;* F^1L have *chori sensu*). As the commentary notes: *Littera saepe choris e. s. s. c., id est quia chorus canentium similitudinem habet O littere,* "Look: I am the letter often signaled by choirs of singers, that is, because a chorus of singers looks like a letter *O*" [in other words, often hold their mouths in an *O* shape, or perhaps there is a reference to the *O*-antiphons commonly sung]. A likely source is Isidore, *Etym.* 6.19.5.

O.2 Note the pun on *manibus . . . manebo.* Compare SYM 13.3 *(Curro vias multas);* BER 11.6 *(currens viam),* BER 59.3 *(currens vias).* As the commentary notes: *curro vias multas, hoc est rota plaustri similis est huic littere,* "I run many ways, that is, a cart wheel is like this letter." A likely source is Isidore, *Etym.* 20.12.1.

ALF P

MANUSCRIPTS: G, fol. 381v; O, fol. 14r–v.
PREVIOUS EDITION: Gl, 736.

The acronym *SPQR* (for *Senatus PopulusQue Romanus,* "the senate and people of Rome") was the official mark of the Roman Republic, and is mentioned in ALF P, R, and S; its lack in ALF Q may signify the lesser status of enclitic *-que*.

P.1 As the commentary notes: *Me sine n. p. h. c. c., hoc est sine P littera PAX non potest dici; et sine pace non erit concordia hominum,* "Without me, no agreement of men can be seen, namely, that 'peace' cannot be said without the letter *P*; and without peace there will be no harmony among people."

P.2 Reading *potentis* (P[3] has *potens*).

P.3 Reading *piorum* (G and L have *priorum*). Compare ALF S.1 *(Nota fui patrum)*. The Latin note *pp* stood for both *papa,* "pope," and *pater patriae,* "father of the nation," or *patres patriae,* "fathers of the nation."

ALF Q

MANUSCRIPTS: G, fol. 381v–82r; O, fol. 14v.
PREVIOUS EDITION: Gl, 737.

Q.1 As the commentary notes: *Sola mihi virtus v. v. q., id est hanc vim habet Q littera, ut ante U tantum scribatur,* "My only power is conquering the fifth vowel, that is, that the letter *Q* has the power to be written only before *U*."

Q.2 As the commentary notes: *qua sine n. n. e., id est quia nunquam Q scribitur, nisi semper V sequatur. Hanc occido nefande, id est quia V perdit naturalem sonum, praecedente Q littera,* "Without which I am not born, that is, because *Q* is never written without *U* always following. I kill it unspeakably, that is, because *U* loses its natural sound when the letter *Q* precedes it." A likely source is Isidore, *Etym.* 1.4.8.

Q.3 Reading *quaternae* (O has *moderni*). As the commentary notes: *quapropter i. m. r. q., hoc est quia Q littera nunquam scribitur ante aliquam vocalem, nisi V intersit,* "Wherefore the four other vowels justly spurn me, namely, that the letter *Q* is never written before a vowel, unless *U* intervenes." A likely source is Isidore, *Etym.* 1.4.13.

ALF R

MANUSCRIPTS: G, fol. 382r; O, fol. 14v.
PREVIOUS EDITION: Gl, 737.

R.1 As the commentary notes: *Est durum nomen, id est durum sonum habet in nomine,* "It is a harsh name, that is, it has a harsh sound in its name." Note that the letter *r* is also called the *littera canina,* "the dog's letter," based on its resemblance to a dog's growl.

R.2 Reading *nam* (F²GLP³ have *non*). As the commentary notes: *idcirco placuit m. n. m. c., id est quia in metro sepe solet liquescere,* "Whereby it was pleasing to soften me in song, that is, because it is metrically often found to become liquid." A likely source is Isidore, *Etym.* 1.4.9.

R.3 Reading *fueram populi* (P³ has *populi fueram*). As the commentary notes: *nota tamen fueram p. v. e. o., hoc est ubi una R littera sola scribitur, significat ROMANOS vel ROMANI,* "Yet I had been the mark of the people who conquered the world, namely, when one *R* is written on its own, it signifies Romans."

ALF S

MANUSCRIPTS: G, fol. 382r; O, fol. 14v.
PREVIOUS EDITION: Gl, 738.

S.1 Compare ALF P.3 *(nota fui patrum).*

S.3 Reading *origine* (GP³ have *ordine*).

AI Г

MANUSCRIPTS: G, fol. 382r; O, fol. .
PREVIOUS EDITION: Gl, 738.

T.1 Reading *en voluit* (P[3] has *as at*).
T.3 Compare ALD 47.9 *(propri nomine)*; TAT 7.1 *(proprio sub nomine)*.

AL

MANUSCRIPTS: G, fol. 382r; O, fol. .
PREVIOUS EDITION: Gl, 739.

V.1 Reading *Forma manet* (F[1]F ve *Formaret*). Note the polysyllabic ending *variatur*; see rther the note at ALD PR.26.
V.2 Compare EUS 54.1 *(DE O NO PISCE*, "about a ship-retaining fish": *forma mane*

AL

MANUSCRIPTS: G, fol. 382r; O, fol.
PREVIOUS EDITION: Gl, 739.

X.1 Compare SYM 52.3 *(forma mihi)*; ALD 80.4; TAT 8.1 and 9.1 (all *mihi forma*), TAT 12 *mihi . . . forma)*.
X.2 Compare SYM 26.1 *(penna volantis)*, 28.2 *(penna volantis)*; ALD 30.4 *(penna volitantis)*

ALF Y

MANUSCRIPTS: not in G or O.
PREVIOUS EDITION: Gl, 740 (Gl also prints an extended poem on the letter *y* that is evidently not part of the original text).

The double power mentioned here is the twin pronounciation of Greek *upsilon* as both /u/ and /i/. The Samian mentioned here is Pythagoras, as Isidore, *Etym*. 1.3.7 explains:

> Υ litteram Pythagoras Samius ad exemplum vitae humanae primus formavit; cuius virgula subterior primam aetatem significat, incertam quippe et quae adhuc se nec vitiis nec virtutibus dedit. Bivium autem, quod superest, ab adolescentia incipit: cuius dextra pars ardua est, sed ad beatam vitam tendens: sinistra facilior, sed ad labem interitumque deducens.

> Pythagoras of Samos first formed the letter Υ as a symbol of human life: the lower stem signifies the first stage of life, certainly an uncertain age, which has not yet given itself to vice or virtue. The branching into two above begins in adolescence: the right part is steep, but leads towards a blessed life, while the left is easier, but heads towards death and destruction.

ALF Z

MANUSCRIPTS: not in G or O.

PREVIOUS EDITION: Gl, 740 (Gl also prints an extended poem on the letter *y* that is evidently not part of the original text).

Z.1 Compare SYM 26.1 (*GRUS*, "crane": *Littera sum caeli . . . perscripta*); ALF C.3 (*Littera sum terrae . . . perscripta*).

Z.3 False quantity: the normal form is *sībilans*. Notice the theme of death here, as at the end of SYM, EUS, and OER, as well as the quadrisyllabic ending, on which see the note at ALD PR.26.

THE OLD ICELANDIC RUNE POEM

Authorship and Date

As Pa (p. 1) characteristically pithily puts it: "The text commonly called the Icelandic rune-poem is only a poem by courtesy," consisting as it does of a series of single sentences, each consisting of a triple interpretation, to form a set of triads that echoes formally the mostly end-stopped three-line aenigmata of SYM and (perhaps more pertinently here) ALF and OER. In the earliest manuscript (Y^1) each of the sixteen constituent riddles is given a Latin solution (equivalent to the individual rune names), as well as a Norse poetic term for "lord" or "ruler" that alliterates with the relevant rune; the whole sequence then offers a kind of mnemonic verse *gradus,* of a kind found elsewhere in Icelandic in both GES (see the headnote to GES 21 below) and the Anglo-Saxon riddle tradition (see the headnote to ALD PR above) that would aid poetic composition.

Manuscript Contexts

OIR survives in two medieval manuscripts, and while neither is of a vintage comparable to most of the texts that make up the Anglo-Saxon riddle tradition, they are both venerable in terms of most extant Old Norse–Icelandic literature. The older, Y^1, from ca. 1500, preserves OIR alongside other similarly arcane lore, notably Latin equivalents to the rune names, cryptic alphabets, and Latin exorcisms and various prayers (see Plate 1 of Pa), while the younger, Y^2, more precisely datable to 1539–58, also includes magical material, particularly the *sator* formula which derives ultimately from the Pater Noster, together with other learned, legal, and religious formulas (see Plate 2 of Pa).

Subject Matter and Solutions

As in OER (and the alphabetic parallels in ALF), each rune has a name, which supplies the solution; as elsewhere in the Anglo-Saxon riddle tradition, such solutions are essentially secondary, even if they are often transmitted along with the riddles and aenigmata proper.

Style

The tripartite structure of each riddle, with the first two elements alliterating with each other and the third alliterating with itself, offers a precise parallel with the Old Norse poetic meter *ljóðaháttr,* "song meter," which is also found commonly though not universally in GES.

Sources and Parallels

The closest echoes are to be found in OER and ONR, as noted below.

This Text and Translation

Here I have principally relied on Pa for establishing the text, though I have also consulted closely Di, which is generally to be preferred over Ha.

Further Reading

Ross, "The Anglo-Saxon and Norse *Rune Poems*"; Page, *Introduction to Old English Runes,* 73–85.

OIR 1

MANUSCRIPTS: Y^1, fol. 1v; Y^2, fol. 15v.
PREVIOUS EDITIONS AND TRANSLATIONS: Di, 28–29; Pa, 27.
SOLUTION: *FÉ* (wealth).

The Latin solution is *aurum,* "gold"; the alliterating mnemonic ruler-word is *fylkir,* "general." The parallel ONR 1 reads: *Fé vældr frænda róge; / føðesk ulfr í skóge,* "Wealth causes strife among kinsmen; / a wolf is brought up in the forest."

OIR 2

MANUSCRIPTS: Y^1, fol. 1v; Y^2, fol. 15v.
PREVIOUS EDITIONS AND TRANSLATIONS: Di, 28–29; Pa, 27.
SOLUTION: *ÚR* (shower).

The Latin solution is *umbre,* "shadows"; the alliterating mnemonic ruler-word is *vísi,* "captain." The parallel ONR 2 reads: *Úr er af illu jarne; / opt løypr ræinn á hjarne,* "Slag is what comes from bad iron; / the reindeer often runs on frozen snow."

OIR 3

MANUSCRIPTS: Y[1], fol. 1v; Y[2], fol. 15v.
PREVIOUS EDITIONS AND TRANSLATIONS: Di, 28–29; Pa, 27.
SOLUTION: *ÞURS* (giant).

The Latin solution is *Saturnus,* "Saturn"; the alliterating mnemonic ruler-word is *þengill,* "prince." The parallel ONR 3 reads: *Þurs vældr kvinna kvillu; / kátr værðr fár af illu,* "Giant is what causes pain to women; / few men are made cheerful by misfortune."

Note the difference here from the parallel rune in OER 3 ("thorn").

OIR 4

MANUSCRIPTS: Y[1], fol. 1v; Y[2], fol. 15v.
PREVIOUS EDITIONS AND TRANSLATIONS: Di, 28–29; Pa, 27.
SOLUTION: *ÓSS* (god).

The Latin solution is *Jupiter,* "Jupiter"; the alliterating mnemonic ruler-word is *odd-viti,* "spear-driver." The parallel ONR 4 reads: *Óss er flæstra færða / fǫr; en skalpr er sværða,* "Mouth [of a river] is the path of most / journeys; but a scabbard of swords."

OIR 5

MANUSCRIPTS: Y[1], fol. 1v; Y[2], fol. 15v.
PREVIOUS EDITIONS AND TRANSLATIONS: Di, 28–29; Pa, 28.
SOLUTION: *REIÐ* (riding).

The Latin solution is *iter,* "path, way"; the alliterating mnemonic ruler-word is *ræsir,* "lord." The parallel ONR 5 reads: *Ræið kveða rossom væsta; / Reginn sló sværðet bæzta,* "Riding, they say, is the worst for horses; / Reginn forged the best of swords."

ᚴ OIR 6 ᚴ

MANUSCRIPTS: Y[1], fol. 1v; Y[2], fol. 15v.
PREVIOUS EDITIONS AND TRANSLATIONS: Di, 28–29; Pa, 28.
SOLUTION: *KAUN* (ulcer).

The Latin solution is *flagella,* "scourges"; the alliterating mnemonic ruler-word is *konungr,* "king." The parallel ONR 6 reads: *Kaun er barna bǫlvan; / bǫl gørver nán fǫlvan,* "Ulcer is baleful for children; / death makes a corpse pale."

ᚴ OIR 7 ᚴ

MANUSCRIPTS: Y[1], fol. 1v; Y[2], fol. 15v.
PREVIOUS EDITIONS AND TRANSLATIONS: Di, 30–31; Pa, 28.
SOLUTION: *HAGALL* (hail).

The Latin solution is *grando,* "hail"; the alliterating mnemonic ruler-word is *hildingr,* "battle-lord." The parallel ONR 7 reads: *Hagall er kaldastr korna; / Kristr skóp hæimenn forna,* "Hail is the coldest of grains; / Christ created the world long ago." There is a further close verbal parallel in the Old English poem *Seafarer* 33a *(corna caldast).*

ᚴ OIR 8 ᚴ

MANUSCRIPTS: Y[1], fol. 1v; Y[2], fol. 15v.
PREVIOUS EDITIONS AND TRANSLATIONS: Di, 30–31; Pa, 28.
SOLUTION: *NAUÐ* (need).

The Latin solution is *opera,* "tasks"; the alliterating mnemonic ruler-word is *niflungr,* "scion." The parallel ONR 8 reads: *Nauðr gerer næppa koste; / nøktan kælr í froste,* "Need makes for a nipped choice; / the naked man is chilled by the frost."

OIR 9

MANUSCRIPTS: Y[1], fol. 1v; Y[2], fol. 15v.
PREVIOUS EDITIONS AND TRANSLATIONS: Di, 30–31; Pa, 28.
SOLUTION: *ÍS* (ice).

The Latin solution is *glacies,* "ice"; the alliterating mnemonic ruler-word is *jǫfurr,* "warrior." The parallel ONR 9 reads: *Ís kǫllum brú bræiða; / blindan þarf at læiða,* "Ice we call a broad bridge; / the blind must be led."

OIR 10

MANUSCRIPTS: Y[1], fol. 1v; Y[2], fol. 15v–16r.
PREVIOUS EDITIONS AND TRANSLATIONS: Di, 28–29; Pa, 29.
SOLUTION: *ÁR* (year).

The Latin solution is *annus,* "year"; the alliterating mnemonic ruler-word is *all-valdr,* "all-ruler." The parallel ONR 10 reads: *Ár er gumna góðe; / get ek at ǫrr var Fróðe,* "Year is a boon to men; / I reckon that Frothi was open-handed."

OIR 11

MANUSCRIPTS: Y[1], fol. 1v; Y[2], fol. 16r.
PREVIOUS EDITIONS AND TRANSLATIONS: Di, 30–31; Pa, 29.
SOLUTION: *SÓL* (sun).

The Latin solution is *rota,* "wheel"; the alliterating mnemonic ruler-word is *siklingr,* "princeling." The parallel ONR 11 reads: *Sól er landa ljóme; / lúti ek helgum dome,* "Sun is the light of the lands; / I bow to divine judgment."

OIR 12

MANUSCRIPTS: Y[1], fol. 1v; Y[2], fol. 16r.
PREVIOUS EDITIONS AND TRANSLATIONS: Di, 30–31; Pa, 29.
SOLUTION: *TÝR* (Týr).

The Latin solution is *Mars,* "Mars"; the alliterating mnemonic ruler-word is *tiggi,* "boss." The parallel ONR 12 reads: *Týr er æin-endr ása; / opt værðr smiðr blása,* "Týr is a one-handed god; / often the smith has to blow."

OIR 13

MANUSCRIPTS: Y[1], fol. 1v; Y[2], fol. 16r.
PREVIOUS EDITIONS AND TRANSLATIONS: Di, 30–31; Pa, 29.
SOLUTION: *BJARKAN* (birch).

The Latin solution is *abies,* "silver fir"; the alliterating mnemonic ruler-word is *buðlungr,* "noble." The parallel ONR 13 reads: *Bjarkan er lauf-grønstr líma; / Loki bar flærða tíma,* "Birch is the most green-leaved of limbs; / Loki took the opportunity for evils."

The form *bjarkan* is rare indeed, and all but restricted to the name of the rune; *bjǫrk* is the common alternative.

OIR 14

MANUSCRIPTS: Y[1], fol. 1v; Y[2], fol. 16r.
PREVIOUS EDITIONS AND TRANSLATIONS: Di, 32–33; Pa, 29.
SOLUTION: *MAÐR* (man).

The Latin solution is *homo,* "man"; the alliterating mnemonic ruler-word is *mildungr,* "generous lord." The parallel ONR 14 reads: *Maðr er moldar auki; / mikil er græip á hauki,* "Man is an increase of earth; / great is the grip of the hawk."

14.1 The phrase *maðr er manns gaman* is also found in *Hávamál* 47.6, as a comment by the god Óðinn, who as the inventor of the runes seems a highly suitable source.

OIR 15

MANUSCRIPTS: Y[1], fol. 1v; Y[2], fol. 16r.
PREVIOUS EDITIONS AND TRANSLATIONS: Di, 32–33; Pa, 30.
SOLUTION: *LÖGR* (liquid).

The Latin solution is *lacus,* "vat, vessel"; the alliterating mnemonic ruler-word is *lofðungr,* "praiseworthy lord." The parallel ONR 15 reads: *Lǫgr er, fællr ór fjalle / foss; en gull ero nosser,* "Liquid is what falls from a mountainside; / but trinkets are gold."

OIR 16

MANUSCRIPTS: Y[1], fol. 1v; not in Y[2].
PREVIOUS EDITIONS AND TRANSLATIONS: Di, 32–33; Pa, 30.
SOLUTION: *ÝR* (yew).

The Latin solution is *arcus,* "bow"; the alliterating mnemonic ruler-word is *ynglingr,* "noble lord." The parallel ONR 16 reads: *Ýr er vetrgrønstr viða; / vænt er, er brennr, at sviða,* "Yew is the winter-greenest of trees; / it is wont, when it burns, to crackle."

THE RIDDLES OF GESTUMBLINDI

Authorship and Date

The so-called *Gestumblindagátur* (Riddles of Gestumblindi) are a group of verse exchanges embedded in the thirteenth-century Icelandic *Hervarar saga ok Heiðreks konungs ins vitra* (The saga of Hervǫr and King Heiðrekr the wise). In the saga, the *Gestumblindagátur* appear as the third of four such verse sequences about which the whole composite text is structured, and are presented as a wisdom contest between the famously wise but implacable king Heiðrekr and a mysterious figure that Heiðrekr believes to be his enemy, but whom the audience know is in fact the even more famously wise and far more implacable god Óðinn. At stake in the contest, we are led to understand, are the lives of the participants, just as they are in similar verse wisdom-contests, notably *Vafþrúðnismál, Grímnismál, Baldrs draumar,* and *Alvíssmál* in the Poetic Edda, the first of which also features Óðinn, who ends that contest by unfairly posing the same unanswerable riddle found here as GES E. In *Vafþrúðnismál* Óðinn only earns the right to put the questions after successfully answering a series posed by his host, the wise giant Vafþrúðnir, whose very name, "mighty weaver," attests to his spider-like ability to ensnare his prey (compare the spider riddle in GES 14), whereas in GES it is exclusively the god who poses the questions, using the name Gestumblindi, a more or less transparent equivalent for "the blind guest," and something of an obvious clue, since the one-eyed Óðinn is celebrated elsewhere not only for his half-blindness, but also for his propensity to wander the various worlds in the guise of a guest (and indeed using the name Gestr, "guest"). Each of the riddles of GES is presented in the same formulaic fashion, concluding with the two-line challenge *Heiðrekr konungr / hyggðu at gátu,* "King Heiðrekr, consider the riddle," and right up until the final riddle the king answers, apparently successfully, in prose. The challenge, which broadly echoes those found elsewhere in the Anglo-Saxon riddle tradition, is heavily abbreviated or indeed omitted in many manuscripts, and here I offer only the riddles themselves, stripped of both challenge and prose solution; the more unusual of those prose solutions are given in the *Notes to the Translations* in the accompanying DOML volume.

Manuscript Contexts

It remains an open question whether all or part of GES was composed at the same time as the saga, and the very different versions of GES in the three main recensions $H^1R^1U^1$ (in other commentators, these manuscripts are designated HRU) only complicate the issue. The earliest manuscript, H^1, also known as *Hauksbók,* includes GES as part of an idiosyncratic collection of old lore, arcane snippets, and wisdom-related material compiled for and mostly written by the Icelandic lawspeaker Haukr Erlendsson; *Hauksbók* is also notable for containing (for example) an Icelandic saga of the Tale of Troy (*Trójumanna saga*), a distinctive version of the eddic poem *Vǫluspá,* and several texts deriving more or less directly from Old English originals. There is a lacuna in H^1 soon after GES begins, as a result of physical damage: it is tempting to suggest that the riddles themselves have been removed as valuable in themselves, as seems to have happened in the case of the Old English version of *Apollonius of Tyre* in Cambridge, Corpus Christi College 201, where there is a similar lacuna precisely where the equivalent Latin text has a series of aenigmata from SYM. The gap in H^1 can be filled thanks to two seventeenth-century paper manuscripts, H^2H^3, and includes seven riddles (GES 7, 10–11, 13, 15, 30, and 33) not found elsewhere, but also lacks a single riddle, GES 23a, that is found in both R and U. There are thirty-six riddles in H^1, thirty in R^1, twenty-eight in U^1, in each case beginning with GES 1–4 and ending with the unanswerable riddle GES E, but otherwise within the three versions the sequence of riddles differs significantly. The riddles of GES combine a variety of meters: *ljóðaháttr* in GES 1–6, 8–11, 13–15, 18–25, 29, 31, 33, and E; *fornyrðislag* in GES 17, 26–28, 30, 32, and 34–35; *fornyrðislag* with a *ljóðaháttr* opening in GES 12 and 16; and the distinctly unusual *greppaminni* in GES 7. It is notable that some conscious effort seems to have been made in U^1 to arrange the riddles by meter, with *ljóðaháttr* overwhelmingly predominating initially, and *fornyrðislag* mostly apparent in the closing riddles of the sequence. U^1 also omits the challenge in all but six of the riddles (whereas by contrast it fails to appear in only one of those in H^2H^3, and in only five of R^1).

Subject Matter and Solutions

Many of the topics in question seem rather mundane, with, as one might expect, a focus on Scandinavian, indeed specifically Icelandic, subjects such as obsidian, angelica, and ptarmigan (GES 16, 18, and 20). It is notable, however, that a number of the solutions given by Heiðrekr seem overly complex or specific, or even unlikely (see, for example, the notes on GES 27 and 34 below), as does a focus on the use of kennings and a general interest in poetic language which in itself offers a broad clue to the identity of the protagonist, Óðinn, the god of poetry. Óðinn is also the god of aristocratic and recreational sex, and it is therefore fitting that there is even a "rude" riddle (GES 30) to match those found in EXE and elsewhere (on which see the introduction to *OEALRT*, under "Shared Themes across the

Collections"). GES as a whole offers a raft of general parallels to the Anglo-Saxon riddle tradition, as the notes below illustrate.

Style

There are a number of formulas sprinkled through GES, several of them in combination, and many with close parallels elsewhere in the Anglo-Saxon riddle tradition. So, for example, the formula *ek sá,* "I saw," occurs in fifteen of the riddles in GES (see the note on GES 2), cognate with the Old English *ic (ge)seah* found in EXE (on which see the note on EXE 11.1a) and parallel to the Latin *vidi* (on which see the note on ps-BED 2); nine of these occur in the context of a more complex formula "What wonder is it / that I saw outside, / just before Delling's door?," *"Hvat er þat undra, / er ek úti sá / fyrir Dellings durum?,"* in the central sequence GES 8–16.

Sources and Parallels

Several of the riddles have close parallels in terms of solution with others in the tradition, as indicated in the notes, although in most cases the treatment here varies considerably from what is found elsewhere. A striking exception is GES 12, which has a very close parallel in ALD 84 (*SCROFA PRAEGNANS,* "pregnant sow"). In more general terms, and leaving aside the obviously mythological themes of the final two riddles (GES 35 and E), as well as the introductory formula in GES 8–16, it is striking the extent to which even when the they have shared solutions with others elsewhere within the tradition, the riddles in GES are consistently idiosyncratic in approach.

This Text and Translation

I have used To as the base, although I have also consulted Bu and Lo closely.

Further Reading

Tomasek, *Das deutsche Rätsel im Mittelalter;* Reifegerste, *Die Hervarar saga;* Hall, "Changing Style and Changing Meaning"; Love, *Reception of "Hervarar saga ok Heiðreks,"* 190–238; Burrows, "Enigma Variations" and *Heiðreks gátur.*

GES 1

MANUSCRIPTS: H[1], 235; also in R[1] and U[1] (no. 1).
EARLIER EDITIONS AND TRANSLATIONS: Fi 31, 365; To 44, 32–33; Bu 1, 410–11.
SOLUTION: *MUNGÁT* (ale).

For other riddles with similar solutions, see for example ALD 78 (*CUPA VINARIA,* "wine cask"); LOR 5 (*COPA VINARIA,* "a wine cup"); EXE 9 (*WIN-FÆT,* "cup of wine"), EXE 25 (*MEDU,* "mead," or *BEOR,* "beer"), EXE 26 (*EALU,* "ale"); BER 50 (*VINUM,* "wine"); ps-BER 1 (*VINUM,* "wine").

The fact that the opening riddle of GES is dedicated to booze points back to the alcoholic haze in which SYM is said to have been composed. The ability of alcohol to trip up the unwary is a common theme, on which see, for example, EXE 9.3–5a, 25.7b–8 and 25.13b–14a; BER 50.5–6. The pseudo-Bede *Collectanea* 252 (BL, 154–55 and 254–56) has the most extensive catalogue, several aspects of which are matched in the texts noted here.

GES 2

MANUSCRIPTS: H[1], 236; also in R[1] and U[1] (no. 2).
EARLIER EDITIONS AND TRANSLATIONS: Fi 32, 365; To 45, 33; Bu 2, 411–12.
SOLUTION: *BRÚ* (bridge).

For another riddle with the same solution, see SYM 62 *(PONS),* although the treatment there is quite different. See further Lo, 212.

2.3 For the formula *sá ek,* "I saw," see too GES 8–16 (twice in GES 11), 24, 30, and 32–34. Similar formulas are found in both Latin and (especially) Old English, as the headnote above makes clear.

GES 3

MANUSCRIPTS: H[1], 237 (part only: the rest supplied from H[2]H[3]); also in R[1] and U[1] (no. 3).

EARLIER EDITIONS AND TRANSLATIONS: Fi 33, 365; To 46, 33; Bu 3, 412–13; Lo, 212–13.

SOLUTION: *DQGG* (dew).

In the H[1] tradition, represented in H[2]H[3], Heiðrekr adds comments that indicate that he begins to suspect who his antagonist is, a dramatic device that is only replicated in the R[1] and U[1] traditions after the bizarre riddle GES 12.

GES 4

MANUSCRIPTS: Lacuna in H[1]: text supplied from H[2]H[3]; also in R[1] and U[1] (no. 4).

EARLIER EDITIONS AND TRANSLATIONS: Fi 34, 365; To 47, 34; Bu 4, 413–14.

SOLUTION: *HAMARR* (hammer).

For another riddle with the same solution, albeit with a rather different treatment, see SYM 87 *(MALLEUS).*

See too Leahy, *Anglo-Saxon Crafts,* 117–19; Riley, *Anglo-Saxon Tools,* 42–43.

GES 5

MANUSCRIPTS: Lacuna in H[1]: text supplied from H[2]H[3]; also in R[1] (no. 15) and U[1] (no. 17).

EARLIER EDITIONS AND TRANSLATIONS: Fi 35, 365; To 58, 38; Bu 5, 414–15; Lo, 214–15.

SOLUTION: *MYRKVI* (fog).

Lo (p. 215), noting that the three recensions here, as later in the series, have quite different explications of the same solution, suggests that the riddles "may well have been exercises in logic . . . with simple, one-word answers . . . which were then expanded."

GES 6

MANUSCRIPTS: Lacuna in H[1]: text supplied from H[2]H[3]; also in R[1] (no. 23) and U[1] (no. 19).

EARLIER EDITIONS AND TRANSLATIONS: Fi 36, 366; To 66, 41–42; Bu 6, 415–16; Lo, 215–17.

SOLUTION: *AKKERI* (anchor).

For other riddles with similar solutions, see SYM 61 (*ANCORA*); EXE 14 (*ANCOR*).

GES 7

MANUSCRIPTS: Lacuna in H[1]: text supplied from H[2]H[3]; not in R[1]U[1].

EARLIER EDITIONS AND TRANSLATIONS: Fi 38, 366; To H7, 80; Bu 7, 416–17.

SOLUTION: *FOSS* (waterfall).

GES 8

MANUSCRIPTS: Lacuna in H[1]: text supplied from H[2]H[3]; also in R[1] (no. 7) and U[1] (no. 10).

EARLIER EDITIONS AND TRANSLATIONS: Fi 37, 366; To 50, 35; Bu 8, 417–19; Lo, 217–18.

SOLUTION: *LAUKR* (leek); U[1] gives *GEIR-LAUKR* (garlic). This is the first of three riddles where U[1] gives a more specific solution: see further the headnotes to GES 18 and 20.

For other riddles with similar solutions, see SYM 44 (*CAEPA,* "onion"); EXE 23 and 63 (*CIPE,* "onion"); BER 51 (*ALIUM,* "garlic"), especially BER 51.6 (*dum natura caput facit succedere plantis,* "while nature places my head below my feet"). This is the first of a sequence of riddles (GES 8–16), all of which begin with the same three-line formula, with a consistent variant in H[1] (as attested in H[2]H[3]), on which see the note at GES 8.3.

8.3 The three main versions appear to differ significantly in the third line of the three-line formula: H[1] (as attested in H[2]H[3]) has the reading there, *Dǫglings,* which refers generically to any descendant of the legendary king Dagr, whose name means "day"; the lower-case form *dǫgling* would also signify any princeling. The reading *Dellings* found in R[1]U[1] relates instead to the name of the dwarf Dellingr, "day-spring" (?), the father of another more literal Dagr, "day," according to the eddic *Vafþrúðnismál* 25; the phrase *fyr Dellings durum* likewise appears elsewhere in the Poetic Edda, in *Hávamál* 160, where the dwarf Þjóðrerir recites a spell "before Delling's door." Despite the discrepancy of names, the sense may in fact be similar: the riddle contest occurs at night, presumably in a court setting, and before dawn; the difference lies in whether the background is the human world or that of mythology, a distinction that is difficult to make. Here I opt for the mythological reading, since it ties in with other examples in eddic verse of verbal contests that conclude at dawn with dire consequences: see further the headnote to EXE 31 above.

GES 9

MANUSCRIPTS: Lacuna in H[1]: text supplied from H[2]H[3]; also in R[1] (no. 5) and U[1] (no. 20).

EARLIER EDITIONS AND TRANSLATIONS: Fi 39, 366; To 48, 34; Bu 9, 419–20; Lo, 218–19.

SOLUTION: *SMIÐ-BELGIR* (bellows).

For other riddles with similar solutions, see SYM 73 (*UTER FOLLIS*); ALD 11 (*POALUM*); EXE 35, 83, and EXE 85 *(BLÆST-BELG).*

9.4 The variant reading of R[1] here (*ókvikvir,* "not living") is tautologous, given the form *andalausir,* "breathless," in the next line.

9.6 The kenning "leek of wounds" (for "sword") represents a riddle within a riddle of the kind found widely in the Anglo-Saxon riddle tradition; see further the note on ALD 44.1 above.

GES 10

MANUSCRIPTS: Lacuna in H^1: text supplied from H^2H^3; not in R^1U^1.
EARLIER EDITIONS AND TRANSLATIONS: Fi 40, 366; To H10, 80; Bu 10, 420–21.
SOLUTION: *HAGL OK REGN* (hail and rain).

For other riddles with similar solutions, see SYM 9 and BER 49 (*PLUVIA*, "rain"), though the treatments there differ considerably from here.

GES 11

MANUSCRIPTS: Lacuna in H^1: text supplied from H^2H^3; not in R^1U^1.
EARLIER EDITIONS AND TRANSLATIONS: Fi, 366; To H11, 80; Bu 11, 421.
SOLUTION: *TORD-ÝFILL* (dung beetle).

GES 12

MANUSCRIPTS: Lacuna in H^1: text supplied from H^2H^3; also in R^1 and U^1 (no. 26).
EARLIER EDITIONS AND TRANSLATIONS: To 69, 43; Bu 12, 422–23; Lo, 219–21.
SOLUTION: *SÚ OK GRÍSIR* (sow and piglets).

For another riddle with a similar solution, see ALD 84 (*SCROFA PRAEGNANS*, "pregnant sow").

GES 13

MANUSCRIPTS: Lacuna in H^1: text supplied from H^2H^3; not in R^1U^1.
EARLIER EDITIONS AND TRANSLATIONS: Fi, 366; To H13, 81; Bu 13, 423–24.
SOLUTION: *ǪR* (arrow).

For other riddles with similar solutions, see SYM 65; BED 14; TAT 32; ALC D85 (all *SAGITTA*).

GES 14

MANUSCRIPTS: Lacuna in H[1]: text supplied from H[2]H[3]; also in R[1] (no. 6) and U[1] (no. 9).
EARLIER EDITIONS AND TRANSLATIONS: To 49, 35; Bu 14, 424–25.
SOLUTION: *KǪNGUR-VÁFA* (spider).

For another riddle with the same solution, see SYM 17 *(ARANEA).*

14.6 Compare ALD 34.6–7 (*LOCUSTA,* "locust"): *Cor mihi sub genibus . . . pectora poplitibus subduntur,* "my heart [lies] under my knees . . . my chest lies under my knees."

GES 15

MANUSCRIPTS: Lacuna in H[1]: text supplied from H[2]H[3]; not in R[1]U[1].
EARLIER EDITIONS AND TRANSLATIONS: Fi 38, 366; To H15, 81; Bu 15, 425–26.
SOLUTION: *SÓL* (sun).

For other riddles with similar solutions, see BER 55–57 *(SOL);* EUS 10 *(SOL);* EXE 4 *(SUNNE).*

GES 16

MANUSCRIPTS: Lacuna in H[1]: text supplied from H[2]H[3]; also in R[1] (no. 8) and U[1] (no. 15).
EARLIER EDITIONS AND TRANSLATIONS: To 51, 35–36; Bu 16, 426–27.
SOLUTION: *HRAFN-TINNA* (obsidian).

Obsidian is a kind of volcanic glass that among the Scandinavian countries is only found in Iceland, a circumstance which perhaps points to the origins of at least this part of GES. This riddle links to the next one through the sharp contrast between the brilliant black of obsidian and the shining white of the female swans.

GES 17

MANUSCRIPTS: Lacuna in H[1]: text supplied from H[2]H[3]; also in R[1] (no. 9) and U[1] (no. 21).

EARLIER EDITIONS AND TRANSLATIONS: To 52, 36; Bu 17, 428–29.

SOLUTION: *SVAN-BRÚÐIR* (female swans).

For another riddle with the same solution, see EXE 5 (*SWAN*, "swan").

This is the first of a sequence of riddles (GES 17–23a), employing a striking variety of terms for "women" with very little repetition of terms *(brúðir . . . ambáttir . . . rýgjar . . . snótir . . . leikur. . . snótir . . . meyjar . . . brúðir . . . ekkjur);* it is notable that all these terms not only take part in alliteration within their individual verses, but employ a range of alliterating options. Old Norse–Icelandic literature is full of such lists *(þulur),* which were apparently intended to be memorized by would-be poets, and employed in much the same way as a Latin *gradus,* which offers synonyms with different scansions (on which see the headnote to ALD PR above). The male swan (also known as a "cob," in contrast to the female "pen") is barely present in this riddle, and only appears in the last two lines, as the aloof "maker" of "the cask of ale" (the egg).

GES 18

MANUSCRIPTS: Lacuna in H[1]: text supplied from H[2]H[3]; also in R[1] (no. 10) and U[1] (no. 11).

EARLIER EDITIONS AND TRANSLATIONS: Fi 38, 366; To 53, 36; Bu 18, 429–30.

SOLUTION: *HVANNIR* (angelica); U[1] gives *FJALL-HVANNIR* (mountain angelica).

On the fuller solution given in U[1], see the headnote on GES 8 above. Angelica is native to Iceland, Norway, Sweden, Greenland, the Faeroes, and Finland.

GES 19

MANUSCRIPTS: Lacuna in H[1]: text supplied from H[2]H[3]; also in R[1] and U[1] (no. 13).

EARLIER EDITION AND TRANSLATION: To 56, 37–38; Bu 19, 430–31.

SOLUTION: *HNEFA-TAFL* (board game).

Various kinds of board games are attested in Norse, of which the most popular and celebrated was *hnefa-tafl,* in which the object was for the attacking side, with twice as many pieces initially situated at the sides of the board, to capture the defending side's chief piece, which starts at the center of the board and has to escape to an edge corner. The descriptions of the martial and heroic women here, even though they are explicitly "weaponless," resemble those of valkyries elsewhere: see the note to EXE 31 above.

GES 20

MANUSCRIPTS: Lacuna in H[1]: text supplied from H[2]H[3]; also in R[1] (no. 18) and U[1] (no. 8).

EARLIER EDITIONS AND TRANSLATIONS: To 61, 39–40; Bu 20, 432–33.

SOLUTION: *RJÚPUR* (ptarmigans) or *UNNIR* (waves) (?); U[1] gives *SKÓGAR-RJÚPUR* (wood ptarmigans). On the fuller solution given in U[1], see the headnote on GES 8 above.

While all three versions agree in general with the avian solution, the appearance of this riddle at the beginning of a sequence that is otherwise solved "waves," as well as significant verbal parallels, may suggest that the given solution is indeed not the only one: while ptarmigans do indeed change color (white in winter, black in summer), so too do waves, buffeted to whitecaps in a windy winter, and dark in the summer's calm. The light/dark imagery here connects this riddle to the one preceding (at least in the order given in the H-recension).

GES 21

MANUSCRIPTS: Lacuna in H[1]: text supplied from H[2]H[3]; also in R[1] (no. 19) and U[1] (no. 7).

EARLIER EDITIONS AND TRANSLATIONS: To 62, 40; Bu 21, 433–34; Lo, 221–26.

SOLUTION: *BYLGJUR* (waves).

This is the first of a sequence of (depending on the manuscript) three or four consecutive riddles with the same general solution, albeit in each case with a different word or phrase, several in the form of kennings. The usefulness of such alternative ways of expressing the same concept for aspiring poets is paralleled in the Anglo-Latin aenigmata which offer a kind of verse *gradus* to their readers (on which see the headnote to ALD PR above), as well as elsewhere in Icelandic (on which see the headnote to OIR). Similar sequences of riddles with the same or similar solutions can be seen elsewhere, for example ALC 7–9 (*FORNAX,* "furnace"); SYM 76 and 76a (both *SILEX,* "flint"); BER 55–59 (all *SOL,* "sun," *LUNA,* "moon," or *SOL ET LUNA,* "sun and moon"). See further Burrows, "Enigma Variations."

GES 22

MANUSCRIPTS: Lacuna in H[1]: text supplied from H[2]H[3]; also in R[1] (no. 20) and U[1] (no. 5).

EARLIER EDITIONS AND TRANSLATIONS: To 63, 40; Bu 22, 435–36; Lo, 221–26.

SOLUTION: *BÁRUR* (waves).

The solution given is an alternative poetic word for the same notion found in GES 21; see the headnote there.

GES 23

MANUSCRIPTS: Lacuna in H[1]: text supplied from H[2]H[3]; also in R[1] (no. 24) and U[1] (no. 18).

EARLIER EDITIONS AND TRANSLATIONS: To 67, 42; Bu 24, 437–38; Lo, 221–26.

SOLUTION: *ÆGIS MEYJAR* (waves; literally "Ægir's girls").

GES 23A

MANUSCRIPTS: This riddle is not found in H^2H^3, and so presumably not in H^1; it is in R^1 (no. 21) and U^1 (no. 6).

EARLIER EDITIONS AND TRANSLATIONS: To 64, 41; Bu 23, 436–37; Lo, 221–26.

SOLUTION: *ÆGIS EKKJUR* (waves; literally "Ægir's women").

GES 24

MANUSCRIPTS: Lacuna in H^1: text supplied from H^2H^3; also in R^1 (no. 11) and U^1 (no. 22).

EARLIER EDITIONS AND TRANSLATIONS: To 54, 37; Bu 25, 438–39.

SOLUTION: *ÍS-JAKA* (ice-floe) or *SKIP* (ship)?

This is another of the "I saw" (*ek sá*) riddles in GES, on which see the note at GES 2.3 above, albeit one of only two (the other is GES 30) that is not part of a longer sequence (as in GES 8–16 and 32–34). The mention of an "ice floe" is common to all three versions, although each gives a series of extra details that are to some extent questionable: U^1 says that the answer is really *STEINN* (a stone), traveling on an ice floe, while R^1 reckons that what is seen is a dead hawk on a dead horse traveling on an ice floe, and U^1 suggests that the travelers are instead a dead horse and a dead snake (reading *naðr* for *nár* in GES 24.3). Given the parallels with certain of the metaphorical ship riddles in EXE (see especially the headnotes to EXE 17, 34, and 62 above), perhaps some kind of a ship may be intended here too? Certainly, Old Norse has a far greater variety of kennings for ships, especially as animated creatures (most often horses), than Old English. See further Olsen "Animated Ships in Old English and Old Norse Poetry," especially pp. 54–64.

GES 25

MANUSCRIPTS: Lacuna in H[1]: text supplied from H[2]H[3]; also in R[1] (no. 16) and U[1] (no. 14).

EARLIER EDITIONS AND TRANSLATIONS: To 59, 39; Bu 26, 440–41.

SOLUTION: *HÚNN* (gaming piece; die).

The Old Norse word *húnn* means "bear cub," and seems here to refer to some kind of gaming piece, perhaps a die, the eight corners of which would then be the eight horns mentioned; such dice games could certainly diminish wealth, while the double sense of *fé* as both money and livestock extends the metaphor: bear cubs are also dangerous to livestock.

GES 26

MANUSCRIPTS: Lacuna in H[1]: text supplied from H[2]H[3]; also in R[1] (no. 17) and U[1] (no. 24).

EARLIER EDITIONS AND TRANSLATIONS: To 60 (p. 39); Bu 27, 441–42.

SOLUTION: *SKJǪLDR* (shield).

For other riddles with similar solutions, see ALD 87 *(CLIPEUS)*; EXE 3 (*BORD*).

GES 27

MANUSCRIPTS: Lacuna in H[1]: text supplied from H[2]H[3]; also in R[1] (no. 22) and U[1] (no. 23).

EARLIER EDITIONS AND TRANSLATIONS: To 65, 41; Bu 28, 442–43.

SOLUTION: *ǪND Í MILLI NAUT-SKJÁLKA* (a duck in an ox skull's jaws).

Such a bizarre and specific solution is not unparalleled in the Anglo-Saxon riddle tradition; see further, for example, TAT 16 (*PRAEPOSITIONES UTRIUSQUE CASUS*); EXE 82 (*AN-EAGEDE GARLEAC-MONGER*); SYM 94 (*LUSCUS ALIUM VENDENS*).

GES 28

MANUSCRIPTS: Lacuna in H[1]: text supplied from H[2]H[3]; also in R[1] (no. 27) and U[1] (no. 28).
EARLIER EDITIONS AND TRANSLATIONS: To 70, 43; Bu 29, 443–44.
SOLUTION: *KÝR* (cow).

For another riddle with the same solution, see EUS 13 *(VACCA).*

GES 29

MANUSCRIPTS: Lacuna in H[1]: text supplied from H[2]H[3]; also in R[1] (no. 14) and U[1] (no. 16).
EARLIER EDITIONS AND TRANSLATIONS: To 57, 38; Bu 30, 444–45.
SOLUTION: *ELDR* (fire).

For other riddles with similar solutions, see ALD 44; TAT 33 (both *IGNIS*); EXE 48 *(FYR).* There are some broad parallels in *Hisperica famina* A426–51 (*DE IGNE,* "on fire"; see further Herren, *Hisperica Famina: The A-Text;* Orchard, "*Hisperica famina* as Literature").

GES 30

MANUSCRIPTS: Lacuna in H[1]: text supplied from H[2]H[3]; not in R[1]U[1].
EARLIER EDITIONS AND TRANSLATIONS: To H30, 81–82; Bu 31, 445–46; Lo, 228.
SOLUTION: *SKEIÐ OK LÍN-VEF* (heddle and weft).

This is another of the "I saw" (*ek sá*) riddles in GES, on which see the note at GES 2.3 above, albeit one of only two (the other is GES 24) that is not part of a longer sequence (as in GES 8–16 and 32–34). No answer is given for this riddle in the saga (which one would think would negate the terms of the contest, although Óðinn, in the guise of Gestumblindi, raises no objections); rather, Heiðrekr offers the same kind of further clue that is found in ALC D76 (*Hoc coqui nostri norunt*), D79 (*Biblos in silva interroga*), and D82 (*Pueri in schola hoc sciunt*), saying *þessa gátu skolo ráða hirðmenn mínir,* "my courtiers must solve that riddle!," so acknowledging the sexual misdirection, before offering the banal or mundane "real" solution; this is another of the so-called rude or double-entendre riddles found throughout the Anglo-Saxon riddle tradition, on which see the introduction to *OEALRT*, under "Shared Themes across the Collections."

GES 31

MANUSCRIPTS: Lacuna in H^1: text supplied from H^2H^3; also in R^1 and U^1 (no. 12).
EARLIER EDITIONS AND TRANSLATIONS: To 55, 37; Bu 32, 446–47.
SOLUTION: *TAFL* (board game).

See further the headnotes to GES 19 and 25 above.

GES 32

MANUSCRIPTS: Lacuna in H^1: text supplied from H^2H^3; also in R^1 and U^1 (no. 25).
EARLIER EDITIONS AND TRANSLATIONS: To 68, 42; Bu 33, 447–48.
SOLUTION: *SÚ OK GRÍSUR* (sow and piglets).

GES 33

MANUSCRIPTS: Lacuna in H^1: text supplied from H^2H^3; not in R^1U^1.
EARLIER EDITIONS AND TRANSLATIONS: To H33, 82; Bu 34, 448–49.
SOLUTION: *GLÆÐUR* (embers).

For another riddle with a similar solution, albeit with a rather different treatment, see TAT 35 (*PRUNA*, "ember"). The twin focus on dark/light imagery and feminine protagonists connects this riddle with several in the sequence GES 8–16, although here the solution is not watery, but rather one of fire.

GES 34

MANUSCRIPTS: Lacuna in H[1]: text supplied from H[2]H[3]; also in R[1] (no. 28) and U[1] (no. 29).
EARLIER EDITIONS AND TRANSLATIONS: To 71, 43–44; Bu 35, 449–50.
SOLUTION: *SKÁLD-SKAPR* (poetry).

This riddle, with its keen focus on the ambiguities of poetic language, not only is a fitting conclusion to the riddle contest proper, but also forms a link to the riddle that follows, which identifies Óðinn, the god of poetry himself, who is of course Gestumblindi in disguise.

GES 35

MANUSCRIPTS: Lacuna in H[1]: text supplied from H[2]H[3]; also in R[1] (no. 29) and U[1] (no. 27).
EARLIER EDITIONS AND TRANSLATIONS: To 72, 44; Bu 36, 450–51.
SOLUTION: *ÓÐINN OK SLEIPNIR* (Óðinn and Sleipnir).

Perhaps the main point to be made is that while this seems at first glance a body-part riddle, it is in fact a simple description that only requires specialized mythological knowledge. As such, it effectively identifies Óðinn as Gestumblindi, and prepares the way for the final, unanswerable riddle (GES E) that follows.

GES E

MANUSCRIPTS: Lacuna in H[1]: text supplied from H[2]H[3]; also in R[1] (no. 30) and U[1] (no. 28).
EARLIER EDITIONS AND TRANSLATIONS: To 73, 44; Bu 37, 451–52.

The same unanswerable riddle (since only Óðinn can possibly know the solution) is used (again by Óðinn) as the capstone to *Vafþrúðnismál;* there too, the unknowable solution is not given.

VARIOUS RIDDLES

The seventeen aenigmata presented here come from seven different manuscripts of various provenance and date, three of which were written or owned in England before 1100, and are therefore described in G–L (P^2SS^1), and the other four of which (P^5XX^1Z) contain texts with strong links to the other material within the Anglo-Saxon riddling tradition, as the notes below highlight.

XMS P1

MANUSCRIPT: P^5, fol. 60v1.
EARLIER EDITIONS AND TRANSLATION: Ve, 46.
SOLUTION: UNKNOWN.

This is a genuinely puzzling aenigma, which nonetheless clearly fits within the Anglo-Saxon riddle tradition, not only because of the close verbal parallels noted below, but also because of its fondness for exactly the same kind of compounds and poetic forms found so widely elsewhere in the same context, for example *ramosus . . . corniger . . . praepes . . . soniger . . . umbrifer,* on which see the introduction to *OEALRT,* under "Style."

1.3 Note the extraordinary amount of alliteration here (*cacumen cuius conscendit corniger*).
1.7 Something is clearly missing after *pausare;* here I supply the bland *per horas,* so as not to prejudice other suggestions for a solution.
1.8 Compare BON 19.4 *(Ob quod semper amavit me Germanica tellus).*
1.9 For the challenge, compare ALD 18.5 *(Scrutetur sapiens, gemino cur nomine fungar),* as well as the more complex ALD 100.80–83.

XMS P2

MANUSCRIPTS: P^5, fol. 60v1 and S^1, fol. 95r.
EARLIER EDITIONS AND TRANSLATION: Ve, 46; *AL* 770 (p. 235).
SOLUTION: *TURTUR* (turtledove).

This is another bird riddle, this time in the form of a logogriph. It is interesting to note that in neither of the two manuscripts is the text formally lineated as verse: in S[1] it appears as a solitary aenigma on the first three lines of the folio, with the *Passio S. Iulianae* beginning at the top of the facing page.

XMS P3

MANUSCRIPT: P[5], fol. 60v1.
EARLIER EDITIONS AND TRANSLATION: *ICUR*, II, 245; *AL* 771 (p. 235).
SOLUTION: *PARIES* → *ARIES* (wall → ram).

Another logogriph, which has a good parallel in ALD 86 (*ARIES*). P[5] simply has the single word *pariete,* presumably the remnant of a title or solution; the text printed here is reproduced from the fuller versions found in other manuscripts and presented in *AL*.

XMS S1

MANUSCRIPT: S, fol. 35v.
EARLIER EDITION: Ve, 46.
SOLUTION: *CORPUS ET ANIMA* (body and soul).

Ve offers a banal solution, based on the notion of three disgruntled students emerging from an inn (!). In fact, this aenigma seems better to fit the soul-and-body nexus exemplified by EXE 41 (*GÆST OND LICHAMA,* "soul and body") and EXE 81 (*FISC OND EA,* "fish and river"), with the first two lines taking up antagonistic positions, while the third expresses the pious hope for the salvation of both. The gateway in question is presumably death.

XMS S2

MANUSCRIPT: S, fol. 60v1.
EARLIER EDITIONS AND TRANSLATION: *ICUR*, 2, 245.
SOLUTION: *REX* (king).

This aenigma brilliantly brings together a number of aspects of the Anglo-Latin riddle tradition, and how they are often combined: if the solution "king" *(REX)* is accepted, then it is a simple logogriph, where reducing the constituent letters of *REX* to a single element does indeed render *X* ("ten" in Latin). The references to a "craftsman," "right hand," and "three limbs" all parallel descriptions elsewhere of the three fingers of a scribe, and so the act of writing itself, in a form of misdirection in a riddle so literally written. There is also an element of challenge here that links this aenigma to others of the Anglo-Saxon riddle tradition.

1 Reading *membris* (S has *menbris*).

XMS S3

MANUSCRIPT: S, fol. 60v1.
EARLIER EDITIONS AND TRANSLATION: *ICUR*, 2, 245.
SOLUTION: *PUGILLARES* (writing tablets).

There are variant forms of this aenigma, as Ve notes, but the general close similarity of theme to ALD 32 suggests the same solution, with the necessary emendation in the second line. There are some broad parallels in *Hisperica famina* A531–46 (*DE TABULA,* "on a writing tablet"; see further Herren, *Hisperica Famina: The A-Text;* Orchard, "*Hisperica famina* as Literature").

3.2 Supplying *aeque* (not in S), for the sake of the meter.

XMS X1

MANUSCRIPT: X, 389.
EARLIER EDITION AND TRANSLATION: BL 197, 144–45 and 245.
SOLUTION: *LEBES* (cauldron).

There is a close parallel in ps-BED 10 (see the note there), which also describes a boiling cauldron extinguishing the fire that heats it; see too ALD 49 and ALC D76, which have the same solution.

This is the first of three aenigmata on a single page of manuscript X (p. 389), all beginning with the familiar Latin formula *Vidi,* "I saw," and all with parallels in ps-BED. These are the only items on an otherwise empty page, following a rubric *Item enigmata vulgaria,* "Popular aenigmata"; it is striking that there is a crudely repaired uneven cut across the whole page immediately after the third aenigma, as if someone had attempted to cut them out. The preceding page (p. 388) has the title *Aenigmata interrogativa,* "Questioning aenigmata," and consists of fifteen questions and answers from the wisdom tradition of a type familiar from elsewhere in the pseudo-Bede *Collectanea,* each preceded in turn by a Δ and M respectively (on which see the headnote to ALC). These two pages of *aenigmata interrogativa* and *aenigmata vulgaria* are the last in the book, and follow a version of SYM (see the headnote there) on 374–87 of X, which also contains on 2–373 a complete text of the eleven books of the *Carmina* of Venantius Fortunatus.

XMS X2

MANUSCRIPT: X, 389.
SOLUTION: *PULLUS* (chick).

There is a very close parallel in ps-BED 2 (see the note there), as well as in EUS 38 *(PULLUS);* see too SYM 14; ALC D78; LOR 8 (all solved *PULLUS IN OVO,* "chick in egg"), as well as EXE 11 (*TEN CICCENU,* "ten chickens").

XMS X3

MANUSCRIPT: X, 389.
EARLIER EDITION AND TRANSLATION: BL 198 (pp. 144–45 and 245).
SOLUTION: *PENNA* (quill pen).

There is a close parallel in ps-BED 11 (see the note there); see too ALD 59 and TAT 6, which have the same solution, as well as EXE 49, where the solution *FEÐER OND FINGRAS* (quill pen and fingers) has been suggested, and is perhaps intended as a blind to the "real" solution accepted here, namely, *SALTERE* (psaltery). The weeping woman is the grammatically feminine quill pen, and her five sons are the grammatically masculine fingers, although parallel riddles generally focus on the three fingers that grip the pen (as in BED 18). I read *vita* (X has *via*), to align this aenigma with others within the tradition, notably EXE 84.31b and 32b *(sped . . . sawle rædes),* that emphasize the enormous spiritual benefits of the written word.

XMS X4

MANUSCRIPT: X[1], fol. 1r.
SOLUTION: *COPA VINARIA* (wine cup).

There is a very close parallel at LOR 5. This manuscript was written in the monastery of St. Gall, and contains mostly liturgical and pastoral works. Here I read *lucidus,* where X[1] has *lucius,* presumably for the proper name Lucius.

XMS Y1

MANUSCRIPT: P[2], fol. 123v.
SOLUTION: *NOE ET COLUMBA* (Noah and the dove). There is a good parallel at ALD 64 *(COLUMBA).*

This aenigma is part of a sequence of five short miscellaneous items; it is preceded by two sayings attributed to Alcuin and Gregory, and followed by two others, the second of which refers to the Creed (see further Brown, "Paris, BN lat. 10861," 121, n. 10). Of more immediate relevance is the text immediately following XMS Y1, which reads simply *Archanum alterius tu numquam scrutaberis umquam,* "you will never ever fathom another's secret." While this becomes a proverbial saying in the later medieval period (and is given as such by *PSLMA* 1.147 [no. 72]), it very clearly derives from Horace, *Epistolae* 1.18.37 *(Arcanum neque tu scrutaberis illius umquam)* and provides a pithy coda to the whole riddling tradition.

XMS Z1

MANUSCRIPT: Z, fol. 70r.

EARLIER EDITION: MS, 13.

SOLUTION: *NUX FATUA* (a bad nut). Note that the solution given is garbled: in the substitution cipher it should be *Nxx fbtxb.*

This is the first of the so-called Reichenau riddles, on which see in general Schmidt, "Die Reichenauer Rätsel"; Bitterli, *Say What I Am Called,* 74–75; Salvador-Bello, *Isidorean Perceptions,* 49–50. These six riddles appear in sequence in the single manuscript Z, immediately following a version of Alcuin's mathematical puzzles, *Propositiones ad acuendos iuvenes* (Propositions for sharpening up young men), on which see Folkerts, "Die Alkuin zugeschriebenen *Propositiones ad acuendos iuvenes*" and *Die älteste mathematische Aufgabensammlung in lateinischer Sprache;* Hadley and Singmaster, "Problems to Sharpen the Young"; Orchard, "Enigma Variations," 284–89. They share many aspects of the Anglo-Saxon riddle tradition, including the use of the same basic substitution cipher as found in EXE 34. The cipher is (partly) exemplified in a title in the manuscript, reading *Aenigmata rkskbklkb* (for *Aenigmata risibilia,* "funny riddles"), although this collection is not notably funnier than the rest.

XMS Z2

MANUSCRIPT: Z, fol. 70r.
EARLIER EDITION: MS, 13.
SOLUTION: *NAVIS* (ship).

XMS Z3

MANUSCRIPT: Z, fol. 70r.
EARLIER EDITION: MS, 13.
SOLUTION: *UMBRA* (shadow). Note that the interpolated solution given seems to offer a further clue: "I have a foot."

XMS Z4

MANUSCRIPT: Z, fol. 70r–v.
EARLIER EDITION: MS, 13.
SOLUTION: *NIX ET SOL* (snow and sun). Note that the solution given is garbled: in the substitution cipher it should perhaps be *Nkx ft Tktbn* (for *nix et Titan*, with Titan as another term for "sun").

XMS Z5

MANUSCRIPT: Z, fol. 70v.
EARLIER EDITION: MS, 13.
SOLUTION: *VITRICUS* (stepfather).

The final two aenigmata are clearly linked by topic, and while dealing with unusual family relationships, do not stray into the areas covered by the incest riddles of (for example) the material pertaining to Apollonius of Tyre (on which see the headnote to SYM) or EXE 44 (*LOTH OND BEARN,* "Lot and his children").

XMS Z6

MANUSCRIPT: Z, fol. 70v.
EARLIER EDITION: MS, 14.
SOLUTION: *FILIUS PRIVIGNI* (the son of a stepson).

Bibliography

Abbott, H. H. *The Riddles of the Exeter Book*. Cambridge, 1968.

Afros, Elena. "Linguistic Ambiguities in Some Exeter Book Riddles." *Notes and Queries* n.s. 52 (2005): 431–37.

———. "*Sindrum Begrunden* in Exeter Book *Riddle 26*: The Enigmatic Dative Case." *Notes and Queries* n.s. 51 (2004): 7–9.

———. "Syntactic Variation in *Riddles 30A* and *30B*." *Notes and Queries* n.s. 52 (2005): 2–5.

Alexander, Michael. *The Earliest English Poems*. Harmondsworth, 1966.

Anderson, James E. "Exeter Latin Riddle 90: A Liturgical Vision." *Viator* 23 (1992): 73–93.

———. *Two Literary Riddles in the Exeter Book: Riddle 1 and the Easter Riddle*. Norman, 1986.

———. "Two Spliced Riddles in the Exeter Book." *In Geardagum* 5 (1983): 57–75.

Anlezark, Daniel, ed. and trans. *The Old English Dialogues of Solomon and Saturn*. Cambridge, 2009.

Archibald, Elizabeth. *Apollonius of Tyre: Medieval and Renaissance Themes and Variations: Including the Text of the 'Historia Apollonii Regis Tyri' with an English Translation*. Cambridge, 1991.

Athenaeus. *The Learned Banqueters*. Ed. and trans. S. Douglas Olson. Cambridge, Mass., 2007–12. 8 vols.

Ball, C. J. E. "The Franks Casket: Right Side—Again." *English Studies* 52 (1974): 512.

Bammesberger, Alfred P. "The Brandon Antler Runic Inscription." *Neophilologus* 86 (2002): 129–31.

Bardowell, Matthew R. "Art and Emotion in Old Norse and Old English Poetry." PhD dissertation, Saint Louis University, 2016.

Barker, Katherine, and Gordon Le Pard. "St Aldhelm and the Chapel at Worth Maltravers: Sea-Mark, Lighthouse, or Bell-Tower?" *Proceedings of the Dorset Natural History and Archaeological Society* 126 (2005): 148–56.

Barley, Nigel F. "Structural Aspects of the Anglo-Saxon Riddle." *Semiotica* 10 (1974): 143–75.

Barnes, Michael P. *Runes: A Handbook*. Woodbridge, Suffolk, 2012.

Barney, Stephen A., W. J. Lewis, J. A. Beach, and Oliver Berghof, trans. *The "Etymologies" of Isidore of Seville*. Cambridge, 2006.

Baum, Paull F. *The Anglo-Saxon Riddles of the Exeter Book*. Durham, N.C., 1963.

Bayless, Martha. "Alcuin's *Disputatio Pippini* and the Early Medieval Riddle Tradition." In *Humour, History and Politics in Late Antiquity and the Early Middle Ages*, ed. Guy Halsall, 157–78. Cambridge, 2002.

———. "The *Collectanea* and Medieval Dialogues and Riddles." In Bayless and Lapidge, *Collectanea Pseudo-Bedae*, 12–24.

Bayless, Martha, and Michael Lapidge. *Collectanea Pseudo-Bedae*. Scriptores Latini Hiberniae 14. Dublin, 1998.

Bergamin, Manuela, ed. and trans. *Aenigmata Symposii: La fondazione dell'enigmistica come genere poetico*. Per Verba. Testi mediolatini con traduzione 22. Florence, 2005.

Bieler, Ludwig. "Some Remarks on the *Aenigmata Laureshamensia*." *Romanobarbarica* 2 (1977): 11–15.

Bierbaumer, Peter, and Elke Wannagat. "Ein neuer Lösungsvorschlag für ein altenglisches Rätsel (Krapp–Dobbie 17)." *Anglia* 99 (1981): 379–82.

Biggam, C. P. "The True Staff of Life: The Multiple Roles of Plants." In Hyer and Owen-Crocker, *Material Culture of Daily Living in the Anglo-Saxon World*, 23–48.

Birkett, Tom. *Reading the Runes in Old English and Old Norse Poetry*. London, 2017.

Bischoff, Bernhard. "Bannita: 1. Syllaba, 2. Littera." In *Latin Script and Letters A.D. 400–900: Festschrift presented to Ludwig Bieler*, ed. J. J. O'Meara and B. Naumann, 207–12. Leiden, 1976.

Bitterli, Dieter. "Alkuin von York und die angelsächsische Rätseldichtung." *Anglia* 128 (2010): 4–20.

———. "The 'Cuckoo' in the *Collectanea* of Pseudo-Bede—An Unnoticed Latin Analogue to Exeter Book *Riddle 9*." *Notes and Queries* 56 (2009): 481–82.

———. "Exeter Book Riddle 15: Some Points for the Porcupine." *Anglia* 120 (2002): 461–87.

———. *Say What I Am Called: The Old English Riddles of the Exeter Book and the Anglo-Latin Riddle Tradition*. Toronto, 2009.

———. "Spur, a New Solution to Exeter Book *Riddle 62*." *Notes and Queries* 66 (2019): 343–47.

———. "The Survival of the Dead Cuckoo: Exeter Book Riddle 9." In Honegger, *Riddles, Knights and Cross-Dressing Saints: Essays on Medieval English Language and Literature*, 95–114.

———. "Two Old English Prose Riddles of the Eleventh Century." *Words, Words, Words: Philology and Beyond; Festschrift for Andreas Fischer on the Occasion of His 65th Birthday*, ed. Sarah Chevalier and Thomas Honegger, 1–11. Tübingen, 2012.

Blakeley, L. "Riddles 22 and 58 of the Exeter Book." *Review of English Studies* 9 (1958): 241–52.

Bliss, A. J. "Single Half-Lines in Old English Poetry." *Notes and Queries* 18 (1971): 442–49.

Bolton, Whitney F. "Tatwine's *De cruce Christi* and *The Dream of the Rood*." *Archiv für das Studium der neueren Sprachen und Literaturen* 200 (1963): 344–46.

Borysławski, Rafał. "The Elements of Anglo-Saxon Wisdom Poetry in the *Exeter Book* Riddles." *Studia Anglica Posnaniensia* 38 (2002): 35–47.

———. *The Old English Riddles and the Riddlic Elements of Old English Poetry*. Studies in English Medieval Language and Literature 9. Frankfurt am Main, 2004.

Bouterwek, Karl Wilhelm. *Cædmons des Angelsachsen biblische Dichtungen*. Elberfeld, 1849–51.

Bradley, Henry. "Two Riddles of the Exeter Book." *Modern Language Review* 6 (1911): 433–40.

Brady, Lindy. "The 'Dark Welsh' as Slaves and Slave Traders in Exeter Book Riddles 51 and 72." *English Studies* 95 (2014): 235–55.

Bragg, Lois. "Runes and Readers: In and around 'The Husband's Message.'" *Studia Neophilologica* 71 (1999): 34–50.

Breeze, Andrew. "Old English *gop* 'Servant' in Riddle 49: Old Irish *gop* 'Snout.'" *Neophilologus* 79 (1995): 671–73.

Bremmer, Rolf H., Jr., and Kees Dekker. "Leiden, Universiteitsbibliotheek, Vossianus Lat. Q. 106." In *Anglo-Saxon Manuscripts in Microfiche Facsimile,* vol. 13, ed. A. N. Doane, 107–11. Tempe, 2006.

Brett, Cyril. "Notes on Old and Middle English." *Modern Language Review* 22 (1927): 257–64.

Brodeur, Arthur G., and Archer Taylor. "The Man, the Horse, and the Canary." *California Folklore Quarterly* 2 (1943): 271–78.

Brooke, Stopford A. *The History of Early English Literature*. New York, 1892.

Brown, M. P. "Paris, B.N., lat. 10861 and the Scriptorium of Christ Church, Canterbury." *Anglo-Saxon England* 15 (1986): 119–37.

Brown, Ray. "The Exeter Book's *Riddle* 2: A Better Solution." *English Language Notes* 29.2 (1991): 1–4.

Buecheler, Franz. "Coniectanea." *Rheinisches Museum* 36 (1881): 329–42.

Bueno Alonso, Jorge Luis. "Actitudes anglosajonas hacia el humor: La caracterización del humor obsceno y sexual en los acertijos del *Exeter Book*." *Cuadernos del CEMYR* 12 (December 2004): 17–36.

Burrows, Hannah. "Enigma Variations: *Hervarar saga*'s Wave-Riddles and Supernatural Women in Old Norse Poetic Tradition." *Journal of English and Germanic Philology* 112 (2013): 194–216.

———. *Heiðreks gátur*. In *Poetry in Fornaldarsögur,* part 1, ed. Margaret Clunies Ross, Skaldic Poetry of the Scandinavian Middle Ages 8, 406–52. Turnhout, 2017.

Burton, Richard. "Nature in Old English Poetry." *Atlantic Monthly* 73 (1894): 476–87.

Butzer, P. L., et al., eds. *Charlemagne and His Heritage: 1200 Years of Civilization and Science in Europe/Karl der Grosse und sein Nachwirken:*

1200 Jahre Kultur und Wissenschaft in Europa, vol. 2: *Mathematical Arts*. Turnhout, 1998.

Cameron, Esther. "Leather-work." In *The Blackwell Encyclopaedia of Anglo-Saxon England*, ed. M. Lapidge et al., 280–81. Oxford, 1999.

Cameron, Esther, and Quita Mould. "Devil's Crafts and Dragon's Skins? Sheaths, Shoes and Other Leatherwork." In Hyer and Owen-Crocker, *Material Culture of Daily Living*, 93–115.

Cameron, M. L. "Aldhelm as Naturalist: A Re-Examination of Some of His *Enigmata*." *Peritia* 4 (1985): 117–33.

Campbell, A. "Some Linguistic Features of Early Anglo-Latin Verse and Its Use of Classical Models." *Transactions of the Philological Society* 52 (1953): 1–20.

Campbell, Jackson J. "A Certain Power." *Neophilologus* 59 (1975): 128–38.

Carmody, Francis J. "*Physiologus Latinus versio Y*." *University of California Publications in Classical Philology* 12, no. 7 (1941): 95–134.

Casiday, Augustine. "St. Aldhelm's Bees (*De virginitate prosa*, cc. iv–vi): Some Observations on a Literary Tradition." *Anglo-Saxon England* 33 (2004): 1–22.

Cassidy, Frederic G., and Richard N. Ringler. *Bright's Old English Grammar and Reader*. New York, 1971.

Cavell, Megan. "The *igil* and Exeter Book *Riddle 15*." *Notes and Queries* 262 (2017): 206–10.

———. "Looming Danger and Dangerous Looms: Violence and Weaving in Exeter Book 'Riddle 56.'" *Leeds Studies in English* 42 (2011): 29–42.

———. "Powerful Patens in the Anglo-Saxon Medical Tradition and Exeter Book *Riddle 48*." *Neophilologus* 101 (2017): 129–38.

———. "Sounding the Horn in Exeter Book Riddle 14." *Explicator* 72 (2014): 324–27.

———. *Weaving Words and Binding Bodies: The Poetics of Human Experience in Old English Literature*. Toronto, 2016.

Cavell, Megan, Victoria Symons, and Matthias Ammon, eds. "The Riddle Ages: Old English Riddles, Translations and Commentaries." https://theriddleages.wordpress.com, accessed November 15, 2019.

Cesario, Marilina. "Ant-lore in Anglo-Saxon England." *Anglo-Saxon England* 40 (2012): 273–91.

Chambers, Raymond W., Max Förster, and Robin Flower, eds. *The Exeter Book of Old English Poetry*. London, 1933.

Charlotte, M. "The Latin Riddle Poets of the Middle Ages." *Classical Journal* 42 (1947): 357–60.

Cherniss, Michael D. "The Cross as Christ's Weapon: The Influence of Heroic Literary Tradition on *The Dream of the Rood*." *Anglo-Saxon England* 2 (1973): 241–52.

Clemoes, Peter. "*Mens absentia cogitans* in *The Seafarer* and *The Wanderer*." In *Medieval Literature and Civilization: Studies in Memory of G. N. Garmonsway*, ed. D. A. Pearsall and R. A. Waldron, 62–77. London, 1969.

———. *Interactions of Thought and Language in Old English Poetry*. Cambridge Studies in Anglo-Saxon England 12. Cambridge, 1995.

Clover, Carol J. "*Vǫlsunga saga* and the Missing Lai of Marie de France." In *Sagnaskemmtun: Studies in Honour of Hermann Pálsson on His 65th Birthday*, ed. Rudolf Simek, Jónas Kristjánsson, and Hans Bekker-Nielsen, 79–84. Philologica Germanica, 8. Vienna, 1986.

Cobbs, Susan Parker. "Prolegomena to the *Ars Grammatica Tatuini*." PhD dissertation, University of Chicago, 1937.

Cochran, Shannon Fern. "The Plough's the Thing: A New Solution to Old English Riddle 4 of the Exeter Book." *Journal of English and Germanic Philology* 108 (2009): 301–9.

Coleman, Julie. "Sexual Euphemism in Old English." *Neuphilologische Mitteilungen* 93 (1992): 93–98.

Colgrave, Bertram. "Some Notes on Riddle 21." *Modern Language Review* 32 (1937): 281–83.

Colgrave, Bertram, and B. M. Griffiths. "A Suggested Solution of Riddle 61." *Modern Language Review* 31 (1936): 545–47.

Combeaud, Bernard, ed. *D. M. Ausonii Burdigalensis Opuscula Omnia*. Paris, 2010.

Conlee, John Wayne. "Artistry in the Riddles of the *Exeter Book*." PhD dissertation, University of Illinois, 1968.

Conner, Patrick W. *Anglo-Saxon Exeter: A Tenth-Century Cultural History*. Studies in Anglo-Saxon History 4. Woodbridge, Suffolk, 1993.

———. "Structure of the Exeter Book Codex." In *Anglo-Saxon Manuscripts: Basic Readings*, ed. Mary P. Richards, 301–15. London, 2001.

Conybeare, John Josias. *Illustrations of Anglo-Saxon Poetry*. London, 1826.

Cook, Albert Stanburrough. "Aldhelm's Legal Studies." *Journal of English and German Philology* 23 (1924): 105–113.

———. *The Old English Elene, Phoenix, and Physiologus*. New Haven, 1919.

Cook, Eleanor. *Enigmas and Riddles in Literature*. Cambridge, 2006.

———. "Riddles of Procreation." *Connotations* 8 (1998–99): 269–82.

Corrigan, Sarah. "Hisperic Enigma Machine: Sea Creatures and Sources in the *Hisperica Famina*." *Peritia* 24–25 (2013–14): 59–73.

Cosijn, Peter J. "Anglosaxonica IV." *Beiträge zur Geschichte der deutschen Sprache und Literatur* 23 (1898): 109–30.

Crane, Susan Lynn. "Describing the World: Aldhelm's *Enigmata* and the *Exeter Riddles* as Examples of Early Medieval Ekphrasis." PhD dissertation, Stony Brook University, 2006.

Crossley-Holland, Kevin, trans. *The Exeter Book Riddles*. Harmondsworth, 1993.

Dale, Corinne. *The Natural World in the Exeter Book Riddles*. Cambridge, 2017.

———. "A New Solution to Exeter Book *Riddle 4*." *Notes and Queries* 262 (2017): 1–3.

Daly, Lloyd William, and Walther Suchier, eds. *Altercatio Hadriani Augusti et Epicteti philosophi*. Illinois Studies in Language and Literature 24. Urbana, 1939.

Dance, Richard. "The Old English Language and the Alliterative Tradition." In *A Companion to Medieval Poetry*, ed. Corinne Saunders, 34–50. Oxford, 2010.

Davidson, H. R. Ellis. *The Sword in Anglo-Saxon England*. Oxford, 1962.

Davis, Adam. "*Agon* and *Gnomon*: Forms and Functions of the Anglo-Saxon Riddles." In *De Gustibus: Essays for Alain Renoir*, ed. John Miles Foley, J. Chris Womack, and Whitney A. Womack, 110–50. Albert Bates Lord Studies in Oral Tradition 11. New York: Garland, 1992.

Davis, Glenn. "The Exeter Book Riddles and the Place of Sexual Idiom in Old English Literature." In *Medieval Obscenities*, ed. Nicola McDonald, 39–54. York, 2006.

Davis, Patricia, and Mary Schlueter. "The Latin Riddle of the Exeter Book." *Archiv für das Studium der neueren Sprachen und Literaturen* 226 (1989): 92–99.

Defour, Tine. "The Use of Memory in the Old English Bookmoth-Riddle: A Different Light on 'Healthy Obscurity.'" *Studia Germanica Gandensia* no. 1/2 (2004): 17–32.

Dennis, Caroline. "Exeter Book Riddle 39: Creature Death." *Medieval Perspectives* 10 (1995): 77–85.

Derolez, René. *Runica Manuscripta: The English Tradition*. Bruges, 1954.

———. "*Runica Manuscripta* Revisited." In *Old English Runes and Their Continental Backgrounds*, ed. A. Bammesberger, 85–106. Anglistische Forschungen 217. Heidelberg, 1991.

Dewa, Roberta. "The Runic Riddles of the Exeter Book: Language Games and Anglo-Saxon Scholarship." *Nottingham Medieval Studies* 39 (1995): 26–36.

Dickins, Bruce. *Runic and Heroic Poems of the Old Teutonic Peoples*. Cambridge, 1915.

Diesenberger, M., and H. Wolfram. "Arn und Alkuin 790 bis 804: Zwei Freunde und ihre Schriften." In *Erzbischof Arn von Salzburg*, ed. M. Niederkorn-Bruck and A. Scharer, 81–106. Veröffentlichungen des Instituts für Österreichische Geschichtsforschung 40. Vienna, 2004.

Dietrich, Franz Eduard. "Die Räthsel des Exeterbuchs. Verfasser, weitere Lösungen." *Zeitschrift für deutsches Altertum* 12 (1865): 232–52.

———. "Die Räthsel des Exeterbuchs. Würdigung, Lösung und Herstellung." *Zeitschrift für deutsches Altertum* 2 (1859): 448–90.

Digan, Laura. "Aspects of Vocabulary in Selected Old English Riddles." MPhil dissertation, University of Glasgow, 2011.

DiNapoli, Robert. "In the Kingdom of the Blind, the One-Eyed Man Is a Seller of Garlic: Depth-Perception and the Poet's Perspective in the Exeter Book Riddles." *English Studies* 81 (2000): 422–55.

———. "Odd Characters: Runes in Old English Poetry." In *Verbal Encounters: Anglo-Saxon and Old Norse Studies for Roberta Frank*, ed. Antonina Harbus and Russell Poole, 145–61. Toronto Old English series. Toronto, 2005.

Doane, A. N. "Spacing, Placing and Effacing: Scribal Textuality and Exeter Riddle 30a/b." In *New Approaches to Editing Old English Verse*, ed. Sarah Larratt Keefer and Katherine O'Brien O'Keeffe, 46–65. Cambridge, 1998.

———. "Three Old English Implement Riddles: Reconsiderations of Numbers 4, 49, and 73." *Modern Philology* 84 (1987): 243–57.

Doležalová, Lucie. "On Mistake and Meaning: *scinderationes fonorum* in Medieval *artes memoriae*, Mnemonic Verses, and Manuscripts." *Language and History* 52 (2009): 26–40.

Donoghue, Daniel. "An *anser* for Exeter Book Riddle 74." In *Words and Works: Studies in Medieval English Language and Literature in Honour of Fred C. Robinson*, ed. Nicholas Howe and Peter S. Baker, 45–58. Toronto Old English series 10. Toronto, 1998.

Douglas Olson, S., ed. and trans. Athenaeus, *The Learned Banqueters; Deipnosophistae*. Cambridge, Mass., 2006–12.

du Bois, Elizabeth Hickman, trans. *The Hundred Riddles of Symphosius*. Woodstock, Vt., 1912.

Dümmler, Ernst, ed. *Aenigmata anglica*, MGH PLAC 1: 20–23. Berlin, 1881.

———, ed. *Aenigmata Bonifatii*, MGH PLAC 1: 1–15. Berlin, 1881.

———. "Lörscher Rätsel." *Zeitschrift für deutsches Altertum* 22 (1878): 258–63.

Ebert, Karl Wilhelm Adolf. "Die Räthselpoesie der Angelsachsen, insbesondere die Ænigmata des Tatwine und Eusebius." *Berichte über die Verhandlung der königlich sächsischen Gesellschaft der Wissenschaften zu Leipzig, phil-hist. Klasse* 29 (1877): 20–56.

Ehwald, Rudolph, ed. *Aldhelmi opera*. MGH AA 15. Berlin, 1913–19.

Eliason, Norman E. "Four Old English Cryptographic Riddles." *Studies in Philology* 49 (1952): 553–65.

Elliott, R. W. V. "Runic Mythology: The Legacy of the Futhark." In *Medieval Studies Conference, Aachen 1983*, ed. Wolf-Dietrich Bald and Horst Weinstock, 37–50. Bamberger Beiträge zur englischen Sprachwissenschaft 15. Frankfurt am Main, 1984.

Erhardt-Siebold, Erika von. "Aldhelm's Chrismal." *Speculum* 10 (1935): 276–80.

———. "The Anglo-Saxon Riddle 74 and Empedokles' Fragment 117." *Medium Ævum* 15 (1946): 48–54.

———. "An Archaeological Find in a Latin Riddle of the Anglo-Saxons." *Speculum* 7 (1932): 252–55.

———. "The Heliotrope Tradition." *Osiris* 3 (1937): 22–46.

———. "History of the Bell in a Riddle's Nutshell." *Englische Studien* 69 (1934): 1–14.

———. *Die lateinischen Rätsel der Angelsachsen: Ein Beitrag zur Kulturgeschichte Altenglands*. Anglistische Forschungen 61. Heidelberg, 1925; repr. Amsterdam, 1974.

———. "Note on Anglo-Saxon Riddle 74." *Medium Ævum* 21 (1952): 36–37.

———. "The Old English Hunt Riddles." *Publications of the Modern Language Association* 63 (1948): 3–6.

———. "The Old English Loom Riddles." In *Philologica: The Malone Anniversary Studies,* ed. Thomas A. Kirby and Henry Bosley Woolf, 9–17. Baltimore, 1949.

———. "Old English Riddle 13." *Modern Language Notes* 65 (1950): 97–100.

———. "Old English Riddle 23: Bow, Old English *Boga.*" *Modern Language Notes* 65 (1950): 93–96.

———. "Old English Riddle No. 4." *Publications of the Modern Language Association* 61 (1946): 620–23.

———. "Old English Riddle No. 39." *Publications of the Modern Language Association* 61 (1946): 910–15.

———. "Old English Riddle No. 57." *Publications of the Modern Language Association* 62 (1947): 1–8.

———. "Old English Riddle No. 95." *Modern Language Notes* 62 (1947): 558–59.

———. "The Old English Storm Riddles." *Publications of the Modern Language Association* 64 (1949): 884–88.

Erlemann, Edmund. "Zu den altenglischen Rätseln." *Archiv* 111 (1903): 49–63.

Erlemann, Fritz. "Zum 90. angelsächsischen Rätseln." *Archiv* 115 (1905): 391–92.

Fanger, Claire. "A Suggestion for a Solution to Exeter Book Riddle 55." *Scintilla* 2–3 (1985–86): 19–28.

Fell, Christine E. "Runes and Riddles in Anglo-Saxon England." In Hough and Lowe, *'Lastworda Betst': Essays in Memory of Christine E. Fell with Her Unpublished Writings,* 264–77.

———. "Some Implications of the Boniface Correspondence." In *New Readings on Women in Old English Literature,* ed. Helen Damico and Alexandra Hennessey Olsen, 29–43. Bloomington, 1990.

———. "Wax Tablets of Stone." In Hough and Lowe, *'Lastworda Betst': Essays in Memory of Christine E. Fell with Her Unpublished Writings,* 249–63.

Finch, Chauncey E. "The Bern Riddles in Codex Vat. Reg. Lat. 1553." *Transactions and Proceedings of the American Philological Association* 92 (1961): 145–55.

———. "Codex Vat. Barb. Lat. 721 as a Source for the Riddles of Symphosius." *Transactions and Proceedings of the American Philological Association* 98 (1967): 173–79.

———. "The Riddles in Cod. Barb. Lat. 1717 and Newberry Case Mediaeval Studies f 11." *Manuscripta* 17 (1973): 3–11.

———. "Symphosius in Codices Pal. lat. 1719, 1753, and Reg. lat. 329, 2078." *Manuscripta* 13 (1969): 3–11.

———. "The Text of the *Aenigmata* of Boniface in Codex Reg. Lat. 1553." *Manuscripta* 6 (1962): 23–28.

Findell, Martin. *Runes.* London, 2014.

Finnur Jónsson, ed., *Heiðreks saga,* in *Hauksbók,* ed. Finnur Jónsson and Eiríkur Jónsson, 350–69. Copenhagen, 1892–96.

Fiocco, Teresa. "Cinque enigmi dall'Exeter Book (Krapp-Dobbie 30, 53, 55, 67 e 73)." *Atti dell'Accademia Peloritana dei Pericolanti, Classe di lettere, filosofia e belle arti* 59 (1983): 145–228.

———. "Gli animali negli enigmi anglo-sassoni dell'*Exeter Book*." In *Simbolismo animale e letteratura*, ed. Dora Faraci, 133–57. Memoria bibliografica 42. Rome, 2003.

———. "Il viaggio della nave nell'enigma 32 dell'Exeter Book." *Blue Guitar* 7–8 (1984–87): 80–89.

Foley, John Miles. "How Genres Leak in Traditional Verse." In *Unlocking the Wordhord: Anglo-Saxon Studies in Memory of Edward B. Irving, Jr.*, ed. Mark C. Amodio and Katherine O'Brien O'Keeffe, 76–108. Toronto, 2003.

———. "'Riddle I' of the *Exeter Book*: The Apocalyptical Storm." *Neuphilologische Mitteilungen* 77 (1976): 347–57.

———. "Riddles 53, 54, and 55: An Archetypal Symphony in Three Movements." *Studies in Medieval Culture* 10 (1977): 25–31.

Folkerts, Menso. "Die Alkuin zugeschriebenen *Propositiones ad acuendos iuvenes*." In *Science in Western and Eastern Civilization in Carolingian Times*, ed. P. L. Butzer and D. Lohrmann, 273–81. Basel, 1993.

———. *Die älteste mathematische Aufgabensammlung in lateinischer Sprache: Die Alcuin zugeschriebenen 'Propositiones ad acuendos iuvenes': Überlieferung, Inhalt, Kritische Edition*. Österreichische Akademie der Wissenschaften, Mathematisch-naturwissenschaftliche Klasse, Denkschriften 116.6. Vienna, 1978.

Forster, Edward Seymour. "Riddles and Problems from the Greek Anthology." *Greece and Rome* 14 (1945): 42–47.

Förster, Max. "Die altenglische Glossenhandschrift Plantinus 32 (Antwerpen) und Additional 32246 (London)." *Anglia* 41 (1917): 94–161.

———. "Ein altenglisches Prosa-Rätsel." *Archiv für das Studium der neueren Sprachen und Literaturen* 115 (1905): 392–93.

———. "Die Lösung des Prosarätsels." *Archiv für das Studium der neueren Sprachen und Literaturen* 116 (1906): 267–71.

Foxhall Forbes, Helen. "Book-Worm or Entomologist? Aldhelm's *Enigma* XXXVI." *Peritia* 19 (2005): 20–29.

Frank, Roberta. "Sex in the *Dictionary of Old English*." In *Unlocking the Wordhord: Anglo-Saxon Studies in Memory of Edward B. Irving, Jr.*, ed. Mark C. Amodio and Katherine O'Brien O'Keeffe, 302–12. Toronto, 2003.

———. "Sharing Words with *Beowulf*." In *Intertexts: Studies in Anglo-Saxon Culture Presented to Paul Szarmach*, ed. Virginia Blanton and Helene Scheck, 3–15. Tempe, Ariz., 2008.

———. "Three 'Cups' and a Funeral in *Beowulf*." In O'Keeffe and Orchard, *Latin Learning and English Lore: Studies in Anglo-Saxon Literature for Michael Lapidge*, vol. 1, 407–20.

Fry, Donald K. "Exeter Book Riddle Solutions." *Old English Newsletter* 15.1 (1981): 22–33.

———. "Exeter Riddle 31: Feather-Pen." *De Gustibus: Essays for Alain Renoir*, ed. John Miles Foley, J. Chris Womack, and Whitney A. Womack, 234–49. Albert Bates Lord Studies in Oral Tradition 11. New York, 1992.

Gameson, Richard. "The Origin of the Exeter Book of Old English Poetry." *Anglo-Saxon England* 25 (1996): 135–85.

Gardner, John. *The Construction of Christian Poetry in Old English*. Carbondale, Ill., 1975.

Garrison, Mary. "An Aspect of Alcuin: 'Tuus Albinus': Peevish Egotist or Parrhesiast?" In *Ego Trouble: Authors and Their Identities in the Early Middle Ages*, ed. R. Coradini, R. McKitterick, M. Gillis, and I. van Renswoude, 137–51. Vienna, 2010.

Garvin, Katharine. "*Nemnað hy sylfe*: A Note on Riddle 57, Exeter Book." *Classica et Mediaevalia* 27 (1966): 294–95.

Gerritsen, Johan. "Leiden Revisited: Further Thoughts on the Text of the Leiden Riddle." In *Medieval Studies Conference, Aachen 1983*, ed. Wolf-Dietrich Bald and Horst Weinstock, 51–59. Bamberger Beiträge zur englischen Sprachwissenschaft 15. Bern, 1984.

———. "*þurh þreata geþræcu*." *English Studies* 35 (1954): 259–62.

Giles, J. A. *Anecdota Bedæ, Lanfranci, et Aliorum*. London, 1851.

Girsch, Elizabeth Stevens. "Metaphorical Usage, Sexual Exploitation, and Divergence in the Old English Terminology for Male and Female Slaves." In *The Work of Work: Servitude, Slavery, and Labor in Medieval England*, ed. Allen J. Frantzen and Douglas Moffat, 30–54. Glasgow, 1994.

Gleason, Raymond Edward. "*Per speculum in enigmate*: Runes, Riddles and Language in Anglo-Saxon Literature." PhD dissertation, Northwestern University, 1997.

Gleissner, Reinhard. "*Leiden Riddle* 3a: [*Ni*] *uaat*, [*Ni*] *uat*, or [*Ni*]*aat*?" *Historical English: On the Occasion of Karl Brunner's 100th Birthday*, ed. Manfred Markus, 99–111. Innsbrucker Beiträge zur Kulturwissenschaft, Anglistische Reihe 1. Innsbruck, 1988.

———. *Die "zweideutigen" altenglischen Rätsel des "Exeter Book" in ihrem zeitgenössischen Kontext*. Sprache und Literatur: Regensburger Arbeiten zur Anglistik und Amerikanistik 23. Bern, 1984.

Glorie, F., ed. *Collectiones aenigmatum merovingicae aetatis*. 2 vols. CCSL 133 and 133A. Turnhout, 1968.

Gneuss, Helmut, and Michael Lapidge. *Anglo-Saxon Manuscripts: A Bibliographical Handlist of Manuscripts and Manuscript Fragments Written or Owned in England up to 1100*. Toronto, 2014.

Göbel, Helga. *Studien zu den altenglischen Schriftwesenrätseln*. Epistemata: Würzburger wissenschaftliche Schriften, Reihe Literaturwissenschaft 7. Würzburg, 1980.

Göbel, Helga, and Rüdiger Göbel. "The Solution of an Old English Riddle." *Studia Neophilologica* 50 (1978): 185–91.

Goolden, Peter, ed. *The Old English "Apollonius of Tyre."* Oxford English Monographs. London, 1958.

Green, Eugene. "Semiotics of Compounds in Old English Riddles." In *New Insights in Germanic Linguistics II*, ed. Irmengard Rauch and Gerald F. Carr, 45–55. Berkeley Insights in Linguistics and Semiotics 38. Bern, 2001.

Green, R. P. H., ed. *The Works of Ausonius*. Oxford, 1991.

Greenfield, Stanley B. *The Interpretation of Old English Poems*. London, 1972.

———. "Old English Riddle 39 Clear and Visible." *Anglia* 98 (1980): 95–100.

Greenfield, Stanley B., and Rüdiger Göbel. "The Solution of an Old English Riddle." *Studia Neophilologica* 50 (1978): 185–91.

Grein, Christian W. M. "Kleine Mitteilungen. 2: Zu den Rätseln des Exeterbuches." *Germania* 10 (1865): 307–9.

Griffith, Mark. "Exeter Book Riddle 74 *Ac* 'Oak' and *Bat* 'Boat.'" *Notes and Queries* n.s. 55 (2008): 393–96.

———. "Riddle 19 of the Exeter Book: *snac*, an Old English Acronym." *Notes and Queries* n.s. 39 (1992): 15–16.

Griffiths, Alan. "Rune-names: The Irish Connection." In *Runes and Their Secrets: Studies in Runology*, ed. Marie Stoklund, Michael Lerche Nielsen, Bente Holmberg, and Gillian Fellows-Jensen, 83–116. Copenhagen, 2006.

Gropp, Harald. "*Propositio de lupo et capra et fasciculo cauli*—On the History of River-Crossing Problems." In Butzer, *Charlemagne and His Heritage: 1200 Years of Civilization and Science in Europe*, 31–41.

Gwara, Scott, and Barbara L. Bolt. "A 'Double Solution' for Exeter Book Riddle 51, 'Pen and Three Fingers.'" *Notes and Queries* n.s. 54 (2007): 16–19.

Hacikyan, Agop. "Emendations for Codex Exoniensis, Folios 101a–115a, 122b–123a, 124b–130b." *Revue de l'Université d'Ottawa* 37 (1967): 46–66, 344–58.

———. "The Exeter Manuscript: Riddle 19." *English Language Notes* 3 (1965–66): 86–88.

———. *A Linguistic and Literary Analysis of Old English Riddles*. Montreal, 1966.

———. "The Literary and the Social Aspects of the Old English Riddles." *Revue de l'Université d'Ottawa* 36 (1966): 107–20.

———. "The Modern English Renditions of Codex Exoniensis, Folios 101a–115a; 122b–123a; 124b–30b." *Revue de l'Université d'Ottawa* 39 (1969): 249–73.

Hadley, John, and David Singmaster. "Problems to Sharpen the Young: An Annotated Translation of *Propositiones ad acuendos iuvenes*, the Oldest Mathematical Problem Collection in Latin, Attributed to Alcuin of York." *Mathematical Gazette* 76 (1992): 102–26.

Hahn, Heinrich. "Die Rätseldichter Tatwin und Eusebius." *Forschungen zur deutschen Geschichte* 26 (1886): 601–31.

Hall, Alaric. "Changing Style and Changing Meaning: Icelandic Historiography and the Medieval Redactions of *Heiðreks saga*." *Scandinavian Studies* 77 (2005): 1–30.

Hall, Thomas, N. "The Portents at Christ's Birth in Vercelli Homilies V and VI: Some Analogues from Medieval Sermons and Biblical Commentaries." In *New Readings in the Vercelli Book*, ed. Samantha

Zacher and Andy Orchard, 62–97. Toronto Anglo-Saxon Studies 4. Toronto, 2009.
Halsall, Maureen. *The Old English Rune Poem: A Critical Edition.* Toronto, 1981.
Harbus, Antonina. "Exeter Book Riddle 39 Reconsidered." *Studia Neophilologica* 70 (1998): 139–48.
Haycock, Marged. *Legendary Poems from the Book of Taliesin.* Aberystwyth, 2007.
Hayes, Mary. "The Talking Dead: Resounding Voices in Old English Riddles." *Exemplaria* 20 (2008): 123–42.
Heikkinen, Seppo. *The Christianisation of Latin Metre: A Study of Bede's 'De arte metrica.'* Helsinki, 2012.
Heist, William W. *The Fifteen Signs before Doomsday.* East Lansing, 1952.
Herren, Michael W., ed. and trans. *The Hisperica Famina I: The A-Text.* Toronto, 1974.
Herzfeld, Georg. *Die Räthsel des Exeterbuches und ihr Verfasser.* Berlin, 1890.
Heyworth, Melanie. "Perceptions of Marriage in *Exeter Book Riddles 20* and *61*." *Studia Neophilologica* 79 (2007): 171–84.
———. "The Devil's in the Detail: A New Solution to Exeter Book Riddle 4." *Neophilologus* 91 (2007): 175–96.
Hickes, George. *Linguarum veterum septentrionalium thesaurum grammatico-criticum et archaeologicum.* Oxford, 1705.
Hicketier, Fritz. "Fünf Rätsel des Exeterbuches." *Anglia* 10 (1888): 564–600.
Higley, Sarah L. "The Wanton Hand: Reading and Reaching into Grammars and Bodies in Old English Riddle 12." In *Naked before God: Uncovering the Body in Anglo-Saxon England,* ed. Benjamin C. Withers and Jonathan Wilcox, 29–59. Medieval European Studies 3. Morgantown, W. Va., 2003.
Hill, David. "Anglo-Saxon Mechanics. 1. *blæstbel(i)g*—the Bellows. 2. *ston mid stel*—the Strikealight." *Medieval Life* 13 (2000): 9–13.
———. "*Cyrn*: The Anglo-Saxon Butter Churn." *Medieval Life* 15 (2001): 19–20.
———. "Prelude: Agriculture Through the Year." In Hyer and Owen-Crocker, *Material Culture of Daily Living in the Anglo-Saxon World,* 9–22.
———. "Riddle 8: A Problem of Identification or a Problem of Translation." *Medieval Life* 11 (1999): 22–23.
Hill, Thomas D. "The Old English Dough Riddle and the Power of Women's Magic: The Traditional Context of Exeter Book Riddle 45." In *Via Crucis: Essays on Early Medieval Sources and Ideas in Memory of J. E. Cross,* ed. Thomas N. Hall, with assistance from Thomas D. Hill and Charles D. Wright, 50–60. Medieval European Studies 1. Morgantown, W.Va., 2002.
———. "A Riddle on the Three Orders in the *Collectanea Pseudo-Bedae*?" *Philological Quarterly* 80 (2001): 205–12.
———. "Saturn's Time Riddle: An Insular Latin Analogue for *Solomon and Saturn II* lines 282–91." *Review of English Studies* 39 (1988): 273–76.
Holthausen, Ferdinand. "Ein altenglisches Rätsel." *Germanisch-Romanische Monatsschrift* 15 (1927): 453–54.
———. "Nochmals die altenglischen Rätsel." *Anglia* 38 (1914): 77–82.

———. "Zu den altenglischen Rätseln." *Anglia Beiblatt* 30 (1919): 50–55.

———. "Zur altenglischen Literatur. 1. Das XI. Rätsel. 2. Zum Neunkräutersegen." *Anglia Beiblatt* 16 (1905): 227–31.

———. "Zur Textkritik altenglischer Dichtungen." *Englische Studien* 37 (1907): 198–211.

Honegger, Thomas, ed. *Riddles, Knights and Cross-Dressing Saints: Essays on Medieval English Language and Literature*. Sammlung/Collection Variations 5. Bern, 2005.

Hoops, Johannes "Die Armbrust im Frühmittelalter." *Wörter und Sachen* 3 (1912): 65–68.

Hough, Carole. "Place-Names and the Provenance of Riddle 49." *Neophilologus* 82 (1998): 617–18.

Hough, Carole, and Kathryn A. Lowe, eds. *'Lastworda Betst': Essays in Memory of Christine E. Fell with Her Unpublished Writings*. Donington, Lincs., 2002.

Howe, Nicholas. "Aldhelm's *Enigmata* and Isidorian Etymology." *Anglo-Saxon England* 14 (1985): 37–59.

Howlett, David. "'Tres Linguae Sacrae' and Threefold Play in Insular Latin." *Peritia* 16 (2002): 94–115.

———. "*Versus cuiusdam Scotti de alphabeto*: An Edition, Translation, and Commentary." *Peritia* 21 (2010): 136–50.

Hudson, John, ed. *Historia Ecclesie Abbendonensis: The History of the Church of Abingdon*. 2 vols. Oxford, 2002–7.

Hull, Vernam E., and Archer Taylor. *A Collection of Irish Riddles*. Folklore Studies 6. Berkeley and Los Angeles, 1955.

———. *A Collection of Welsh Riddles*. University of California Publications in Modern Philology 26. Berkeley and Los Angeles, 1942.

Hyer, Maren Clegg, and Gale R. Owen-Crocker. "Woven Works: Making and Using Textiles." In Hyer and Owen-Crocker, *The Material Culture of Daily Living in the Anglo-Saxon World*, 157–84.

———, eds. *The Material Culture of Daily Living in the Anglo-Saxon World*. Exeter, 2011.

Igarashi, Michelle Michie Yoshimori. "A Contextual Study of the Exeter Book Riddles." PhD dissertation, State University of New York at Stony Brook, 1999.

Irvine, Martin. *The Making of Textual Culture: "Grammatica" and Literary Theory (350–1100)*. Cambridge, 1994.

Irving, Edward B., Jr. "Heroic Experience in the Old English Riddles." In *Old English Shorter Poems: Basic Readings*, ed. Katherine O'Brien O'Keeffe, 199–212. Basic Readings in Anglo-Saxon England 3. New York, 1994.

Jacobs, Nicolas. "The Old English 'Book-Moth' Riddle Reconsidered." *Notes and Queries* n.s. 35 (1988): 290–92.

Jember, Gregory K. "A Generative Method for the Study of Anglo-Saxon Riddles." *Studies in Medieval Culture* 11 (1977): 33–39.

———. "Proposed Restoration in *Riddle 48*." *In Geardagum* 3 (1979): 91–93.

———. "*Riddle* 57: A New Proposal." *In Geardagum* 2 (1977): 68–73.

———, trans. *The Old English Riddles: A New Translation*. Denver, 1976.

Jonassen, Frederick B. "The Pater Noster Letters in the Poetic *Solomon and Saturn.*" *Modern Language Review* 83 (1988): 1–9.

Joyce, John H. "Natural Process in *Exeter Book* Riddle #29: 'Sun and Moon.'" *Annuale Mediaevale* 14 (1974): 5–13.

Juster, A. M., trans. *Saint Aldhelm's Riddles.* Toronto, 2015.

Kaske, Robert E. "A Poem of the Cross in the Exeter Book: 'Riddle 60' and 'The Husband's Message.'" *Traditio* 23 (1967): 41–71.

Kay, Donald. "Riddle 20: A Revaluation." *Tennessee Studies in Literature* 13 (1968): 133–39.

Kendall, Calvin B., ed. *Bede: Libri II De arte metrica et de schematibus et tropis; The Art of Poetry and Rhetoric.* Saarbrücken, 1991.

Kennedy, Christopher B. "Old English Riddle No. 39." *English Language Notes* 13 (1975): 81–85.

Ker, Neil R. *Catalogue of Manuscripts Containing Anglo-Saxon.* Oxford, 1957.

Kiernan, K. S. "Cwene: The Old Profession of Exeter Riddle 95." *Modern Philology* 72 (1975): 384–90.

———. "The Mysteries of the Sea-Eagle in Exeter Riddle 74." *Philological Quarterly* 54 (1975): 518–22.

Kirby, Ian J. "The Exeter Book, *Riddle 60.*" *Notes and Queries* n.s. 48 (2001): 219–20.

Kitson, Peter. "Old English Bird-Names." *English Studies* 78 (1997): 481–505; *English Studies* 79 (1998): 2–22.

———. "Swans and Geese in Old English Riddles." *Anglo-Saxon Studies in Archaeology and History* 7 (1994): 79–84.

Klaeber, Frederick. "Das 9. altenglische Rätsel." *Archiv* 182 (1942–43): 107–8.

———. "Emendations in Old English Poems." *Modern Philology* 2 (1904): 141–46.

Klein, Thomas. "Of Water and the Spirit: Metaphorical Focus in Exeter Book Riddle 74." *Review of English Studies* 66 (2014): 1–19.

———. "The Old English Translation of Aldhelm's Riddle *Lorica.*" *Review of English Studies* 48 (1997): 345–49.

Klipstein, Louis F. *Analecta Anglo-Saxonica.* New York, 1849.

Knappe, Gabriele. "On Rhetoric and Grammar in the *Hisperica Famina.*" *Journal of Medieval Latin* 4 (1994): 130–62.

Konick, Marcus. "Exeter Book Riddle 41 as a Continuation of Riddle 40." *Modern Language Notes* 54 (1939): 259–62.

Kopár, Lilla. "The Anglo-Saxon Scribe in the Light of the Exeter Book Riddles." In *English Studies and the Curriculum: Proceedings of the Second TEMPUS-JEN Mini Conference,* ed. István Rácz, 29–37. Debrecen, Hungary, 1997.

Korhammer, Michael. "The Last of the Exeter Book Riddles." In *Bookmarks from the Past: Studies in Early English Language and Literature in Honour of Helmut Gneuss,* ed. Lucia Kornexl and Ursula Lenker, 69–80. Münchener Universitäts-Schriften, Texte und Untersuchungen zur englischen Philologie 30. Bern, 2003.

Krapp, George Philip, and Elliot Van Kirk Dobbie, eds. *The Exeter Book. Anglo-Saxon Poetic Records* 3. London, 1936.

Kries, Susanne. "*Fela í rúnum eða í skáldskap*: Anglo-Saxon and Scandinavian Approaches to Riddles and Poetic Disguises." In Honegger, *Riddles, Knights and Cross-Dressing Saints: Essays on Medieval English Language and Literature*, 139–64.

Kwapisz, Jan, David Petrain, and Mikołaj Szymański, eds. *The Muse at Play: Riddles and Wordplay in Greek and Latin Poetry*. Berlin, 2013.

Lagorio, V. M. "Aldhelm's *Aenigmata* in Codex Vaticanus Palatinus latinus 1719." *Manuscripta* 15 (1971): 23–27.

Lapidge, Michael. "Aldhelmus Malmesberiensis Abb. et Sciretburnensis ep." In *La trasmissione dei testi latini del medioevo/Medieval Latin Texts and Their Transmission: Te. Tra 4*, ed. P. Chiesa and L. Castaldi, 14–38. Florence, 2012.

———. *Anglo-Latin Literature*. Vol. 1, *600–899*. London, 1996. Vol. 2, *900–1066*. London, 1993.

———. *The Anglo-Saxon Library*. Oxford, 2006.

———. *Bede the Poet*. Jarrow Lecture. Jarrow, 1993. Repr. in Lapidge, *Anglo-Latin Literature*, vol. 1, *600–899*, 313–38.

———. *Bede's Latin Poetry*. Oxford Medieval Texts. Oxford, 2019.

———. "The Career of Aldhelm." *Anglo-Saxon England* 36 (2007): 15–69.

———. "The Hermeneutic Style in Tenth-Century Anglo-Latin Literature." *Anglo-Saxon England* 4 (1975): 67–111. Repr. in Lapidge, *Anglo-Latin Literature*, vol. 2, *900–1066*, 105–49.

———. "How 'English' Is Pre-Conquest Anglo-Latin?" In *Britannia Latina: Latin in the Culture of Great Britain from the Middle Ages to the Twentieth Century*, ed. Charles Burnett and Nicholas Mann, 1–13. Warburg Institute Colloquia 8. London, 2005.

———. "Some Remnants of Bede's Lost *Liber Epigrammatum*." *English Historical Review* 90 (1975): 798–820. Repr. in Lapidge, *Anglo-Latin Literature*, vol. 1, *600–899*, 357–80.

———. "Stoic Cosmology and the Source of the First Old English Riddle." *Anglia* 112 (1994): 1–25.

Lapidge, Michael, and James L. Rosier. *Aldhelm: The Poetic Works*. Cambridge, 1985.

Laszlo, Renate. *Köcherfliege und Seidenraupe in den altenglischen Rätseln*. Marburg, 1997.

———. *Die Sonne bringt es an den Tag: Ein altenglisches Rätsel des siebten Jahrhunderts und seine Lösung*. Marburg, 1998.

Law, Vivien. *Grammar and Grammarians in the Early Middle Ages*. London, 1997.

Leahy, Kevin. *Anglo-Saxon Crafts*. Stroud, Glos., 2012.

Leary, T. J., ed. and trans. *Symphosius, The "Aenigmata": An Introduction, Text, and Commentary*. London, 2014.

Leff, Gordon. "Alcuin of York (ca. 730–804)." In *Charlemagne and His Heritage: 1200 Years of Civilization and Science in Europe/Karl der Grosse und sein Nachwirken: 1200 Jahre Kultur und Wissenschaft in Europa*. Vol. 2: *Mathematical Arts*, ed. P. L. Butzer et al., 3–9. Turnhout, 1998.

Lendinara, Patrizia. "Ags. *wlanc*: Alcune annotazioni." *Annali dell'Istituto Universitario Orientale Napoli: Filologia germanica* 19 (1976): 53–81.

———. "Aspetti della società germanica negli enigmi del Codice Exoniense." In *Antichità germaniche: I Parte. I Seminario avanzato in Filologia germanica*, ed. Vittoria Dolcetti Corazza and Renato Gendre, 3–41. Bibliotheca Germanica, Studi e Testi 10. Alessandria, Italy, 2001.

———. "E se B stesse per *bana*? Una nuova interpretazione dell'enigma n. 17 del Codice Exoniense." *Annali dell'Istituto Universitario Orientale Napoli: Filologia germanica* 18 (1975): 161–81.

———. "Gli *Aenigmata Laureshamensia*." *PAN: Studi dell'Istituto di Filologia Latina* 7 (1981 for 1979): 73–90.

———. "Gli enigmi del Codice Exoniense: Una ricerca bibliografica." *Annali dell'Istituto Universitario Orientale Napoli: Filologia germanica* 19 (1976): 231–329.

———. "'In a Grove': Old English *bearu* in the Exeter Book Riddles." In *MedieVaria: Un liber amicorum per Giuseppe Brunetti*, ed. Alessandra Petrina, 49–87. Padua, 2011.

———. "L'Enigma n. 8 del Codice Exoniense." *Annali dell'Istituto Universitario Orientale Napoli: Filologia germanica* 13 (1970): 225–34.

———. "*Poculum mortis*: Una nota." *Annali dell'Istituto Universitario Orientale Napoli: Filologia germanica* 18 (1975): 131–41.

Lerer, Seth. *Literacy and Power in Anglo-Saxon Literature*. Norman, Neb., 1991.

———. "The Riddle and the Book: Exeter Book Riddle 42 in Its Contexts." *Papers on Language and Literature* 25 (1989): 3–18.

Leslie, Roy F. "The Integrity of Riddle 60." *Journal of English and Germanic Philology* 67 (1968): 451–57.

Lester, G. A. "*Sindrum begrunden* in Exeter Riddle No. 26." *Notes and Queries* n.s. 38 (1991): 13–15.

Levison, Wilhelm. *England and the Continent in the Eighth Century*. Oxford, 1946.

Liebermann, Felix. "Das ags. Rätsel 56: 'Galgen' als Waffenständer." *Archiv* 114 (1905): 163–64.

Lindow, John. "Riddles, Kennings, and the Complexity of Skaldic Poetry." *Scandinavian Studies* 47 (1975): 311–27.

Lindsay, W. M., ed. *Isidori Hispalensis episcopi Etymologiarum sive originum libri XX*. 2 vols. Oxford, 1911.

Liuzza, Roy M., ed. and trans. *Anglo-Saxon Prognostics: An Edition and Translation of Texts from London, British Library, MS Cotton Tiberius A.iii*. Cambridge, 2011.

———. "The Texts of the Old English *Riddle 30*." *Journal of English and Germanic Philology* 87 (1988): 1–15.

Lockett, Leslie. *Anglo-Saxon Psychologies in the Vernacular and Latin Traditions*. Toronto, 2011.

Lockhart, Jessica, "Everyday Wonders and Enigmatic Structures: Riddles from Symphosius to Chaucer." PhD dissertation, University of Toronto, 2017.

Love, Jeffrey Scott. *The Reception of "Hervarar saga ok Heiðreks" from the Middle Ages to the Seventeenth Century*. Munich, 2013.

Löwenthal, Fritz. *Studien zum germanischen Rätsel*. Heidelberg, 1914.

Luo, Shu-han. "Prosody and Literary Play: A Metrical Study of the Exeter Book Riddles." MSt dissertation, University of Oxford, 2011.

Machan, Tim William, and Robyn G. Peterson. "The Crux of Riddle 53." *English Language Notes* 24, no. 3 (1987): 7–14.

Mackie, W. S., ed. *The Exeter Book. Part II: Poems IX–XXXII*. Early English Text Society o.s. 194. London, 1934.

MacLean, George E. *An Old and Middle English Reader*. New York, 1893.

Manitius, Maximilian. "Zu Aldhelm und Beda." *Sitzungsberichte der kaiserlichen Akademie der Wissenschaften in Wien, philosophisch-historische Classe* 92 (1886): 535–634.

Marco, Maria de, ed. *Tatwine: Ars Grammatica*. CCSL 133, 1–141. Turnhout, 1968.

Marino, Matthew. "The Literariness of the Exeter Book Riddles." *Neuphilologische Mitteilungen* 79 (1978): 258–65.

Marsden, Richard. "'Ask What I Am Called': The Anglo-Saxons and Their Bibles." In *The Bible as Book: The Manuscript Tradition*, ed. John L. Sharpe III and Kimberly Van Kampen, 145–76. London, 1998.

Maxims I. In *Old English Shorter Poems*, vol. 2, *Wisdom and Lyric*, ed. and trans. Robert E. Bjork. DOML 32. Washington, DC, 2014.

McCarthy, Marcella. "A Solution to Riddle 72 in the Exeter Book." *Review of English Studies* 44 (1993): 204–10.

McFadden, Brian. "Raiding, Reform, and Reaction: Wondrous Creatures in the Exeter Book Riddles." *Texas Studies in Literature and Language* (2008): 329–51.

Meaney, Audrey L. "Birds on the Stream of Consciousness: Riddles 7 to 10 of the Exeter Book." In *Medieval Animals*, ed. Aleks Pluskowski, 120–52. Cambridge, 2002.

———. "Exeter Book Riddle 57 (55): A Double Solution?" *Anglo-Saxon England* 25 (1996): 187–200.

Meccariello, Chiara. "An Echo of Nonius Marcellus in Aldhelm's *Enigmata*." *Classica et Mediaevalia* 61 (2010): 257–65.

Menninger, K. *Number Words and Number Symbols: A Cultural History of Numbers*. Trans. P. Broneer. Cambridge, Mass., 1969.

Merkelbach, Reinhold. "Zwei Gespensternamen: Aelafius und Symphosius." *Zeitschrift für Papyrologie und Epigraphik* 51 (1983): 228–29.

Meyvaert, Paul. "The Solution to Old English Riddle 39." *Speculum* 51 (1976): 195–201.

Milanović-Barham, Čelica. "Aldhelm's *Enigmata* and Byzantine Riddles." *Anglo-Saxon England* 22 (1993): 51–64.

Mitchell, Stephen A. "Ambiguity and Germanic Imagery in Old English Riddle 1: 'Army.'" *Studia Neophilologica* 54 (1982): 39–52.

Moorman, F. W. *The Interpretation of Nature in English Poetry from Beowulf to Shakespeare*. Quellen und Forschungen zur Sprach- und Kulturgeschichte der germanischen Völker 95. Strasbourg, 1905.

Morgan, Gwendolyn, and Brian McAllister. "Reading *Riddles 30A* and *30B* as Two Poems." *In Geardagum* 14 (1993): 67–77.

Morley, Henry Foster. *English Writers*, vol. 2. London, 1864.
Muir, Bernard J., ed. *The Exeter Anthology of Old English Poetry*. 2 vols. Exeter, 1994. Rev. ed. 2000; 2nd rev. ed. 2006 with DVD.
Müllenhof, K., and W. Scherer. *Denkmäler deutscher Poesie und Prosa aus dem VIII–IX Jahrhundert*. 2nd ed. Berlin, 1873.
Müller, Eduard. *Die Rätsel des Exeterbuches*. Cöthen, Germany, 1861.
Müller, Ludvig Christian. *Collectanea Anglo-Saxonica*. Copenhagen, 1835.
Murphy, Patrick J. "The Riders of the Celestial Wain in Exeter Book *Riddle* 22." *Notes and Queries* n.s. 53 (2006): 401–7.
———. *Unriddling the Exeter Riddles*. University Park, Penn., 2011.
Musgrave, Elaine K. "Cithara as the Solution to Riddle 31 of the Exeter Book." *Pacific Coast Philology* 37 (2002): 69–84.
Nelson, Marie. "Four Social Functions of the Exeter Book Riddles." *Neophilologus* 75 (1991): 445–50.
———. "Old English Riddle 18 (20): A Description of Ambivalence." *Neophilologus* 66 (1982): 291–300.
———. "Old English Riddle No. 15: The 'Badger': An Early Example of the Mock Heroic." *Neophilologus* 59 (1975): 447–50.
———. "The Paradox of Silent Speech in the Exeter Book Riddles." *Neophilologus* 62 (1978): 609–15.
———. "Plus Animate: Two Possible Transformations of Riddles by Symphosius." *Germanic Notes* 18 (1987): 46–48.
———. "The Rhetoric of the Exeter Book Riddles." *Speculum* 49 (1974): 421–40.
———. "Time in the Exeter Book Riddles." *Philological Quarterly* 54 (1975): 511–18.
Neville, Jennifer. "Fostering the Cuckoo: Exeter Book Riddle 9." *Review of English Studies* 58 (2007): 431–36.
———. *Representations of the Natural World in Old English Poetry*. Cambridge Studies in Anglo-Saxon England 27. Cambridge, 1999.
———. "Speaking the Unspeakable: Appetite for Deconstruction in *Exeter Book* Riddle 12." *English Studies* (2012): 519–28.
———. "The Unexpected Treasure of the 'Implement Trope': Hierarchical Relationships in the Old English Riddles." *Review of English Studies* 62 (2011): 505–19.
Niles, John D. "Exeter Book Riddle 74 and the Play of the Text." *Anglo-Saxon England* 27 (1998): 169–207.
———. *Old English Enigmatic Poems and the Play of the Texts*. Studies in the Early Middle Ages 13. Turnhout, 2006.
Nuck, R. "Zu Trautmanns Deutung des ersten und neunundachtzigsten Rätsels." *Anglia* 10 (1888): 390–94.
O'Brien O'Keeffe, Katherine. "Exeter Riddle 40: The Art of an Old English Translator." *Proceedings of the PMR Conference* 5 (1983 for 1980): 107–17.
———. "The Text of Aldhelm's *Enigma* no. c in Oxford, Bodleian Library, Rawlinson C.697 and Exeter Riddle 40." *Anglo-Saxon England* 14 (1985): 61–73.

———. *Visible Song: Transitional Literacy in Old English Verse*. Cambridge Studies in Anglo-Saxon England 4. Cambridge, 1990.
Oda, Takuji. *A Concordance to the Riddles of the Exeter Book*. Tokyo, 1982.
Ohl, Raymond Theodore. *The Enigmas of Symphosius*. Philadelphia, 1928.
———. "Symphosius and the Latin Riddle." *Classical World* 25 (1932): 209–12.
Ohlert, Konrad. *Rätsel und Rätselspiele der alten Griechen*. Berlin, 1912.
———. "Zur antiken Rathselpoesie." *Philologus* 57 (1898): 596–602.
Okasha, Elisabeth. "Old English *hring* in Riddles 48 and 59." *Medium Ævum* 62 (1993): 61–69.
Okasha, Elisabeth, and Jennifer O'Reilly. "An Anglo-Saxon Portable Altar: Inscription and Iconography." *Journal of the Warburg and Courtauld Institutes* 47 (1984): 32–51.
O'Keeffe, Katherine O'Brien, and Andy Orchard, eds. *Latin Learning and English Lore: Studies in Anglo-Saxon Literature for Michael Lapidge*. Toronto Old English series. 2 vols. Toronto, 2005.
Olsen, Karin. "Animated Ships in Old English and Old Norse Poetry." In *Animals and the Symbolic in Mediaeval Art and Literature,* ed. L. A. J. R. Houwen, 53–66. Mediaevalia Groningana 20. Groningen, 1997.
Ooi, S. Elizabeth Newman. "The Speaking Objects of Anglo-Saxon England." PhD dissertation, Catholic University of America, 2018.
Orchard, Andy. "After Aldhelm: The Teaching and Transmission of the Anglo-Latin Hexameter." *Journal of Medieval Latin* 2 (1992): 96–133.
———. "Alcuin's Educational Dispute: The Riddle of Teaching and the Teaching of Riddles." In *Childhood and Adolescence in Anglo-Saxon Literary Culture,* ed. Susan Irvine and Winfried Rudolf, 167–201. Toronto, 2018.
———. *A Critical Companion to Beowulf*. Cambridge, 2003.
———. "*The Dream of the Rood*: Cross-References." In *New Readings in the Vercelli Book,* ed. Samantha Zacher and Andy Orchard, 225–53. Toronto Old English Series. Toronto, 2009.
———. "Enigma Variations: The Anglo-Saxon Riddle-Tradition." In O'Keeffe and Orchard, *Latin Learning and English Lore: Studies in Anglo-Saxon Literature for Michael Lapidge,* vol. 1, 284–304.
———. "The *Hisperica famina* as Literature." *Journal of Medieval Latin* 10 (2000): 1–45.
———. "Old English and Latin Poetic Traditions." In *A Companion to Medieval Poetry,* ed. Corinne Saunders, 65–82. Oxford, 2010.
———. "Old Sources, New Resources: Finding the Right Formula for Boniface." *Anglo-Saxon England* 30 (2001): 15–38.
———. "Oral Tradition." In *Reading Old English Texts,* ed. Katherine O'Brien O'Keeffe, 101–23. Cambridge, 1997.
———. "Performing Writing and Singing Silence in the Anglo-Saxon Riddle-Tradition." In *Or Words to That Effect: Orality and the Writing of Literary History,* ed. Daniel F. Chamberlain and J. Edward Chamberlin, 73–91. Amsterdam, 2016.

———. *The Poetic Art of Aldhelm.* Cambridge Studies in Anglo-Saxon England 8. Cambridge, 1994.
———. *Pride and Prodigies: Studies in the Monsters of the 'Beowulf'-Manuscript.* Cambridge, 1995.
———. "The Riddle of Anglo-Saxon Lewdness and Learning," *Anglo-Saxon England*, forthcoming.
———. "Wish You Were Here: Alcuin's Courtly Verse and the Boys Back Home." In *Courts and Regions in Medieval Europe*, ed. Sarah Rees Jones, Richard Marks, and A. J. Minnis, 21–43. Woodbridge, Suffolk, 2000.
Orton, Peter. "The Exeter Book *Riddles*: Authorship and Transmission." *Anglo-Saxon England* 44 (2016): 131–62.
———. "The Technique of Object-Personification in *The Dream of the Rood* and a Comparison with the Old English Riddles." *Leeds Studies in English* n.s. 11 (1980): 1–18.
Osborn, Marijane. "Anglo-Saxon Tame Bees: Some Evidence for Beekeeping from Riddles and Charms." *Neuphilologische Mitteilungen* 107 (2006): 271–83.
———. "Old English Ing and His *Wain.*" *Neuphilologische Mitteilungen* 81 (1980): 388–89.
———. "'Skep' (*Beinenkorb, *beoleap*) as a Culture-Specific Solution to *Exeter Book* Riddle 17." *American Notes and Queries* 18, no. 1 (2005): 7–18.
———. "Vixen as Hero: Solving Exeter Book Riddle 15." In *The Hero Recovered: Essays on Medieval Heroism in Honor of George Clark*, ed. Robin Waugh and James Weldon, 173–87. Kalamazoo, Mich., 2010.
Owen-Crocker, Gale R. "'Seldom . . . does the deadly spear rest for long': Weapons and Armour." In Hyer and Owen-Crocker, *Material Culture of Daily Living in the Anglo-Saxon World*, 201–30.
Padelford, Frederick Morgan. "Old English Musical Terms." *Bonner Beiträge zur Anglistik* 4 (1899): 1–112.
Page, R. I. "The Icelandic Rune Poem." *Nottingham Medieval Studies* 42 (1998): 1–37. [Reprinted as a booklet by the Viking Society for Northern Research.]
———. *An Introduction to English Runes.* London, 1973.
———. *Runes and Runic Inscriptions.* Woodbridge, Suffolk, 1995.
———. "The Study of Latin Texts (2): The Evidence of English Glosses." In *Latin and the Vernacular Languages in Early Medieval Britain*, ed. Nicholas Brooks, 141–65. Leicester, 1982.
Parkes, M. B. "The Manuscript of the Leiden Riddle." *Anglo-Saxon England* 1 (1972): 207–17.
Parsons, David N. *Recasting the Runes: The Reform of the Anglo-Saxon 'Futhorc.'* Uppsala, 1999.
Patch, Howard R. "Anglo-Saxon Riddle 56." *Modern Language Notes* 35 (1920): 181–82.
Paton, W. P., ed. *The Greek Anthology.* 5 vols. London, 1916–18.
Pavlovskis, Zoja. "The Riddler's Microcosm: from Symphosius to St. Boniface." *Classica et Mediaevalia* 39 (1988): 219–51.

Perkins, Richard. *Thor the Wind-Raiser and the Eyrarland Image*. London, 2001.

Perrello, Tony. "An Undiscovered Riddle in *Brussels, Bibliothèque Royale* Mediaeval Studies 1828–1830." *English Language Notes* 43, no. 2 (2005): 8–14.

Pezzini, Giuseppe. "Contraction of *est* in Latin." *Transactions of the Philological Society* 109 (2011): 327–41.

Pinsker, Hans. "Bemerkungen zum ae. Sturmrätsel." *Arbeiten aus Anglistik und Amerikanistik* 6 (1981): 221–26.

———. "Neue Deutungen für zwei altenglische Rätsel." *Anglia* 91 (1973): 11–17.

———. "Ein verschollenes altenglisches Rätsel?" In *A Yearbook of Studies in English Language and Literature*, ed. Siegfried Korninger, 53–59. Beiträge zur englischen Philologie 78. Vienna, 1981.

Pinsker, Hans, and Waltraud Ziegler, ed. and trans. *Die altenglischen Rätsel des Exeterbuchs*. Anglistische Forschungen 183. Heidelberg, 1985.

Pitman, James H., trans. *The Riddles of Aldhelm*. Yale Studies in English 67. New Haven, 1925.

PL = J.-P. Migne, ed., Patrologiae cursus completus, Series latina. Paris, 1844–80.

Poole, Russell. *Old English Wisdom Poetry*. Annotated Bibliographies of Old and Middle English Literature 5. Cambridge, 1998.

Pope, John C. "Palaeography and Poetry: Some Solved and Unsolved Mysteries of the Exeter Book." In *Medieval Scribes, Manuscripts and Libraries: Essays Presented to N. R. Ker*, ed. M. B. Parkes and Andrew G. Watson, 25–65. London, 1978.

———. "An Unsuspected Lacuna in the Exeter Book: Divorce Proceedings for an Ill-Matched Couple in the Old English Riddles." *Speculum* 49 (1974): 615–22.

Porter, David W. "Æthelwold's Bowl and *The Chronicle of Abingdon*." *Neuphilologische Mitteilungen* 97 (1996): 163–67.

———. "A Double Solution to the Latin Riddle in MS. Antwerp, Plantin-Moretus Museum M16.2." *American Notes and Queries* 9, no. 1 (1996): 3–9.

Porter, John, trans. *Anglo-Saxon Riddles*. Hockwold-cum-Wilton, 1995.

Postgate, J. P. "Etymological Studies." *American Journal of Philology* 3 (1882): 329–39.

Prehn, August. "Komposition und Quellen der Rätsel des Exeterbuches." *Neuphilologische Studien* (1883): 145–285.

Prescott, Andrew. *The Benedictional of St Æthelwold: A Masterpiece of Anglo-Saxon Art; A Facsimile*. London, 2002.

Preston, Todd. "An Alternative Solution to *Exeter Book* Riddle 77." *Viator* 42, no. 1 (2011): 25–34.

Price, Helen. "A Hive of Activity: Realigning the Figure of the Bee in the Mead-Making Network of *Exeter Book* Riddle 27." *Postmedieval: A Journal of Medieval Cultural Studies* 8 (2016): 444–62.

Pujalte, Julián Solana. "Análisis métrico-prosódico de la poesía de Alcuino de York." PhD dissertation, University of Seville, 1987.

Pulsiano, Phillip. "Abbot Ælfwine and the Date of the Vitellius Psalter." *American Notes and Queries* 11 (1998): 3–12.

Pulsiano, Phillip, and Kirsten Wolf. "*Exeter Book* Riddle 57: Those Damned Souls, Again." *Germanic Notes* 22 (1991): 2–5.

Rahtz, Philip, and Donald Bullough. "The Parts of an Anglo-Saxon Mill." *Anglo-Saxon England* 6 (1977): 15–37.

Reifegerste, E. Matthias. *Die Hervarar saga: Eine kommentierte Übersetzung und Untersuchungen zur Herkunft und Integration ihrer Überlieferungsschichten*. Berlin, 1999.

Reuschel, Helga. "Kenningar bei Alcuin. Zur 'Disputatio Pippini cum Albino.'" *Beiträge zur Geschichte der deutschen Sprache und Literatur* 62 (1938): 143–55.

Riddler, Ian, and Nicola Trzaska-Nartowski. "Chanting upon a Dunghill: Working Skeletal Materials." In Hyer and Owen-Crocker, *Material Culture of Daily Living in the Anglo-Saxon World*, 116–41.

Riedinger, Anita R. "The Formulaic Style in the Old English Riddles." *Studia Neophilologica* 76 (2004): 30–43.

Riese, Alexander, ed., "Bern Riddles." In *Anthologia Latina*, Part 1, fasc. 1, 351–70. Leipzig, 1894; repr. Amsterdam, 1964.

Rigg, A. G., and G. R. Wieland. "A Canterbury Classbook of the Mid-Eleventh Century (the 'Cambridge Songs' Manuscript)." *Anglo-Saxon England* 4 (1975): 113–30.

Riley, Dennis. *Anglo-Saxon Tools*. Ely, 2014.

Rissanen, Matti. "*Nathwæt* in the *Exeter Book Riddles*." *American Notes and Queries* 24 (1986): 116–20.

Ritzke-Rutherford, Jean. *Light and Darkness in Anglo-Saxon Thought and Writing*. Frankfurt, 1979.

Robinson, Fred C. "Artful Ambiguities in the Old English 'Book-Moth' Riddle." *Anglo-Saxon Poetry: Essays in Appreciation, For John C. McGalliard*, ed. Lewis E. Nicholson and Dolores Warwick Frese, 355–62. Notre Dame, 1975.

Robson, Peter. "'Feorran Broht': Exeter Book Riddle 12 and the Commodification of the Exotic." In *Authority and Subjugation in Writing of Medieval Wales*, ed. Ruth Kennedy and Simon Meecham-Jones, 71–84. New York, 2008.

Ross, Margaret Clunies. "The Anglo-Saxon and Norse *Rune Poems*: A Comparative Approach." *Anglo-Saxon England* 19 (1990): 23–39.

Rudolf, Winfried. "Riddling and Reading: Iconicity and Logogriphs in Exeter Book *Riddles* 23 and 45." *Anglia* 130 (2012): 499–525.

Ruff, Carin. "The Place of Metrics in Anglo-Saxon Latin Education: Aldhelm and Bede." *Journal of English and Germanic Philology* 104 (2005): 149–70.

Rügamer, Antje. *Die Poetizität der altenglischen Rätsel des Exeter Book*. Hamburg, 2008.

Rulon-Miller, Nina. "Sexual Humor and Fettered Desire in Exeter Book Riddle 12." In Wilcox, *Humour in Anglo-Saxon Literature*, 99–126.

Rusche, Philip. "Isidore's *Etymologiae* and the Canterbury Aldhelm Scholia." *Journal of English and German Philology* 104 (2005): 437–55.

Russom, Geoffrey. "Exeter Riddle 47: A Moth Laid Waste to Fame." *Philological Quarterly* 56 (1977): 129–36.

Salvador-Bello, Mercedes. "Allegorizing and Moralizing Zoology in Aldhelm's *Enigmata*." *Revista canaria de estudios ingleses* 68 (2014): 209–18.

———. "A Case of Editorial Hypercorrection in Exeter Riddle 35 (8b)." *American Notes and Queries* 14 (2001): 5–11.

———. "The Compilation of the Old English Riddles of the *Exeter Book*." PhD dissertation, University of Seville, 1997.

———. "Direct and Indirect Clues: Exeter Riddle No. 74 Reconsidered." *Neuphilologische Mitteilungen* 99 (1998): 17–29.

———. "The Evening Singer of Riddle 8 (K–D)." *SELIM* 9 (1999): 57–68.

———. "Exeter Book Riddle 90 under a New Light: a School Drill in Hisperic Robes." *Neophilologus* 102 (2018): 107–23.

———. *Isidorean Perceptions of Order: the Exeter Book Riddes and Medieval Latin Enigmata*. Medieval European Studies 17. Morgantown, W.Va. 2015.

———. "The Key to the Body: Unlocking Riddles 42–46." In *Naked before God: Uncovering the Body in Anglo-Saxon England*, ed. Benjamin C. Withers and Jonathan Wilcox, 60–96. Medieval European Studies 3. Morgantown, W.Va., 2003.

———. "The Oyster and the Crab: A Riddle Duo (nos. 77 and 78) in the *Exeter Book*." *Modern Philology* 101 (2004): 400–19.

———. "Patterns of Compilation in Anglo-Latin Enigmata and the Evidence of a Source-Collection in Riddles 1–40 of the Exeter Book." *Viator* 43 (2012): 339–74.

———. "The Sexual Riddle Type in Aldhelm's *Enigmata*, the Exeter Book, and Early Medieval Latin." *Philological Quarterly* 90 (2012): 357–85.

Sanford, Eva Matthews. "*De loquela digitorum*." *Classical Journal* 23 (1928): 588–93.

Sayers, William. "*Exeter Book* Riddle 17 and the L-Rune: British **lester* 'Vessel, Oat-Straw Hive'?" *American Notes and Queries* 19, no. 2 (2006): 5–9.

———. "Exeter Book Riddle No. 5: Whetstone?" *Neuphilologische Mitteilungen* 97 (1996): 387–92.

Scattergood, John. "Eating the Book: *Riddle* 47 and Memory." In *Text and Gloss: Studies in Insular Learning and Literature Presented to Joseph Donovan Pheifer*, ed. Helen Conrad O'Brian, Anne Marie D'Arcy, and John Scattergood, 119–27. Dublin, 1999.

Schlutter, Otto B. "Afog 'peruersus.' im 24ten Rätsel, die Balliste bezeichnend." *Englische Studien* 41 (1910): 435–34.

Schmidt, Arno. "Die Reichenauer Rätsel." *Zeitschrift für deutsches Altertum und deutsche Literatur* 73 (1936): 197–200.

Schneider, Karl. "Zu vier ae. Rätseln." In *Gedenkschrift für Jost Trier*, ed. Hartmut Beckers and Hans Schwarz, 330–54. Cologne, 1975.

Schneider, Robert. *Satzbau und Wortschatz der altenglischen Rätsel des Exeterbuches: Ein Beitrag zur Lösung der Verfasserfrage*. Breslau, 1913.

Scott, Peter Dale. "Rhetorical and Symbolic Ambiguity: The Riddles of Symphosius and Aldhelm." In *Saints, Scholars and Heroes: Studies in Medieval Culture in Honour of Charles W. Jones*, vol. 1, ed. Margot H. King and Wesley M. Stevens, 117–44. Collegeville, Minn., 1979.

Scull, C. "Scales and Weights in Early Anglo-Saxon England." *Archaeological Journal* 147 (1990): 183–215.

Sebo, Erin. *In Enigmate: The History of a Riddle, 400–1500*. Dublin, 2018.

———. "Symphosius 93.2: A New Interpretation." *Harvard Studies in Classical Philology* 106 (2011): 315–20.

———. "Was Symphosius an African? A Contextualizing Note on Two Textual Clues in the *Aenigmata Symphosii*." *Notes and Queries* 56 (2009): 323–24.

Shaw, Philip. "Hair and Heathens: Picturing Pagans and the Carolingian Connection in the Exeter Book and the *Beowulf*-Manuscript." In *Texts and Identities in the Early Middle Ages*, ed. Richard Corradini, Rob Meens, Christine Pössel, and Philip Shaw, 345–57. Österreichische Akademie der Wissenschaften, Phil.-Hist. Klasse, Denkschriften 344. Vienna, 2006.

Shook, Laurence K. "Old English Riddle 28: Testudo (Tortoise-Lyre)." *Mediaeval Studies* 20 (1958): 93–97.

———. "Old English Riddle I: 'Fire.'" *Mediaeval Studies* 8 (1946): 316–18.

———. "Old English Riddle No. 20: *Heoruswealwe*." In *Franciplegius: Medieval and Linguistic Studies in Honor of Francis Peabody Magoun, Jr*, ed. Jess B. Bessinger and Robert P. Creed, 194–204. New York, 1965.

———. "Riddling Relating to the Anglo-Saxon Scriptorium." In *Essays in Honour of Anton Charles Pegis*, ed. J. Reginald O'Donnell, 215–36. Toronto, 1974.

Simms, Douglas P. A. "Exeter Book *Riddle 19*: Its Runes and Transmission." *Notes and Queries* 261 (2016): 351–54.

Sims-Williams, Patrick. "Riddling Treatment of the 'Watchman Device' in *Branwen* and *Togail Bruidne Da Derga*." *Studia Celtica* 12–13 (1977–78): 83–117.

Singmaster, David. "The History of Some of Alcuin's Propositions." In Butzer, *Charlemagne and His Heritage: 1200 Years of Civilization and Science in Europe*, 11–29.

Smith, A. H. *Three Northumbrian Poems*. Exeter, 1978.

Smith, D. K. "Humor in Hiding: Laughter between the Sheets in the Exeter Book Riddles." In Wilcox, *Humour in Anglo-Saxon Literature*, 79–98.

Sonke, Emma. "Zu dem 25. Rätsel des Exeterbuches." *Englische Studien* 37 (1907): 313–18.

Soper, Harriet. "A Count of Days: The Life Course in Old English Poetry." PhD dissertation, Cambridge University, 2017.

———. "Reading the Exeter Book Riddles as Life-Writing." *Review of English Studies* 68 (2017): 841–65.

Sorrell, Paul. "A Bee in My Bonnet: Solving Riddle 17 of the Exeter Book." In *New Windows on a Woman's World: Essays for Jocelyn Harris*, ed. Cohn Gibson and Lisa Marr, 544–53. Dunedin, New Zealand, 2005.

———. "Alcuin's 'Comb' Riddle." *Neophilologus* 80 (1996): 311–18.

———. "Like a Duck to Water: Representations of Aquatic Animals in Early Anglo-Saxon Literature and Art." *Leeds Studies in English* n.s. 25 (1994): 29–68.

———. "Oaks, Ships, Riddles and the Old English *Rune Poem*." *Anglo-Saxon England* 19 (1990): 103–16.

Spallone, Maddalena. "Symphosius o Symposius? Un problema di fonetica nell'Anthologia Latina." *Quaderni dell'Isituto di Lingua e Letterature Latina. Università 'La Sapienza.' Facoltà di Magisterio* 4 (1982): 41–48.

Stanley, E. G. "Exeter Book *Riddle 11*: 'Alcohol' and its Effects." *Notes and Queries* n.s. 61 (2014): 182–85.

———. "Exeter Book *Riddles*, I: *Riddles 60* and *17*." *Notes and Queries* n.s. 64 (2017): 213–17.

———. "Exeter Book *Riddles*, II: The Significant but Often Misleading Opening Word." *Notes and Queries* n.s. 64 (2017): 355–65.

———. "Heroic Aspects of the Exeter Book Riddles." In *Prosody and Poetics in the Early Middle Ages: Essays in Honour of C. B. Hieatt*, ed. M. J. Toswell, 197–218. Toronto, 1995.

———. "Notes on the Text of *Christ and Satan*; and on *The Riming Poem* and the *Rune Poem*, chiefly on *wynn*, *wēn*, and *wenne*." *Notes and Queries* n.s. 31 (1984): 443–53.

———. "Riddling: A Serious Pursuit through the Ages and in Many Languages." In *Proceedings of the Sixth International Conference 'Language, Culture, and Society Russian/English Studies,'* ed. Jane Roberts and Emma Volodarskaya, 16–36. London, 2016.

———. "Stanley B. Greenfield's Solution of *Riddle* (ASPR) 39: 'Dream.'" *Notes and Queries* n.s. 38 (1991): 148–49.

Steen, Janie. *Verse and Virtuosity: The Adaptation of Latin Rhetoric in Old English Poetry*. Toronto, 2008.

Stephens, Win. "The Bright Cup: Early Medieval Vessel Glass." In Hyer and Owen-Crocker, *Material Culture of Daily Living in the Anglo-Saxon World*, 275–92.

Stephenson, I. P. *The Anglo-Saxon Shield*. Stroud, 2002.

Stévanovitch, Colette. "Exeter Book Riddle 70a: Nose?" *Notes and Queries* n.s. 42 (1995): 8–10.

Stevenson, Jane. "The Beginnings of Literacy in Ireland." *Proceedings of the Royal Irish Academy* 89C (1989): 127–65.

Stewart, Ann Harleman. "The Diachronic Study of Communicative Competence." In *Current Topics in English Historical Linguistics*, ed. Michael Dayenport, et al, 123–36. Odense, 1983.

———. "Double Entendre in the Old English Riddles." *Lore and Language* 3, no. 8 (1983): 39–52.

———. "Inference in Socio-Historical Linguistics: The Example of Old English Word-Play." *Folia Linguistica Historica* 6 (1985): 63–85.

———. "Kenning and Riddle in Old English." *Papers on Language and Literature* 15 (1979): 115–36.

———. "Old English Riddle 47 as Stylistic Parody." *Papers on Language and Literature* 11 (1975): 227–41.

———. "The Solution to Old English Riddle 4." In *Eight Anglo-Saxon Studies*, ed. J. Wittig, 52–61. Chapel Hill, 1981.

Stoklund, Marie, Michael Lerche Nielsen, Bente Holmberg, and Gillian Fellows-Jensen. *Runes and Their Secrets: Studies in Runology.* Copenhagen, 2006.

Stork, Nancy Porter. *Through a Gloss Darkly: Aldhelm's Riddles in the British Library MS Royal 12.C.xxiii.* Studies and Texts 98. Toronto, 1990.

Strecker, Karl, ed. *Aenigmata hexasticha.* MGH PLAC 4.2, 732–59. Berlin, 1923.

Suchier, Walther, ed. "Disputatio Pippini cum Albino." In *Die Altercatio Hadriani Augusti et Epicteti Philosophi, nebst einigen verwandten Texten,* ed. L. W. Daly and W. Suchier, 134–46. Studies in Language and Literature 24. Urbana, 1939.

Sutherland, Alexander Christian. "The Paradoxes in the Riddles of the Anglo-Saxons." PhD dissertation, Cambridge University, 1983.

Swaen, A. E. H. "Het 18e Oudengelsche Raadsel." *Neophilologus* 4 (1919): 258–62.

———. "Het Angelsaksische Raadsel 58." *Neophilologus* 13 (1928): 293–96.

———. "The Anglo-Saxon Horn Riddles." *Neophilologus* 26 (1941): 298–302.

———. "Notes on Anglo-Saxon Riddles." *Neophilologus* 31 (1947): 145–48.

———. "Riddle 8 (10,11)." *Neophilologus* 30 (1946): 126–27.

———. "Riddle 9 (6, 8)." *Studia Neophilologica* 14 (1941–2): 67–70.

———. "Riddle 9 (12)." *Neophilologus* 30 (1946): 126.

———. "Riddle 63 (60, 62)." *Neophilologus* 27 (1942): 220.

———. "Riddle xiii (xvi)." *Neophilologus* 26 (1941): 228–31.

Symons, Victoria. *Runes and Roman Letters in Anglo-Saxon Manuscripts.* Berlin, 2016.

Talentino, Arnold. "Riddle 30: The Vehicle of the Cross." *Neophilologus* 65 (1981): 129–36.

Tangl, Michael, ed. *Epistolae Bonifatii et Lullii,* MGH ES 1. Berlin, 1916.

Tanke, John W. "The Bachelor-Warrior of Exeter Book Riddle 20." *Philological Quarterly* 79 (2000): 409–27.

———. "*Wonfeax wale*: Ideology and Figuration in the Sexual Riddles of the Exeter Book." In *Class and Gender in Early English Literature,* ed. Britton J. Harwood and Gillian R. Overing, 21–42. Bloomington, Ind., 1994.

Taylor, Anita. "Enigma Variations: The Literary Pragmatics of the Riddle in Early English Literature." PhD dissertation, Indiana University, 2015.

Taylor, Archer. *English Riddles from Oral Tradition.* Berkeley, 1948.

———. *The Literary Riddle before 1600.* Berkeley, 1948.

———. "Riddles Dealing with Family Relationships." *The Journal of American Folklore* 51 (1938): 25–37.

———. "The Varieties of Riddles." In *Philologica: The Malone Anniversary Studies,* ed. Thomas A. Kirby and Henry Bosley Woolf, 1–8. Baltimore, 1949.

Taylor, Keith P. "Mazers, Mead, and the Wolf's-head Tree: A Reconsideration of Old English *Riddle 55.*" *Journal of English and Germanic Philology* 94 (1995): 497–512.

Teele, Elinor Bartlet. "The Heroic Tradition in the Old English *Riddles*." PhD dissertation, Cambridge University, 2004.

Teviotdale, E. C. "Latin Verse Inscriptions in Anglo-Saxon Art." *Gesta* 35 (1996): 99–110.

Thier, Katrin. "Steep Vessel, High Horn-ship: Water Transport." In Hyer and Owen-Crocker, *Material Culture of Daily Living in the Anglo-Saxon World*, 49–72.

Thornbury, Emily. "Aldhelm's Rejection of the Muses and the Mechanics of Poetic Inspiration in Early Anglo-Saxon England." *Anglo-Saxon England* 36 (2007): 71–92.

Thorpe, Benjamin, ed. *Codex Exoniensis: A Collection of Anglo-Saxon Poetry, from a Manuscript in the Library of the Dean and Chapter of Exeter, with an English Translation, Notes, and Indexes*. London, 1842.

Tigges, Wim. "Signs and Solutions: A Semiotic Approach to the Exeter Book Riddles." In *This Noble Craft*, ed. Erik Kooper, 59–82. Amsterdam, 1991.

———. "Snakes and Ladders: Ambiguity and Coherence in the Exeter Book Riddles and Maxims." In *Companion to Old English Poetry*, ed. Henk Aertsen and Rolf H. Bremmer, Jr., 95–118. Amsterdam, 1994.

Tolkien, Christopher, ed. and trans. *The Saga of King Heidrek the Wise*. New York, 1960.

Tomasek, Tomas. *Das deutsche Rätsel im Mittelalter*. Tübingen, 1994.

Trautmann, Moritz. *Die altenglischen Rätsel (die Rätsel des Exeterbuchs), herausgegeben, erläutert und mit Wörterverzeichnis versehen*. Heidelberg, 1915.

———. "Alte und neue Antworten auf altenglischen Rätsel." *Bonner Beiträge zur Anglistik* 19 (1905): 167–215.

———. " Die Auflösungen der altenglischen Rätsel." *Anglia Beiblatt* 5 (1894): 46–51.

———. "Cynewulf und die Rätsel." *Anglia Anzeiger* 6 (1883): 158–69.

———. "Weiteres zu den altenglischen Rätseln und Metrisches." *Anglia* 43 (1919): 245–60.

———. "Zeit, Heimat und Verfasser der altenglischen Rätsel." *Anglia* 38 (1914): 365–73.

———. "Zu den altenglischen Rätseln." *Anglia* 17 (1895): 396–400.

———. "Zu den Lösungen der Rätsel des Exeterbuchs." *Beiblatt* 25 (1914): 273–79.

———. "Zu meiner Ausgabe der altenglischen Rätsel." *Anglia* 42 (1918): 125–41.

Tripp, Raymond P., Jr. "The Effect of the Occult and the Supernatural upon the Way We Read Old English Poetry." In *Literature and the Occult: Essays in Comparative Literature*, ed. Luanne Frank, 255–63. Arlington, Tex., 1977.

Tristram, Hildegard L. C. "In Support of Tupper's Solution of the Exeter Book Riddle (Krapp-Dobbie) 55." In *Germanic Dialects: Linguistic and Philological Investigations*, ed. Bela Brogyanyi and Thomas Krömmelbein, 585–98. Current Issues in Linguistic Theory 38. Amsterdam, 1986.

Tucker, Susie I. "The Comparative Study of Riddles." *Modern Language Notes* 18 (1903): 1–8.

———. "'Sixty' as an Indefinite Number in Middle English." *Review of English Studies* 25 (1949): 152–53.
Tupper, Frederick M., Jr. "Originals and Analogues of the *Exeter Book Riddles*." *Modern Language Notes* 18 (1903): 97–106.
———. "Riddles of the Bede Tradition: The *Flores* of pseudo-Bede." *Modern Philology* 2 (1905): 561–72.
———, ed. *The Riddles of the Exeter Book*. Boston, 1910. Repr. 1968.
———. "Solutions of the Exeter Book Riddles." *Modern Language Notes* 21 (1906): 97–105.
Turner, J. Hilton. "Roman Elementary Mathematics: The Operations." *The Classical Journal* 47 (1951): 63–74 and 106–8.
Vernet, André. "Notice et extraits d'un manuscrit d'Edimbourg (Adv. Mss. 18.6.12, 18.7.8, 18.7.7)." *Bibliothèque de l'École des Chartes* 107 (1948): 33–51.
Waxenberger, Gaby. "The *yew*-rune and the Runes ᚻ, ᚷ, ᛡ, and ᛁ in the Old English Corpus (Epigraphical Material)." In Stoklund et al., *Runes and Their Secrets: Studies in Runology*, 385–414.
Weber, Benjamin. "The Isidorian Context of Aldhelm's 'Lorica' and Exeter Riddle 35." *Neophilologus* 96 (2012): 1–10.
Webster, Leslie. *The Franks Casket*. London, 2012.
Weiskott, Eric. "Old English Poetry, Verse by Verse." *Anglo-Saxon England* 44 (2016): 95–130.
Wells, Richard. "The Old English Riddles and Their Ornithological Content." *Lore and Language* 2, no. 9 (1978): 57–67.
Welsh, Andrew. "Swallows Name Themselves: Exeter Book Riddle 55." *American Notes and Queries* n.s. 3 (1990): 90–93.
Whitbread, Leslie. "The Latin Riddle in the Exeter Book." *Notes and Queries* 190 (1946): 156–58.
———. "The Latin Riddle in the Exeter Book." *Notes and Queries* 194 (1949): 80–82.
Whitman, Charles Huntington. "The Birds of Old English Literature." *Journal of English and Germanic Philology* 2 (1898): 149–98.
Whitman, Frank H. "Aenigmata Tatwini." *Neuphilologische Mitteilungen* 88 (1987): 8–17.
———. "Old English Riddle 74." *English Language Notes* 6 (1968–69): 1–5.
———. *Old English Riddles*. Canadian Federation for the Humanities, Monograph Series 3. Port Credit, Ont., 1982.
———. "The Origin of Old English 'Riddle LXV.'" *Notes and Queries* 213 (1968): 203–4.
———. "Riddle 60 and Its Source." *Philological Quarterly* 50 (1971): 108–15.
———. "Significant Motifs in Riddle 53." *Medium Ævum* 46 (1977): 1–11.
Wilbur, Richard. "Some Riddles from Symphosius." *Yale Review* 91 (2003): 25–26.
———. "Some Riddles in Symphosius." *The Hopkins Review* 1 (2008): 152–54.
———. "Three Riddles from Symphosius." *Poetry* 152 (1988): 1.
Wilcox, Jonathan, ed. *Humour in Anglo-Saxon Literature*. Cambridge, 2000.
———. "Mock-Riddles in Old English: Exeter Riddles 86 and 19." *Studies in Philology* 93 (1996): 180–87.

———. "New Solutions to Old English Riddles: Riddles 17 and 53." *Philological Quarterly* 69 (1990): 393–408.

———. "'Tell Me What I Am': The Old English Riddles." In *Readings in Medieval Texts: Interpreting Old and Middle English Literature*, ed. David F. Johnson and Elaine Treharne, 46–59. Oxford, 2005.

Williams, Edith Whitehurst. "*Hwa mec rære?... Hwa mec stæðþe?*: The Quest for Certainty in the Old English Storm Riddle." *Medieval Perspectives* 14 (1999): 255–72.

———. "The Relation between Pagan Survivals and Diction in Two Old English Riddles." *Philological Quarterly* 54 (1975): 664–70.

———. "What's So New about the Sexual Revolution? Some Comments on Anglo-Saxon Attitudes toward Sexuality in Women Based on Four Exeter Book Riddles." *Texas Quarterly* 18 (1975): 46–55.

Williams, Mary Jane MacDonald. "The Riddles of Tatwine and Eusebius." PhD dissertation, University of Michigan, 1974.

Williamson, Craig, ed. *The Complete Old English Poems*. Philadelphia, 2017.

———. *A Feast of Creatures: Anglo-Saxon Riddle-Songs Translated with Introduction, Notes and Commentary*. Philadelphia, 1982.

———. *The Old English Riddles of the 'Exeter Book.'* Chapel Hill, 1977.

Wilmanns, W., ed. "Disputatio regalis et nobilissimi iuvenis Pippini cum Albino scholastico." *Zeitschrift fur deutsches Altertum* 14 (1869): 530–55.

Wilson, David M. *Anglo-Saxon Ornamental Metalwork, 700–1100, in the British Museum*. London, 1964.

Wilson, John. "Old English Riddle No. 39: 'Comet.'" *Notes and Queries* n.s. 38 (1991): 442–43.

Winterbottom, M. "Aldhelm's Prose Style and Its Origins." *Anglo-Saxon England* 6 (1977): 39–76.

Wrenn, C. L. "Two Anglo-Saxon Harps." *Comparative Literature* 14 (1962): 118–28.

Wright, Charles D. "The Persecuted Church and the *Mysterium Lunae*." In O'Keeffe and Orchard, *Latin Learning and English Lore: Studies in Anglo-Saxon Literature for Michael Lapidge*, vol. 2, 293–314.

———. "The Three 'Victories' of the Wind: A Hibernicism in the *Hisperica Famina, Collectanea Bedae*, and the Old English Prose *Solomon and Saturn* Pater Noster Dialogue." *Ériu* 41 (1990): 13–25.

Wright, Thomas. *Biographia Britannica Literaria I: Anglo-Saxon Period*. London, 1842.

Wülker, Richard P. "Die Bedeutung einer neuen Entdeckung für die angelsächsische Literaturgeschichte." *Berichte über die Verhandlungen der königlichen sächsischen Gesellschaft der Wissenschaften zu Leipzig, philologisch-historische Klasse* 40 (1888): 209–18.

Wyatt, Alfred J. *Old English Riddles*. Boston, 1912.

Young, Jean I. "Riddle 8 of the *Exeter Book*." *Review of English Studies* 18 (1942): 308–12.

———. "Riddle 15 of the *Exeter Book*." *Review of English Studies* 20 (1944): 304–6.

Zehnder, Ursula. "Hypermetrical Verse Patterns in the *Riddles* of the Exeter Book." *Notes and Queries* n.s. 47 (2000): 405–9.

———. "A Metrical Comparison of *Beowulf* and the *Old English Riddles* of the Exeter Book." In *Authors, Heroes and Lovers: Essays on Medieval English Literature and Language; Selected Papers from the Studientage zum englischen Mittelalter SEM I and II (Potsdam 1999 and 2000)/Liebhaber, Helden und Autoren: Studien zur alt- und mittelenglischen Literatur und Sprache; Ausgewählte Beiträge der Studientage zum englischen Mittelalter SEM I and II (Potsdam 1999 and 2000)*, ed. Thomas Honegger, 27–46. Sammlung/Collection Variations 2. Bern, 2001.

Ziegler, Waltraud. "Ein neuer Lösungsversuch für das altenglische Rätsel Nr. 28." *Arbeiten aus Anglistik und Amerikanistik* 7 (1982): 185–90.

Zimmermann, Gunhild. *The Four Old English Poetic Manuscripts: Texts, Contexts, and Historical Background*. Heidelberg, 1995.

Ziolkowski, Jan M. "Classical Influences on Medieval Latin Views of Poetic Inspiration." In *Latin Poetry and the Classical Tradition: Essays in Medieval and Renaissance Literature*, ed. Peter Godman and Oswyn Murray, 15–38. Oxford, 1990.

———. *Talking Animals: Medieval Latin Beast Poetry, 750–1150*. Philadelphia, 1993.

Zironi, A. "Reading and Writing Gothic in the Carolingian Age." In *Teaching to Write, Learning to Write: Proceedings of the XVIth Colloquium of the Comité Internationale de Paléographie Latine*, ed. P. R. Robinson, 103–10. Kings College London Medieval Studies 22. London, 2010.

Zupitza, Julius, ed. *Ælfrics Grammatik und Glossar*, 3rd ed. with a preface by H. Gneuss. Berlin, 2001.

Zweck, Jordan. "Silence in the Exeter Book Riddles." *Exemplaria* 28 (2016): 319–36.

Index of Solutions

The symbol † marks riddles where the solution is one that has sometimes been suggested, but for which another is preferred.

abduction of Venus, †EXE 27
absence of harm, ALC D9
Adam, TAT 22; with Eve, two sons, and a daughter, †EXE 44; with Enoch/Elias and Lazarus ALC D84
adder. *See* bird of prey eating ring-shaped adder
Ægir. *See* waves
age of man, BED 16, ps-BED 4, SOL 2
air, ALC D4. *See also* breath
alchemy, †EXE 8, †EXE 49
ale (and its ingredients), †EXE 26, GES 1
allegory, four senses of, TAT 3
alpha (Greek letter), EUS 9
alphabet. *See* letter(s) of the alphabet
altar, TAT 8, †EXE 47. *See also* sacrificial altar
amphora, EXE 16
anagogical sense. *See* allegory, four senses of
anchor, †EXE 1.16–30 (taken as a separate riddle), †EXE 8, EXE 14, SYM 61, GES 6
anchorite, EXE 14
angel, EUS 2. *See also* fallen angel
angelica, GES 18
anger, BON 12, †EXE 48
ant, SYM 22
ant lion, ALD 18
antler, †EXE 84, †EXE 89
anvil, TAT 28
apocalyptic storm, †EXE 1
apple, SYM 85; tree ALD 76
archetypal feminine, †EXE 31
Arcturus, ALD 53. *See also* Charles's Wain
arithmetic, BIB 3
armor, ALD 33
army, †EXE 1.1–15 (taken as a separate riddle)
arrow, BED 14, TAT 32, ALC D85, SYM 65, GES 13. *See also* bow; burning arrow
ash, OER 26; tree †EXE 88. *See also* spear: made of ash
astronomy, BIB 6
atmosphere, †EXE 1
auger, †EXE 60
Augustine and Tertullian, †EXE 86
aurelia of the butterfly, †EXE 11
aurochs, OER 2
auspicious dream, †EXE 37
autumn, ALC D58
axle and wheel, †EXE 70. See also wheel(s)

baby. *See* crying baby
bad nut, XMS Z1
badger, †EXE 13
bagpipes, †EXE 29
baker's boy and oven, †EXE 52
baking oven, EXE 47
ball, SYM 59
ballista, †EXE 15
baptism, †EXE 8
Barleycorn, John. *See* John Barleycorn
barm, †EXE 39
barnacle goose, EXE 8, †EXE 72
barrel. *See* mead barrel and drinking bowl

barrow. *See* wheelbarrow
barrow (burial mound), †EXE 26, †EXE 47
bat, SYM 28
battering ram, †EXE 51, †EXE 71, †EXE 88. *See also* beechwood: battering ram
beaker. *See* glass: beaker
beam, EXE 28
beard, ALC D13
beaver, ALD 56, OER 28
bee(s), ALD 20, †EXE 32, †EXE 43, †EXE 55, BER 21. *See also* lion: and bee; Samson's lion and bees
bee skep. *See* beehive
beech tree, †EXE 88. *See also* book(s): and beech tree
beechwood: battering ram, †EXE 88; shield †EXE 88
beehive, †EXE 15
beer, †EXE 26
beer mug, ps-BED 13
beet, SYM 42
bell(s), TAT 7, ALC D74, EXE 2, †EXE 6, †EXE 46, EXE 67, SYM 80
bellows, ALD 11, EXE 35, EXE 83, EXE 85, SYM 73, GES 9
belly, ALC D31
bench, BER 4
Bible, †EXE 24, †EXE 65, †EXE 91
birch, OER 13, OIR 18
bird: and wind, †EXE 27; of prey eating a ring-shaped adder †EXE 62. *See also* barnacle goose; blackbird; brown bird; chick; cock; cockerel; crane; crow(s); cuckoo; diving bird; dove; eagle; falcon; female swan(s); green woodpecker; hawk; hen; horned owl; jackdaw; jay; magpie; martins; mute swan; night raven; nightingale; peacock; ptarmigans; ring-tailed peacock; rooks; song thrush; swallow(s); swan(s); ten chickens; ten pheasants; turtledove; twelve chickens; whooper swan; woodpecker
birth. *See* conception and birth
bissextile day, EUS 26
bivalve mollusc, ALD 17
blackbird, †EXE 6, †EXE 55
blind. *See* man: born blind
blood, ALC D36
board. *See* chopping board
board game, GES 19, GES 3
board-gaming piece, OER 14, GES 25
boastfulness. *See* vainglory
boat, EXE 34. *See also* merchant ship; ship
body, ALC D11; and soul XMS S1, EXE 4, †EXE 81, †EXE 84
boiler. *See* double boiler
bone(s), ALC D32; and mouth, BED 3. *See also* mouth or bone
book(s), EXE 91, SOL 1; and beech tree, EXE 88. *See also* Gospel book; riddle or riddle book
book chest, ALD 89, †EXE 47
book moth, EXE 45
book wallet, EUS 33
bookworm, SYM 16
boot, SYM 56
borer, †EXE 60
bottle. *See* leather: bottle
bow, EXE 21, †EXE 71, OER 27. *See also* arrow; burning arrow
bowl. *See* mead barrel and drinking bowl
brain, ALC D14
bread: and oven, †EXE 47. *See also* loaf of bread
breath, ALC D4. *See also* air
bridge, †EXE 20, SYM 62, GES 2. *See also* ice bridge
bronze strigil, SYM 88
broom, †EXE 50, SYM 79, BER 18
brown bird, †EXE 55
bubble, ALD 62, †EXE 8, BER 7
bucket of water, †EXE 2. *See also* two buckets; well: buckets
buffoon. *See* devil: as buffoon
bulb, BER 51
bull, SYM 32, EUS 12
bullock (young bull), ALD 83, ps-BED 7, EUS 37, LOR 11, EXE 36
burden. *See* load
burning arrow, †EXE 60. *See also* arrow; bow
butter-churning servant, †EXE 52
butterfly. *See* aurelia of the butterfly

cage. *See* falcon: cage
camel, ALD 99
candle, ALD 52, EUS 28, †EXE 68

cases, grammatical. *See* prepositions taking two cases
cask, †EXE 16; and cooper, †EXE 83. *See also* wine: cask
cat, ps-SYM 1. *See also* mouser
caterpillar. *See* looper caterpillar
Catholic faith, BON 2
cauldron, ALD 49, ps-BED 10, ALC D76, XMS X1
cedar tree, BER 16
centaur, SYM 39
chain, SYM 5
chalice, †EXE 46, EXE 57
chameleon, EUS 45
charcoal, TAT 38
charity. *See* hope: Hope, Faith, Charity
Charles's Wain, EXE 20
chestnut tree, LOR 7, BER 48
chick, ps-BED 2, EUS 38, XMS X2; in egg, ALC D78, SYM 14. *See also* fetus; hatchling chicks
chickens. *See* ten chickens; twelve chickens
children. *See* Lot and his children
Chimera, EUS 52
chive, †EXE 63
chopping board, EXE 3
chough (bird). *See* jackdaw
chrismal, ALD 55, †EXE 46
Christ, ps-ALC 1; walking on the sea, †EXE 66; cross of, TAT 9. *See also* God; Lamb of God; savior
Christian virtues. *See* faith; four virtues; hope; humility; mercy; patience; peace
churn, EXE 52
cithara, †EXE 29
clock. *See* water clock
cloud, ALD 3, ALC D45, †EXE 37, SYM 8; and wind, †EXE 27. *See also* storm: cloud(s)
cock: and hen, EXE 40, †EXE 73. *See also* weathercock
cockerel (young cock), ALD 26
cold, ALC D52
Colossus, ALD 72
comb, ALC 1
comet, †EXE 37
conception and birth, †EXE 7
conch, BER 47
conscience. *See* guilt
cooper. *See* cask: and cooper
corn. *See* grain of corn
cornfield, †EXE 28
counting. *See* finger-counting
cow, EUS 13, GES 28. *See also* bull; ox; yoke of oxen led by female slave
crab, ALD 37, EXE 75, EXE 78
crane, SYM 26
creation, ALD 100, EXE 38, EXE 64, EXE 90
creature. *See* water-dwelling creature
crocus, BER 36
cross, EUS 17, †EXE 28, †EXE 53, †EXE 56, †EXE 65, †EXE 71; reliquary, †EXE 53. *See also* Christ: cross of; gallows
crossbow, †EXE 21
crow(s), †EXE 55, SYM 27
crying baby, †EXE 6
cuckoo, ps-BED 9, EXE 7, ps-SYM 1
cup, BER 6. *See also* wine: cup
cupping glass, †EXE 69
curiosity, ALC D60
cuttlefish, †EXE 72
cycle and the moon's leap, EUS 29
Cynewulf, †EXE 86

dagger, ALD 6, †EXE 69
dagger sheath, †EXE 42
damned souls, †EXE 55
day, ALC D40, †EXE 37, OER 24; and night EUS 48
days of the month, †EXE 20
death, ALC D6, EXE 37. *See also* life: and death; threefold death
demon, EUS 3, †EXE 2, †EXE 45
devil: as buffoon †EXE 6. *See also* Lamb of God: and the devil
dew, GES 3
dialectic, BIB 12
diamond, ALD 9
die, SYM 90, GES 25
divine power, †EXE 64
diving bird, †EXE 72
dog, †EXE 48, †EXE 73.1 (taken as a separate riddle). *See also* fox: and hound; horseman: with woman, dog, and ship; hound and hind; watchdog
double boiler, ALD 54
double flute, †EXE 67
dough, EXE 43. *See also* barm

dove, ALD 64, XMS Y1. *See also* turtledove
draconite, ALD 24
dragon, EUS 42, †EXE 49
dragon stone. *See* draconite
drawing of a horse, ps-BED 3
dream, ALC D72. *See also* auspicious dream; figure in a dream
drinking bowl. *See* mead barrel and drinking bowl
drunkenness, BON 16
duck in an ox skull's jaws, GES 27
dung beetle, GES 11
dwarf elder tree, ALD 94

eagle, ALD 57
ears, ALC D17
earth, ALD 1, EUS 6, ALC D47, †EXE 39, OER 29, BER 45
earthenware jar, SYM 81. *See also* jar
earthquake. *See* submarine earthquake
Easter fire, †EXE 28
echo, ALC D79, SYM 98
egg(s), BED 13, BER 8. *See also* chick: in egg
elephant, ALD 96
elk hunter, †EXE 73.1 (taken as a separate riddle)
elk sedge, OER 15
ember(s), TAT 35, GES 33
embroidery needle, TAT 13
embryo. *See* fetus
envy, BON 18
epistle. *See* letter (epistle)
ethics, BIB 7
Eve, OEP. *See also* Adam
evening star, ALD 58
evil, TAT 21, ALC 2
execution, †EXE 54
eyes, TAT 18, ALC D15. *See also* squinting eyes

face, ALC D18
faith, ALC D70. *See also* Catholic faith; Hope, Faith, Charity
falcon, †EXE 18, †EXE 76.1 (taken as a separate riddle); cage, †EXE 47
falconry, †EXE 17, †EXE 62
fallen angel. *See* demon
family. *See* Adam: with Eve, two sons, and a daughter; Lot and his children
fate, ALD 7
feather pen, †EXE 29. *See also* pen
feet, ALC D35
female genitalia, †EXE 74
female masturbation, †EXE 10
female swan(s), GES 17
feminine. *See* archetypal feminine
fetus, LOR 8
fiddle, †EXE 29
field of grain, BED 6. *See also* cornfield
fig tree, ALD 77
figure in a dream, ALC D81
figurehead. *See* ship's figurehead
file, ALD 21
finger-counting, ALC D82, SYM 96
fingers, ALC D24. *See also* pen: and fingers; quill pen and fingers; scribe's fingers; ten fingers (with gloves)
fire, ALD 44, TAT 31, TAT 33, ALC D51, ALC D73, †EXE 1.1–15 (taken as a separate riddle), †EXE 28, †EXE 39, EXE 48, GES 29. *See also* Easter fire; wind: and fire
fire and water, EUS 15
fish, ALD 71, EUS 40, BER 30; and river, ALC D80, EXE 81, SYM 12. *See also* flatfish; pike; remora; torpedo fish
five senses, TAT 26
flail, †EXE 2, EXE 50, †EXE 54
flask, EUS 16, †EXE 61
flatfish, †EXE 74
flint, ALC D75, SYM 76–76a
flour, SYM 52
flute, †EXE 6, †EXE 61. *See also* double flute; reed: flute; rye flute
fly, SYM 23
fog, GES 5
foot. *See* feet
forge, †EXE 15
fork. *See* winnowing fork
fortress, †EXE 15
four virtues, BIB 8
fox, †EXE 13, SYM 34; and hound, †EXE 13
friendship, ALC D69
frog, †EXE 6, SYM 19
frozen pond, †EXE 66
furnace, ALC 7–9
furrow. *See* ocean furrow

gallbladder, ALC D28
gallows, EXE 51. *See also* Yggdrasill
garlic, †BER 51. *See also* one-eyed garlic seller
garment. *See* shirt
gem. *See* ring with gem
genitalia. *See* female genitalia; penis; vagina
geometry, BIB 4
giant, OIR 3
gift, OER 7
gimlet. *See* borer
giraffe, EUS 45
glass: beaker, ALD 80, EXE 61, BER 50a. *See also* cupping glass
glory, OER 17
gloves. *See* ten fingers (with gloves)
gnats, †EXE 55
goat. *See* she-goat
God (Christian), †EUS 1, EXE 1.16–104 (taken as a separate riddle), †EXE 64. *See also* Christ; Lamb of God; wind: and God; word: of God
god (pagan), OIR 4. *See also* Ing; Odin and Sleipnir; Tir; Týr
gold, †EXE 9, EXE 79
goose. *See* barnacle goose
Gospel book, EXE 24, EXE 65, †EXE 46
gourd, SYM 43
gouty soldier, SYM 93
grain of corn, BER 12. *See also* field of grain
grammar, BIB 10. *See also* prepositions taking two cases
grass, ALC D63
greed, BON 13
green woodpecker, †EXE 22
guilt, †EXE 3, †EXE 4

hail, OER 9, OIR 7; hailstones, †EXE 55. *See also* snow: with hail and ice
hair, ALC D12, SYM 58
ham, SYM 85
hammer, SYM 86, GES 4
hand(s), ALC 5, ALC D23
hand mill, †EXE 2
harm. *See* absence of harm
harp, †EXE 26, †EXE 29, †EXE 53, †EXE 67
harrow, †EXE 78
harrowing of Hell, †EXE 32
harvest, OER 12
hatchling chicks, †EXE 11
hatred, †EXE 31
hawk, †EXE 18, †EXE 76.1 (taken as a separate riddle). *See also* horseman
hay, SYM 50
head, ALC D10
heart, ALC D26, LOR 2
heaven, EUS 5, ALC D38. *See also* sphere of the heavens
heddle and weft, GES 30
hedgehog, EXE 13, SYM 29
heliotrope, ALD 51
Hell. *See* harrowing of Hell
hellebore, ALD 98
helmet, †EXE 59; with visor, †EXE 77. *See also* iron: helmet
hemp, †EXE 23
hen, †EXE 73.3 (taken as a separate riddle). *See also* cock: and hen
herbs, ALC D64
hide, †EXE 10, †EXE 24. *See also* ox: and its hide; oxhide
hind. *See* hound and hind
hippopotamus, EUS 53
hips, ALC D33
historical sense. *See* allegory, four senses of
hive. *See* bee skep
hobnail, SYM 57
holy scripture. *See* Bible
homeland, OER 23
honey, BER 20
hood, †EXE 59
hook, SYM 54
hope, BON 3, ALC D68
Hope, Faith, Charity, TAT 2
horn, EXE 12, EXE 76, †EXE 84, †EXE 89, OER 27. *See also* inkhorn; yew horn
horned owl, EUS 60
hornet, ALD 75
horns. *See* ox: and its horns
horse, OER 19; and wagon, †EXE 49. *See also* drawing of a horse; pregnant horse and two women

horseman: and hawk, †EXE 17, †EXE 62; and woman, †EXE 34; with servant and hawk, †EXE 17, †EXE 62; with wagon and hawk, †EXE 17; with woman, dog, and ship, †EXE 34
hound and hind, †EXE 73. *See also* dog; fox: and hound
house, EUS 20
humility, TAT 24, BON 9; and pride, EUS 27
hunger, ALC D65
hunt. *See* waterfowl hunt
hunter. *See* elk hunter
hurricane, †EXE 1
hyena, †EXE 72

ice, ps-BED 6, ALC D53, LOR 4, EXE 31, EXE 66, OER 11, SYM 10, ps-SYM 1, BER 38, BER 42, OIR 9; bridge, †EXE 20; floe, EXE 31, GES 24. *See also* snow: with hail and ice
iceberg, †EXE 31; †EXE 66
ignorance, BON 19
incense, ALC 3, SYM 47
Ing, OER 22. *See also* god (pagan)
iniquity and justice, EUS 18
ink, LOR 12
inkhorn, EUS 30, EXE 84, EXE 89
inkwell, †EXE 15, †EXE 16
inscription ring on a chalice, †EXE 46, †EXE 57
instrument. *See* musical instrument; stringed instrument
intercourse. *See* sexual intercourse
iron: helmet, †EXE 69; shield, †EXE 69; weapon, †EXE 69
ivory, SYM 49
ivy, BER 39

jackdaw, †EXE 6, †EXE 55
jar, BER 1. *See also* earthenware jar
javelin, †EXE 71
jaws. *See* duck in an ox skull's jaws
jay, †EXE 6, EXE 22
jetty. *See* letter beam cut from old jetty
John Barleycorn, †EXE 26
joy, OER 8
jug of wine, †EXE 16
justice, BON 6. *See also* iniquity and justice

kelp weed, †EXE 58
key, EXE 42, EXE 87, SYM 4; and lock, †EXE 42, †EXE 87
king, XMS S2

ladder, SYM 78, BER 10
lamb, ALC 5
Lamb of God, EXE 86; and the devil, †EXE 86
lamp, LOR 10, BER 2. *See also* lantern; torch
lamprey, †EXE 75
lance, †EXE 60
land and sea, EUS 21
lantern, SYM 67. *See also* lamp
lathe. *See* pole lathe
leather, †EXE 10; bottle, †EXE 16, †EXE 85
lectern, TAT 10
leech, ALD 43
leek, †EXE 23, †EXE 63, GES 8. *See also* onion
legs, ALC D34
leopard, EUS 46
letter (epistle), ALC D88
letter beam cut from old jetty, †EXE 58
letter(s) of the alphabet, ALD 30, TAT 4, EUS 7, ALC D1, †EXE 11, EXE 55, BER 25; *a*, BED 7, ALF A; *b*, ALF B; *c*, ALF C; *d*, ALF D; *e*, ALF E; *f*, BED 2, ALF F; *g*, ALF G; *h*, ALF H; *i*, BED 8, EUS 39, ALF I; *k*, ALF K; *l*, ALF L; *m*, ALF M; *n*, ALF N; *o* BED 9, ALF O; *p*, ALF P; *q*, ALF Q; *r*, ALF R; *s*, ALF S; *t*, ALF T; *u/v*, BED 10, EUS 19, ALF V; *x*, EUS 14, ALF X; *y*, ALF Y; *z*, ALF Z. *See also* alpha (Greek letter)
lice, ALC D77, SYM 30
life, ALC D5, †EXE 72; and death, EUS 24
light, ALC D39
light warship, EXE 17
lighthouse, ALD 92, EXE 68
lily, BER 35. *See also* water lily
lime, SYM 75
lion, ALD 39; and bee, †EXE 15.
lips, ALC D21
liquid, OIR 15
liquor. *See* malt liquor
liver, ALC D27
lizard, EUS 50

load, BED 11
loaf of bread, ALD 70. *See also* bread
lock, †EXE 2. *See also* key: and lock
locust, ALD 34
logic, BIB 9
loom, †EXE 54. *See also* tapestry and loom; web and loom
looper caterpillar, †EXE 11
Lot and his children, EXE 44
love, BED 4; TAT 14; BON 5. *See also* Hope, Faith, Charity
lung, ALC D25
luxury, BON 17

maggot and psalter, †EXE 45
magician, ALC 5
magnet, ALD 25
magpie, EXE 22
mail: mailcoat, EXE 33; mailshirt, †EXE 59
male masturbation, †EXE 52
mallow, SYM 41
malt liquor, †EXE 26
man, ALC 3, †EXE 36, †EXE 77, OER 20, OIR 14; born blind, ALD 85; called *-wulf*, †EXE 86; on a stool, ps-BED 8. *See also* age of man; one-eyed man; sword: or man; white-haired man
mankind, EUS 4, ALC D7, LOR 1
Mars, OER 17. *See also* god (pagan)
martins, †EXE 55
mastiff, ALD 10
masturbation. *See* female masturbation; male masturbation
matter. *See* primordial matter
me. *See* you: and me
mead, EXE 25, †EXE 26
mead barrel and drinking bowl, †EXE 53
merchant ship, EXE 30
mercy, BON 4
metal, †EXE 79
midge(s), ALD 36, †EXE 55
milfoil (yarrow), ALD 50
mill. *See* hand mill
millpond and its sluice, †EXE 47
millstone, ALD 66, †EXE 2, †EXE 30, SYM 51, BER 9
mimic of animal and bird noises. *See* magpie; jay
mine and yours, ALC 6
Minotaur, ALD 28
mirror, SYM 69, BER 29
mole, SYM 21
mollusc. *See* bivalve mollusc
money, †EXE 79, SYM 91. *See also* wealth
monster, †EXE 34
month. *See* days of the month
moon, ALD 6, EUS 11, ALC D42, †EXE 37, †EXE 91, BER 58, BER 59; and sun, ALD 79, EXE 27. *See also* cycle and the moon's leap
moral sense. *See* allegory, four senses of
morning star, ALD 81
moth. *See* book moth
mouse, ALC 5, SYM 25
mouser, ALD 65. *See also* cat
mousetrap, BER 40
mouth or bone, BED 3, ALC D19, OER 4. *See also* bone(s)
moving pole, †EXE 56
mug. *See* beer mug
mule, ALC 2, SYM 37
music, BIB 5
musical instrument, †EXE 29
musical notes in manuscript, †EXE 55
mustard, †EXE 23, BER 26
mute swan, †EXE 5
myrrh, SYM 4

nail. *See* hobnail
natural science, BIB 2
nature, ALD 4, †EXE 38, †EXE 64, †EXE 72, †EXE 90. *See also* power: of Nature
need, OER 10, OIR 8
needle, TAT 11, SYM 55. *See also* embroidery needle
negligence, BON 11
nettle, ALD 46
neumes. *See* musical notes in manuscript
night, ALD 97, †EXE 9. *See also* day: and night
night raven, ALD 35
nightingale, ALD 22, EXE 6
no. *See* yes and no
Noah and dove, XMS Y1
nose, †EXE 68
nostrils, ALC D16
notes. *See* musical notes in manuscript
nothing, ALC D87
nut. *See* bad nut

oak, EXE 73, OER 25. *See also* ship: made of oak
obsidian, GES 16
ocean, EUS 23
ocean furrow, †EXE 8
Odin and Sleipnir, GES 35. *See also* god (pagan); Yggdrasill
old age. *See* age of man
old woman, ALC 4, ALC 5
olive tree, BER 14
omen, BED 5
one-eyed garlic seller, EXE 82, SYM 94
one-eyed man, TAT 20
onion, EXE 23, EXE 63, SYM 44, BER 51. *See also* leek
ore, †EXE 69, †EXE 79
organ, ALD 13, †EXE 82. *See also* portable organ
organistrum, †EXE 29, †EXE 67
ostrich, ALD 42, EUS 57
oven, †EXE 15. *See also* baker's boy and oven; baking oven; bread: and oven
oven rake, †EXE 60
overindulgence, BON 15
owl, †EXE 6. *See also* horned owl
owlet, EUS 58
ox, EXE 10, EXE 70; and its hide, †EXE 10; and its horns, †EXE 12. *See also* duck in an ox skull's jaws; yoke of oxen led by female slave
oxhide, †EXE 10
oyster, EXE 74, †EXE 75

pair of scales, ALD 23, BED 1, ABI, BER 53
pair of tongs, TAT 27
palm tree, ALD 91, BER 15
pane. *See* windowpane
panther, EUS 44
paper, †BER 50a
papyrus, BER 27
parchment, TAT 5, EUS 32, EXE 24, BER 24
parrot, EUS 59
party. *See* raiding party
paten, TAT 12, EXE 46
patience, BON 7
pattern-welded sword, †EXE 26
peace, BON 8
peacock, ALD 14. *See also* ring-tailed peacock
pearl, BER 44
pen, ALD 59, TAT 6, †EXE 71, †EXE 72; and fingers, †EXE 17. *See also* feather pen; quill pen; reed: pen; stylus
penis, †EXE 2, †EXE 9, †EXE 15, †EXE 16, †EXE 18, †EXE 19, †EXE 21, †EXE 23, †EXE 28, †EXE 32, †EXE 35, †EXE 42, †EXE 43, †EXE 48, †EXE 51, †EXE 52, †EXE 56, EXE 60, †EXE 76, †EXE 83, †EXE 85, †EXE 87
pepper, ALD 40, BER 37
pestle, SYM 87, BER 46
petrifaction, †EXE 66
pheasants. *See* ten pheasants
philosophy, TAT 1
phoenix, SYM 31
piebald serpent, EUS 47
pig, SYM 36. *See also* pregnant sow; sow and piglets; swine
piglet, GES 32
pike, †EXE 86
pillow, ALD 41, ALC D83
pipe, SYM 72. *See also* shepherd's pipe
piss, †EXE 73
Pleiades, ALD 8
plow, EXE 19
plow team, †EXE 2
pneuma. *See* Stoic conception of *pneuma*
poetry, GES 34
poker, †EXE 60
pole. *See* moving pole
pole lathe, EXE 54, †EXE 56
pond. *See* frozen pond
poplar, OER 18
poppy, SYM 40
porcupine, EXE 13
portable organ, †EXE 29
power, ALC 3; of Nature, †EXE 1. *See also* divine power
pregnant horse and two women, †EXE 34
pregnant sow, ALD 84, †EXE 34, GES 12. *See also* pig; sow and piglets
prepositions taking two cases, TAT 16
pride, TAT 25, BON 14. *See also* humility: and pride
priest, ALC 5
primordial matter, †EXE 38

prostitute, †EXE 91
psalter. *See* maggot and psalter
ptarmigans, GES 20

quill pen, ps-BED 11, EUS 35, LOR 9, †EXE 2, †EXE 49, †EXE 91, XMS X3; and fingers, EXE 29, EXE 49. *See also* pen
quiver, TAT 34, EXE 15

rack. *See* weapon rack
raiding party, †EXE 1.1–15 (taken as a separate riddle)
rain, ALC D44, †EXE 28, †EXE 55, †EXE 72, SYM 9, †BER 49, GES 10
rainbow, ALD 5
rake, EXE 32. *See also* oven rake
ram (animal), ALD 86, XMS P3
ram (siege engine). *See* battering ram
raven, ALD 63. *See also* night raven
rays of the sun, TAT 40
reed, EXE 58, SYM 2; flute, †EXE 6, †EXE 58; pen, †EXE 58
reflection in water, ALC D71
reliquary. *See* cross: reliquary
remora, EUS 54
revenant, †EXE 1, †EXE 2, †EXE 7, †EXE 37, †EXE 58, †EXE 63, †EXE 69, †EXE 71, †EXE 79
rhetoric, BIB 11
riddle or riddle book, †EXE 91
riding, OER 5, OIR 5
ring. *See* inscription ring on a chalice
ring with gem, SYM 3
ring-tailed peacock, †EXE 62. *See also* peacock
rite of passage, †EXE 20
river(s), EUS 34, ALC D49. *See also* fish: and river
robin, †EXE 6
roof tile, SYM 6
rooks, †EXE 55
rose, SYM 45, BER 34, BER 52
rose hip, †EXE 23
running water, †EXE 66
rye flute, †EXE 67

sacramental vessel, †EXE 46
sacrificial altar, †EXE 47
salamander, ALD 15
salt, ALD 19, BER 3
Samson's lion and bees, †EXE 15
sandy shore, ALC D62
savior, †EXE 73.1 (taken as a separate riddle). *See also* Christ
saw, SYM 60
scabbard, †EXE 53
scales. *See* pair of scales
scorpion, EUS 51
scribe's fingers, BED 18. *See also* fingers
scripture. *See* Bible
Scylla, ALD 95
sea, BED 15, ALC D48. *See also* Christ: walking on the sea; land and sea
sea-steed, EXE 62. *See also* ship
sedge. See elk sedge
senses. See five senses
serpent, ALD 88. *See also* piebald serpent; two-headed serpent; water serpent
servant. *See* butter-churning servant; horseman: with servant and hawk
sexual intercourse, †EXE 52
shadow, SYM 97, BER 61, XMS Z3
shawm (musical instrument), †EXE 67
sheath. *See* dagger sheath; sword: and sheath
sheep, BER 22
she-goat, SYM 35
shepherd's pipe, †EXE 67
shield, ALD 87, EXE 3, †EXE 53, GES 26. *See also* beechwood: shield; iron: shield
ship, BED 12, ALC D61, †EXE 17, †EXE 30, †EXE 62, †EXE 77, SYM 13, BER 11, GES 24, XMS Z2; made of oak, EXE 72. *See also* boat; horseman: with woman, dog, and ship; merchant ship
ship's figurehead, †EXE 72
shirt, EXE 59
shower, OIR 2
shuttle, †EXE 67
sickle, †EXE 87
sieve, ALD 67, BER 17
silkworm(s), ALD 12, BER 28, BER 43
singer. *See* wandering singer
siphon, BER 31
siren, †EXE 72
skep. *See* bee skep
sky, BER 60
slave, †EXE 70. *See also* yoke of oxen led by female slave
sleep, ALC D8, †EXE 25, SYM 99

Sleipnir. *See* Odin and Sleipnir
sling, ALD 74
sluice. *See* millpond and its sluice
smoke, SYM 7
snail, SYM 18
snow, ALC D54, LOR 6, †EXE 28, SYM 11, ps-SYM 4; and sun, XMS Z4; with hail and ice, TAT 15
soldier, ALC D86. *See also* gouty soldier
son of a stepson, XMS Z6
song thrush, †EXE 6
soul, †EXE 5, †EXE 7, †EXE 15, †EXE 91. *See also* body: and soul; damned souls; trial of the soul
sow and piglets, GES 32. *See also* pig; pregnant sow
sower, TAT 37
spark, ALD 93, †TAT 31, †BER 23
sparrow. *See* swallow(s): and sparrow
spear, †EXE 51, †EXE 60, †EXE 76; made of ash, EXE 71
speech, EUS 22, †EXE 37
sphere of the heavens, ALD 48
spiced wine, SYM 82
spider, SYM 17, GES 14
spindle, ALD 45
spirit, EUS 25, †EXE 63, †EXE 71, †EXE 79, †EXE 91
spleen, ALC D29
sponge, SYM 63, BER 32
spring (season), ALC D56
spring of water, ALD 73
spur, EXE 60
squid, ALD 16
squinting eyes, TAT 19
squirrel, TAT 17
stand. *See* sword stand
star(s), ALC D43, OER 16, BER 62. *See also* Arcturus; Charles's Wain; evening star; morning star
starlings, †EXE 55
steed. *See* sea-steed
stepfather, XMS Z5
steps, SYM 78
stepson. *See* son of a stepson
Stoic conception of *pneuma*, †EXE 1
stomach, ALC D30
stone, SYM 74. *See also* tombstone, whetstone
stool. *See* man: on a stool
stork, ALD 31, EUS 56
storm, †EXE 1; cloud(s), †EXE 55, BER 49. *See also* apocalyptic storm
strider. *See* water strider
strigil. *See* bronze strigil
stringed instrument, †EXE 26
stylus, SYM 1. *See also* pen
submarine earthquake, †EXE 1.16–104 (taken as a separate riddle)
summer, ALC D57
sun, ALC D41, EUS 10, †EXE 1.31–104 (taken as a separate riddle), EXE 4, †EXE 17, †EXE 28, †EXE 72, BER 55, BER 56, BER 57, OIR 11, GES 15. *See also* moon: and sun; rays of the sun; snow: and sun
swallow(s), ALD 47, †EXE 55; and sparrow, †EXE 27
swan(s), EXE 5, †EXE 55, †EXE 72, GES 17. *See also* female swan(s); mute swan; whooper swan
sweep. *See* well: sweep
swine, ALC 4. *See also* pig
sword, EUS 36, †EXE 2, †EXE 76; and sheath, TAT 30, †EXE 76.1 (taken as a separate riddle); or man, EXE 18, EXE 69. *See also* pattern-welded sword
sword stand, †EXE 53
sword-swallower, †EXE 18

table, TAT 29, BER 5
tablets. *See* writing: tablets
tapestry and loom, †EXE 54
team. *See* plow team
teeth, ALC D20
ten chickens, EXE 11
ten fingers (with gloves), †EXE 11
ten pheasants, †EXE 11
Tertullian. *See* Augustine and Tertullian
tetractys, †EXE 53
thorn, OER 3
thought, †EXE 91
threefold death, TAT 23
throat, ALC D22
thrush. *See* song thrush
tightrope walker, SYM 95
tigress, EUS 43, SYM 38
tile. *See* roof tile
time, †EXE 37
Tir, OER 17. *See also* god (pagan); Týr
tombstone, SYM 100

tongs. *See* pair of tongs
tongue, ALC D3
tooth. *See* teeth
torch, OER 6. *See also* lamp
torpedo fish, EUS 55
tortoise, †EXE 26, SYM 20
town, †EXE 15
trap. *See* mousetrap
treadle. *See* weaver's treadle
tree. *See* apple: tree; ash: tree; beech tree; birch; cedar tree; chestnut tree; dwarf elder tree; fig tree; olive tree; palm tree; poplar; yew: tree
trial of the soul, †EXE 26
trident, SYM 64
trumpet, ALD 68
truth, BON 1
turtledove, XMS P2
twelve chickens, †EXE 11
twins. *See* woman: bearing twins
two buckets, †EXE 50
two-headed serpent, EUS 49
Týr, OIR 12. *See also* god (pagan); Tir

ulcer, OIR 6
unicorn, ALD 60
unknown (no solution), XMS P1
Ursa Major, †EXE 20
us. *See* you: and us

vagina, †EXE 59. *See also* female genitalia
vainglory, BON 20
veins, ALC D37
venom, ALC 3
Venus. *See* abduction of Venus
vessel. *See* sacramental vessel
vine, SYM 53, BER 13
vinegar. *See* wine: turned to vinegar
violet, SYM 46, BER 33
viper, SYM 15
virginity, BON 10
virtues. *See* faith; four virtues; hope; Hope, Faith, Charity; humility; mercy; patience; peace
visor. *See* helmet: with visor

wagon, †EXE 30, †EXE 35. *See also* horse: and wagon; horseman: with wagon and hawk
wall, XMS P3
wallet. *See* book wallet
wandering singer, †EXE 91
warship. *See* light warship
watchdog, †EXE 2
water, ALD 29, ALC D50, LOR 3, †EXE 38, EXE 39, †EXE 64, †EXE 72, EXE 80, OER 21. *See also* fire and water; reflection in water; running water
water clock, SYM 70
water lily, †EXE 8
water serpent, EUS 41
water strider, ALD 38
water-dwelling creature, †EXE 75
waterfall, GES 7
waterfowl hunt, †EXE 34
waves, GES 21, GES 22, GES 23, GES 23a
wax, EUS 31, BER 19. *See also* writing: tablets
wealth, ALC D66, OER 1, OIR 1. *See also* money
weapon. *See* iron: weapon
weapon rack, EXE 53
weasel, ALD 82, †EXE 13
weathercock, EXE 77
weaver's treadle, BER 54
web and loom, †EXE 54, †EXE 86
weed. *See* kelp weed
weevil, SYM 24
weft. *See* heddle and weft
well, †EXE 54, †EXE 56, SYM 71; buckets, †EXE 50; sweep, EXE 56
whale, BED 17
wheel(s), †EXE 30, SYM 77. *See also* axle and wheel
wheelbarrow, †EXE 30
whetstone, ALD 27, TAT 39, †EXE 3
whip, †EXE 25, SYM 66
white-haired man, ALC 4
whooper swan, †EXE 72
wind, ALD 2, ps-BED 5, ALC D46, BER 41; and fire, EUS 8; and God, EXE 1. *See also* bird: and wind; cloud: and wind
windowpane, SYM 68
wine, †EXE 9, BER 50, ps-BER 1; cask, ALD 78, LOR 5; †EXE 26, XMS X4; cup, EXE 9; turned to vinegar, SYM 83. *See also* jug of wine; spiced wine
winnowing fork, TAT 36
winter, ALC D55, †EXE 66

wisdom, ps-BED 1, BIB 1, †EXE 39
wolf, †EXE 86, SYM 33
woman, †EXE 26; bearing twins, ALD 90, ps-BED 12, SYM 92. *See also* horseman; old woman; pregnant horse and two women
wooden cross, †EXE 28
woodpecker, †EXE 22. *See also* green woodpecker
word(s), ALC D2, SYM 96; of God, †EXE 91
worm(s). *See* bookworm; silkworm(s)
writing, †EXE 17, †EXE 45, †EXE 62, †EXE 71; tablets, ALD 32, XMS S3
-wulf. See man: called *-wulf*
yarrow. *See* milfoil
year, ALC D59, OIR 10
yes and no, ALC 6
yew: horn, †EXE 26; tree, ALD 69, †EXE 58, OER 13, OIR 16
Yggdrasill (horse of Odin), †EXE 88. *See also* gallows
yoke of oxen led by female slave, †EXE 50
you: and me, ALC 6; and us, ALC 6

Concordance of Parallels with Isidore's *Etymologiae*

See further Salvador-Bello, *Isidorean Perceptions*, esp. pp. 88–117 and 456.

Etymologiae	Riddles
1.2.1–3	BIB 10
1.3.4	ALF A.2
1.3.7	ALF Y.2–3
1.3.10	ALF B.3
1.4.4	ALF E.1
1.4.8	EUS 19, ALF Q.2
1.4.9	ALF L.2, ALF R.2
1.4.10	ALD 30
1.4.11	ALF H.1
1.4.12	ALF K.1
1.4.13	ALF Q.3
1.4.14	EUS 14
1.4.15	ALF 1.1
1.4.16	EUS 9, ALF A.1
1.4.17	ALF 1.1
1.9.1	ALC D2
1.15	ALC D1
1.17.1	ALD 84
1.19.9–11	ALF H.1
1.27.10	ALF H.3
1.27.11	ALF 1.1
1.27.14	ALF K.1
1.35.5	ALF M.1
1.40.4	EUS 52

Etymologiae	Riddles
2.22	BIB 12
2.23	BIB 11
2.24.3–4	BIB 2
2.24.5	BIB 7, BIB 8
2.24.7	BIB 9
2.24.14–15	BIB 3
2.24.15	BIB 4, BIB 5, BIB 6
3.21.13	ALC D74
3.47–52	ALC D41
3.53–57	ALC D42
3.60–71	ALC D43
3.71.1	ALC D41, ALC D42
3.71.6	ALD 53
3.71.13	ALD 8
3.71.23–32	ALC D59
4.11.4	BER 45
5.30.1	ALC D40
5.31.1–14	ALD 97
5.35.3	ALC D56
5.35.4	ALC D57
5.35.5	ALC D58
5.35.6	ALD 1, ALC D55

Etymologiae	Riddles
5.36.1	ALC D59
6.8.17	ALC D88
6.11.1	TAT 5
6.19.5	ALF O.1
7.2.25–26	BIB 1
7.3.18	ALC D69
7.3.22	ALD 64
7.8.34	ALC D8, ALC D69, ALC D72
8.2.5	ALC D68
8.2.6	ALC D69
8.9.93	ALD 89
8.11.27	ALD PR
8.11.93	ALD 45
9.2.40	ALD 12
9.5.23–24	ALD 28
10.L.163	ALF L.1
11.1.4	ALC D5, ALC D7
11.1.14	ALC D11
11.1.25	ALC D10
11.1.30	ALC D12
11.1.31	ALC D15
11.1.35	ALC D18
11.1.45	ALC D13
11.1.46	ALC D17
11.1.47	ALC D16
11.1.49	ALC D19
11.1.50	ALC D3
11.1.50	ALC D21
11.1.52	ALC D20
11.1.58 and 60	ALC D22
11.1.61	ALC D14
11.1.66	ALC D23
11.1.70	ALC D24
11.1.81	ALD 14
11.1.86	ALC D32

Etymologiae	Riddles
11.1.107	ALC D33
11.1.110	ALC D34
11.1.112	ALC D35
11.1.118	ALC D26
11.1.121	ALC D37
11.1.122	ALC D36
11.1.124	ALC D25
11.1.125	ALC D14, ALC D27
11.1.127	ALC D29
11.1.128	ALC D28, ALC D30
11.1.132	ALC D31
11.2.31	ALC D6
11.2.31–32	TAT 23
11.3.32	ALD 95
11.3.34–35	EUS 41
11.3.36	EUS 52
11.3.38	ALD 28
11.4.3	ALD 37
12.1.8	ALD 28
12.1.11	ALD 86
12.1.15	SYM 35
12.1.18	ALD 88
12.1.25	SYM 36
12.1.27	ALD 88
12.1.29	SYM 32
12.1.35	ALD 99
12.1.43	SYM 39
12.1.57	SYM 37
12.2.3–5	ALD 39
12.2.7	EUS 43, SYM 38
12.2.8–9	EUS 44
12.2.10–11	EUS 46
12.2.12–13	ALD 60
12.2.14	ALD 96
12.2.18–19	EUS 45
12.2.21	ALD 56
12.2.23	SYM 33
12.2.29	SYM 34
12.2.38	ALD 65

Etymologiae	Riddles
12.3.1	SYM 25
12.3.3	ALD 82
12.3.5	SYM 21
12.3.9	SYM 22
12.3.10	ALD 18
12.4.4	EUS 42
12.4.11	SYM 15
12.4.19	EUS 47
12.4.20	EUS 49
12.4.24	EUS 41
12.4.36	ALD 15
12.4.37	EUS 50
12.5.1	SYM 17
12.5.3	ALD 43
12.5.4	EUS 51
12.5.8	ALD 12
12.5.14	ALC D77, SYM 30
12.6.1	EUS 39
12.6.7	ALD 100
12.6.21	EUS 53
12.6.34	EUS 54
12.6.45	EUS 55
12.6.47	ALD 16
12.6.48	BER 47
12.6.48–50	SYM 18
12.6.50	ALD 17
12.6.51–52	ALD 37
12.6.56	SYM 20
12.6.57	SYM 29
12.6.58	SYM 19
12.7.5	ALC D78
12.7.15	SYM 26
12.7.16	ALD 31
12.7.16–17	EUS 56
12.7.20	ALD 42, EUS 57
12.7.24	EUS 59, SYM 31
12.7.36	SYM 28
12.7.39	EUS 60
12.7.39–42	ALD 35
12.7.40	EUS 58
12.7.41	ALD 35

Etymologiae	Riddles
12.7.42	EUS 60
12.7.43	ALD 63
12.7.46	EXE 22
12.7.80	ALC D78
12.8.1	ALD 20, BED 7
12.8.11	SYM 23
12.8.14	ALD 36
12.8.17	SYM 24
13.2.1–4	ALD 100
13.4.1	ALC D38
13.5.6	ALD 4
13.6.1–7	ALD 100
13.7.1	ALC D4
13.10.1	ALD 5
13.10.2	ALC D44
13.10.3	BER 49
13.10.6	ALC D54
13.10.7	ALC D53
13.10.8	TAT 35
13.10.10	ALC D45
13.10.14	ALC D39
13.11.1	ALC D46
13.12.1	ALC D50
13.14.1	ALC D48
13.21.1	ALC D49
14.1.1	ALD 1
14.1.1	ALC D47
14.6.14	ALD 25
14.8.11	ALD PR
15.1.30	ALF K.3
15.1.31	ALD 36
15.2.37	ALD 92
15.4.13–14	TAT 8
16.2.3	BER 3
16.3.1	ALC D75
16.3.6	ALD 27, TAT 39
16.3.11	ALD 88, ALC D62

Etymologiae	Riddles
16.4.1	ALD 25
16.5.19	SYM 49
16.13.2–3	ALD 9
16.13.3	ALD 25
16.14.7	ALD 24
16.25.4	ALD 23
17.5.2	SYM 53
17.5.10	ALD 78
17.5.13–14	ALD 78
17.7.1	ALD 91
17.7.17	ALD 77
17.7.25	LOR 7
17.7.26–47	ALD 84
17.7.28	ALD 100
17.7.65	BER 14
17.8.3	SYM 47
17.8.4	SYM 48
17.8.8	ALD 40
17.9.17	SYM 45
17.9.19	SYM 46
17.9.24	ALD 98
17.9.31	SYM 40
17.9.36	ALD 4
17.9.37	ALD 51
17.9.44	ALD 46
17.9.104	ALC D63
17.9.106	SYM 50
17.10	ALC D64
17.10.5	SYM 41
17.10.12	SYM 44
17.10.15	SYM 42
17.10.16	SYM 43
18.4.5	ALD 13, ALD 96
18.6.6	ALD 61
18.8	ALC D85
18.11.1–4	ALD 86
18.12.1–6	ALD 70
18.13.1–2	ALD 33
18.69.2	SYM 59
19.1.5	ALC D61
19.2.15	SYM 61
19.3.3	ALF C.2
19.6.3–5	TAT 33
19.6.5	ALC D51
19.6.7	TAT 38
19.19.9	SYM 60
19.20.3	ALD 41, ALC D83
19.26.1	ALD 45
19.31.2	BER 49
19.31.9	SYM 55
19.34.12	SYM 56
20.2.18	SYM 52
20.8.3–4	ALD 49, ALC D76
20.8.4	ALD 50
20.8.6	SYM 51, BER 9
20.10.2	BER 2
20.10.7	SYM 67
20.12.1	ALF O.2
20.13.5	ALD 100
20.14.4–5	ALF L.3

General Index

Abingdon, 300–1
Acca of Hexham, 174, 186
acrostics, 9–11, 133–37, 163, 167, 172, 174, 230, 234–37, 239, 240–42, 244–45, 249, 251, 253–56, 606
Adam, 157–58, 184, 232, 288, 417, 506
Adonis, 545
Aediluulf, *De abbatibus*, 58, 98
Ægir, 643
Ælfric of Canterbury, 300
Ælfric of Eynsham, 207, 300, 463; *De temporibus anni*, 374, 386; *Grammar*, 413
Ælfwine of Winchester, 505–7
Aeneas, 52, 513
Aeolus, 329, 338, 595
Aesop, *Fables*, 45
Æthelbald of Mercia, 131
Æthelstan, King, 127
Æthelwold of Winchester, 467, 480; Abbot of Abingdon, 300–1
Alcuin of York, 14, 25, 32, 46, 52, 67, 76, 257, 259–62, 264–65, 284, 400, 490, 569, 614, 619, 652–53
Aldfrith of Northumbria, 2, 318
Aldhelm of Malmesbury, 1–3, 5–7, 9–30, 33–37, 39, 41–53, 55–58, 60–70, 72, 74–86, 88–92, 94–112, 114–15, 117, 134–42, 150, 153–54, 160–61, 164, 166–67, 171–72, 177, 179–80, 183, 191, 203, 205–6, 225, 230–56, 296, 318, 327, 330–31, 338–41, 354, 358, 365, 393, 397, 406, 416, 420, 422, 434, 444, 463, 470, 509–10, 528, 563, 572, 582, 585, 608; *Carmen de virginitate*, 2, 12–15, 21, 24–25, 27, 29, 33, 35–36, 37, 39, 41, 43–47, 49, 51–53, 55–58, 63–67, 69–70, 72, 75, 77–86, 88–92, 94–95, 97–102, 104–12, 117, 137, 142, 150, 154, 160–61, 164, 166–67, 171, 179–80, 191, 203, 205–6, 233–56, 296, 528, 582; *Carmina ecclesiastica*, 2, 12, 14, 22, 24, 35, 44–45, 49, 52, 55, 65, 70, 79, 81–84, 86, 88, 90, 95, 97, 99, 100, 102, 104–5, 107–8, 233, 235, 238, 240, 242, 244, 247–48, 254, 420; *Carmen rhythmicum*, 16, 237, 330, 338–41; *De metris*, 2–3, 6, 11, 138, 290, 510, 563, 572; *De pedum regulis*, 2–3, 6, 10–11, 90, 290, 510; *Epistola ad Acircium*, 2, 11, 20, 318; prose *De virginitate*, 25, 95, 96, 365; *Prose Preface to the Aenigmata*, 3, 6, 8
Alexander the Great, 323, 595
Alfred Jewel, 316
alliteration, 19, 23, 42, 63, 69, 76, 78, 91–92, 100, 110, 112, 125, 153, 158, 162, 164, 166, 180, 196, 202, 208, 212–14, 216, 222, 229, 233, 243–44, 254, 293, 295, 297, 300, 340, 343, 346, 357, 375, 385, 390, 419, 428, 442, 451, 460, 473, 475, 483, 485, 520, 539, 543–44, 549, 550, 555–56, 561, 640
Altercatio Hadriani Augusti et Epicteti philosophi, 260
Alvíss, 394
Alvíssmál, 394, 631
Amalthea, 538
Ambrose, *De fide*, 206
anacoluthon, 176, 181
anaphora, 320, 324, 336–37, 355, 359, 374–75, 378, 397–98, 405, 436, 485, 547

Andreas (*And*), 50, 326, 337, 339–40, 344, 357, 360, 372, 375, 377, 382, 388, 394–96, 401, 407, 410, 430, 432, 444–45, 455, 457, 463, 471–72, 474, 497
Anglian, 317–18, 498
Anglo-Saxon Chronicle, 132, 368, 500
Anthologia Latina, 517
Antiochus, 510
antiphons, 263, 519, 619
aphaeresis, 517
Aphrodite, 563
Apocalypse, 207, 609. *See also* Revelation
Apollo, 84, 619
Apollonius of Tyre, 507, 510–11, 514, 632, 654–55
Appendix Vergiliana, 105
Arator, *Ad Parthenium*, 296; *De actibus apostolorum*, 45, 55, 64, 70, 74, 80, 95, 98, 101, 106
Arcturus, 62, 374
Aristotle, 3, 313, 323
Arius, 190–91
Asculum, 532
Asia, Asia Minor, 223, 492, 536
assonance, 92, 147, 347
Athena, Pallas, 511, 527, 563
Atli, 394
Augustine of Hippo, 185; *Confessiones*, 157; *De civitate Dei*, 21, 25
Augustus, Emperor, 186–88
Aulus Gellius, 516
Ausonius, 515–17; *Griphus ternarii numeri*, 513
Auzon Casket. *See* Franks Casket
Avianus, *Fabulae*, 45

b- for -*f*-/*v*- spellings, 37, 71–72, 167, 203, 227, 233
Bacchus, 595
Baldrs draumar, 631
Battle of Vesuvius, 532
Battle of Brunanburh (Brun), 343
Beaduhild, 315
Bede, 51, 66–67, 79, 96–97, 110–111, 113–17, 121–22, 128–32, 134, 172, 174, 185–86, 195–97, 223, 257, 262, 297, 350, 510, 516; *De arte metrica*, 117, 121, 176, 178, 185, 196, 203–4, 308; *De die iudicii*, 15, 85, 111; *De scematibus et tropis*, 165, 190, 199; *De temporum ratione*, 173–74, 183, 185, 193, 569; *Explanatio Apocalypsis*, 172; *Expositio Actuum Apostolorum*, 173; *Historia abbatum*, 173; *Historia ecclesiastica*, 131; *In primam partem Samuhelis*, 173; *Vita S. Cudbercti*, 13, 15, 66–67, 79, 97, 223, 297
Behemoth, 11–12, 318
Bellerophon, 217–18
Benedict Biscop, 113
Beowulf, 96, 117, 316, 339–40, 344–45, 360, 362–63, 375, 380, 382, 390–92, 394–96, 401–2, 410, 440, 448–50, 453, 455–57, 459, 472, 477–78, 482, 488, 493, 499–500
Bible, 3, 418, 607
Bible, New Testament:
  1 Corinthians, 169, 180
  1 Timothy, 249
  2 Peter, 86
  Acts, 174
  John, 17, 94, 113, 168–69, 190, 199, 384, 582, 609
  Luke, 159, 168, 196, 240, 340, 418
  Mark, 156
  Matthew, 82, 152, 156, 159, 168, 204, 247, 329, 418, 616
Bible, Old Testament:
  1 Kings, 82
  1 Samuel, 79
  Baruch, 418
  Deuteronomy, 159
  Ecclesiasticus, 140
  Genesis, 12, 19, 38, 69, 71, 73, 82, 92, 106, 262, 417, 469
  Isaiah, 86, 145, 418
  Job, 11–12, 20, 53, 159, 418
  Psalms, 13–14, 45–46, 159, 177, 185, 189, 198, 319, 409, 234, 505
  Song of Songs, 293
"biter bitten" motif, 77, 125, 139, 146, 158, 542, 593–95
"black on white" motif, 67, 142–43, 182, 199–201, 299, 425, 434, 587
body-part riddles, 31, 54, 89, 100, 149, 211, 258, 268, 323, 333, 405, 435–36, 467, 474, 647
Boniface, 18, 33, 74, 134, 171, 173, 230–34, 236–39, 242, 246, 251–54, 256, 290
Brandon antler, 317
Branwen Ferch Lŷr, 155
Breedon-on-the-Hill, 131
Brussels Reliquary Cross, 316

Caelius Sedulius, *Carmen paschale*, 13, 19, 41, 51–53, 62–64, 66, 72–74, 76, 79, 82–83, 86, 95, 100–1, 104, 107–8, 111, 117, 191, 223, 296, 510
Caesar, 145–46, 226, 492, 564, 614
caesura, 10–11, 96, 145, 152, 178, 187, 212, 308, 512, 549
Camillus, 7, 104
Cancer, 7, 10, 27, 47, 463
Candidus, 490
Canterbury, 1, 56, 131, 134, 150, 264, 300, 303, 502
Carian fruit, 82
Carmen Flavii Felicis, 90
Cassian, 160
Castalian nymphs, 11
Cato, Marcius Porcus, the Elder (or Cato the Younger?), 512, 564
Ceadwalla of Wessex, 1
Celtic, 365, 612
Centwine of Wessex, 1
Ceolfrith, 173
Ceres, 511
challenge, 6, 112, 167, 255, 259, 261–62, 264, 320, 329, 333, 336, 338, 342, 349, 352, 355, 360, 364, 369, 377, 383–85, 391–92, 397–98, 401, 404, 406–7, 412, 427, 443, 448, 450, 458, 465, 470, 475, 631–32, 648, 650
Charles's Wain, 62, 326, 354, 373, 386
Charybdis, 99
charms, 420, 506
Chaucer, *House of Fame*, 409
chiasmus, 67, 185, 194–95, 518, 538, 558
Chimera, 217–18
China, 42
Christ, 17, 19, 50, 66, 148, 186, 187, 189, 191, 205, 258, 265, 288, 304, 315, 317, 329, 333–34, 347, 426, 429, 432, 437, 450, 472, 583, 627
Christ A (ChristA), 333, 335, 411–12, 471
Christ C (ChristC), 50, 337, 339–40, 347, 382, 415, 432, 450, 471, 472
Christ and Satan (XSt), 449
Christological, 67, 83, 134, 205, 207, 304, 579, 582, 584
Cilicia, 218, 512
Cinyras, 545
Circe, 50
Ciris, 83, 105
classical, 11, 19–20, 62, 77, 84, 139, 217–18, 229, 244, 329, 501, 511, 513–14, 519, 521, 538, 557, 561, 595
Claudian, *Epithalamium Laurentii*, 51, 107; *In Rufinum*, 70
colophon, 145, 424
Colossus, 78
companion piece, 236, 239, 355
compounds, poetic, 5–6, 23, 26, 115, 135, 176, 230, 291, 294, 316, 333, 335, 337–39, 343–45, 347, 349–51, 353, 355–56, 358–59, 361–63, 365–67, 369–72, 374, 377–78, 380, 382–83, 385–86, 388, 390, 392–97, 400, 402–4, 407, 412–17, 419–20, 422–24, 426–28, 430, 432, 434, 436–37, 439–42, 444, 446–49, 451–55, 457, 459, 461–63, 465, 467–70, 472–74, 476–77, 479, 482–83, 485, 487–88, 494, 503–4, 506–7, 512, 528, 550, 567, 574–75, 648
computus, 173–74, 195, 197, 506
consonant clusters, 235, 238, 242–43, 245, 247, 250
Continent, 230, 399, 574
Corippus, 12, 39, 81, 104–6
Cornwall, 330
Coronation of Edgar (CEdg), 405
Cos, 171
Crediton, 230
Creed, 653
Crete, 38, 225, 538
Cross, 148, 317, 387, 429–30, 438
cross references
ABI, 116
ALC, 15–16, 52, 59, 62, 71–72, 89, 103, 123, 128, 130, 136, 143, 165, 179, 201, 253, 255, 257–89, 303, 325, 359, 434, 502, 523, 525, 535, 550, 553, 559, 569, 571, 579, 638, 642, 645, 651
ALD, 2–95, 97–116, 119, 125–26, 128–31, 133–35, 138–56, 159–60, 162–67, 171–72, 174, 176–77, 180–90, 192–93, 196, 198–206, 208–9, 211–14, 216, 218–25, 227, 233–57, 260, 262–63, 265, 275–78, 284–85, 288, 290–95, 297–304, 307, 309, 311, 313, 317–21, 325, 330–32, 337, 341, 344, 345, 351, 354, 356, 358–60, 365, 374, 381, 388, 393, 395, 397–400, 403–4, 406–12, 419, 422–25, 434, 444, 446, 448, 453, 455, 463, 467, 470, 502–5, 509–10,

512, 515, 519, 521, 522, 523, 525, 527–28, 531–34, 536–40, 542–43, 546, 549–50, 553–54, 557–59, 565, 568, 569, 571–74, 576, 578, 583, 585–91, 594–95, 597, 599–600, 602–4, 606–9, 613, 618, 622–24, 633–34, 637–40, 642, 644–45, 648–52

ALF, 4, 40, 43, 45, 58, 60, 65, 72, 85, 114, 119, 147–48, 151, 183, 201, 204, 219, 303, 309, 321, 332, 490, 524, 533–34, 546, 563, 581, 605, 607–24

BED, 13–15, 18–19, 40, 59, 71, 80, 89, 114–26, 128–31, 136–37, 140, 149, 165, 173, 188, 203, 233, 257, 260–62, 270, 273, 277, 279, 281, 285, 289, 297, 299–300, 321–22, 325, 350, 356–57, 502–3, 505, 572, 577, 590, 601, 603, 633, 638, 651–52

BER, 15, 19, 22, 24, 29–30, 40, 43, 54, 62, 67, 73, 85, 93–94, 98, 107, 111, 116, 121, 129, 136, 144–47, 154, 163, 169, 178, 184–85, 188, 199, 203, 217, 225, 245–46, 254, 264, 266, 275–77, 279, 281, 286, 292–94, 296, 297, 300, 303–4, 307, 311, 326, 345, 422–23, 475–76, 480, 507, 524–25, 536, 539, 543, 564–65, 568, 571, 574–606, 619, 634, 636, 638–39, 642

BIB, 12, 30, 33, 43, 65, 67, 90, 94, 102, 114, 128, 137–38, 151, 235–36, 248, 249, 296, 302–13, 321, 568, 585, 603, 614

BON, 4–6, 12–16, 18, 20, 22, 29–31, 33–34, 37, 41, 43, 49, 52, 54–55, 59, 63–67, 69–70, 72–77, 79, 81–82, 84–86, 89, 91, 93, 95, 98, 100–3, 105, 107–10, 121, 123, 139, 143, 148, 152, 159, 172, 176, 195, 204, 209, 230–57, 261, 265, 282, 291, 293, 295, 298, 300, 303–4, 307, 309, 311, 318, 326, 357, 502, 512, 519, 549, 568, 574, 599, 606, 613–14, 648

EUS, 5–6, 10, 13, 19, 23, 26–27, 29, 31, 35–37, 39, 41, 45, 48, 50, 53–54, 59–60, 65–67, 69, 71–72, 74, 77–78, 88–89, 92, 94–95, 97, 100, 102, 105, 112, 114, 119–21, 132–36, 139, 143–44, 147–49, 156, 159, 161, 163–64, 166, 169, 172–227, 229, 236, 252, 255, 257, 262–63, 266–67, 275–78, 293, 297–99, 302, 318, 321, 325, 329–30, 345, 354, 356, 358–59, 403, 425, 433, 440, 449, 455, 459, 470, 485–86, 488, 501–2, 512, 518–19, 524, 527, 540, 557, 559, 587, 589, 593, 595, 603, 622–23, 639, 645, 651

EXE, 5, 15, 17, 19, 22–23, 27, 30–32, 36, 38, 40, 42, 48–49, 55–56, 62, 67, 85, 87, 89, 92, 104–11, 118–19, 123, 128–30, 132, 134, 136, 138–39, 143–44, 147–49, 163, 167, 175, 178–79, 186, 189, 192, 194–95, 198–200, 203, 222, 229, 233, 261, 263, 265–66, 275–79, 284–85, 287, 294, 296, 300, 316–489, 496–97, 500–1, 503–5, 507, 509, 511, 514, 518, 523–24, 526, 529, 534, 548, 550–51, 557, 568, 573, 579, 586–89, 595, 598, 602, 606, 633–34, 636–37, 639–41, 643–45, 649, 651–54

FRA, 125, 315–16, 318, 376

GES, 85, 89, 189, 264, 275–76, 278, 284, 289, 326, 344, 352, 357, 394, 447, 502–4, 606, 624–25, 631–47

LEI, 9, 37, 42, 71–72, 107, 167, 203, 227, 233, 316–19, 397–98, 537

LOR, 4, 6, 16, 19, 20, 25, 32, 37, 39, 43, 53–55, 58, 67, 71, 85, 89, 102, 110, 119, 128–29, 139, 143, 150, 152, 160, 163–64, 166, 171, 178, 180, 194, 199, 201, 203, 218, 234, 247, 249, 252, 267, 272, 278–79, 290–300, 434, 573, 576, 578, 591, 595, 598, 600, 634, 651–52

OEP, 502, 505–6, 511, 603

OER, 229, 303, 332, 393, 454, 457, 459, 461, 464, 489–501, 572, 607, 623–26

OIR, 303, 489–499, 607, 624–30, 642

ONR, 489–91, 493–95, 607, 625–30

SOL, 15, 17, 264, 275, 345, 484, 501–5, 507, 578, 592, 602–4, 639, 642, 654

SYM, 4–7, 9, 15–16, 19, 22–23, 32, 38–40, 42–45, 47, 55–56, 58–61, 63, 66–67, 69, 71–72, 74, 78, 80, 83, 85–86, 89, 94, 98, 101–2, 104–5, 107, 112–14, 123, 128–29, 133–36, 143, 146–49, 151–52, 154, 156, 162, 164–65, 174, 177–79, 194, 200, 203, 205, 209, 214, 223, 229, 234, 242, 249–50, 256, 260, 264, 267–68,

276, 279, 281–82, 285–87, 289–90, 292–93, 296–97, 303–4, 307–8, 318, 321, 326, 328, 344, 352, 354, 361, 363, 374, 379, 393–95, 400, 402, 417–18, 436, 439, 447, 469, 473–74, 481, 501, 507, 509–15, 517–75, 579, 581–82, 584, 587–91, 593–95, 597, 599, 603, 605, 607, 611, 615, 619, 622, 623–24, 632, 634–39, 642, 644, 651, 654
TAT, 5–6, 14–16, 19, 22, 24, 28, 36–37, 39–41, 43, 46–47, 51, 54–55, 58–60, 67, 69, 71–72, 74–75, 78, 80, 85, 89, 91, 93, 98, 100–3, 105, 107–12, 114, 116, 123, 131–72, 174–78, 180, 184–85, 187–89, 192, 195, 199, 201–3, 207, 217, 225, 227, 234–35, 237, 240, 244, 249–50, 252–53, 256–57, 262–63, 266, 269, 278, 282, 284–85, 288–89, 292, 294–95, 298, 301–2, 304, 306–7, 318, 321, 325, 328, 345, 381, 424, 433, 502, 519, 525, 533, 539, 541, 543, 546, 564, 576, 586–87, 595, 603, 606, 622, 638, 644–46, 652
XMS, 29, 72–73, 91, 112, 128, 130, 255, 295, 300, 505, 648–54
Cynewulf, 10, 247, 321, 334, 368, 479, 487; *Christ B (ChristB)*, 336, 396, 401, 445, 448–49, 471, 482; *Elene*, 337, 353, 384, 389, 392, 401, 405, 438, 455, 471, 498–99; *Fates of the Apostles*, 456, 482, 494; *Juliana (Jul)*, 247, 353, 384, 408, 414, 430, 448, 482, 494
Cynthia, 84, 511, 521
Cynthus, 11
Cyprianus Gallus, 12, 14, 38, 69, 75, 78, 80, 83, 88, 94, 97, 99, 101, 106, 112

dactylic, 50, 152, 154–55
Dagr, 394, 637
Damasus, Pope, 610; *Epigrammata* 84
Damoetas, 261
Daniel (Dan), 396, 401, 471, 497
Darraðarljóð, 431
David, 10–11, 14, 79, 234, 519
Death of Edgar (DEdg), 459
Dellingr, 633, 637
Delphic, 619
Deor, 355, 456
Deucalion, 512
direct quotations, 19, 65, 72, 103, 395, 403
Disputatio Hadriani cum Secundo philosopho, 260
Domberht, 290
Doomsday, 124, 334
double entendre, 119, 163, 322–23, 355, 372, 379–80, 416, 426, 428, 441–44, 447, 467, 475, 479, 481, 483, 577, 592, 598, 646
double sense of individual words, 18, 74, 86, 97, 103, 241, 244, 250, 359, 644
double solution, 175, 182, 214, 300–1
Dracontius, *De laude Dei*, 74, 81, 83
dragons, 34, 206–8, 210, 218, 424
Drahmal, 316
Dream of the Rood (Dream), 148, 316–17, 388, 442, 477
drinking formulas, 323, 360, 371, 430, 432, 444, 450, 465, 474
Dunstan of Canterbury, 160, 502

earth/sea/sky, 58, 205, 329, 503
East, 34, 323, 499, 536
Easter, 197, 387
Eastern Church, 150
Ecgburg, 252
Echo, 49, 109, 571
eddic verse, 259, 394, 631, 637
Eden, 158, 262
Egypt, Egyptians, 42, 44–46, 251
elegiac couplets, 265, 303
Elijah, 288
elision, 5, 11, 115, 135, 139, 146–48, 152, 160, 163, 166–67, 172, 176, 178, 187, 199, 201, 204, 227, 233, 237, 246, 512, 517, 547, 555, 557, 564, 608, 618
end-stopped verse, 5, 115, 176, 624
enjambment, 176, 185, 203, 224
Enoch, 12, 288
enumerative pattern, 89, 94, 401, 467, 474, 480
envelope pattern, 20, 258, 292, 334, 355–56, 372, 405, 418, 420, 422, 437
Epictetus, 260
Ethiopia, 211
etymological, etymology, 7–8, 17, 19–20, 28, 30, 38, 41, 44, 48, 60–61, 68, 75, 81, 84, 88, 158, 209, 213, 217, 308, 476, 504, 531–532, 547, 552, 584, 603
Europe, 492, 498

Eusebius, 136, 139, 172–77, 179, 181–83, 186, 194, 196, 206, 213, 223, 226–27, 229, 354, 358, 403, 449, 470, 477, 485
Eve, 158, 417, 505, 506, 579–80, 613
Exeter, 20, 30, 46, 60, 62, 66, 80, 85, 105, 372, 383, 387–89, 397, 401, 409, 427, 520–21, 523, 525, 532, 542, 557, 561, 568, 585, 606
Exeter Book, 36, 101, 138–39, 144, 210, 229, 321–22, 326–28, 333, 342–43, 346–55, 358, 360–61, 364–65, 367–70, 373–74, 376, 378–79, 381, 386, 388, 396, 402–4, 406–7, 411–13, 415–18, 421, 423–26, 428–29, 433–36, 438–39, 441, 443, 446–50, 452–56, 458–59, 462, 464, 466, 469–71, 473–75, 477–81, 483–85, 487–88, 584, 592
Exeter Cathedral, 321
Exodus, 12, 14, 44, 46, 75, 83, 97, 112, 147, 151, 388, 401, 449, 477, 494
Expositio Actuum Apostolorum, 173
eye-skip, 98, 473, 614

Fabulae, 45
Faeroes, 640
Fall of Man, 92, 158
false quantity, 18, 29, 35, 38, 40, 47, 55, 61–62, 66, 84, 91, 100, 104, 109, 135, 139, 145, 157, 159, 163, 169–70, 172, 181–84, 189, 191–93, 196–200, 203, 207–10, 212–14, 218–19, 224, 229, 232–35, 241, 245–46, 249–50, 252, 254, 293, 296, 526, 528, 565, 610–12, 614, 617–18, 623
Finland, 640
first recension of ALD, 3–4, 9, 18, 23, 25, 32, 38, 29, 40, 53, 55, 61–63, 66, 69, 80, 83, 87, 100, 109
five senses, 134, 161
Flood, 71, 73, 331–32
formula, 336, 343–44, 351, 357, 359–60, 362, 365, 367, 371, 375, 377–78, 380, 383–88, 391–92, 396, 398, 400–4, 406, 412, 414–16, 420, 422, 432, 436, 440, 442, 447–52, 454, 456, 459, 461, 465, 467–68, 471, 473, 479, 483, 488, 493, 504–5, 521–22, 539, 558, 572, 624, 633–34, 636–37, 651
formulaic, 5, 259, 303, 320, 324, 331, 336, 338, 342, 349, 352, 355, 357, 360, 364, 369, 377, 383–84, 390, 392, 401, 406, 413, 424, 427, 430, 437, 441, 443, 446, 448, 458, 465, 470, 472, 475–76, 490, 534, 608, 631
fornyrðislag, 632
France, 230
Franks Casket, 315, 317
Frithegod, *Breviloquium S. Wilfridi*, 15, 21, 61, 74, 84, 106
Fulgentius, 117

Gallican Psalter, 506
Ganymede, 65
Genesis A (GenA), 353, 355, 362, 371, 382, 387, 396, 405, 417, 430, 432, 437, 448, 456, 471
Germanic, 293, 315, 328, 490, 492, 494, 498
Gestr, 631. *See also* Óðinn
Gestumblindi, 502, 630–31, 645, 647
Glastonbury, 502
glossaries, 48, 107, 142, 180
glosses, 5, 8, 12, 15, 17, 20–28, 30–36, 38–39, 45–49, 51–53, 55–60, 62–65, 68–70, 78, 81, 83, 87, 92–93, 95–96, 99, 103–4, 109–12, 114, 116–27, 137–42, 144–45, 147–69, 172, 178–82, 184–200, 202, 206–9, 211, 217, 219, 221–24, 227, 229, 233–41, 243–57, 263, 300, 340, 349, 399–400, 402, 453, 456, 498
God, 10–11, 15, 119, 138, 156, 177, 180, 186, 191–92, 292, 324–27, 329–31, 333, 346, 448, 457, 466, 479–80, 487, 506, 609
golden line, 23, 167, 243, 294–95
Goliath, 79
Gospel, 144, 323, 325, 381, 423–25, 440, 449–50, 484, 486, 488, 587, 610, 616
Gothic, 316, 490–91, 493–500
Gradus, Latin, 10, 624, 640, 642
grammarian, 117, 131, 133, 142, 146, 154, 162
grammatical gender, 24, 143, 164, 168, 228
grammatically, 15, 39, 162, 263, 293, 317, 416, 539, 575–76, 582, 585, 590, 652
Grateley, 127
Great Bear, 373
Greece, 29, 43
Greek, Greeks, 1, 3, 5, 7, 13, 21, 28–29, 32, 44, 59–60, 68, 70, 74, 87, 92, 168, 171, 178, 183, 191, 206, 208–9, 217, 224, 226, 259, 263, 288, 297, 305–6, 311–12,

323, 356, 509, 512, 529, 542, 563, 607, 609–11, 617, 619, 623
Greenland, 640
Gregory I, the Great, Pope, 28, 614
Gregory II, Pope, 230
Grendel, 493
greppaminni, 632
Grímnismál, 631
Guthlac A (GuthA), 344, 347, 388, 448, 450
Guthlac B (GuthB), 349, 377, 388, 392, 414–15, 423, 440, 445, 488

Hades, 77
Hadrian, Abbot, 2
Hadrian, Emperor, 260
Hamartigenia, 44, 106
hanging nominative, 176, 181
haplography, 122, 358, 400
Haukr Erlendsson, Lawspeaker, 631
Hauksbók, 631
Hávamál, 629, 637
Heahfrith, 69
Hebrew, 3, 10, 288, 506, 607, 609, 614
Heiðrekr, 502, 630–32, 635, 645
Helgakviða Hjǫrvarðssonar, 394
Hell, 293, 396
Hera, 563
Hercules, 206–7, 217, 595
Hervarar saga ok Heiðreks konungs ins vitra, 630
Hervǫr, 630
Herwagen, 113, 510
Hexham, 174, 186
hiatus, 11, 40, 53, 55, 183, 213, 231, 233, 237, 241, 243, 246–47, 249–50
Hiberno-Latin, 332
"high/low" motif, 139, 177–78, 195
Hisperica famina, 15, 26, 41, 54, 93, 124, 129, 165, 200, 202, 277–78, 284, 331, 423, 594, 605, 608, 645, 650
Historia Apollonii Regis Tyri, 510, 518, 523–24, 550–52, 555, 560, 566
Historia ecclesie Abbendonensis, 301
hnefa-tafl, 641
holy scripture, 144, 381
homoeoteleuton, 187, 473
homographs, 262, 422, 494
Horace, 513; *Carmina*, 525; *Epistolae*, 653; *Sermones*, 111, 117, 515, 542
Hrímgerd, Hrímgerðr, 394
Hronesness, 453
Husband's Message, 438–39, 441
Hwætberht, 133, 172–74, 185, 193, 195
hyperbaton, 236
Hydra, 205–7, 217, 252

"I saw" motif, 123, 131, 245, 296, 324, 461, 480–81, 633–34, 643, 645, 651
Iceland, Icelandic, 393, 431, 491, 609, 624, 630–32, 639–40, 642
ictus, 235, 238, 242–43, 245, 247, 250
incest, 417, 505, 507, 510–11, 603, 654
India, 226, 536
Indian Ocean, 221
interpolation, 175, 178, 245,369, 377, 399–400, 456, 460, 512, 654
Irish, 1, 155, 365, 502–3, 574, 610
Isidore of Seville, 3, 138, 303, 463, 574; *De natura rerum*, 62, 374; *Etymologiae (Etym.)*, 8–9, 12, 15, 17, 20–21, 23–28, 30, 33–35, 37–40, 42, 45–51, 53, 56–60, 62, 65, 68, 70–73, 77, 82–83, 87, 89–94, 97, 99–100, 102, 104–105, 110–112, 143, 146, 158, 165, 168, 170–71, 175–76, 183, 187–88, 191, 201, 205–7, 209–13, 215–22, 224–29, 258, 266–86, 288–89, 297, 302, 304–6, 308–13, 361, 378, 514, 525–548, 550–51, 554, 558, 564, 576, 580, 583, 597–99, 602, 608–11, 613–21, 623; *Liber numerorum*, 138
Italy, 574

Jerome, 137, 506
Jerusalem, 504
John Barleycorn, 384
John the Baptist, 168
Jorvík Museum, 347
Judices, 75, 78, 83, 88
Judith (Jud), 117, 450
Judgement Day I (JDayI), 449, 497
Julian calendar, 195
Julius Caesar, 564; *De bello Gallico*, 492
Juno, 563
Jupiter, 512–13, 626
Juvenal, 514
Juvencus, *Evangelia*, 14, 22, 28, 30, 35, 39, 45, 52, 58, 65, 66–67, 70, 73–75, 77–78, 82, 84, 88, 93, 95, 97–99, 101, 105–106, 110–11, 221, 223, 254, 294
juxtaposition, 157–58, 166, 381, 385

Kanu y cwrwf, 333
Kanu y gwynt, 333
kennings, 50, 324–25, 327, 340, 345, 359, 368, 445, 457, 497, 499–500, 632, 637, 642–43
kisses, kissing, 85, 239, 295, 358, 388, 577–78, 592, 597

Lactantius, *De ave phoenice*, 536
Leicestershire, 131
Leiden Riddle, 4, 317, 320, 397
Leland, John, 113–14
lengthening by position, 30, 49, 52, 61, 70, 82, 86, 88, 91–92, 106, 107, 111, 154, 178, 196, 204, 210, 212, 221, 224–25, 235, 237–38, 242–43, 245, 247, 249, 252, 299–300, 306, 308, 512, 549
Leoba/Leofgyth, 230
Leofric of Exeter, 321
Liber monstrorum, 21, 26, 38, 50, 78, 99–100, 215
Limoges, 230
Lindisfarne Gospels, 356
Livy, *Ab urbe condita*, 532
ljóðaháttr, 447, 607, 625, 632
logogriphs, 8, 71–72, 91, 114, 122, 142–43, 167–68, 201, 210, 258, 262–63, 539, 558, 613, 618, 649, 650
Lorsch, 289–90
Lot, 380, 417, 505, 507, 511, 654
Lucan, 510; *Bellum civile*, 14, 17, 22, 34, 36, 49, 69, 73, 81, 98–99, 101, 106, 112, 213–15, 229
Lucius, 652
Lucretius, 514, 547; *De rerum natura*, 25, 193, 218, 247

Magi, 315
Mainz, 261
Malmesbury, 1, 113
Manes, 512, 536
Manilius, 514
manuscripts (sigla)
- Aberystwyth, National Library of Wales, 735 C (A1), 230–31, 234–37, 239–45, 249, 251, 253–56
- Antwerp, Plantin-Moretus Museum, M. 16. 2 (Q), 300, 302
- Berlin, Staatsbibliothek zu Berlin, Preussischer Kulturbesitz, Phillipps 1825 (I), 574, 600
- Bern, Burgerbibliothek 611 (H), 574
- Brussels, Bibliothèque royale: MS 10615–729 (F1), 3–4, 607, 609, 611–12, 617, 622; MS 9799–809 (F2), 3–4, 607, 613, 617, 622–23
- Cambridge, Corpus Christi College, MS 201, 510, 632; MS 422 (C1), 502, 504–5
- Cambridge, University Library, Gg. 5. 35 (G), 4, 9, 14–31, 33–44, 46–62, 64–66, 68–95, 97–100, 102–5, 114, 116–26, 132–33, 136–37, 139–72, 174–75, 177–205, 207–24, 226–27, 229, 231, 233–49, 251–53, 302, 304–6, 308–13, 515, 517–72, 607, 609–23
- Copenhagen, GKS 2845 4° (R1), 631–32, 634–47
- Edinburgh, National Library of Scotland, Advocates 18. 6. 12 (S), 648–49
- Exeter, Cathedral Library, MS 3501 (E), 321, 327–28, 333, 335–46, 348–60, 362–64, 366–67, 369–73, 376–77, 379–92, 395–96, 398–99, 401–32, 435–38, 439–52, 454–60, 462–65, 467–89
- Grand Haven, Michigan, The Scriptorium, VK 861 (M), 264
- Karlsruhe, Badische Landesbibliothek, Aug. perg. 205 (Z), 653–54
- Leiden, Universiteitsbibliotheek: Vossianus Lat. O. 15, 4 (K); Vossianus Lat. Q. 106 (D), 4, 9, 33–44, 46–62, 64–66, 68–95, 97–100, 102–5, 317, 319, 510, 515, 517–72
- London, British Library: Add. 32246, 301, 302; Cotton Otho B. 10, 490; Cotton Vitellius E. 505–6 (C), 511; Harley 3020 (S1), 648; Royal 12. C. XXIII (L), 4, 9, 14–44, 46–62, 64–66, 68–95, 97–100, 102–5, 109–12, 114, 132–33, 136–37, 139–46, 148–72, 174–75, 177–205, 207–18, 220–24, 226–27, 515, 517–72, 607, 609–21; Royal 15. A. XVI (B), 4, 9, 14–31, 33–44, 46–62, 64–66, 68–95, 97–100, 102–5; Royal 15. B. XIX, 231 (L2), 234–37, 239–42, 527–73

Oxford, Bodleian Library, Rawlinson C. 697 (O), 4, 9, 33–44, 46–62, 64–66, 68–95, 97–100, 102–5, 607, 609–23
Paris, Bibliothèque nationale de France: lat. 10861 (P2), 648, 652; lat. 2773 (P3), 4, 607, 609, 613–16, 618–22; lat. 8071 (P5), 648–49; lat. 8440 (P4), 4; lat. 13048 (R), 4
Reykjavík, Stofnun Árna Magnússonar: AM 281 4° (H2), 632, 635–47; AM 544, 4° (H1), 631–32, 634–47; AM 597b 4° (H3), 632, 635–47; AM 687d (Y), 4°, 624–30
[Rome], Città del Vaticano, Biblioteca Apostolica Vaticana: Pal. lat. 1719 (T), 4; Pal. lat. 1753 (U), 4, 289–90, 292–99; Reg. lat. 1553 (N), 4, 249–50, 253, 574–606; Reg. lat. 2078 (V), 4
St. Gallen, Stiftsbibliothek: MS 196 (X), 515, 517–72, 648, 651–52; MS 446 (X1), 648, 652
St. Petersburg, Russian National Library: F. v. XIV. 1, 4 (R); St. Petersburg, Russian National Library, Q. v. I. 15 (A), 4
Uppsala, University Library, R715 (U1), 631–47
Wolfenbüttel, Herzog August Bibliothek, Gud. lat. 331 (W), 4
Marie de France, *Eliduc*, 88
Mars, 139, 159, 498, 512, 629
Martial, *Apophoreta*, 513; *Epigrammata* 226–27; *Xenia* 513
Martyrology, 186
Mary, 506, 579
Maxims 1, 50
Mediterranean, 113, 512
Menalcas, 261
Menologium (Men), 388, 472, 488
Mercia, 131
Mercury, 41, 493
Mermedonians, 463
Meters of Boethius (Met), 20, 339, 386, 393, 396, 423, 471–72, 478, 482
Metrical Charm 4 (MCharm4), 468
Milred of Worcester, 113, 132, 255
Minerva, 563
Minos, 536
Minotaur, 7, 38, 536
Miracula S. Nyniae, 13–14, 22, 35, 49, 52, 62, 79, 84, 99, 101, 106
misdirection, 201, 352, 370, 379, 402, 416, 426, 428, 433–34, 462, 506, 573, 579, 646, 650
mnemonic, 175, 490, 607, 624–30
mock-heroic, 65, 80, 87, 154, 324, 344, 567
molossus, 96, 232
Monkwearmouth-Jarrow, 113, 133, 173, 195
monosyllables, monosyllabic, 11–13, 75, 109, 114, 118, 146–48, 151, 153, 160, 163, 166, 178, 187, 199, 204, 214, 293, 374
Moralia in Iob, 28
Moses, 11
motifs, 49, 54, 62, 77, 139, 141–42, 145–49, 153, 158, 162, 177–78, 185, 199, 200, 205, 309, 356, 358, 385, 402, 422, 455, 467, 520, 543, 577, 579–80, 582, 584, 588–89, 591–93, 595
Muses, 9, 11–13, 511
mute and liquid, combination of, 30, 49, 52, 61, 70, 82, 86, 88, 91–92, 106, 107, 111, 235, 238, 242–43, 245, 247
Myrrha, 545

Narcissus, 571
Natural History. *See* Pliny, *Natural History*
Nidhad, 315
Nile, 45, 219
Njáls saga, 431
Noah, 73, 652
nominativum pendens, 176, 181
Nonius Marcellus, 49; *De compendiosa doctrina*, 50, 109
North Africa, 492
Northumbria, Northumbrian, 2, 257, 317, 318, 421, 425
Norway, 640

Oak Eggar, 24
Obsidian, 632, 639
Odin. *See* Óðinn, Woden
Óðinn, 259, 502, 629–32, 645, 647. *See also* Woden
Old English Martyrology, 186
Old High German, 349, 357, 476, 490
Old Minster, 466
Old Norse, 88, 259, 357, 431, 494, 501–4, 624–25, 640, 643–44

Old Testament, 3, 11, 81, 323, 505
opening formula, 343, 357, 387
opening line, 20, 36, 41, 45, 75, 135–37, 140, 172, 192, 198, 263, 265, 299, 312, 322, 333–34, 357, 376, 385, 394, 471, 504, 552, 562, 581, 589, 598
opening word, 15, 37, 135, 140, 178, 181, 245, 318, 377, 434
Ops, 568
Order of the World (OrW), 450, 472
Ovid, *Metamorphoses*, 12, 18, 20, 30–31, 33, 36, 38–39, 41, 44, 49, 50–51, 55, 60–61, 65–66, 70, 80, 92, 94, 99–100, 105, 107, 109–11, 228–29, 518, 525, 527, 533, 536, 540, 545, 568, 571
oxymoron, 193, 202–3, 296, 419, 545

pagan, 11, 19, 83, 138, 145–46, 218, 353, 493, 501–2
Pan, 518
Panther (Pan), 210, 345–46
paradox, 152, 177, 179, 182, 188, 194, 347, 351, 354, 435, 518, 580, 590
parallelism, 205, 232, 355, 405, 518, 550
Paris Psalter (PPs), 319, 396, 407, 470
Parnassus, 11–12
paronomasia, 160–61, 165, 190, 199, 539, 545, 549, 556
Pasiphaë, 536
Passio S. Iulianae, 649
Passover, 197
Pater Noster, 502, 505, 624
Paul, 606
Paul the Deacon, 606
Paulinus of Nola, 12, 24, 47, 64, 88, 90, 101, 104–5, 112
Paulinus of Périgueux, 105–6
pentasyllabic, 13, 188
Persian, 209, 540
Persius, 11–12
Peter, 86, 152
phallic, 57, 371, 415, 442
Philosophy, 137, 139, 307
Phoebus, 139
Phoenix, 326, 340, 346–47, 349, 396, 405, 413–15, 452, 471, 536
Physiologus, 101, 210, 218, 222, 327, 346, 361
Pippin, 259, 284
Pisces, 27, 78
Plato, Platonic, 305, 306, 311, 404
Plautus, *Casina*, 116
Pleiades, 17, 19–20, 62
Pliny, *Natural History (Nat. Hist.)*, 27, 53, 57, 60, 65, 68, 78, 93, 163, 186, 212, 221, 526–29, 533, 536–37, 540, 542–44, 556, 558–59
Poetic Edda, 394, 631, 637
polyptoton, 19, 155, 158, 188, 208, 210, 240, 519, 520, 522, 529–30, 548, 550, 556
polysyllabic, 13, 40, 116, 140, 160, 184, 187, 192, 622
pride, 21, 26, 38, 50, 78, 99–100, 160–61
prodelision, 517
productio ob caesuram, 194, 196, 300
Prometheus, 512, 561
Prosper of Aquitaine, 510
Prudentius, 35–36, 44, 101, 106, 112, 246; *Apotheosis*, 12, 26, 76, 98; *Contra Symmachum*, 35, 78, 94; *Peristephanon*, 72; *Psychomachia*, 36, 79, 160, 191
pseudo-Bede, *Collectanea*, 4, 113, 116, 123, 126, 130–31, 140, 145, 158, 343, 350, 510, 518–19, 521–23, 634, 651
Publius Decius Mus, 512, 532
pun, 7, 18, 36, 38, 40, 46, 56–57, 75, 81, 86, 97, 104, 146, 202, 205, 225, 242, 263, 293, 297, 313, 344, 359, 419–20, 513, 537, 543, 556, 563, 567, 595, 619
Pythagoras, 623
Pythian, 619

quadrisyllabic, 11, 13–14, 115, 117, 140, 172, 301, 561, 623
quotation, 102, 215, 395, 403

Red Sea, 251
Reichenau Riddles, 400, 653
repetition, 115, 121, 157, 202, 211, 222–23, 250, 264, 386, 463, 478, 525, 531, 567, 640
Revelation, 148, 174, 504, 609
rhyme, 32, 222, 337, 353, 355, 362, 385, 480–81, 522, 535, 565
Riculf of Mainz, 261
riddles within riddles, 54, 77, 82, 325, 336, 345, 353, 382, 423, 455, 457, 465–66, 469, 475–76, 488, 550, 552, 586–87, 637
Roman, 7, 45, 77, 96, 104, 145, 190, 195, 204, 315–16, 338, 346, 357, 368–69,

375, 378, 399–400, 461, 475, 482, 489, 498, 536, 558, 563, 568–69, 607, 620
Romans, 7, 96, 104, 139, 171, 621
Rome, 1, 43, 113, 118, 174, 186, 620
Ruin, 436, 439, 441
Rune Poem (Run), 454, 459, 482, 489, 491, 609
runes, runic, 10, 175, 315–16, 317, 343, 345–46, 355, 358, 365, 368–69, 371, 378, 395, 400, 413, 436, 439, 445–46, 454–55, 457, 459–61, 464, 482–83, 489–90, 493–96, 498–99, 501, 624, 626, 629
Ruthwell Cross, 316

Samos, Samian, 623
Sapientia, 14, 128, 137, 139–40, 149, 163, 177, 304, 603. *See also* wisdom
Saturn, 15, 129, 501–5, 568, 626
Saturnalia, 513, 515, 568
Scandinavia, Scandinavian, 393, 489–90, 632, 639
scansion, 9–10, 13, 18, 29, 38, 40, 47, 51, 55, 61, 62, 66, 77, 81, 97, 100, 104, 152, 172, 187, 193, 209, 210, 235, 238, 242–43, 245, 247, 249, 296, 607
scriptorium, 39, 41, 67, 93, 130, 133, 142, 144, 149, 181, 183, 187, 190, 198, 204, 298–99, 381, 421, 458, 504
Scylla, 8, 99, 206, 227
Seafarer (Sea), 450, 457–58
second recension of ALD, 3, 9, 17–18, 20, 22–34, 37, 39–40, 47, 49, 52–53, 55, 59–64, 66, 68–70, 75, 78, 80–81, 87, 92, 95, 99–100, 109
Secundus, 221, 260
Sentinum, 532
Sergius, Pope, 174
Seven Sages, 306
Severus, 96
Sextus, 515
Sherborne, 1
Sicily, 99
Silius Italicus, 514
Sleipnir, 647
Socrates, 310
Solomon, 15, 129, 501–4
Solomon and Saturn, 15, 129, 501–4
solution given (as opposed to the preferred solution), 18, 32, 137, 141–42, 146, 151, 160, 162, 164, 167, 170, 180–81, 189, 192, 194, 196, 198–99, 205, 208–10, 213–16, 219–20, 222, 227, 524–25, 474, 570, 576, 578, 580, 584, 585, 588–90, 592, 593–94, 596–99, 603, 605, 640–42, 653–54
solution preferred (as opposed to the given solution), 37, 151, 167, 171, 196, 199, 201, 209, 434, 452, 454, 462, 466, 484, 571
Somniale Danielis, 123
soundplay, 40, 71, 101, 164, 188–89, 223, 228–29, 347, 349, 363, 464, 494, 515, 528–29, 602, 610, 612, 615, 618, 620–21
spondaic verses, 115, 146, 155
Statius, *Thebaid*, 16, 36, 64–65, 78, 107
Stoic, 328, 331, 564
"suffering servant" motif, 144, 185, 385, 467, 577, 582, 584, 588, 592
suffix, 5, 135, 176, 230, 291
Sweden, 640
Symmachus, 515
Symphosius, 3, 5–6, 134, 177, 229, 323, 354, 379, 447, 473–74, 509–10, 513–16, 518–19, 522, 531, 547, 565, 568, 573, 607
syncopation, 121, 601
synizesis, 178, 193, 232–33, 251, 254, 257, 597
synonyms, 2–3, 26, 77, 81, 83, 153, 373–74, 607, 640
Syrinx, 518

Taliesin, 333
Tarsia, 510
Tarsus, 2
Tatwine, 131–37, 139–42, 144–48, 150–51, 153–54, 157, 159–60, 162, 167, 172–77, 230; *Ars de partibus orationis*, 132; *Ars Tatuini*, 153, 182
Taurus, 512, 536
telestichs, 9–11, 133–37, 167, 172, 174
Thales of Miletus, 306
Thaumas, 18
Theodore of Canterbury, 1, 150
Þjóðrerir, 637
Thor, 329, 394
"three fingers" motif, 126, 145, 424, 650, 652
Tigris, 209, 512
Tir. *See* Týr
tironian nota, 480
Titan, 18, 66, 86, 139, 341, 654

titles/solutions, 3, 132–33, 142, 147, 150, 162, 164, 167–68, 170, 199, 206–210, 290
tmesis, 146, 148, 158, 197, 203, 234
tres linguae sacrae, 3, 607
triads, 58, 182, 258, 283, 353, 374, 446, 503, 624
trisyllabic, 233, 254, 297, 597, 612
Trojan War, Troy, 563, 631
Trójumanna saga, 631
Tubal-Cain, 469
Týr, 628–29

unanswerable riddle, 631–32, 639
ungrammatical, 19, 185, 198, 208, 216, 596
Ursa Major, 373

Vafþrúðnir, 259, 631
Vafþrúðnismál, 259, 631, 637, 647
Vainglory (Vain), 414, 448, 472
valkyries, 641
Venantius Fortunatus, 29, 51, 81, 84, 88, 98, 106–9, 111–12, 152, 651; *Carminum appendix*, 57, 108; *Vita S. Martini*, 12, 35, 65, 76, 100, 104–6, 109, 111, 191
Venus, 386, 563
Versus Sibyllae, 24, 64
Viking, 63, 347, 400
Virgil, 29, 47, 51–53, 138, 152, 261, 510, 520–21, 524, 527–28, 548–49; *Aeneid*, 18–20, 27–28, 36, 38, 43–44, 47, 52, 55, 57–58, 60–67, 69–70, 73–74, 76–77, 80–81, 83–84, 89, 94–95, 97–98, 102–4, 106, 108–10, 112, 117, 124, 164, 214, 225, 228, 239, 244–46, 294–95, 297, 329, 338, 513, 515, 521, 524, 528, 535, 541, 548–49, 551, 567, 569, 595, 598; *Georgics*, 27, 32, 34, 36, 51, 53, 57–58, 74, 89–90, 104, 106, 140, 152, 239, 263, 513, 520, 527, 545, 559
Virgilius Maro Grammaticus, 183, 378
viscera, 23–24, 61, 70, 79, 83, 88, 93, 99, 110, 150, 152, 164, 166–67, 208, 253, 294, 298, 341, 486, 590. *See also* womb
Vita S. Ceolfrithi, 173
Vǫlsunga saga, 88
Vǫluspá, 632
Vulcan, 37, 77, 409
Vulgate, 17, 45, 151, 263, 418, 580

Waldere, 499
Weland, 315
Welsh, 155, 332–33, 355, 365, 413, 425–26, 433, 455–56
Wessex, 1, 230, 317, 432, 498
Whale, 346, 411, 445, 462, 471
Widsith, 472
Wife's Lament, 322, 439
Winchester, 466, 480, 506
wisdom, 14, 93, 128, 137, 139–40, 142–43, 149, 160, 163, 177–78, 183, 200, 302, 304–5, 327, 412, 421, 449, 485, 489, 501–3, 527–28, 574, 577, 603, 630–31. *See also Sapientia*
Woden, 493; *See also* Óðinn
womb, 13, 23, 153, 341, 365–67, 401–2, 442, 467, 475–76, 478–79, 486, 526, 591. *See also viscera*
Wonders of the East, 323
wordplay, 18, 72, 74, 97, 103, 125, 160, 171, 180, 188–90, 199, 208, 210, 219, 226, 229, 232, 370–71, 388, 430, 518–20, 537–38, 542, 549, 559–60, 580
Worth Matravers, Dorset, 96
Wulf and Eadwacer, 321, 322, 355, 439
Wulfgar, 300
Wulfstan Cantor of Winchester, 17, 24–25, 101, 466
Wynfrith, 230. *See also* Boniface

Yggdrasill, 483
York, 259, 261, 347

Zeeland, 499
Zeus, 65, 538